COMPUTER GRAPHICS PROGRAMMING IN OPENGL WITH C++

Third Edition

COMPUTER GRAPHICS PROGRAMMING IN OpenGL WITH C++

Third Edition

V. Scott Gordon, Ph.D.
California State University, Sacramento

John Clevenger, Ph.D.
California State University, Sacramento

MERCURY LEARNING AND INFORMATION
Boston, Massachusetts

Publisher: David Pallai
MERCURY LEARNING AND INFORMATION
121 High Street
Boston, MA 02110
info@merclearning.com
www.merclearning.com
(800) 232-0223

Computer Graphics Programming in OpenGL with C++, Third Edition.
V. Scott Gordon & John Clevenger.
ISBN: 978-1-50152-259-8

Library of Congress Control Number: 2023951965

242526321   Printed on acid-free paper in the United States of America.

Contents

Preface

This updated edition is designed primarily as a textbook for a typical computer science undergraduate course in OpenGL 3D graphics programming. However, we have also endeavored to create a text that could be used to teach oneself, without an accompanying course. With both of those aims in mind, we have tried to explain things as clearly and as simply as we can. All of the programming examples are stripped down and simplified as much as possible, but they are still complete so that the reader may run them all as presented.

One of the things that we hope is unique about this book is that we have strived to make it accessible to someone new to 3D graphics programming. While there is by no means a lack of information available on the topic—quite the contrary—many students are initially overwhelmed. This text is our attempt to write the book we wish we had had when we were starting out, with step-by-step explanations of the basics, progressing in an organized manner up through advanced topics. We considered titling the book "shader programming made easy"; however, we don't think that there really is any way of making shader programming "easy." We hope that we have come close.

This book teaches OpenGL programming in *C++*. There are several advantages to learning graphics programming in C++:

- OpenGL's native language is C, so a C++ program can make direct OpenGL function calls.
- OpenGL applications written in C++ typically exhibit very high performance.
- C++ offers modern programming constructs (classes, polymorphism, etc.) not available in C.
- C++ is a popular language choice for using OpenGL, and a large number of instructional resources for OpenGL are available in C++.

It is worth mentioning that there do exist other language bindings for OpenGL. Popular alternatives exist for Java, C#, Python, and many others. This textbook focuses only on C++.

Another thing that makes this book unique is that it has a "sister" textbook: *Computer Graphics Programming in OpenGL With Java*. The two books are organized in lockstep, with the same chapter and section numbers and topics, figures, exercises, and theoretical descriptions. Wherever possible, the code is organized similarly. Of course, the use of C++ versus Java leads to considerable programming differences (although all of the shader code is identical). Still, we believe that we have provided virtually identical learning paths, even allowing a student to choose either option within a single classroom.

An important point of clarification is that there exist both different *versions* of OpenGL (briefly discussed later) and different *variants* of OpenGL. For example, in addition to "standard OpenGL" (sometimes called "desktop OpenGL"), there exists a variant called "OpenGL ES," which is tailored for development of *embedded systems* (hence the "ES"). "Embedded systems" include devices such as mobile phones, game consoles, automobiles, and industrial control systems. OpenGL ES is mostly a subset of standard OpenGL, eliminating a large number of operations that are typically not needed for embedded systems. OpenGL ES also adds some additional functionality, typically application-specific operations for particular target environments. This book focuses on standard OpenGL.

Yet another variant of OpenGL is called "WebGL." Based on OpenGL ES, WebGL is designed to support the use of OpenGL in web browsers. WebGL allows an application to use JavaScript[1] to invoke OpenGL ES operations, which makes it easy to embed OpenGL graphics into standard HTML (web) documents. Most modern web browsers support WebGL, including Apple Safari, Google Chrome, Microsoft Edge, Microsoft Internet Explorer, Mozilla Firefox, and Opera. Since web programming is outside the scope of this book, we will not cover any WebGL specifics. Note however that because WebGL is based on OpenGL ES, which in turn is based on standard OpenGL, much of what *is* covered in this book can be transferred directly to learning about these OpenGL variants.

The very topic of 3D graphics lends itself to impressive, even beautiful images. Indeed, many popular textbooks on the topic are filled with breathtaking scenes, and it is enticing to leaf through their galleries. While we acknowledge the motivational utility of such examples, our aim is to teach, not to impress. The images in this book are simply the outputs of the example programs, and since this is an introductory text, the resulting scenes are unlikely to impress an expert. However, the techniques presented do constitute the foundational elements for producing today's stunning 3D effects.

---

[1] JavaScript is a scripting language that can be used to embed code in webpages. It has strong similarities to Java, but also includes many important differences.

We also have not tried to create an OpenGL "reference." Our coverage of OpenGL represents only a tiny fraction of its capabilities. Rather, our aim is to use OpenGL as a vehicle for teaching the fundamentals of modern shader-based 3D graphics programming, and provide the reader with a sufficiently deep understanding for further study.

What's New in This Edition

There are two major additions in this 3rd edition of Computer Graphics Programming in OpenGL Using C++:

- Chapter 17 – *Ray Tracing of Complex Models*
- Appendix D – *Building a Simple Camera Controller*

Ray Tracing is a hot topic in computer graphics, and Chapter 17 expands on our coverage to include: (1) ray tracing models stored in OBJ files, and (2) using *bounding volume hierarchies* to improve performance and make the ray tracing of complex models feasible. We are excited to finally be able to include this important material in our book.

Appendix D addresses the most common difficulty students have reported when using our book – moving the virtual camera around a 3D scene. In earlier editions, we purposely avoided including code for controlling the camera because writing a camera controller is an excellent instructional exercise for students. Instead, we had described the basic elements and mathematical formulas for doing this (in Chapter 3), leaving the implementation as an exercise. It turned out that for most of our students, this was not enough, and so we have been providing our own students with supplemental material describing, step by step, how to implement a camera controller. This new material is now included in the book as Appendix D. Although we still have avoided providing fully implemented code for this task, we think that the new appendix will give students all the information they need to complete the task without confusion.

We overhauled our coverage of *refraction* in Chapter 16, expanding both the explanation and the examples. We think that the reader will find our revised examples of refraction to be more comprehensive and more realistic.

Stereoscopy, which was Chapter 17 in the 2nd edition, has become Chapter 18 in this 3rd edition.

Besides the new material, there are important revisions throughout the book. A small but important correction that we made was to change all of our lighting computations so that they are done in world space rather than camera space – this makes it easier to build applications that require being able to move the camera around. We had previously made this lighting computation change in our "sister" Java book, and implementing the same changes in this C++ book aligns the two volumes so that all of their shaders are now identical.

We beefed up our installation instructions (Appendices A and B). Configuring the libraries remains more arduous than it really ought to be, but we have tried to explain it more thoroughly than we did in our previous edition. Macintosh support for OpenGL continues to worsen, making library installation even more difficult on that platform. We strove to list all of the steps as carefully as possible – as of November 2023, the steps we list in Appendix B worked correctly.

NVIDIA's Nsight debugger, the topic of Appendix C, now has a standalone application that is easier to use than previous versions that required integration with Visual Studio. We revised Appendix C to utilize the newer standalone version.

There are dozens of small changes in every chapter that the reader might not even notice: fixing typos, cleaning up code inconsistencies, updating the installation instructions, making slight wording changes, sprucing up figures, updating references, and so on Great effort has been made to stay up to date and error free in a book about an ever-changing technology. As a result, this 3rd edition is slightly larger than the previous edition.

Intended Audience

This book is targeted at students of computer science. This could mean undergraduates pursuing a BS degree, but it could also mean anyone who studies computer science. As such, we are assuming that the reader has at least a solid background in object-oriented programming, at the level of someone who is, for example, a computer science major at the junior or senior level.

There are also some specific things that we use in this book that we don't cover, because we assume the reader already has sufficient background in the following:

- C++ and its most commonly used libraries, such as the Standard Template Library;
- familiarity with using an *Integrated Development Environment* (IDE), such as Visual Studio;
- basic data structures and algorithms, such as linked lists, stacks and queues, and so on;
- recursion;

- event-driven programming concepts;
- basic matrix algebra and trigonometry;
- basic analytic geometry, such as for defining points, lines, vectors, planes, and circles, and
- awareness of color models, such as RGB, RGBA, and so on.

It is hoped that the potential audience for this new book is further bolstered by the existence of its "sister" textbook, *Computer Graphics Programming in OpenGL With Java*. In particular, we envision a learning environment where students are free to utilize either C++ or Java *in the same classroom*, selecting one or the other book. The two texts cover the material sufficiently in lockstep that we have been able to conduct our graphics programming course successfully in this manner.

How to Use This Book

This book is designed to be read from front to back. That is, material in later chapters frequently relies on information learned in earlier chapters. So it probably won't work to jump back and forth in the chapters; rather, work your way forward through the material.

This is also intended mostly as a practical, hands-on guide. While there is plenty of theoretical material included, the reader should treat this text as a sort of "workbook," in which you learn basic concepts by actually programming them yourself. We have provided code for all of the examples, but to really learn the concepts you will want to "play" with those examples—extend them to build your own 3D scenes.

At the end of each chapter are a few exercises to solve. Some are very simple, involving merely making small modifications to the provided code. The problems that are marked "*(PROJECT)*," however, are expected to take some time to solve, and require writing a significant amount of code, or combining techniques from various examples. There are also a few marked "*(RESEARCH)*"—those are problems that encourage independent study because this textbook doesn't provide sufficient detail to solve them.

OpenGL calls often involve long lists of parameters. While writing this book, the authors debated whether or not to, in each case, describe all of the parameters. We decided that in the early chapters we would describe every detail. Further into the book, as the topics progress, we decided to avoid getting bogged down in every piece of minutiae in the OpenGL calls (and there are *many*), for fear of the reader losing sight of the big picture. For this reason, it is essential when working through the examples to have ready access to reference material for OpenGL and the various libraries being used.

For this, there are a number of excellent online resources that we recommend using in conjunction with this book. The documentation for OpenGL is absolutely essential; details on the various commands are available either by simply using Google to search for the command in question, or by visiting:

https://www.khronos.org/registry/OpenGL-Refpages/gl4/

Our examples utilize a mathematics library called GLM. After installing GLM (described in the appendices), the reader should locate the accompanying online documentation and bookmark it. At press time, the current link is:

https://glm.g-truc.net/0.9.9/index.html

Another library used throughout the book for which the reader may wish to periodically consult its documentation is SOIL2, which is used for loading and processing texture image files. Documentation for SOIL2, and the image loading library stb on which it is based, can be found on its repository:

https://github.com/SpartanJ/soil2

There are many other books on 3D graphics programming that we recommend reading in parallel with this book (such as for solving the "research" problems). Here are five that we often refer to:

- (Sellers et al.) *OpenGL SuperBible* [SW15]
- (Kessenich et al.) *OpenGL Programming Guide* [KS16] (the "red book")
- (Wolff) *OpenGL 4 Shading Language Cookbook* [WO18]
- (Angel and Shreiner) *Interactive Computer Graphics* [AS20]
- (Luna) *Introduction to 3D Game Programming with DirectX 12* [LU16]

Companion Files

There is a set of companion files available for this book that contain the following items:

- All of the C++/OpenGL programs and related utility class files and GLSL shader code presented in the book
- The models and texture files used in the various programs and examples
- The cubemap and skydome image files used to make the skies and horizons
- Normal maps and height maps for lighting and surface detail effects
- All of the figures in the book, as image files

The companion files are available for downloading by writing to the publisher at info@merclearning.com.

Instructor Ancillaries

Instructors in a college or university setting are encouraged to obtain the *instructor ancillary package* that is available for this book. It contains the following additional items:

- A complete set of PowerPoint slides covering all topics in the book
- Solutions to most of the exercises at the ends of the chapters, including code where applicable
- Sample syllabus for a course based on the book
- Additional hints for presenting the material, chapter-by-chapter

This instructor ancillary package is available by writing to the publisher at info@merclearning.com.

Acknowledgments

A lot of the content in this book is built off of our first book *Computer Graphics Programming in OpenGL With Java*, which we drafted in 2016 for the CSc-155 (3D Graphics and Shader Programming) course at California State University Sacramento. Many CSc-155 students actively contributed suggestions and bug fixes to an early draft during that year, including Mitchell Brannan, Tiffany Chiapuzio-Wong, Samson Chua, Anthony Doan, Kian Faroughi, Cody Jackson, John Johnston, Zeeshan Khaliq, Raymond Rivera, Oscar Solorzano, Darren Takemoto, Jon Tinney, James Womack, and Victor Zepeda. The following year our colleague Dr. Pinar Muyan-Ozcelik used the first edition of the Java book while teaching CSc-155 for her first time, and kept a running log of questions and corrections for each chapter, which led to many improvements for subsequent editions..

In spring 2020 we tested our idea of allowing students (in our CSc-155 course) to select either C++ or Java, using the respective edition of this textbook. It was a sort of acid test of our "sister" textbook idea, and we were pleased with how things went. We have been teaching the course in this manner ever since. Again, students noted typos – Paul McHugh in particular caught and fixed an important memory leak in our 3D texture code.

Early versions of the implementations described in Chapters 15, 16, and 17 were developed by three California State University alumni: Chris Swenson (Havalo LLP), Luis Gutierrez (Lawrence Livermore National Security), and Robin O'Connell, respectively. They all did an excellent job of distilling these complex topics into nicely coherent solutions.

We continue to receive a steady stream of great feedback from instructors around the world who adopt our books for their courses, and from professionals and enthusiasts – Dr. Mauricio Papa (University of Tulsa), Dr. Fuhua "Frank" Cheng (University of Kentucky), Dan Asimov (NASA Ames), Sean McCrory, Michael Hiatt, Scott Anderson, Reydalto Hernandez, and Bill Crupi, just to name a few.

Dr. Alan Mills, over the course of several months starting in early 2020, sent us over two hundred suggestions and corrections from his notes as he worked through our Java edition. About half of his notes were also applicable to the C++ edition. Among his many finds was a significant correction to the texture coordinates in the torus model. Alan's attention to detail is amazing and we greatly appreciate the positive impact of his efforts on both books.

Jay Turberville of Studio 522 Productions in Scottsdale (Arizona) built the dolphin model shown on the cover and used throughout all of our books. Our students love it. Studio 522 Productions does incredibly high-quality 3D animation and video production, as well as custom 3D modeling. We are thrilled that Mr. Turberville kindly offered to build such a wonderful model just for these books.

Martín Lucas Golini, who developed and maintains the SOIL2 texture image handling library, has been very supportive and enthusiastic about our book, and has been quickly responsive whenever any problems have arisen. His continued availability to us has been much appreciated.

We wish to thank a few other artists and researchers who were gracious enough to allow us to utilize their models and textures. James Hastings-Trew of Planet Pixel Emporium provided many of the planetary surface textures. Paul Bourke allowed us to use his wonderful star field. Dr. Marc Levoy of Stanford University granted us permission to use the famous "Stanford Dragon" model. Paul Baker's bump-mapping tutorial formed the basis of the "torus" model we used in many examples. We also thank Mercury Learning and Information for allowing us to use some of the textures from *Introduction to 3D Game Programming With DirectX 12*, [LU16].

The late Dr. Danny Kopec connected us with Mercury Learning and introduced us to its publisher, David Pallai. Being a chess enthusiast, Dr. Gordon (one of the authors) was originally familiar with Dr. Kopec as a well-known international chess master and prolific chess book author. He was also a computer science professor, and his textbook, *Artificial Intelligence in the 21st Century*, inspired us to consider Mercury Learning for our book project. We had several telephone conversations with Dr. Kopec which were extremely informative. We were deeply saddened by Dr. Kopec's untimely passing in 2016, and regret that he didn't have the chance to see our books, which he had helped jump start, come to fruition.

Finally, we wish to thank David Pallai and Jennifer Blaney of Mercury Learning for their ongoing enthusiasm and support for this project and for guiding us through the textbook publishing process.

Errata

Should you find any errors in our book, please let us know. We will do our best to post corrections as soon as errors are reported to us. We have established a webpage for collecting errata and posting corrections:

http://athena.ecs.csus.edu/~gordonvs/textC3E.html

About the Authors

Dr. V. Scott Gordon has been a professor in the California State University system for thirty years, and currently teaches graphics and game engineering courses at CSU Sacramento. He has authored or coauthored over thirty publications in a variety of areas including artificial intelligence, neural networks, evolutionary computation, computer graphics, compiler optimization, software engineering, video and strategy game programming, and computer science education. Dr. Gordon obtained his PhD at Colorado State University. He is also a jazz drummer and a competitive table tennis player.

Dr. John Clevenger is a professor with over forty years of experience teaching a wide variety of courses including advanced graphics, game architecture, operating systems, VLSI chip design, system simulation, and other topics. He is the developer of several software frameworks and tools for teaching graphics and game architecture, including the graphicslib3D library used in the first edition of our Java-based textbook. He is the technical director of the International Collegiate Programming Contest (ICPC), and oversees the ongoing development of PC^2, the most widely used programming contest support system in the world. Dr. Clevenger obtained his PhD at the University of California, Davis. He is also a performing jazz musician, and spends summer vacations in his mountain cabin.

References

[AS20]   E. Angel and D. Shreiner, *Interactive Computer Graphics: A Top-Down Approach with WebGL*, 8th ed. (Pearson, 2020).

[KS16]   J. Kessenich, G. Sellers, and D. Shreiner, *OpenGL Programming Guide: The Official Guide to Learning OpenGL, Version 4.5 with SPIR-V*, 9th ed. (Addison-Wesley, 2016).

[LU16]   F. Luna, *Introduction to 3D Game Programming with DirectX 12*, 2nd ed. (Mercury Learning, 2016).

[SW15]   G. Sellers, R. Wright Jr., and N. Haemel, *OpenGL SuperBible: Comprehensive Tutorial and Reference*, 7th ed. (Addison-Wesley, 2015).

[WO18]   D. Wolff, *OpenGL 4 Shading Language Cookbook*, 3rd ed. (Packt Publishing, 2018).

GETTING STARTED

Graphics programming has a reputation for being among the most challenging computer science topics to learn. These days, graphics programming is *shader based*—that is, some of the program is written in a standard language such as C++ or Java for running on the CPU and some is written in a special-purpose *shader* language for running directly on the graphics card (GPU). Shader programming has a steep learning curve, so that even drawing something simple requires a convoluted set of steps to pass graphics data down a "pipeline." Modern graphics cards are able to process this data in *parallel*, and so the graphics programmer must understand the parallel architecture of the GPU, even when drawing simple shapes.

The payoff, however, is extraordinary power. The blossoming of stunning virtual reality in videogames and increasingly realistic effects in Hollywood movies can be greatly attributed to advances in shader programming. If reading this book is your entrée into 3D graphics, you are taking on a personal challenge that will reward you not only with pretty pictures but with a level of control over your machine that you never imagined was possible. Welcome to the exciting world of computer graphics programming!

■1.1■ LANGUAGES AND LIBRARIES

Modern graphics programming is done using a *graphics library*. That is, the programmer writes code which invokes functions in a predefined library (or set of libraries) that provide support for lower-level graphical operations. There are many graphics libraries in use today, but the most common library for platform-independent graphics programming is called *OpenGL (Open Graphics Library)*. This book describes how to use OpenGL for 3D graphics programming in C++.

Using OpenGL with C++ requires configuring several libraries. At this time there is a dizzying array of options, depending on one's individual needs. In this section, we describe which libraries are needed, some common options for each, and the option(s) that we will use throughout the book. Details on how to install and configure these libraries for use on your specific platform can be found in the Appendices.

In summary, you will need languages and libraries for the following functions:

- C++ development environment
- OpenGL / GLSL
- window management
- extension library
- math library
- texture management

It is likely that the reader will need to do several preparatory steps to ensure that each of these are installed and properly accessible on his/her system. In the following subsections we briefly describe each of them; see the Appendices for details on how to install and/or configure them for use.

1.1.1 C++

C++ is a general-purpose programming language that first appeared in the mid-1980s. Its design, and the fact that it is generally compiled to native machine code, make it an excellent choice for systems that require high performance, such as 3D graphics computing. Another advantage of C++ is that the OpenGL call library is C based.

Many C++ development environments are available. In this textbook we recommend using *Microsoft Visual Studio* [VS22] if using a PC, and *Xcode* [XC18] if using a Macintosh. Descriptions for installing and configuring each of them, depending on your platform, are given in the Appendices.

1.1.2 OpenGL / GLSL

Version 1.0 of OpenGL appeared in 1992 as an "open" alternative to vendor-specific Application Programming Interfaces (APIs) for computer graphics.

Its specification and development was managed and controlled by the *OpenGL Architecture Review Board (ARB)*, a then newly formed group of industry participants. In 2006 the ARB transferred control of the OpenGL specification to the *Khronos Group*, a nonprofit consortium which manages not only the OpenGL specification but a wide variety of other open industry standards.

Since its beginning OpenGL has been revised and extended regularly. In 2004, version 2.0 introduced the OpenGL Shading Language (GLSL), allowing "shader programs" to be installed and run directly in graphics pipeline stages.

In 2009, version 3.1 removed a large number of features that had been deprecated, to enforce the use of shader programming as opposed to earlier approaches (referred to as "immediate mode").[1] Among the more recent features, version 4.0 (in 2010) added a *tessellation* stage to the programmable pipeline.

This textbook assumes that the user is using a machine with a graphics card that supports at least version 4.3 of OpenGL. If you are not sure which version of OpenGL your GPU supports, there are free applications available on the web that can be used to find out. One such application is GLView, by a company named "realtech-vr" [GV23].

1.1.3 Window Management

OpenGL doesn't actually draw to a computer screen. Rather, it renders to a *frame buffer*, and it is the job of the individual machine to then draw the contents of the frame buffer onto a window on the screen. There are various libraries that support doing this. One option is to use the windowing capabilities provided by the operating system, such as the ***Microsoft Windows API***. This is generally impractical and requires a lot of low-level coding. **GLUT** is a historically popular option; however, it is deprecated. A modernized extension is **freeglut**. Other related options are **CPW**, **GLOW**, and **GLUI**.

One of the most popular options, and the one used in this book, is **GLFW**, which has built-in support for Windows, Macintosh, Linux, and other systems [GF22]. It can be downloaded from www.glfw.org, and it must be compiled on the machine where it is to be used (we describe those steps in the Appendices).

---

[1] Despite this, many graphics card manufacturers (notably NVIDIA) continue to support deprecated functionality.

1.1.4 Extension Library

OpenGL is organized around a set of base functions and an *extension* mechanism used to support new functionality as technologies advance. Modern versions of OpenGL, such as those found in version 4+ as we use in this book, require identifying the extensions available on the GPU. There are commands built into core OpenGL for doing this, but they involve several rather convoluted lines of code that would need to be performed for each modern command used—and in this book we use such commands constantly. Therefore, it has become standard practice to use an *extension library* to take care of these details, and to make modern OpenGL commands available to the programmer directly. Examples are **Glee**, **GLLoader**, **GLEW**, and more recently **GL3W** and **GLAD**.

A commonly used library among those listed is **GLEW**, which stands for *Open__GL__ __E__xtension __W__rangler*. It is available for a variety of operating systems including Windows, Macintosh, and Linux [GE17]. **GLEW** is not a perfect choice; for example, it requires an additional DLL. Recently, many developers are choosing **GL3W** or **GLAD**. They have the advantage of being automatically updated. However, **GLEW** is simple to install, and our students have been using it without problems for many years. For this reason, in this book we have opted to use **GLEW**. It can be downloaded at glew.sourceforge.net. Complete instructions for installing and configuring **GLEW** are given in the appendices.

1.1.5 Math Library

3D graphics programming makes heavy use of vector and matrix algebra. For this reason, use of OpenGL is greatly facilitated by accompanying it with a function library or class package to support common mathematical tasks. Two such libraries that are frequently used with OpenGL are **Eigen** and **vmath**, the latter being used in the popular *OpenGL SuperBible* [SW15].

Arguably the most popular, and the one used in this book, is *OpenGL Mathematics*, usually called **GLM**. It is a header-only C++ library compatible with Windows, Macintosh, and Linux [GM20]. **GLM** commands conveniently use the same naming conventions as those in GLSL, making it easy to go back and forth when reading C++ and GLSL code used in a particular application. **GLM** is available for download at https://github.com/g-truc/glm and at https://glm.g-truc.net/0.9.9/index.html.

GLM provides classes and basic math functions related to graphics concepts, such as *vector*, *matrix*, and *quaternion*. It also contains a variety of utility classes for creating and using common 3D graphics structures, such as perspective and look-at matrices. It was first released in 2005, and it is maintained by Christophe Riccio [GM20]. Instructions for installing **GLM** are given in the appendices.

`1.1.6` Texture Management

Starting with Chapter 5, we will use image files to add "texture" to the objects in our graphics scenes. This means that we will frequently need to load such image files into our C++/OpenGL code. It is possible to code a texture image loader from scratch; however, given the wide variety of image file formats, it is generally preferable to use a texture loading library. Some examples are **FreeImage**, **DevIL**, OpenGL Image (**GLI**), and **Glraw**. Probably the most commonly used OpenGL image loading library is Simple OpenGL Image Loader (**SOIL**), although it has become somewhat outdated.

The texture image loading library used in this book is **SOIL2**, an updated fork of **SOIL**. Like the previous libraries we have chosen, **SOIL2** is compatible with a wide variety of platforms [SO23], and detailed installation and configuration instructions are given in the appendices.

`1.1.7` Optional Libraries

There are many other helpful libraries that the reader may wish to utilize. For example, in this book we show how to implement a simple "OBJ" model loader from scratch. However, as we will see, it doesn't handle many of the options available in the OBJ standard. Some examples of more sophisticated OBJ importers are **Assimp** and **tinyobjloader**. For our examples, we will just use our simple model loader described and implemented in this book.

`1.2` INSTALLATION AND CONFIGURATION

While developing the C++ edition of this book, we wrestled with the best approach for including the platform-specific configuration information necessary to run the example programs. Configuring a system for using OpenGL with C++ is considerably more complicated than the equivalent configuration using Java, which can be described in just a few short paragraphs (as can be seen in the Java edition of the book [GC21]). Ultimately, we opted to separate installation and configuration information into individual platform-specific Appendices. We hope that this will provide each reader with a single relevant place to look for information regarding his/her specific system, while at the same time avoiding bogging down the rest of the text with platform-specific details which may not be relevant to every reader. In this edition, we provide detailed configuration instructions for Microsoft Windows in Appendix A, and for the Apple Macintosh in Appendix B.

Continually updated library installation instructions will be maintained on this textbook's website, available at: *http://athena.ecs.csus.edu/~gordonvs/textC3E.html*

References

[GC21] V. Gordon and J. Clevenger, *Computer Graphics Programming in OpenGL with Java*, 3rd ed. (Mercury Learning, 2021).

[GE17] OpenGL Extension Wrangler (GLEW), accessed November 2023, http://glew.sourceforge.net/

[GF22] Graphics Library Framework (GLFW), accessed November 2023, http://www.glfw.org/

[GM20] OpenGL Mathematics (GLM), accessed November 2023, https://github.com/g-truc/glm

[GV23] GLView, realtech-vr, accessed November 2023, https://www.realtech-vr.com/home/glview

[SO23] Simple OpenGL Image Library 2 (SOIL2), *SpartanJ*, accessed November 2023, https://github.com/SpartanJ/SOIL2

[SW15] G. Sellers, R. Wright Jr., and N. Haemel, *OpenGL SuperBible: Comprehensive Tutorial and Reference*, 7th ed. (Addison-Wesley, 2015).

[VS22] Microsoft Visual Studio downloads, accessed November 2023, https://visualstudio.microsoft.com/downloads/

[XC23] Apple Developer site for Xcode, accessed November 2023, https://developer.apple.com/xcode

THE OPENGL PIPELINE

OpenGL (Open Graphics Library) is a multi-platform 2D and 3D graphics API that incorporates both hardware and software. Using OpenGL requires a graphics card (GPU) that supports a sufficiently up-to-date version of OpenGL (as described in Chapter 1).

On the hardware side, OpenGL provides a multi-stage *graphics pipeline* that is partially programmable using a language called **GLSL** (OpenGL Shading Language).

On the software side, OpenGL's API is written in C, and thus the calls are directly compatible with C and C++. Stable language *bindings* (or "wrappers") are available for more than a dozen other popular languages (Java, Perl, Python, Visual Basic, Delphi, Haskell, Lisp, Ruby, etc.) with virtually equivalent performance. This textbook uses C++, probably the most popular language choice. When using C++, the programmer writes code that runs on the CPU (compiled, of course) and includes OpenGL calls. We will refer to a C++ program that contains OpenGL calls as a *C++/OpenGL application*. One important task of a C++/OpenGL application is to install the programmer's GLSL code onto the GPU.

An overview of a C++-based graphics application is shown in Figure 2.1, with the software components highlighted in pink.

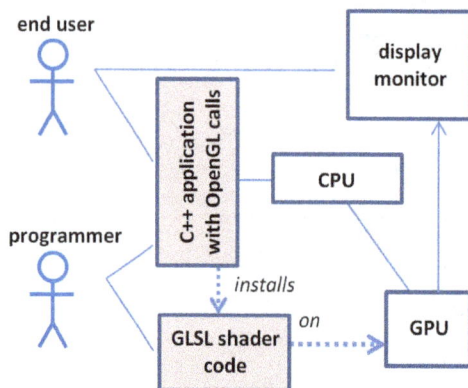

Figure 2.1
Overview of a C++-based graphics application.

Some of the code we will write will be in C++, with OpenGL calls, and some will be written in GLSL. Our C++/OpenGL application will work together with our GLSL modules, and the hardware, to create our 3D graphics output. Once our application is complete, the end user will interact with the C++ application.

GLSL is an example of a *shader language*. Shader languages are intended to run on a GPU, in the context of a graphics pipeline. There are other shader languages, such as HLSL, which works with Microsoft's 3D framework *DirectX*. GLSL is the specific shader language that is compatible with OpenGL, and thus we will write shader code in GLSL, in addition to our C++/OpenGL application code.

For the rest of this chapter, we will take a brief "tour" of the OpenGL pipeline. The reader is not expected to understand every detail thoroughly but should just get a feel for how the stages work together.

▨ 2.1 ▨ THE OPENGL PIPELINE

Modern 3D graphics programming utilizes a *pipeline*, in which the process of converting a 3D scene to a 2D image is broken down into a series of steps. OpenGL and DirectX both utilize similar pipelines.

A simplified overview of the OpenGL graphics pipeline is shown in Figure 2.2 (not every stage is shown, just the major ones we will study). The C++/OpenGL application sends graphics data into the vertex shader—processing proceeds through the pipeline, and pixels emerge for display on the monitor.

The stages shaded in blue (vertex, tessellation, geometry, and fragment) are *programmable* in GLSL. It is one of the responsibilities of the C++/OpenGL application to load GLSL programs into these shader stages, as follows:

1. It uses C++ to obtain the GLSL shader code, either from text files or hard-coded as strings.

2. It then creates OpenGL shader objects and loads the GLSL shader code into them.

3. Finally, it uses OpenGL commands to compile and link objects and install them on the GPU.

In practice, it is usually necessary to provide GLSL code for at least the *vertex* and *fragment* stages, whereas the tessellation and geometry stages are optional. Let's walk through the entire process and see what takes place at each step.

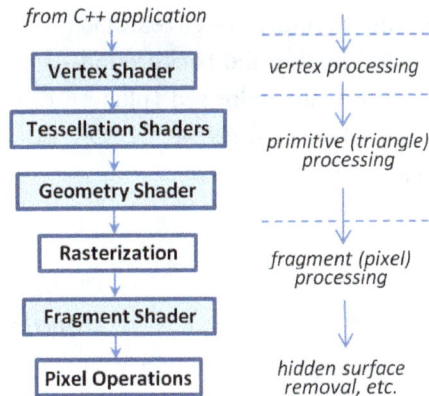

Figure 2.2
Overview of the OpenGL pipeline.

2.1.1 C++/OpenGL Application

The bulk of our graphics application is written in C++. Depending on the purpose of the program, it may interact with the end user using standard C++ libraries. For tasks related to 3D rendering, it uses OpenGL calls. As described in the previous chapter, we will be using several additional libraries: GLEW (OpenGL Extension Wrangler), GLM (OpenGL Mathematics), SOIL2 (Simple OpenGL Image Loader), and GLFW (Graphics Library Framework).

The GLFW library includes a class called GLFWwindow on which we can draw 3D scenes. As already mentioned, OpenGL also gives us commands for installing GLSL programs onto the programmable shader stages and compiling them. Finally, OpenGL uses *buffers* for sending 3D models and other related graphics data down the pipeline.

Before we try writing shaders, let's write a simple C++/OpenGL application that instantiates a GLFWwindow and sets its background color. Doing that won't require any shaders at all! The code is shown in Program 2.1. The main() function shown in Program 2.1 is the same one that we will use throughout this textbook. Among the significant operations in main() are: (a) initializes the GLFW library, (b) instantiates a GLFWwindow, (c) initializes the GLEW library, (d) calls the function "init()" once, and (e) calls the function "display()" repeatedly.

The "init()" function is where we will place application-specific initialization tasks. The display() method is where we place code that draws to the GLFWwindow.

In this example, the glClearColor() command specifies the color value to be applied when clearing the background—in this case (1,0,0,1), corresponding to the RGB values of the color red (plus a "1" for the opacity component). We then use the OpenGL call glClear(GL_COLOR_BUFFER_BIT) to actually fill the color buffer with that color.

Program 2.1 First C++/OpenGL Application

```
#include <GL/glew.h>
#include <GLFW/glfw3.h>
#include <iostream>

using namespace std;

void init(GLFWwindow* window) { }

void display(GLFWwindow* window, double currentTime) {
    glClearColor(1.0, 0.0, 0.0, 1.0);
    glClear(GL_COLOR_BUFFER_BIT);
}

int main(void) {
    if (!glfwInit()) { exit(EXIT_FAILURE); }
    glfwWindowHint(GLFW_CONTEXT_VERSION_MAJOR, 4);
    glfwWindowHint(GLFW_CONTEXT_VERSION_MINOR, 3);
    GLFWwindow* window = glfwCreateWindow(600, 600, "Chapter2 - program1", NULL, NULL);
    glfwMakeContextCurrent(window);
    if (glewInit() != GLEW_OK) { exit(EXIT_FAILURE); }
    glfwSwapInterval(1);

    init(window);

    while (!glfwWindowShouldClose(window)) {
        display(window, glfwGetTime());
        glfwSwapBuffers(window);
        glfwPollEvents();
    }

    glfwDestroyWindow(window);
    glfwTerminate();
    exit(EXIT_SUCCESS);
}
```

The output of Program 2.1 is shown in Figure 2.3.

The mechanism by which these functions are deployed is as follows: the GLFW and GLEW libraries are initialized using the commands glfwInit() and glewInit() respectively. The GLFW window and an associated OpenGL *context*[1] are created with the glfwCreateWindow() command, with options set by any preceding *window hints*. Our window hints specify that the machine must be com-

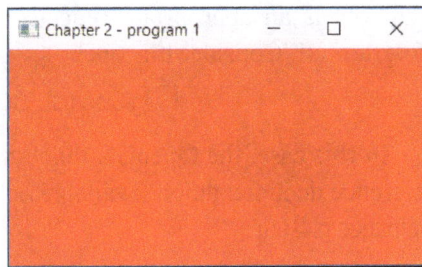

Figure 2.3
Output of Program 2.1.

patible with OpenGL version 4.3 ("major"=4. and "minor"=3). The parameters on the glfwCreateWindow() command specify the width and height of the window (in pixels) and the title placed at the top of the window. (The additional two parameters which are set to NULL, and which we aren't using, allow for full screen mode and resource sharing.) Vertical synchronization (VSync) is enabled by using the glfwSwapInterval() and glfwSwapBuffers() commands—GLFW windows are by default double-buffered.[2] Note that creating the GLFW window doesn't automatically make the associated OpenGL context current—for that reason we also call glfwMakeContextCurrent().

Our main() includes a very simple rendering loop that calls our display() function repeatedly. It also calls glfwSwapBuffers(), which paints the screen, and glfwPollEvents(), which handles other window-related events (such as a key being pressed). The loop terminates when GLFW detects an event that should close the window (such as the user clicking the "X" in the upper right corner). Note that we have included a reference to the GLFW window object on the init() and display() calls; those functions may in certain circumstances need access to it. We have also included the current time on the call to display(), which will be useful for ensuring that our animations run at the same speed regardless of the computer being used. For this purpose, we use glfwGetTime(), which returns the elapsed time since GLFW was initialized.

---

[1] The term "context" refers to an OpenGL instance and its state information, which includes items such as the color buffer.

[2] "Double buffering" means that there are two color buffers—one that is displayed, and one that is being rendered to. After an entire frame is rendered, the buffers are swapped. Double buffering is used to reduce undesirable visual artifacts.

Now is an appropriate time to take a closer look at the OpenGL calls in Program 2.1. Consider this one:

glClear(GL_COLOR_BUFFER_BIT);

In this case, the OpenGL function being called, as described in the OpenGL reference documentation (available on the web at https://registry.khronos.org/OpenGL-Refpages/gl4/), is:

void glClear(GLbitfield mask);

The parameter references a "GLbitfield" called "GL_COLOR_BUFFER_BIT". OpenGL has many predefined constants (some of them are called *enums*); this one references the *color buffer* that contains the pixels as they are rendered. OpenGL has several color buffers, and this command clears all of them—that is, it fills them with a predefined color called the "clear color." Note that "clear" in this context doesn't mean "a color that is clear"; rather, it refers to the color that is applied when a color buffer is reset (cleared).

Immediately before the call to glClear() is a call to glClearColor(). This allows us to specify the value placed in the elements of a color buffer when it is cleared. Here we have specified (1,0,0,1), which corresponds to the RGBA color *red*.

Finally, our render loop exits when the user attempts to close the GLFW window. At that time, our main() asks GLFW to destroy the window and terminate, via calls to glfwDestroyWindow() and glfwTerminate() respectively.

2.1.2 Vertex and Fragment Shaders

Our first OpenGL program didn't actually draw anything—it simply filled the color buffer with a single color. To actually draw something, we need to include a *vertex shader* and a *fragment shader.*

You may be surprised to learn that OpenGL is capable of drawing only a few kinds of very simple things, such as *points*, *lines*, or *triangles*. These simple things are called *primitives*, and for this reason, most 3D models are made up of lots and lots of primitives, usually triangles.

Primitives are made up of *vertices*—for example, a triangle consists of three vertices. The vertices can come from a variety of sources—they can be read from files and then loaded into buffers by the C++/OpenGL application, or they can be hardcoded in the C++ code or even in the GLSL code.

Before any of this can happen, the C++/OpenGL application must compile and link appropriate GLSL vertex and fragment shader programs, and then load them into the pipeline. We will see the commands for doing this shortly.

The C++/OpenGL application also is responsible for telling OpenGL to construct triangles. We do this by using the following OpenGL function:

glDrawArrays(GLenum mode, GLint first, GLsizei count);

The mode is the type of primitive—for triangles we use GL_TRIANGLES. The parameter "first" indicates which vertex to start with (generally vertex number 0, the first one), and count specifies the total number of vertices to be drawn.

When glDrawArrays() is called, the GLSL code in the pipeline starts executing. Let's now add some GLSL code to that pipeline.

Regardless of where they originate, all of the vertices pass through the vertex shader. They do so *one by one*; that is, the shader is executed *once per vertex*. For a large and complex model with a lot of vertices, the vertex shader may execute hundreds, thousands, or even millions of times, often in parallel.

Let's write a simple program with only one vertex, hardcoded in the vertex shader. That's not enough to draw a triangle, but it is enough to draw a point. For it to display, we also need to provide a *fragment shader*. For simplicity we will declare the two shader programs as arrays of strings.

Program 2.2 Shaders, Drawing a POINT

(.....#includes are the same as before)

```
#define numVAOs 1                          ⎫
                                           ⎬  new declarations
GLuint renderingProgram;                    ⎭
GLuint vao[numVAOs];

GLuint createShaderProgram() {
   const char *vshaderSource =
      "#version 430   \n"
      "void main(void) \n"
      "{ gl_Position = vec4(0.0, 0.0, 0.0, 1.0); }";

   const char *fshaderSource =
      "#version 430   \n"
      "out vec4 color; \n"
```

```
    "void main(void) \n"
    "{ color = vec4(0.0, 0.0, 1.0, 1.0); }";

    GLuint vShader = glCreateShader(GL_VERTEX_SHADER);
    GLuint fShader = glCreateShader(GL_FRAGMENT_SHADER);

    glShaderSource(vShader, 1, &vshaderSource, NULL);
    glShaderSource(fShader, 1, &fshaderSource, NULL);
    glCompileShader(vShader);
    glCompileShader(fShader);

    GLuint vfProgram = glCreateProgram();
    glAttachShader(vfProgram, vShader);
    glAttachShader(vfProgram, fShader);
    glLinkProgram(vfProgram);

    return vfProgram;
}

void init(GLFWwindow* window) {
    renderingProgram = createShaderProgram();
    glGenVertexArrays(numVAOs, vao);
    glBindVertexArray(vao[0]);
}

void display(GLFWwindow* window, double currentTime) {
    glUseProgram(renderingProgram);
    glDrawArrays(GL_POINTS, 0, 1);
}

. . . main() same as before
```

The program appears to have output a blank window (see Figure 2.4). But close examination reveals a tiny blue dot in the center of the window (assuming that this printed page is of sufficient resolution). The default size of a point in OpenGL is one pixel.

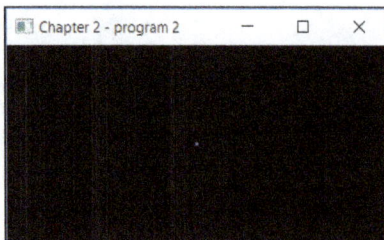

Figure 2.4
Output of Program 2.2.

There are many important details in Program 2.2 (color-coded in the program, for convenience) for us to discuss. First, note the frequent use of "GLuint"—this is a platform-independent shorthand for "unsigned int", provided by OpenGL (many OpenGL constructs have integer references). Next, note that init() is no longer empty—it now calls another function named "createShaderProgram()" (that we wrote). This function starts by declaring two shaders as character strings called vshaderSource and fshaderSource. It then calls glCreateShader() twice, which generates the two shaders of types GL_VERTEX_ SHADER and GL_FRAGMENT_SHADER. OpenGL creates each shader object (initially empty), and returns an integer ID for each that is an index for referencing it later— our code stores this ID in the variables vShader and fShader. It then calls glShader-Source(), which loads the GLSL code from the strings into the empty shader objects. The shaders are then each compiled using glCompileShader(). glShaderSource() has four parameters: (a) the shader object in which to store the shader, (b) the number of strings in the shader source code, (c) an array of pointers to strings containing the source code, and (d) an additional parameter we aren't using (it will be explained later, in the supplementary chapter notes). Note that the two calls specify the number of lines of code in each shader as being "1"—this too is explained in the supplementary notes.

The application then creates a *program* object named vfProgram, and saves the integer ID that points to it. An OpenGL "program" object contains a series of compiled shaders, and here we see the following commands: glCreateProgram() to create the program object, glAttachShader() to attach each of the shaders to it, and then glLinkProgram() to request that the GLSL compiler ensure that they are compatible.

As we saw earlier, after init() finishes, display() is called. One of the first things display() does is call glUseProgram(), which loads the program containing the two compiled shaders into the OpenGL pipeline stages (onto the GPU!). Note that glUseProgram() *doesn't run the shaders*, it just loads them onto the hardware.

As we will see later in Chapter 4, ordinarily at this point the C++/OpenGL program would prepare the vertices of the model being drawn for sending down the pipeline. But not in this case, because for our first shader program we simply hardcoded a single vertex in the vertex shader. Therefore in this example the display() function next proceeds to the glDrawArrays() call, which initiates pipeline processing. The primitive type is GL_POINTS, and there is just one point to display.

Now let's look at the shaders themselves, shown in green earlier (and duplicated in the explanations that follow). As we saw, they have been declared in the C++/OpenGL program as arrays of strings. This is a clumsy way to code, but it is sufficient in this very simple case. The vertex shader is:

```
#version 430
void main(void)
{   gl_Position = vec4(0.0,  0.0,  0.0,  1.0); }
```

The first line indicates the OpenGL version, in this case 4.3. There follows a "main" function (as we will see, GLSL is somewhat C++-like in syntax). The primary purpose of any vertex shader is to send a vertex down the pipeline (which, as mentioned before, it does for every vertex). The built-in variable gl_Position is used to set a vertex's coordinate position in 3D space, and is sent to the next stage in the pipeline. The GLSL datatype vec4 is used to hold a 4-tuple, suitable for such coordinates, with the associated four values representing X, Y, Z, and a fourth value set here to 1.0 (we will learn the purpose of this fourth value in Chapter 3). In this case, the vertex is hardcoded to the origin location (0,0,0).

The vertices move through the pipeline to the *rasterizer*, where they are transformed into pixel locations (or more accurately *fragments*—this is described later). Eventually, these pixels (fragments) reach the fragment shader:

```
#version 430
out vec4 color;
void main(void)
{   color = vec4(0.0,  0.0,  1.0,  1.0); }
```

The purpose of any fragment shader is to set the RGB color of a pixel to be displayed. In this case the specified output color (0, 0, 1) is blue (the fourth value 1.0 specifies the level of opacity). Note the "out" tag indicating that the variable color is an output. (It wasn't necessary to specify an "out" tag for gl_Position in the vertex shader, because gl_Position is a predefined output variable.)

There is one detail in the code that we haven't discussed, in the last two lines in the init() function (shown in red). They probably appear a bit cryptic. As we will see in Chapter 4, when sets of data are prepared for sending down the pipeline, they are organized into *buffers*. Those buffers are in turn organized into *Vertex Array Objects* (VAOs). In our example, we hardcoded a single point in the vertex shader, so we didn't need any buffers. However, OpenGL still requires that at least one VAO be created whenever shaders are being used, even if the application isn't using any buffers. So the two lines create the required VAO.

Finally, there is the issue of how the *vertex* that came out of the vertex shader became a *pixel* in the fragment shader. Recall from Figure 2.2 that between vertex processing and pixel processing is the *rasterization* stage. It is there that primitives (such as points or triangles) are converted into sets of pixels. The default size of an OpenGL "point" is one pixel, so that is why our single point was rendered as a single pixel.

Let's add the following command in display(), right before the glDrawArrays() call:

glPointSize(30.0f);

Now, when the rasterizer receives the vertex from the vertex shader, it will set pixel color values that form a point having a size of 30 pixels. The resulting output is shown in Figure 2.5.

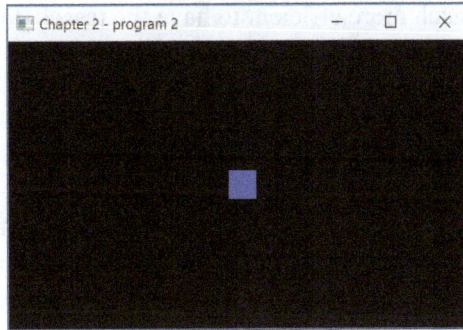

Figure 2.5
Changing glPointSize.

Let's now continue examining the remainder of the OpenGL pipeline.

2.1.3 Tessellation

We cover tessellation in Chapter 12. The programmable tessellation stage is one of the most recent additions to OpenGL (in version 4.0). It provides a *tessellator* that can generate a large number of triangles, typically as a grid, and also some tools to manipulate those triangles in a variety of ways. For example, the programmer might manipulate a tessellated grid of triangles as shown in Figure 2.6.

Tessellation is useful when a lot of vertices are needed on what is otherwise a simple shape, such as on a square area or curved surface. It is also very useful for generating complex terrain, as we will see later. In such instances, it is sometimes

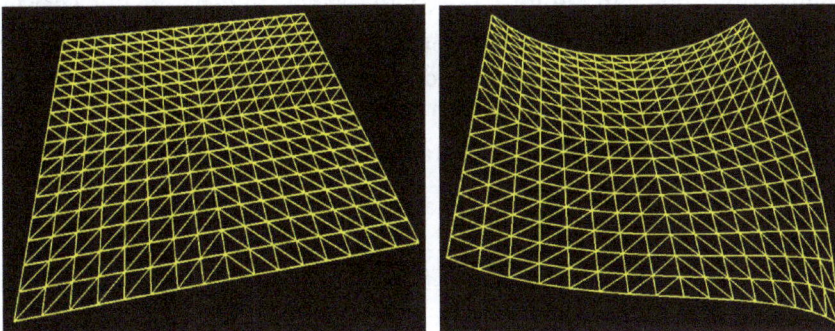

Figure 2.6
Grid produced by tessellator.

much more efficient to have the tessellator in the GPU generate the triangle mesh in hardware, rather than doing it in C++.

2.1.4 Geometry Shader

We cover the geometry shader stage in Chapter 13. Whereas the *vertex shader* gives the programmer the ability to manipulate one *vertex* at a time (i.e., "per-vertex" processing), and the *fragment shader* (as we will see) allows manipulating one *pixel* at a time ("per-fragment" processing), the *geometry shader* provides the capability to manipulate one *primitive* at a time—"per-primitive" processing.

Recalling that the most common primitive is the *triangle*, by the time we have reached the geometry stage, the pipeline must have completed grouping the vertices into triangles (a process called *primitive assembly*). The geometry shader then makes all three vertices in each triangle accessible to the programmer simultaneously.

There are a number of uses for per-primitive processing. The primitives could be altered, such as by stretching or shrinking them. Some of the primitives could be deleted, thus putting "holes" in the object being rendered—this is one way of turning a simple model into a more complex one.

The geometry shader also provides a mechanism for generating additional primitives. Here too, this opens the door to many possibilities for turning simple models into more complex ones.

An interesting use for the geometry shader is for adding surface texture such as bumps or scales—even "hair" or "fur"—to an object. Consider for example the simple torus shown in Figure 2.7 (we will see how to generate this later in the book). The surface of this torus is built out of many hundreds of triangles. If at each triangle we use a geometry shader to add additional triangles that face outward, we get the result shown in Figure 2.8. This "scaly torus" would be computation-ally expensive to try and model from scratch in the C++/OpenGL application side.

It might seem redundant to provide a per-primitive shader stage when the tes-sellation stage(s) give the programmer access to *all* of the vertices in an entire model simultaneously. The difference is that tessellation only offers this capability in very limited circumstances—specifically when the model is a grid of triangles generated by the tessellator. It does not provide such simultaneous access to all the vertices of, say, an arbitrary model being sent in from C++ through a buffer.

Figure 2.7
Torus model.

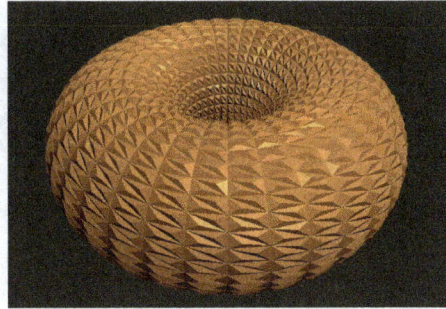

Figure 2.8
Torus modified in geometry shader.

2.1.5 Rasterization

Ultimately, our 3D world of vertices, triangles, colors, and so on needs to be displayed on a 2D monitor. That 2D monitor screen is made up of a *raster*—a rectangular array of pixels.

When a 3D object is *rasterized*, OpenGL converts the primitives in the object (usually triangles) into *fragments*. A fragment holds the information associated with a pixel. Rasterization determines the locations of pixels that need to be drawn in order to produce the triangle specified by its three vertices.

Rasterization starts by interpolating, pairwise, between the three vertices of the triangle. There are some options for doing this interpolation; for now it is sufficient to consider simple linear interpolation as shown in Figure 2.9. The original three vertices are shown in red.

If rasterization were to stop here, the resulting image would appear as wireframe. This is an option in OpenGL, by adding the following command in the display() function, before the call to glDrawArrays():

glPolygonMode(GL_FRONT_AND_BACK,
      GL_LINE);

If the torus shown previously in Section 2.1.4 is rendered with the addition of this line of code, it appears as shown in Figure 2.10.

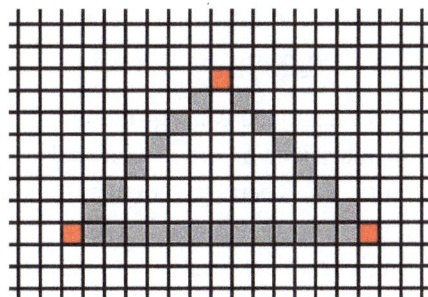

Figure 2.9
Rasterization (step 1).

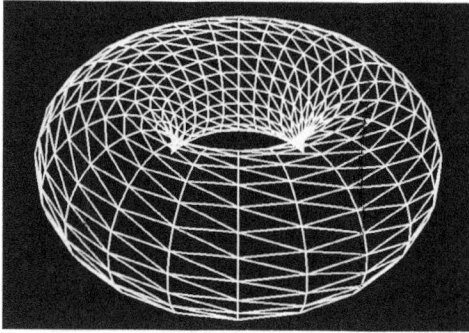

Figure 2.10
Torus with wireframe rendering.

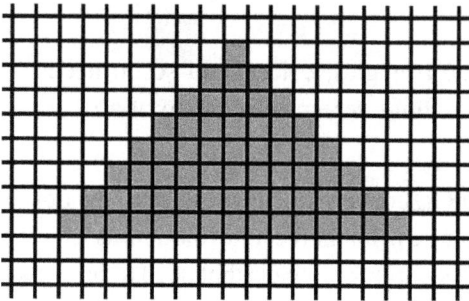

Figure 2.11
Fully rasterized triangle.

If we didn't insert the preceding line of code (or if GL_FILL had been specified instead of GL_LINE), interpolation would continue along raster lines and fill the interior of the triangle, as shown in Figure 2.11. When applied to the torus, this results in the fully rasterized or "solid" torus shown in Figure 2.12 (on the left). Note that in this case the overall shape and curvature of the torus is not evident—that is because we haven't included any texturing or lighting techniques, so it appears "flat." At the right, the same "flat" torus is shown with the wireframe rendering superimposed. The torus shown earlier in Figure 2.7 included lighting effects, and thus revealed the shape of the torus much more clearly. We will study lighting in Chapter 7.

As we will see in later chapters, the rasterizer can interpolate more than just pixels. *Any* variable that is output by the vertex shader and input by the fragment shader will be interpolated based on the corresponding pixel position. We will use this capability to generate smooth color gradations, achieve realistic lighting, and many more effects.

2.1.6 Fragment Shader

As mentioned earlier, the purpose of the fragment shader is to assign colors to the rasterized pixels. We have already seen an example of a fragment shader in Program 2.2. There, the fragment shader simply hardcoded its output to a specific value, so every generated pixel had the same color. However, GLSL affords us virtually limitless creativity to calculate colors in other ways.

One simple example would be to base the output color of a pixel on its location. Recall that in the vertex shader, the outgoing coordinates of a vertex are

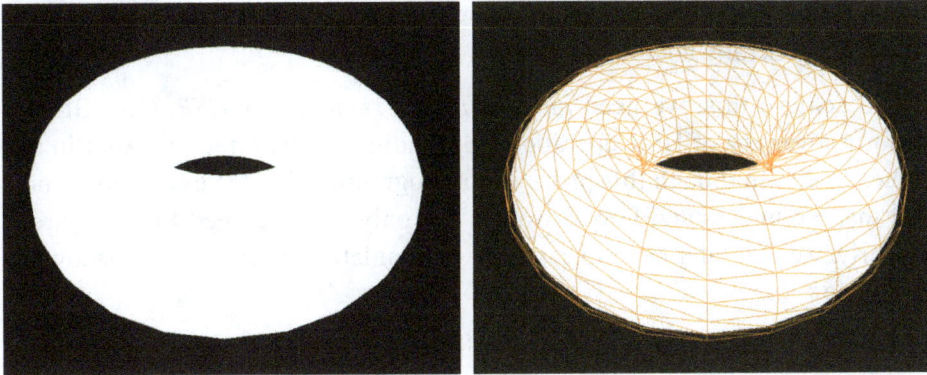

Figure 2.12
Torus with fully rasterized primitives (left), and with wireframe grid superimposed (right).

specified using the predefined variable gl_Position. In the fragment shader, there is a similar variable available to the programmer for accessing the coordinates of an incoming *fragment*, called gl_FragCoord. We can modify the fragment shader from Program 2.2 so that it uses gl_FragCoord (in this case referencing its x component using the GLSL *field selector* notation) to set each pixel's color based on its location, as shown here:

```
#version 430
out vec4 color;
void main(void)
{   if (gl_FragCoord.x < 295) color = vec4(1.0, 0.0, 0.0, 1.0); else color = vec4(0.0, 0.0, 1.0, 1.0);
}
```

Assuming that we increase the GL_PointSize as we did at the end of Section 2.1.2, the pixel colors will now vary across the rendered point—red where the x coordinates are less than 200, and blue otherwise, as seen in Figure 2.13.

2.1.7 Pixel Operations

As objects in our scene are drawn in the display() function using the glDrawArrays() command, we usually expect objects in front to block our view of objects behind them. This

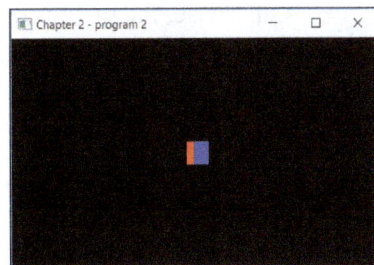

Figure 2.13
Fragment shader color variation.

also extends to the objects themselves, wherein we expect to see the front of an object, but generally not the back.

To achieve this, we need *hidden surface removal*, or *HSR*. OpenGL can perform a variety of HSR operations, depending on the effect we want in our scene. And even though this phase is not programmable, it is extremely important that we understand how it works. Not only will we need to configure it properly, we will later need to carefully manipulate it when we add shadows to our scene.

Hidden surface removal is accomplished by OpenGL through the cleverly coordinated use of two buffers: the *color buffer* (which we have discussed previously), and the *depth buffer* (sometimes called the *Z-buffer*). Both of these buffers are the same size as the raster—that is, there is an entry in each buffer for every pixel on the screen.

As various objects are drawn in a scene, pixel colors are generated by the fragment shader. The pixel colors are placed in the color buffer—it is the color buffer that is ultimately written to the screen. When multiple objects occupy some of the same pixels in the color buffer, a determination must be made as to which pixel color(s) are retained, based on which object is nearest the viewer.

Hidden surface removal is done as follows:

- Before a scene is rendered, the depth buffer is filled with values representing maximum depth.
- As a pixel color is output by the fragment shader, its distance from the viewer is calculated.
- If the computed distance is *less than* the distance stored in the depth buffer (for that pixel), then: (a) the pixel color replaces the color in the color buffer, and (b) the distance replaces the value in the depth buffer. Otherwise, the pixel is discarded.

This procedure is called the *Z-buffer algorithm*, as expressed in Figure 2.14.

2.2 ■ DETECTING OPENGL AND GLSL ERRORS

The workflow for compiling and running GLSL code differs from standard coding, in that *GLSL compilation happens at C++ runtime*. Another complication is that GLSL code doesn't run on the CPU (it runs on the GPU), so *the operating*

```
Color [ ] [ ] colorBuf = new Color [pixelRows][pixelCols];
double [ ] [ ] depthBuf = new double [pixelRows][pixelCols];
for (each row and column)   // initialize color and depth buffers
{    colorBuf [row][col] = backgroundColor;
     depthBuf [row][col] = far away;
}

for (each shape)      // update buffers when new pixel is closer
{    for (each pixel in the shape)
     {    if (depth at pixel < depthBuf value)
          {    depthBuf [pixel.row][pixel.col] = depth at pixel;
               colorBuf [pixel.row][pixel.col] = color at pixel;
}   }   }
return colorBuf;
```

Figure 2.14
Z-buffer algorithm.

system cannot always catch OpenGL runtime errors. This makes debugging difficult, because it is often hard to detect if a shader failed, and why.

Program 2.3 (which follows) presents some modules for catching and displaying GLSL errors. They make use of the OpenGL functions glGetShaderiv() and glGetProgramiv(), which are used to provide information about compiled GLSL shaders and programs. Accompanying them is the createShaderProgram() function from the previous Program 2.2, but with the error-detecting calls added.

Program 2.3 contains the following three utilities:

- **checkOpenGLError** – checks the OpenGL error flag for the occurrence of an OpenGL error
- **printShaderLog** – displays the contents of OpenGL's log when GLSL compilation failed
- **printProgramLog** – displays the contents of OpenGL's log when GLSL linking failed

The first, checkOpenGLError(), is useful for detecting both GLSL compilation errors and OpenGL runtime errors, so it is highly recommended to use it throughout a C++/OpenGL application during development. For example, in the prior example (Program 2.2), the calls to glCompileShader() and glLinkProgram() could easily be augmented with the code shown in Program 2.3 to ensure that any typos or other compile errors would be caught and their cause reported. Calls to checkOpenGLError() could be added after runtime OpenGL calls, such as immediately after the call to glDrawArrays().

Another reason that it is important to use these tools is that *a GLSL error does not cause the C++ program to stop.* So unless the programmer takes steps to catch errors at the point that they happen, debugging will be very difficult.

Program 2.3 Modules to Catch GLSL Errors

```
void printShaderLog(GLuint shader) {
    int len = 0;
    int chWrittn = 0;
    char *log;
    glGetShaderiv(shader, GL_INFO_LOG_LENGTH, &len);
    if (len > 0) {
        log = (char *)malloc(len);
        glGetShaderInfoLog(shader, len, &chWrittn, log);
        cout << "Shader Info Log: " << log << endl;
        free(log);
    } }

void printProgramLog(int prog) {
    int len = 0;
    int chWrittn = 0;
    char *log;
    glGetProgramiv(prog, GL_INFO_LOG_LENGTH, &len);
    if (len > 0) {
        log = (char *)malloc(len);
        glGetProgramInfoLog(prog, len, &chWrittn, log);
        cout << "Program Info Log: " << log << endl;
        free(log);
    } }

bool checkOpenGLError() {
    bool foundError = false;
    int glErr = glGetError();
    while (glErr != GL_NO_ERROR) {
        cout << "glError: " << glErr << endl;
        foundError = true;
        glErr = glGetError();
    }
    return foundError;
}
```

Example of checking for OpenGL errors:

```
GLuint createShaderProgram() {
    GLint vertCompiled;
    GLint fragCompiled;
    GLint linked;
    . . .
    // catch errors while compiling shaders

    glCompileShader(vShader);
    checkOpenGLError();
    glGetShaderiv(vShader, GL_COMPILE_STATUS, &vertCompiled);
    if (vertCompiled != 1) {
        cout << "vertex compilation failed" << endl;
        printShaderLog(vShader);
    }

    glCompileShader(fShader);
    checkOpenGLError();
    glGetShaderiv(fShader, GL_COMPILE_STATUS, &fragCompiled);
    if (fragCompiled != 1) {
        cout << "fragment compilation failed" << endl;
        printShaderLog(fShader);
    }

    // catch errors while linking shaders

    glAttachShader(vfProgram, vShader);
    glAttachShader(vfProgram, fShader);

    glLinkProgram(vfProgram);
    checkOpenGLError();
    glGetProgramiv(vfProgram, GL_LINK_STATUS, &linked);
    if (linked != 1) {
        cout << "linking failed" << endl;
        printProgramLog(vfProgram);
    }
    return vfProgram;
}
```

There are other tricks for deducing the causes of runtime errors in shader code. A common result of shader runtime errors is for the output screen to be completely blank, essentially with no output at all. This can happen even if the error is a very small typo in a shader, yet it can be difficult to tell at which stage of the pipeline the error occurred. With no output at all, it's like looking for a needle in a haystack.

One useful trick in such cases is to temporarily replace the fragment shader with the one shown in Program 2.2. Recall that in that example, the fragment shader simply output a particular color—solid blue, for example. If the subsequent output is of the correct geometric form (but solid blue), the vertex shader is probably correct, and there is an error in the original fragment shader. If the output is still a blank screen, the error is more likely earlier in the pipeline, such as in the vertex shader.

In Appendix C, we show how to use yet another useful debugging tool called *Nsight*, which is available for machines equipped with certain Nvidia graphics cards.

2.3 ■ READING GLSL SOURCE CODE FROM FILES

So far, our GLSL shader code has been stored inline in strings. As our programs grow in complexity, this will become impractical. We should instead store our shader code in files and read them in.

Reading text files is a basic C++ skill, and won't be covered here. However, for practicality, code to read shaders is provided in readShaderSource(), shown in Program 2.4. It reads the shader text file and returns an array of strings, where each string is one line of text from the file. It then determines the size of that array based on how many lines were read in. Note that here, createShaderProgram() replaces the version from Program 2.2.

In this example, the vertex and fragment shader code is now placed in the text files "vertShader.glsl" and "fragShader.glsl" respectively.

Program 2.4 Reading GLSL Source from Files

(....#includes same as before, main(), display(), init() as before, plus the following...)

```
#include <string>
#include <iostream>
#include <fstream>

. . .

string readShaderSource(const char *filePath) {
    string content;
    ifstream fileStream(filePath, ios::in);
    string line = "";
```

```
    while (!fileStream.eof()) {
        getline(fileStream, line);
        content.append(line + "\n");
    }
    fileStream.close();
    return content;
}
GLuint createShaderProgram() {
    (...... as before plus....)
    string vertShaderStr = readShaderSource("vertShader.glsl");
    string fragShaderStr = readShaderSource("fragShader.glsl");

    const char *vertShaderSrc = vertShaderStr.c_str();
    const char *fragShaderSrc = fragShaderStr.c_str();

    glShaderSource(vShader, 1, &vertShaderSrc, NULL);
    glShaderSource(fShader, 1, &fragShaderSrc, NULL);

    (....etc., building rendering program as before)
}
```

2.4 ■ BUILDING OBJECTS FROM VERTICES

Ultimately we want to draw more than just a single point. We'd like to draw objects that are constructed of *many* vertices. Large sections of this book will be devoted to this topic. For now we just start with a simple example—we will define *three* vertices and use them to draw a *triangle*.

We can do this by making two small changes to Program 2.2 (actually, the version in Program 2.4 which reads the shaders from files): (a) modify the vertex shader so that *three different* vertices are output to the subsequent stages of the pipeline, and (b) modify the glDrawArrays() call to specify that we are using *three* vertices.

In the C++/OpenGL application (specifically in the glDrawArrays() call) we specify GL_TRIANGLES (rather than GL_POINTS), and also specify that there are *three* vertices sent through the pipeline. This causes the vertex shader to run *three times*, and at each iteration, the built-in variable gl_VertexID is automatically incremented (it is initially set to 0). By testing the value of gl_VertexID, the shader is designed to output a different point each of the three times it is executed. Recall that the three points then pass through the *rasterization* stage, producing a filled-in triangle. The modifications are shown in Program 2.5 (the remainder of the code is the same as previously shown in Program 2.4).

Program 2.5 Drawing a Triangle

Vertex Shader

```
#version 430
void main(void)
{   if (gl_VertexID == 0) gl_Position = vec4( 0.25, -0.25, 0.0, 1.0);
    else if (gl_VertexID == 1) gl_Position = vec4(-0.25, -0.25, 0.0, 1.0);
    else gl_Position = vec4( 0.25, 0.25, 0.0, 1.0);
}
```

C++/OpenGL application—in display()

```
. . .
glDrawArrays(GL_TRIANGLES, 0, 3);
```

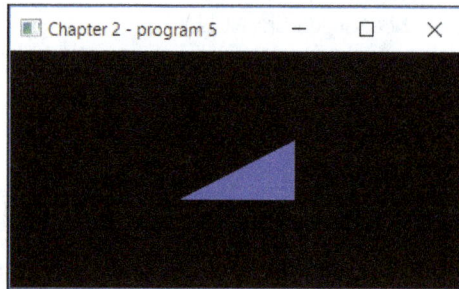

Figure 2.15
Drawing a simple triangle.

2.5 ANIMATING A SCENE

Many of the techniques in this book can be *animated*. This is when things in the scene are moving or changing, and the scene is rendered repeatedly to reflect these changes in real time.

Recall from Section 2.1.1 that we have constructed our main() to make a single call to init(), and then to call display() repeatedly. Thus, while each of the preceding examples may have appeared to be a single fixed rendered scene, in actuality the loop in the main was causing it to be drawn over and over again.

For this reason, our main() is already structured to support animation. We simply design our display() function to alter what it draws over time. Each rendering of our scene is then called a *frame*, and the frequency of the calls to display() is the *frame rate*. Handling the rate of movement within the application logic can be controlled using the elapsed time since the previous frame (this is the reason for including "currentTime" as a parameter on the display() function).

An example is shown in Program 2.6. We have taken the triangle from Program 2.5 and animated it so that it moves to the right, then moves to the left, back and forth. In this example, we don't consider the elapsed time, so the triangle may move more or less quickly depending on the speed of the computer. In future examples, we will use the elapsed time to ensure that our animations run at the same speed regardless of the computer on which they are run.

In Program 2.6, the application's display() method maintains a variable "x" used to offset the triangle's X coordinate position. Its value changes each time display() is called (and thus is different for each frame), and it reverses direction each time it reaches 1.0 or -1.0. The value in x is copied to a corresponding variable called "offset" in the vertex shader. The mechanism that performs this copy uses something called a *uniform variable*, which we will study later in Chapter 4. It isn't necessary to understand the details of uniform variables yet. For now, just note that the C++/OpenGL application first calls glGetUniformLocation() to get a pointer to the "offset" variable, and then calls glProgramUniform1f() to copy the value of x into offset. The vertex shader then adds the offset to the X coordinate of the triangle being drawn. Note also that the background is cleared at each call to display(), to avoid the triangle leaving a trail as it moves. Figure 2.16 illustrates the display at three time instances (of course, the movement can't be shown in a still figure).

Program 2.6 Simple Animation Example

C++/OpenGL application:

```
//  same #includes and declarations as before, plus the following:

float x = 0.0f;              // location of triangle on x axis
float inc = 0.01f;           // offset for moving the triangle

void display(GLFWwindow* window, double currentTime) {
    glClear(GL_DEPTH_BUFFER_BIT);
    glClearColor(0.0, 0.0, 0.0, 1.0);
    glClear(GL_COLOR_BUFFER_BIT);          // clear the background to black, each time

    glUseProgram(renderingProgram);

    x += inc;                              // move the triangle along x axis
    if (x > 1.0f) inc = -0.01f;            // switch to moving the triangle to the left
```

```
    if (x < -1.0f) inc = 0.01f;                              // switch to moving the triangle to the right
    GLuint offsetLoc = glGetUniformLocation(renderingProgram, "offset");    // get ptr to "offset"
    glProgramUniform1f(renderingProgram, offsetLoc, x);                     // send value in "x" to "offset"

    glDrawArrays(GL_TRIANGLES,0,3);
  }
  ... // remaining functions, same as before
}
```

Vertex shader:

```
#version 430
uniform float offset;
void main(void)
{   if (gl_VertexID == 0) gl_Position = vec4( 0.25 + offset, -0.25, 0.0, 1.0);
    else if (gl_VertexID == 1) gl_Position = vec4(-0.25 + offset, -0.25, 0.0, 1.0);
    else gl_Position = vec4( 0.25 + offset, 0.25, 0.0, 1.0);
}
```

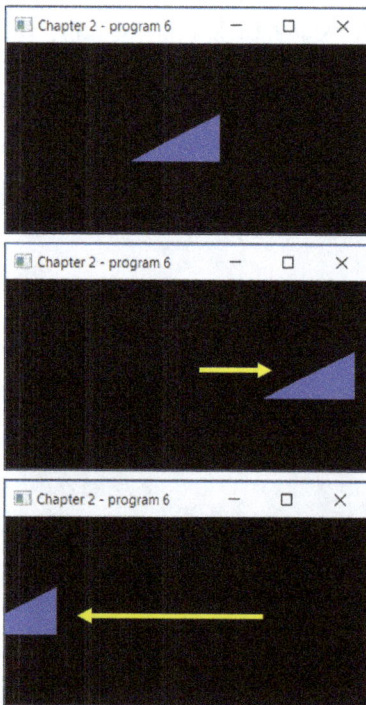

Figure 2.16
An animated, moving triangle.

Note that in addition to adding code to animate the triangle, we have also added the following line at the beginning of the display() function:

```
glClear(GL_DEPTH_BUFFER_BIT);
```

While not strictly necessary in this particular example, we have added it here and it will continue to appear in most of our applications. Recall from the discussion in Section 2.1.7 that *hidden surface removal* requires both a color buffer and a depth buffer. As we proceed to drawing progressively more complex 3D scenes, it will be necessary to initialize (clear) the depth buffer each frame, especially for scenes that are animated, to ensure that depth comparisons aren't affected by old depth data. It should be apparent from the previous example that the command for clearing the depth buffer is essentially the same as for clearing the color buffer.

2.6 ORGANIZING THE C++ CODE FILES

So far, we have been placing all of the C++/OpenGL application code in a single file called "main.cpp", and the GLSL shaders into files called "vertShader. glsl" and "fragShader.glsl". While we admit that stuffing a lot of application code into main.cpp isn't a best practice, we have adopted this convention in this book so that it is absolutely clear in every example which file contains the main block of C++/OpenGL code relevant to the example being discussed. Throughout this text-book, it will always be called "main.cpp". In practice, applications should of course be modularized to appropriately reflect the tasks performed by the application.

However, as we proceed, there will be circumstances in which we create mod-ules that will be useful in many different applications. Wherever appropriate, we will move those modules into separate files to facilitate reuse. For example, later we will define a Sphere class that will be useful in many different examples, and so it will be separated into its own files (Sphere.cpp and Sphere.h).

Similarly, as we encounter *functions* that we wish to reuse, we will place them in a file called "Utils.cpp" (and an associated "Utils.h"). We have already seen several functions that are appropriate to move into "Utils.cpp": the error-detecting modules described in Section 2.2, and the functions for reading in GLSL shader programs described in Section 2.3. The latter is particularly well-suited to overloading, such that a "createShaderProgram()" function can be defined for each possible combina-tion of pipeline shaders assembled in a given application:

- GLuint Utils::createShaderProgram(const char *vp, const char *fp)
- GLuint Utils::createShaderProgram(const char *vp, const char *gp, const char *fp)
- GLuint Utils::createShaderProgram(const char *vp, const char *tCS, const char* tES, const char *fp)
- GLuint Utils::createShaderProgram(const char *vp, const char *tCS, const char* tES, const char *gp, const char *fp)

The first case in the previous list supports shader programs which utilize only a vertex and fragment shader. The second supports those utilizing vertex, geometry, and fragment shaders. The third supports those using vertex, tessellation, and fragment shaders. The fourth supports those using vertex, tessellation, geometry, and fragment shaders. The parameters accepted in each case are pathnames for the GLSL files containing the shader code. For example, the following call uses one of the overloaded functions to compile and link a shader pipeline program that includes a vertex and fragment shader. The completed program is placed in the variable "renderingProgram":

```
renderingProgram = Utils::createShaderProgram("vertShader.glsl", "fragShader.glsl");
```

These createShaderProgram() implementations can all be found in the companion files (specifically in the "Utils.cpp" file), and all of them incorporate the error-detecting modules from Section 2.2 as well. There is nothing new about them; they are simply organized in this way for convenience. As we move forward in the book, other similar functions will be added to Utils.cpp as we go along. The reader is strongly encouraged to examine the Utils.cpp file in the companion files, and even add to it as desired. The programs found there are built from the methods as we learn them in the book, and studying their organization should serve to strengthen one's own understanding.

Regarding the functions in the "Utils.cpp" file, we have implemented them as static methods so that it isn't necessary to instantiate the Utils class. Readers may prefer to implement them as instance methods rather than static methods, or even as freestanding functions, depending on the architecture of the particular system being developed.

All of our shaders will be named with a ".glsl" extension.

SUPPLEMENTAL NOTES

There are many details of the OpenGL pipeline that we have not discussed in this introductory chapter. We have skipped a number of internal stages and have completely omitted how *textures* are processed. Our goal was to map out, as simply as possible, the framework in which we will be writing our code. As we proceed we will continue to learn additional details.

We have also deferred presenting code examples for tessellation and geometry. In later chapters, we will build complete systems that show how to write practical shaders for each of the stages.

There are more sophisticated ways to organize the code for animating a scene, especially with respect to managing threads. Some language bindings such as JOGL and LWJGL (for Java) offer classes to support animation. Readers interested in designing a render loop (or "game loop") appropriate for a particular application are encouraged to consult some of the more specialized books on game engine design (e.g., [NY14]), and to peruse the related discussions on gamedev.net [GD23].

We glossed over one detail on the glShaderSource() command. The fourth parameter is used to specify a "lengths array" that contains the integer string lengths of each line of code in the given shader program. If this parameter is set to null, as we have done, OpenGL will build this array automatically if the strings are null-terminated. While we have been careful to ensure that our strings sent to glShaderSource() are null-terminated (by calling the c_str() function in createShaderProgram()), it is not uncommon to encounter applications that build these arrays manually rather than sending null.

Throughout this book, the reader may at times wish to know one or more of OpenGL's upper limits. For example, the programmer might need to know the maximum number of outputs that can be produced by the geometry shader, or the maximum size that can be specified for rendering a point. Many such values are implementation-dependent, meaning that they can vary between different machines. OpenGL provides a mechanism for retrieving such limits using the glGet() command, which takes various forms depending on the type of the parameter being queried. For example, to find the maximum allowable point size, the following call will place the minimum and maximum values (for your machine's OpenGL implementation) into the first two elements of the float array named "size":

glGetFloatv(GL_POINT_SIZE_RANGE, size)

Many such queries are possible. Consult the OpenGL reference [OP22] documentation for examples.

In this chapter, we have tried to describe each parameter on each OpenGL call. However, as the book proceeds, this will become unwieldy and we will sometimes not bother describing a parameter when we believe that doing so would complicate matters unnecessarily. This is because many OpenGL functions have a large number of parameters that are irrelevant to our examples. The reader should get used to using the OpenGL documentation to fill in such details when necessary.

Exercises

2.1 Modify Program 2.2 to add animation that causes the drawn point to grow and shrink, in a cycle. Hint: use the glPointSize() function, with a variable as the parameter.

2.2 Modify Program 2.5 so that it draws an isosceles triangle (rather than the right triangle shown in Figure 2.15).

2.3 *(PROJECT)* Modify Program 2.5 to include the error-checking modules shown in Program 2.3. After you have that working, try inserting various errors into the shaders and observing both the resulting behavior and the error messages generated.

2.4 Modify Program 2.6 so that it calculates the amount of movement for the triangle using the "currentTime" variable passed into the display() function. Hint: the "currentTime" variable contains the total time that has elapsed since the program began. Your solution will need to determine the time that has elapsed since the last frame, and compute the increment amount based on that. Computing animations in this way will ensure that they move at the same speed regardless of the speed of the computer.

References

[GD23] Game Development Network, accessed November 2023, https://www.gamedev.net/

[NY14] R. Nystrom, "Game Loop," in *Game Programming Patterns* (Genever Benning, 2014), and accessed November 2023, http://gameprogrammingpatterns.com/game-loop.html

[OP22] OpenGL 4.5 Reference Pages, accessed November 2023, https://registry.khronos.org/OpenGL-Refpages/gl4/

[SW15] G. Sellers, R. Wright Jr., and N. Haemel, *OpenGL SuperBible: Comprehensive Tutorial and Reference*, 7th ed. (Addison-Wesley, 2015).

MATHEMATICAL FOUNDATIONS

Computer graphics makes heavy use of mathematics, particularly matrices and matrix algebra. Although we tend to consider 3D graphics programming to be among the most contemporary of technical fields (and in many respects it is), many of the techniques that are used actually date back hundreds of years. Some of them were first understood and codified by the great philosophers of the Renaissance era.

Virtually every facet of 3D graphics, every effect—movement, scale, perspective, texturing, lighting, shadows, and so on—will be accomplished largely mathematically. Therefore, this chapter lays the groundwork upon which every subsequent chapter relies.

It is assumed the reader has a basic knowledge of matrix operations; a full coverage of basic matrix algebra is beyond the scope of this text. Therefore, if at any point a particular matrix operation is unfamiliar, it may be necessary to do some supplementary background reading to ensure full understanding before proceeding.

3.1 3D COORDINATE SYSTEMS

3D space is generally represented with three axes: X, Y, and Z. The three axes can be arranged into two configurations, *right-handed* or *left-handed*. (The name derives from the orientation of the axes as if constructed by pointing the thumb and first two fingers of the right versus the left hand, at right angles.)

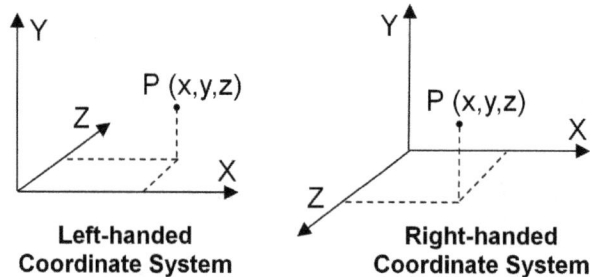

Figure 3.1
3D coordinate systems.

It is important to know which coordinate system your graphics programming environment uses. For example, the majority of coordinate systems in OpenGL are right-handed, whereas in Direct3D the majority are left-handed. Throughout this book, we will assume a right-handed configuration unless otherwise stated.

3.2 POINTS

Points in 3D space can be specified by listing the X, Y, Z values, using a notation such as (2, 8, -3). However, it turns out to be much more useful to specify points using *homogeneous* notation, a representation first described in the early 1800s. Points in homogeneous notation contain four values. The first three correspond to X, Y, and Z, and the fourth, W, is always a fixed nonzero value, usually 1. Thus, we represent this point as (2, 8, -3, 1). As we will see shortly, homogeneous notation will make many of our graphics computations more efficient.

The appropriate GLSL data type for storing points in homogeneous 3D notation is vec4 ("vec" refers to *vector*, but it can also be used for a point). The GLM library includes classes appropriate for creating and storing 3-element and 4-element (homogeneous) points in the C++/OpenGL application, called vec3 and vec4 respectively.

3.3 ■ MATRICES

A *matrix* is a rectangular array of values, and its elements are typically accessed by means of subscripts. The first subscript refers to the row number, and the second subscript refers to the column number, with the subscripts starting at 0. Most of the matrices that we will use for 3D graphics computations are of size 4x4, as shown in Figure 3.2:

$$\begin{bmatrix} A_{00} & A_{01} & A_{02} & A_{03} \\ A_{10} & A_{11} & A_{12} & A_{13} \\ A_{20} & A_{21} & A_{22} & A_{23} \\ A_{30} & A_{31} & A_{32} & A_{33} \end{bmatrix}$$

Figure 3.2
4x4 matrix.

The GLSL language includes a data type called mat4 that can be used for storing 4x4 matrices. Similarly, GLM includes a *class* called mat4 for instantiating and storing 4x4 matrices.

The *identity matrix* contains all zeros, with ones along the diagonal:

$$\begin{bmatrix} 1 & 0 & 0 & 0 \\ 0 & 1 & 0 & 0 \\ 0 & 0 & 1 & 0 \\ 0 & 0 & 0 & 1 \end{bmatrix}$$

Any point or matrix multiplied by the identity matrix is unchanged. In GLM, the constructor call glm::mat4 m(1.0f) builds the identity matrix in the variable m.

The *transpose* of a matrix is computed by interchanging its rows and columns. For example:

$$\begin{bmatrix} A_{00} & A_{01} & A_{02} & A_{03} \\ A_{10} & A_{11} & A_{12} & A_{13} \\ A_{20} & A_{21} & A_{22} & A_{23} \\ A_{30} & A_{31} & A_{32} & A_{33} \end{bmatrix} = \begin{bmatrix} A_{00} & A_{10} & A_{20} & A_{30} \\ A_{01} & A_{11} & A_{21} & A_{31} \\ A_{02} & A_{12} & A_{22} & A_{32} \\ A_{03} & A_{13} & A_{23} & A_{33} \end{bmatrix}^T$$

The GLM library and GLSL both have transpose functions: glm::transpose(mat4) and transpose(mat4) respectively.

Matrix addition is straightforward:

$$
\begin{bmatrix} A+a & B+b & C+c & D+d \\ E+e & F+f & G+g & H+h \\ I+i & J+j & K+k & L+l \\ M+m & N+n & O+o & P+p \end{bmatrix} = \begin{bmatrix} A & B & C & D \\ E & F & G & H \\ I & J & K & L \\ M & N & O & P \end{bmatrix} + \begin{bmatrix} a & b & c & d \\ e & f & g & h \\ i & j & k & l \\ m & n & o & p \end{bmatrix}
$$

In GLSL the **+** operator is overloaded on mat4 to support matrix addition.

There are various multiplication operations that can be done with matrices that are useful in 3D graphics. Matrix multiplication in general can be done either *left to right* or *right to left* (note that since these operations are different, it follows that matrix multiplication is not commutative). Most of the time we will use right-to-left multiplication.

In 3D graphics, multiplying a point by a matrix is in most cases done right to left, and produces a point, as follows:

$$
\begin{pmatrix} AX + BY + CZ + D \\ EX + FY + GZ + H \\ IX + JY + KZ + L \\ MX + NY + OZ + P \end{pmatrix} = \begin{bmatrix} A & B & C & D \\ E & F & G & H \\ I & J & K & L \\ M & N & O & P \end{bmatrix} * \begin{pmatrix} X \\ Y \\ Z \\ 1 \end{pmatrix}
$$

Note that we represent the point (X,Y,Z) in homogeneous notation as a 1-column matrix.

GLSL and GLM both support multiplying a point (a vec4, to be exact) by a matrix with the * operator.

Multiplying a 4x4 Matrix by another 4x4 matrix is done as follows:

$$
\begin{bmatrix} A & B & C & D \\ E & F & G & H \\ I & J & K & L \\ M & N & O & P \end{bmatrix} * \begin{bmatrix} a & b & c & d \\ e & f & g & h \\ i & j & k & l \\ m & n & o & p \end{bmatrix} =
$$

$$
\begin{bmatrix} Aa+Be+Ci+Dm & Ab+Bf+Cj+Dn & Ac+Bg+Ck+Do & Ad+Bh+Cl+Dp \\ Ea+Fe+Gi+Hm & Eb+Ff+Gj+Hn & Ec+Fg+Gk+Ho & Ed+Fh+Gl+Hp \\ Ia+Je+Ki+Lm & Ib+Jf+Kj+Ln & Ic+Jg+Kk+Lo & Id+Jh+Kl+Lp \\ Ma+Ne+Oi+Pm & Mb+Nf+Oj+Pn & Mc+Ng+Ok+Po & Md+Nh+Ol+Pp \end{bmatrix}
$$

Matrix multiplication is frequently referred to as ***concatenation***, because as will be seen, it is used to combine a set of matrix transforms into a single matrix. This ability to combine matrix transforms is made possible because of the ***associative*** property of matrix multiplication. Consider the following sequence of operations:

$$\text{New Point} = \text{Matrix}_1 * (\text{Matrix}_2 * (\text{Matrix}_3 * \text{Point}))$$

Here, we multiply a point by Matrix_3, then multiply that result by Matrix_2, and that result finally by Matrix_1. The result is a new point. The associative property ensures that the previous computation is equivalent to:

$$\text{New Point} = (\text{Matrix}_1 * \text{Matrix}_2 * \text{Matrix}_3) * \text{Point}$$

Here, we first multiply the three matrices together, forming the *concatenation* of Matrix_1, Matrix_2, and Matrix_3 (which itself is also a 4x4 matrix). If we refer to this concatenation as Matrix_C, we can rewrite the previous operation as:

$$\text{New Point} = \text{Matrix}_C * \text{Point}$$

The advantage here, as we will see in Chapter 4, is that we will frequently need to apply the same sequence of matrix transformations to every point in our scene. By pre-computing the concatenation of all of those matrices once, it turns out that we can reduce the total number of matrix operations needed manyfold.

GLSL and GLM both support matrix multiplication with the overloaded * operator.

The ***inverse*** of a 4x4 matrix M is another 4x4 matrix, denoted M^{-1}, that has the following property under matrix multiplication:

$$M*(M^{-1}) = (M^{-1})*M = \textit{identity matrix}$$

We won't present the details of computing the inverse here. However, it is worth knowing that determining the inverse of a matrix can be computationally expensive; fortunately, we will rarely need it. In the rare instances when we do, it is available in both GLSL and GLM through the mat4.inverse() function.

3.4 ■ TRANSFORMATION MATRICES

In graphics, matrices are typically used for performing *transformations* on objects. For example, a matrix can be used to move a point from one location to another. In this chapter, we will learn several useful transformation matrices:

- *Translation*
- *Rotation*
- *Scale*
- *Projection*
- *Look-At*

An important property of our transformation matrices is that they are all of size 4x4. This is made possible by our decision to use the *homogeneous* notation. Otherwise, some of the transforms would be of diverse and incompatible dimensions. As we have seen, ensuring they are the same size is not just for convenience; it also makes it possible to combine them arbitrarily, and pre-compute groups of transforms for improved performance.

3.4.1 Translation

A *translation* matrix is used to move items from one location to another. It consists of an identity matrix, with the X, Y, and Z movement(s) given in locations A_{03}, A_{13}, A_{23}. Figure 3.3 shows the form of a translation matrix and its effect when multiplied by a homogeneous point; the result is a new point "moved" by the translate values.

$$\begin{pmatrix} X + T_X \\ Y + T_Y \\ Z + T_Z \\ 1 \end{pmatrix} = \begin{bmatrix} 1 & 0 & 0 & T_X \\ 0 & 1 & 0 & T_Y \\ 0 & 0 & 1 & T_Z \\ 0 & 0 & 0 & 1 \end{bmatrix} * \begin{pmatrix} X \\ Y \\ Z \\ 1 \end{pmatrix}$$

Figure 3.3
Translation matrix transform.

Note that point (X,Y,Z) is translated (or moved) to location $(X+T_x, Y+T_y, Z+T_z)$ as a result of being multiplied by the translation matrix. Also note that multiplication is specified *right to left*.

For example, if we wish to move a group of points upward 5 units along the positive Y direction, we could build a translation matrix by taking an identity matrix and placing the value 5 in the T_y position. Then we simply multiply each of the points we wish to move by the matrix.

There are several functions in GLM for building translation matrices and for multiplying points by matrices. Some relevant operations are:

- *glm::translate(Tx,Ty,Tz)*   *builds a matrix that translates by (Tx,Ty,Tz)*
- *mat4 * vec4*

3.4.2 Scaling

A scale matrix is used to change the size of objects or move points toward or away from the origin. Although it may initially seem strange to scale a point, objects in OpenGL are defined by groups of points. So, scaling an object involves expanding or contracting its set of points.

The scale matrix transform consists of an identity matrix with the X, Y, and Z scale factors given in locations A_{00}, A_{11}, A_{22}. Figure 3.4 shows the form of a scale matrix and its effect when multiplied by a homogeneous point; the result is a new point modified by the scale values.

$$
\begin{pmatrix} X * S_X \\ Y * S_Y \\ Z * S_Z \\ 1 \end{pmatrix} = \begin{bmatrix} S_X & 0 & 0 & 0 \\ 0 & S_Y & 0 & 0 \\ 0 & 0 & S_Z & 0 \\ 0 & 0 & 0 & 1 \end{bmatrix} * \begin{pmatrix} X \\ Y \\ Z \\ 1 \end{pmatrix}
$$

Figure 3.4
Scale matrix transform.

There are several functions in GLM for building scale matrices and multiplying points by scale matrix transforms. Some relevant operations are:

- *glm::scale(Sx,Sy,Sz)*   *builds a matrix that scales by (Sx,Sy,Sz)*
- *mat4 * vec4*

Scaling can be used to switch coordinate systems. For example, we can use scale to determine what the left-hand coordinates would be, given a set of right-hand coordinates. From Figure 3.1, we see that negating the Z coordinate would toggle between right-hand and left-hand systems, so the scale matrix transform to accomplish this is:

$$
\begin{bmatrix} 1 & 0 & 0 & 0 \\ 0 & 1 & 0 & 0 \\ 0 & 0 & -1 & 0 \\ 0 & 0 & 0 & 1 \end{bmatrix}
$$

3.4.3 Rotation

Rotation is a bit more complex, because rotating an item in 3D space requires specifying (a) an axis of rotation and (b) a rotation amount in degrees or radians.

In the mid-1700s, the mathematician Leonhard Euler showed that a rotation around any desired axis could be specified instead as a combination of rotations around the X, Y, and Z axes [EU76]. These three rotation angles around the respective axes have come to be known as *Euler angles*. The discovery, known as *Euler's Theorem*, is very useful to us, because rotations around each of the three axes can be specified using matrix transforms.

The three rotation transforms, around the X, Y, and Z axes respectively, are shown in Figure 3.5. There are several functions in GLM for building and using rotation matrices as well:

- *glm::rotate(mat4, θ, x, y, z)*   *builds a rotation matrix for an angle θ around an axis x,y,z.*

- *mat4 * vec4*

Rotation around X by θ:

$$
\begin{pmatrix} X \\ Y' \\ Z' \\ 1 \end{pmatrix} = \begin{bmatrix} 1 & 0 & 0 & 0 \\ 0 & cos\theta & -sin\theta & 0 \\ 0 & sin\theta & cos\theta & 0 \\ 0 & 0 & 0 & 1 \end{bmatrix} * \begin{pmatrix} X \\ Y \\ Z \\ 1 \end{pmatrix}
$$

Rotation around Y by θ:

$$
\begin{pmatrix} X' \\ Y \\ Z' \\ 1 \end{pmatrix} = \begin{bmatrix} cos\theta & 0 & sin\theta & 0 \\ 0 & 1 & 0 & 0 \\ -sin\theta & 0 & cos\theta & 0 \\ 0 & 0 & 0 & 1 \end{bmatrix} * \begin{pmatrix} X \\ Y \\ Z \\ 1 \end{pmatrix}
$$

Rotation around Z by θ:

$$
\begin{pmatrix} X' \\ Y' \\ Z \\ 1 \end{pmatrix} = \begin{bmatrix} cos\theta & -sin\theta & 0 & 0 \\ sin\theta & cos\theta & 0 & 0 \\ 0 & 0 & 1 & 0 \\ 0 & 0 & 0 & 1 \end{bmatrix} * \begin{pmatrix} X \\ Y \\ Z \\ 1 \end{pmatrix}
$$

Figure 3.5
Rotation transform matrices.

In practice, using Euler angles to rotate an item around an arbitrary line in 3D space takes a couple of additional steps if the line doesn't pass through the origin. In general:

1. Translate the axis of rotation so that it goes through the origin.
2. Rotate by appropriate Euler angles around X, Y, and Z.
3. Undo the translation of Step 1.

The three rotation transforms shown in Figure 3.5 each have the interesting property that the inverse rotation happens to equal the transpose of the matrix. This can be verified by examining the previous matrices, recalling that $\cos(-\theta) = \cos(\theta)$, and $\sin(-\theta) = -\sin(\theta)$. This property will become useful later.

Euler angles can cause certain artifacts in some 3D graphics applications. For that reason it is often advisable to use *quaternions* for computing rotations. Many resources exist for those readers interested in exploring quaternions (e.g., [KU02]). Euler angles will suffice for most of our needs.

3.5 VECTORS

Vectors specify a *magnitude* and *direction*. They are not bound to a specific location; a vector can be "moved" without changing what it represents.

There are various ways to notate a vector, such as a line segment with an arrowhead at one end, or as a pair (magnitude, direction), or as the difference between two points. In 3D graphics, vectors are frequently represented as a single point in space, where the vector is the distance and direction from the origin to that point. In Figure 3.6, vector V (shown in red) can be specified either as the

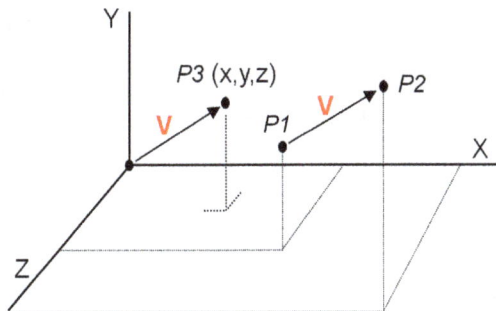

Figure 3.6
Two representations for a vector V.

difference between points P1 and P2, or as an equivalent distance from the origin to P3. In all of our applications, we specify V as simply (x,y,z), the same notation used to specify the point P3.

It is convenient to represent a vector the same way as a point, because we can use our matrix transforms on points or vectors interchangeably. However, it also can be confusing. For this reason we sometimes will notate a vector with a small arrow above it (such as $\vec{V}$). Many graphics systems do not distinguish between a point and a vector at all, such as in GLSL and GLM, which provide data types vec3/vec4 that can be used to hold either points or vectors. Some systems (such as the graphicslib3D library used in an earlier Java-based edition of this book) have separate point and vector classes, and enforce appropriate use of one or the other depending on the operation being done. It is an open debate as to whether it is clearer to use one data type for both, or separate data types.

There are several vector operations that are used frequently in 3D graphics, for which there are functions available in GLM and GLSL. For example, assuming vectors A(u,v,w) and B(x,y,z):

Addition and Subtraction:

$A \pm B = (u \pm x, v \pm y, w \pm z)$
glm: vec3 ± vec3
GLSL: vec3 ± vec3

Normalize (change to length=1):

$\hat{A} = A/|A| = A/sqrt(u^2+v^2+w^2)$, where $|A| \equiv$ *length of vector A*
glm: normalize(vec3) *or* normalize(vec4)
GLSL: normalize(vec3) *or* normalize(vec4)

Dot Product:

$A \bullet B = ux + vy + wz$
glm: dot(vec3,vec3) *or* dot(vec4,vec4)
GLSL: dot(vec3,vec3) *or* dot(vec4,vec4)

Cross Product:

$A \times B = (vz-wy, wx-uz, uy-vx)$
glm: cross(vec3,vec3)
GLSL: cross(vec3,vec3)

Other useful vector functions are *magnitude* (which is available in both GLSL and GLM as length()), and *reflection* and *refraction* (both are available in GLSL and GLM).

We shall now take a closer look at the functions *dot product* and *cross product*.

3.5.1 Uses for *Dot Product*

Throughout this book, our programs make heavy use of the dot product. The most important and fundamental use is for finding the *angle between two vectors*. Consider two vectors $\vec{V}$ and $\vec{W}$, and say we wish to find the angle θ separating them.

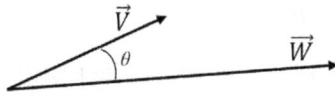

$$\vec{V} \bullet \vec{W} = |\vec{V}| * |\vec{W}| * \cos(\theta)$$

$$\cos(\theta) = \frac{\vec{V} \bullet \vec{W}}{|\vec{V}| * |\vec{W}|}$$

Therefore, if $\vec{V}$ and $\vec{W}$ are normalized (i.e., of unit length—here we use the "^" notation for normalization, as shown earlier), then:

$$\cos(\theta) = \hat{V} \bullet \hat{W}$$
$$\theta = \arccos(\hat{V} \bullet \hat{W})$$

Interestingly, we will later see that often it is *cos(θ)* that we need, rather than θ itself. So, both of the previous derivations will be directly useful.

The dot product also has a variety of other uses:

- Finding a vector's magnitude: $\sqrt{\vec{V} \bullet \vec{V}}$
- Finding whether two vectors are perpendicular, if: $\vec{V} \bullet \vec{W} = 0$
- Finding whether two vectors are parallel, if: $\vec{V} \bullet \vec{W} = |\vec{V}| * |\vec{W}|$
- Finding whether two vectors are parallel but pointing in opposite directions, if: $\vec{V} \bullet \vec{W} = -|\vec{V}| * |\vec{W}|$

- Finding whether the angle between vectors lies in the range (-90°..+90°): $\hat{V} \bullet \hat{W} > 0$
- Finding the minimum signed distance from point $P=(x,y,z)$ to plane $S=(a,b,c,d)$. First, find unit vector normal to S:

$\hat{n} = (\frac{a}{\sqrt{a^2+b^2+c^2}}, \frac{b}{\sqrt{a^2+b^2+c^2}}, \frac{c}{\sqrt{a^2+b^2+c^2}})$, and shortest distance

$D = \frac{d}{\sqrt{a^2+b^2+c^2}}$ from the origin to the plane. Then, the minimum signed distance from P to S is: $(\hat{n} \bullet \vec{P}) + D$ and the sign of this distance determines on which side of the plane S point P lies.

3.5.2 Uses for *Cross Product*

An important property of the cross product of two vectors, which we will make heavy use of throughout this book, is that it produces a vector that is *normal* (perpendicular) to the plane defined by the original two vectors.

Any two non-collinear vectors define a plane. For example, consider two arbitrary vectors $\vec{V}$ and $\vec{W}$. Since vectors can be moved without changing their meaning, they can be moved so that their origins coincide. Figure 3.8 shows a plane defined by $\vec{V}$ and $\vec{W}$, and the normal vector resulting from their cross product. The direction of the resulting normal obeys the *right-hand rule*, wherein curling the fingers of one's right hand from $\vec{V}$ to $\vec{W}$ causes the thumb to point in the direction of the normal vector $\vec{R}$.

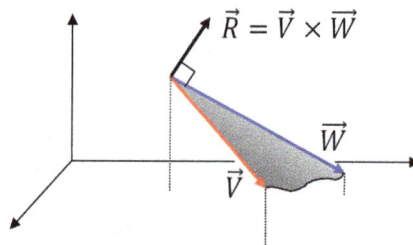

Figure 3.7
Cross product produces normal vector.

Note that the order is significant; $\vec{W} \times \vec{V}$ would produce a vector in the opposite direction from $\vec{R}$.

The ability to find normal vectors by using the cross product will become extremely useful later when we study *lighting*. In order to determine lighting effects, we will need to know *outward normals* associated with the model we are rendering. Figure 3.8 shows an example of a simple model made up of six points (vertices) and the computation employing cross product that determines the outward normal of one of its faces.

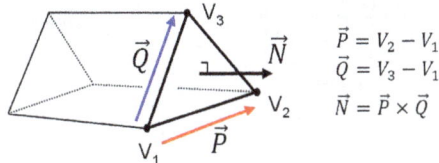

$$\vec{P} = V_2 - V_1$$
$$\vec{Q} = V_3 - V_1$$
$$\vec{N} = \vec{P} \times \vec{Q}$$

Figure 3.8
Computing outward normals.

3.6 LOCAL AND WORLD SPACE

The most common use for 3D graphics (with OpenGL or any other framework) is to simulate a three-dimensional world, place objects in it, and then view that simulated world on a monitor. The objects placed in the 3D world are usually modeled as collections of triangles. Later, in Chapter 6, we will dive into modeling. But we can start looking at the overall process now.

When building a 3D model of an object, we generally orient the model in the most convenient manner for describing it. For example, when modeling a sphere, we might orient the model with the sphere's center at the origin (0,0,0) and give it a convenient radius, such as 1. The space in which a model is defined is called its *local space*, or *model space*. OpenGL documentation uses the term *object space*.

The sphere might then be used as a piece of a larger model, such as becoming the head on a robot. The robot would, of course, be defined in its own local/model space. Positioning the sphere model into the robot model space can be done using the matrix transforms for scale, rotation, and translation, as illustrated in Figure 3.9. In this manner, complex models can be built hierarchically (this is developed further in Section 4.8 of Chapter 4 using a stack of matrices).

In the same manner, modeled objects are placed in a simulated world by deciding on the orientation and dimensions of that world, called *world space*. The matrix that positions and orients an object into world space is called a *model matrix*, or M.

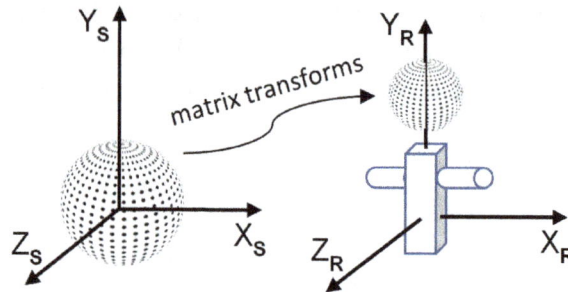

Figure 3.9
Model spaces for a sphere and a robot.

3.7 ■ EYE SPACE AND THE SYNTHETIC CAMERA

So far, the transform matrices we have seen all operate in 3D space. Ultimately, however, we will want to display our 3D space—or a portion of it—on a 2D monitor. In order to do this, we need to decide on a vantage point. Just as we see our real world through our eyes from a particular point in a particular direction, so too must we establish a position and orientation as the window into our virtual world. This vantage point is called "view" or "eye" space, or the "synthetic camera."

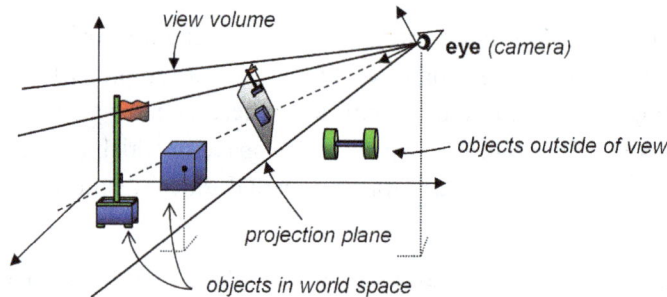

Figure 3.10
Positioning a camera in the 3D world.

As shown in Figures 3.10 and 3.12, viewing involves: (a) placing the camera at some world location; (b) orienting the camera, which usually requires maintaining its own set of orthogonal axes $\vec{U}/\vec{V}/\vec{N}$; (c) defining a *view volume*; and (d) projecting objects within the volume onto a *projection plane*.

OpenGL includes a camera that is permanently fixed at the origin (0,0,0) and faces down the negative Z-axis, as shown in Figure 3.11.

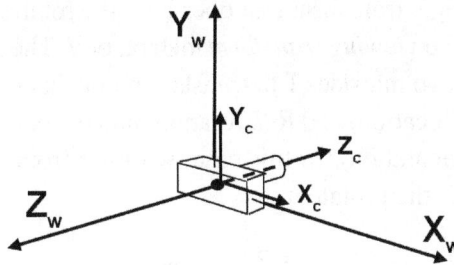

Figure 3.11
OpenGL fixed camera.

In order to use the OpenGL camera, one of the things we need to do is *simulate* moving it to some desired location and orientation. This is done by figuring out where our objects in the world are located relative to the desired camera position (i.e., where they are located in "camera space," as defined by the U, V, and N axes of the camera as illustrated in Figure 3.12). Given a point at world space location P_W, we need a transform to convert it to the equivalent point in camera space, making it *appear* as though we are viewing it from the desired camera location C_W. We do this by computing its camera space position P_C. Knowing that the OpenGL camera location is always at the fixed position (0,0,0), what transform would achieve this?

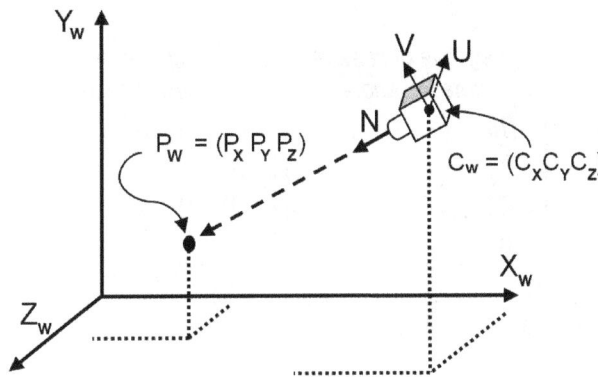

Figure 3.12
Camera orientation.

The necessary transforms are determined as follows:

1. Translate P_W by the negative of the desired camera location.
2. Rotate P_W by the negative of the desired camera orientation Euler angles.

We can build a single transform that does both the rotation and the translation in one matrix, called the *viewing transform* matrix, or **V**. The matrix **V** is produced by concatenating the two matrices **T** (a translation matrix containing the negative of the desired camera location) and **R** (a rotation matrix containing the negative of the desired camera orientation). In this case, working from right to left, we first translate world point P, then rotate it:

$$P_C = R * (T * P_W)$$

As we saw earlier, the associative rule allows us to group the operations instead thusly:

$$P_C = (R * T) * P_W$$

If we save the concatenation R*T in the matrix V, the operation now looks like:

$$P_C = V * P_W$$

The complete computation, and the exact contents of matrices T and R, are shown in Figure 3.13 (we omit the derivation of matrix R—a derivation is available in [FV95]).

$$
\begin{pmatrix} X_C \\ Y_C \\ Z_C \\ 1 \end{pmatrix} =
\overset{\overset{\textit{negative of camera}}{\textit{rotation angles}}}{\begin{bmatrix} \hat{U}_X & \hat{U}_Y & \hat{U}_Z & 0 \\ \hat{V}_X & \hat{V}_Y & \hat{V}_Z & 0 \\ -\hat{N}_X & -\hat{N}_Y & -\hat{N}_Z & 0 \\ 0 & 0 & 0 & 1 \end{bmatrix}} *
\overset{\overset{\textit{negative of}}{\textit{camera location}}}{\begin{bmatrix} 1 & 0 & 0 & -C_X \\ 0 & 1 & 0 & -C_Y \\ 0 & 0 & 1 & -C_Z \\ 0 & 0 & 0 & 1 \end{bmatrix}} *
\begin{pmatrix} P_X \\ P_Y \\ P_Z \\ 1 \end{pmatrix}
$$

point P_C in eye space   **R** *(rotation)*   **T** *(translation)*   world point P_W

V *(viewing transform)*

Figure 3.13
Deriving a view matrix.

More commonly, the V matrix is concatenated with the model matrix M to form a single *model-view* (MV) matrix:

$$MV = V * M$$

Then, a point P_M in its own model space is transformed directly to camera space in one step as follows:

$$P_C = MV * P_M$$

The advantage of this approach becomes clear when one considers that, in a complex scene, we will need to perform this transformation not on just one point, but *on every vertex in the scene*. By pre-computing MV, transforming each point into view space will require us to do just *one* matrix multiplication per vertex, rather than two. Later, we will see that we can extend this process to pre-computing several matrix concatenations, reducing the per-vertex computations considerably.

3.8 PROJECTION MATRICES

Now that we have established the camera, we can examine *projection matrices.* Two important projection matrices that we will now examine are (a) *perspective* and (b) *orthographic.*

3.8.1 The Perspective Projection Matrix

Perspective projection attempts to make a 2D picture appear 3D, by utilizing the concept of perspective to mimic what we see when we look at the real world. Objects that are close appear larger than objects that are far away, and in some cases, lines that are parallel in 3D space are no longer parallel when drawn with perspective.

Perspective was one of the great discoveries of the Renaissance era in the 1400–1500s, when artists started painting with more realism than did their predecessors.

An excellent example can be seen in Figure 3.14, "The Annunciation, with Saint Emidius" by Carlo Crivelli, painted in 1486 (currently held at the National Gallery in London [CR86]). The intense use of perspective is clear—the receding lines of the left-facing wall of the building on the right are slanted toward each other dramatically. This creates the illusion of depth and 3D space, and in the process lines that are parallel in reality are not parallel in the picture. Also, the people in the foreground are larger than the people in the background. While today we take these devices for granted, finding a transformation matrix to accomplish this requires some mathematical analysis.

We achieve this effect by using a matrix transform that converts parallel lines into appropriate non-parallel lines. Such a matrix is called a *perspective matrix* or *perspective transform*, and is built by defining the four parameters of a *view volume*. Those parameters are (a) *aspect ratio*, (b) *field of view*, (c) *projection plane* or *near clipping plane*, and (d) *far clipping plane*.

Only objects between the *near* and *far* clipping planes are rendered. The near clipping plane also serves as the plane on which objects are *projected*, and is generally positioned close to the eye or camera (shown on the left in Figure 3.15). Selection of an appropriate value for the far clipping plane is discussed in Chapter 4.

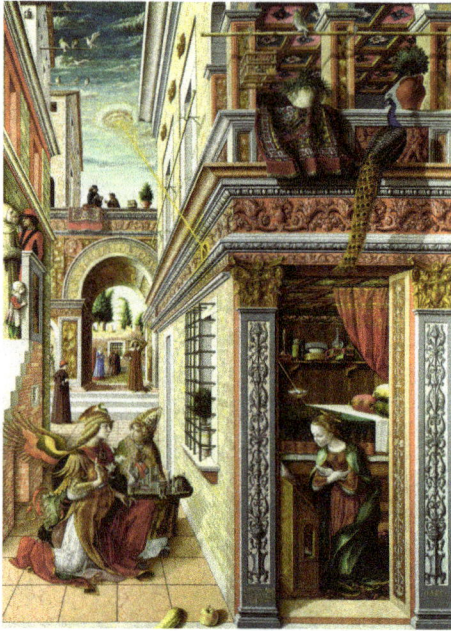

Figure 3.14
The Annunciation, with Saint Emidius (Crivelli – 1486).

The *field of view* is the vertical angle of viewable space. The *aspect ratio* is the ratio width/height of the near and far clipping planes. The shape formed by these elements and shown in Figure 3.15 is called a *frustum*.

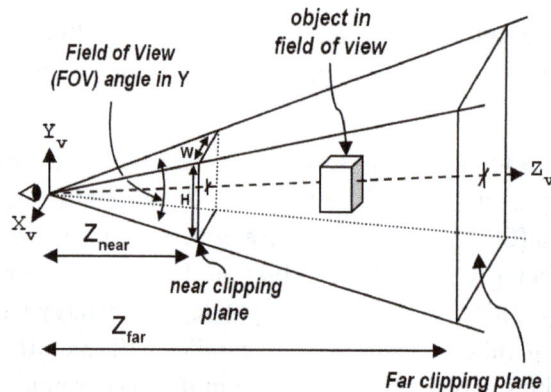

Figure 3.15
Perspective view volume or frustum.

The perspective matrix is used to transform points in 3D space to their appropriate position on the near clipping plane, and it is built by first computing values q, A, B, and C, and then using those values to construct the matrix, as shown in Figure 3.16 (and derived in [FV95]).

$$q = \frac{1}{\tan(\frac{fieldOfView}{2})}$$

$$A = \frac{q}{aspectRatio}$$

$$B = \frac{Z_{near} + Z_{far}}{Z_{near} - Z_{far}}$$

$$C = \frac{2 * (Z_{near} * Z_{far})}{Z_{near} - Z_{far}}$$

$$\begin{bmatrix} A & 0 & 0 & 0 \\ 0 & q & 0 & 0 \\ 0 & 0 & B & C \\ 0 & 0 & -1 & 0 \end{bmatrix}$$

Figure 3.16
Building a perspective matrix.

Generating a perspective transform matrix is a simple matter, by simply inserting the described formulas into the cells of a 4x4 matrix. The GLM library also includes a function glm::perspective() for building a perspective matrix.

3.8.2 The Orthographic Projection Matrix

In *orthographic* projection, parallel lines remain parallel; that is, perspective isn't employed. Instead, objects that are within the view volume are projected directly, without any adjustment of their sizes due to their distances from the camera.

An orthographic projection is a parallel projection in which all projections are at right angles with the projection plane. An orthographic matrix is built by defining the following parameters: (a) the distance Z_{near} from the camera to the projection plane, (b) the distance Z_{far} from the camera to the far clipping plane, and (c) values

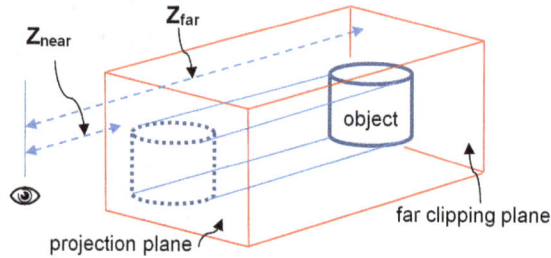

Figure 3.17
Orthographic projection.

for L, R, T, and B, with L and R corresponding to the X coordinates of the left and right boundaries of the projection plane respectively, and T and B corresponding to the Y coordinates of the top and bottom boundaries of the projection plane respectively. The orthographic projection matrix as derived in [WB15] is shown in Figure 3.18.

$$\begin{bmatrix} \dfrac{2}{R-L} & 0 & 0 & -\dfrac{R+L}{R-L} \\ 0 & \dfrac{2}{T-B} & 0 & -\dfrac{T+B}{T-B} \\ 0 & 0 & \dfrac{-2}{Z_{far}-Z_{near}} & -\dfrac{Z_{far}+Z_{near}}{Z_{far}-Z_{near}} \\ 0 & 0 & 0 & 1 \end{bmatrix}$$

Figure 3.18
Orthographic projection matrix.

Not all parallel projections are orthographic, but others are out of the scope of this textbook.

Parallel projections don't match what the eye sees when looking at the real world. But they are useful in a variety of situations, such as in casting shadows, performing 3D clipping, and in CAD (computer aided design)—the latter because they preserve measurement regardless of the placement of the objects. However, the great majority of examples in this book use perspective projection.

3.9 ■ LOOK-AT MATRIX

The final transformation we will examine is the *look-at* matrix. This is handy when you wish to place the camera at one location and look toward a particular other location, as illustrated in Figure 3.19. Of course, it would be possible to achieve this using the methods we have already seen, but it is such a common operation that building one matrix transform to do it is often useful.

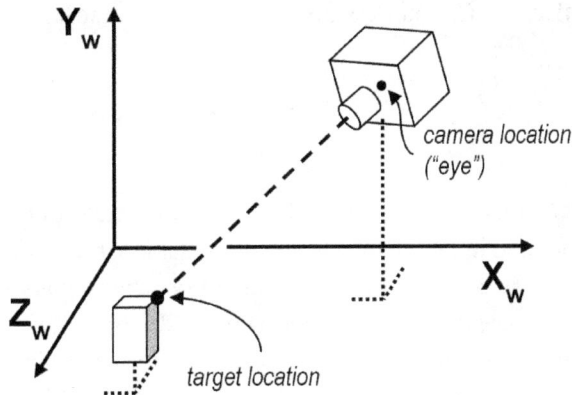

Figure 3.19
Elements of look-at.

A look-at transform still requires deciding on a camera orientation. We do this by specifying a vector approximating the general orientation desired (such as the world $\vec{Y}$ axis). Typically, a sequence of cross products can be used to then generate a suitable set of forward, side, and up vectors for the desired camera orientation. Figure 3.20 shows the computations, starting with the camera location (eye), target location, and initial up vector $\vec{Y}$, to build the look-at matrix, as derived in [FV95].

$$\overrightarrow{fwd} = normalize(eye - target)$$

$$\overrightarrow{side} = normalize(-\overrightarrow{fwd} \times \vec{Y})$$

$$\overrightarrow{up} = normalize(\overrightarrow{side} \times -\overrightarrow{fwd})$$

The look-at matrix then equals:

$$\begin{bmatrix} \overrightarrow{side}_X & \overrightarrow{side}_Y & \overrightarrow{side}_Z & -(\overrightarrow{side} \bullet \overrightarrow{eye}) \\ \overrightarrow{up}_X & \overrightarrow{up}_Y & \overrightarrow{up}_Z & -(\overrightarrow{up} \bullet \overrightarrow{eye}) \\ -\overrightarrow{fwd}_X & -\overrightarrow{fwd}_Y & -\overrightarrow{fwd}_Z & -(-\overrightarrow{fwd} \bullet \overrightarrow{eye}) \\ 0 & 0 & 0 & 1 \end{bmatrix}$$

Figure 3.20
Look-At matrix.

We could encode this as a simple C++/OpenGL utility function that builds a look-at matrix, given specified values for camera location, target location, and the initial "up" vector $\vec{Y}$. Since GLM includes the function glm::lookAt() for building a look-at matrix, we will simply use that. This function will be useful later in this textbook, particularly in Chapter 8 when we generate shadows.

3.10 GLSL FUNCTIONS FOR BUILDING MATRIX TRANSFORMS

Although GLM includes predefined functions for performing many of the 3D transformations covered in this chapter, such as translation, rotation, and scale, GLSL only includes basic matrix operations such as addition, concatenation, and so on. It is therefore sometimes necessary to write our own GLSL utility functions for building 3D transformation matrices when we need them to perform certain 3D computations in a shader. The appropriate datatype to hold such a matrix in GLSL is mat4.

The syntax for initializing mat4 matrices in GLSL loads values by columns. The first four values are put into the first column, the next four into the next column, and so forth, as illustrated in the following example:

```
mat4 translationMatrix =
    mat4(1.0, 0.0, 0.0, 0.0, // note this is the leftmost column, not the top row
         0.0, 1.0, 0.0, 0.0,
         0.0, 0.0, 1.0, 0.0,
         tx, ty, tz, 1.0 );
```

which builds the translation matrix described previously in Figure 3.3.

Program 3.1 includes five GLSL functions for building 4x4 translation, rotation, and scale matrices, each corresponding to formulas given earlier in this chapter. We will use some of these functions later in the book.

Program 3.1 Building Transformation Matrices in GLSL

```
// builds and returns a translation matrix
mat4 buildTranslate(float x, float y, float z)
{   mat4 trans = mat4(1.0, 0.0, 0.0, 0.0,
                      0.0, 1.0, 0.0, 0.0,
                      0.0, 0.0, 1.0, 0.0,
                      x, y, z, 1.0 );
    return trans;
}
```

```
// builds and returns a matrix that performs a rotation around the X axis
mat4 buildRotateX(float rad)
{   mat4 xrot = mat4(1.0, 0.0, 0.0, 0.0,
                     0.0, cos(rad), -sin(rad), 0.0,
                     0.0, sin(rad), cos(rad), 0.0,
                     0.0, 0.0, 0.0, 1.0 );
    return xrot;
}

// builds and returns a matrix that performs a rotation around the Y axis
mat4 buildRotateY(float rad)
{   mat4 yrot = mat4(cos(rad), 0.0, sin(rad), 0.0,
                     0.0, 1.0, 0.0, 0.0,
                     -sin(rad), 0.0, cos(rad), 0.0,
                     0.0, 0.0, 0.0, 1.0 );
    return yrot;
}

// builds and returns a matrix that performs a rotation around the Z axis
mat4 buildRotateZ(float rad)
{   mat4 zrot = mat4(cos(rad), -sin(rad), 0.0, 0.0,
                     sin(rad), cos(rad), 0.0, 0.0,
                     0.0, 0.0, 1.0, 0.0,
                     0.0, 0.0, 0.0, 1.0 );
    return zrot;
}

// builds and returns a scale matrix
mat4 buildScale(float x, float y, float z)
{   mat4 scale = mat4(x, 0.0, 0.0, 0.0,
                      0.0, y, 0.0, 0.0,
                      0.0, 0.0, z, 0.0,
                      0.0, 0.0, 0.0, 1.0 );
    return scale;
}
```

SUPPLEMENTAL NOTES

In this chapter, we have seen examples of applying matrix transformations to points. Later, we will also want to apply these same transforms to vectors. In order to accomplish a transform on a vector V equivalent to applying some matrix transform M to a point, it is necessary in the general case to compute the *inverse transpose* of M, denoted $(M^{-1})^T$, and multiply V by that matrix. In some cases, $M=(M^{-1})^T$, and in those cases it is possible to simply use M. For example, the basic rotation matrices we have seen in this chapter are equal to their own inverse transpose and can be applied directly to vectors (and therefore also to points). Thus, the examples in this book sometimes use $(M^{-1})^T$ when applying a transform to a vector, and sometimes simply use M.

One of the things we haven't discussed in this chapter is techniques for moving the camera smoothly through space. This is very useful, especially for games and CGI movies, but also for visualization, virtual reality, and for 3D modeling. Code that does this is called a *camera controller*, and details for implementing a simple camera controller are described in Appendix D. There are also many resources available online for this topic [TR15].

We didn't include complete derivations for all of the matrix transforms that were presented (they can be found in other sources, such as [FV95]). We strove instead for a concise summary of the point, vector, and matrix operations necessary for doing basic 3D graphics programming. As this book proceeds, we will encounter many practical uses for the methods presented.

Exercises

3.1 Modify Program 2.5 so that the vertex shader includes one of the buildRotate() functions from Program 3.1 and applies it to the points comprising the triangle. This should cause the triangle to be rotated from its original orientation. You don't need to animate the rotation.

3.2 *(RESEARCH)* At the end of Section 3.4 we indicated that Euler angles can in some cases lead to undesirable artifacts. The most common is called "gimbal lock." Describe gimbal lock, give an example, and explain why gimbal lock can cause problems.

3.3 *(RESEARCH)* One way of avoiding the artifacts that can manifest when using Euler angles is to use *quaternions*. We didn't study quaternions; however, GLM includes several quaternion classes and functions. Do some independent study on quaternions and familiarize yourself with the related GLM quaternion capabilities.

References

[CR86] C. Crivelli, *The Annunciation, with Saint Emidius*, (National Gallery, London, England, 1486), accessed November 2023, https://www .nationalgallery.org.uk/paintings/carlo-crivelli-the-annunciation-with-saint-emidius

[EU76] L. Euler, *Formulae generals pro translatione quacunque coporum rigidorum* (General formulas for the translation of arbitrary rigid bodies), (Novi Commentarii academiae scientiarum Petropolitanae 20, 1776).

[FV95] J. Foley, A. van Dam, S. Feiner, and J. Hughes, *Computer Graphics – Principles and Practice*, 2nd ed. (Addison-Wesley, 1995).

[KU02] J. B. Kuipers, *Quaternions and Rotation Sequences* (Princeton University Press, 2002).

[TR15] T. Reed, OpenGL Part 3B: Camera Control (blog). Accessed November 2023, https://www.trentreed.net/blog/qt5-opengl-part-3b-camera-control

[WB15] W. Brown, LearnWebGL (2015), chapter 8.2 (Orthographic Projections), Accessed November 2023, http://learnwebgl.brown37.net/08_projections/projections_ortho.html

MANAGING 3D GRAPHICS DATA

Using OpenGL to render 3D images generally involves sending several datasets through the OpenGL shader pipeline. For example, to draw a simple 3D object such as a *cube*, you will need to at least send the following items:

- the vertices for the cube model
- some transformation matrices to control the appearance of the cube's orientation in 3D space

To complicate matters a bit, there are *two* ways of sending data through the OpenGL pipeline:

- through a *buffer* to a *vertex attribute* or
- directly to a *uniform variable*.

It is important to understand exactly how these two mechanisms work, so as to use the appropriate method for each item we are sending through.

Let's start by rendering a simple cube.

4.1 ■ BUFFERS AND VERTEX ATTRIBUTES

For an object to be drawn, its vertices must be sent to the vertex shader. Vertices are usually sent by putting them in a *buffer* on the C++ side and associating that buffer with a *vertex attribute* declared in the shader. There are several steps to accomplish this, some of which only need to be done once, and some of which—if the scene is animated—must be done at every frame:

Done once—typically in init():

1. create a buffer
2. copy the vertices into the buffer

Done at each frame—typically in display():

1. enable the buffer containing the vertices
2. associate the buffer with a vertex attribute
3. enable the vertex attribute
4. use glDrawArrays(...) to draw the object

Buffers are typically created all at once at the start of the program, either in init() or in a function called by init(). In OpenGL, a buffer is contained in a *Vertex Buffer Object*, or *VBO*, which is declared and instantiated in the C++/OpenGL application. A scene may require many VBOs, so it is customary to generate and then fill several of them in init() so that they are available whenever your program needs to draw one or more of them.

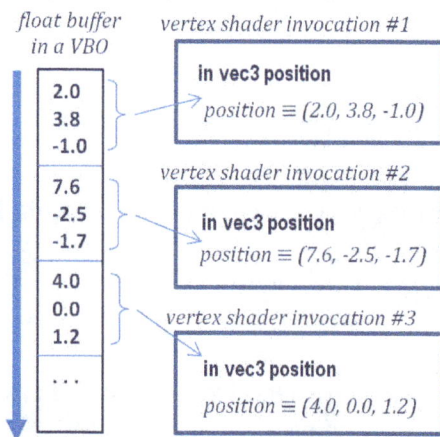

Figure 4.1
Data transmission between a VBO and a vertex attribute.

A buffer interacts with a vertex attribute in a specific way. When glDrawArrays() is executed, the data in the buffer starts flowing, sequentially from the beginning of the buffer, through the vertex shader. As described in Chapter 2, the vertex shader executes *once per vertex*. A vertex in 3D space requires three values, so an appropriate vertex attribute in the shader to receive these three values would be of type vec3. Then, for each *three values* in the buffer, the shader is invoked, as illustrated in Figure 4.1.

A related structure in OpenGL is called a *Vertex Array Object*, or *VAO*. VAOs were introduced in version 3.0 of OpenGL and are provided as a way of organizing buffers and making them easier to manipulate in complex scenes. OpenGL requires that at least one VAO be created, and for our purposes one will be sufficient.

For example, suppose that we wish to display two objects. On the C++ side, we could do this by declaring a single VAO and an associated set of two VBOs (one per object), as follows:

```
GLuint vao[1];   // OpenGL requires these values be specified in arrays
GLuint vbo[2];
...
glGenVertexArrays(1, vao);
glBindVertexArray(vao[0]);
glGenBuffers(2, vbo);
```

The two OpenGL commands glGenVertexArrays() and glGenBuffers() create VAOs and VBOs respectively, and produce integer IDs for these items that are stored in the arrays vao and vbo. The two parameters on each of them refer to how many IDs are created, and an array to hold the returned IDs. The purpose of glBindVertexArrays() is to make the specified VAO "active" so that the generated buffers[1] will be associated with that VAO.

A buffer needs to have a corresponding *vertex attribute* variable declared in the vertex shader. Vertex attributes are generally the first variables declared in a shader. In our cube example, a vertex attribute to receive the cube vertices could be declared in the vertex shader as follows:

```
layout (location = 0) in vec3 position;
```

The keyword in means "input" and indicates that this vertex attribute will be receiving values from a buffer (as we will see later, vertex attributes can also be used for "output"). As seen before, the "vec3" means that each invocation of the shader will grab *three* float values (presumably *x*, *y*, *z*, comprising a single vertex). The variable name is "position". The "layout (location=0)" portion of the command is called a "layout qualifier" and is how we will associate the vertex attribute with a particular buffer. Thus this vertex attribute has an identifier 0 that we will use later for this purpose.

---

[1] Throughout this example, two buffers are declared, to emphasize that *usually* we will use several buffers. Later we will use the additional buffer(s) to store other information associated with the vertex, such as color. In the current case we are using only one of the declared buffers, so it would have been sufficient to declare just one VBO.

The manner in which we load the vertices of a model into a buffer (VBO) depends on where the model's vertex values are stored. In Chapter 6, we will see how models are commonly built in a modeling tool (such as *Blender* [BL23] or *Maya* [MA23]), exported to a standard file format (such as .obj—also described in Chapter 6), and imported into the C++/OpenGL application. We will also see how a model's vertices can be calculated on the fly or generated inside the pipeline using a tessellation shader.

For now, let's say that we wish to draw a *cube*, and let's presume that the vertices of our cube are hardcoded in an array in the C++/OpenGL application. In that case, we need to copy those values into one of our two buffers that we previously generated. To do that, we need to (a) make that buffer (say, the 0th buffer) "active" with the OpenGL glBindBuffer() command, and (b) use the glBufferData() command to copy the array containing the vertices into the active buffer (the 0th VBO in this case). Presuming that the vertices are stored in a float array named vPositions, the following C++ code[2] would copy those values into the 0th VBO:

```
glBindBuffer(GL_ARRAY_BUFFER, vbo[0]);
glBufferData(GL_ARRAY_BUFFER, sizeof(vPositions), vPositions, GL_STATIC_DRAW);
```

Next, we add code to display() that will cause the values in the buffer to be sent to the vertex attribute in the shader. We do this with the following three steps: (a) make that buffer "active" with the glBindBuffer() command as we did above, (b) associate the active buffer with a vertex attribute in the shader, and (c) enable the vertex attribute. The following lines of code accomplish these steps:

```
glBindBuffer(GL_ARRAY_BUFFER, vbo[0]);                    // make the 0th buffer "active"
glVertexAttribPointer(0, 3, GL_FLOAT, GL_FALSE, 0, 0);   // associate 0th attribute with buffer
glEnableVertexAttribArray(0);                             // enable the 0th vertex attribute
```

Now when we execute glDrawArrays(), data in the 0th VBO will be transmitted to the vertex attribute that has a layout qualifier with location 0. This sends the cube vertices to the shader.

---

[2] Note that here, for the first time, we are refraining from describing every parameter in one or more OpenGL calls. As mentioned in Chapter 2, the reader is encouraged to utilize the OpenGL documentation for such details as needed.

4.2 UNIFORM VARIABLES

Rendering a scene so that it appears 3D requires building appropriate transformation matrices, such as those described in Chapter 3, and applying them to each of the models' vertices. It is most efficient to apply the required matrix operations in the vertex shader, and it is customary to send these matrices from the C++/OpenGL application to the shader in a *uniform variable*.

Uniform variables are declared in a shader by using the "uniform" keyword. The following example, which declares variables to hold model-view and projection matrices, will be suitable for our cube program:

```
uniform mat4 mv_matrix;
uniform mat4 p_matrix;
```

The keyword "mat4" indicates that these are 4x4 matrices. Here we have named the variable mv_matrix to hold the model-view matrix and the variable p_matrix to hold the projection matrix. Since 3D transformations are 4x4, *mat4* is a commonly used datatype in GLSL shader uniforms.

Sending data from a C++/OpenGL application to a uniform variable requires the following steps: (a) acquire a reference to the uniform variable and (b) associate a pointer to the desired values with the acquired uniform reference. Assuming that the linked rendering program is saved in a variable called "renderingProgram", the following lines of code would specify that we will be sending model-view and projection matrices to the two uniforms mv_matrix and p_matrix in our cube example:

```
mvLoc = glGetUniformLocation(renderingProgram,"mv_matrix");   // get locations of uniforms
pLoc = glGetUniformLocation(renderingProgram,"p_matrix");     // in the shader program
glUniformMatrix4fv(mvLoc, 1, GL_FALSE, glm::value_ptr(mvMat)); // send matrix data to the
glUniformMatrix4fv(pLoc, 1, GL_FALSE, glm::value_ptr(pMat));   // uniform variables
```

The above example assumes that we have utilized the GLM utilities to build model-view and projection matrix transforms mvMat and pMat, as will be discussed in greater detail shortly. They are of type mat4 (a GLM class). The GLM function call value_ptr() returns a reference to the matrix data, which is needed by glUniformMatrix4fv() to transfer those matrix values to the uniform variable.

4.3 ■ INTERPOLATION OF VERTEX ATTRIBUTES

It is important to understand how *vertex attributes* are processed in the OpenGL pipeline, versus how *uniform variables* are processed. Recall that immediately before the fragment shader is *rasterization*, where primitives (e.g., triangles) defined by vertices are converted to fragments. Rasterization *linearly interpolates vertex attribute* values so that the displayed pixels seamlessly connect the modeled surfaces.

By contrast, *uniform* variables behave like initialized constants and remain unchanged across each vertex shader invocation (i.e., for each vertex sent from the buffer). A uniform variable is not interpolated; it always contains the same value regardless of the number of vertices.

The interpolation done on vertex attributes by the rasterizer is useful in many ways. Later, we will use rasterization to interpolate colors, texture coordinates, and surface normals. It is important to understand that *all values sent through a buffer to a vertex attribute will be interpolated* further down the pipeline.

We have seen vertex attributes in a vertex shader declared as "in" to indicate that they receive values from a buffer. Vertex attributes may instead be declared as "out", meaning that they send their values forward toward the next stage in the pipeline. For example, the following declaration in a vertex shader specifies a vertex attribute named "color" that outputs a vec4:

out vec4 color;

It is not necessary to declare an "out" variable for the vertex positions, because OpenGL has a built-in out vec4 variable named gl_Position for that purpose. In the vertex shader, we apply the matrix transformations to the incoming vertex (declared earlier as position), assigning the result to gl_Position:

gl_Position = p_matrix * mv_matrix * position;

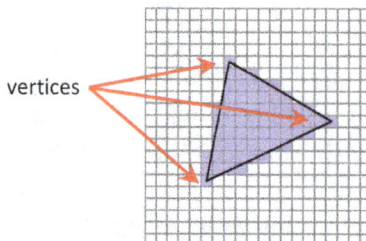

Figure 4.2
Rasterization of vertices.

The transformed vertices will then be automatically output to the rasterizer, with corresponding pixel locations ultimately sent to the fragment shader.

The rasterization process is illustrated in Figure 4.2. When specifying GL_TRIANGLES in the glDrawArrays() function, rasterization is done per triangle. Interpolation starts along the lines connecting the vertices, at a level of precision corresponding to the pixel display density. The pixels in the interior space of the triangle are then filled by interpolating along the horizontal lines connecting the edge pixels.

4.4 MODEL-VIEW AND PERSPECTIVE MATRICES

A fundamental step in rendering an object in 3D is to create appropriate transformation matrices and send them to uniform variables like we did in Section 4.2. We start by defining three matrices:

1. a *Model* matrix
2. a *View* matrix
3. a *Perspective* (*Projection*) matrix

The *Model* matrix positions and orients the object in the world coordinate space. Each model has its own model matrix, and that matrix would need to be continuously rebuilt if the model moves.

The *View* matrix moves and rotates the models in the world to simulate the effect of a camera at a desired location. Recall from Chapter 3 that the OpenGL camera exists at location (0,0,0) and faces down the negative Z axis. To simulate the appearance of that camera being moved a certain way, we will need to move the objects themselves in the opposite direction. For example, moving a camera to the right would cause the objects in the scene to appear to move to the left; although the OpenGL camera is fixed, we can make it appear as though we have moved it to the right by moving the objects to the left.

The *Perspective* matrix is a transform that provides the 3D effect according to the desired frustum, as described earlier in Chapter 3.

It is also important to understand when to compute each type of matrix. Matrices that never change can be built in init(), but those that change would need to be built in display() so that they are rebuilt for each frame. Let's assume that the models are animated and the camera is movable. Then:

- A model matrix needs to be created *for each model* and *at each frame*.
- The view matrix needs to be created *once per frame* (because the camera can be moved), but it is the same for all objects rendered during that frame.

• The perspective matrix is created once (in init()), using the screen window's width and height (and desired frustum parameters), and it usually remains unchanged unless the window is resized.

Generating model and view transformation matrices then happens in the display() function, as follows:

1. Build the view matrix based on the desired camera location and orientation.
2. For each model, do the following:
   i. Build a model matrix based on the model's location and orientation.
   ii. Concatenate the model and view matrices into a single "MV" matrix.
   iii. Send the MV and P matrices to the corresponding shader uniforms.

Technically, it isn't necessary to combine the model and view matrices into a single matrix. That is, they could be sent to the vertex shader in individual, separate matrices. However, there are certain advantages to combining them, while keeping the perspective matrix separate. For example, in the vertex shader, each vertex in the model is multiplied by the matrices. Since complex models may have hundreds or even thousands of vertices, performance can be improved by premultiplying the model and view matrices once before sending them to the vertex shader. Later, we will see the need to keep the perspective matrix separate for lighting purposes.

4.5 OUR FIRST 3D PROGRAM – A 3D CUBE

It's time to put all the pieces together! In order to build a complete C++/OpenGL/GLSL system to render our cube in a 3D "world," all of the mechanisms described so far will need to be put together and perfectly coordinated. We can reuse some of the code that we have seen previously in Chapter 2. Specifically, we won't repeat the following functions for reading in files containing shader code, compiling and linking them, and detecting GLSL errors; in fact, recall that we have moved them to a "Utils.cpp" file:

• createShaderProgram()
• readShaderSource()
• checkOpenGLError()
• printProgramLog()
• printShaderLog()

We will also need a utility function that builds a perspective matrix, given a specified field-of-view angle for the Y axis, the screen aspect ratio, and the desired near and far clipping planes (selecting appropriate values for near and far clipping planes is discussed in Section 4.9). While we could easily write such a function ourselves, GLM already includes one:

glm::perspective(*<field of view>*, *<aspect ratio>*, *<near plane>*, *<far plane>*);

We now build the complete 3D cube program, shown as follows in Program 4.1:

Program 4.1 Plain Red Cube

C++/OpenGL Application

```
#include <GL/glew.h>
#include <GLFW/glfw3.h>
#include <string>
#include <iostream>
#include <fstream>
#include <cmath>
#include <glm/glm.hpp>
#include <glm/gtc/type_ptr.hpp>
#include <glm/gtc/matrix_transform.hpp>
#include "Utils.h"
using namespace std;

#define numVAOs 1
#define numVBOs 2

float cameraX, cameraY, cameraZ;
float cubeLocX, cubeLocY, cubeLocZ;
GLuint renderingProgram;
GLuint vao[numVAOs];
GLuint vbo[numVBOs];

// allocate variables used in display() function, so that they won't need to be allocated during rendering
GLuint mvLoc, pLoc;
int width, height;
float aspect;
glm::mat4 pMat, vMat, mMat, mvMat;

void setupVertices(void) {      // 36 vertices, 12 triangles, makes 2x2x2 cube placed at origin
    float vertexPositions[108] = {
        -1.0f,  1.0f, -1.0f, -1.0f, -1.0f, -1.0f,  1.0f, -1.0f, -1.0f,
         1.0f, -1.0f, -1.0f,  1.0f,  1.0f, -1.0f, -1.0f,  1.0f, -1.0f,
```

```
        1.0f, -1.0f, -1.0f, 1.0f, -1.0f,  1.0f, 1.0f,  1.0f, -1.0f,
        1.0f, -1.0f,  1.0f, 1.0f,  1.0f,  1.0f, 1.0f,  1.0f, -1.0f,
        1.0f, -1.0f,  1.0f, -1.0f, -1.0f,  1.0f, 1.0f,  1.0f,  1.0f,
       -1.0f, -1.0f,  1.0f, -1.0f,  1.0f,  1.0f, 1.0f,  1.0f,  1.0f,
       -1.0f, -1.0f,  1.0f, -1.0f, -1.0f, -1.0f, -1.0f,  1.0f,  1.0f,
       -1.0f, -1.0f, -1.0f, -1.0f,  1.0f, -1.0f, -1.0f,  1.0f,  1.0f,
       -1.0f, -1.0f,  1.0f,  1.0f, -1.0f,  1.0f, 1.0f, -1.0f, -1.0f,
        1.0f, -1.0f, -1.0f, -1.0f, -1.0f, -1.0f, -1.0f, -1.0f,  1.0f,
       -1.0f,  1.0f, -1.0f, 1.0f,  1.0f, -1.0f, 1.0f,  1.0f,  1.0f,
        1.0f,  1.0f,  1.0f, -1.0f,  1.0f,  1.0f, -1.0f,  1.0f, -1.0f
    };
    glGenVertexArrays(1, vao);
    glBindVertexArray(vao[0]);
    glGenBuffers(numVBOs, vbo);

    glBindBuffer(GL_ARRAY_BUFFER, vbo[0]);
    glBufferData(GL_ARRAY_BUFFER, sizeof(vertexPositions), vertexPositions, GL_STATIC_DRAW);
}

void init(GLFWwindow* window) {
    renderingProgram = Utils::createShaderProgram("vertShader.glsl", "fragShader.glsl");
    cameraX = 0.0f; cameraY = 0.0f; cameraZ = 8.0f;
    cubeLocX = 0.0f; cubeLocY = -2.0f; cubeLocZ = 0.0f;    // shift down Y to reveal perspective
    setupVertices();
}

void display(GLFWwindow* window, double currentTime) {
    glClear(GL_DEPTH_BUFFER_BIT);
    glUseProgram(renderingProgram);

    // get the uniform variables for the MV and projection matrices
    mvLoc = glGetUniformLocation(renderingProgram, "mv_matrix");
    pLoc = glGetUniformLocation(renderingProgram, "p_matrix");

    // build perspective matrix
    glfwGetFramebufferSize(window, &width, &height);
    aspect = (float)width / (float)height;
    pMat = glm::perspective(1.0472f, aspect, 0.1f, 1000.0f); // 1.0472 radians = 60 degrees

    // build view matrix, model matrix, and model-view matrix
    vMat = glm::translate(glm::mat4(1.0f), glm::vec3(-cameraX, -cameraY, -cameraZ));
    mMat = glm::translate(glm::mat4(1.0f), glm::vec3(cubeLocX, cubeLocY, cubeLocZ));
    mvMat = vMat * mMat;
```

```
    // copy perspective and MV matrices to corresponding uniform variables
    glUniformMatrix4fv(mvLoc, 1, GL_FALSE, glm::value_ptr(mvMat));
    glUniformMatrix4fv(pLoc, 1, GL_FALSE, glm::value_ptr(pMat));

    // associate VBO with the corresponding vertex attribute in the vertex shader
    glBindBuffer(GL_ARRAY_BUFFER, vbo[0]);
    glVertexAttribPointer(0, 3, GL_FLOAT, GL_FALSE, 0, 0);
    glEnableVertexAttribArray(0);

    // adjust OpenGL settings and draw model
    glEnable(GL_DEPTH_TEST);
    glDepthFunc(GL_LEQUAL);
    glDrawArrays(GL_TRIANGLES, 0, 36);
}

int main(void) {                              // main() is unchanged from before
    if (!glfwInit()) { exit(EXIT_FAILURE); }
    glfwWindowHint(GLFW_CONTEXT_VERSION_MAJOR, 4);
    glfwWindowHint(GLFW_CONTEXT_VERSION_MINOR, 3);
    GLFWwindow* window = glfwCreateWindow(600, 600, "Chapter 4 - program 1", NULL, NULL);
    glfwMakeContextCurrent(window);
    if (glewInit() != GLEW_OK) { exit(EXIT_FAILURE); }
    glfwSwapInterval(1);

    init(window);

    while (!glfwWindowShouldClose(window)) {
        display(window, glfwGetTime());
        glfwSwapBuffers(window);
        glfwPollEvents();
    }
    glfwDestroyWindow(window);
    glfwTerminate();
    exit(EXIT_SUCCESS);
}
```

Vertex shader (file name: "vertShader.glsl")

```
#version 430

layout (location=0) in vec3 position;

uniform mat4 mv_matrix;
uniform mat4 p_matrix;

void main(void)
{   gl_Position = p_matrix * mv_matrix * vec4(position,1.0);
}
```

Fragment shader (file name: "fragShader.glsl")

```
#version 430

out vec4 color;

uniform mat4 mv_matrix;
uniform mat4 p_matrix;

void main(void)
{   color = vec4(1.0, 0.0, 0.0, 1.0);
}
```

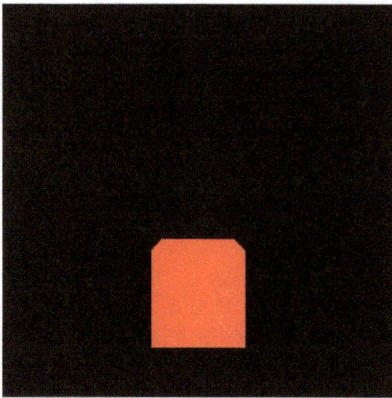

Figure 4.3
Output of Program 4.1. red cube positioned at (0,-2,0) viewed from (0,0,8).

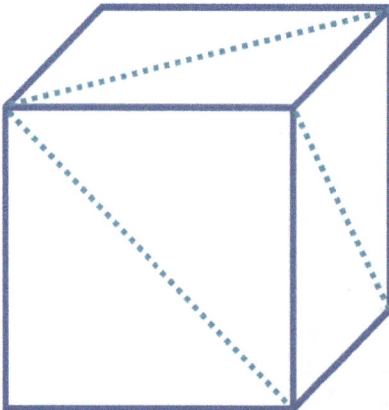

Figure 4.4
Cube made of triangles.

Let's take a close look at the code in Program 4.1. It is important that we understand how *all* of the pieces work, *and how they work together.*

Start by examining the function setupVertices(), called by init(). At the start of this function, an array is declared called vertexPositions that contains the 36 vertices comprising the cube. At first you might wonder why this cube has 36 vertices, when logically a cube should only require eight. The answer is that we need to build our cube out of triangles, and so each of the six cube faces needs to be built of two triangles, for a total of 6x2=12 triangles (see Figure 4.4). Since each triangle is specified by three vertices, this totals 36 vertices. Since each vertex has three values (*x,y,z*), there are a total of 36x3=108 values in the array. It is true that each vertex participates in multiple triangles, but we still specify each vertex separately because for now we are sending each triangle's vertices down the pipeline separately.

The cube is defined in its own coordinate system, with (0,0,0) at its center, and with its corners ranging from -1.0 to +1.0 along the *x*, *y*, and *z* axes. The rest of the setupVertices() function sets up the VAO and two VBOs (although only one is used) and loads the cube vertices into the 0th VBO buffer.

Note that the init() function performs tasks that only need to be done once: reading in shader code and building the rendering program, and loading cube vertices into the VBO (by calling setupVertices()). Note that it also positions the cube and the camera in the world. Later we will animate the cube and also see how to move the camera around, at which point we may need to remove this hardcoded positioning.

Now let's look at the display() function. Recall that display() may be called repeatedly and the rate at which it is called is referred to as the *frame rate*. That is, animation works by continually drawing and redrawing the scene, or frame, very quickly. It is usually necessary to clear the depth buffer before rendering a frame so that hidden surface removal occurs properly (not clearing the depth buffer can sometimes result in every surface being removed, resulting in a completely black screen). By default, depth values in OpenGL range from 0.0 to 1.0. Clearing the depth buffer is done by calling glClear(GL_DEPTH_BUFFER_BIT), which fills the depth buffer with the default value (usually 1.0).

Next, display() enables the shaders by calling glUseProgram(), installing the GLSL code on the GPU. Recall this doesn't run the shader program, but it does enable subsequent OpenGL calls to determine the shader's *vertex attribute* and *uniform* locations. The display() function next gets the uniform variable locations, builds the perspective, view, and model matrices[3], concatenates the view and model matrices into a single MV matrix, and assigns the perspective and MV matrices to their corresponding uniforms. Here, it is worth noting also the form of the GLM call to the translate() function:

```
vMat = glm::translate(glm::mat4(1.0f), glm::vec3(-cameraX, -cameraY, -cameraZ));
```

The somewhat cryptic-looking call builds a translation matrix by (a) starting with an identity matrix (using the glm::mat4(1.0f) constructor) and (b) specifying translation values in the form of a vector (with the glm::vec3(*x,y,z*) constructor). Many of the GLM transform operations utilize this approach.

---

[3] An astute reader may notice that it shouldn't be necessary to build the perspective matrix every time display() is called, because its value doesn't change. This is partially true—the perspective matrix *would* need to be recomputed if the user were to *resize* the window while the program was running. In Section 4.11 we will handle this situation more efficiently, and in the process we will move the computation of the perspective matrix out of display() and into the init() function.

Next, display() enables the buffer containing the cube vertices and attaches it to 0th vertex attribute to prepare for sending the vertices to the shader.

The last thing display() does is draw the model by calling glDrawArrays(), specifying that the model is composed of triangles and has 36 total vertices. The call to glDrawArrays() is typically preceded by additional commands that adjust rendering settings for this model.[4] In this example there are two such commands, both of which are related to depth testing. Recall from Chapter 2 that depth testing is used by OpenGL to perform hidden surface removal. Here, we enable depth testing and specify the particular depth test we wish OpenGL to use. The settings shown here correspond to the description in Chapter 2; later in the book we will see other uses for these commands.

Finally, consider the shaders. First, note that they both include the same block of uniform variable declarations. Although this is not always required, it is often a good practice to include the same block of uniform variable declarations in all of the shaders within a particular rendering program.

Note also in the vertex shader the presence of the layout qualifier on the incoming vertex attribute position. Since the location is specified as "0", the display() function can reference this variable simply by using 0 in the first parameter of the glVertexAttribPointer() function call and in the glEnableVertexAttribArray() function call. Note also that the position vertex attribute is declared as a vec3, and so it needs to be converted to a vec4 in order to be compatible with the 4x4 matrices with which it will be multiplied. This conversion is done with vec4(position,1.0), which builds a vec4 out of the variable named "position", putting a value of 1.0 in the newly added 4th spot.

The multiplication in the vertex shader applies the matrix transforms to the vertex, converting it to camera space (note the right-to-left concatenation order). Those values are put in the built-in OpenGL output variable gl_Position, and then proceed through the pipeline and are interpolated by the rasterizer.

The interpolated pixel locations (referred to as *fragments*) are then sent to the *fragment shader*. Recall that the primary purpose of the fragment shader is to set the color of an outputted pixel. In a manner similar to the vertex shader, the fragment shader processes the pixels one by one, with a separate invocation for each pixel. In this case, it outputs a hardcoded value corresponding to red. For reasons

---

4 Often, these calls may be placed in init() rather than in display(). However, it is necessary to place one or more of them in display() when drawing multiple objects with different properties. For simplicity, we always place them in display().

indicated earlier, the uniform variables have been included in the fragment shader even though they aren't being used there in this example.

An overview of the flow of data starting with the C++/OpenGL application and passing through the pipeline is shown in Figure 4.5.

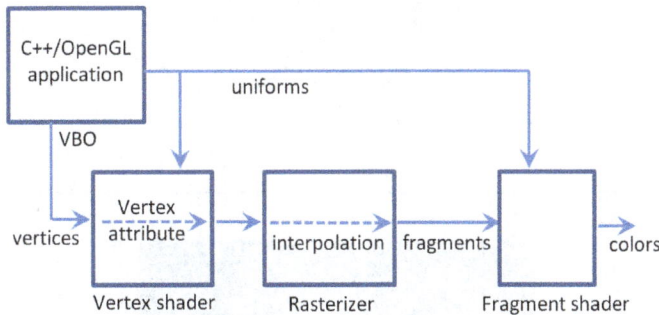

Figure 4.5
Data flow through Program 4.1.

Let's make a slight modification to the shaders. In particular, we will assign a color to each vertex according to its location, and put that color in the outgoing vertex attribute varyingColor. The fragment shader is similarly revised to accept the incoming color (interpolated by the rasterizer) and use that to set the color of the output pixel. Note that the code also multiplies the location by 1/2 and then adds 1/2 to convert the range of values from [-1..+1] to [0..1]. Note also the use of the common convention of assigning variable names that include the word "varying" to programmer-defined interpolated vertex attributes. The changes in each shader are highlighted, and the resulting output is as follows.

Revised vertex shader:

```
#version 430

layout (location=0) in vec3 position;
uniform mat4 mv_matrix;
uniform mat4 p_matrix;

out vec4 varyingColor;

void main(void)
{   gl_Position = p_matrix * mv_matrix * vec4(position,1.0);
    varyingColor = vec4(position,1.0) * 0.5 + vec4(0.5, 0.5, 0.5, 0.5);
}
```

Revised fragment shader:

```
#version 430
in vec4 varyingColor;
out vec4 color;
uniform mat4 mv_matrix;
uniform mat4 p_matrix;

void main(void)
{   color = varyingColor;
}
```

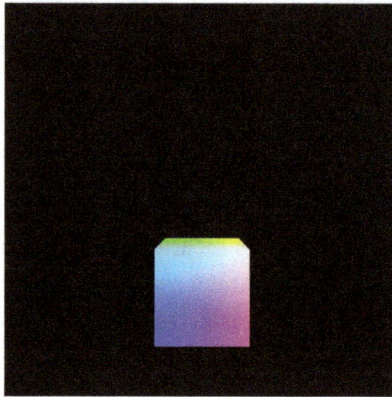

Figure 4.6
Cube with interpolated colors.

Note that because the colors are sent out from the vertex shader in a vertex attribute (varyingColor), *they too are interpolated* by the rasterizer! The effect of this can be seen in Figure 4.6, where the colors from corner to corner are clearly interpolated smoothly throughout the cube.

Note also that the "out" variable varyingColor in the vertex shader is also the "in" variable in the fragment shader. The two shaders know which variable from the vertex shader feeds which variable in the fragment shader because they have the same name "varyingColor" in both shaders.

Since our main() includes a render loop, we can animate our cube as we did in Program 2.6, by building the model matrix using a varying translation and rotation based on the time. For example, the code in the display() function in Program 4.1 could be modified as follows (changes are highlighted):

```
glClear(GL_DEPTH_BUFFER_BIT);
glClear(GL_COLOR_BUFFER_BIT);

. . .
// use current time to compute different translations in x, y, and z
tMat = glm::translate(glm::mat4(1.0f),
    glm::vec3(sin(0.35f*currentTime)*2.0f, cos(0.52f*currentTime)*2.0f, sin(0.7f*currentTime)*2.0f));
rMat = glm::rotate(glm::mat4(1.0f), 1.75f*(float)currentTime, glm::vec3(0.0f, 1.0f, 0.0f));
rMat = glm::rotate(rMat, 1.75f*(float)currentTime, glm::vec3(1.0f, 0.0f, 0.0f));
rMat = glm::rotate(rMat, 1.75f*(float)currentTime, glm::vec3(0.0f, 0.0f, 1.0f));
// the 1.75 adjusts the rotation speed

mMat = tMat * rMat;
```

The use of current time (and a variety of trigonometric functions) in the model matrix causes the cube to appear to tumble around in space. Note that adding this animation illustrates the importance of clearing the depth buffer each time through display() to ensure correct hidden surface removal. It also necessitates clearing the *color* buffer as shown; otherwise, the cube will leave a trail as it moves.

The translate() and rotate() functions are part of the GLM library. Also, note the matrix multiplication in the last line—the order in which tMat and rMat are listed in the operation is significant. It computes a concatenation of the two transforms, with translation on the left and rotation on the right. When a vertex is subsequently multiplied by this matrix, the computation is right to left, meaning that the rotation is done first, followed by the translation. The order of application of transforms is significant, and changing the order would result in different behavior. Figure 4.7 shows some of the frames that are displayed after animating the cube.

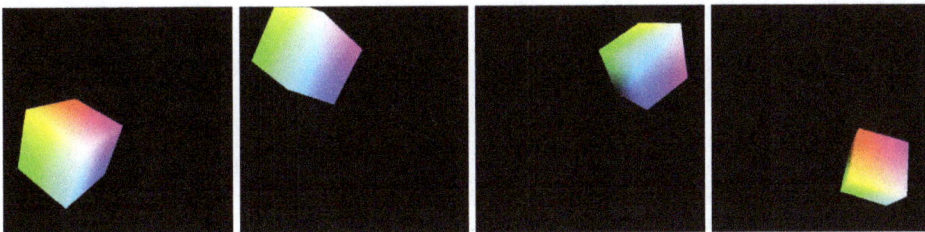

Figure 4.7
Animated ("tumbling") 3D cube.

4.6 ■ RENDERING MULTIPLE COPIES OF AN OBJECT

We now extend what we have learned to rendering multiple objects. Before we tackle the general case of rendering a variety of models in a single scene, let's consider the simpler case of *multiple occurrences of the same model*. Suppose, for instance, that we wish to expand the previous example so that it renders a "swarm" of 24 tumbling cubes. We can do this by moving the portions of the code in display() that build the MV matrix and that draw the cube (shown as follows in blue) into a loop that executes 24 times. We incorporate the loop variable into the cube's rotation and translation so that each time the cube is drawn, a different model matrix is built. (We also positioned the camera further down the positive Z axis so we can see all of the cubes.) A frame from the resulting animated scene is shown in Figure 4.8.

```
void display(GLFWwindow* window, double currentTime) {
    . . .
    for (i=0; i<24; i++)
    {   tf = currentTime + i;     // tf == "time factor", declared as type float
        tMat = glm::translate(glm::mat4(1.0f), glm::vec3(sin(.35f*tf)*8.0f, cos(.52f*tf)*8.0f,
                                                                  sin(.70f*tf)*8.0f));
        rMat = glm::rotate(glm::mat4(1.0f), 1.75f*tf, glm::vec3(0.0f, 1.0f, 0.0f));
        rMat = glm::rotate(rMat, 1.75f*tf, glm::vec3(1.0f, 0.0f, 0.0f));
        rMat = glm::rotate(rMat, 1.75f*tf, glm::vec3(0.0f, 0.0f, 1.0f));
        mMat = tMat * rMat;
        mvMat = vMat * mMat;

        glUniformMatrix4fv(mvLoc, 1, GL_FALSE, glm::value_ptr(mvMat));
        glUniformMatrix4fv(pLoc, 1, GL_FALSE, glm::value_ptr(pMat));

        glBindBuffer(GL_ARRAY_BUFFER, vbo[0]);
        glVertexAttribPointer(0, 3, GL_FLOAT, GL_FALSE, 0, 0);
        glEnableVertexAttribArray(0);

        glEnable(GL_DEPTH_TEST);
        glDepthFunc(GL_LEQUAL);
        glDrawArrays(GL_TRIANGLES, 0, 36);
    }
}
```

Figure 4.8
Multiple tumbling cubes.

4.6.1 Instancing

Instancing provides a mechanism for telling the graphics card to render multiple copies of an object using only a single C++/OpenGL call. This can result in a significant performance benefit, particularly when there are thousands or millions of copies of the object being drawn—such as when rendering many flowers in a field, or many zombies in an army.

We start by changing the glDrawArrays() call in our C++/OpenGL application to glDrawArraysInstanced(). Now, we can ask OpenGL to draw as many copies as we want. We can specify drawing 24 cubes as follows:

glDrawArraysInstanced(GL_TRIANGLES, 0, 36, 24);

When using instancing, the vertex shader has access to a built-in variable gl_InstanceID, an integer that refers to which numeric instance of the object is currently being processed.

To replicate our previous tumbling cubes example using instancing, we will need to move the computations that build the different model matrices (previously inside a loop in display()) into the vertex shader. Since GLSL does not provide translate or rotate functions, and we cannot make calls to GLM from inside a shader, we will need to use the utility functions from Program 3.1. We will also need to pass the "time factor" from the C++/OpenGL application to the vertex shader in a uniform. We also need to pass the view matrix in its own uniform variable because the rotation computations have been moved to the vertex shader. The revisions, including those in the C++/OpenGL application and those in the new vertex shader, are shown in Program 4.2.

Program 4.2 Instancing – Twenty-Four Animated Cubes

Vertex Shader:

```glsl
#version 430
layout (location=0) in vec3 position;

uniform mat4 v_matrix;
uniform mat4 p_matrix;
uniform float tf;                   // time factor for animation and placement of cubes

out vec4 varyingColor;

mat4 buildRotateX(float rad);       // declaration of matrix transformation utility functions
mat4 buildRotateY(float rad);       // (GLSL requires functions to be declared prior to invocation)
mat4 buildRotateZ(float rad);
mat4 buildTranslate(float x, float y, float z);

void main(void)
{   float i = gl_InstanceID + tf;   // value based on time factor, but different for each cube instance
    float a = sin(2.0 * i) * 8.0;   // these are the x, y, and z components for the translation, below
    float b = sin(3.0 * i) * 8.0;
    float c = sin(4.0 * i) * 8.0;

    // build the rotation and translation matrices to be applied to this cube's model matrix
    mat4 localRotX = buildRotateX(1000*i);
    mat4 localRotY = buildRotateY(1000*i);
    mat4 localRotZ = buildRotateZ(1000*i);
    mat4 localTrans = buildTranslate(a,b,c);

    // build the model matrix and then the model-view matrix
    mat4 newM_matrix = localTrans * localRotX * localRotY * localRotZ;
    mat4 mv_matrix = v_matrix * newM_matrix;

    gl_Position = p_matrix * mv_matrix * vec4(position,1.0);
    varyingColor = vec4(position,1.0) * 0.5 + vec4(0.5, 0.5, 0.5, 0.5);
}
```

```
// utility function to build a translation matrix (from Chapter 3)
mat4 buildTranslate(float x, float y, float z)
{   mat4 trans = mat4(1.0, 0.0, 0.0, 0.0,
                      0,0, 1.0, 0.0, 0.0,
                      0.0, 0.0, 1.0, 0.0,
                      x, y, z, 1.0 );
    return trans;
}

// similar functions included for rotation around the X, Y, and Z axes (also from Chapter 3)
. . .
```

C++/OpenGL Application (in display())

```
    . . .
    // computations that build (and transform) mMat have been moved to the vertex shader.
    // there is no longer any need to build an MV matrix in the C++ application.
    glUniformMatrix4fv(vLoc, 1, GL_FALSE, glm::value_ptr(vMat));   // shader needs the V matrix
    timeFactor = ((float)currentTime);                            // uniform for the time factor
    tfLoc = glGetUniformLocation(renderingProgram, "tf");         // (the shader needs that too)
    glUniform1f(tfLoc, (float)timeFactor);

    . . .
    glDrawArraysInstanced(GL_TRIANGLES, 0, 36, 24);
```

The resulting output of Program 4.2 is identical to that for the previous example, and can be seen in the previous Figure 4.8.

Instancing makes it possible to greatly expand the number of copies of an object; in this example animating *100,000* cubes is still feasible even for a modest GPU. The changes to the code—mainly just a few modified constants to spread the large number of cubes further apart—are as follows:

Vertex Shader:

```
    . . .
    float a = sin(203.0 * i/8000.0) * 403.0;
    float b = cos(301.0 * i/4001.0) * 401.0;
    float c = sin(400.0 * i/6003.0) * 405.0;
    . . .
```

C++/OpenGL Application

```
    . . .
    cameraZ = 420.0f;   // move camera further down the Z axis to view the increased number of cubes
    . . .
    glDrawArraysInstanced(GL_TRIANGLES, 0, 36, 100000);
```

The resulting output is shown in Figure 4.9.

Figure 4.9
Instancing: 100,000 animated cubes.

4.7 ■ RENDERING MULTIPLE DIFFERENT MODELS IN A SCENE

To render more than one model in a single scene, a simple approach is to use a separate buffer for each model. Each model will need its own model matrix, and thus a new model-view matrix will be generated for each model that we render. There will also need to be separate calls to glDrawArrays() for each model. Thus there will need to be changes both in init() and in display().

Another consideration is whether or not we will need different shaders—or a different rendering program—for each of the objects we wish to draw. As it turns out, *in many cases we can use the same shaders* (and thus the same rendering program) for the various objects we are drawing. We usually only need to employ different rendering programs for the various objects if they are built of different primitives (such as lines instead of triangles), or if there are complex lighting or other effects involved. For now, that isn't the case, so we can reuse the same vertex and fragment shaders, and just modify our C++/OpenGL application to send each model down the pipeline when display() is called.

Let's proceed by adding a simple pyramid, so our scene includes both a single cube and a pyramid. The relevant modifications to the code are shown in Program 4.3. A few of the key details are highlighted, such as where we specify one or the other buffer, and where we specify the number of vertices contained in the model. Note that the pyramid is composed of six triangles—four on the sides and two on the bottom, totaling 6×3=18 vertices.

The resulting scene, containing both the cube and the pyramid, is then shown in Figure 4.10.

Program 4.3 Cube and Pyramid

```
void setupVertices() {
    float cubePositions[108] =
    { -1.0f,  1.0f, -1.0f, -1.0f, -1.0f, -1.0f,  1.0f, -1.0f, -1.0f,
       1.0f, -1.0f, -1.0f,  1.0f,  1.0f, -1.0f, -1.0f,  1.0f, -1.0f,
            ... same as before, for the rest of the cube vertices
    };

    // pyramid with 18 vertices, comprising 6 triangles (four sides, and two on the bottom)
    float pyramidPositions[54] =
    {   -1.0f, -1.0f, 1.0f, 1.0f, -1.0f, 1.0f, 0.0f, 1.0f, 0.0f,    // front face
         1.0f, -1.0f, 1.0f, 1.0f, -1.0f, -1.0f, 0.0f, 1.0f, 0.0f,   // right face
         1.0f, -1.0f, -1.0f, -1.0f, -1.0f, -1.0f, 0.0f, 1.0f, 0.0f, // back face
        -1.0f, -1.0f, -1.0f, -1.0f, -1.0f, 1.0f, 0.0f, 1.0f, 0.0f,  // left face
        -1.0f, -1.0f, -1.0f, 1.0f, -1.0f, 1.0f, -1.0f, -1.0f, 1.0f, // base – left front
         1.0f, -1.0f, 1.0f, -1.0f, -1.0f, 1.0f, 1.0f, -1.0f, -1.0f  // base – right back
    };
    glGenVertexArrays(numVAOs, vao);                     // we need at least 1 VAO
    glBindVertexArray(vao[0]);
    glGenBuffers(numVBOs, vbo);                          // we need at least 2 VBOs

    glBindBuffer(GL_ARRAY_BUFFER, vbo[0]);
    glBufferData(GL_ARRAY_BUFFER, sizeof(cubePositions), cubePositions, GL_STATIC_DRAW);

    glBindBuffer(GL_ARRAY_BUFFER, vbo[1]);
    glBufferData(GL_ARRAY_BUFFER, sizeof(pyramidPositions), pyramidPositions, GL_STATIC_DRAW);
}
void display(GLFWwindow* window, double currentTime) {
    . . .
    // clear the color and depth buffers as before (not shown here)
    // use rendering program and obtain uniform locations as before (not shown here)
    // projection matrix computed as before (not shown here)
    . . .
```

```
// the view matrix is computed once and used for both objects

vMat = glm::translate(glm::mat4(1.0f), glm::vec3(-cameraX, -cameraY, -cameraZ));

// draw the cube (use buffer #0)

mMat = glm::translate(glm::mat4(1.0f), glm::vec3(cubeLocX, cubeLocY, cubeLocZ));
mvMat = vMat * mMat;

glUniformMatrix4fv(mvLoc, 1, GL_FALSE, glm::value_ptr(mvMat));
glUniformMatrix4fv(pLoc, 1, GL_FALSE, glm::value_ptr(pMat));

glBindBuffer(GL_ARRAY_BUFFER, vbo[0]);
glVertexAttribPointer(0, 3, GL_FLOAT, GL_FALSE, 0, 0);
glEnableVertexAttribArray(0);

glEnable(GL_DEPTH_TEST);
glDepthFunc(GL_LEQUAL);
glDrawArrays(GL_TRIANGLES, 0, 36);

// draw the pyramid (use buffer #1)

mMat = glm::translate(glm::mat4(1.0f), glm::vec3(pyrLocX, pyrLocY, pyrLocZ));
mvMat = vMat * mMat;

glUniformMatrix4fv(mvLoc, 1, GL_FALSE, glm::value_ptr(mvMat));
glUniformMatrix4fv(pLoc, 1, GL_FALSE, glm::value_ptr(pMat));

glBindBuffer(GL_ARRAY_BUFFER, vbo[1]);
glVertexAttribPointer(0, 3, GL_FLOAT, GL_FALSE, 0, 0);
glEnableVertexAttribArray(0);

glEnable(GL_DEPTH_TEST);
glDepthFunc(GL_LEQUAL);
glDrawArrays(GL_TRIANGLES, 0, 18);
}
```

Figure 4.10
3D cube and pyramid.

A few other minor details to note regarding Program 4.3:

- The variables pyrLocX, pyrLocY, and pyrLocZ need to be declared and then initialized in init() to the desired pyramid location, as was done for the cube location.

- The view matrix vMat is built at the top of display() and then used in both the cube's and the pyramid's model-view matrices.

- The vertex and fragment shaders are not shown—they are unchanged from Section 4.5.

4.8 MATRIX STACKS

So far, the models we have rendered have each been constructed of a single set of vertices. It is often desired, however, to build complex models by assembling smaller, simple models. For example, a model of a "robot" could be created by separately drawing the head, body, legs, and arms, where each of those is a separate model. An object built in this manner is often called a *hierarchical model*. The tricky part of building hierarchical models is keeping track of all the model-view matrices and making sure they stay perfectly coordinated—otherwise the robot might fly apart into pieces!

Hierarchical models are useful not only for building complex objects—they can also be used to generate complex scenes. For example, consider how our planet Earth revolves around the sun, and in turn how the moon revolves around the Earth. Such a scene is shown in Figure 4.11.[5] Computing the moon's actual

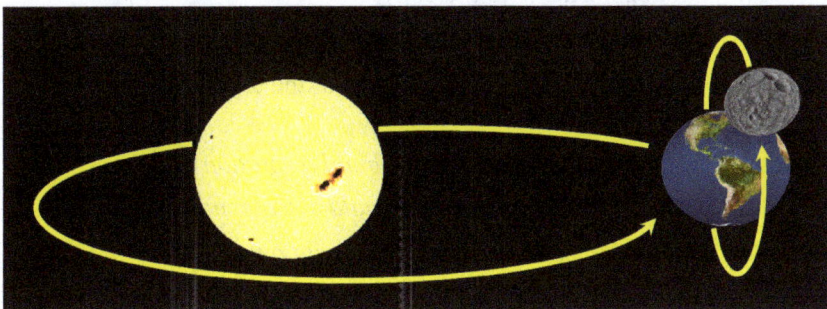

Figure 4.11
Animated planetary system (sun and earth textures from [HT23], moon texture from [NA23]).

---

[5] Yes, we know that the moon doesn't revolve in this "vertical" trajectory around the earth, but rather in one that is more co-planar with the earth's revolution around the sun. We chose this orbit to make our program's execution clearer.

path through space could be complex. However, if we can *combine* the transforms representing the two simple circular paths—the moon's path around the Earth and the Earth's path around the sun—we avoid having to explicitly compute the moon's trajectory.

It turns out that we can do this fairly easily with a *matrix stack*. A matrix stack is, as its name implies, a stack of transformation matrices. As we will see, matrix stacks make it easy to create and manage complex hierarchical objects and scenes, where transforms can be built upon (and removed from) other transforms.

OpenGL has a built-in matrix stack, but as part of the older fixed-function (non-programmable) pipeline it has long been deprecated [OL16]. However, the C++ Standard Template Library (STL) has a class called "stack" that is relatively straightforward to adapt as a matrix stack, by using it to build a stack of mat4s. As we will see, many of the model, view, and model-view matrices that would normally be needed in a complex scene can be replaced by a single instance of stack<glm::mat4>.

We will first examine the basic commands for instantiating and utilizing a C++ stack, then use one to build a complex animated scene. We will use the C++ stack class in the following ways:

- push() – makes available a new entry on the top of the stack. We will typically use this command by pushing a copy of the matrix that is currently at the top of the stack, with the intent of concatenating additional transforms onto the copy.
- pop() – removes (and returns) the top matrix.
- top() – returns a reference to the matrix at the top of the stack, without removing it.
- <stack>.top() *= rotate(*parameters to build a rotation matrix*) ⎫ apply
- <stack>.top() *= scale(*parameters to build a scale matrix*) ⎬ transforms directly to the top
- <stack>.top() *= translate(*parameters to build a translation matrix*) ⎭ matrix in the stack

As shown in the previous list, the "*=" operator is overloaded in mat4 so that it can be used to concatenate matrices. Therefore, we will typically use it in one of the forms shown to add translations, rotations, and so on to the matrix at the top of the matrix stack.

Now, rather than building transforms by creating instances of mat4, we instead use the push() command to create new matrices at the top of the stack. Desired transforms are then applied as needed to the newly created matrix on the top of the stack.

The first matrix pushed on the stack is frequently the VIEW matrix. The matrices above it are model-view matrices of increasing complexity; that is, they have an increasing number of model transforms applied to them. These transforms can either be applied directly or by first concatenating other matrices.

In our planetary system example, the matrix positioned immediately above the VIEW matrix would be the sun's MV matrix. The matrix on top of that matrix would be the earth's MV matrix, *which consists of a copy of the sun's MV matrix with the Earth's model matrix transforms applied to it*. That is, the Earth's MV matrix is built by incorporating the planet's transforms into the sun's transforms. Similarly, the moon's MV matrix sits on top of the planet's MV matrix and is constructed by applying the moon's model matrix transforms to the planet's MV matrix immediately below it.

After rendering the moon, a second "moon" could be rendered by "popping" the first moon's matrix off of the stack (restoring the top of the stack to the planet's model-view matrix) and then repeating the process for the second moon.

The basic approach is as follows:

1. We declare our stack, giving it the name "mvStack".
2. When a new object is created relative to a parent object, call "mvStack .push(mvStack.top())".
3. Apply the new object's desired transforms; i.e., multiply a desired transform onto it.
4. When an object or sub-object has finished being drawn, call "mvStack .pop()" to remove its model-view matrix from atop the matrix stack.

In later chapters, we will learn how to create spheres and make them look like planets and moons. For now, to keep things simple, we will build a "planetary system" using our pyramid and a couple of cubes.

Here is an overview of how a display() function using a matrix stack is typically organized:

Setup	• Instantiate the matrix stack.
Camera	• Push a new matrix onto the stack. (this will instantiate an empty VIEW matrix).
	• Apply transform(s) to the view matrix on the top of the stack.
Parent	• Push a new matrix onto the stack (this will be the parent MV matrix—for the first parent, it duplicates the view matrix).
	• Apply transforms to incorporate the parent's M matrix into the duplicated view matrix.
	• Send the topmost matrix (i.e., use "glm::value_ptr()") to the MV uniform variable in the vertex shader.
	• Draw the parent object.
Child	• Push a new matrix onto the stack. This will be the child's MV matrix, duplicating the parent MV matrix.
	• Apply transforms to incorporate the child's M matrix into the duplicated parent MV matrix.
	• Send the topmost matrix (i.e., use "glm::value_ptr()") to the MV uniform variable in the vertex shader.
	• Draw the child object.
Cleanup	• Pop the child's MV matrix off the stack.
	• Pop the parent's MV matrix off the stack.
	• Pop the VIEW matrix off the stack.

Note that the pyramid ("sun") rotation on its axis is in its own local coordinate space, and should not be allowed to affect the "children" (the planet and moon, in this case). Therefore, the sun's rotation (shown in the image below) is pushed onto the stack, but then after drawing the sun, it must be removed (popped) from the stack.

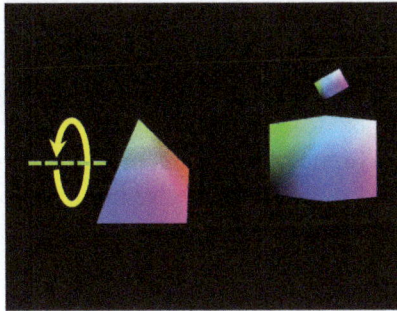

The big cube's (planet) revolution around the sun (left image, below) will affect the moon's movement, and so it is pushed on the stack and remains there when drawing the moon as well. By contrast, the planet's rotation on its axis (right image, below) is local and does not affect the moon, so it is popped off the stack before drawing the moon.

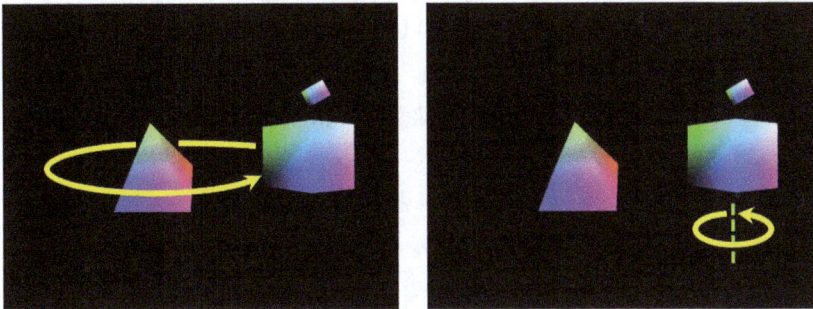

Similarly, we would push transforms onto the stack for the moon's rotations (around the planet, and on its axis), indicated in the following images.

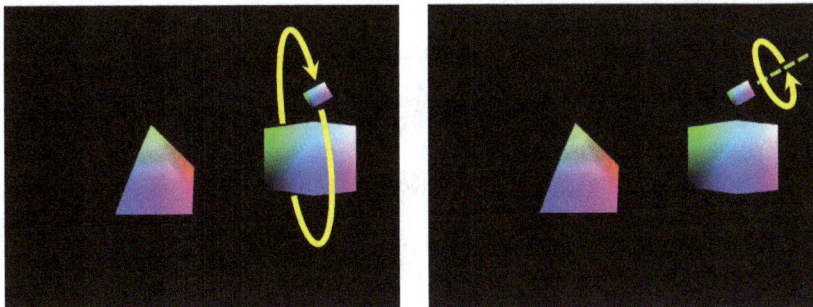

Here is the sequence of steps for the "planet":

- **push()** This will be the portion of the planet's MV matrix that will also affect children.
- **translate(...)** To incorporate the planet movement around the sun into the planet's MV matrix. In this example we use trigonometry to calculate the planet movement as a translation.
- **push()** This will be the planet's complete MV matrix, also including its axis rotation.
- **rotate(...)** To incorporate the planet's axis rotation (this will later be popped and not affect children).
- **glm::value_ptr(mvStack.top())** To obtain the MV matrix and then send it to the MV uniform.
- Draw the planet.
- **pop()** This removes the planet MV matrix off the stack, exposing underneath it an earlier copy of the planet MV matrix that doesn't include the planet's axis rotation (so that only the planet's translation will affect the moon).

We now can write the complete display() routine, shown in Program 4.4.

Program 4.4 Simple Solar System Using Matrix Stack

```
stack<glm::mat4> mvStack;
void display(GLFWwindow* window, double currentTime) {
    // setup of background, depth buffer, rendering program, and P matrices unchanged
    . . .
    // push view matrix onto the stack
    vMat = glm::translate(glm::mat4(1.0f), glm::vec3(-cameraX, -cameraY, -cameraZ));
    mvStack.push(vMat);

    // --------------------- pyramid == sun ---------------------------------------
    mvStack.push(mvStack.top());
    mvStack.top() *= glm::translate(glm::mat4(1.0f), glm::vec3(0.0f, 0.0f, 0.0f));   // sun position
    mvStack.push(mvStack.top());
    mvStack.top() *= glm::rotate(glm::mat4(1.0f), (float)currentTime, glm::vec3(1.0f, 0.0f, 0.0f));
                                                                              // sun rotation
    glUniformMatrix4fv(mvLoc, 1, GL_FALSE, glm::value_ptr(mvStack.top()));
    glBindBuffer(GL_ARRAY_BUFFER, vbo[1]);
```

```
glVertexAttribPointer(0, 3, GL_FLOAT, GL_FALSE, 0, 0);
glEnableVertexAttribArray(0);
glEnable(GL_DEPTH_TEST);
glEnable(GL_LEQUAL);
glDrawArrays(GL_TRIANGLES, 0, 18);        // draw the sun
mvStack.pop();                            // remove the sun's axial rotation from the stack

//---------------------- cube == planet ----------------------------------------
mvStack.push(mvStack.top());
mvStack.top() *=
    glm::translate(glm::mat4(1.0f), glm::vec3(sin((float)currentTime)*4.0, 0.0f, cos((float)currentTime)*4.0));
mvStack.push(mvStack.top());
mvStack.top() *= glm::rotate(glm::mat4(1.0f), (float)currentTime, glm::vec3(0.0, 1.0, 0.0));
                                                                    // planet rotation
glUniformMatrix4fv(mvLoc, 1, GL_FALSE, glm::value_ptr(mvStack.top()));
glBindBuffer(GL_ARRAY_BUFFER, vbo[0]);
glVertexAttribPointer(0, 3, GL_FLOAT, GL_FALSE, 0, 0);
glEnableVertexAttribArray(0);
glDrawArrays(GL_TRIANGLES, 0, 36);        // draw the planet
mvStack.pop();                            // remove the planet's axial rotation from the stack

//---------------------- smaller cube == moon ----------------------------------
mvStack.push(mvStack.top());
mvStack.top() *=
    glm::translate(glm::mat4(1.0f), glm::vec3(0.0f, sin((float)currentTime)*2.0,
                                                cos((float)currentTime)*2.0));
mvStack.top() *= glm::rotate(glm::mat4(1.0f), (float)currentTime, glm::vec3(0.0, 0.0, 1.0));
                                                                    // moon rotation
mvStack.top() *= glm::scale(glm::mat4(1.0f), glm::vec3(0.25f, 0.25f, 0.25f));   // make the moon smaller
glUniformMatrix4fv(mvLoc, 1, GL_FALSE, glm::value_ptr(mvStack.top()));
glBindBuffer(GL_ARRAY_BUFFER, vbo[0]);
glVertexAttribPointer(0, 3, GL_FLOAT, GL_FALSE, 0, 0);
glEnableVertexAttribArray(0);
glDrawArrays(GL_TRIANGLES, 0, 36);        // draw the moon

// remove moon scale/rotation/position, planet position, sun position, and view matrices from stack
mvStack.pop();  mvStack.pop();  mvStack.pop();  mvStack.pop();
}
```

The matrix stack operations have been highlighted. There are several details worth noting:

- We have introduced a *scale* operation in a model matrix. We want the moon to be a smaller cube than the planet, so we use a call to scale() when building the MV matrix for the moon.

- In this example, we are using the trigonometric operations sin() and cos() to compute the revolution of the planet around the sun (as a translation), and also for the moon around the planet.

- The two buffers #0 and #1 contain cube and pyramid vertices respectively.

- Note the use of the glm::value_ptr(mvMatrix.top()) function call within the glUniformMatrix() command. This call retrieves the values in the matrix on top of the stack, and those values are then sent to the uniform variable (in this case, the sun, the planet, and then the moon's MV matrices).

The vertex and fragment shaders are not shown—they are unchanged from the previous example. We also moved the initial position of the pyramid (sun) and the camera to center the scene on the screen.

4.9 COMBATING "Z-FIGHTING" ARTIFACTS

Recall that when rendering multiple objects, OpenGL uses the *Z-buffer algorithm* (shown earlier in Figure 2.14) for performing hidden surface removal. Ordinarily, this resolves which object surfaces are visible and rendered to the screen, versus which surfaces lie behind other objects and thus should not be rendered, by choosing a pixel's color to be that of the corresponding fragment closest to the camera.

However, there can be occasions when two object surfaces in a scene overlap and lie in coincident planes, making it problematic for the Z-buffer algorithm to determine which of the two surfaces should be rendered (since neither is "closest" to the camera). When this happens, floating point rounding errors can lead to some portions of the rendered surface using the color of one of the objects, and other portions using the color of the other object. This artifact is known as *Z-fighting* or *depth-fighting*, because the effect is the result of rendered fragments "fighting" over mutually corresponding pixel entries in the Z-buffer. Figure 4.12 shows an example of Z-fighting between two boxes with overlapping coincident (top) faces.

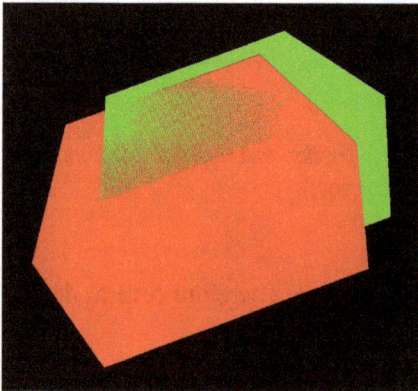

Figure 4.12
Z-fighting example.

Situations like this often occur when creating terrain or shadows. It is some-times possible to predict Z-fighting in such instances, and a common way of cor-recting it in these cases is to move one object slightly, so that the surfaces are no longer coplanar. We will see an example of this in Chapter 8.

Z-fighting can also occur due to limited precision of the values in the depth buffer. For each pixel processed by the Z-buffer algorithm, the accuracy of its depth information is limited by the number of bits available for storing it in the depth buffer. The greater the range between near and far clipping planes used to build the perspective matrix, the more likely two objects' points with similar (but not equal) actual depths will be represented by the same numeric value in the depth buffer. Therefore, it is up to the programmer to select near and far clipping plane values to minimize the distance between the two planes, while still ensuring that all objects essential to the scene lie within the viewing frustum.

It is also important to understand that, due to the effect of the perspective transform, changing the near clipping plane value can have a greater impact on the likelihood of Z-fighting artifacts than making an equivalent change in the far clipping plane. Therefore, it is advisable to avoid selecting a near clipping plane that is too close to the eye.

Previous examples in this book have simply used values of 0.1 and 1000 (in our calls to perspective()) for the near and far clipping planes. These may need to be adjusted for your scene.

4.10 ■ OTHER OPTIONS FOR PRIMITIVES

OpenGL supports a number of primitive types—so far we have seen two: GL_TRIANGLES and GL_POINTS. In fact, there are several others. All of the avail-able primitive types supported in OpenGL fall into the categories of *triangles*, *lines*, *points*, and *patches*. Here is a complete list:

Triangle primitives:

GL_TRIANGLES	The most common primitive type in this book. Vertices that pass through the pipeline form distinct triangles: *vertices:* `0 1 2` `3 4 5` `6 7 8` etc. *triangles:* ✓ ✓ ✓

GL_TRIANGLE_STRIP	Each vertex that passes through the pipeline efficiently forms a triangle with the previous two vertices:
GL_TRIANGLE_FAN	Each pair of vertices that passes through the pipeline forms a triangle with the very first vertex:
GL_TRIANGLES_ADJACENCY	Intended only for use with geometry shaders. Allows the shader to access the vertices in the current triangle, plus additional adjacent vertices.
GL_TRIANGLE_STRIP_ ADJACENCY	Intended only for use with geometry shaders. Similar to GL_TRIANGLES_ADJACENCY, except that triangle vertices overlap as for GL_TRIANGLE_STRIP.

Line primitives:

GL_LINES	Vertices that pass through the pipeline form distinct lines:
GL_LINE_STRIP	Each vertex that passes through the pipeline efficiently forms a line with the previous vertex:
GL_LINE_LOOP	Same as GL_LINE_STRIP, except a line is also formed between the very first and very last vertices.

GL_LINES_ADJACENCY	Intended only for use with geometry shaders. Allows the shader to access the vertices in the current line, plus additional adjacent vertices.
GL_LINE_STRIP_ADJACENCY	Similar to GL_LINES_ADJACENCY, except that line vertices overlap as for GL_LINE_STRIP.

Point primitives:

GL_POINTS	Each vertex that passes through the pipeline is a point.

Patch primitives:

GL_PATCHES	Intended only for use with tessellation shaders. Indicates that a set of vertices passes from the vertex shader to the tessellation control shader, where they are typically used to shape a tessellated grid into a curved surface.

4.11 CODING FOR PERFORMANCE

As the complexity of our 3D scenes grows, we will become increasingly concerned with performance. We have already seen a few instances where coding decisions were made in the interest of speed, such as when we used instancing, and when we moved expensive computations into the shaders.

Actually, the code we have presented has already also included some additional optimizations that we haven't yet discussed. We now explore these and other important techniques.

4.11.1 Minimizing Dynamic Memory Allocation

The critical section of our C++ code, with respect to performance, is clearly the display() function. This is the function that is called repeatedly during any animation or real-time rendering, and it is thus in this function (or in any function that it calls) where we must strive for maximum efficiency.

One important way of keeping overhead in the display() function to a minimum is by avoiding any steps that require memory allocation. Obvious examples of things to avoid thus would include:

- instantiating objects
- declaring variables

The reader is encouraged to review the programs that we have developed so far, and observe that virtually every variable used in the display() function was declared, and its space allocated, *before* the display() function was ever actually called. Declarations or instantiations almost never appear in display(). For example, Program 4.1 included the following block of code early in its listing:

```
// allocate variables used in display() function, so that they won't need to be allocated during rendering
GLuint mvLoc, pLoc;
int width, height;
float aspect;
glm::mat4 pMat, vMat, mMat, mvMat;
```

Note that we purposely placed a comment at the top of the block indicating that these variables are pre-allocated for later use in the display() function (although we are only explicitly pointing that out now).

One case of a variable that wasn't pre-allocated occurred in our matrix stack example. By using the C++ stack class, each "push" operation results in a dynamic memory allocation. Interestingly in *Java*, the JOML library provides a MatrixStack class intended for use with OpenGL that allows one to pre-allocate space for a matrix stack! We utilize it in our Java-based "sister" book *Computer Graphics Programming in OpenGL with Java, Second Edition.*

There are other, more subtle examples. For example, function calls that convert data from one type to another may in some cases instantiate and return the newly converted data. It is thus important to understand the behaviors of any library functions called from display(). The math library, GLM, was not specifically designed with speed in mind. As a result, some of the operations can lead to dynamic allocation. We have tried to use GLM functions that operate directly onto (or into) variables whose space has already been allocated, when possible. The reader is encouraged to explore alternative methods when performance is critical.

4.11.2 Pre-Computing the Perspective Matrix

Another optimization that can be done to reduce overhead in the display() function is to move the computation of the perspective matrix into the init() function. We mentioned this possibility earlier in Section 4.5 (well, in a footnote). While this is certainly easy to do, there is one slight complication. Although it is not normally necessary to recompute the perspective matrix, it *would* be necessary if the user running the application *resizes* the window (such as by dragging the window corner resize handle).

Fortunately, GLFW can be configured to automatically make a callback to a specified function whenever the window is resized. We add the following to the main(), just before the call to init():

glfwSetWindowSizeCallback(window, window_reshape_callback);

The first parameter is the GLFW window, and the second is the name of a function that GLFW calls whenever the window is resized. We then move the code that computes the perspective matrix into init(), and also copy it into a new function called window_reshape_callback().

Consider for example Program 4.1. If we reorganize the code so as to remove the computation of the perspective matrix from display(), then the revised versions of the main(), init(), display(), and the new function window_reshape_callback() would be as follows:

```
void init(GLFWwindow* window) {
    . . .
    // same as earlier, plus the following three lines:
    glfwGetFramebufferSize(window, &width, &height);
    aspect = (float)width / (float)height;
    pMat = glm::perspective(1.0472f, aspect, 0.1f, 1000.0f);         // 1.0472 radians = 60 degrees
}
void display(GLFWwindow* window, double currentTime) {
    . . .
    // same as earlier, except with the following lines removed:

    // build perspective matrix
    glfwGetFramebufferSize(window, &width, &height);
    aspect = (float)width / (float)height;
    pMat = glm::perspective(1.0472f, aspect, 0.1f, 1000.0f);
    // the rest of the function is unchanged

    . . .
}
```

```
void window_reshape_callback(GLFWwindow* window, int newWidth, int newHeight) {
    aspect = (float)newWidth / (float)newHeight;    // new width&height provided by the callback
    glViewport(0, 0, newWidth, newHeight);          // sets screen region associated with framebuffer
    pMat = glm::perspective(1.0472f, aspect, 0.1f, 1000.0f);
}
int main(void) {
    . . .
    // same as earlier, plus the following additional call:

    glfwSetWindowSizeCallback(window, window_reshape_callback);

    init(window)

    while (!glfwWindowShouldClose(window)) {
        // etc. as before
    }
```

The implementations of the programs found in this book's companion files are all organized in this manner with respect to perspective matrix computation, starting with the single tumbling cube version of Program 4.1.

4.11.3 Back-Face Culling

Another way of improving rendering efficiency is to take advantage of OpenGL's ability to do *back-face culling*. When a 3D model is entirely "closed," meaning the interior is never visible (such as for the cube and for the pyramid), then it turns out that those portions of the outer surface that are angled away from the viewer will always be obscured by some other portion of the same model. That is, those triangles that face away from the viewer cannot possibly be seen (they would be overwritten by hidden surface removal anyway), and thus there is no reason to rasterize or render them.

We can ask OpenGL to identify and "cull" (not render) back-facing triangles with the command glEnable(GL_CULL_FACE). We can also disable face culling with glDisable(GL_CULL_FACE). By default, face culling is disabled, so if you want OpenGL to cull back-facing triangles, you must enable it.

When face culling is enabled, by default triangles are rendered only if they are *front-facing*. Also by default a triangle is considered front-facing if its three vertices progress in a *counter-clockwise* direction (based on the order that they were defined in the buffer) as viewed from the OpenGL camera. Triangles whose vertices progress in a clockwise direction (as viewed from the OpenGL camera) are *back-facing*, and are not rendered. This counter-clockwise definition of "front-facing" is sometimes called the *winding order*, and can be set explicitly using the function call glFrontFace(GL_CCW) for counter-clockwise (the default) or glFrontFace(GL_CW) for clockwise. Similarly, whether it is the front-facing or the back-facing triangles that are rendered can also be set explicitly. Actually, for this purpose we specify which ones are *not* to be rendered—that is, which ones are "culled." We can specify that the back-facing triangles be culled (although this would be unnecessary because it is the default) by calling glCullFace(GL_BACK). Alternatively, we can specify instead that the front-facing triangles be culled, or even that all of the triangles be culled, by replacing the parameter GL_BACK with either GL_FRONT or GL_FRONT_AND_BACK respectively.

As we will see in Chapter 6, 3D models are typically designed so that the outer surface is constructed of triangles with the same winding order—most commonly counter-clockwise—so that if culling is enabled, then by default the portion of the model's outer surface that faces the camera is rendered. Since by default OpenGL assumes the winding order is counter-clockwise, if a model is designed to be displayed with a *clockwise* winding order, it is up to the programmer to call gl_FrontFace(GL_CW) to account for this if back-face culling is enabled.

Note that in the case of GL_TRIANGLE_STRIP, the winding order of each triangle alternates. OpenGL compensates for this by "flipping" the vertex sequence when building each successive triangle, as follows: 0-1-2, then 2-1-3, 2-3-4, 4-3-5, 4-5-6, and so on.

Back-face culling improves performance by ensuring that OpenGL doesn't spend time rasterizing and rendering surfaces that are never intended to be seen. Most of the examples we have seen in this chapter are so small that there is little motivation to enable face culling (an exception is the example shown in Figure 4.9, with the 100,000 instanced animated cubes, which may pose a performance challenge on some systems). In practice, it is common for most 3D models to be "closed," and so it is customary to routinely enable back-face culling. For example, we can add back-face culling to Program 4.3 by modifying the display() function as follows:

```
void display(GLFWwindow* window, double currentTime) {
    . . .
    glEnable(GL_CULL_FACE);

    // draw the cube
    . . .
```

```
glEnable(GL_DEPTH_TEST);
glDepthFunc(GL_LEQUAL);
glFrontFace(GL_CW);              // the cube vertices have clockwise winding order
glDrawArrays(GL_TRIANGLES, 0, 36);

//  draw the pyramid
. . .

glEnable(GL_DEPTH_TEST);
glDepthFunc(GL_LEQUAL);
glFrontFace(GL_CCW);            // the pyramid vertices have counter-clockwise winding order
glDrawArrays(GL_TRIANGLES, 0, 18);
}
```

Properly setting the winding order is important when using back-face culling. An incorrect setting, such as GL_CW when it should be GL_CCW, can lead to the interior of an object being rendered rather than its exterior, which in turn can produce distortion similar to that of an incorrect perspective matrix.

Efficiency isn't the only reason for doing face culling. In later chapters, we will see other uses, such as for those circumstances when we want to see the *inside* of a 3D model, or when using transparency.

SUPPLEMENTAL NOTES

There is a myriad of other capabilities and structures available for managing and utilizing data in OpenGL/GLSL, and we have only scratched the surface in this chapter. We haven't, for example, described a *uniform block*, which is a mechanism for organizing uniform variables similar to a *struct* in C. Uniform blocks can even be set up to receive data from buffers. Another powerful mechanism is a *shader storage block*, which is essentially a buffer into which a shader can write.

An excellent reference on the many options for managing data is the *OpenGL SuperBible* [SW15], particularly the chapter entitled "Data" (Chapter 5 in the 7th edition). It also describes many of the details and options for the various commands that we have covered. The first two example programs in this chapter, Program 4.1 and Program 4.2, were inspired by similar examples in the *SuperBible*.

There are other types of data that we will need to learn how to manage, and how to send down the OpenGL pipeline. One of these is a *texture*, which contains color image data (such as in a photograph) that can be used to "paint" the objects in our scene. We will study texture images in Chapter 5. Another important buffer that we will study further is the *depth buffer* (or Z-buffer). This will become important when we study shadows in Chapter 8. We still have much to learn about managing graphics data in OpenGL!

Exercises

4.1 *(PROJECT)* Modify Program 4.1 to replace the cube with some other simple 3D shape of your own design. Be sure to properly specify the number of vertices in the glDrawArrays() command.

4.2 *(PROJECT)* In Program 4.1, the "view" matrix is defined in the display() function simply as the negative of the camera location.

```
vMat = glm::translate(glm::mat4(1.0f), glm::vec3(-cameraX, -cameraY, -cameraZ));
```

Replace this code with an implementation of the computation shown in Figure 3.13. This will allow you to position the camera by specifying a camera position and three orientation axes. You will find it necessary to store the vectors U,V,N described in Section 3.7. Then, experiment with different camera viewpoints, and observe the resulting appearance of the rendered cube. Refer to Appendix D for more details on completing these changes.

4.3 *(PROJECT)* Modify Program 4.4 to include a second "planet," which is your custom 3D shape from Exercise 4.1. Make sure that your new "planet" is in a different orbit than the existing planet so that they don't collide.

4.4 *(PROJECT)* Modify Program 4.4 so that the "view" matrix is constructed using the "look-at" function (as described in Section 3.9). Then experiment with setting the "look-at" parameters to various locations, such as looking at the sun (in which case the scene should appear normal), looking at the planet, or looking at the moon.

4.5 *(RESEARCH)* Propose a practical use for glCullFace(GL_FRONT_AND_BACK).

References

[BL23] Blender, The Blender Foundation, accessed November 2023, https://www.blender.org/

[HT23] J. Hastings-Trew, *JHT's Planetary Pixel Emporium*, accessed November 2023, http://planetpixelemporium.com/

[MA23] Maya, AutoDesk, Inc., accessed November 2023, http://www.autodesk .com/products/maya/overview

[NA23] NASA 3D Resources, accessed November 2023, http://nasa3d.arc.nasa.gov/

[OL16] Legacy OpenGL, accessed November 2023, https://www.khronos.org/ opengl/wiki/Legacy_OpenGL

[SW15] G. Sellers, R. Wright Jr., and N. Haemel, *OpenGL SuperBible: Comprehensive Tutorial and Reference*, 7th ed. (Addison-Wesley, 2015).

TEXTURE MAPPING

■ ■ ■ ■ ■

Texture mapping is the technique of overlaying an image across a rasterized model surface. It is one of the most fundamental and important ways of adding realism to a rendered scene.

Texture mapping is so important that there is hardware support for it, allowing for very high performance resulting in real-time photorealism. *Texture Units* are hardware components designed specifically for texturing, and modern graphics cards typically come with several texture units included.

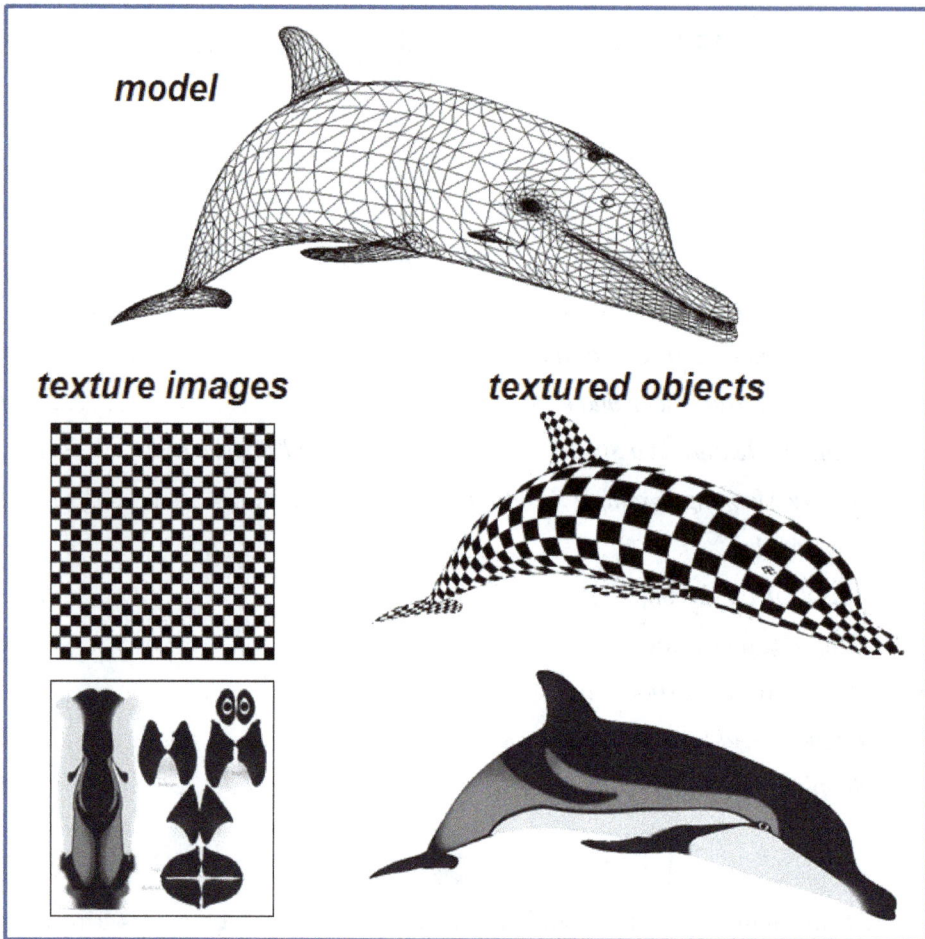

Figure 5.1
Texturing a dolphin model with two different images [TU18].

5.1 LOADING TEXTURE IMAGE FILES

There are a number of datasets and mechanisms that need to be coordinated to accomplish texture mapping efficiently in OpenGL/GLSL:

- a *texture object* to hold the texture image (in this chapter we consider only 2D images)
- a special uniform *sampler* variable so that the vertex shader can access the texture

- a buffer to hold the *texture coordinates*
- a vertex attribute for passing the texture coordinates down the pipeline
- a *texture unit* on the graphics card

A texture image can be a picture of anything. It can be a picture of something man-made or occurring in nature, such as cloth, grass, or a planetary surface; or, it could be a geometric pattern, such as the checkerboard in Figure 5.1. In video-games and animated movies, texture images are commonly used to paint faces and clothing on characters or paint skin on creatures such as the dolphin in Figure 5.1.

Images are typically stored in image files, such as .jpg, .png, .gif, or .tiff. In order to make a texture image available to shaders in the OpenGL pipeline, we need to extract the colors from the image and put them into an OpenGL *texture object* (a built-in OpenGL structure for holding a texture image).

Many C++ libraries are available for reading and processing image files. Among the popular choices are Cimg, Boost GIL, and Magick++. We have opted to use a library designed particularly for OpenGL called SOIL2 [SO23], which is based on the very popular but now outdated library SOIL. The installation steps for SOIL2 are given in Appendices A and B.

The general steps we will use for loading a texture into an OpenGL application are: (a) use SOIL2 to instantiate an OpenGL texture object and read the data from an image file into it, (b) call glBindTexture() to make the newly created texture object active, and (c) adjust the texture settings using the glTexParameter() function. The result is an integer ID for the now available OpenGL texture object.

Texturing an object starts by declaring a variable of type GLuint. As we have seen, this is an OpenGL type for holding integer IDs referencing OpenGL objects. Next, we call SOIL_load_OGL_texture() to actually generate the texture object. The SOIL_load_OGL_texture() function accepts an image file name as one of its parameters (some of the other parameters will be described later). These steps are implemented in the following function:

```
GLuint loadTexture(const char *texImagePath) {
    GLuint textureID;
    textureID = SOIL_load_OGL_texture(texImagePath,
        SOIL_LOAD_AUTO, SOIL_CREATE_NEW_ID, SOIL_FLAG_INVERT_Y);
    if (textureID == 0) cout << "could not find texture file" << texImagePath << endl;
    return textureID;
}
```

We will use this function often, so we add it our Utils.cpp utility class. The C++ application then simply calls the above loadTexture() function to create the OpenGL texture object as follows:

GLuint myTexture = Utils::loadTexture("image.jpg");

where image.jpg is a texture image file, and myTexture is an integer ID for the resulting OpenGL texture object. Several image file types are supported, including the ones listed previously.

■5.2■ TEXTURE COORDINATES

Now that we have a means for loading a texture image into OpenGL, we need to specify how we want the texture to be applied to the rendered surface of an object. We do this by specifying *texture coordinates* for each vertex in our model.

Texture coordinates are references to the pixels in a (usually 2D) texture image. Pixels in a texture image are referred to as *texels*, in order to differentiate them from the pixels being rendered on the screen. Texture coordinates are used to map points on a 3D model to locations in a texture. Each point on the surface of the model has, in addition to (x,y,z) coordinates that place it in 3D space, texture coordinates (s,t) that specify which texel in the texture image provides its color. Thus, the surface of the object is "painted" by the texture image. The orientation of a texture across the surface of an object is determined by the assignment of texture coordinates to object vertices.

In order to use texture mapping, *it is necessary to provide texture coordinates for every vertex* in the object to be textured. OpenGL will use these texture coordinates to determine the color of each rasterized pixel in the model by looking up the color stored at the referenced texel in the texure image. In order to ensure that every pixel in a rendered model is painted with an appropriate texel from the texture image, *the texture coordinates are put into a vertex attribute so that they are also interpolated by the rasterizer*. In that way the texture image is interpolated, or filled in, along with the model vertices.

For each set of vertex coordinates (x,y,z) passing through the vertex shader, there will be an accompanying set of texture coordinates (s,t). We will thus set up two buffers, one for the vertices (with three components x, y, and z in each entry) and one for the corresponding texture coordinates (with two components s and t in each entry). Each vertex shader invocation thus receives one vertex, now comprised of both its spatial coordinates and its corresponding texture coordinates.

Texture coordinates are most often 2D (OpenGL does support some other dimensionalities, but we won't cover them in this chapter). It is assumed that the image is rectangular, with location (0,0) at the lower left and (1,1) at the upper right.[1] Texture coordinates, then, should ideally have values in the range [0..1].

Consider the example shown in Figure 5.2. The cube model, recall, is constructed of triangles. The four corners of one side of the cube are highlighted, but remember that it takes two triangles to specify each square side. The texture coordinates for each of the *six* vertices that specify this one cube side are listed alongside the four corners, with the corners at the upper left and lower right each composed of a pair of vertices. A texture image is also shown. The texture coordinates (indexed by s and t) have mapped portions of the image (the texels) onto the rasterized pixels of the front face of the model. Note that all of the intervening pixels in between the vertices have been painted with the intervening texels in the image. This is achieved because the texture coordinates are sent to the fragment shader in a *vertex attribute*, and thus are *also interpolated* just like the vertices themselves.

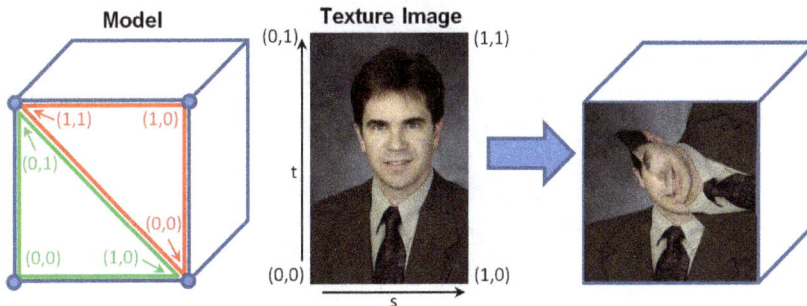

Figure 5.2
Texture coordinates.

---

[1] This is the orientation that OpenGL texture objects assume. However, this is different from the orientation of an image stored in many standard image file formats, in which the origin is at the upper left. Reorienting the image by flipping it vertically so that it corresponds to OpenGL's expected format is accomplished by specifying the SOIL_FLAG_INVERT_Y parameter as was done in the call that we made to SOIL_load_OGL_texture() in our loadTexture() function.

In this example, for purposes of illustration, we deliberately specified texture coordinates that result in an oddly painted surface. If you look closely, you can also see that the image appears slightly stretched—that is because the aspect ratio of the texture image doesn't match the aspect ratio of the cube face relative to the given texture coordinates.

For simple models like cubes or pyramids, selecting texture coordinates is relatively easy. But for more complex curved models with lots of triangles, it isn't practical to determine them by hand. In the case of curved geometric shapes, such as a sphere or torus, texture coordinates can be computed algorithmically or mathematically. In the case of a model built with a modeling tool such as Maya [MA23] or Blender [BL23], such tools offer "UV-mapping" (outside of the scope of this book) to make this task easier.

Let us return to rendering our pyramid, only this time texturing it with an image of bricks. We will need to specify: (a) the integer ID referencing the texture image, (b) texture coordinates for the model vertices, (c) a buffer for holding the texture coordinates, (d) vertex attributes so that the vertex shader can receive and forward the texture coordinates through the pipeline, (e) a texture unit on the graphics card for holding the texture object, and (f) a *uniform sampler* variable for accessing the texture unit in GLSL, which we will see shortly. These are each described in the next sections.

5.3 CREATING A TEXTURE OBJECT

Suppose the image shown here is stored in a file named "brick1.jpg" [LU16].

As shown previously, we can load this image by calling our loadTexture() function, as follows:

```
GLuint brickTexture = Utils::loadTexture("brick1.jpg");
```

Recall that texture objects are identified by integer IDs, so brickTexture is of type GLuint.

5.4 CONSTRUCTING TEXTURE COORDINATES

Our pyramid has four triangular sides and a square on the bottom. Although geometrically this only requires five (5) points, we have been rendering it with triangles. This requires four triangles for the sides, and two triangles for the square bottom, for a total of six triangles. Each triangle has three vertices, for a total of 6x3=18 vertices that must be specified in the model.

We already listed the pyramid's geometric vertices in Program 4.3 in the float array pyramidPositions[ ]. There are many ways that we could orient our texture coordinates so as to draw our bricks onto the pyramid. One simple (albeit imperfect) way would be to make the top center of the image correspond to the peak of the pyramid, as follows:

We can do this for all four of the triangle sides. We also need to paint the bottom square of the pyramid, which is comprised of two triangles. A simple and reasonable approach would be to texture it with the entire area from the picture (the pyramid has been tipped back and is sitting on its side):

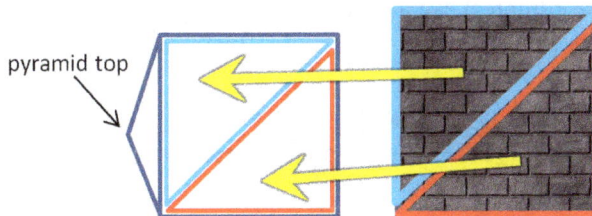

Using this very simple strategy for the first nine of the pyramid vertices from Program 4.3, the corresponding set of vertex and texture coordinates is shown in Figure 5.3.

```
          vertices              texture coordinates
     (-1.0,-1.0,  1.0)          (0,   0)    // front face
     ( 1.0,-1.0,  1.0)          (1,   0)
     (   0, 1.0,    0)          (.5,  1)
     ( 1.0,-1.0,  1.0)          (0,   0)    // right face
     ( 1.0,-1.0,-1.0)          (1,   0)
     (   0, 1.0,    0)          (.5,  1)
     ( 1.0,-1.0,-1.0)          (0,   0)    // back face
     (-1.0,-1.0,-1.0)          (1,   0)
     (   0, 1.0,    0)          (.5,  1)
     etc.
```

Figure 5.3
Texture coordinates for the pyramid (partial list).

5.5 ■ LOADING TEXTURE COORDINATES INTO BUFFERS

We can load the texture coordinates into a VBO in a similar manner as seen previously for loading the vertices. In setupVertices(), we add the following declaration of the texture coordinate values:

```
float pyrTexCoords[36] =
{   0.0f, 0.0f, 1.0f, 0.0f, 0.5f, 1.0f,   0.0f, 0.0f, 1.0f, 0.0f, 0.5f, 1.0f,   // top and right faces
    0.0f, 0.0f, 1.0f, 0.0f, 0.5f, 1.0f,   0.0f, 0.0f, 1.0f, 0.0f, 0.5f, 1.0f,   // back and left faces
    0.0f, 0.0f, 1.0f, 1.0f, 0.0f, 1.0f,   1.0f, 1.0f, 0.0f, 0.0f, 1.0f, 0.0f }; // base triangles
```

Then, after the creation of at least two VBOs (one for the vertices, and one for the texture coordinates), we add the following lines of code to load the texture coordinates into VBO #1:

```
glBindBuffer(GL_ARRAY_BUFFER, vbo[1]);
glBufferData(GL_ARRAY_BUFFER, sizeof(pyrTexCoords), pyrTexCoords, GL_STATIC_DRAW);
```

▪5.6▪ USING THE TEXTURE IN A SHADER: SAMPLER VARIABLES AND TEXTURE UNITS

To maximize performance, we will want to perform the texturing in hardware. This means that our fragment shader will need a way of accessing the texture object that we created in the C++/OpenGL application. The mechanism for doing this is via a special GLSL tool called a *uniform sampler variable*. This is a variable designed for instructing a texture unit on the graphics card as to which texel to extract or "sample" from a loaded texture object.

Declaring a sampler variable in the shader is easy—just add it to your set of uniforms:

```
layout (binding=0) uniform sampler2D samp;
```

Ours is named "samp". The "layout (binding=0)" portion of the declaration specifies that this sampler is to be associated with texture unit 0.

A texture unit (and associated sampler) can be used to sample whichever texture object you wish, and that can change at runtime. Your display() function will need to specify which texture object you want the texture unit to sample for the current frame. So each time you draw an object, you will need to activate a texture unit and bind it to a particular texture object, for example:

```
glActiveTexture(GL_TEXTURE0);
glBindTexture(GL_TEXTURE_2D, brickTexture);
```

The number of available texture units depends on how many are provided on the graphics card. According to the OpenGL API documentation, OpenGL version 4.5 requires that this be at least 16 per shader stage, and at least 80 total units across all stages [OP23]. In this example, we have made the 0th texture unit active by specifying GL_TEXTURE0 in the glActiveTexture() call.

To actually perform the texturing, we will need to modify how our fragment shader outputs colors. Previously, our fragment shader either output a constant color, or it obtained colors from a vertex attribute. This time instead, we need to use the interpolated texture coordinates received from the vertex shader (through the rasterizer) to sample the texture object, by calling the texture() function as follows:

```
in vec2 tc;          // texture coordinates
. . .
color = texture(samp, tc);
```

5.7 TEXTURE MAPPING: EXAMPLE PROGRAM

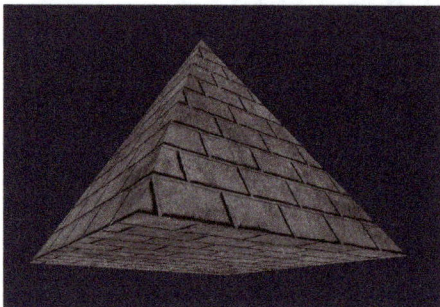

Figure 5.4
Pyramid texture mapped with brick image.

Program 5.1 combines the previous steps into a single program. The result, showing the pyramid textured with the brick image, appears in Figure 5.4. Two rotations (not shown in the code listing) were added to the pyramid's model matrix to expose the underside of the pyramid.

It is now a simple matter to replace the brick texture image with other texture images, as desired, simply by changing the filename in the loadTexture() call. For example, if we replace "brick1.jpg" with the image file "ice.jpg" [LU16], we get the result shown in Figure 5.5.

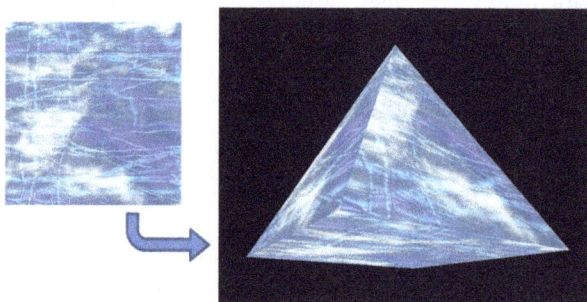

Figure 5.5
Pyramid texture mapped with "ice" image.

Program 5.1 Pyramid with Brick Texture

C++/OpenGL Application

```
#include <SOIL2/soil2.h>
// other #includes as before

. . .

#define numVAOs 1
#define numVBOs 2

// variables for camera and object location, rendering program, VAOs and VBOs as before

. . .
```

```
// variable allocation for display function same as before
...
GLuint brickTexture;

void setupVertices(void) {
    float pyramidPositions[54] = { /* data as listed previously in Program 4.2 */ }

    float pyrTexCoords[36] = {
        0.0f, 0.0f, 1.0f, 0.0f, 0.5f, 1.0f,    0.0f, 0.0f, 1.0f, 0.0f, 0.5f, 1.0f,
        0.0f, 0.0f, 1.0f, 0.0f, 0.5f, 1.0f,    0.0f, 0.0f, 1.0f, 0.0f, 0.5f, 1.0f,
        0.0f, 0.0f, 1.0f, 1.0f, 0.0f, 1.0f,    1.0f, 1.0f, 0.0f, 0.0f, 1.0f, 0.0f
    };

    // ... generate the VAO as before, and at least two VBOs, then load the two buffers as follows:
    glBindBuffer(GL_ARRAY_BUFFER, vbo[0]);
    glBufferData(GL_ARRAY_BUFFER, sizeof(pyramidPositions), pyramidPositions, GL_STATIC_DRAW);

    glBindBuffer(GL_ARRAY_BUFFER, vbo[1]);
    glBufferData(GL_ARRAY_BUFFER, sizeof(pyrTexCoords), pyrTexCoords, GL_STATIC_DRAW);
}

void init(GLFWwindow* window) {
    // setup of rendering program, camera and object location unchanged

    ...
    brickTexture = Utils::loadTexture("brick1.jpg");
}

void display(GLFWwindow* window, double currentTime) {

    ...
    // setup of background color, depth buffer, rendering program, M, V, MV, and P matrices unchanged

    ...
    glBindBuffer(GL_ARRAY_BUFFER, vbo[0]);
    glVertexAttribPointer(0, 3, GL_FLOAT, GL_FALSE, 0, 0);
    glEnableVertexAttribArray(0);

    glBindBuffer(GL_ARRAY_BUFFER, vbo[1]);
    glVertexAttribPointer(1, 2, GL_FLOAT, GL_FALSE, 0, 0);
    glEnableVertexAttribArray(1);

    glActiveTexture(GL_TEXTURE0);
    glBindTexture(GL_TEXTURE_2D, brickTexture);

    glEnable(GL_DEPTH_TEST);
    glDepthFunc(GL_LEQUAL);

    glDrawArrays(GL_TRIANGLES, 0, 18);
}

// main() same as before
```

Vertex shader

```
#version 430
layout (location=0) in vec3 pos;
layout (location=1) in vec2 texCoord;
out vec2 tc;            // texture coordinate output to rasterizer for interpolation
uniform mat4 mv_matrix;
uniform mat4 p_matrix;
layout (binding=0) uniform sampler2D samp;      // not used in vertex shader

void main(void)
{   gl_Position = p_matrix * mv_matrix * vec4(pos,1.0);
    tc = texCoord;
}
```

Fragment shader

```
#version 430
in vec2 tc;            // interpolated incoming texture coordinate
out vec4 color;
uniform mat4 mv_matrix;
uniform mat4 p_matrix;
layout (binding=0) uniform sampler2D samp;

void main(void)
{   color = texture(samp, tc);
}
```

5.8 MIPMAPPING

Texture mapping commonly produces a variety of undesirable artifacts in the rendered image. This is because the resolution or aspect ratio of the texture image rarely matches that of the region in the scene being textured.

A very common artifact occurs when the image resolution is *less than* that of the region being drawn. In this case, the image would need to be stretched to cover the region, becoming blurry (and possibly distorted). This can sometimes be combated, depending on the nature of the texture, by assigning the texture coordinates differently so that applying the texture requires less stretching. Another solution is to use a higher resolution texture image.

The reverse situation is when the resolution of the image texture is *greater than* that of the region being drawn. It is probably not at all obvious why this would pose a problem, but it does! In this case, noticeable *aliasing* artifacts can occur, giving rise to strange-looking false patterns, or "shimmering" effects in moving objects.

Aliasing is caused by *sampling errors*. It is most often associated with signal processing, where an inadequately sampled signal appears to have different properties (such as wavelength) than it actually does when it is reconstructed. An example is shown in Figure 5.6. The original waveform is shown in red. The yellow dots along the waveform represent the samples. If they are used to reconstruct the wave, and if there aren't enough of them, they can define a different wave (shown in blue).

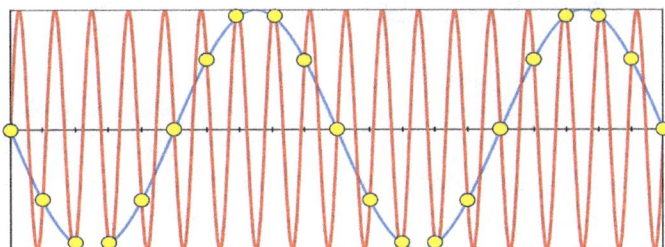

Figure 5.6
Aliasing due to inadequate sampling.

Similarly, in texture-mapping, when a high-resolution (and highly detailed) image is sparsely sampled (such as when using a uniform sampler variable), the colors retrieved will be inadequate to reflect the actual detail in the image, and may instead seem random. If the texture image has a repeated pattern, aliasing can result in a *different* pattern being produced than the one in the original image. If the object being textured is moving, rounding errors in texel lookup can result in constant changes in the sampled pixel at a given texture coordinate, producing an unwanted sparkling effect across the surface of the object being drawn.

Figure 5.7 shows a tilted, close-up rendering of the top of a cube which has been textured by a large, high-resolution image of a checkerboard.

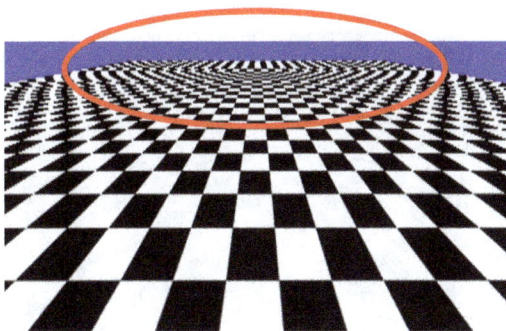

Figure 5.7
Aliasing in a texture map.

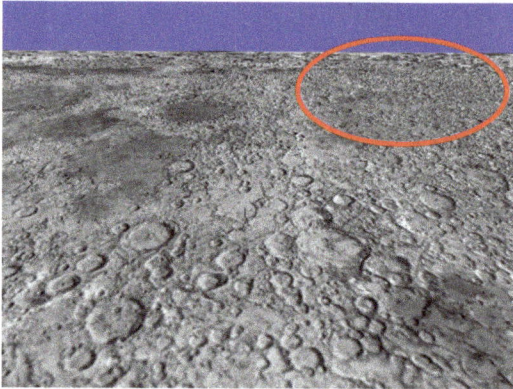

Figure 5.8
"Sparkling" in a texture map.

Aliasing is evident near the top of the image, where the under-sampling of the checkerboard has produced a "striped" effect. Although we can't show it here in a still image, if this were an animated scene, the patterns would likely undulate between various incorrect patterns such as this one.

Another example appears in Figure 5.8, in which the cube has been textured with an image of the surface of the moon [HT23]. At first glance, this image appears sharp and full of detail. However, some of the detail at the upper right of the image is false and causes "sparkling" as the cube object (or the camera) moves. (Unfortunately, we can't show the sparkling effect clearly in a still image.)

These and similar sampling error artifacts can be largely corrected by a technique called *mipmapping*, in which different versions of the texture image are created at various resolutions. OpenGL then uses the texture image that most closely matches the resolution at the point being textured. Even better, colors can be averaged between the images closest in resolution to that of the region being textured. Results of applying mipmapping to the images in Figure 5.7 and Figure 5.8 are shown in Figure 5.9.

Figure 5.9
Mipmapped results.

Mipmapping works by a clever mechanism for storing a series of successively lower-resolution copies of the same image in a texture image one-third larger than the original image. This is achieved by storing the R, G, and B components of the image separately in three-quarters of the texture image space, then repeating the process in the remaining one-quarter of the image space for the same image at one-quarter the original resolution. This subdividing repeats until the remaining quadrant is too small to contain any useful image data. An example image and a visualization of the resulting mipmap is shown in Figure 5.10.

Figure 5.10
Mipmapping an image.

This method of stuffing several images into a small space (well, just a bit bigger than the space needed to store the original image) is how mipmapping got its name. MIP stands for *Multum In Parvo* [WI83], which is Latin for "much in a small space."

When actually texturing an object, the mipmap can be sampled in several ways. In OpenGL, the manner in which the mipmap is sampled can be chosen by setting the GL_TEXTURE_MIN_FILTER parameter to the desired *minification* technique, which is one of the following:

- **GL_NEAREST_MIPMAP_NEAREST**
  chooses the mipmap with the resolution most similar to that of the region of pixels being textured. It then obtains the nearest texel to the desired texture coordinates.

- **GL_LINEAR_MIPMAP_NEAREST**

  chooses the mipmap with the resolution most similar to that of the region of pixels being textured. It then interpolates the four texels nearest to the texture coordinates. This is called "linear filtering."

- **GL_NEAREST_MIPMAP_LINEAR**

  chooses the two mipmaps with resolutions nearest to that of the region of pixels being textured. It then obtains the nearest texel to the texture coordinates from each mipmap and interpolates them. This is called "bilinear filtering."

- **GL_LINEAR_MIPMAP_LINEAR**

  chooses the two mipmaps with resolutions nearest to that of the region of pixels being textured. It then interpolates the four nearest texels in each mipmap and interpolates those two results. This is called "trilinear filtering" and is illustrated in Figure 5.11.

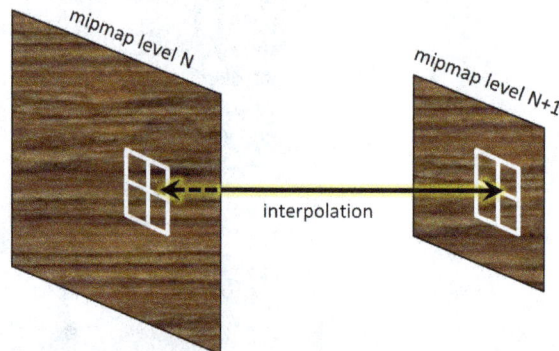

Figure 5.11
Trilinear filtering.

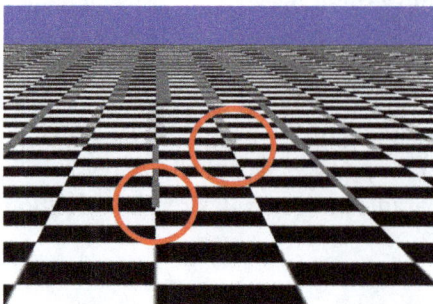

Figure 5.12
Linear filtering artifacts.

Trilinear filtering is usually preferable, as lower levels of blending often produce artifacts, such as visible separations between mipmap levels. Figure 5.12 shows a close-up of the checkerboard using mipmapping with only linear filtering enabled. Note the circled artifacts where the vertical lines suddenly change from thick to thin at a mipmap boundary. By contrast, the example in Figure 5.9 used trilinear filtering.

Mipmapping is richly supported in OpenGL. There are mechanisms provided for building your own mipmap levels or having OpenGL build them for you. In most cases, the mipmaps built automatically by OpenGL are sufficient. This is done by adding the following lines of code to the Utils::loadTexture() function (described earlier in Section 5.1), immediately after the getTextureObject() function call:

```
glBindTexture(GL_TEXTURE_2D, textureID);
glTexParameteri(GL_TEXTURE_2D, GL_TEXTURE_MIN_FILTER, GL_LINEAR_MIPMAP_LINEAR);
glGenerateMipmap(GL_TEXTURE_2D);
```

This tells OpenGL to generate the mipmaps. The brick texture is made active with the glBindTexture() call, and then the glTexParameteri() function call enables one of the minification factors listed previously, such as GL_LINEAR_MIPMAP_LINEAR shown in the above call, which enables trilinear filtering.

Once the mipmap is built, the filtering option can be changed (although this is rarely necessary) by calling glTexParameteri() again, such as in the display function. Mipmapping can even be disabled by selecting GL_NEAREST or GL_LINEAR.

For critical applications, it is possible to build the mipmaps yourself, using whatever is your preferred image editing software. They can then be added as mipmap levels when creating the texture object by repeatedly calling OpenGL's glTexImage2D() function for each mipmap level. Further discussion of this approach is outside the scope of this book.

■5.9■ ANISOTROPIC FILTERING

Mipmapped textures can sometimes appear more blurry than non-mipmapped textures, especially when the textured object is rendered at a heavily tilted viewing angle. We saw an example of this back in Figure 5.9, where reducing artifacts with mipmapping led to reduced detail (compared with Figure 5.8).

This loss of detail occurs because when an object is tilted, its primitives appear smaller along one axis (i.e., width vs. height) than along the other. When OpenGL textures a primitive, it selects the mipmap appropriate for the *smaller* of the two axes (to avoid "sparkling" artifacts). In Figure 5.9, the surface is tilted heavily away from the viewer, so each rendered primitive will utilize the mipmap appropriate for its reduced *height*, which is likely to have a resolution lower than appropriate for its *width*.

One way of restoring some of this lost detail is to use *anisotropic filtering* (AF). Whereas standard mipmapping samples a texture image at a variety of square resolutions (e.g., 256x256, 128x128, etc.), AF samples the textures at a number of rectangular resolutions as well, such as 256x128, 64x128, and so on. This enables viewing at various angles while retaining as much detail in the texture as possible.

Anisotropic filtering is more computationally expensive than standard mipmapping and is not a required part of OpenGL. However, most graphics cards support AF (this is referred to as an *OpenGL extension*), and OpenGL does provide both a way of querying the card to see if it supports AF, and a way of accessing AF if it does. The code is added immediately after generating the mipmap:

```
. . .
// if mipmapping
glBindTexture(GL_TEXTURE_2D, textureID);
glTexParameteri(GL_TEXTURE_2D, GL_TEXTURE_MIN_FILTER, GL_LINEAR_MIPMAP_LINEAR);
glGenerateMipmap(GL_TEXTURE_2D);

// if also anisotropic filtering
if (glewIsSupported("GL_EXT_texture_filter_anisotropic")) {
    GLfloat anisoSetting = 0.0f;
    glGetFloatv(GL_MAX_TEXTURE_MAX_ANISOTROPY_EXT, &anisoSetting);
    glTexParameterf(GL_TEXTURE_2D, GL_TEXTURE_MAX_ANISOTROPY_EXT, anisoSetting);
}
```

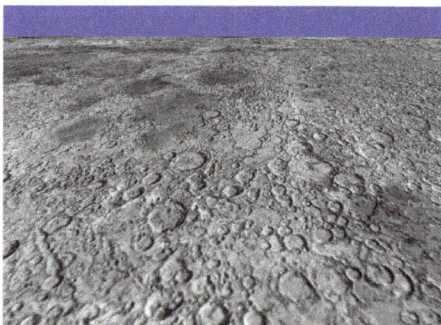

Figure 5.13
Anisotropic filtering.

The call to glewIsSupported() tests whether the graphics card supports AF. If it does, we set it to the maximum degree of sampling supported, a value retrieved using glGetFloatv() as shown. It is then applied to the active texture object using glTexParameterf(). The result is shown in Figure 5.13. Note that much of the lost detail from Figure 5.8 has been restored, while still removing the sparkling artifacts.

5.10 WRAPPING AND TILING

So far we have assumed that texture coordinates all fall in the range [0..1]. However, OpenGL actually supports texture coordinates of any value. There are several options for specifying what happens when texture coordinates fall outside the range [0..1]. The desired behavior is set using glTexParameteri(), and some of the options are as follows:

- **GL_REPEAT**: The integer portion of the texture coordinates are ignored, generating a repeating or "tiling" pattern. This is the default behavior.
- **GL_MIRRORED_REPEAT**: The integer portion is ignored, except that the coordinates are reversed when the integer portion is odd, so the repeating pattern alternates between normal and mirrored.
- **GL_CLAMP_TO_EDGE**: Coordinates less than 0 and greater than 1 are set to 0 and 1 respectively.
- **GL_CLAMP_TO_BORDER**: Texels outside of [0..1] will be assigned some specified border color.

For example, consider a pyramid in which the texture coordinates have been defined in the range [0..5] rather than the range [0..1]. The default behavior (GL_REPEAT), using the texture image shown previously in Figure 5.2, would result in the texture repeating five times across the surface (sometimes called "tiling"), as shown in Figure 5.14:

Figure 5.14
Texture coordinate wrapping with GL_REPEAT.

To make the tiles' appearance alternate between normal and mirrored, we can specify the following:

```
glTexParameteri(GL_TEXTURE_2D, GL_TEXTURE_WRAP_S, GL_MIRRORED_REPEAT);
glTexParameteri(GL_TEXTURE_2D, GL_TEXTURE_WRAP_T, GL_MIRRORED_REPEAT);
```

Specifying that values less than 0 and greater than 1 be set to 0 and 1 respectively can be done by replacing GL_MIRRORED_REPEAT with GL_CLAMP_TO_EDGE.

Specifying that values less than 0 and greater than 1 result in a "border" color can be done as follows:

```
glTexParameteri(GL_TEXTURE_2D, GL_TEXTURE_WRAP_S, GL_CLAMP_TO_BORDER);
glTexParameteri(GL_TEXTURE_2D, GL_TEXTURE_WRAP_T, GL_CLAMP_TO_BORDER);
float redColor[4] = { 1.0f, 0.0f, 0.0f, 1.0f };
glTexParameterfv(GL_TEXTURE_2D, GL_TEXTURE_BORDER_COLOR, redColor);
```

The effect of each of these options (mirrored repeat, clamp to edge, and clamp to border), with texture coordinates ranging from -2 to +3, are shown respectively (left to right) in Figure 5.15.

Figure 5.15
Textured pyramid with various wrapping options.

In the center example (clamp to edge), the pixels along the edges of the texture image are replicated outward. Note that as a side effect, the lower-left and lower-right regions of the pyramid faces obtain their color from the lower-left and lower-right pixels of the texture image respectively.

5.11 PERSPECTIVE DISTORTION

We have seen that as texture coordinates are passed from the vertex shader to the fragment shader, they are interpolated as they pass through the rasterizer. We have also seen that this is the result of the automatic linear interpolation that is always performed on vertex attributes.

However, in the case of texture coordinates, linear interpolation can lead to noticeable distortion in a 3D scene with perspective projection.

Consider a rectangle made of two triangles, textured with a checkerboard image, facing the camera. As the rectangle is rotated around the X axis, the top part of the rectangle tilts away from the camera, while the lower part of the rectangle swings closer to the camera. Thus, we would expect the squares at the top to become smaller and the squares at the bottom to become larger. However, linear interpolation of the texture coordinates will instead cause the height of *all* squares to be equal. The distortion is exacerbated along the diagonal defining the two triangles that make up the rectangle. The resulting distortion is shown in Figure 5.16.

Fortunately, there are algorithms for correcting perspective distortion, and by default, OpenGL applies a *perspective correction* algorithm [OP14, SP16] during rasterization. Figure 5.17 shows the same rotating checkerboard, properly rendered by OpenGL.

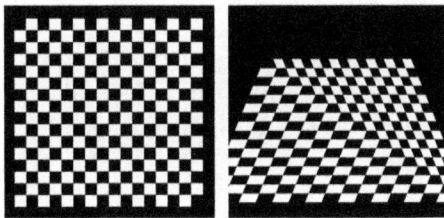

Figure 5.16
Texture perspective distortion.

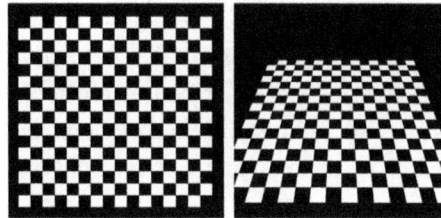

Figure 5.17
OpenGL perspective correction.

Although not common, it is possible to disable OpenGL's perspective correction by adding the keyword "noperspective" in the declaration of the vertex attribute containing the texture coordinates. This has to be done in both the vertex and fragment shaders. For example, the vertex attribute in the vertex shader of Program 5.1 would be declared as follows:

```
noperspective out vec2 tc;
```

The corresponding attribute in the fragment shader would be declared:

```
noperspective in vec2 tc;
```

This syntax was in fact used to produce the distorted checkerboard in Figure 5.16.

5.12 TEXTURES – ADDITIONAL OPENGL DETAILS

The SOIL2 texture image loading library that we are using throughout this book has the advantage that it is relatively easy and intuitive to use. However, when learning OpenGL, using SOIL2 has the unintended consequence of shielding the user from some important OpenGL details that are useful to learn. In this section, we describe some of those details a programmer would need to know in order to load and use textures in the absence of a texture loading library such as SOIL2.

It is possible to load texture image file data into OpenGL directly, using C++ and OpenGL functions. While it is quite a bit more complicated, it is commonly done. The general steps are:

1. Read the image file using C++ tools.
2. Generate an OpenGL texture object.
3. Copy the image file data into the texture object.

We won't describe the first step in detail—there are numerous methods. One approach is described nicely at opengl-tutorials.org (the specific tutorial page is [OT18]), and uses C++ functions fopen() and fread() to read in data from a .bmp image file into an array of type unsigned char.

Steps 2 and 3 are more generic and involve mostly OpenGL calls. In step 2, we create one or more texture objects using the OpenGL glGenTextures() command. For example, generating a single OpenGL texture object (with an integer reference ID) can be done as follows:

```
GLuint textureID;        // or an array of GLuint if making more than one texture object
glGenTextures(1, &textureID);
```

In step 3, we associate the image data from step 1 into the texture object created in step 2. This is done using the OpenGL glTexImage2D() command. The following example loads the image data from the unsigned char array described in step 1 (and denoted here as "data") into the texture object created in step 2:

```
glBindTexture(GL_TEXTURE_2D, textureID)
glTexImage2D(GL_TEXTURE_2D, 0,GL_RGB, width, height, 0, GL_BGR,
                                        GL_UNSIGNED_BYTE, data);
```

At this point, the various glTexParameteri() calls described earlier in this chapter for setting up mipmaps and so forth can be applied to the texture object. We also now use the integer reference (textureID) in the same manner as was described throughout the chapter.

SUPPLEMENTAL NOTES

Researchers have developed a number of uses for texture units beyond just texturing models in a scene. In later chapters, we will see how texture units can be used for altering the way light reflects off an object, making it appear bumpy. We can also use a texture unit to store "height maps" for generating terrain, and for storing "shadow maps" to efficiently add shadows to our scenes. These uses will be described in subsequent chapters.

Shaders can also *write to textures*, allowing shaders to modify texture images, or even copy part of one texture into some portion of another texture.

Mipmaps and anisotropic filtering are not the only tools for reducing aliasing artifacts in textures. *Full-scene anti-aliasing* (FSAA) and other supersampling methods, for example, can also improve the appearance of textures in a 3D scene. Although not part of the OpenGL core, they are supported on many graphics cards through OpenGL's extension mechanism [OE22].

There is an alternative mechanism for configuring and managing textures and samplers. Version 3.3 of OpenGL introduced *sampler objects* (sometimes called "*sampler states*"—not to be confused with sampler variables) that can be used to hold a set of texture settings independent of the actual texture object. Sampler objects are attached to texture units and allow for conveniently and efficiently changing texture settings. The examples shown in this textbook are sufficiently simple that we decided to omit coverage of sampler objects. For interested readers, usage of sampler objects is easy to learn, and there are many excellent online tutorials (such as [GE11]).

Exercises

5.1 Modify Program 5.1 by adding the "noperspective" declaration to the texture coordinate vertex attributes, as described in Section 5.11. Then rerun the program and compare the output with the original. Is any perspective distortion evident?

5.2 Using a simple "paint" program (such as Windows "Paint" or GIMP [GI23]), draw a freehand picture of your own design. Then use your image to texture the pyramid in Program 5.1.

5.3 *(PROJECT)* Modify Program 4.4 so that the "sun," "planet," and "moon" are textured. You may continue to use the shapes already present, and you may use any texture you like. This will require you to build texture coordinates for the cube.

References

[BL23]   Blender, The Blender Foundation, accessed November 2023, https://www.blender.org/

[GE11]   Geeks3D, "OpenGL Sampler Objects: Control Your Texture Units," September 8, 2011, accessed November 2023, http://www.geeks3d.com/20110908/

[GI23]   GNU Image Manipulation Program, accessed November 2023, http://www.gimp.org

[HT23]   J. Hastings-Trew, *JHT's Planetary Pixel Emporium*, accessed November 2023, http://planetpixelemporium.com/

[LU16]   F. Luna, *Introduction to 3D Game Programming with DirectX 12*, 2nd ed. (Mercury Learning, 2016) [accompanying disk].

[MA23]   Maya, AutoDesk, Inc., accessed November 2023, http://www.autodesk.com/products/maya/overview

[OE22]   OpenGL Registry, The Khronos Group, accessed November 2023, https://registry.khronos.org/OpenGL/index_gl.php

[OP14]   OpenGL Graphics System: A Specification (version 4.4), M. Segal and K. Akeley, March 19, 2014, accessed November 2023, https://registry.khronos.org/OpenGL/specs/gl/glspec44.core.pdf

[OP23]   OpenGL 4.5 Reference Pages, accessed November 2023, https://registry.khronos.org/OpenGL-Refpages/gl4/

[OT18]   OpenGL Tutorial, "Loading BMP Images Yourself," opengl-tutorial.org, accessed November 2023, http://www.opengl-tutorial.org/beginners-tutorials/tutorial-5-a-textured-cube/#loading-bmp-images-yourself

[SO23] Simple OpenGL Image Library 2 (SOIL2), *SpartanJ*, accessed November 2023, https://github.com/SpartanJ/SOIL2

[SP16] Perspective Correct Interpolation and Vertex Attributes. Scratchapixel, c.2016, Accessed November 2023. https://www.scratchapixel.com/lessons/3d-basic-rendering/rasterization-practical-implementation/overview-rasterization-algorithm.html

[TU18] J. Turberville, Studio 522 Productions, Scottsdale, AZ, accessed November 2023, www.studio522.com (dolphin model developed 2016).

[WI83] L. Williams, "Pyramidal Parametrics," *Computer Graphics* 17, no. 3 (July 1983).

3D MODELS

So far we have dealt only with very simple 3D objects, such as cubes and pyramids. These objects are so simple that we have been able to explicitly list all of the vertex information in our source code and place it directly into buffers.

However, most interesting 3D scenes include objects that are too complex to continue building them as we have, by hand. In this chapter, we will explore more complex object models, how to build them, and how to load them into our scenes.

3D modeling is itself an extensive field, and our coverage here will necessarily be very limited. We will focus on the following two topics:

*   *building models procedurally*
*   *loading models produced externally*

While this only scratches the surface of the rich field of 3D modeling, it will give us the capability to include a wide variety of complex and realistically detailed objects in our scenes.

6.1   PROCEDURAL MODELS – BUILDING A SPHERE

Some types of objects, such as spheres, cones, and so forth, have mathematical definitions that lend themselves to algorithmic generation. Consider for example a circle of radius R—coordinates of points around its perimeter are well defined (Figure 6.1).

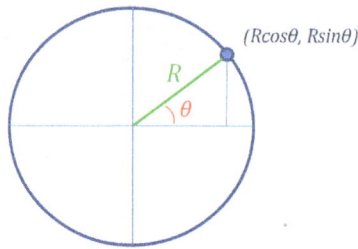

Figure 6.1
Points on a circle.

We can systematically use our knowledge of the geometry of a circle to algorithmically build a sphere model. Our strategy is as follows:

1. Select a *precision* representing a number of circular regions the sphere is divided into. In the left side Figure 6.2, the sphere is sliced into four regions.

2. Subdivide the circumference of each circular slice into some number of points. See the right side of Figure 6.2. More points and horizontal slices produces a more accurate and smoother model of the sphere. In our model, *each slice will have the same number of points, including at the very top and bottom (where those points are coincident).*

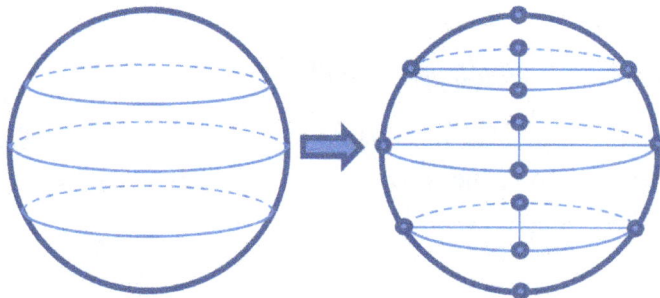

Figure 6.2
Building vertices for a sphere.

3. Group the vertices into triangles. One approach is to step through the vertices, building two triangles at each step. For example, as we move along the row of the five colored vertices on the sphere in Figure 6.3, for each of those five vertices we build the two triangles shown in the corresponding color (the steps are described in greater detail below).

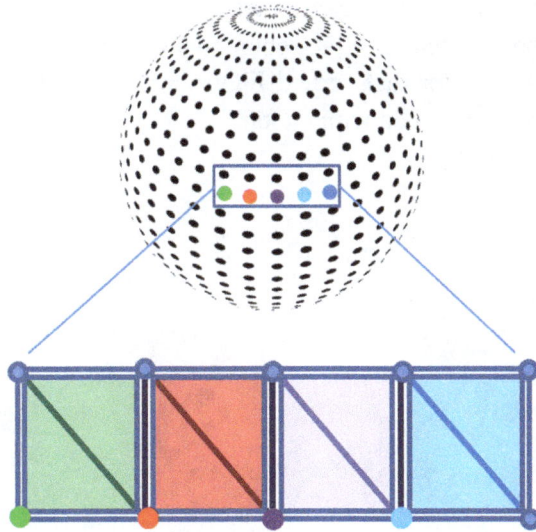

Figure 6.3
Grouping vertices into triangles.

4. Select texture coordinates depending on the nature of our texture images. In the case of a sphere, there exist many topographical texture images, such as the one shown in Figure 6.4 [VE23] for planet Earth. If we assume this sort of texture image, then by imagining the image "wrapped" around the sphere as shown in Figure 6.5, we can assign texture coordinates to each vertex according to the resulting corresponding positions of the texels in the image.

Figure 6.4
Topographical texture image [VE16].

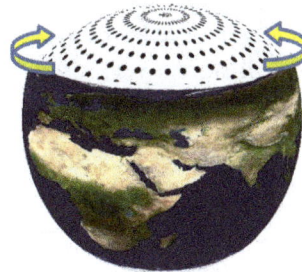

Figure 6.5
Sphere texture coordinates.

5. It is also often desirable to generate *normal vectors*—vectors that are *perpendicular to the model's surface*—for each vertex. We will use them soon, in Chapter 7, for *lighting*.

Determining normal vectors can be tricky, but in the case of a sphere, the vector pointing from the center of the sphere to a vertex happens to conveniently equal the normal vector for that vertex! Figure 6.6 illustrates this property (the center of the sphere is indicated with a "star").

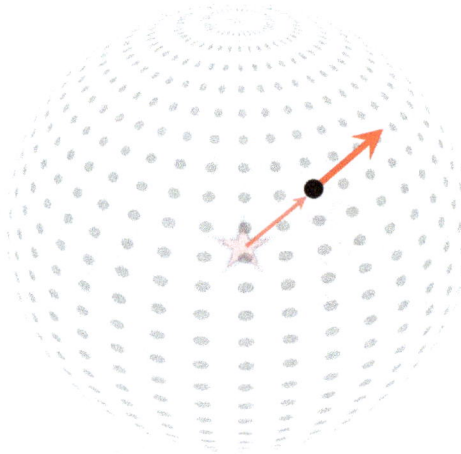

Figure 6.6
Sphere vertex normal vectors.

Some models define triangles using *indices*. Note in Figure 6.3 that each vertex appears in multiple triangles, which would lead to each vertex being specified multiple times. Rather than doing this, we instead store each vertex once, and then specify indices for each corner of a triangle, referencing the desired vertices. Since we will store a vertex's location, texture coordinates, and normal vector, this can facilitate memory savings for large models.

The vertices are stored in a one-dimensional array, starting with the vertices in the bottommost horizontal slice. When using indexing, the associated array of indices includes an entry for each triangle corner. The contents are integer references (specifically, subscripts) into the vertex array. Assuming that each slice contains n vertices, the vertex array would look as shown in Figure 6.7, along with an example portion of the corresponding index array.

We can then traverse the vertices in a circular fashion around each horizontal slice, starting at the bottom of the sphere. As we visit each vertex, we build

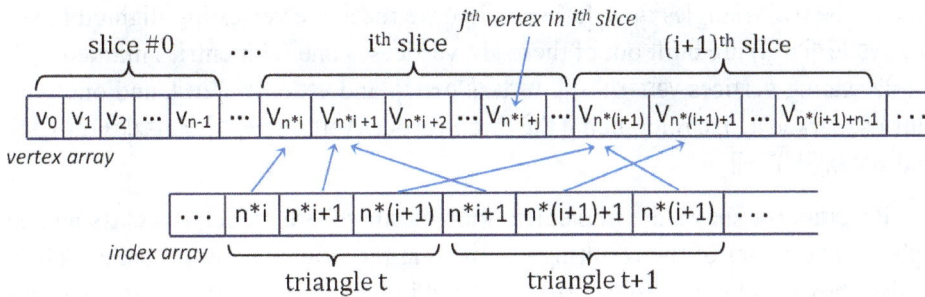

Figure 6.7
Vertex array and corresponding index array.

two triangles forming a square region above and to its right, as shown earlier in Figure 6.3. The processing is thus organized into nested loops, as follows:

for each horizontal slice i in the sphere (i ranges from 0 through all the slices in the sphere)
{ for each vertex j in slice i (j ranges from 0 through all the vertices in the slice)
*   {   calculate indices for two triangles which point to neighboring vertices to the right,*
*   above, and to the above-right of vertex j*
} }

For example, consider the "red" vertex from Figure 6.3 (repeated in Figure 6.8). The vertex in question is at the lower left of the yellow triangles shown in Figure 6.8, and given the loops just described, would be indexed by $i*n+j$, where i is the slice currently being processed (the outer loop), j is the vertex currently being processed within that slice (the inner loop), and n is the number of vertices per slice. Figure 6.8 shows this vertex (in red) along with its three relevant neighboring vertices, each with formulas showing how they would be indexed.

These four vertices are then used to build the two triangles (shown in yellow) generated for this (red) vertex. The six entries in the index table for these two triangles are indicated in the figure in the order shown by the numbers 1 through 6. Note that entries 3 and 6 both refer to the same vertex, which is also the case for entries 2

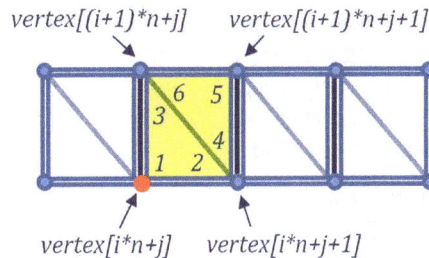

Figure 6.8
Indices generated for the jth vertex in the ith slice (*n = number of vertices per slice*).

and 4. The two triangles thus defined when we reach the vertex highlighted in red (i.e., vertex[i*n+j]) are built out of these six vertices—one with entries marked 1, 2, 3 referencing vertices vertex[i*n+j], vertex[i*n+j+1], and vertex[(i+1)*n+j], and one with entries marked 4, 5, 6 referencing the three vertices vertex[i*n+j+1], vertex[(i+1)*n+j+1], and vertex[(i+1)*n+j].

Program 6.1 shows the implementation of our sphere model as a class named Sphere. The center of the resulting sphere is at the origin. Code for using Sphere is also shown. Note that each vertex is stored in C++ vectors containing instances of the GLM classes vec2 and vec3 (this is different from previous examples, where vertices were stored in float arrays). vec2 and vec3 include methods for obtaining the desired x, y, and z components as float values, which are then put into float buffers as before. We store these values in variable-length C++ vectors because the size depends on the number of slices specified at runtime.

Note the calculation of triangle indices in the Sphere class, as described earlier in Figure 6.8. The variable "prec" refers to the "precision," which in this case is used both for the number of sliced sphere regions and the number of desired points per slice. Because the texture map wraps completely around the sphere, we will need an extra coincident vertex at each of the points where the left and right edges of the texture map meet. Thus, the total number of vertices is (prec+1)*(prec+1). Since six triangle indices are generated per vertex, the total number of indices is prec*prec*6.

Program 6.1 Procedurally Generated Sphere

Sphere class (Sphere.cpp)

```
#include <cmath>
#include <vector>
#include <iostream>
#include <glm/glm.hpp>
#include "Sphere.h"
using namespace std;

Sphere::Sphere() {
    init(48);
}

Sphere::Sphere(int prec) {      // prec is precision, or number of slices
    init(prec);
}
```

```
float Sphere::toRadians(float degrees) { return (degrees * 2.0f * 3.14159f) / 360.0f; }

void Sphere::init(int prec) {
    numVertices = (prec + 1) * (prec + 1);
    numIndices = prec * prec * 6;
    for (int i = 0; i < numVertices; i++) { vertices.push_back(glm::vec3()); }      // std::vector::push_back()
    for (int i = 0; i < numVertices; i++) { texCoords.push_back(glm::vec2()); }     // inserts new element at
    for (int i = 0; i < numVertices; i++) { normals.push_back(glm::vec3()); }       // the end of a vector and
    for (int i = 0; i < numIndices; i++) { indices.push_back(0); }                  // increases the vector size by 1

    // calculate triangle vertices
    for (int i = 0; i <= prec; i++) {
        for (int j = 0; j <= prec; j++) {
            float y = (float)cos(toRadians(180.0f - i * 180.0f / prec));
            float x = -(float)cos(toRadians(j*360.0f / prec)) * (float)abs(cos(asin(y)));
            float z = (float)sin(toRadians(j*360.0f / prec)) * (float)abs(cos(asin(y)));
            vertices[i*(prec + 1) + j] = glm::vec3(x, y, z);
            texCoords[i*(prec + 1) + j] = glm::vec2(((float)j / prec), ((float)i / prec));
            normals[i*(prec + 1) + j] = glm::vec3(x,y,z);
        }
    }

    // calculate triangle indices
    for (int i = 0; i<prec; i++) {
        for (int j = 0; j<prec; j++) {
            indices[6 * (i*prec + j) + 0] = i*(prec + 1) + j;
            indices[6 * (i*prec + j) + 1] = i*(prec + 1) + j + 1;
            indices[6 * (i*prec + j) + 2] = (i + 1)*(prec + 1) + j;
            indices[6 * (i*prec + j) + 3] = i*(prec + 1) + j + 1;
            indices[6 * (i*prec + j) + 4] = (i + 1)*(prec + 1) + j + 1;
            indices[6 * (i*prec + j) + 5] = (i + 1)*(prec + 1) + j;
        }
    }
}

// accessors
int Sphere::getNumVertices() { return numVertices; }
int Sphere::getNumIndices() { return numIndices; }
std::vector<int> Sphere::getIndices() { return indices; }
std::vector<glm::vec3> Sphere::getVertices() { return vertices; }
std::vector<glm::vec2> Sphere::getTexCoords() { return texCoords; }
std::vector<glm::vec3> Sphere::getNormals() { return normals; }
```

Sphere header file (Sphere.h)

```
#include <cmath>
#include <vector>
#include <glm/glm.hpp>

class Sphere
{
private:
    int numVertices;
    int numIndices;
    std::vector<int> indices;
    std::vector<glm::vec3> vertices;
    std::vector<glm::vec2> texCoords;
    std::vector<glm::vec3> normals;
    void init(int);
    float toRadians(float degrees);

public:
    Sphere(int prec);
    int getNumVertices();
    int getNumIndices();
    std::vector<int> getIndices();
    std::vector<glm::vec3> getVertices();
    std::vector<glm::vec2> getTexCoords();
    std::vector<glm::vec3> getNormals();
};
```

Using the Sphere class

```
. . .

#include "Sphere.h"

. . .

Sphere mySphere(48);

. . .

void setupVertices(void) {
    std::vector<int> ind = mySphere.getIndices();
    std::vector<glm::vec3> vert = mySphere.getVertices();
    std::vector<glm::vec2> tex = mySphere.getTexCoords();
    std::vector<glm::vec3> norm = mySphere.getNormals();

    std::vector<float> pvalues;          // vertex positions
    std::vector<float> tvalues;          // texture coordinates
    std::vector<float> nvalues;          // normal vectors
```

```
int numIndices = mySphere.getNumIndices();
for (int i = 0; i < numIndices; i++) {
    pvalues.push_back((vert[ind[i]]).x);
    pvalues.push_back((vert[ind[i]]).y);
    pvalues.push_back((vert[ind[i]]).z);

    tvalues.push_back((tex[ind[i]]).s);
    tvalues.push_back((tex[ind[i]]).t);

    nvalues.push_back((norm[ind[i]]).x);
    nvalues.push_back((norm[ind[i]]).y);
    nvalues.push_back((norm[ind[i]]).z);
}
glGenVertexArrays(1, vao);
glBindVertexArray(vao[0]);
glGenBuffers(3, vbo);

// put the vertices into buffer #0
glBindBuffer(GL_ARRAY_BUFFER, vbo[0]);
glBufferData(GL_ARRAY_BUFFER, pvalues.size()*4, &pvalues[0], GL_STATIC_DRAW);

// put the texture coordinates into buffer #1
glBindBuffer(GL_ARRAY_BUFFER, vbo[1]);
glBufferData(GL_ARRAY_BUFFER, tvalues.size()*4, &tvalues[0], GL_STATIC_DRAW);

// put the normals into buffer #2
glBindBuffer(GL_ARRAY_BUFFER, vbo[2]);
glBufferData(GL_ARRAY_BUFFER, nvalues.size()*4, &nvalues[0], GL_STATIC_DRAW);
}
```

in display()

```
. . .
glDrawArrays(GL_TRIANGLES, 0, mySphere.getNumIndices());
. . .
```

When using the Sphere class, we will need three values for each vertex position and normal vector, but only two values for each texture coordinate. This is reflected in the declarations for the vectors (vertices, texCoords, and normals) shown in the Sphere.h header file, and from which the data is later loaded into the buffers.

It is important to note that although indexing is used in the process of building the sphere, the ultimate sphere vertex data stored in the VBOs doesn't utilize indexing. Rather, as setupVertices() loops through the sphere indices, it generates

Figure 6.9
Textured sphere model.

Figure 6.10
OpenGL GLUT teapot.

separate (often redundant) vertex entries in the VBO for each of the index entries. OpenGL does have a mechanism for indexing vertex data; for simplicity we didn't use it in this example, but we will use OpenGL's indexing in the next example.

Figure 6.9 shows the output of Program 6.1, with a precision of 48. The view has been slightly rotated for clarity. The texture from Figure 6.5 has been loaded as described in Chapter 5.

Many other models can be created procedurally, from geometric shapes to real-world objects. One of the most well-known is the *"Utah teapot"* [CH23], which was developed in 1975 by Martin Newell, using a variety of Bézier curves and surfaces. The *OpenGL Utility Toolkit* (or *"GLUT"*) [GL23] even includes procedures for drawing teapots(!) (see Figure 6.10). We don't cover GLUT in this book, but Bézier surfaces are covered in Chapter 11.

6.2 ■ OPENGL INDEXING – BUILDING A TORUS

6.2.1 ■ The Torus

Algorithms for producing a *torus* can be found on various websites. Paul Baker gives a step-by-step description for defining a circular slice, and then rotating the slice around a circle to form a donut, in his OpenGL bump mapping tutorial [PP07]. Figure 6.11 shows two views, from the side and from above.

The way that the torus vertex positions are generated is rather different from what was done to build the sphere. For the torus, the algorithm positions a vertex to the right of the origin and then rotates that vertex in a circle on the XY plane using a rotation around the Z axis to form a "ring." The ring is then moved outward by the "inner radius" distance. Texture coordinates and normal vectors are computed for

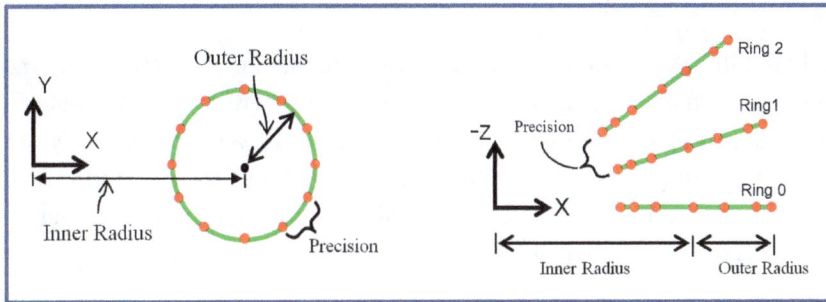

Figure 6.11
Building a torus.

each of these vertices as they are built. An additional vector tangent to the surface of the torus (called the *tangent vector*) is also generated for each vertex.

Vertices for additional torus rings are formed by rotating the original ring around the Y axis. Tangent and normal vectors for each resulting vertex are computed by also rotating the tangent and normal vectors of the original ring around the Y axis. After the vertices are created, they are traversed from ring to ring, and for each vertex two triangles are generated. The generation of six index table entries comprising the two triangles is done in a similar manner as we did for the sphere.

Our strategy for choosing texture coordinates for the remaining rings will be to arrange them so that the S axis of the texture image wraps halfway around the horizontal perimeter of the torus and then repeats for the other half. As we rotate around the Y axis generating the rings, we specify a variable ring that starts at 1 and increases up to the specified precision (again dubbed "prec"). We then set the S texture coordinate value to ring*2.0/prec, causing S to range between 0.0 and 2.0, then set the texture's tiling mode to GL_REPEAT as described in Section 5.10. The motivation for this approach is to avoid having the texture image appear overly "stretched" horizontally. If instead we did want the texture to stretch completely around the torus, we would simply remove the "*2.0" multiplier from the texture coordinate computation.

Building a torus class in C++/OpenGL could be done in a virtually identical manner as for the Sphere class. However, we have the opportunity to take advantage of the indices that we created while building the torus by using OpenGL's support for vertex indexing (we could have also done this for the sphere, but we didn't). For very large models with thousands of vertices, using OpenGL indexing can result in improved performance, and so we will describe how to do that next.

6.2.2 Indexing in OpenGL

In both our sphere and torus models, we generate an array of integer indices referencing into the vertex array. In the case of the sphere, we use the list of indices to build a complete set of individual vertices and load them into a VBO just as we did for examples in earlier chapters. Instantiating the torus and loading its vertices, normals, and so on into buffers could be done in a similar manner as was done in Program 6.1, but instead we will use OpenGL's indexing.

When using OpenGL indexing, we also load the indices themselves into a VBO. We generate one additional VBO for holding the indices. Since each index value is simply an integer reference, we first copy the index array into a C++ vector of integers, and then use glBufferData() to load the vector into the added VBO, specifying that the VBO is of type GL_ELEMENT_ARRAY_BUFFER (this tells OpenGL that the VBO contains indices). The code that does this can be added to setupVertices():

```
std::vector<int> ind = myTorus.getIndices();   // torus index accessor returns indices as an int vector
. . .
glBindBuffer(GL_ELEMENT_ARRAY_BUFFER, vbo[3]);      // vbo #3 is the additional added vbo
glBufferData(GL_ELEMENT_ARRAY_BUFFER, ind.size()*4, &ind[0], GL_STATIC_DRAW);
```

In the display() method, we replace the glDrawArrays() call with a call to glDrawElements(), which tells OpenGL to utilize the index VBO for looking up the vertices to be drawn. We also enable the VBO that contains the indices by using glBindBuffer(), specifying which VBO contains the indices and that it is a GL_ELEMENT_ARRAY_BUFFER. The code is as follows:

```
numTorusIndices = myTorus.getNumIndices();
glBindBuffer(GL_ELEMENT_ARRAY_BUFFER, vbo[3]);
glDrawElements(GL_TRIANGLES, numTorusIndices, GL_UNSIGNED_INT, 0);
```

Interestingly, the shaders used for drawing the sphere continue to work, unchanged, for the torus, even with the changes that we made in the C++/OpenGL application to implement indexing. OpenGL is able to recognize the presence of a GL_ELEMENT_ARRAY_BUFFER and utilize it to access the vertex attributes.

Program 6.2 shows a class named Torus based on Baker's implementation. The "inner" and "outer" variables refer to the corresponding inner and outer radius in Figure 6.11. The prec ("precision") variable has a similar role as in the sphere, with analogous computations for number of vertices and indices. By contrast, determining normal vectors is much more complex than it was for the sphere. We have used the strategy given in Baker's description, wherein two tangent vectors are computed (dubbed *sTangent* and *tTangent* by Baker, although more commonly referred to as "tangent" and "bitangent"), and their cross-product forms the normal.

We will use this torus class (and the sphere class described earlier) in many examples throughout the remainder of the textbook.

Program 6.2 Procedurally Generated Torus

Torus class (Torus.cpp)

```cpp
#include <cmath>
#include <vector>
#include <iostream>
#include "Torus.h"
using namespace std;

Torus::Torus() {
    prec = 48;
    inner = 0.5f;
    outer = 0.2f;
    init();
}

Torus::Torus(float innerRadius, float outerRadius, int precIn) {
    prec = precIn;
    inner = innerRadius;
    outer = outerRadius;
    init();
}

float Torus::toRadians(float degrees) { return (degrees * 2.0f * 3.14159f) / 360.0f; }

void Torus::init() {
    numVertices = (prec + 1) * (prec + 1);
    numIndices = prec * prec * 6;
    for (int i = 0; i < numVertices; i++) { vertices.push_back(glm::vec3()); }
    for (int i = 0; i < numVertices; i++) { texCoords.push_back(glm::vec2()); }
    for (int i = 0; i < numVertices; i++) { normals.push_back(glm::vec3()); }
    for (int i = 0; i < numVertices; i++) { sTangents.push_back(glm::vec3()); }
    for (int i = 0; i < numVertices; i++) { tTangents.push_back(glm::vec3()); }
    for (int i = 0; i < numIndices; i++) { indices.push_back(0); }

    // calculate first ring
    for (int i = 0; i < prec + 1; i++) {
        float amt = toRadians(i*360.0f / prec);
```

```
    // build the ring by rotating points around the origin, then moving them outward
    glm::mat4 rMat = glm::rotate(glm::mat4(1.0f), amt, glm::vec3(0.0f, 0.0f, 1.0f));
    glm::vec3 initPos(rMat * glm::vec4(0.0f, outer, 0.0f, 1.0f));
    vertices[i] = glm::vec3(initPos + glm::vec3(inner, 0.0f, 0.0f));

    // compute texture coordinates for each vertex on the ring
    texCoords[i] = glm::vec2(0.0f, ((float)i / (float)prec));

    // compute tangents and normals -- first tangent is Y-axis rotated around Z
    rMat = glm::rotate(glm::mat4(1.0f), amt+(3.14159f/2.0f), glm::vec3(0.0f, 0.0f, 1.0f));
    tTangents[i] = glm::vec3(rMat * glm::vec4(0.0f, -1.0f, 0.0f, 1.0f));
    sTangents[i] = glm::vec3(glm::vec3(0.0f, 0.0f, -1.0f));          // second tangent is -Z.
    normals[i] = glm::cross(tTangents[i], sTangents[i]);            // their X-product is the normal.
}
// rotate the first ring about Y to get the other rings
for (int ring = 1; ring < prec + 1; ring++) {
    for (int vert = 0; vert < prec + 1; vert++) {

        // rotate the vertex positions of the original ring around the Y axis
        float amt = (float)( toRadians(ring * 360.0f / prec));
        glm::mat4 rMat = glm::rotate(glm::mat4(1.0f), amt, glm::vec3(0.0f, 1.0f, 0.0f));
        vertices[ring*(prec + 1) + i] = glm::vec3(rMat * glm::vec4(vertices[i], 1.0f));

        // compute the texture coordinates for the vertices in the new rings
        texCoords[ring*(prec + 1) + vert] = glm::vec2((float)ring*2.0f / (float)prec, texCoords[vert].t);

        // rotate the tangent and bitangent vectors around the Y axis
        rMat = glm::rotate(glm::mat4(1.0f), amt, glm::vec3(0.0f, 1.0f, 0.0f));
        sTangents[ring*(prec + 1) + i] = glm::vec3(rMat * glm::vec4(sTangents[i], 1.0f));
        rMat = glm::rotate(glm::mat4(1.0f), amt, glm::vec3(0.0f, 1.0f, 0.0f));
        tTangents[ring*(prec + 1) + i] = glm::vec3(rMat * glm::vec4(tTangents[i], 1.0f));

        // rotate the normal vector around the Y axis
        rMat = glm::rotate(glm::mat4(1.0f), amt, glm::vec3(0.0f, 1.0f, 0.0f));
        normals[ring*(prec + 1) + i] = glm::vec3(rMat * glm::vec4(normals[i], 1.0f));
} }
// calculate triangle indices corresponding to the two triangles built per vertex
for (int ring = 0; ring < prec; ring++) {
    for (int vert = 0; vert < prec; vert++) {
        indices[((ring*prec + vert) * 2) * 3 + 0] = ring*(prec + 1) + vert;
        indices[((ring*prec + vert) * 2) * 3 + 1] = (ring + 1)*(prec + 1) + vert;
        indices[((ring*prec + vert) * 2) * 3 + 2] = ring*(prec + 1) + vert + 1;
        indices[((ring*prec + vert) * 2 + 1) * 3 + 0] = ring*(prec + 1) + vert + 1;
        indices[((ring*prec + vert) * 2 + 1) * 3 + 1] = (ring + 1)*(prec + 1) + vert;
        indices[((ring*prec + vert) * 2 + 1) * 3 + 2] = (ring + 1)*(prec + 1) + vert + 1;
} } }
```

```
// accessors for the torus indices and vertices
int Torus::getNumVertices() { return numVertices; }
int Torus::getNumIndices() { return numIndices; }
std::vector<int> Torus::getIndices() { return indices; }
std::vector<glm::vec3> Torus::getVertices() { return vertices; }
std::vector<glm::vec2> Torus::getTexCoords() { return texCoords; }
std::vector<glm::vec3> Torus::getNormals() { return normals; }
std::vector<glm::vec3> Torus::getStangents() { return sTangents; }
std::vector<glm::vec3> Torus::getTtangents() { return tTangents; }
```

Torus header file (Torus.h)

```
#include <cmath>
#include <vector>
#include <glm/glm.hpp>
class Torus
{
private:
    int numVertices;
    int numIndices;
    int prec;
    float inner;
    float outer;
    std::vector<int> indices;
    std::vector<glm::vec3> vertices;
    std::vector<glm::vec2> texCoords;
    std::vector<glm::vec3> normals;
    std::vector<glm::vec3> sTangents;
    std::vector<glm::vec3> tTangents;
    void init();
    float toRadians(float degrees);

public:
    Torus();
    Torus(float innerRadius, float outerRadius, int prec);
    int getNumVertices();
    int getNumIndices();
    std::vector<int> getIndices();
    std::vector<glm::vec3> getVertices();
    std::vector<glm::vec2> getTexCoords();
    std::vector<glm::vec3> getNormals();
    std::vector<glm::vec3> getStangents();
    std::vector<glm::vec3> getTtangents();
};
```

Using the Torus class (with OpenGL indexing)

. . .

#include "Torus.h"

. . .

Torus myTorus(0.5f, 0.2f, 48);

. . .

```
void setupVertices(void) {
    std::vector<int> ind = myTorus.getIndices();
    std::vector<glm::vec3> vert = myTorus.getVertices();
    std::vector<glm::vec2> tex = myTorus.getTexCoords();
    std::vector<glm::vec3> norm = myTorus.getNormals();

    std::vector<float> pvalues;
    std::vector<float> tvalues;
    std::vector<float> nvalues;

    int numVertices = myTorus.getNumVertices();
    for (int i = 0; i < numVertices; i++) {
        pvalues.push_back(vert[i].x);
        pvalues.push_back(vert[i].y);
        pvalues.push_back(vert[i].z);

        tvalues.push_back(tex[i].s);
        tvalues.push_back(tex[i].t);

        nvalues.push_back(norm[i].x);
        nvalues.push_back(norm[i].y);
        nvalues.push_back(norm[i].z);
    }
    glGenVertexArrays(1, vao);
    glBindVertexArray(vao[0]);
    glGenBuffers(4, vbo);                      // generate VBOs as before, plus one for indices

    glBindBuffer(GL_ARRAY_BUFFER, vbo[0]);              // vertex positions
    glBufferData(GL_ARRAY_BUFFER, pvalues.size() * 4, &pvalues[0], GL_STATIC_DRAW);

    glBindBuffer(GL_ARRAY_BUFFER, vbo[1]);              // texture coordinates
    glBufferData(GL_ARRAY_BUFFER, tvalues.size() * 4, &tvalues[0], GL_STATIC_DRAW);

    glBindBuffer(GL_ARRAY_BUFFER, vbo[2]);              // normal vectors
    glBufferData(GL_ARRAY_BUFFER, nvalues.size() * 4, &nvalues[0], GL_STATIC_DRAW);

    glBindBuffer(GL_ELEMENT_ARRAY_BUFFER, vbo[3]);  // indices
    glBufferData(GL_ELEMENT_ARRAY_BUFFER, ind.size() * 4, &ind[0], GL_STATIC_DRAW);
}
```

in display()

```
. . .
glBindBuffer(GL_ELEMENT_ARRAY_BUFFER, vbo[3]);
glDrawElements(GL_TRIANGLES, myTorus.getNumIndices(), GL_UNSIGNED_INT, 0);
```

Note in the code that uses the Torus class that the loop in setupVertices() now stores the data associated with each vertex once, rather than once for each index entry (as was the case in the sphere example). This difference is also reflected in the declared array sizes for the data being entered into the VBOs. Also note that in the torus example, rather than using the index values when retrieving vertex data, they are simply loaded into VBO #3. Since that VBO is designated as a GL_ELEMENT_ARRAY_BUFFER, OpenGL knows that that VBO contains vertex indices.

Figure 6.12 shows the result of instantiating a torus and texturing it with the brick texture.

Figure 6.12
Procedurally generated torus.

6.3 ■ LOADING EXTERNALLY PRODUCED MODELS

Complex 3D models, such as characters found in videogames or computer-generated movies, are typically produced using modeling tools. Such "DCC" (digital content creation) tools make it possible for people (such as artists) to build arbitrary shapes in 3D space and automatically produce the vertices, texture coordinates, vertex normals, and so on. There are too many such tools to list, but some examples are Maya, Blender, Lightwave, Cinema4D, and many others. Blender is free and open source. Figure 6.13 shows an example Blender screen during the editing of a 3D model.

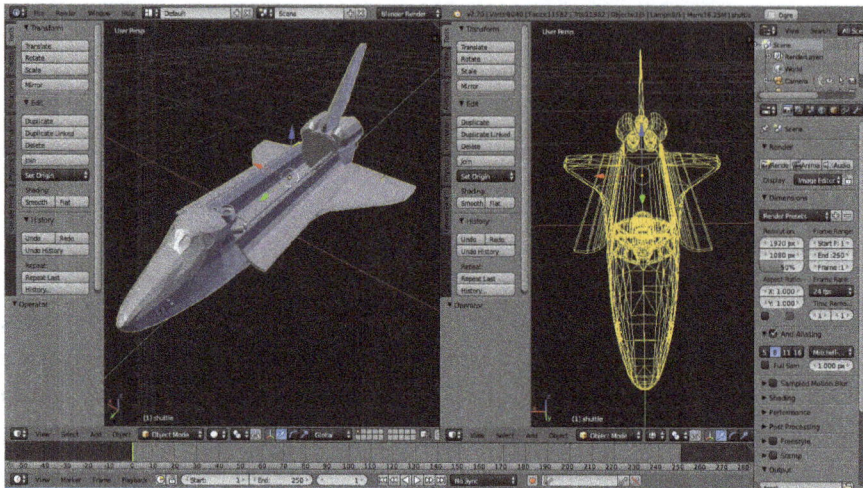

Figure 6.13
Example Blender model creation [BL23].

In order for us to use a DCC-created model in our OpenGL scenes, that model needs to be saved (exported) in a format that we can read (import) into our program. There are several standard 3D model file formats; again, there are too many to list, but some examples are Wavefront (.obj), 3D Studio Max (.3ds), Stanford Scanning Repository (.ply), Ogre3D (.mesh), to name a few. Arguably the simplest is Wavefront (usually dubbed OBJ), so we will examine that one.

OBJ files are simple enough that we can develop a basic importer relatively easily. In an OBJ file, lines of text specify vertex geometric data, texture coordinates, normals, and other information. It has some limitations—for example, OBJ files have no way of specifying model animation.

Lines in an OBJ file start with a character tag indicating what kind of data is on that line. Some common tags include:

- v – geometric (vertex location) data
- vt – texture coordinates
- vn – vertex normal
- f – face (typically vertices in a triangle)

Other tags make it possible to store the object name, materials it uses, curves, shadows, and many other details. We will limit our discussion to the four tags listed above, which are sufficient for importing a wide variety of complex models.

Suppose we use Blender to build a simple pyramid such as the one we developed for Program 4.3. Figure 6.14 is a screenshot of a similar pyramid being created in Blender:

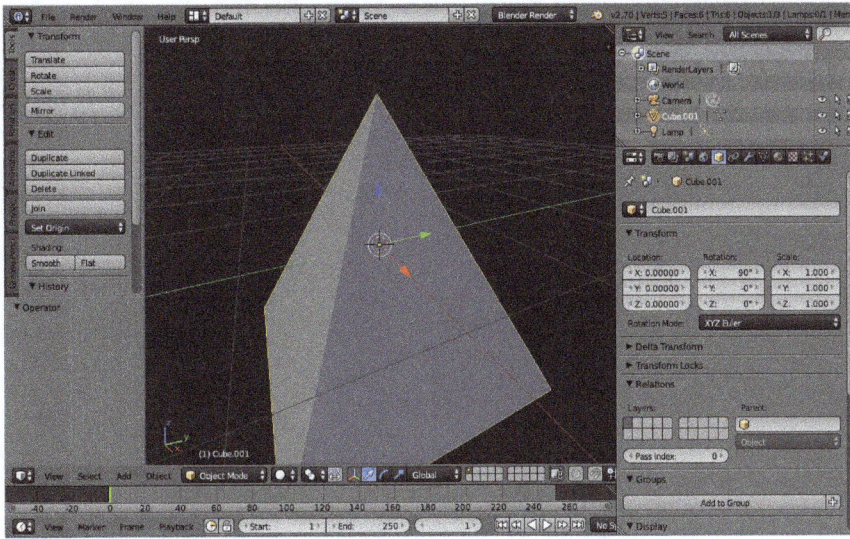

Figure 6.14
Pyramid built in Blender.

In Blender, if we now *export* our pyramid model, specify the .obj format, and also set Blender to output texture coordinates and vertex normals, an OBJ file is created that includes all of this information. The resulting OBJ file is shown in Figure 6.15. (The actual values of the texture coordinates can vary depending on how the model is built.)

We have color-coded the important sections of the OBJ file for reference. The lines at the top beginning with "#" are comments placed there by Blender, which our importer ignores. This is followed by a line beginning with "o" giving the name of the object. Our importer can ignore this line as well. Later, there is a line beginning with "s" that specifies that the faces shouldn't be smoothed. Our code will also ignore lines starting with "s".

The first substantive set of lines in the OBJ file are those starting with "v", colored blue. They specify the X, Y, and Z local spatial coordinates of the five vertices of our pyramid model relative to the origin, which in this case is at the center of the pyramid.

```
# Blender v2.70 (sub 0) OBJ File: ''
# www.blender.org
o Pyramid
v 1.000000 -1.000000 -1.000000
v 1.000000 -1.000000 1.000000
v -1.000000 -1.000000 1.000000
v -1.000000 -1.000000 -1.000000
v 0.000000 1.000000 0.000000
vt 0.515829 0.258220
vt 0.515829 0.750612
vt 0.023438 0.750612
vt 0.370823 0.790246
vt 0.820312 0.388210
vt 0.820312 0.991264
vt 0.566135 0.988689
vt 0.015625 0.742493
vt 0.566135 0.496298
vt 0.015625 0.250102
vt 0.566135 0.003906
vt 1.000000 0.000000
vt 1.000000 0.603054
vt 0.550510 0.402036
vt 0.023438 0.258220
vn 0.000000 -1.000000 0.000000
vn 0.894427 0.447214 0.000000
vn -0.000000 0.447214 0.894427
vn -0.894427 0.447214 -0.000000
vn 0.000000 0.447214 -0.894427
s off
f 2/1/1 3/2/1 4/3/1
f 1/4/2 5/5/2 2/6/2
f 2/7/3 5/8/3 3/9/3
f 3/9/4 5/10/4 4/11/4
f 5/12/5 1/13/5 4/14/5
f 1/15/1 2/1/1 4/3/1
```

Figure 6.15
Exported OBJ file for the pyramid.

The values colored red (starting with "vt") are the various texture coordinates. The reason that the list of texture coordinates is longer than the list of vertices is that some of the vertices participate in more than one triangle, and in those cases different texture coordinates might be used.

The values colored green (starting with "vn") are the various normal vectors. This list too is often longer than the list of vertices (although not in this example), again because some of the vertices participate in more than one triangle, and in those cases different normal vectors might be used.

The values colored purple (starting with "f"), near the bottom of the file, specify the triangles (i.e., "faces"). In this example, each face (triangle) has three elements, each with three values separated by "/" (OBJ allows other formats as well). The values for each element are indices into the lists of vertices, texture coordinates, and normal vectors respectively. For example, the third face is:

f 2/7/3 5/8/3 3/9/3

This indicates that the second, fifth, and third vertices from the list of vertices (in blue) comprise a triangle (note that OBJ indices start at 1). The corresponding texture coordinates are the seventh, eighth, and ninth from the list of texture coordinates in the section colored red. All three vertices have the same normal vector, the third in the list of normals in the section colored green.

Models in OBJ format are not required to have normal vectors, or even texture coordinates. If a model does not have texture coordinates or normals, the face values would specify only the vertex indices:

f 2 5 3

If a model has texture coordinates, but not normal vectors, the format would be as follows:

f 2/7 5/8 3/9

And, if the model has normals but not texture coordinates, the format would be:

f 2//3 5//3 3//3

It is not unusual for a model to have tens of thousands of vertices. There are hundreds of such models available for download on the Internet for nearly every conceivable application, including models of animals, buildings, cars, planes, mythical creatures, people, and so on.

Programs of varying sophistication that can import an OBJ model are available on the Internet. Alternatively, it is relatively easy to write a very simple OBJ loader function that can handle the basic tags we have seen (v, vt, vn, and f). Program 6.3 shows one such loader, albeit a *very* limited one. It incorporates a class to hold an arbitrary imported model, which in turn calls the importer.

Before we describe the code in our simple OBJ importer, we must warn the reader of its limitations:

- It only supports models that include *all three* face attribute fields. That is, vertex positions, texture coordinates, and normals *must all* be present and in the form: f #/#/# #/#/# #/#/#.

- The material tag, often used to specify a texture file, is ignored— texturing must be done using the methods described in Chapter 5.

- Only OBJ models composed of a single triangle mesh are supported (the OBJ format supports models comprised of multiple meshes, but our simple importer does not).

- It assumes that elements on each line are separated by exactly one space.

If you have an OBJ model that doesn't satisfy all of the above criteria, and you wish to import it using the simple loader in Program 6.3, it *may* still be feasible to do so. It is often possible to load such a model into Blender, and then export it to another OBJ file that accommodates the loader's limitations. For instance, if the model doesn't include normal vectors, it is possible to have Blender produce normal vectors while it exports the revised OBJ file.

Another limitation of our OBJ loader has to do with indexing. Observe in the previous descriptions that the "face" tag allows for the possibility of mix-and-matching vertex positions, texture coordinates, and normal vectors. For example, two different "face" rows may include indices which point to the same v entry, but different vt entries. Unfortunately, OpenGL's indexing mechanism does not support this level of flexibility—index entries in OpenGL can only point to a particular vertex *along with its attributes*. This complicates writing an OBJ model loader somewhat, as we cannot simply copy the references in the triangle face entries into an index array. Rather, using OpenGL indexing would require ensuring that entire *combinations* of v, vt, and vn values for a face entry each have their own references in the index array. A simpler, albeit less efficient, alternative is to create a new vertex for every triangle face entry. We opt for this simpler approach here in the interest of clarity, despite the space-saving advantage of using OpenGL indexing (especially when loading larger models).

The ModelImporter class includes a parseOBJ() function that reads in each line of an OBJ file one by one, handling separately the four cases v, vt, vn, and f. In each case, the subsequent numbers on the line are extracted, first by using erase()

to skip the initial v, vt, vn, or f character(s), and then using the "»" operator in the C++ **stringstream** class to extract each subsequent parameter value, and then storing them in a C++ float vector. As the face (f) entries are processed, the vertices are built with corresponding entries in C++ float vectors for vertex positions, texture coordinates, and normal vectors.

The ModelImporter class is included in the file containing the ImportedModel class, which simplifies loading and accessing the vertices of an OBJ file by putting the imported vertices into vectors of **vec2** and **vec3** objects. Recall these are GLM classes; we use them here to store vertex positions, texture coordinates, and normal vectors. The accessors in the ImportedModel class then make them available to the C++/OpenGL application in much the same manner as was done in the Sphere and Torus classes.

Following the ModelImporter and ImportedModel classes is an example sequence of calls for loading an OBJ file and then transferring the vertex information into a set of VBOs for subsequent rendering.

Figure 6.16 shows a rendered model of the space shuttle downloaded as an OBJ file from the NASA website [NA23], imported using the code from Program 6.3, and textured using the code from Program 5.1 with the associated NASA texture image file with anisotropic filtering. This texture image is an example of the use of *UV-mapping*, where texture coordinates in the model are carefully mapped to particular regions of the texture image. (As mentioned in Chapter 5, the details of UV-mapping are outside the scope of this book.)

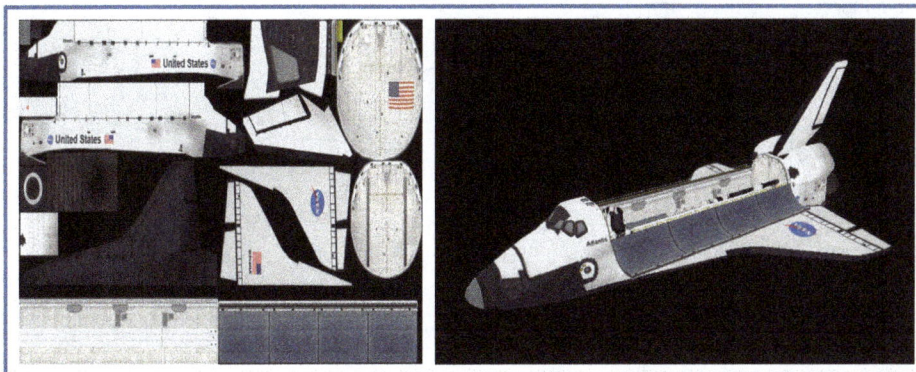

Figure 6.16
NASA space shuttle model with texture.

Program 6.3 Simple (Limited) OBJ Loader

ImportedModel and ModelImporter classes (ImportedModel.cpp)

```cpp
#include <fstream>
#include <sstream>
#include <glm/glm.hpp>
#include "ImportedModel.h"
using namespace std;

// ----------- Imported Model class

ImportedModel::ImportedModel(const char *filePath) {
    ModelImporter modelImporter = ModelImporter();
    modelImporter.parseOBJ(filePath);              // uses modelImporter to get vertex information
    numVertices = modelImporter.getNumVertices();
    std::vector<float> verts = modelImporter.getVertices();
    std::vector<float> tcs = modelImporter.getTextureCoordinates();
    std::vector<float> normals = modelImporter.getNormals();

    for (int i = 0; i < numVertices; i++) {
        vertices.push_back(glm::vec3(verts[i*3], verts[i*3+1], verts[i*3+2]));
        texCoords.push_back(glm::vec2(tcs[i*2], tcs[i*2+1]));
        normalVecs.push_back(glm::vec3(normals[i*3], normals[i*3+1], normals[i*3+2]));
} }

int ImportedModel::getNumVertices() { return numVertices; }          // accessors
std::vector<glm::vec3> ImportedModel::getVertices() { return vertices; }
std::vector<glm::vec2> ImportedModel::getTextureCoords() { return texCoords; }
std::vector<glm::vec3> ImportedModel::getNormals() { return normalVecs; }

// ------------- Model Importer class

ModelImporter::ModelImporter() {}

void ModelImporter::parseOBJ(const char *filePath) {
    float x, y, z;
    string content;
    ifstream fileStream(filePath, ios::in);
    string line = "";
    while (!fileStream.eof()) {
        getline(fileStream, line);
        if (line.compare(0, 2, "v ") == 0) {                // vertex position ("v" case)
            stringstream ss(line.erase(0, 1));
            ss >> x; ss >> y; ss >> z;                      // extract the vertex position values
            vertVals.push_back(x);
            vertVals.push_back(y);
            vertVals.push_back(z);
        }
```

```cpp
if (line.compare(0, 2, "vt") == 0) {                    // texture coordinates ("vt" case)
    stringstream ss(line.erase(0, 2));
    ss >> x; ss >> y;                                   // extract texture coordinate values
    stVals.push_back(x);
    stVals.push_back(y);
}
if (line.compare(0, 2, "vn") == 0) {                    // vertex normals ("vn" case)
    stringstream ss(line.erase(0, 2));
    ss >> x; ss >> y; ss >> z;                          // extract the normal vector values
    normVals.push_back(x);
    normVals.push_back(y);
    normVals.push_back(z);
}
if (line.compare(0, 2, "f") == 0) {                     // triangle faces ("f" case)
    string oneCorner, v, t, n;
    stringstream ss(line.erase(0, 2));
    for (int i = 0; i < 3; i++) {
        getline(ss, oneCorner, ' ');                    // extract triangle face references
        stringstream oneCornerSS(oneCorner);
        getline(oneCornerSS, v, '/');
        getline(oneCornerSS, t, '/');
        getline(oneCornerSS, n, '/');

        int vertRef = (stoi(v) - 1) * 3;                // "stoi" converts string to integer
        int tcRef = (stoi(t) - 1) * 2;
        int normRef = (stoi(n) - 1) * 3;

        triangleVerts.push_back(vertVals[vertRef]);     // build vector of vertices
        triangleVerts.push_back(vertVals[vertRef + 1]);
        triangleVerts.push_back(vertVals[vertRef + 2]);

        textureCoords.push_back(stVals[tcRef]);         // build vector of texture coords
        textureCoords.push_back(stVals[tcRef + 1]);

        normals.push_back(normVals[normRef]);           //... and normals
        normals.push_back(normVals[normRef + 1]);
        normals.push_back(normVals[normRef + 2]);
} } } }

int ModelImporter::getNumVertices() { return (triangleVerts.size()/3); }        // accessors
std::vector<float> ModelImporter::getVertices() { return triangleVerts; }
std::vector<float> ModelImporter::getTextureCoordinates() { return textureCoords; }
std::vector<float> ModelImporter::getNormals() { return normals; }
```

ImportedModel and ModelImporter header file (ImportedModel.h)

```
#include <vector>

class ImportedModel
{
private:
    int numVertices;
    std::vector<glm::vec3> vertices;
    std::vector<glm::vec2> texCoords;
    std::vector<glm::vec3> normalVecs;
public:
    ImportedModel(const char *filePath);
    int getNumVertices();
    std::vector<glm::vec3> getVertices();
    std::vector<glm::vec2> getTextureCoords();
    std::vector<glm::vec3> getNormals();
};

class ModelImporter
{
private:
    // values as read in from OBJ file
    std::vector<float> vertVals;
    std::vector<float> stVals;
    std::vector<float> normVals;

    // values stored for later use as vertex attributes
    std::vector<float> triangleVerts;
    std::vector<float> textureCoords;
    std::vector<float> normals;

public:
    ModelImporter();
    void parseOBJ(const char *filePath);
    int getNumVertices();
    std::vector<float> getVertices();
    std::vector<float> getTextureCoordinates();
    std::vector<float> getNormals();
};
```

Using the Model Importer

```
. . .
ImportedModel myModel("shuttle.obj");            // in top-level declarations
. . .
```

```
void setupVertices(void) {
    std::vector<glm::vec3> vert = myModel.getVertices();
    std::vector<glm::vec2> tex = myModel.getTextureCoords();
    std::vector<glm::vec3> norm = myModel.getNormals();
    int numObjVertices = myModel.getNumVertices();

    std::vector<float> pvalues;        // vertex positions
    std::vector<float> tvalues;        // texture coordinates
    std::vector<float> nvalues;        // normal vectors

    for (int i = 0; i < numObjVertices(); i++) {
        pvalues.push_back((vert[i]).x);
        pvalues.push_back((vert[i]).y);
        pvalues.push_back((vert[i]).z);
        tvalues.push_back((tex[i]).s);
        tvalues.push_back((tex[i]).t);
        nvalues.push_back((norm[i]).x);
        nvalues.push_back((norm[i]).y);
        nvalues.push_back((norm[i]).z);
    }
    glGenVertexArrays(1, vao);
    glBindVertexArray(vao[0]);
    glGenBuffers(numVBOs, vbo);

    // VBO for vertex locations
    glBindBuffer(GL_ARRAY_BUFFER, vbo[0]);
    glBufferData(GL_ARRAY_BUFFER, pvalues.size() * 4, &pvalues[0], GL_STATIC_DRAW);

    // VBO for texture coordinates
    glBindBuffer(GL_ARRAY_BUFFER, vbo[1]);
    glBufferData(GL_ARRAY_BUFFER, tvalues.size() * 4, &tvalues[0], GL_STATIC_DRAW);

    // VBO for normal vectors
    glBindBuffer(GL_ARRAY_BUFFER, vbo[2]);
    glBufferData(GL_ARRAY_BUFFER, nvalues.size() * 4, &nvalues[0], GL_STATIC_DRAW);
}
```

in display():
. . .
```
glDrawArrays(GL_TRIANGLES, 0, myModel.getNumVertices());
```

SUPPLEMENTAL NOTES

Although we discussed the use of DCC tools for creating 3D models, we didn't discuss how to use such tools. While such instruction is outside the scope of this text, there is a wealth of tutorial video material documentation for all of the popular tools such as Blender and Maya.

The topic of 3D modeling is itself a rich field of study. Our coverage in this chapter has been just a rudimentary introduction, with emphasis on its relationship to OpenGL. Many universities offer entire courses in 3D modeling, and readers interested in learning more are encouraged to consult some of the popular resources that offer greater detail (e.g., [BL23], [CH11], [VA12]).

We reiterate that the OBJ importer we presented in this chapter is limited, and can only handle a subset of the features supported by the OBJ format. Although sufficient for our needs, it will fail on some OBJ files. In those cases it would be necessary to first load the model into Blender (or Maya, etc.) and re-export it as an OBJ file that complies with the importer's limitations as described earlier in this chapter.

Exercises

6.1 Modify Program 4.4 so that the "sun," "planet," and "moon" are textured *spheres*, such as the ones shown in Figure 4.11.

6.2 *(PROJECT)* Modify your program from Exercise 6.1 so that the imported NASA shuttle object from Figure 6.16 also orbits the "sun." You'll want to experiment with the scale and rotation applied to the shuttle to make it look realistic.

6.3 *(RESEARCH & PROJECT)* Learn the basics of how to use Blender to create a 3D object of your own. To make full use of Blender with your OpenGL applications, you'll want to learn how to use Blender's UV-unwrapping tools to generate texture coordinates and an associated texture image. You can then export your object as an OBJ file and load it using the code from Program 6.3.

References

[BL23] Blender, The Blender Foundation, accessed November 2023, https://www.blender.org/

[CH11] A. Chopine, *3D Art Essentials: The Fundamentals of 3D Modeling, Texturing, and Animation* (Focal Press, 2011).

[CH23] Computer History Museum, accessed November 2023, http://www
.computerhistory.org/revolution/computer-graphics-music-and-art/15/206

[GL23] GLUT and OpenGL Utility Libraries, accessed November 2023, https://
www.opengl.org/resources/libraries/

[NA23] NASA 3D Resources, accessed November 2023, http://nasa3d.arc.nasa.gov/

[PP07] P. Baker, *Paul's Projects*, 2007, accessed November 2023, www
.paulsprojects.net

[VA12] V. Vaughan, *Digital Modeling* (New Riders, 2012).

[VE23] Visible Earth, NASA Goddard Space Flight Center Image, accessed
November 2023, http://visibleearth.nasa.gov

LIGHTING

Light affects the appearance of our world in varied and sometimes dramatic ways. When a flashlight shines on an object, we expect it to appear brighter on the side facing the light. The earth on which we live is itself brightly lit where it faces the sun at noon, but as it turns, that daytime brightness gradually fades into evening, until becoming completely dark at midnight.

Objects also respond differently to light. Besides having different colors, objects can have different reflective characteristics. Consider two objects, both green, but where one is made of cloth versus another made of polished steel—the latter will appear more "shiny."

7.1 LIGHTING MODELS

Light is the product of photons being emitted by high energy sources and subsequently bouncing around until some of the photons reach our eyes. Unfortunately, it is computationally infeasible to emulate this natural process, as it would require simulating and then tracking the movement of a huge number of photons, adding many objects (and matrices) to our scene. What we need is a *lighting model*.

Lighting models are sometimes called *shading models*, although in the presence of shader programming, that can be a bit confusing. Sometimes the term *reflection model* is used, complicating the terminology further. We will try to stick to whichever terminology is simple and most practical.

The most common lighting models today are called "ADS" models, because they are based on three types of reflection labeled A, D, and S:

- **A**mbient reflection simulates a low-level illumination that equally affects everything in the scene.
- **D**iffuse reflection brightens objects to various degrees depending on the light's angle of incidence.
- **S**pecular reflection conveys the shininess of an object by strategically placing a highlight of appropriate size on the object's surface where light is reflected most directly toward our eyes.

ADS models can be used to simulate different lighting effects and a variety of materials.

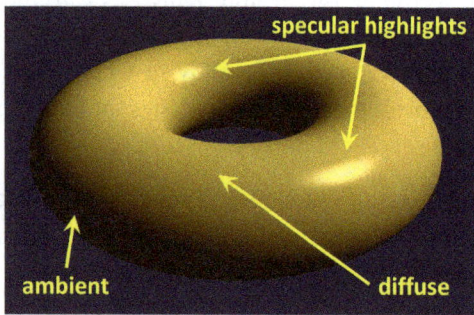

Figure 7.1
ADS Lighting contributions.

Figure 7.1 illustrates the ambient, diffuse, and specular contributions of a positional light on a shiny gold torus.

Recall that a scene is ultimately drawn by having the fragment shader output a color for each pixel on the screen. Using an ADS lighting model requires specifying contributions due to lighting on a pixel's RGBA output value. Factors include:

- The type of light source and its ambient, diffuse, and specular characteristics
- The object's material's ambient, diffuse, and specular characteristics
- The object's material's specified "shininess"
- The angle at which the light hits the object
- The angle from which the scene is being viewed

■7.2■ LIGHTS

There are many types of lights, each with different characteristics and requiring different steps to simulate their effects. Some types include:

- Global (usually called "global ambient" because it includes only an ambient component)
- Directional (or "distant")
- Positional (or "point source")
- Spotlight

Global ambient light is the simplest type of light to model. Global ambient light has no source position—the light is equal everywhere, at each pixel on every object in the scene, regardless of where the objects are. Global ambient lighting simulates the real-world phenomenon of light that has bounced around so many times that its source and direction are undeterminable. Global ambient light has only an ambient component, specified as an RGBA value; it has no diffuse or specular components. For example, global ambient light can be defined as follows:

```
float globalAmbient[4] = { 0.6f, 0.6f, 0.6f, 1.0f };
```

RGBA values range from 0 to 1, so global ambient light is usually modeled as dim white light, where each of the RGB values is set to the same fractional value between 0 and 1 and the alpha is set to 1.

Directional or *distant* light also doesn't have a source location, but it does have a *direction*. It is useful for situations where the source of the light is so far away that the light rays are effectively parallel, such as light coming from the sun. In many such situations we may only be interested in modeling the light and not the object that produces the light. The effect of directional light on an object depends on the light's angle of impact; objects are brighter on the side facing a directional light than on a tangential or opposite side. Modeling directional light requires specifying its direction (as a vector) and its ambient, diffuse, and specular characteristics (as RGBA values). A red directional light pointing down the negative Z axis might be specified as follows:

```
float dirLightAmbient[4] = { 0.1f, 0.0f, 0.0f, 1.0f };
float dirLightDiffuse[4] = { 1.0f, 0.0f, 0.0f, 1.0f };
float dirLightSpecular[4] = { 1.0f, 0.0f, 0.0f, 1.0f };
float dirLightDirection[3] = { 0.0f, 0.0f, -1.0f };
```

It might seem redundant to include an ambient contribution for a light when we already have global ambient light. The separation of the two, however, is intentional and noticeable when the light is "on" or "off." When "on," the total ambient contribution would be increased, as expected. In the above example, we have included only a small ambient contribution for the light. It is important to balance the two contributions depending on the needs of your scene.

A *Positional* light has a specific location in the 3D scene. Light sources that are near the scene, such as lamps, candles, and so forth, are examples. Like directional lights, the effect of a positional light depends on angle of impact; however, its direction is not specified, as it is different for each vertex in our scene. Positional lights may also incorporate *attenuation factors* in order to model how their intensity diminishes with distance. As with the other types of lights we have seen, positional lights have ambient, diffuse, and specular properties specified as RGBA values. A red positional light at location (5, 2, -3) could for example be specified as follows:

```
float posLightAmbient[4] = { 0.1f, 0.0f, 0.0f, 1.0f };
float posLightDiffuse[4] = { 1.0f, 0.0f, 0.0f, 1.0f };
float posLightSpecular[4] = { 1.0f, 0.0f, 0.0f, 1.0f };
float posLightLocation[3] = { 5.0f, 2.0f, -3.0f };
```

Attenuation factors can be modeled in a variety of ways. One way is to include tunable non-negative parameters for *constant*, *linear*, and *quadratic* attenuation (k_c, k_l, and k_q respectively). These parameters are then combined, taking into account the distance (d) from the light source:

$$attenuation\ Factor = \frac{1}{k_c + k_l d + k_q d^2}$$

Multiplying this factor by the light intensity causes the intensity to be decreased the greater the distance is to the light source. Note that k_c should always be set greater than or equal to 1.0, and at least one of the other parameters greater than 0.0, so that the attenuation factor will always be in the range [0..1] and approach 0 as the distance d increases.

Spotlights have both a position and a direction. The effect of the spotlight's "cone" can be simulated using a *cutoff angle* θ between 0° and 90° specifying the half-width of the light beam, and a *falloff exponent* to model the variation of intensity across the angle of the beam. As shown in Figure 7.2, we determine the angle ϕ between the spotlight's direction and a vector from the spotlight to the pixel. We then compute an *intensity factor* by raising the cosine of ϕ to the fall-off exponent when ϕ is less than θ (when ϕ is greater than θ, the intensity factor is set to 0). The result is an intensity factor that ranges from 0 to 1. The falloff exponent adjusts the rate at which the intensity factor tends to 0 as the angle ϕ increases. The intensity factor is then multiplied by the light's intensity to simulate the cone effect.

A red spotlight at location (5,2,-3) pointing down the negative Z axis could be specified as:

```
float spotLightAmbient[4] = { 0.1f, 0.0f, 0.0f, 1.0f };
float spotLightDiffuse[4] = { 1.0f, 0.0f, 0.0f, 1.0f };
float spotLightSpecular[4] = { 1.0f,0.0f, 0.0f, 1.0f };
float spotLightLocation[3] = { 5.0f, 2.0f, -3.0f };
float spotLightDirection[3] = { 0.0f, 0.0f, -1.0f };
float spotLightCutoff = 20.0f;
float spotLightExponent = 10.0f;
```

Spotlights also can include attenuation factors. We haven't shown them in the above settings, but defining them can be done in the same manner as described earlier for positional lights.

Historically, spotlights have been iconic in computer graphics since Pixar's popular animated short "Luxo Jr." appeared in 1986 [Dl23].

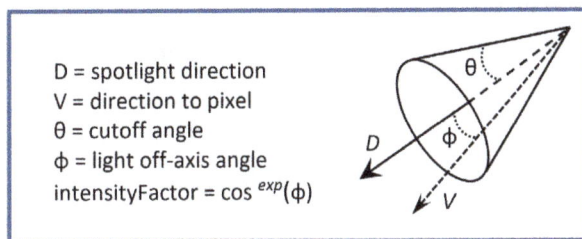

D = spotlight direction
V = direction to pixel
θ = cutoff angle
ϕ = light off-axis angle
intensityFactor = $\cos^{exp}(ϕ)$

Figure 7.2
Spotlight components.

When designing a system containing many types of lights, a programmer should consider creating a class hierarchy, such as defining a "Light" class and subclasses for "Global Ambient," "Directional," "Positional," and "Spotlight." Because spotlights share characteristics of both directional and positional lights, it is worth considering utilizing C++'s *multiple inheritance* capability, and to design a Spotlight class that inherits from both directional and positional light classes. Our examples are sufficiently simple that we omit building such a class hierarchy for lighting in this edition.

◾7.3◾ MATERIALS

The "look" of the objects in our scene has so far been handled exclusively by color and texture. The addition of lighting allows us to also consider the *reflectance* characteristics of the surfaces. By that we mean how the object interacts with our ADS lighting model. This can be modeled by considering each object to be "made of" a certain *material*.

Materials can be simulated in an ADS lighting model by specifying four values, three of which we are already familiar with—*ambient*, *diffuse*, and *specular* RGB colors. The fourth is called *shininess*, which, as we will see, is used to build an appropriate specular highlight for the intended material. ADS and shininess values have been developed for many different types of common materials. For example, "pewter" can be specified as follows:

```
float pewterMatAmbient[4] = { .11f, .06f, .11f, 1.0f };
float pewterMatDiffuse[4] = { .43f, .47f, .54f, 1.0f };
float pewterMatSpecular[4] = { .33f, .33f, .52f, 1.0f };
float pewterMatShininess = 9.85f;
```

ADS RGBA values for a few other materials are given in Figure 7.3 (from [BA21]).

Sometimes other properties are included in the material properties. *Transparency* is handled in the RGBA specifications in the fourth (or "alpha") channel, which specifies an opacity; a value of 1.0 represents completely opaque and 0.0 represents completely transparent. For most materials it is simply set to 1.0, although for certain materials a slight transparency plays a role. For example, in Figure 7.3, note that the materials "jade" and "pearl" include a small amount of transparency (values slightly less than 1.0) to add realism.

Emission is also sometimes included in an ADS material specification. This is useful when simulating a material that emits its own light, such as phosphorescent materials.

material	ambient RGBA diffuse RGBA specular RGBA	shininess
Gold	0.2473, 0.1995, 0.0745, 1.0 0.7516, 0.6065, 0.2265, 1.0 0.6283, 0.5558, 0.3661, 1.0	51.200
Jade	0.1350, 0.2225, 0.1575, 0.95 0.5400, 0.8900, 0.6300, 0.95 0.3162, 0.3162, 0.3162, 0.95	12.800
Pearl	0.2500, 0.2073, 0.2073, 0.922 1.0000, 0.8290, 0.8290, 0.922 0.2966, 0.2966, 0.2966, 0.922	11.264
Silver	0.1923, 0.1923, 0.1923, 1.0 0.5075, 0.5075, 0.5075, 1.0 0.5083, 0.5083, 0.5083, 1.0	51.200

Figure 7.3
Material ADS and shininess coefficients.

When an object is rendered that doesn't have a texture, it is often desirable to specify material characteristics. For that reason, it will be very convenient to have a few predefined materials available to us. We thus add the following lines of code to our "Utils.cpp" file:

```
// GOLD material - ambient, diffuse, specular, and shininess
float* Utils::goldAmbient() { static float a[4] = { 0.2473f, 0.1995f, 0.0745f, 1 }; return (float*)a; }
float* Utils::goldDiffuse() { static float a[4] = { 0.7516f, 0.6065f, 0.2265f, 1 }; return (float*)a; }
float* Utils::goldSpecular() { static float a[4] = { 0.6283f, 0.5558f, 0.3661f, 1 }; return (float*)a; }
float Utils::goldShininess() { return 51.2f; }

// SILVER material - ambient, diffuse, specular, and shininess
float* Utils::silverAmbient() { static float a[4] = { 0.1923f, 0.1923f, 0.1923f, 1 }; return (float*)a; }
float* Utils::silverDiffuse() { static float a[4] = { 0.5075f, 0.5075f, 0.5075f, 1 }; return (float*)a; }
float* Utils::silverSpecular() { static float a[4] = { 0.5083f, 0.5083f, 0.5083f, 1 }; return (float*)a; }
float Utils::silverShininess() { return 51.2f; }

// BRONZE material - ambient, diffuse, specular, and shininess
float* Utils::bronzeAmbient() { static float a[4] = { 0.2125f, 0.1275f, 0.0540f, 1 }; return (float*)a; }
float* Utils::bronzeDiffuse() { static float a[4] = { 0.7140f, 0.4284f, 0.1814f, 1 }; return (float*)a; }
float* Utils::bronzeSpecular() { static float a[4] = { 0.3935f, 0.2719f, 0.1667f, 1 }; return (float*)a; }
float Utils::bronzeShininess() { return 25.6f; }
```

This makes it very easy to specify that an object has, say, a "gold" material, in either the init() function or in the top level declarations, as follows:

```
float* matAmbient = Utils::goldAmbient();
float* matDiffuse = Util::goldDiffuse();
float* matSpecular = util.goldSpecular();
float matShininess = util.goldShininess();
```

Note that our code for light and material properties described so far in these sections does not actually perform lighting. It merely provides a way to specify and store desired light and material properties for elements in a scene. We still need to actually compute the lighting ourselves. This is going to require some serious mathematical processing in our shader code. So let's now dive into the nuts and bolts of implementing ADS lighting in our C++/OpenGL and GLSL graphics programs.

7.4 ■ ADS LIGHTING COMPUTATIONS

As we draw our scene, recall that each vertex is transformed so as to simulate a 3D world on a 2D screen. Pixel colors are the result of rasterization as well as texturing and interpolation. We must now incorporate the additional step of adjusting those rasterized pixel colors to effect the lighting and materials in our scene. The basic ADS computation that we need to perform is to determine the reflection intensity *(I)* for each pixel. This computation takes the following form:

$$I_{observed} = I_{ambient} + I_{diffuse} + I_{specular}$$

That is, we need to compute and sum the ambient, diffuse, and specular reflection contributions for each pixel, for each light source. This will of course depend on the type of light(s) in our scene and the type of material associated with the rendered model.

Ambient contribution is the simplest. It is the product of the specified ambient light and the specified ambient coefficient of the material:

$$I_{ambient} = Light_{ambient} * Material_{ambient}$$

Keeping in mind that light and material intensities are specified via RGB values, the computation is more precisely:

$$I_{ambient}^{red} = Light_{ambient}^{red} * Material_{ambient}^{red}$$
$$I_{ambient}^{green} = Light_{ambient}^{green} * Material_{ambient}^{green}$$
$$I_{ambient}^{blue} = Light_{ambient}^{blue} * Material_{ambient}^{blue}$$

Diffuse contribution is more complex because it depends on the angle of incidence between the light and the surface. Lambert's Cosine Law (published in 1760) specifies that the amount of light that reflects from a surface is proportional to the cosine of the light's angle of incidence. This can be modeled as follows:

$$I_{diffuse} = Light_{diffuse} * Material_{diffuse} * cos(\theta)$$

As before, the actual computations involve red, green, and blue components.

Determining the angle of incidence θ requires us to (a) find a vector from the pixel being drawn to the light source (or, similarly, a vector opposite the light direction), and (b) find a vector that is normal (perpendicular) to the surface of the object being rendered. Let's denote these vectors $\vec{L}$ and $\vec{N}$ respectively, as shown in Figure 7.4:

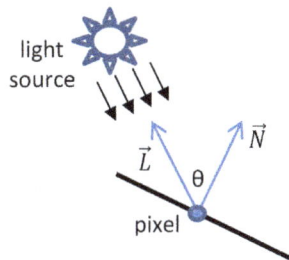

Figure 7.4
Angle of light incidence.

Depending on the nature of the lights in the scene, $\vec{L}$ could be computed by negating the light direction vector or by computing a vector from the location of the pixel to the location of the light source. Determining vector $\vec{N}$ may be trickier— normal vectors may be available for the vertices in the model being rendered, but if the model doesn't include normals, $\vec{N}$ would need to be estimated geometrically based on the locations of neighboring vertices. For the rest of the chapter, we will assume that the model being rendered includes normal vectors for each vertex (this is common in models constructed with modeling tools such as Maya or Blender).

It turns out that in this case, it isn't necessary to compute θ itself. What we really desire is $\cos(\theta)$, and recall from Chapter 3 that this can be found using the *dot product*. Thus, the diffuse contribution can be computed as follows:

$$I_{diffuse} = Light_{diffuse} * Material_{diffuse} * (\widehat{N} \bullet \widehat{L})$$

The diffuse contribution is only relevant when the surface is exposed to the light, which occurs when $-90 \leq \theta \leq 90$; that is, when $\cos(\theta) \geq 0$. Thus, we must replace the rightmost term in the previous equation with:

$$max\,((\widehat{N} \bullet \widehat{L}),\, 0)$$

Specular contribution determines whether the pixel being rendered should be brightened because it is part of a "specular highlight." It involves not only the angle of incidence of the light source, but also the angle between the reflection of the light on the surface and the viewing angle of the "eye" relative to the object's surface.

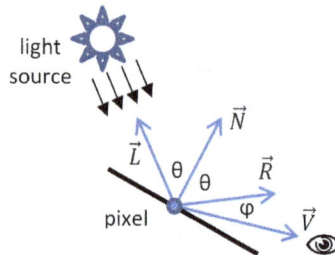

Figure 7.5
View angle incidence.

In Figure 7.5, $\vec{R}$ represents the direction of reflection of the light, and $\vec{V}$ (called the *view vector*) is a vector from the pixel to the eye. Note that $\vec{V}$ is the negative of the vector from the eye to the pixel (in world space, the negative of the translation component of the view vector minus the pixel location). The smaller the angle φ between $\vec{R}$ and $\vec{V}$, the more the eye is on-axis or "looking into" the reflection, and the more this pixel contributes to the specular highlight (and thus the brighter it should appear).

The manner in which φ is used to compute the specular contribution depends on the desired "shininess" of the object being rendered. Objects that are extremely shiny, such as a mirror, have very small specular highlights—that is, they reflect the incoming light to the eye exactly. Materials that are less shiny have specular highlights that are more "spread out," and thus more pixels are a part of the highlight.

Shininess is generally modeled with a *falloff* function that expresses how quickly the specular contribution reduces to zero as the angle φ grows. We can use *cos(φ)* to model falloff, and increase or decrease the shininess by using powers of the cosine function, such as $cos(φ)$, $cos^2(φ)$, $cos^3(φ)$, $cos^{10}(φ)$, $cos^{50}(φ)$, and so on, as illustrated in Figure 7.6.

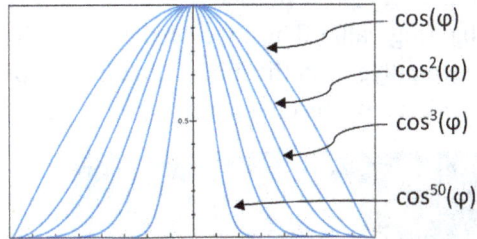

$cos(φ)$

$cos^2(φ)$

$cos^3(φ)$

$cos^{50}(φ)$

Figure 7.6
Shininess modeled as cosine exponent.

Note that the higher the value of the exponent, the faster the falloff, and thus the smaller the specular contribution of pixels with light reflections that are off-axis from the viewing angle.

We call the exponent *n*, as used in the $cos^n(φ)$ falloff function, the *shiness factor* for a specified material. Note back in Figure 7.3 that shininess factors for each of the materials listed are specified in the rightmost column.

We now can specify the full specular calculation:

$$I_{specular} = Light_{specular} * Material_{specular} * \max(0, (\hat{R} \bullet \hat{V})^n)$$

Note that we use the max() function in a similar manner as we did for the diffuse computation. In this case, we need to ensure that the specular contribution does not ever utilize negative values for cos(φ), which could produce strange artifacts such as "darkened" specular highlights.

And of course as before, the actual computations involve red, green, and blue components.

7.5 IMPLEMENTING ADS LIGHTING

The computations described in Section 7.4 have so far been mostly theoretical, as they have assumed that we can perform them for every pixel. This is complicated by the fact that normal ($\vec{N}$) vectors are typically available to us only for the vertices that define the models, not for each pixel. Thus, we need to either compute normals for each pixel, which could be time-consuming, or find some way of estimating the values that we need to achieve a sufficient effect.

One approach is called "faceted shading" or "flat shading." Here we assume that every pixel in each rendered primitive (i.e., polygon or triangle) has the same lighting value. Thus, we need only do the lighting computations for one vertex in each polygon in the model, and then copy those lighting values across the nearby rendered pixels on a per-polygon or per-triangle basis.

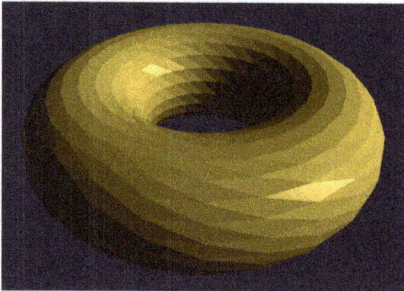

Faceted shading is rarely used today, because the resulting images tend to not look very realistic, and because modern hardware makes more accurate computations feasible. An example of a faceted-shaded torus, in which each triangle behaves as a flat reflective surface, is shown in Figure 7.7.

Figure 7.7
Torus with faceted shading.

Although faceted shading can be adequate in some circumstances (or used as a deliberate effect), usually a better approach is "smooth shading," in which the lighting intensity is computed for each pixel. Smooth shading is feasible because of the parallel processing done on modern graphics cards, and because of the interpolated rendering that takes place in the OpenGL graphics pipeline.

We will examine two popular methods for smooth shading: *Gouraud shading* and *Phong shading*.

7.5.1 Gouraud Shading

The French computer scientist Henri Gouraud published a smooth shading algorithm in 1971 that has come to be known as *Gouraud shading* [GO71]. It is particularly well suited to modern graphics cards, because it takes advantage of the automatic interpolated rendering that is available in 3D graphics pipelines such as OpenGL. The process for Gouraud shading is as follows:

1. Determine the color of each *vertex*, incorporating the lighting computations.

2. Allow those colors to be interpolated across intervening pixels through the normal rasterization process (which will also in effect interpolate the lighting contributions).

In OpenGL, this means that most of the lighting computations will be done in the vertex shader. The fragment shader will simply be a pass-through, so as to reveal the automatically interpolated lighted colors.

Figure 7.8 outlines the strategy we will use to implement our Gouraud shader in OpenGL, for a scene with a torus and one positional light. The strategy is then implemented in Program 7.1.

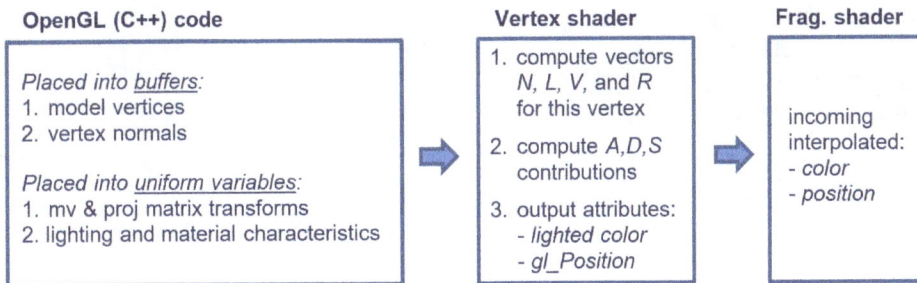

OpenGL (C++) code

Placed into *buffers*:
1. model vertices
2. vertex normals

Placed into *uniform variables*:
1. mv & proj matrix transforms
2. lighting and material characteristics

Vertex shader

1. compute vectors N, L, V, and R for this vertex
2. compute A,D,S contributions
3. output attributes:
   - lighted color
   - gl_Position

Frag. shader

incoming interpolated:
- color
- position

Figure 7.8
Implementing Gouraud shading.

Program 7.1 Torus with Positional Light and Gouraud Shading

C++/OpenGL application

```
. . .
#include "Torus.h"
#include "Utils.h"

. . .

// declarations for building shaders and rendering program, as before.
// declaration of one VAO, and two VBOs, and Torus as before.
// declaration and assignment of torus and camera location as before.
// Utils.cpp now has gold, silver, and bronze material accessors added.

. . .
// allocate variables for display() function
GLuint mLoc, vLoc, pLoc, nLoc;

// locations for shader uniform variables
GLuint globalAmbLoc, ambLoc, diffLoc, specLoc, posLoc, mAmbLoc, mDiffLoc, mSpecLoc, mShiLoc;
```

```
glm::mat4 pMat, vMat, mMat, invTrMat;
glm::vec3 currentLightPos, lightPosV;    // light position as Vector3f, in both model and view space
float lightPos[3];                       // light position as float array

// initial light location
glm::vec3 initialLightLoc = glm::vec3(5.0f, 2.0f, 2.0f);

// white light properties
float globalAmbient[4] = { 0.7f, 0.7f, 0.7f, 1.0f };
float lightAmbient[4] = { 0.0f, 0.0f, 0.0f, 1.0f };
float lightDiffuse[4] = { 1.0f, 1.0f, 1.0f, 1.0f };
float lightSpecular[4] = { 1.0f, 1.0f, 1.0f, 1.0f };

// gold material properties
float* matAmb = Utils::goldAmbient();
float* matDif = Utils::goldDiffuse();
float* matSpe = Utils::goldSpecular();
float matShi = Utils::goldShininess();

void setupVertices(void) {
    // This function is unchanged from the previous chapter
    // The following portion is repeated for clarity, because we now will actually use the normals:

    . . .
    glBindBuffer(GL_ARRAY_BUFFER, vbo[2]);
    glBufferData(GL_ARRAY_BUFFER, nvalues.size() * 4, &nvalues[0], GL_STATIC_DRAW);
}

void display(GLFWwindow* window, double currentTime) {
    // clear the depth buffer, and load rendering program as in earlier examples

    . . .
    // uniforms for model-view, projection, and inverse-transpose (normal) matrices
    mLoc = glGetUniformLocation(renderingProgram, "m_matrix");
    vLoc = glGetUniformLocation(renderingProgram, "v_matrix");
    pLoc = glGetUniformLocation(renderingProgram, "p_matrix");
    nLoc = glGetUniformLocation(renderingProgram, "norm_matrix");

    // setup of projection and view matrices as in earlier examples
    . . .
    // build the MODEL matrix based on the torus location
    mMat = glm::translate(glm::mat4(1.0f), glm::vec3(torLocX, torLocY, torLocZ));
    // rotate the torus to make it easier to see
    mMat *= glm::rotate(mMat, toRadians(35.0f), glm::vec3(1.0f, 0.0f, 0.0f));
```

```
    // set up lights based on the current light's position
    currentLightPos = glm::vec3(initialLightLoc.x, initialLightLoc.y, initialLightLoc.z);
    installLights();

    // build the inverse-transpose of the M matrix, for transforming normal vectors
    invTrMat = glm::transpose(glm::inverse(mMat));

    // put the M, V, P, and Inverse-transpose(normal) matrices into the corresponding uniforms
    glUniformMatrix4fv(mLoc, 1, GL_FALSE, glm::value_ptr(mMat));
    glUniformMatrix4fv(vLoc, 1, GL_FALSE, glm::value_ptr(vMat));
    glUniformMatrix4fv(pLoc, 1, GL_FALSE, glm::value_ptr(pMat));
    glUniformMatrix4fv(nLoc, 1, GL_FALSE, glm::value_ptr(invTrMat));

    // bind the vertices buffer (VBO #0) to vertex attribute #0 in the vertex shader
    glBindBuffer(GL_ARRAY_BUFFER, vbo[0]);
    glVertexAttribPointer(0, 3, GL_FLOAT, false, 0, 0);
    glEnableVertexAttribArray(0);

    // bind the normals buffer (in VBO #2) to vertex attribute #1 in the vertex shader
    glBindBuffer(GL_ARRAY_BUFFER, vbo[2]);
    glVertexAttribPointer(1, 3, GL_FLOAT, false, 0, 0);
    glEnableVertexAttribArray(1);

    glEnable(GL_CULL_FACE);
    glFrontFace(GL_CCW);
    glEnable(GL_DEPTH_TEST);
    glDepthFunc(GL_LEQUAL);

    glBindBuffer(GL_ELEMENT_ARRAY_BUFFER, vbo[3]);
    glDrawElements(GL_TRIANGLES, myTorus.getNumIndices(), GL_UNSIGNED_INT, 0);
}

void installLights() {
    // save the light position in a float array
    lightPos[0] = currentLightPos.x;
    lightPos[1] = currentLightPos.y;
    lightPos[2] = currentLightPos.z;

    // get the locations of the light and material fields in the shader
    globalAmbLoc = glGetUniformLocation(renderingProgram, "globalAmbient");
    ambLoc = glGetUniformLocation(renderingProgram, "light.ambient");
    diffLoc = glGetUniformLocation(renderingProgram, "light.diffuse");
    specLoc = glGetUniformLocation(renderingProgram, "light.specular");
    posLoc = glGetUniformLocation(renderingProgram, "light.position");
    mAmbLoc = glGetUniformLocation(renderingProgram, "material.ambient");
    mDiffLoc = glGetUniformLocation(renderingProgram, "material.diffuse");
    mSpecLoc = glGetUniformLocation(renderingProgram, "material.specular");
    mShiLoc = glGetUniformLocation(renderingProgram, "material.shininess");
```

```
// set the uniform light and material values in the shader
glProgramUniform4fv(renderingProgram, globalAmbLoc, 1, globalAmbient);
glProgramUniform4fv(renderingProgram, ambLoc, 1, lightAmbient);
glProgramUniform4fv(renderingProgram, diffLoc, 1, lightDiffuse);
glProgramUniform4fv(renderingProgram, specLoc, 1, lightSpecular);
glProgramUniform3fv(renderingProgram, posLoc, 1, lightPos);
glProgramUniform4fv(renderingProgram, mAmbLoc, 1, matAmb);
glProgramUniform4fv(renderingProgram, mDiffLoc, 1, matDif);
glProgramUniform4fv(renderingProgram, mSpecLoc, 1, matSpe);
glProgramUniform1f(renderingProgram, mShiLoc, matShi);
}
// init() and main() are the same as before
```

Most of the elements of Program 7.1 should be familiar. The Torus, light, and materials properties are defined. Torus vertices and associated normals are loaded into buffers. The display() function is similar to that in previous programs, except that it also sends the light and material information to the vertex shader. To do this, it calls installLights(), which loads the light location and the light and material ADS characteristics into corresponding uniform variables to make them available to the shaders. Note that we declared these uniform location variables ahead of time, for performance reasons.

An important detail is that the transformation matrix M, used to move vertex positions into world space, doesn't always properly adjust *normal vectors* into world space. Simply applying the M matrix to the normals doesn't guarantee that they will remain perpendicular to the object surface. The correct transformation is the *inverse transpose* of M, as described earlier in the supplemental notes to Chapter 3. In Program 7.1, this additional matrix, named "invTrMat", is sent to the shaders in a uniform variable.

The variable lightPos contains the light's position, but as a float array. This facilitates sending the light's world location to the vertex shader as a uniform.

The shaders are shown in the following continuation of program 7.1. The vertex shader utilizes some notations that we haven't yet seen. Note for example the vector addition done at the end of the vertex shader—vector addition was described in Chapter 3, and is available as shown here in GLSL. We will discuss some of the other notations after presenting the shaders.

(Program 7.1, continued)

Vertex Shader

```
#version 430
layout (location=0) in vec3 vertPos;
layout (location=1) in vec3 vertNormal;
out vec4 varyingColor;

struct PositionalLight
{   vec4 ambient;
    vec4 diffuse;
    vec4 specular;
    vec3 position;
};
struct Material
{   vec4 ambient;
    vec4 diffuse;
    vec4 specular;
    float shininess;
};
uniform vec4 globalAmbient;
uniform PositionalLight light;
uniform Material material;
uniform mat4 m_matrix;
uniform mat4 v_matrix;
uniform mat4 p_matrix;
uniform mat4 norm_matrix;    // for transforming normals

void main(void)
{   vec4 color;

    // convert vertex position to world space,
    // convert normal to world space, and
    // calculate world space light vector (from vertex to light)
    vec4 P = m_matrix * vec4(vertPos, 1.0);
    vec3 N = normalize((norm_matrix * vec4(vertNormal,1.0)).xyz);
    vec3 L = normalize(light.position - P.xyz);

    // view vector is from vertex to camera, camera loc is extracted from view matrix
    vec3 V = normalize(-v_matrix[3].xyz - P.xyz);

    // R is reflection of -L with respect to surface normal N
    vec3 R = reflect(-L,N);

    // ambient, diffuse, and specular contributions
    vec3 ambient = ((globalAmbient * material.ambient) + (light.ambient * material.ambient)).xyz;
    vec3 diffuse = light.diffuse.xyz * material.diffuse.xyz * max(dot(N,L), 0.0);
```

```
    vec3 specular =
        material.specular.xyz * light.specular.xyz * pow(max(dot(R,V), 0.0f), material.shininess);

    // send the color output to the fragment shader
    varyingColor = vec4((ambient + diffuse + specular), 1.0);

    // send the position to the fragment shader, as before
    gl_Position = p_matrix * v_matrix * m_matrix * vec4(vertPos,1.0);
}
```

Fragment Shader

```
#version 430
in vec4 varyingColor;
out vec4 fragColor;

// uniforms match those in the vertex shader,
// but are not used directly in this fragment shader

struct PositionalLight
{   vec4 ambient;
    vec4 diffuse;
    vec4 specular;
    vec3 position;
};
struct Material
{   vec4 ambient;
    vec4 diffuse;
    vec4 specular;
    float shininess;
};
uniform vec4 globalAmbient;
uniform PositionalLight light;
uniform Material material;
uniform mat4 m_matrix;
uniform mat4 v_matrix;
uniform mat4 p_matrix;
uniform mat4 norm_matrix;

void main(void)
{   fragColor = varyingColor;
}
```

The output of Program 7.1 is shown in Figure 7.9.

The vertex shader contains our first example of using the struct notation. A GLSL "struct" is like a datatype; it has a name and a set of fields. When a variable is declared using the name of a struct, it then contains those fields, which are accessed using the "." notation. For example, variable "light" is declared of type "PositionalLight", so we can thereafter refer to its fields light.ambient, light.diffuse, and so forth.

Figure 7.9
Torus with Gouraud shading.

Also note the field selector notation ".xyz", used in several places in the vertex shader. This is a shortcut for converting a vec4 to an equivalent vec3 containing only its first three elements.

The vertex shader is where most of the lighting computations are performed. For each vertex, the appropriate matrix transforms are applied to the vertex position and associated normal vector, and vectors for light direction ($\vec{L}$) and reflection ($\vec{R}$) are computed. The ADS computations described in Section 7.4 are then performed, resulting in a color for each vertex (called varyingColor in the code). The colors are interpolated as part of the normal rasterization process. The fragment shader is then a simple pass-through. The lengthy list of uniform variable declarations is also present in the fragment shader (for reasons described earlier in Chapter 4), but none of them are actually used there.

Note the use of the GLSL functions normalize(), which converts a vector to unit length and is necessary for proper application of the dot product, and reflect(), which computes the reflection of one vector about another.

Artifacts are evident in the output torus shown in Figure 7.9. Specular highlights have a blocky, faceted appearance. This artifact is more pronounced if the object is in motion (we can't illustrate that here).

Gouraud shading is susceptible to other artifacts. If the specular highlight is entirely contained within one of the model's triangles—that is, if it doesn't contain at least one of the model vertices—then it may disappear entirely. The specular component is calculated per-vertex, so if a model vertex with a specular contribution does not exist, none of the rasterized pixels will include specular light either.

7.5.2 Phong Shading

Bui Tuong Phong developed a smooth shading algorithm while a graduate student at the University of Utah, and described it in his 1973 dissertation [PH73] and published it in [PH75]. The structure of the algorithm is similar to the algorithm for Gouraud shading, except that the lighting computations are done *per-pixel* rather than per-vertex. Since the lighting computations require a normal vector $\vec{N}$ and a light vector $\vec{L}$, which are only available in the model on a per-vertex basis, Phong shading is often implemented using a clever "trick," whereby $\vec{N}$ and $\vec{L}$ are computed in the vertex shader and *interpolated* during rasterization. Figure 7.10 outlines the strategy:

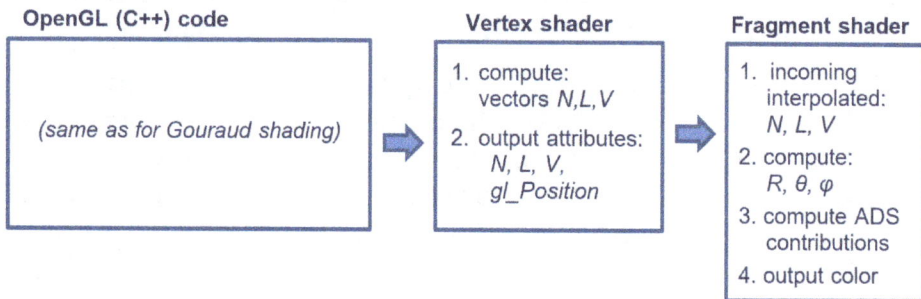

OpenGL (C++) code	Vertex shader	Fragment shader
(same as for Gouraud shading)	1. compute: vectors *N,L,V* 2. output attributes: *N, L, V, gl_Position*	1. incoming interpolated: *N, L, V* 2. compute: *R, θ, φ* 3. compute ADS contributions 4. output color

Figure 7.10
Implementing Phong shading.

The C++/OpenGL code is completely unchanged. Some of the computations previously done in the vertex shader are now moved into the fragment shader. The effect of interpolating normal vectors is illustrated in Figure 7.11:

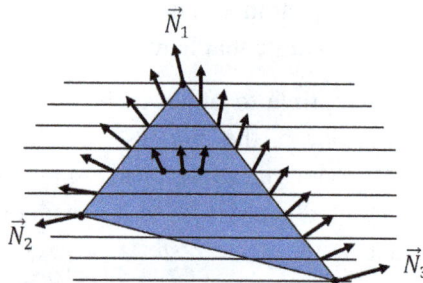

Figure 7.11
Interpolation of normal vectors.

We now are ready to implement our torus with positional lighting, using Phong shading. Most of the code is identical to that used for Gouraud shading. Since the C++/OpenGL code is unchanged, we present only the revised vertex and fragment shaders, shown in Program 7.2. Examining the output of Program 7.2, as shown in Figure 7.12, Phong shading corrects the artifacts present in Gouraud shading.

Figure 7.12
Torus with Phong shading.

Program 7.2 Torus with Phong Shading

Vertex Shader

```
#version 430
layout (location=0) in vec3 vertPos;
layout (location=1) in vec3 vertNormal;
out vec3 varyingNormal;      // world-space vertex normal
out vec3 varyingLightDir;    // vector pointing to the light
out vec3 varyingVertPos;     // vertex position in world space

// structs and uniforms same as for Gouraud shading
. . .
void main(void)
{   // output vertex position, light direction, and normal to the rasterizer for interpolation
    varyingVertPos=(m_matrix * vec4(vertPos,1.0)).xyz;
    varyingLightDir = light.position - varyingVertPos;
    varyingNormal=(norm_matrix * vec4(vertNormal,1.0)).xyz;

    gl_Position = p_matrix * v_matrix * m_matrix * vec4(vertPos,1.0);
}
```

Fragment Shader

```
#version 430
in vec3 varyingNormal;
in vec3 varyingLightDir;
in vec3 varyingVertPos;
out vec4 fragColor;

// structs and uniforms same as for Gouraud shading
. . .
```

```
void main(void)
{   // normalize the light, normal, and view vectors:
    vec3 L = normalize(varyingLightDir);
    vec3 N = normalize(varyingNormal);
    vec3 V = normalize(-v_matrix[3].xyz - varyingVertPos);

    // compute light reflection vector with respect to N:
    vec3 R = normalize(reflect(-L, N));
    // get the angle between the light and surface normal:
    float cosTheta = dot(L,N);
    // angle between the view vector and reflected light:
    float cosPhi = dot(V,R);

    // compute ADS contributions (per pixel), and combine to build output color:
    vec3 ambient = ((globalAmbient * material.ambient) + (light.ambient * material.ambient)).xyz;
    vec3 diffuse = light.diffuse.xyz * material.diffuse.xyz * max(cosTheta,0.0);
    vec3 specular =
        light.specular.xyz * material.specular.xyz * pow(max(cosPhi,0.0), material.shininess);

    fragColor = vec4((ambient + diffuse + specular), 1.0);
}
```

Although Phong shading offers better realism than Gouraud shading, it does so while incurring a performance cost. One optimization to Phong shading was proposed by James Blinn in 1977 [BL77], and is referred to as the *Blinn-Phong* reflection model. It is based on the observation that one of the most expensive computations in Phong shading is determining the reflection vector $\vec{R}$.

Blinn observed that the vector $\vec{R}$ itself actually is not needed—$\vec{R}$ is only produced as a means of determining the angle φ. It turns out that φ can be found without out computing $\vec{R}$, by instead computing a vector $\vec{H}$ that is halfway between $\vec{L}$ and $\vec{V}$. As shown in Figure 7.13, the angle α between $\vec{H}$ and $\vec{N}$ is usually close to $\frac{1}{2}(\varphi)$. Although α isn't identical to φ, Blinn showed that good results can be obtained by using α instead of φ.

The "halfway" vector $\vec{H}$ is most easily determined by finding $\vec{L}$ $\vec{V}$ (see Figure 7.14), after which $\cos(\alpha)$ can be found using the dot product $\widehat{H}$ $\widehat{N}$.

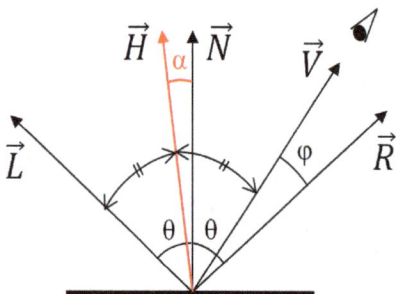

Figure 7.13
Blinn-Phong reflection.

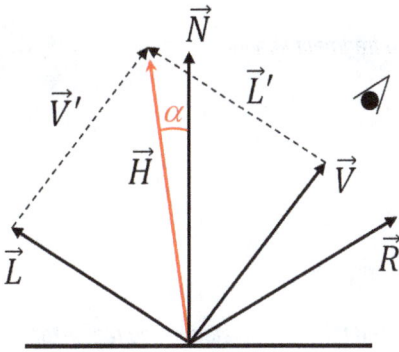

Figure 7.14
Blinn-Phong computation.

Figure 7.15
Torus with Blinn-Phong shading.

The computations can be done in the fragment shader, or even in the vertex shader (with some tweaks) if necessary for performance. Figure 7.15 shows the torus rendered using Blinn-Phong shading; the quality is largely indistinguishable from Phong shading, with substantial performance cost savings.

Program 7.3 shows the revised vertex and fragment shaders for converting the Phong shading example shown in Program 7.2 to Blinn-Phong shading. As before, there is no change to the C++/OpenGL code.

Program 7.3 Torus with Blinn-Phong Shading

Vertex Shader

```
. . .
// half-vector "H" is an additional output varying
out vec3 varyingHalfVector;
. . .
void main(void)
{   // computations same as before, plus the following that computes L+V
    varyingHalfVector = (varyingLightDir + (-varyingVertPos)).xyz;

    // (the rest of the vertex shader is unchanged)
}
```

Fragment Shader

```
. . .
in vec3 varyingHalfVector;
. . .
```

```
void main(void)
{   // note that it is no longer necessary to compute R in the fragment shader
    vec3 L = normalize(varyingLightDir);
    vec3 N = normalize(varyingNormal);
    vec3 V = normalize(-v_matrix[3].xyz - varyingVertPos);
    vec3 H = normalize(varyingHalfVector);

    . . .

    // get angle between the normal and the halfway vector
    float cosPhi = dot(H,N);

    // halfway vector H was computed in the vertex shader, and then interpolated by the rasterizer
    vec3 ambient = ((globalAmbient * material.ambient) + (light.ambient * material.ambient)).xyz;
    vec3 diffuse = light.diffuse.xyz * material.diffuse.xyz * max(cosTheta,0.0);
    vec3 specular =
        light.specular.xyz * material.specular.xyz * pow(max(cosPhi,0.0), material.shininess*3.0);
        // the multiplication by 3.0 at the end is a "tweak" to improve the specular highlight.
    fragColor = vec4((ambient + diffuse + specular), 1.0);
}
```

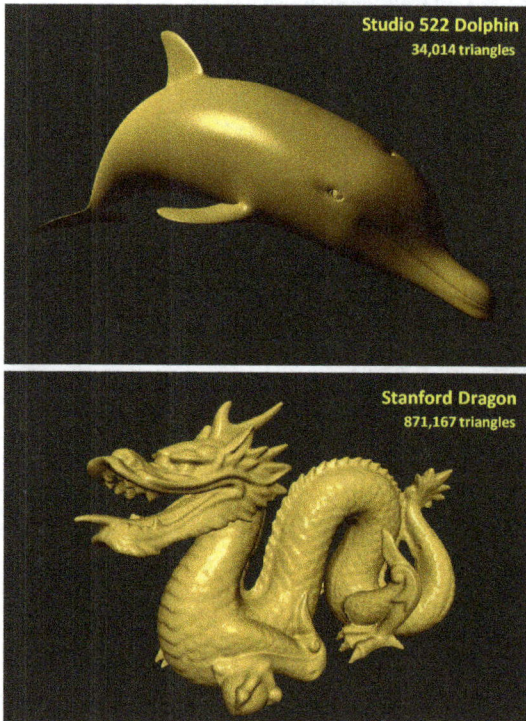

Studio 522 Dolphin
34,014 triangles

Stanford Dragon
871,167 triangles

Figure 7.16
External models with Phong shading.

Figure 7.16 shows two examples of the effect of Phong shading on more complex externally generated models. The top image shows a rendering of an OBJ model of a dolphin created by Jay Turberville at Studio 522 Productions [TU18]. The bottom image is a rendering of the well-known "Stanford Dragon," the result of a 3D scan of an actual figurine, done in 1996 [ST23]. Both models were rendered using the "gold" material we placed in our "Utils.cpp" file. The Stanford dragon is widely used for testing graphics algorithms and hardware because of its size—it contains over 800,000 triangles.

7.6 ■ COMBINING LIGHTING AND TEXTURES

So far, our lighting model has assumed that we are using lights with specified ADS values to illuminate objects made of material that has also been defined with ADS values. However, as we saw in Chapter 5, some objects may instead have surfaces defined by texture images. Therefore, we need a way of combining colors retrieved by sampling a texture and colors produced from a lighting model.

The manner in which we combine lighting and textures depends on the nature of the object and the purpose of its texture. There are several scenarios, a few of which include:

- The texture image very closely reflects the actual appearance of the object's surface.
- The object has both a material and a texture.
- The texture contains shadow or reflection information (covered in Chapters 8 and 9).
- There are multiple lights and/or multiple textures involved.

Let's consider the first case, where we have a simple textured object and we wish to add lighting to it. One simple way of accomplishing this in the fragment shader is to remove the material specification entirely, and to use the texel color returned from the texture sampler in place of the material ADS values. The following is one such strategy (expressed in pseudocode):

fragColor = textureColor * (ambientLight + diffuseLight) + specularLight

Here the texture color contributes to the ambient and diffuse computation, while the specular color is defined entirely by the light. It is common to set the specular contribution solely based on the light color, especially for metallic or "shiny" surfaces. However, some less shiny surfaces, such as cloth or unvarnished wood (and even a few metals, such as gold) have specular highlights that include the color of the object surface. In those cases, a suitable slightly modified strategy would be:

fragColor = textureColor * (ambientLight + diffuseLight + specularLight)

There are also cases in which an object has an ADS material that is supplemented by a texture image, such as an object made of silver that has a texture that adds some tarnish to the surface. In those situations, the standard ADS model with both light and material, as described in previous sections, can be combined with the texture color using a weighted sum. For example:

```
textureColor = texture(sampler, texCoord)
lightColor = (ambLight * ambMaterial) + (diffLight * diffMaterial) + specLight
fragColor = 0.5 * textureColor + 0.5 * lightColor
```

This strategy for combining lighting, materials, and textures can be extended to scenes involving multiple lights and/or multiple textures. For example:

```
texture1Color = texture(sampler1, texCoord)
texture2Color = texture(sampler2, texCoord)

light1Color = (ambLight1 * ambMaterial) + (diffLight1 * diffMaterial) + specLight1
light2Color = (ambLight2 * ambMaterial) + (diffLight2 * diffMaterial) + specLight2

fragColor  = 0.25 * texture1Color
           + 0.25 * texture2Color
           + 0.25 * light1Color
           + 0.25 * light2Color
```

Figure 7.17 shows the Studio 522 Dolphin with a UV-mapped texture image (produced by Jay Turberville [TU18]), and the NASA shuttle model we saw earlier in Chapter 6. Both textured models are enhanced with Blinn-Phong lighting, without the inclusion of materials, and with specular highlights that utilize light only. In both cases, the relevant output color computation in the fragment shader is:

```
vec4 texColor = texture(sampler, texCoord);
fragColor = texColor * (globalAmbient + lightAmb + lightDiff * max(dot(L,N),0.0))
          + lightSpec * pow(max(dot(H,N),0.0), matShininess*3.0);
```

Note that it is possible for the computation that determines fragColor to produce values greater than 1.0. When that happens, OpenGL clamps the computed value to 1.0.

SUPPLEMENTAL NOTES

The faceted-shaded torus shown in Figure 7.7 was created by adding the "flat" interpolation qualifier to the corresponding normal vector vertex attribute declarations in the vertex and fragment shaders. This instructs the rasterizer to *not*

Figure 7.17
Combining lighting and textures.

perform interpolation on the specified variable and instead assign the same value for each fragment (by default it chooses the value associated with the first vertex in the triangle). In the Phong shading example, this could be done as follows:

```
flat out vec3 varyingNormal;      in the vertex shader, and
flat in vec3 varyingNormal;       in the fragment shader.
```

An important kind of light source that we haven't discussed is a *distributed light* or *area light*, which is a light that is characterized by having a source that occupies an area rather than being a single point location. A real-world example would be a fluorescent tube-style light commonly found in an office or classroom. Interested readers can learn about such lighting details in [MH18].

HISTORICAL NOTE

We took the liberty of over-simplifying some of the terminology in this chapter with respect to the contributions of Gouraud and Phong. Gouraud is credited with *Gouraud shading*—the notion of generating a smoothly curved surface appearance by computing light intensities at vertices and allowing the rasterizer to interpolate these values (sometimes called "smooth shading"). Phong is credited with *Phong shading*, another form of smooth shading that instead interpolates normals and computes lighting per pixel. Phong is also credited with pioneering the successful incorporation of specular highlights into smooth shading. For this reason, the ADS lighting model, when applied to computer graphics, is often referred to as the *Phong Reflection Model*. So, our example of Gouraud shading is, more accurately, Gouraud shading with a Phong reflection model. Since Phong's reflection model has become so ubiquitous in 3D graphics programming, it is common to demonstrate Gouraud shading in the presence of Phong reflection, although it is a bit misleading because Gouraud's original 1971 work did not, for example, include any specular component.

Exercises

7.1 *(PROJECT)* Modify Program 7.1 so that the light can be positioned by moving the mouse. After doing this, move the mouse around and note the movement of the specular highlight and the appearance of the Gouraud shading artifacts. You may find it convenient to render a point (or small object) at the location of the light source.

7.2 Repeat Exercise 7.1, but applied to Program 7.2. This should only require substituting the shaders for Phong shading into your solution to Exercise 7.1. The improvement from Gouraud to Phong shading should be even more apparent here, when the light is being moved around.

7.3 *(PROJECT)* Modify Program 7.2 so that it incorporates TWO positional lights placed in different locations. The fragment shader will need to blend the diffuse and specular contributions of each of the lights. Try using a weighted sum, similar to the one shown in Section 7.6. You can also try simply adding them and clamping the result so it doesn't exceed the maximum light value.

7.4 *(RESEARCH AND PROJECT)* Replace the positional light in Program 7.2 with a "spot" light as described in Section 7.2. Experiment with the settings for *cutoff angle* and *falloff exponent* and observe the effects.

References

[BA21]   N. Barradeu, accessed November 2023, http://www.barradeau.com/nicoptere/dump/materials.html

[BL77]   J. Blinn, "Models of Light Reflection for Computer Synthesized Pictures," *Proceedings of the 4th Annual Conference on Computer Graphics and Interactive Techniques*, 1977.

[DI23]   *Luxo Jr.* (Pixar – copyright held by Disney), accessed November 2023, https://www.pixar.com/luxo-jr/#luxo-jr-main

[GO71]   H. Gouraud, "Continuous Shading of Curved Surfaces," *IEEE Transactions on Computers* C-20, no. 6 (June 1971).

[MH18]   T. Akenine-Möller, E. Haines, N. Hoffman, A. Pesce, M. Iwanicki, and S. Hillaire, *Real-Time Rendering*, 4th ed. (A. K. Peters / CRC Press 2018).

[PH73]   B. Phong, "Illumination of Computer-Generated Images" (PhD thesis, University of Utah, 1973).

[PH75]   B. Phong, "Illumination for Computer Generated Pictures," *Communications of the ACM* 18, no. 6 (June 1975): 311–317.

[ST23]   The Stanford 3D Scanning Repository, accessed November 2023, http://graphics.stanford.edu/data/3Dscanrep/

[TU18]   J. Turberville, Studio 522 Productions, Scottsdale, AZ, accessed November 2023, www.studio522.com (dolphin model developed 2016).

SHADOWS

8.1 THE IMPORTANCE OF SHADOWS

In Chapter 7, we learned how to add lighting to our 3D scenes. However, we didn't actually add light; instead, we simulated the effects of light on objects—using the ADS model—and modified how we drew those objects accordingly.

The limitations of this approach become apparent when we use it to light more than one object in the same scene. Consider the scene in Figure 8.1, which includes both our brick-textured torus and a ground plane (the ground plane is the top of a giant cube with a grass texture from [LU16]).

Figure 8.1
Scene without shadows.

At first glance our scene may appear reasonable. However, closer examination reveals that there is something very important missing. In particular, it is impossible to discern the distance between the torus and the large textured cube below it. Is the torus floating above the cube, or is it resting on top of the cube?

The reason we cannot answer this question is due to the lack of *shadows* in the scene. We expect to see shadows, and our brain uses shadows to help build a more complete mental model of the objects we see and where they are located.

Consider the same scene, shown in Figure 8.2, with shadows incorporated. It is now obvious that the torus is resting on the ground plane in the left example and floating above it in the right example.

Figure 8.2
Lighting with shadows.

8.2 ■ PROJECTIVE SHADOWS

A variety of interesting methods have been devised for adding shadows to 3D scenes. One method that is well-suited to drawing shadows on a ground plane (such as our image in Figure 8.1), and relatively computationally inexpensive, is called *projective shadows*. Given a point light source position (X_L, Y_L, Z_L), an object to render, and a plane on which the object's shadow is to be cast, it is possible to derive a transformation matrix that will convert points (X_W, Y_W, Z_W) on the object to corresponding shadow points $(X_S, 0, Z_S)$ on the plane. The resulting "shadow polygon" is then drawn, typically as a dark object blended with the texture on the ground plane, as illustrated in Figure 8.3.

The advantages of projective shadow casting are that it is efficient and simple to implement. However, it only works on a flat plane—the method can't be used to cast shadows on a curved surface or on other objects. It is still useful for performance-intensive applications involving outdoor scenes, such as in many video games.

Development of projective shadow transformation matrices is discussed in [BL88], [AS14], and [KS16].

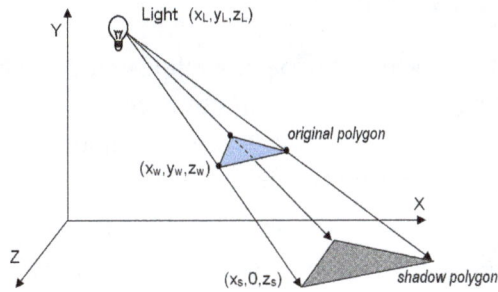

Figure 8.3
Projective shadow.

8.3 ■ SHADOW VOLUMES

Another important method, proposed by Crow in 1977, is to identify the spatial volume shadowed by an object and reduce the color intensity of polygons inside the intersection of the shadow volume with the view volume [CR77]. Figure 8.4 shows a cube in a shadow volume, so the cube would be drawn darker.

Shadow volumes have the advantage of being highly accurate, with fewer artifacts than other methods. However, finding the shadow volume and then computing whether each polygon is inside of it is computationally expensive even on modern GPU hardware. Geometry shaders can be used to generate shadow volumes, and the *stencil buffer*[1] can be used to determine whether a pixel is within the volume. Some graphics cards include hardware support for optimizing certain shadow volume operations.

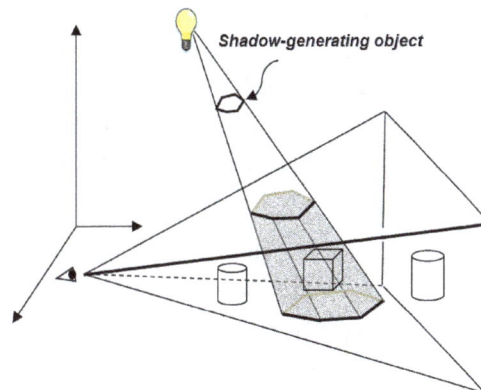

Figure 8.4
Shadow volume.

---

[1] The *stencil buffer* is a third buffer—along with the color buffer and the z-buffer—accessible through OpenGL. The stencil buffer is not described in this textbook.

8.4 SHADOW MAPPING

One of the most practical and popular methods for casting shadows is called *shadow mapping.* Although it is not always as accurate as shadow volumes (and is often accompanied by pesky artifacts), shadow mapping is easier to implement, can be used in a wide variety of situations, and enjoys powerful hardware support.

We would be remiss if we failed to clarify our use of the word "easier" in the previous paragraph. Although shadow mapping is simpler than shadow volumes (both conceptually and in practice), it is by no means "easy"! Students often find shadow mapping among the most difficult techniques to implement in a 3D graphics course. Shader programs are by nature difficult to debug, and shadow mapping requires the perfect coordination of several components and shader modules. *Be advised that successful implementation of shadow mapping will be greatly facilitated by liberal use of the debugging tools described earlier in Section 2.2.*

Shadow mapping is based on a very simple and clever idea: namely, anything that cannot be seen by the *light* is in shadow. That is, if object #1 blocks the light from reaching object #2, it is the same as the light not being able to "see" object #2.

The reason this idea is so powerful is that we already have a method for determining if something can be "seen"—the hidden surface removal algorithm (HSR) using the Z-buffer, as described in Section 2.1.7. So, a strategy for finding shadows is to temporarily move the camera to the location of the light, apply the Z-buffer HSR algorithm, and then use the resulting depth information to find shadows.

Rendering our scene will require two passes: one to render the scene from the point of view of the light (but not actually drawing it to the screen), and a second pass to render it from the point of view of the camera. The purpose of pass one is to generate a Z-buffer from the light's point of view. After completing pass one, we need to retain the Z-buffer and use it to help us generate shadows in pass two. Pass two actually draws the scene.

Our strategy is now becoming more refined:

- *(Pass 1) Render the scene from the light's position. The depth buffer then contains, for each pixel, the distance between the light and the nearest object to it.*
- *Copy the depth buffer to a separate "shadow buffer."*

- *(Pass 2) Render the scene normally. For each pixel, look up the corresponding position in the shadow buffer. If the distance to the point being rendered is greater than the value retrieved from the shadow buffer, then the object being drawn at this pixel is further from the light than the object nearest the light, and therefore this pixel is in shadow.*

When a pixel is found to be in shadow, we need to make it darker. One simple and effective way of doing this is to render only its ambient lighting, ignoring its diffuse and specular components.

The method described above is often called "shadow buffering." The term "shadow mapping" arises when, in the second step, we instead copy the depth buffer into a *texture*. When a texture object is used in this way, we will refer to it as a *shadow texture*, and OpenGL has support for shadow textures in the form of a sampler2DShadow type (discussed below). This allows us to leverage the power of hardware support for texture units and sampler variables (i.e., "texture mapping") in the fragment shader to quickly perform the depth lookup in pass 2. Our revised strategy now is:

- *(Pass 1) as before.*
- *Copy the depth buffer into a <u>texture</u>.*
- *(Pass 2) as before, except that the shadow buffer is now a <u>shadow</u> <u>texture</u>.*

Let's now implement these steps.

⬛8.4.1⬛ Shadow Mapping (PASS ONE) – "Draw" Objects from Light Position

In step one, we first move our camera to the light's position and then render the scene. Our goal here is *not* to actually draw the scene on the display, but to complete just enough of the rendering process that the depth buffer is properly filled. Thus, it will not be necessary to generate colors for the pixels, and so our first pass will utilize a vertex shader, but the fragment shader does nothing.

Of course, moving the camera involves constructing an appropriate *view* matrix. Depending on the contents of the scene, we will need to decide on an appropriate *direction* to view the scene from the light. Typically, we would want this direction to be toward the region that is ultimately rendered in pass 2.

This is often application specific—in our scenes, we will generally be pointing the camera from the light to the origin.

Several important details need to be handled in pass one:

- Configure the buffer and shadow texture.
- Disable color output.
- Build a look-at matrix from the light toward the objects in view.
- Enable the GLSL pass one shader program, containing only the simple vertex shader shown in Figure 8.5 that expects to receive an MVP matrix. In this case, the MVP matrix will include the object's model matrix M, the look-at matrix computed in the previous step (serving as the view matrix V), and the perspective matrix P. We call this MVP matrix "shadowMVP" because it is based on the point of view of the light rather than the camera. Since the view from the light isn't actually being displayed, the pass one shader program's fragment shader doesn't do anything.
- For each object, create the shadowMVP matrix and call glDrawArrays(). It is not necessary to include textures or lighting in pass one, because objects are not rendered to the screen.

```
#version 430              // vertex shader
layout (location=0) in vec3 vertPos;
uniform mat4 shadowMVP;

void main(void)
{    gl_Position = shadowMVP * vec4(vertPos,1.0);
}
```
```
#version 430              // fragment shader
void main(void)  { }
```

Figure 8.5
Shadow mapping pass 1 vertex and fragment shaders.

8.4.2 Shadow Mapping (Intermediate Step) – Copying the Z-Buffer to a Texture

OpenGL offers two methods for putting Z-buffer depth data into a texture unit. The first method is to generate an empty shadow texture and then use the command glCopyTexImage2D() to copy the active depth buffer into the shadow texture.

The second method is to build a "custom framebuffer" back in pass one (rather than use the default Z-buffer) and attach the shadow texture to it using the command glFrameBufferTexture(). This command was introduced into OpenGL in version 3.0 to further support shadow mapping. When using this approach, it isn't necessary to "copy" the Z-buffer into a texture, because the buffer already has a texture attached to it, and so the depth information is put into the texture by OpenGL automatically. This is the method we will use in our implementation.

8.4.3 Shadow Mapping (PASS TWO) – Rendering the Scene with Shadows

Much of pass two will resemble what we saw in Chapter 7. Namely, it is here that we render our complete scene and all of the items in it, along with the lighting, materials, and any textures adorning the objects in the scene. We also need to add the necessary code to determine, for each pixel, whether or not it is in shadow.

An important feature of pass two is that it utilizes two MVP matrices. One is the standard MVP matrix that transforms object coordinates into screen coordinates (as seen in most of our previous examples). The other is the shadowMVP matrix that was generated in pass one for use in rendering from the light's point of view—this will now be used in pass two for looking up depth information from the shadow texture.

A complication arises in pass two when we try to look up pixels in a texture map. The OpenGL camera utilizes a [-1..+1] coordinate space, whereas texture maps utilize a [0..1] space. A common solution is to build an additional matrix transform, typically called B, that converts (or "biases," hence the name) from camera space to texture space. Deriving B is fairly simple—a scale by one-half followed by a translate by one-half.

The B matrix is as follows:

$$B = \begin{bmatrix} 0.5 & 0 & 0 & 0.5 \\ 0 & 0.5 & 0 & 0.5 \\ 0 & 0 & 0.5 & 0.5 \\ 0 & 0 & 0 & 1 \end{bmatrix}$$

B is then concatenated onto the shadowMVP matrix for use in pass two, as follows:

shadowMVP2 = [B] [shadowMVP$_{(pass1)}$]

Assuming that we use the method whereby a shadow texture has been attached to our custom framebuffer, OpenGL provides some relatively simple tools for determining whether each pixel is in shadow as we draw the objects. Here is a summary of the details handled in pass two:

- Build the "B" transform matrix for converting from light to texture space (actually, this is more appropriately done in init()).
- Enable the shadow texture for lookup.
- Enable color output.
- Enable the GLSL pass two rendering program, containing both vertex and fragment shaders.
- Build the MVP matrix for the object being drawn based on the camera position (as normal).
- Build the shadowMVP2 matrix (incorporating the B matrix, as described earlier)—the shaders will need it to look up pixel coordinates in the shadow texture.
- Send the matrix transforms to shader uniform variables.
- Enable buffers containing vertices, normal vectors, and texture coordinates (if used), as usual.
- Call glDrawArrays().

In addition to their rendering duties, the vertex and fragment shaders have additional tasks:

- The vertex shader converts vertex positions from camera space to light space and sends the resulting coordinates to the fragment shader in a vertex attribute so that they will be interpolated. This makes it possible to retrieve the correct values from the shadow texture.
- The fragment shader calls the textureProj() function, which returns a 0 or 1 indicating whether or not the pixel is in shadow (this mechanism is explained later). If it is in shadow, the shader outputs a darker pixel by not including its diffuse and specular contributions.

Shadow mapping is such a common task that GLSL provides a special type of sampler variable called a sampler2DShadow (as previously mentioned) that can be attached to a shadow texture in the C++/OpenGL application. The textureProj() function is used to look up values from a shadow texture, and it is similar to texture() that we saw previously in Chapter 5, except that it uses a vec3 to index the texture rather than the usual vec2. Since a pixel coordinate is a vec4, it is necessary to project that onto 2D texture space in order to look up the depth value in the shadow texture map. As we will see in the following, textureProj() does all of this for us.

The remainder of the vertex and fragment shader code implements Blinn-Phong shading. These shaders are shown in Figures 8.6 and 8.7, with the added code for shadow mapping highlighted.

Let's examine more closely how we use OpenGL to perform the depth comparison between the pixel being rendered and the value in the shadow texture. We start in the vertex shader with vertex coordinates in model space, which we multiply by shadowMVP2 to produce shadow texture coordinates that correspond to vertex coordinates projected into light space, previously generated from the light's

```
#version 430
layout (location=0) in vec3 vertPos;
layout (location=1) in vec3 vertNormal;

out vec3 varyingNormal, varyingLightDir, varyingVertPos, varyingHalfVec;
out vec4 shadow_coord;

struct PositionalLight  { vec4 ambient, diffuse, specular;  vec3 position; };
struct Material  { vec4 ambient, diffuse, specular;  float shininess; };
uniform vec4 globalAmbient;
uniform PositionalLight light;        // light's position is assumed to be in eye space
uniform Material material;
uniform mat4 m_matrix;
uniform mat4 v_matrix;
uniform mat4 p_matrix;
uniform mat4 norm_matrix;
uniform mat4 shadowMVP2;
layout (binding=0) uniform sampler2DShadow shTex;

void main(void)
{     varyingVertPos = (m_matrix * vec4(vertPos,1.0)).xyz;
      varyingLightDir = light.position - varyingVertPos;
      varyingNormal = (norm_matrix * vec4(vertNormal,1.0)).xyz;
      varyingHalfVec = (varyingLightDir - varyingVertPos).xyz;
      shadow_coord = shadowMVP2 * vec4(vertPos,1.0);
      gl_Position = p_matrix * v_matrix * m_matrix * vec4(vertPos,1.0);
}
```

Figure 8.6
Shadow mapping pass 2 vertex shader.

```
#version 430
in vec3 varyingNormal, varyingLightDir, varyingVertPos, varyingHalfVec;
in vec4 shadow_coord;
out vec4 fragColor;
// same structs and uniforms as in the vertex shader

void main(void)
{    vec3 L = normalize(varyingLightDir);
     vec3 N = normalize(varyingNormal);
     vec3 V = normalize(-v.matrix[3].xyz - varyingVertPos);
     vec3 H = normalize(varyingHalfVec);

     float inShadow = textureProj(shTex, shadow_coord);

     fragColor = globalAmbient * material.ambient +  light.ambient * material.ambient;
     If (notInShadow == 1.0)
     {    fragColor += light.diffuse * material.diffuse * max(dot(L,N),0.0)
          + light.specular * material.specular
          * pow(max(dot(H,N),0.0),material.shininess*3.0);
     }
}
```

Figure 8.7
Shadow mapping pass 2 fragment shader.

point of view. The interpolated (3D) light space coordinates (x,y,z) are used in the fragment shader as follows. The z component represents the distance from the light to the pixel. The (x,y) components are used to retrieve the depth information stored in the (2D) shadow texture. This retrieved value (the distance to the object nearest the light) is compared with z. This comparison produces a "binary" result that tells us whether the pixel we are rendering is further from the light than the object nearest the light (i.e., whether the pixel is in shadow).

If in OpenGL we use glFrameBufferTexture() as described earlier, and we enable *depth testing*, then using a sampler2DShadow and textureProj() as shown in the fragment shader (Figure 8.7) will do exactly what we need. That is, textureProj() will output either 0.0 or 1.0 depending on the depth comparison. Based on this value, we can then in the fragment shader omit the diffuse and specular contributions when the pixel is further from the light than the object nearest the light, effectively creating the shadow when appropriate. An overview is shown in Figure 8.8.

We are now ready to build our C++/OpenGL application to work with the previously described shaders.

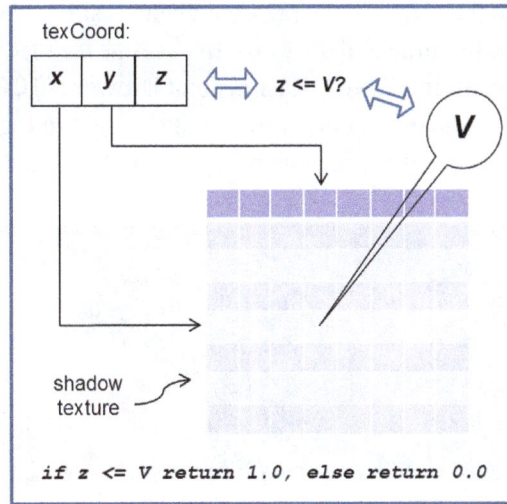

Figure 8.8
Automatic depth comparison.

8.5 ■ A SHADOW MAPPING EXAMPLE

Consider the scene in Figure 8.9 that includes a torus and a pyramid. A positional light has been placed on the left (note the specular highlights).

The pyramid *should* be casting a shadow on the torus.

To clarify the development of the example, our first step will be to *render pass one to the screen* to make sure it is working properly. To do this, we will temporarily add a

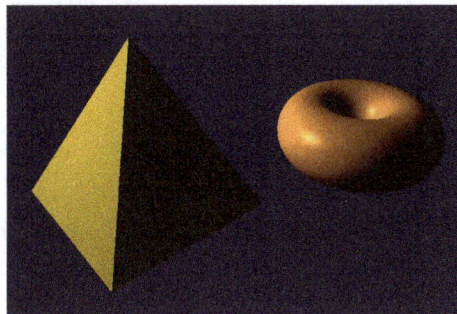

Figure 8.9
Lighted scene without shadows.

simple fragment shader (it will not be included in the final version) to pass one that just outputs a constant color (e.g., red); for example:

```
#version 430
out vec4 fragColor;
void main(void)
{   fragColor = vec4(1.0, 0.0, 0.0, 0.0);
}
```

Let's assume that the origin of the previous scene is situated at the center of the figure, in between the pyramid and the torus. In pass one we place the camera at the light's position (at the left in Figure 8.10) and point it toward (0,0,0). If we then draw the objects in red, it produces the output shown at the right in Figure 8.10. Note the torus near the top—from this vantage point it is partially behind the pyramid.

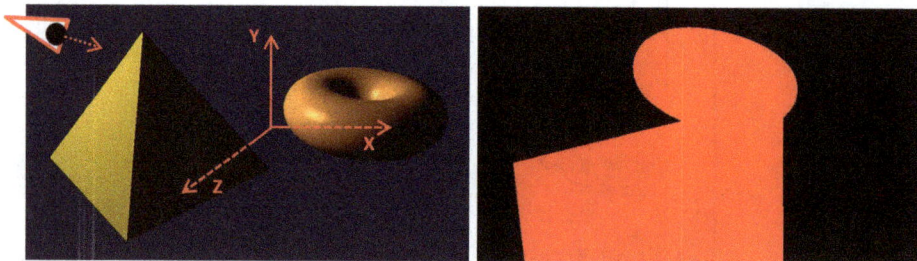

Figure 8.10
Pass one: Scene (left) from light's point of view (right).

The complete two-pass C++/OpenGL code with lighting and shadow mapping is shown in Program 8.1.

Program 8.1 Shadow Mapping

```
// Much is the same as we have seen before. New sections to support shadows are highlighted.
// The imports necessary for lighting, etc., would be included at the start, are the same as before,
// and are not shown here.

// variable declarations for rendering programs, buffers, shader sources, etc., would go here.
...
ImportedModel pyramid("pyr.obj");              // define the pyramid
Torus myTorus(0.6f, 0.4f, 48);                 // define the torus
int numPyramidVertices, numTorusVertices, numTorusIndices;

...
// locations of torus, pyramid, camera, and light
glm::vec3 torusLoc(1.6f, 0.0f, -0.3f);
glm::vec3 pyrLoc(-1.0f, 0.1f, 0.3f);
glm::vec3 cameraLoc(0.0f, 0.2f, 6.0f);
glm::vec3 lightLoc(-3.8f, 2.2f, 1.1f);

// properties of white light (global and positional) used in this scene
float globalAmbient[4] = { 0.7f, 0.7f, 0.7f, 1.0f };
float lightAmbient[4] = { 0.0f, 0.0f, 0.0f, 1.0f };
float lightDiffuse[4] = { 1.0f, 1.0f, 1.0f, 1.0f };
float lightSpecular[4] = { 1.0f, 1.0f, 1.0f, 1.0f };
```

```
// gold material for the pyramid
float* goldMatAmb = Utils::goldAmbient();
float* goldMatDif = Utils::goldDiffuse();
float* goldMatSpe = Utils::goldSpecular();
float goldMatShi = Utils::goldShininess();

// bronze material for the torus
float* bronzeMatAmb = Utils::bronzeAmbient();
float* bronzeMatDif = Utils::bronzeDiffuse();
float* bronzeMatSpe = Utils::bronzeSpecular();
float bronzeMatShi = Utils::bronzeShininess();

// variables used in display() for transfering light to shaders
float curAmb[4], curDif[4], curSpe[4], matAmb[4], matDif[4], matSpe[4];
float curShi, matShi;

// shadow-related variables
int screenSizeX, screenSizeY;
GLuint shadowTex, shadowBuffer;
glm::mat4 lightVmatrix;
glm::mat4 lightPmatrix;
glm::mat4 shadowMVP1;
glm::mat4 shadowMVP2;
glm::mat4 b;

// light and camera view matrix transforms are all declared here (mMat, vMat, etc.) of type mat4.
// Other variables used in display() are also declared here.

    . . .

int main(void) {
    // unchanged from previous examples
}

// The init() routine performs the usual calls to compile shaders and initialize objects.
// It also calls setupShadowBuffers() to instantiate the buffers related to shadow-mapping.
// Lastly, it builds the B matrix for converting from light space to texture space.

void init(GLFWwindow* window) {

    renderingProgram1 = Utils::createShaderProgram("./vert1Shader.glsl", "./frag1Shader.glsl");
    renderingProgram2 = Utils::createShaderProgram("./vert2Shader.glsl", "./frag2Shader.glsl");

    setupVertices();
    setupShadowBuffers();

    b = glm::mat4(
        0.5f, 0.0f, 0.0f, 0.0f,
        0.0f, 0.5f, 0.0f, 0.0f,
        0.0f, 0.0f, 0.5f, 0.0f,
        0.5f, 0.5f, 0.5f, 1.0f);
}
```

```
void setupShadowBuffers(GLFWwindow* window) {
    glfwGetFramebufferSize(window, &width, &height);
    screenSizeX = width;
    screenSizeY = height;

    // create the custom frame buffer
    glGenFramebuffers(1, &shadowBuffer);

    // create the shadow texture and configure it to hold depth information.
    // these steps are similar to those in Program 5.2
    glGenTextures(1, &shadowTex);
    glBindTexture(GL_TEXTURE_2D, shadowTex);
    glTexImage2D(GL_TEXTURE_2D, 0, GL_DEPTH_COMPONENT32,
        screenSizeX, screenSizeY, 0, GL_DEPTH_COMPONENT, GL_FLOAT, 0);
    glTexParameteri(GL_TEXTURE_2D, GL_TEXTURE_MIN_FILTER, GL_LINEAR);
    glTexParameteri(GL_TEXTURE_2D, GL_TEXTURE_MAG_FILTER, GL_LINEAR);
    glTexParameteri(GL_TEXTURE_2D, GL_TEXTURE_COMPARE_MODE,
                                        GL_COMPARE_REF_TO_TEXTURE);
    glTexParameteri(GL_TEXTURE_2D, GL_TEXTURE_COMPARE_FUNC, GL_LEQUAL);
}

void setupVertices(void) {
    // same as in earlier examples. This function creates the VAO, the VBOs, and then
    // loads vertices and normal vectors for the torus and pyramid into the buffers.
}

// The display() function manages the setup of the custom frame buffer and the shadow texture
// in preparation for pass 1 and pass 2 respectively. New shadow-related features are highlighted.

void display(GLFWwindow* window, double currentTime) {
    glClear(GL_COLOR_BUFFER_BIT);
    glClear(GL_DEPTH_BUFFER_BIT);

    // set up view and perspective matrix from the light point of view, for pass 1
    lightVmatrix = glm::lookAt(currentLightPos, origin, up);   // vector from light to origin
    lightPmatrix = glm::perspective(toRadians(60.0f), aspect, 0.1f, 1000.0f);

    // make the custom frame buffer current, and associate it with the shadow texture
    glBindFramebuffer(GL_FRAMEBUFFER, shadowBuffer);
    glFramebufferTexture(GL_FRAMEBUFFER, GL_DEPTH_ATTACHMENT, shadowTex, 0);

    // disable drawing colors, but enable the depth computation
    glDrawBuffer(GL_NONE);
    glEnable(GL_DEPTH_TEST);

    passOne();
```

```
    // restore the default display buffer, and re-enable drawing
    glBindFramebuffer(GL_FRAMEBUFFER, 0);
    glActiveTexture(GL_TEXTURE0);
    glBindTexture(GL_TEXTURE_2D, shadowTex);
    glDrawBuffer(GL_FRONT);                    // re-enables drawing colors

    passTwo();
}
```

```
// What follows now are the methods for the first and second passes.
// They are largely identical to things we have seen before.
// Shadow-related additions are highlighted.
```

```
void passOne(void) {

    // renderingProgram1 includes the pass one vertex and fragment shaders
    glUseProgram(renderingProgram1);

    . . .

    // the following blocks of code render the torus to establish the depth buffer from the light point of view

    mMat = glm::translate(glm::mat4(1.0f), torusLoc);
    // slight rotation for viewability
    mMat = glm::rotate(mMat, toRadians(25.0f), glm::vec3(1.0f, 0.0f, 0.0f));

    // we are drawing from the light's point of view, so we use the light's P and V matrices
    shadowMVP1 = lightPmatrix * lightVmatrix * mMat;
    sLoc = glGetUniformLocation(renderingProgram1, "shadowMVP");
    glUniformMatrix4fv(sLoc, 1, GL_FALSE, glm::value_ptr(shadowMVP1));

    // we only need to set up torus vertices buffer – we don't need its textures or normals for pass one.
    glBindBuffer(GL_ARRAY_BUFFER, vbo[0]);
    glVertexAttribPointer(0, 3, GL_FLOAT, GL_FALSE, 0, 0);
    glEnableVertexAttribArray(0);

    glClear(GL_DEPTH_BUFFER_BIT);
    glEnable(GL_CULL_FACE);
    glFrontFace(GL_CCW);
    glEnable(GL_DEPTH_TEST);
    glDepthFunc(GL_LEQUAL);

    glBindBuffer(GL_ELEMENT_ARRAY_BUFFER, vbo[4]);     // vbo[4] contains torus indices
    glDrawElements(GL_TRIANGLES, numTorusIndices, GL_UNSIGNED_INT, 0);

    // repeat for the pyramid (but don't clear the GL_DEPTH_BUFFER_BIT)
    // The pyramid is not indexed, so we use glDrawArrays() rather than glDrawElements()
    . . .
    glDrawArrays(GL_TRIANGLES, 0, numPyramidVertices);
}
```

```
void passTwo(void) {
    glUseProgram(renderingProgram2);              // pass two vertex and fragment shaders

    // draw the torus – this time we need to include lighting, materials, normals, etc.
    // We also need to provide MVP tranforms for BOTH camera space and light space.
    mLoc = gl.glGetUniformLocation(renderingProgram2, "m_matrix");
    vLoc = gl.glGetUniformLocation(renderingProgram2, "v_matrix");
    pLoc = gl.glGetUniformLocation(renderingProgram2, "p_matrix");
    nLoc = glGetUniformLocation(renderingProgram2, "norm_matrix");
    sLoc = glGetUniformLocation(renderingProgram2, "shadowMVP");

    // the torus is bronze
    curAmb[0] = bronzeMatAmb[0];    curAmb[1] = bronzeMatAmb[1];    curAmb[2] = bronzeMatAmb[2];
    curDif[0] = bronzeMatDif[0];    curDif[1] = bronzeMatDif[1];    curDif[2] = bronzeMatDif[2];
    curSpe[0] = bronzeMatSpe[0];    curSpe[1] = bronzeMatSpe[1];    curSpe[2] = bronzeMatSpe[2];
    curShi = bronzeMatShi;

    vMat = glm::translate(glm::mat4(1.0f), glm::vec3(-cameraLoc.x, -cameraLoc.y, -cameraLoc.z));

    currentLightPos = glm::vec3(lightLoc);
    installLights(renderingProgram2);

    mMat = glm::translate(glm::mat4(1.0f), torusLoc);
    // slight rotation for viewability
    mMat = glm::rotate(mMat, toRadians(25.0f), glm::vec3(1.0f, 0.0f, 0.0f));

    // build the inverse-transpose matrix for the normal vectors
    invTrMat = glm::transpose(glm::inverse(mMat));

    // build the MVP matrix for the torus from the light's point of view
    shadowMVP2 = b * lightPmatrix * lightVmatrix * mMat;

    // put the M, V and P matrices into the corresponding uniforms
    glUniformMatrix4fv(mLoc, 1, GL_FALSE, glm::value_ptr(mMat));
    glUniformMatrix4fv(vLoc, 1, GL_FALSE, glm::value_ptr(vMat));
    glUniformMatrix4fv(pLoc, 1, GL_FALSE, glm::value_ptr(pMat));
    glUniformMatrix4fv(nLoc, 1, GL_FALSE, glm::value_ptr(invTrMat));
    glUniformMatrix4fv(sLoc, 1, GL_FALSE, glm::value_ptr(shadowMVP2));

    // set up torus vertices and normals buffers (and texture coordinates buffer if used)
    glBindBuffer(GL_ARRAY_BUFFER, vbo[0]);             // torus vertices
    glVertexAttribPointer(0, 3, GL_FLOAT, GL_FALSE, 0, 0);
    glEnableVertexAttribArray(0);

    glBindBuffer(GL_ARRAY_BUFFER, vbo[2]);             // torus normals
    glVertexAttribPointer(1, 3, GL_FLOAT, GL_FALSE, 0, 0);
    glEnableVertexAttribArray(1);

    glClear(GL_DEPTH_BUFFER_BIT);
    glEnable(GL_CULL_FACE);
    glFrontFace(GL_CCW);
```

```
glEnable(GL_DEPTH_TEST);
glDepthFunc(GL_LEQUAL);

glBindBuffer(GL_ELEMENT_ARRAY_BUFFER, vbo[4]);        // vbo[4] contains torus indices
glDrawElements(GL_TRIANGLES, numTorusIndices, GL_UNSIGNED_INT, 0);
. . .
// repeat for the gold pyramid
}
```

Program 8.1 shows the relevant portions of the C++/OpenGL application that interact with the pass one and pass two shaders previously detailed. Not shown are the usual modules for reading in and compiling the shaders, building the models and their related buffers, installing the positional light's ADS characteristics in the shaders, and performing the perspective and look-at matrix computations. Those are unchanged from previous examples.

8.6 ■ SHADOW MAPPING ARTIFACTS

Although we have implemented all of the basic requirements for adding shadows to our scene, running Program 8.1 produces mixed results, as shown in Figure 8.11.

Figure 8.11
Shadow "acne."

The good news is that our pyramid is now casting a shadow on the torus! Unfortunately, this success is accompanied by a severe artifact. There are wavy lines covering many of the surfaces in the scene. This is a common by-product of shadow mapping, and is called *shadow acne* or *erroneous self-shadowing*.

Shadow acne is caused by rounding errors during depth testing. The texture coordinates computed when looking up the depth information in a shadow texture often don't exactly match the actual coordinates. Thus, the lookup may return the depth for a neighboring pixel, rather than the one being rendered. If the distance to the neighboring pixel is further, then our pixel will appear to be in shadow even if it isn't.

Shadow acne can also be caused by differences in precision between the texture map and the depth computation. This too can lead to rounding errors and subsequent incorrect assessment of whether or not a pixel is in shadow.

Fortunately, fixing shadow acne is fairly easy. Since shadow acne typically occurs on surfaces that are *not* in shadow, a simple trick is to move every pixel slightly closer to the light during pass one, and then move them back to their normal positions for pass two. This is usually sufficient to compensate for either type of rounding error. An easy way is to call glPolygonOffset() in the display() function, as shown in Figure 8.12 (highlighted).

Adding these few lines of code to our display() function improves the output of our program considerably, as shown in Figure 8.13. Note also that with the artifacts gone, we can now see that the inner circle of the torus displays a small correctly cast shadow on itself.

```
void display(GLFWwindow* window, double currentTime) {
    // clearing the depth and color buffers as before goes here
    . . .
    // setting up matrices for camera and light points of view as before goes here
    . . .
    glBindFramebuffer(GL_FRAMEBUFFER, shadowBuffer);
    glFramebufferTexture(GL_FRAMEBUFFER, GL_DEPTH_ATTACHMENT, shadowTex, 0);

    glDrawBuffer(GL_NONE);
    glEnable(GL_DEPTH_TEST);

    // for reducing shadow artifacts
    glEnable(GL_POLYGON_OFFSET_FILL);
    glPolygonOffset(2.0f, 4.0f);

    passOne();

    glDisable(GL_POLYGON_OFFSET_FILL);

    glBindFramebuffer(GL_FRAMEBUFFER, 0);
    glActiveTexture(GL_TEXTURE0);
    glBindTexture(GL_TEXTURE_2D, shadowTex);
    glDrawBuffer(GL_FRONT);

    passTwo();
}
```

Figure 8.12
Combating shadow acne.

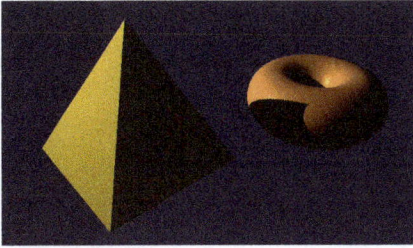

Figure 8.13
Rendered scene with shadows.

Figure 8.14
"Peter Panning."

Although fixing shadow acne is easy, sometimes the repair causes new artifacts. The "trick" of moving the object before pass one can sometimes cause a gap to appear inside an object's shadow. An example of this is shown in Figure 8.14. This artifact is often called "Peter Panning," because sometimes it causes the shadow of a resting object to inappropriately separate from the object's base (thus making portions of the object's shadow detach from the rest of the shadow, reminiscent of J. M. Barrie's character Peter Pan [PP23]). Fixing this artifact requires adjusting the glPolygonOffset() parameters. If they are too small, shadow acne can appear; if too large, Peter Panning happens.

There are many other artifacts that can happen during shadow mapping. For example, shadows can *repeat* as a result of the region of the scene being rendered in pass one (into the shadow buffer) being different from the region of the scene rendered in pass two (they are from different vantage points). Because of this difference, those portions of the scene rendered in pass two that fall outside the region rendered in pass one will attempt to access the shadow texture using texture coordinates outside of the range [0..1]. Recall that the default behavior in this case is GL_REPEAT, which can result in incorrectly duplicated shadows.

One possible solution is to add the following lines of code to setupShadowBuffers(), to set the texture wrap mode to "clamp to edge":

```
glTexParameteri(GL_TEXTURE_2D, GL_TEXTURE_WRAP_S, GL_CLAMP_TO_EDGE);
glTexParameteri(GL_TEXTURE_2D, GL_TEXTURE_WRAP_T, GL_CLAMP_TO_EDGE);
```

This causes values outside of a texture edge to be clamped to the value at edge (instead of repeating). Note that this approach can introduce its own artifacts, namely, when a shadow exists at the edge of the shadow texture, clamping to the edge can produce a "shadow bar" extending to the edge of the scene.

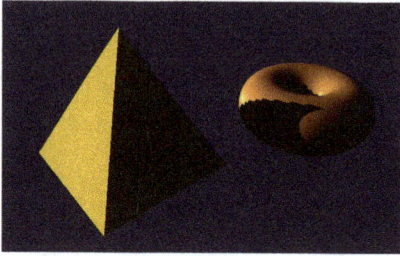

Figure 8.15
Jagged shadow edges.

Another common error is *jagged shadow edges*. This can happen when the shadow being cast is significantly larger than the shadow buffer can accurately represent. This usually depends on the location of the objects and light(s) in the scene. In particular, it commonly occurs when the light source is relatively distant from the objects involved. An example is shown in Figure 8.15.

Eliminating jagged shadow edges is not as simple as for the previous artifacts. One technique is to move the light position closer to the scene during pass one, and then return it to the correct position in pass two. Another approach that is often effective is to employ one of the "soft shadow" methods that we will discuss next.

8.7 SOFT SHADOWS

The methods presented thus far are limited to producing *hard shadows*. These are shadows with sharp edges. However, most shadows that occur in the real world are *soft shadows*. That is, their edges are blurred to various degrees. In this section, we will explore the appearance of soft shadows as they occur in the real world and then describe a commonly used algorithm for simulating them in OpenGL.

8.7.1 Soft Shadows in the Real World

There are many causes of soft shadows, and there are many types of soft shadows. One thing that commonly causes soft shadows in nature is that real-world

Figure 8.16
Soft shadow real-world example.

light sources are rarely points—more often they occupy some area. Another cause is the accumulation of imperfections in materials and surfaces, and the role that the objects themselves play in generating ambient light through their own reflective properties.

Figure 8.16 shows a photograph of an object casting a soft shadow on a table top. Note that this is *not* a 3D computer rendering, but an actual photograph of an object, taken in the home of one of the authors.

There are two aspects to note about the shadow in Figure 8.16:

- The shadow is "softer" the further it is from the object and "harder" the closer it is to the object. This is apparent when comparing the shadow near the legs of the object versus the wider portion of the shadow at the right region of the image.

- The shadow appears slightly darker the closer it is to the object.

The dimensionality of the light source itself can lead to soft shadows. As shown in Figure 8.17, the various regions across the light source cast slightly different shadows. The lighter areas at the edges of the shadow — where only a portion of the light is blocked by the object — are collectively called the *penumbra*.

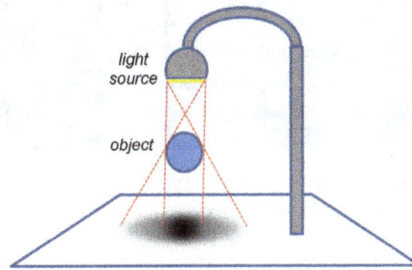

Figure 8.17
Soft shadow penumbra effect.

8.7.2 Generating Soft Shadows – Percentage Closer Filtering (PCF)

There are various ways of simulating the penumbra effect to generate soft shadows in software. One of the simplest and most common is called *Percentage Closer Filtering* (PCF). In PCF (proposed in 1987 by Reeves et al. [RS87]), we sample the shadow texture at several surrounding locations to estimate what percentage of nearby locations are in shadow. Depending on how many of the nearby locations are in shadow, we increase or decrease the degree of lighting contribution for the pixel being rendered. The entire computation can be done in the fragment shader, and that is the only place where we have to change any of the code. PCF also can be used to reduce jagged line artifacts.

Before we study the actual PCF algorithm, let's first look at a simple similar motivating example to illustrate the goal of PCF. Consider the set of output fragments (pixels) shown in Figure 8.18, whose colors are being computed by the fragment shader.

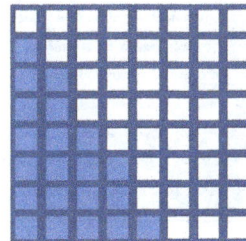

Figure 8.18
Hard shadow rendering.

Suppose that the darkened pixels are in shadow, as computed using shadow mapping. Instead of simply rendering the pixels as shown (i.e., with or without the diffuse and specular components included), suppose that we had access to neighboring pixel information, so that we could see how many of the neighboring pixels are in shadow. For example, consider the particular pixel highlighted in yellow in Figure 8.19, which according to Figure 8.18 is not in shadow.

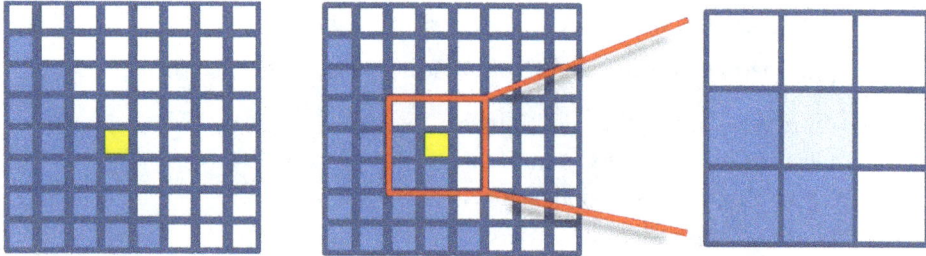

Figure 8.19
PCF sampling for a particular pixel.

In the nine-pixel neighborhood of the highlighted pixel, three of the pixels are in shadow and six are not. Thus, the color of the rendered pixel could be computed as the sum of the ambient contribution at that pixel, plus six-ninths of the diffuse and specular contributions, resulting in a fairly (but not completely) brightened pixel. Repeating this process throughout the grid would produce pixel colors approximately as shown in Figure 8.20. Note that for those pixels whose neighborhoods are entirely in (or out of) shadow, the resulting color is the same as for standard shadow-mapping.

Unlike the example just shown, implementations of PCF do not sample every pixel within a certain vicinity of the pixel being rendered. There are two reasons for this: (a) we'd like to perform this computation in the fragment shader, but the fragment shader does not have access to other pixels; and (b) obtaining a sufficiently broad penumbra effect (say, ten to twenty pixels wide) would require sampling hundreds of nearby pixels for each pixel being rendered.

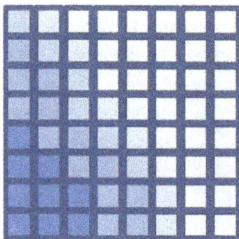

Figure 8.20
Soft shadow rendering.

PCF addresses these two issues as follows. First, rather than attempting to access nearby pixels, we instead sample nearby *texels* in the shadow map. The fragment shader can do this because even though it doesn't have access to nearby pixel values, it does have access to the entire shadow map. Second, to achieve a sufficiently broad penumbra effect, a moderate number of nearby shadow map texels are sampled, each at some modest distance from the texel corresponding to the pixel being rendered.

The width of the penumbra and the number of points sampled can be tuned depending on the scene and the performance requirements. For example, the

Figure 8.21
Soft shadow rendering – 64 samples per pixel.

image shown in Figure 8.21 was generated using PCF, with each pixel's brightness determined by sampling 64 nearby shadow map texels at various distances from the pixel's texel.

The accuracy or smoothness of our soft shadows depends on the number of nearby texels sampled. Thus, there is a tradeoff between performance and quality—the more points sampled, the better the results, but the more computational overhead is incurred. Depending on the complexity of the scene and the framerate required for a given application, there is often a corresponding practical limit to the quality that can be achieved. Samping 64 points per pixel, such as in Figure 8.21, is usually impractical.

A commonly used algorithm for implementing PCF is to sample four nearby texels per pixel, with the samples selected at specified offset distances from the texel which corresponds to the pixel. As we process each pixel, we alter the offsets used to determine which four texels are sampled. Altering the offsets in a staggered manner is sometimes called *dithering*, and aims to make the soft shadow boundary appear less "blocky" than it ordinarily would given the small number of sample points.

A common approach is to assume one of four different offset patterns—we can choose which pattern to use for a given pixel by computing the pixel's glFragCoord mod 2. Recall that glFragCoord is of type vec2, containing the x and y coordinates of the pixel location; the result of the mod computation is then one of four values: (0,0), (0,1), (1,0), or (1,1). We use this result to select one of our four different offset patterns in texel space (i.e., in the shadow map).

The offset patterns are typically specified in the x and y directions with different combinations of -1.5, -0.5, +0.5, and +1.5 (these can also be scaled as desired).

More specifically, the four usual offset patterns for each of the cases resulting from the glFragCoord mod 2 compuation are:

case (0,0)	case (0,1)	case (1,0)	case (1,1)
sample points:	sample points:	sample points:	sample points:
$(s_x-1.5, s_y+1.5)$	$(s_x-1.5, s_y+0.5)$	$(s_x-0.5, s_y+1.5)$	$(s_x-0.5, s_y+0.5)$
$(s_x-1.5, s_y-0.5)$	$(s_x-1.5, s_y-1.5)$	$(s_x-0.5, s_y-0.5)$	$(s_x-0.5, s_y-1.5)$
$(s_x+0.5, s_y+1.5)$	$(s_x+0.5, s_y+0.5)$	$(s_x+1.5, s_y+1.5)$	$(s_x+1.5, s_y+0.5)$
$(s_x+0.5, s_y-0.5)$	$(s_x+0.5, s_y-1.5)$	$(s_x+1.5, s_y-0.5)$	$(s_x+1.5, s_y-1.5)$

S_x and S_y refer to the location (S_x, S_y) in the shadow map corresponding to the pixel being rendered, identified as shadow_coord in the code examples throughout this chapter. These four offset patterns are illustrated in Figure 8.22, with each case shown in a different color. In each case, the texel corresponding to the pixel being rendered is at the origin of the graph for that case. Note that when shown together in Figure 8.23, the staggering/dithering of the offsets is apparent.

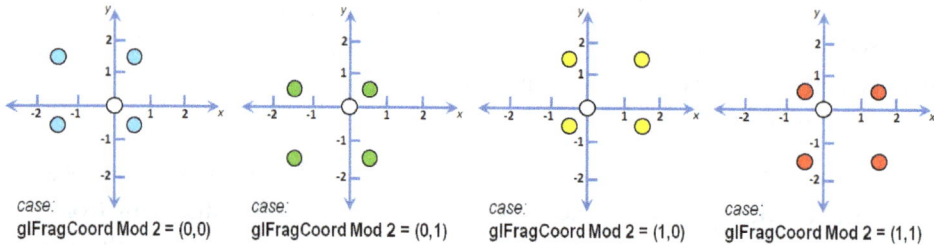

Figure 8.22
Dithered four-pixel PCF sampling cases.

Let's walk through the entire computation for a particular pixel. Assume the pixel being rendered is located at glFragCoord = (48,13). We start by determining the four shadow map sample points for the pixel. To do that, we would compute vec2(48,13) mod 2, which equals (0,1). From that we would choose the offsets shown for case (0,1), shown in green in Figure 8.22, and the specific points to be sampled in the shadow map (assuming that no scaling of the offsets has been specified) would be:

- (shadow_coord.x–1.5, shadow_coord.y+0.5)
- (shadow_coord.x–1.5, shadow_coord.y–1.5)

- (shadow_coord.x+0.5, shadow_coord.y+0.5)
- (shadow_coord.x+0.5, shadow_coord.y−1.5)

(Recall that shadow_coord is the location of the texel in the shadow map corresponding to the pixel being rendered—shown as a white circle in Figures 8.22 and 8.23.)

We next call textureProj() on each of these four points, which in each case returns either 0.0 or 1.0 depending on whether or not that sampled point is in shadow. We sum the four results and divide by 4.0 to determine the percentage of sam-

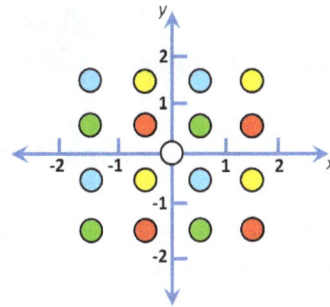

Figure 8.23
Dithered four-pixel PCF sampling (four cases shown together).

pled points which are in shadow. This percentage is then used as a multiplier to determine the amount of diffuse and specular lighting to be applied when rendering the current pixel.

Despite the small sampling size—only four samples per pixel—this dithered approach can often produce surprisingly good soft shadows. Figure 8.24 was generated using four-point dithered PCF. While not quite as good as the 64-point sampled version shown previously in Figure 8.21, it renders considerably faster.

In the next section, we develop the GLSL fragment shader that produced both this four-sample dithered PCF soft shadow and the previously shown 64-sample PCF soft shadow.

Figure 8.24
Soft shadow rendering – four samples per pixel, dithered.

8.7.3 A Soft Shadow/PCF Program

As mentioned earlier, the soft shadow computation can be done entirely in the fragment shader. Program 8.2 shows the fragment shader that replaces the one in Figure 8.7. The PCF additions are highlighted.

Program 8.2 Percentage Closer Filtering (PCF)

Fragment Shader

```glsl
#version 430
// all variable declarations are unchanged
. . .

// Returns the shadow depth value for a texel at distance (x,y) from shadow_coord.  Recall that
// shadow_coord is the location in the shadow map corresponding to the current pixel being rendered.

float lookup(float ox, float oy)
{   float t = textureProj(shadowTex,
        shadow_coord + vec4(ox * 0.001 * shadow_coord.w, oy * 0.001 * shadow_coord.w,
        -0.01, 0.0));   // the third parameter (-0.01) is an offset to counteract shadow acne
    return t;
}

void main(void)
{   float shadowFactor = 0.0;
    vec3 L = normalize(vLightDir);
    vec3 N = normalize(vNormal);
    vec3 V = normalize(-v_matrix[3].xyz - vVertPos);
    vec3 H = normalize(vHalfVec);

    // ----- this section produces a 4-sample dithered soft shadow
    float swidth = 2.5;            // tunable amount of shadow spread
    // produces one of 4 sample patterns depending on glFragCoord mod 2
    vec2 offset = mod(floor(gl_FragCoord.xy), 2.0) * swidth;
    shadowFactor += lookup(-1.5*swidth + offset.x,  1.5*swidth - offset.y);
    shadowFactor += lookup(-1.5*swidth + offset.x, -0.5*swidth - offset.y);
    shadowFactor += lookup( 0.5*swidth + offset.x,  1.5*swidth - offset.y);
    shadowFactor += lookup( 0.5*swidth + offset.x, -0.5*swidth - offset.y);
    shadowFactor = shadowFactor / 4.0;    // shadowFactor is an average of the four sampled points

    // ----- this section, if un-commented, produces a 64-sample hi resolution soft shadow
    //   float swidth = 2.5;       // tunable amount of shadow spread
    //   float endp = swidth*3.0 +swidth/2.0;
    //   for (float m=-endp ; m<=endp ; m=m+swidth)
    //   {   for (float n=-endp ; n<=endp ; n=n+swidth)
    //       {        shadowFactor += lookup(m,n);
    //   }   }
    //   shadowFactor = shadowFactor / 64.0;

    vec4 shadowColor = globalAmbient * material.ambient + light.ambient * material.ambient;
```

```
vec4 lightedColor = light.diffuse * material.diffuse * max(dot(L,N),0.0)
                  + light.specular * material.specular
                  * pow(max(dot(H,N),0.0),material.shininess*3.0);
fragColor = vec4((shadowColor.xyz + shadowFactor*(lightedColor.xyz)),1.0);
}
```

The fragment shader shown in Program 8.2 contains code for both the four-sample and 64-sample PCF soft shadows. First, a function lookup() is defined to make the sampling process more convenient. It makes a call to the GLSL function textureProj() that does a lookup in the shadow texture, but is offset by a specified amount (ox,oy). The offset is multiplied by 1/windowsize, which here we have simply hardcoded to .001, assuming a window size of 1000×1000 pixels.[2]

The four-sample dithered computation appears highlighted in main(), and it follows the algorithm described in the previous section. A scale factor swidth has been added that can be used to adjust the size of the "soft" region at the edge of the shadows.

The 64-sample code follows and is commented out. It can be used instead of the four-sample computation by un-commenting it and instead commenting out the four-sample code. The swidth scale factor in the 64-sample code is used as a step size in the nested loop that samples points at various distances from the pixel being rendered. For example, using the value of swidth shown (2.5), points would be sampled along each axis at distances of 1.25, 3.75, 6.25, and 8.25 in both directions—then scaled based on the window size (as described earlier) and used as texture coordinates into the shadow texture. With this many samples, dithering is generally not necessary to obtain good results.

Figure 8.25 shows our running torus/pyramid shadow-mapping example, incorporating PCF soft shadowing with the fragment shader from Program 8.2, for both four-sample and 64-sample approaches. The value chosen for swidth is scene dependent; for the torus/pyramid example it was set to 2.5, whereas for the dolphin example shown previously in Figure 8.21, swidth was set to 8.0.

---

[2] We have also multiplied the offset by the w component of the shadow coordinate, because OpenGL automatically divides the input coordinate by w during texture lookup. This operation, called *perspective divide*, is one which we have ignored up to this point. It must be accounted for here. For more information on *perspective divide*, see [LO12].

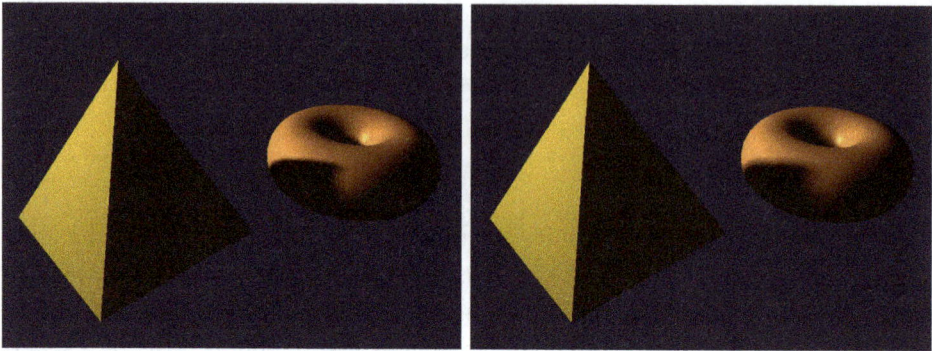

Figure 8.25
PCF Soft shadow rendering—4 samples per pixel, dithered (left), and 64 samples per pixel, not dithered (right).

SUPPLEMENTAL NOTES

In this chapter, we have only given the most basic of introductions to the world of shadows in 3D graphics. Even using the basic shadow mapping methods presented here will likely require further study if used in more complex scenes.

For example, when adding shadows to a scene in which some of the objects are textured, it is necessary to ensure that the fragment shader properly distinguishes between the shadow texture and other textures. A simple way of doing this is to bind them to different texture units, such as:

```
layout (binding = 0) uniform sampler2DShadow shTex;
layout (binding = 1) uniform sampler2D otherTexture;
```

Then, the C++/OpenGL application can refer to the two samplers by their binding values.

When a scene utilizes multiple lights, multiple shadow textures are necessary—one for each light source. In addition, a *pass one* will need to be performed for each one, with the results blended in pass two.

Although we have used perspective projection at each phase of shadow mapping, it is worth noting that *orthographic* projection is often preferred when the light source is distant and directional, rather than the positional light we utilized.

Generating realistic shadows is a rich and complex area of computer graphics, and many of the available techniques are outside the scope of this text. Readers interested in more detail are encouraged to investigate more specialized resources such as [ES12], [GP10], and [MI20].

The second fragment shader of Program 8.2 contains an example of a GLSL function, lookup(). As in the C language, functions must be defined before (or "above") where they are called, or else a forward declaration must be provided. In the example, a forward declaration isn't required because the function has been defined above the call to it.

Exercises

8.1 In Program 8.1, experiment with different settings for glPolygonOffset(), and observe the effects on shadow artifacts such as Peter Panning.

8.2 *(PROJECT)* Modify Program 8.1 so that the *light* can be positioned by moving the mouse, similar to Exercise 7.1. You will probably notice that some lighting positions exhibit shadow artifacts, while others look fine.

8.3 *(PROJECT)* Add animation to Program 8.1, such that either the objects or the light (or both) move around on their own—such as one revolving around the other. The shadow effects will be more pronounced if you add a ground plane to the scene, such as the one illustrated in Figure 8.14.

8.4 *(PROJECT)* Modify Program 8.2 to replace the hardcoded values 0.001 in the lookup() function with the more accurate values of 1.0/shadowbufferwidth and 1.0/shadowbufferheight. Observe to what degree this change makes a difference (or not) for various window sizes.

8.5 *(RESEARCH)* More sophisticated implementations of Percentage Closer Filtering (PCF) take into account the relative distance between the light and the shadow versus the light and the occluder. Doing this can make soft shadows more realistic, by allowing their penumbra to change in size as the light moves closer or further from the occluder (or as the occluder moves closer or further from the shadow). Study existing methods for incorporating this capability, and add it to Program 8.2.

References

[AS14] E. Angel and D. Shreiner, *Interactive Computer Graphics: A Top-Down Approach with WebGL*, 7th ed. (Pearson, 2014).

[BL88] J. Blinn, "Me and My (Fake) Shadow," *IEEE Computer Graphics and Applications* 8, no. 2 (1988).

[CR77] F. Crow, "Shadow Algorithms for Computer Graphics," *Proceedings of SIGGRAPH '77* 11, no. 2 (1977).

[ES12] E. Eisemann, M. Schwarz, U. Assarsson, and M. Wimmer, *Real-Time Shadows* (CRC Press, 2012).

[GP10] *GPU Pro* (series), ed. Wolfgang Engel (A. K. Peters, 2010–2016).

[KS16] J. Kessenich, G. Sellers, and D. Shreiner, *OpenGL Programming Guide: The Official Guide to Learning OpenGL, Version 4.5 with SPIR-V*, 9th ed. (Addison-Wesley, 2016).

[LO12] *Understanding OpenGL's Matrices*, Learn OpenGL ES (2012), accessed November 2023, http://www.learnopengles.com/tag/perspective-divide/

[LU16] F. Luna, *Introduction to 3D Game Programming with DirectX 12*, 2nd ed. (Mercury Learning, 2016).

[MI20] *Common Techniques to Improve Shadow Depth Maps* (Microsoft Corp., 2018), accessed November 2023, https://learn.microsoft.com/en-us/windows/win32/dxtecharts/common-techniques-to-improve-shadow-depth-maps

[PP23] Peter Pan, Wikipedia, accessed November 2023, https://en.wikipedia.org/wiki/Peter_Pan

[RS87] Rendering Antialiased Shadows with Depth Maps, *Computer Graphics*, Volume 21, Number 4, July 1987.

SKY AND BACKGROUNDS

■ ■ ■ ■ ■

The realism in a 3D scene can often be improved by generating a realistic effect at the distant horizon. As we look beyond our nearby buildings and trees, we are accustomed to seeing large distant objects such as clouds, mountains, or the sun (or at night, the moon and stars). However, adding such objects to our scene as individual models may come at an unacceptable performance cost. A *skybox* or *skydome* provides a relatively simple way of efficiently generating a convincing horizon.

9.1   SKYBOXES

The concept of a *skybox* is a remarkably clever and simple one:

1.   Instantiate a cube object.
2.   Texture the cube with the desired environment.
3.   Position the cube so it surrounds the camera.

We already know how to do all of these steps. There are a few additional details, however.

•   *How do we make the texture for our horizon?*

A cube has six faces, and we will need to texture all of them. One way is to use six image files and six texture units. Another common (and efficient) way is to use a single image that contains textures for all six faces, such as shown in Figure 9.1.

Figure 9.1
Six-faced skybox texture cube map.

An image that can texture all six faces of a cube with a single texture unit is an example of a *texture cube map*. The six portions of the cube map correspond to the top, bottom, front, back, and two sides of the cube. When "wrapped" around the cube, it acts as a horizon for a camera placed inside the cube, as shown in Figure 9.2.

Figure 9.2
Texture cube map wrapping around the camera.

Texturing the cube with a texture cube map requires specifying appropriate texture coordinates. Figure 9.3 shows the distribution of texture coordinates that are in turn assigned to each of the cube vertices.

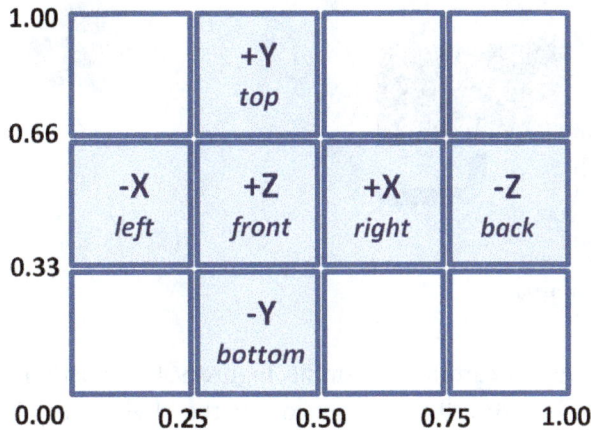

Figure 9.3
Cube map texture coordinates.

- *How do we make the skybox appear "distant"?*

Another important factor in building a skybox is ensuring that the texture appears as a distant horizon. At first, one might assume this would require making the skybox very large. However, it turns out that this isn't desirable because it would stretch and distort the texture. Instead, it is possible to make the skybox *appear* very large (and thus distant), by using the following two-part trick:

- ○ Disable depth testing and render the skybox first (re-enabling depth testing when rendering the other objects in the scene).
- ○ Move the skybox with the camera (if the camera moves).

By drawing the skybox first with depth testing disabled, the depth buffer will still be filled completely with 1.0s (i.e., maximally far away). Thus, all other objects in the scene will be fully rendered; that is, none of the other objects will be blocked by the skybox. This causes the walls of the skybox to appear farther away than every other object, *regardless of the actual size of the skybox*. The actual skybox cube itself can be quite small, as long as it is moved along with the camera whenever the camera moves. Figure 9.4 shows viewing a simple scene (actually just a brick-textured torus) from inside a skybox.

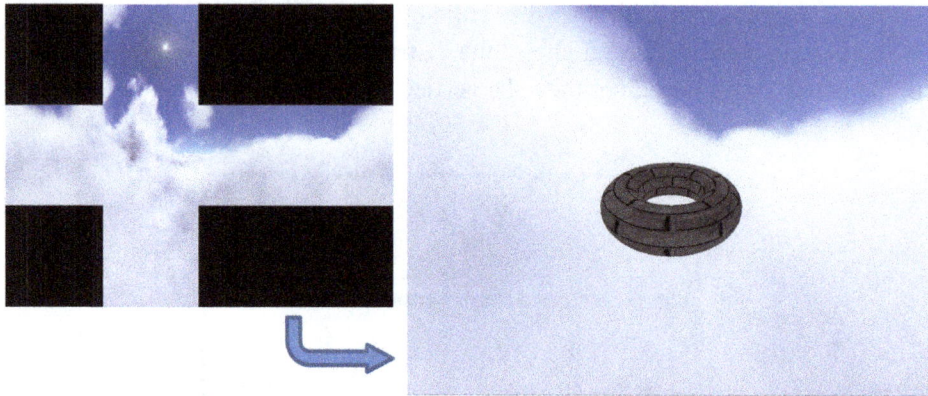

Figure 9.4
Viewing a scene from inside a skybox.

It is instructive to carefully examine Figure 9.4 in relation to the previous Figures 9.2 and 9.3. Note that the portion of the skybox that is visible in the scene is the rightmost section of the cube map. This is because the camera has been placed in the default orientation, facing in the negative Z direction, and is therefore looking at the *back* of the skybox cube (and so labeled in Figure 9.3). Also note that this back portion of the cube map appears horizontally reversed when rendered in the scene, because the cube map is being viewed from the inside of the cube. For example, see how the "back" (-Z) portion of the cube map has been folded around the camera and thus appears flipped sideways, as shown in Figure 9.2.

• *How do we construct the texture cube map?*

Building a texture cube map image, from artwork or photos, requires care to avoid "seams" at the cube face junctions and to create proper perspective so that the skybox will appear realistic and undistorted. Many tools exist for assisting in this regard: Terragen, Autodesk 3ds Max, Blender, and Adobe Photoshop have tools for building or working with cube maps. There are also many websites offering a variety of off-the-shelf cube maps, some for a price, some for free.

9.2 SKYDOMES

Another way of building a horizon effect is to use a *skydome*. The basic idea is the same as for a skybox, except that instead of using a textured cube, we use a textured *sphere* (or half a sphere). As was done for the skybox, we render the skydome first (with depth testing disabled), and keep the camera positioned at

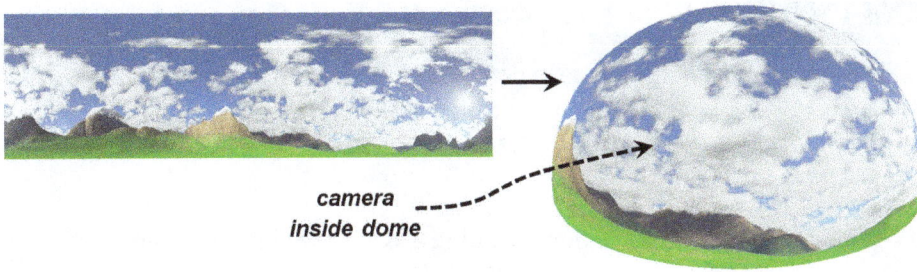

Figure 9.5
Skydome with camera placed inside.

the center of the skydome. (The skydome texture in Figure 9.5 was made using Terragen [TE22].)

Skydomes have some advantages over skyboxes. For example, they are less susceptible to distortion and seams (although spherical distortion at the poles must be accounted for in the texture image). One disadvantage of a skydome is that a sphere or dome is a more complex model than a cube, with many more vertices and a potentially varying number of vertices depending on the desired precision.

When using a skydome to represent an outdoor scene, it is usually combined with a ground plane or some sort of terrain. When using a skydome to represent a scene in space, such as a starfield, it is often more practical to use a sphere such as is shown in Figure 9.6 (a dashed line has been added for clarity in visualizing the sphere).

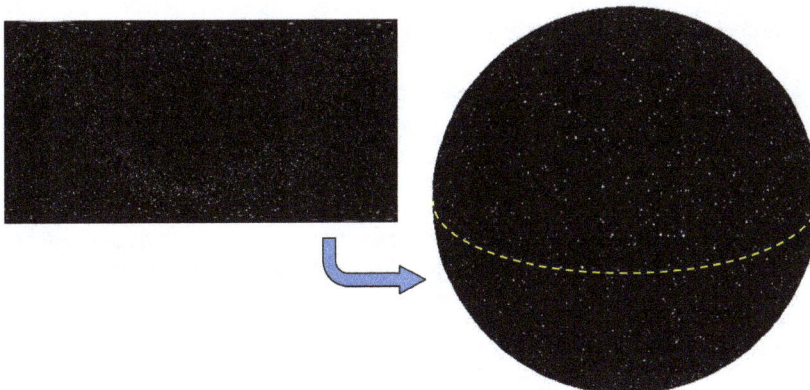

Figure 9.6
Skydome of stars using a sphere (starfield from [BO11]).

9.3 ■ IMPLEMENTING A SKYBOX

Despite the advantages of a skydome, skyboxes are still more common. They also are better supported in OpenGL, which is advantageous when doing *environment mapping* (covered later in this chapter). For these reasons, we will focus on skybox implementation.

There are two methods of implementing a skybox: building a simple one from scratch, and using the cube map facilities in OpenGL. Each has its advantages, so we will cover them both.

9.3.1 ■ Building a Skybox from Scratch

We have already covered almost everything needed to build a simple skybox. A cube model was presented in Chapter 4; we can assign the texture coordinates as shown earlier in this chapter in Figure 9.3. We saw how to read in textures using the SOIL2 library and how to position objects in 3D space. We will see how to easily enable and disable depth testing (it's a single line of code).

Program 9.1 shows the code organization for our simple skybox, with a scene consisting of just a single textured torus. Texture coordinate assignments and calls to enable/disable depth testing are highlighted.

Program 9.1 Simple Skybox

C++/OpenGL application

```
// all variable declarations, constructor, and init() same as before
...
void display(GLFWwindow* window, double currentTime) {
    // clear color and depth buffers, and create projection and camera view matrix as before
    ...
    glUseProgram(renderingProgram);

    // Prepare to draw the skybox first. The M matrix places the skybox at the camera location
    mMat = glm::translate(glm::mat4(1.0f), glm::vec3(cameraX, cameraY, cameraZ));

    // build the MODEL-VIEW matrix
    mvMat = vMat * mMat;

    // put MV and P matrices into uniforms, as before
    ...
```

```
    // set up buffer containing vertices
    glBindBuffer(GL_ARRAY_BUFFER, vbo[0]);
    glVertexAttribPointer(0,3, GL_FLOAT, GL_FALSE, 0, 0);
    glEnableVertexAttribArray(0);

    // set up buffer containing texture coordinates
    glBindBuffer(GL_ARRAY_BUFFER, vbo[1]);
    glVertexAttribPointer(1,2, GL_FLOAT, GL_FALSE, 0, 0);
    glEnableVertexAttribArray(1);

    // activate the skybox texture
    glActiveTexture(GL_TEXTURE0);
    glBindTexture(GL_TEXTURE_2D, skyboxTexture);

    glEnable(GL_CULL_FACE);
    glFrontFace(GL_CCW);          // cube has CW winding order, but we are viewing its interior

    glDisable(GL_DEPTH_TEST);
    glDrawArrays(GL_TRIANGLES, 0, 36);       // draw the skybox without depth testing
    glEnable(GL_DEPTH_TEST);

    // now draw desired scene objects as before
    . . .
    glDrawElements( . . . );    // as before for scene objects
}
void setupVertices(void) {
    // cube_vertices defined same as before
    // cube texture coordinates for the skybox as they appear in Figure 9.3
    float cubeTextureCoord[72] = {
        1.00f, 0.66f, 1.00f, 0.33f, 0.75f, 0.33f,     // back face lower right
        0.75f, 0.33f, 0.75f, 0.66f, 1.00f, 0.66f,     // back face upper left
        0.75f, 0.33f, 0.50f, 0.33f, 0.75f, 0.66f,     // right face lower right
        0.50f, 0.33f, 0.50f, 0.66f, 0.75f, 0.66f,     // right face upper left
        0.50f, 0.33f, 0.25f, 0.33f, 0.50f, 0.66f,     // front face lower right
        0.25f, 0.33f, 0.25f, 0.66f, 0.50f, 0.66f,     // front face upper left
        0.25f, 0.33f, 0.00f, 0.33f, 0.25f, 0.66f,     // left face lower right
        0.00f, 0.33f, 0.00f, 0.66f, 0.25f, 0.66f,     // left face upper left
        0.25f, 0.33f, 0.50f, 0.33f, 0.50f, 0.00f,     // bottom face upper right
        0.50f, 0.00f, 0.25f, 0.00f, 0.25f, 0.33f,     // bottom face lower left
        0.25f, 1.00f, 0.50f, 1.00f, 0.50f, 0.66f,     // top face upper right
        0.50f, 0.66f, 0.25f, 0.66f, 0.25f, 1.00f      // top face lower left
    };
    // set up buffers for cube and scene objects as usual
}
// modules for loading shaders, textures, main(), etc. as before
```

Standard texturing shaders are now used for all objects in the scene, including the cube map:

Vertex Shader

```
#version 430
layout (location = 0) in vec3 position;
layout (location = 1) in vec2 tex_coord;
out vec2 tc;
uniform mat4 mv_matrix;
uniform mat4 p_matrix;
layout (binding = 0) uniform sampler2D s;

void main(void)
{   tc = tex_coord;
    gl_Position = p_matrix * mv_matrix * vec4(position,1.0);
}
```

Fragment Shader

```
#version 430
in vec2 tc;
out vec4 fragColor;
uniform mat4 mv_matrix;
uniform mat4 p_matrix;
layout (binding = 0) uniform sampler2D s;

void main(void)
{   fragColor = texture(s,tc);
}
```

The output of Program 9.1 is shown in Figure 9.7, for each of two different cube map textures.

As mentioned earlier, skyboxes are susceptible to image distortion and *seams*. Seams are lines that are sometimes visible where two texture images meet, such as along the edges of the cube. Figure 9.8 shows an example of a seam in the upper part of the image that is an artifact of running Program 9.1. Avoiding seams requires careful construction of the cube map image and assignment of precise texture coordinates. There exist tools for reducing seams along image edges (such as [Gl23]); this topic is outside the scope of this book.

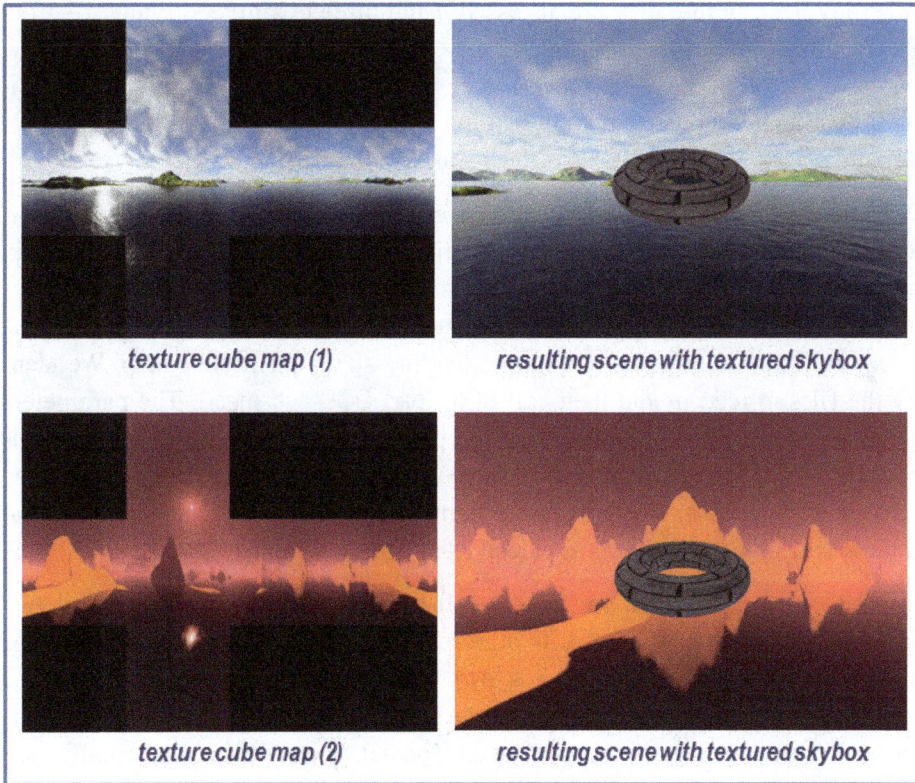

Figure 9.7
Simple skybox results.

9.3.2 Using OpenGL Cube Maps

Another way to build a sky-box is to use an OpenGL *texture cube map*. OpenGL cube maps are a bit more complex than the simple approach we saw in the previous section. There are advantages, how-ever, to using OpenGL cube maps, such as seam reduction and support for environment mapping.

OpenGL texture cube maps are similar to *3D textures* that we

Figure 9.8
Skybox "seam" artifact.

will study later, in that they are accessed using three texture coordinates—often labeled *(s,t,r)*—rather than two as we have been doing thus far. Another unique characteristic of OpenGL texture cube maps is that the images in them are oriented with texture coordinate (0,0,0) at the upper left (rather than the usual lower left) of the texture image; this is often a source of confusion.

Whereas the method shown in Program 9.1 reads in a single image for texturing the cube map, the loadCubeMap() function shown in Program 9.2 reads in six separate cube face image files. As we learned in Chapter 5, there are many ways to read in texture images; we chose to use the SOIL2 library. Here too, SOIL2 is very convenient for instantiating and loading an OpenGL cube map. We identify the files to read in and then call SOIL_load_OGL_cubemap(). The parameters include the six image files and additional parameters that are similar to the ones for SOIL_load_OGL_texture() that we saw in Chapter 5. In the case of OpenGL cube maps, it isn't necessary to flip the textures vertically, since OpenGL does that automatically. Note that we have placed loadCubeMap() in our "Utils.cpp" file.

The init() function now includes a call to enable GL_TEXTURE_CUBE_MAP_ SEAMLESS, which tells OpenGL to attempt to blend adjoining edges of the cube to reduce or eliminate seams. In display(), the cube's vertices are sent down the pipeline as before, but this time it is unnecessary to send the cube's texture coordinates. As we will see, this is because an OpenGL texture cube map usually uses the cube's vertex positions as its texture coordinates. After disabling depth testing, the cube is drawn. Depth testing is then re-enabled for the rest of the scene.

The completed OpenGL texture cube map is referenced by an int identifier. As was the case for shadow-mapping, artifacts along a border can be reduced by setting the texture wrap mode to "clamp to edge." In this case it can help further reduce seams. Note that this is set for all three texture coordinates: s, t, and r.

The texture is accessed in the fragment shader with a special type of sampler called a samplerCube. In a texture cube map, the value returned from the sampler is the texel "seen" from the origin as viewed along the direction vector *(s,t,r)*. As a result, we can usually simply use the incoming interpolated vertex positions as the texture coordinates. In the vertex shader, we assign the cube vertex positions into the outgoing texture coordinate attribute so that they will be interpolated when they reach the fragment shader. Note also in the vertex shader that we convert the incoming view matrix to 3x3, and then back to 4x4. This "trick" effectively removes the translation component while retaining the rotation (recall that translation values are found in the fourth column of a transformation matrix). This fixes the cube map at the camera location, while still allowing the synthetic camera to "look around." The output of Program 9.2 is the same as for Program 9.1.

Program 9.2 OpenGL Cube Map Skybox

C++/OpenGL application

```
. . .
int brickTexture, skyboxTexture;
int renderingProgram, renderingProgramCubeMap;
. . .
void init(GLFWwindow* window) {
    renderingProgram = Utils::createShaderProgram("vertShader.glsl", "fragShader.glsl");
    renderingProgramCubeMap = Utils::createShaderProgram("vertCShader.glsl", "fragCShader.glsl");

    setupVertices();

    brickTexture = Utils::loadTexture("brick1.jpg");          // for the torus in the scene
    skyboxTexture = Utils::loadCubeMap("cubeMap");            // folder containing the skybox textures
    glEnable(GL_TEXTURE_CUBE_MAP_SEAMLESS);
}
void display(GLFWwindow* window, double currentTime) {
    // clear color and depth buffers, projection and camera view matrix as before.
    . . .
    // draw cube map first – note that it now requires a different rendering program
    glUseProgram(renderingProgramCubeMap);

    // put the P and V matrices into their corresponding uniforms.
    . . .
    // set up vertices buffer for cube (buffer for texture coordinates not necessary)
    glBindBuffer(GL_ARRAY_BUFFER, vbo[0]);
    glVertexAttribPointer(0, 3, GL_FLOAT, GL_FALSE, 0, 0);
    glEnableVertexAttribArray(0);

    // make the cube map the active texture
    glActiveTexture(GL_TEXTURE0);
    glBindTexture(GL_TEXTURE_CUBE_MAP, skyboxTexture);

    // disable depth testing, and then draw the cube map
    glEnable(GL_CULL_FACE);
    glFrontFace(GL_CCW);
    glDisable(GL_DEPTH_TEST);
    glDrawArrays(GL_TRIANGLES, 0, 36);
    glEnable(GL_DEPTH_TEST);
```

```
    // draw remainder of the scene
    . . .
}

GLuint Utils::loadCubeMap(const char *mapDir) {
    GLuint textureRef;

    // assumes that the six texture image files are named xp, xn, yp, yn, zp, zn and are JPG
    string xp = mapDir; xp = xp + "/xp.jpg";
    string xn = mapDir; xn = xn + "/xn.jpg";
    string yp = mapDir; yp = yp + "/yp.jpg";
    string yn = mapDir; yn = yn + "/yn.jpg";
    string zp = mapDir; zp = zp + "/zp.jpg";
    string zn = mapDir; zn = zn + "/zn.jpg";

    textureRef = SOIL_load_OGL_cubemap(xp.c_str(), xn.c_str(), yp.c_str(), yn.c_str(),
        zp.c_str(), zn.c_str(), SOIL_LOAD_AUTO, SOIL_CREATE_NEW_ID, SOIL_FLAG_MIPMAPS);

    if (textureRef == 0) cout << "didnt find cube map image file" << endl;

    glBindTexture(GL_TEXTURE_CUBE_MAP, textureRef);

    // reduce seams
    glTexParameteri(GL_TEXTURE_CUBE_MAP, GL_TEXTURE_WRAP_S, GL_CLAMP_TO_EDGE);
    glTexParameteri(GL_TEXTURE_CUBE_MAP, GL_TEXTURE_WRAP_T, GL_CLAMP_TO_EDGE);
    glTexParameteri(GL_TEXTURE_CUBE_MAP, GL_TEXTURE_WRAP_R, GL_CLAMP_TO_EDGE);

    return textureRef;
}
```

Vertex shader

```
#version 430
layout (location = 0) in vec3 position;
out vec3 tc;

uniform mat4 v_matrix;
uniform mat4 p_matrix;
layout (binding = 0) uniform samplerCube samp;

void main(void)
{
    tc = position;                          // texture coordinates are simply the vertex coordinates
    mat4 vrot_matrix = mat4(mat3(v_matrix));   // removes translation from view matrix
    gl_Position = p_matrix * vrot_matrix * vec4(position, 1.0);
}
```

Fragment shader

```
#version 430
in vec3 tc;
out vec4 fragColor;

uniform mat4 v_matrix;
uniform mat4 p_matrix;
layout (binding = 0) uniform samplerCube samp;

void main(void)
{   fragColor = texture(samp,tc);
}
```

9.4 ENVIRONMENT MAPPING

When we looked at lighting and materials, we considered the "shininess" of objects. However, we never modeled *very* shiny objects, such as a mirror or something made out of chrome. Such objects don't just have small specular highlights; they actually reflect their surroundings. When we look at them, we see things in the room, or sometimes even our own reflection. The ADS lighting model doesn't provide a way of simulating this effect.

Texture cube maps, however, offer a relatively simple way to simulate reflective surfaces—at least partially. The trick is to *use the cube map to texture the reflective object itself.*[1] Doing this so that it appears realistic requires finding texture coordinates that correspond to which part of the surrounding environment we should see reflected in the object from our vantage point.

Figure 9.9 illustrates the strategy of using a combination of the view vector and the normal vector to calculate a *reflection vector* which is then used to look up a texel from the cube map. The reflection vector can thus be used to access the texture cube map directly. When the cube map performs this function, it is referred to as an *environment map.*

We computed reflection vectors earlier when we studied Blinn-Phong lighting. The concept here is similar, except that now we are using the reflection vector to look up a value from a texture map. This technique is called *environment mapping* or *reflection mapping.* If the cube map is implemented using the second method

---

[1] This same trick is also possible in those cases where a skydome is being used instead of a skybox, by texturing the reflective object with the skydome texture image.

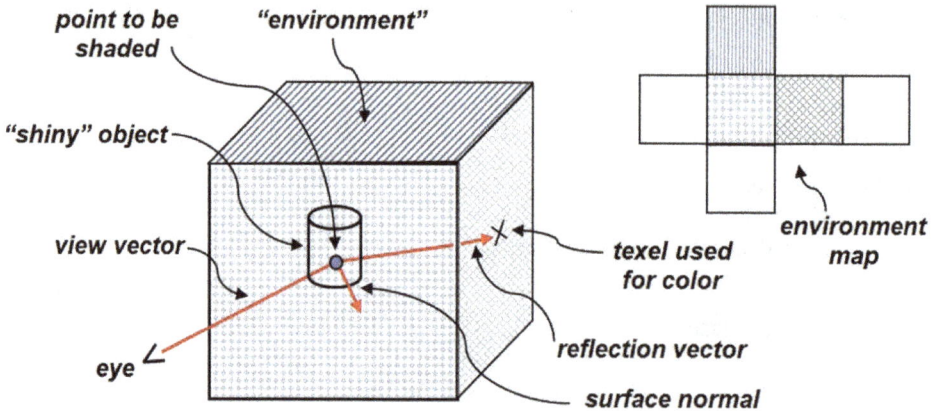

Figure 9.9
Environment mapping overview.

we described (in Section 9.3.2; that is, as an OpenGL GL_TEXTURE_CUBE_MAP), then OpenGL can perform the environment mapping lookup in the same manner as was done for texturing the cube map itself. We use the view vector and the surface normal to compute a reflection of the view vector off the object's surface. The reflection vector can then be used to sample the texture cube map image directly. The lookup is facilitated by the OpenGL samplerCube; recall from the previous section that the samplerCube is indexed by a view direction vector. The reflection vector is thus well suited for looking up the desired texel.

The implementation requires a relatively small amount of additional code. Program 9.3 shows the changes that would be made to the display() and init() functions and the relevant shaders for rendering a "reflective" torus using environment mapping. The changes are highlighted. It is worth noting that if Blinn-Phong lighting is present, many of these additions would likely already be present. The only truly new section of code is in the fragment shader (in the main() method).

In fact, it might at first appear as if the highlighted code in Program 9.3 (i.e., the yellow sections) isn't really new at all. Indeed, we have seen nearly identical code before, when we studied lighting. However, in this case, the normal and reflection vectors are used for an entirely different purpose. Previously they were used to implement the ADS lighting model. Here they are instead used to compute texture coordinates for environment mapping. We highlighted these lines of code so that the reader can more easily track the use of normals and reflection computations for this new purpose.

The result, showing an environment-mapped "chrome" torus, is shown in Figure 9.10.

Figure 9.10
Example of environment mapping to create a reflective torus.

Program 9.3 Environment Mapping

```
void display(GLFWwindow* window, double currentTime) {
    // the code for drawing the cube map is unchanged.

    . . .

    // the changes are all in drawing the torus:

    glUseProgram(renderingProgram);

    // uniform locations for matrix transforms, including the transform for normals
    mvLloc = glGetUniformLocation(renderingProgram, "mv_matrix");
    pLoc = glGetUniformLocation(renderingProgram, "p_matrix");
    nLoc = glGetUniformLocation(renderingProgram, "norm_matrix");

    // build the MODEL matrix, as before
    mMat = glm::translate(glm::mat4(1.0f), glm::vec3(torLocX, torLocY, torLocZ));

    // build the MODEL-VIEW matrix, as before
    mvMat = vMat * mMat;
    invTrMat = glm::transpose(glm::inverse(mvMat));
```

```
// the normals transform is now included in the uniforms:
glUniformMatrix4fv(mvLoc, 1, GL_FALSE, glm::value_ptr(mvMat));
glUniformMatrix4fv(pLoc, 1, GL_FALSE, glm::value_ptr(pMat));
glUniformMatrix4fv(nLoc, 1, GL_FALSE , glm::value_ptr(invTrMat));

// activate the torus vertices buffer, as before
glBindBuffer(GL_ARRAY_BUFFER, vbo[1]);
glVertexAttribPointer(0, 3, GL_FLOAT, GL_FALSE, 0, 0);
glEnableVertexAttribArray(0);

// we need to activate the torus normals buffer:
glBindBuffer(GL_ARRAY_BUFFER, vbo[2]);
glVertexAttribPointer(1, 3, GL_FLOAT, GL_FALSE, 0, 0);
glEnableVertexAttribArray(1);

// the torus texture is now the cube map
glActiveTexture(GL_TEXTURE0);
glBindTexture(GL_TEXTURE_CUBE_MAP, skyboxTexture);

// drawing the torus is otherwise unchanged
glClear(GL_DEPTH_BUFFER_BIT);
glEnable(GL_CULL_FACE);
glFrontFace(GL_CCW);
glDepthFunc(GL_LEQUAL);

glBindBuffer(GL_ELEMENT_ARRAY_BUFFER, vbo[3]);
glDrawElements(GL_TRIANGLES, numTorusIndices, GL_UNSIGNED_INT, 0);
}
```

Vertex shader

```
#version 430
layout (location = 0) in vec3 position;
layout (location = 1) in vec3 normal;
out vec3 varyingNormal;
out vec3 varyingVertPos;
uniform mat4 mv_matrix;
uniform mat4 p_matrix;
uniform mat4 norm_matrix;
layout (binding = 0) uniform samplerCube tex_map;

void main(void)
{   varyingVertPos = (mv_matrix * vec4(position,1.0)).xyz;
    varyingNormal = (norm_matrix * vec4(normal,1.0)).xyz;
    gl_Position = p_matrix * mv_matrix * vec4(position,1.0);
}
```

Fragment shader

```
#version 430
in vec3 varyingNormal;
in vec3 varyingVertPos;
out vec4 fragColor;
uniform mat4 mv_matrix;
uniform mat4 p_matrix;
uniform mat4 norm_matrix;
layout (binding = 0) uniform samplerCube tex_map;

void main(void)
{   vec3 r = -reflect(normalize(-varyingVertPos), normalize(varyingNormal));
    fragColor = texture(tex_map, r);
}
```

Although two sets of shaders are required for this scene—one set for the cube map and another set for the torus—only the shaders used to draw the torus are shown in Program 9.3. This is because the shaders used for rendering the cube map are unchanged from Program 9.2. The changes made to Program 9.2, resulting in Program 9.3, are summarized as follows:

*in **init()**:*

- A buffer of normals for the torus is created (actually done in setupVertices(), called by init()).
- The buffer of texture coordinates for the torus is no longer needed.

*in **display()**:*

- The matrix for transforming normals (dubbed "norm_matrix" in Chapter 7) is created and linked to the associated uniform variable.
- The torus normal buffer is activated.
- The texture cube map is activated as the texture for the torus (rather than the "brick" texture).

*in the **vertex shader**:*

- The normal vectors and norm_matrix are added.
- The transformed vertex and normal vector are output in preparation for computing the reflection vector, similar to what was done for lighting and shadows.

in the **fragment shader***:*

- The reflection vector is computed in a similar way to what was done for lighting.
- The output color is retrieved from the texture (now the cube map), with the lookup texture coordinate now being the reflection vector.

The resulting rendering shown in Figure 9.10 is an excellent example of how a simple trick can achieve a powerful illusion. By simply painting the background on an object, we have made the object look "metallic," when no such ADS material modeling has been done at all. It has also given the appearance that light is reflecting off of the object, even though no ADS lighting whatsoever has been incorporated into the scene. In this example, there even seems to be a specular highlight on the lower left of the torus, because the cube map includes the sun's reflection off of the water.

SUPPLEMENTAL NOTES

As was the case in Chapter 5 when we first studied textures, while using SOIL2 makes building and texturing a cube map easy, it can have the unintended conseqence of shielding a user from some OpenGL details that are useful to learn. Of course, it is possible to instantiate and load an OpenGL cube map in the absence of SOIL2. It is still advisable to use an image handling library, such as stb_image.h [SB23]. The basic steps are detailed in [dV14] and are summarized as follows:

1. Copy the stb_image.h header file into your project directory.
2. Use glGenTextures() to create a texture for the cube map and its integer reference.
3. Call glBindTexture(), specifying the texture's ID and GL_TEXTURE_CUBE_ MAP.
4. Read the six image files using stbi_load().
5. Use glTexImage2D() to assign the images to cube faces.

The stb_image.h header file is already included with SOIL2, or it can be installed separately. For more details, see [dV14] or [GE16].

A major limitation of environment mapping, as presented in this chapter, is that it is only capable of constructing objects that reflect the cube map. Other objects rendered in the scene are not reflected in the reflection-mapped object. Depending on the nature of the scene, this might or might not be acceptable. If other objects are present that must be reflected in a mirror or chrome object, other methods must be used. A common approach utilizes the stencil buffer (mentioned earlier in Chapter 8) and is described in various web tutorials ([OV12], [NE14], and [GR97], for example), but it is outside the scope of this text.

We didn't include an implementation of skydomes, although they are in some ways arguably simpler than skyboxes and can be less susceptible to distortion. Even environment mapping is simpler—at least the math—but the OpenGL support for cube maps often makes skyboxes more practical.

Of the topics covered in the later sections of this textbook, skyboxes and skydomes are arguably among the simplest conceptually. However, getting them to look convincing can consume a lot of time. We have dealt only briefly with some of the issues that can arise (such as seams), but depending on the texture image files used, other issues can occur, requiring additional repair. This is especially true when the scene is animated, or when the camera can be moved interactively.

We also glossed over the generation of usable and convincing texture cube map images. There are excellent tools for doing this, one of the most popular being Terragen [TE22]. All of the cube maps in this chapter were made by the authors (except for the star field in Figure 9.6) using Terragen.

Exercises

9.1 *(PROJECT)* In Program 9.2, add the ability to move the camera around with the mouse or the keyboard. To do this, you will need to utilize the code you developed earlier in Exercise 4.2 for constructing a view matrix. You'll also need to assign mouse or keyboard actions to functions that move the camera forward and backward, and functions that rotate the camera on one or more of its axes (refer to Appendix D for instructions on doing this). After doing this, you should be able to "fly around" in your scene, noting that the skybox always appears to remain at the distant horizon.

9.2 Draw labels on the six cube map image files to confirm that the correct orientation is being achieved. For example, you could draw axis labels on the images, such as these:

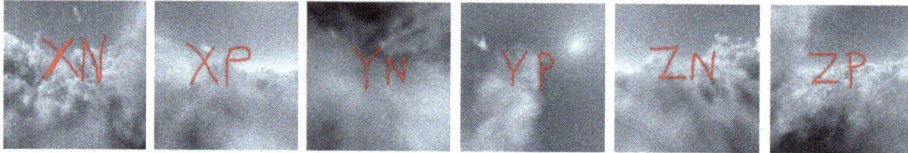

Also use your "labeled" cube map to verify that the reflections in the environment-mapped torus are being rendered correctly.

9.3 *(PROJECT)* Modify Program 9.3 so that the object in the scene blends environment-mapping with a texture. Use a weighted sum in the fragment shader, as described in Chapter 7.

9.4 *(RESEARCH & PROJECT)* Learn the basics of how to use Terragen [TE22] to create a simple cube map. This generally entails making a "world" with the desired terrain and atmospheric patterns (in Terragen), and then positioning Terragen's synthetic camera to save six images representing the views front, back, right, left, top, and bottom. Use your images in Programs 9.2 and 9.3 to see their appearance as cube maps and with environment mapping. The free version of Terragen is quite sufficient for this exercise.

References

[BO11] P. Bourke, "Representing Star Fields," October 2011, accessed November 2023, http://paulbourke.net/miscellaneous/astronomy/

[dV14] J. de Vries, "Learn OpenGL – Cubemaps," 2014, accessed November 2023, https://learnopengl.com/Advanced-OpenGL/Cubemaps

[GE16] A. Gerdelan, "Cube Maps: Sky Boxes and Environment Mapping," 2016, accessed November 2023, http://antongerdelan.net/opengl/cubemaps.html

[GI23] GNU Image Manipulation Program, accessed November 2023, https://www.gimp.org

[GR97] OpenGL Resources, "Planar Reflections and Refractions Using the Stencil Buffer," accessed November 2023, https://www.opengl.org/archives/resources/code/samples/advanced/advanced97/notes/node90.html

[NE14] NeHeProductions, "Clipping and Reflections Using the Stencil Buffer," 2014, accessed November 2023, http://nehe.gamedev.net/tutorial/clipping__reflections_using_the_stencil_buffer/17004/

[OV12] A. Overvoorde, "Depth and Stencils," 2012, accessed November 2023, https://open.gl/depthstencils

[SB23] S. Barrett, stbi_image.h, Accessed November 2023, https://github.com/nothings/stb

[TE22] Terragen, Planetside Software, LLC, accessed November 2023, http://planetside.co.uk/

ENHANCING SURFACE DETAIL

Suppose we want to model an object with an irregular surface—like the bumpy surface of an orange, the wrinkled surface of a raisin, or the cratered surface of the moon. How would we do it? So far, we have learned two potential methods: (a) we could model the entire irregular surface, which would often be impractical (a highly cratered surface would require a huge number of vertices); or (b) we could apply a texture-map image of the irregular surface to a smooth version of the object. The second option is often effective. However, if the scene includes lights, and the lights (or camera angle) move, it becomes quickly obvious that the object is statically textured (and smooth), because the light and dark areas on the texture wouldn't change as they would if the object was actually bumpy.

In this chapter, we are going to explore several related methods for using lighting effects to make objects *appear* to have realistic surface texture, even if the underlying object model is smooth. We will start by examining *bump mapping* and *normal mapping*, which can add considerable realism to the objects in our scenes when it would be too computationally expensive to include tiny surface details in the object models. We will also look at ways of actually perturbing the vertices in a smooth surface through *height mapping*, which is useful for generating *terrain* (and other uses).

10.1 BUMP MAPPING

In Chapter 7, we saw how surface normals are critical to creating convincing lighting effects. Light intensity at a pixel is determined largely by the reflection angle,

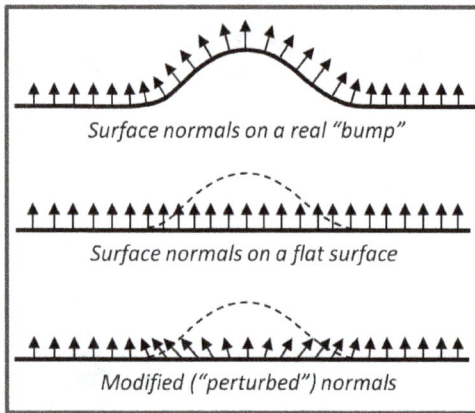

Figure 10.1
Perturbed normal vectors for bump mapping.

Figure 10.2
Procedural bump mapping example.

taking into account the light source location, camera location, and the normal vector at the pixel. Thus, we can avoid generating detailed vertices corresponding to a bumpy or wrinkled surface if we can find a way of generating the corresponding normals.

Figure 10.1 illustrates the concept of modified normals corresponding to a single "bump."

Thus, if we want to make an object look as though it has bumps (or wrinkles, craters, etc.), one way is to compute the *normals* that would exist on such a surface. Then when the scene is lit, the lighting would produce the desired illusion. This was first proposed by Blinn in 1978 [BL78], and it became practical with the advent of the capability of performing per-pixel lighting computations in a fragment shader.

An example is illustrated in the vertex and fragment shaders shown in Program 10.1, which produces a torus with a "golf-ball" surface as shown in Figure 10.2. The code is almost identical to what we saw previously in Program 7.2. The only significant change is in the fragment shader—the incoming interpolated normal vectors (named "varyingNormal" in the original program) are altered with bumps calculated using a sine wave function in the X, Y, and Z axes applied to the original (untransformed) vertices of the torus model. Note that the vertex shader therefore now needs to pass these untransformed vertices down the pipeline.

Altering the normals in this manner, with a mathematical function computed at runtime, is called *procedural bump mapping*.

Program 10.1 Procedural Bump Mapping

Vertex Shader

```
#version 430
//  same as Phong shading, but add this output vertex attribute:
out vec3 originalVertex;

. . .
void main(void)
{   // include this pass-through of original vertex for interpolation:
    originalVertex = vertPos;
    . . .
}
```

Fragment Shader

```
#version 430
//  same as Phong shading, but add this input vertex attribute:
in vec3 originalVertex;

. . .
void main(void)
{  . . .
    // add the following to perturb the incoming normal vector:
    float a = 0.25;    // a controls height of bumps
    float b = 100.0;   // b controls width of bumps
    float x = originalVertex.x;
    float y = originalVertex.y;
    float z = originalVertex.z;
    N.x = varyingNormal.x + a*sin(b*x);    // perturb incoming normal using sine function
    N.y = varyingNormal.y + a*sin(b*y);
    N.z = varyingNormal.z + a*sin(b*z);
    N = normalize(N);
    // lighting computations and output fragColor (unchanged) now utilize the perturbed normal N
    . . .
}
```

10.2 NORMAL MAPPING

An alternative to bump mapping is to replace the normals using a lookup table. This allows us to construct bumps for which there is no mathematical function, such as the bumps corresponding to the craters on the moon. A common way of doing this is called *normal mapping*.

To understand how this works, we start by noting that a vector can be stored to reasonable precision in three bytes, one for each of the X, Y, and Z components. This makes it possible to store normals in a color image file, with the R, G, and B components corresponding to X, Y, and Z. RGB values in an image are stored in bytes and are usually interpreted as values in the range [0..1], whereas vectors can have positive or negative component values. If we restrict normal vector components to the range [-1..+1], a simple conversion to enable storing a normal vector N as a pixel in an image file is:

$$R = (N_X + 1) / 2$$
$$G = (N_Y + 1) / 2$$
$$B = (N_Z + 1) / 2$$

Normal mapping utilizes an image file (called a *normal map*) that contains normals corresponding to a desired surface appearance in the presence of lighting. In a normal map, the vectors are represented relative to an arbitrary plane X-Y, with their X and Y components representing deviations from "vertical" and their Z component set to 1. A vector strictly perpendicular to the X-Y plane (i.e., with no deviation) would be represented (0,0,1), whereas non-perpendicular vectors would have non-zero X and/or Y components. We use the above formulae to convert to RGB space; for example, (0,0,1) would be stored as (.5,.5,1), since actual offsets range [-1..+1], but RGB values range [0..1].

We can make use of such a normal map through yet another clever application of texture units: instead of storing colors in the texture unit, we store the desired normal vectors. We can then use a sampler to look up the value in the normal map for a given fragment, and then rather than applying the returned value to the output pixel color (as we did in texture mapping), we instead use it as the normal vector.

Figure 10.3
Normal mapping image file example [LU16].

One example of such a normal map image file is shown in Figure 10.3. It was generated by applying the GIMP normal mapping plugin [GN12] to a texture from Luna [LU16]. Normal-mapping image files are not intended for viewing; we show this one to point out that such images end up being largely blue. This is because every entry in the image file has a B value of 1 (maximum blue), making the image appear "bluish" if viewed.

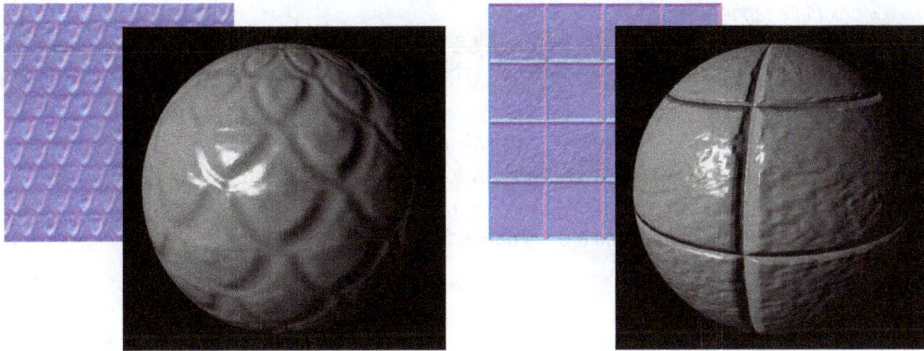

Figure 10.4
Normal mapping examples.

Figure 10.4 shows two different normal map image files (both are built out of textures from Luna [LU16]) and the result of applying them to a sphere in the presence of Blinn-Phong lighting.

Normal vectors retrieved from a normal map cannot be utilized directly, because they are defined relative to an arbitrary X-Y plane as described previously, without taking into account their position on the object and their orientation in world space. Our strategy for addressing this will be to build a transformation matrix for converting the normals into world space, as follows.

At each vertex on an object, we consider a plane that is tangent to the object. The object normal at that vertex is perpendicular to this plane. We define two mutually perpendicular vectors in that plane, also perpendicular to the normal, called the *tangent* and *bitangent* (sometimes called the *binormal*). Constructing our desired transformation matrix requires that our models include a tangent vector for each vertex (the bitangent can be built by computing the cross product of the tangent and the normal). If the model does not already have tangent vectors defined, they could be computed. In the case of a sphere they can be computed exactly, as shown in the following modifications to Program 6.1:

. . .

```
for (int i=0; i<=prec; i++) {
    for (int j=0; j<=prec; j++) {
        float y = (float)cos(toRadians(180.0f - i*180.0f / prec));
        float x = -(float)cos(toRadians(j*360.0f / prec)) * (float)abs(cos(asin(y)));
        float z = (float)sin(toRadians(j*360.0f / prec)) * (float)abs(cos(asin(y)));
        vertices[i*(prec+1)+j] = glm::vec3(x, y, z);
```

```
// calculate tangent vector
if (((x==0) && (y==1) && (z==0)) || ((x==0) && (y==-1) && (z==0)))   // if north or south pole,
{    tangent[i*(prec+1)+j] = glm::vec3(0.0f, 0.0f, -1.0f);              // set tangent to -Z axis
}

else                        // otherwise, calculate tangent
{    tangent[i*(prec+1)+j] = glm::cross(glm::vec3(0.0f, 1.0f, 0.0f), glm::vec3(x,y,z));
}
    . . . // remaining computations are unchanged
    }
}
```

For models that don't lend themselves to exact analytic derivation of surface tangents, the tangents can be approximated, for example by drawing vectors from each vertex to the next as they are constructed (or loaded). Note that such an approximation can lead to tangent vectors that are not strictly perpendicular to the corresponding vertex normals. Implementing normal mapping that works across a variety of models therefore needs to take this possibility into account (our solution will).

The tangent vectors are sent from a buffer (VBO) to a vertex attribute in the vertex shader, as is done for the vertices, texture coordinates, and normals. The vertex shader then processes them the same as is done for normal vectors, by applying the inverse-transpose of the M matrix and forwarding the result down the pipeline for interpolation by the rasterizer and ultimately into the fragment shader. The application of the inverse transpose converts the normal and tangent vectors into world space, after which we construct the bitangent using the cross product.

Once we have the normal, tangent, and bitangent vectors in world space, we can use them to construct a matrix (called the "TBN" matrix, after its components) which transforms the normals retrieved from the normal map into their corresponding orientation in world space relative to the surface of the object.

In the fragment shader, the computing of the new normal is done in the calcNewNormal() function. The computation in the third line of the function (the one containing dot(tangent, normal)) ensures that the tangent vector is perpendicular to the normal vector. A cross product between the new tangent and the normal produces the bitangent.

We then create the TBN as a 3×3 mat3 matrix. The mat3 constructor takes three vectors and generates a matrix containing the first vector in the top row, the second vector in the middle row, and the third in the bottom row (similar to building a view matrix from a camera position—see Figure 3.13).

The shader uses the fragment's texture coordinates to extract the normal map entry corresponding to the current fragment. The sampler variable "normMap" is used for this, and in this case is bound to texture unit 0 (note: the C++/OpenGL application must therefore have attached the normal map image to texture unit 0). To convert the color component from the stored range [0..1] to its original range [-1..+1], we multiply by 2.0 and subtract 1.0.

The TBN matrix is then applied to the resulting normal to produce the final normal for the current pixel. The rest of the shader is identical to the fragment shader used for Phong lighting. The fragment shader is shown in Program 10.2 and is based on a version by Etay Meiri [ME11].

A variety of tools exist for developing normal map images. Some image editing tools, such as GIMP [GI23] and Photoshop [PH23], have such capabilities. Such tools analyze the edges in an image, inferring peaks and valleys, and produce a corresponding normal map.

Figure 10.5 shows a texture map of the surface of the moon created by Hastings-Trew [HT23] based on NASA satellite data. The corresponding normal map was generated by applying the GIMP normal map plugin [GN12] to a black and white reduction also created by Hastings-Trew.

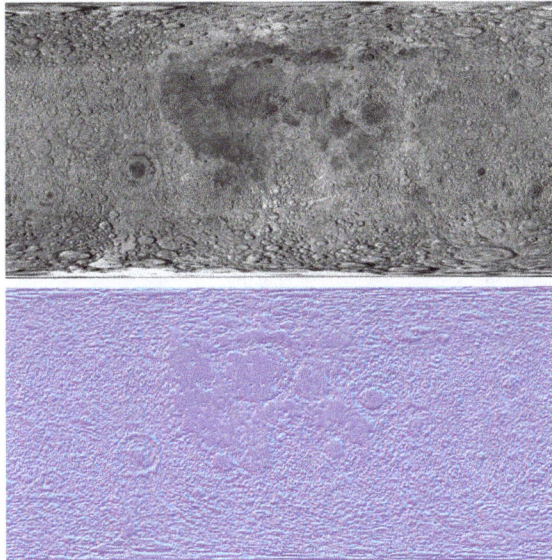

Figure 10.5
Moon, texture and normal map.

Program 10.2 Normal Mapping Fragment Shader

```glsl
#version 430
in vec3 varyingLightDir;
in vec3 varyingVertPos;
in vec3 varyingNormal;
in vec3 varyingTangent;
in vec3 originalVertex;
in vec2 tc;
out vec4 fragColor;

layout (binding=0) uniform sampler2D normMap;
// remaining uniforms same as before

. . .

vec3 calcNewNormal()
{   vec3 normal = normalize(varyingNormal);
    vec3 tangent = normalize(varyingTangent);
    tangent = normalize(tangent - dot(tangent, normal) * normal);    // tangent is perpendicular to normal
    vec3 bitangent = cross(tangent, normal);
    mat3 tbn = mat3(tangent, bitangent, normal);        // TBN matrix to convert to camera space
    vec3 retrievedNormal = texture(normMap,tc).xyz;
    retrievedNormal = retrievedNormal * 2.0 - 1.0;        // convert from RGB space
    vec3 newNormal = tbn * retrievedNormal;
    newNormal = normalize(newNormal);
    return newNormal;
}

void main(void)
{   // normalize the light, normal, and view vectors:
    vec3 L = normalize(varyingLightDir);
    vec3 V = normalize(-v_matrix[3].xyz - varyingVertPos);
    vec3 N = calcNewNormal();

    // get the angle between the light and surface normal:
    float cosTheta = dot(L,N);

    // compute light reflection vector, with respect N:
    vec3 R = normalize(reflect(-L, N));

    // angle between the view vector and reflected light:
    float cosPhi = dot(V,R);

    // compute ADS contributions (per pixel):
    fragColor = globalAmbient * material.ambient
    + light.ambient * material.ambient
    + light.diffuse * material.diffuse * max(cosTheta,0.0)
    + light.specular * material.specular * pow(max(cosPhi,0.0), material.shininess);
}
```

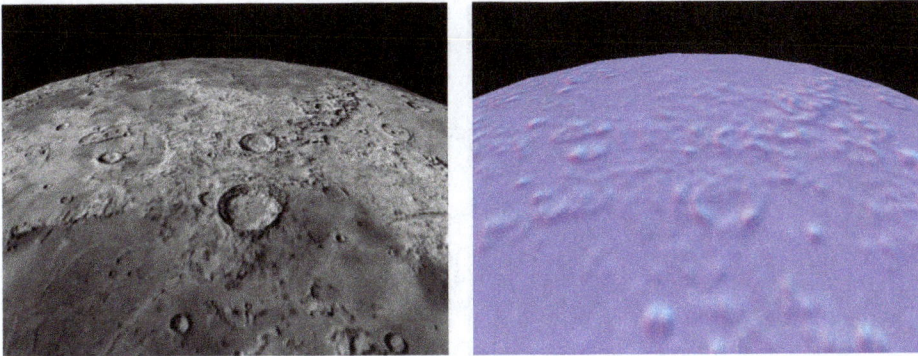

Figure 10.6
Sphere textured with moon texture (left) and normal map (right).

Figure 10.6 shows a sphere with the moon surface rendered in two different ways. On the left, it is simply textured with the original texture map; on the right, it is textured with the image normal map (for reference). Normal mapping has not been applied in either case. As realistic as the textured "moon" is, close examination reveals that the texture image was apparently taken when the moon was being lit from the left, because ridge shadows are cast to the right (most clearly evident in the crater near the bottom center). If we were to add lighting to this scene with Phong shading, and then animate the scene by moving the moon, the camera, or the light, those shadows would not change as we would expect them to.

Furthermore, as the light source moves (or as the camera moves), we would expect many specular highlights to appear on the ridges. But a plain textured sphere such as at the left of Figure 10.6 would produce only one specular highlight, corresponding to what would appear on a smooth sphere, which would look very unrealistic. Incorporation of the normal map can improve the realism of lighting on objects such as this considerably.

If we use normal mapping on the sphere (rather than applying the texture), we obtain the results shown in Figure 10.7. Although not as realistic (yet) as standard texturing, it now *does* respond to lighting changes. The first image is lit from the left, and the second is lit from the right. Note the blue and yellow arrows showing the change in diffuse lighting around ridges and the movement of specular highlights.

Figure 10.8 shows the effect of combining normal mapping with standard texturing in the presence of Phong lighting. The image of the moon is enhanced with diffuse-lit regions and specular highlights that respond to the movement of the

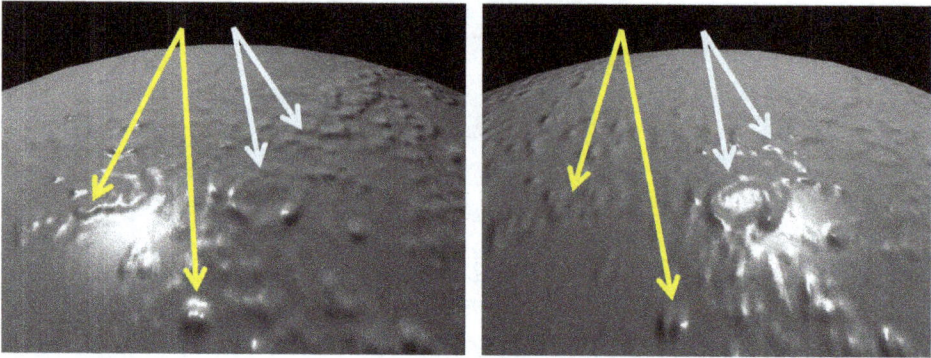

Figure 10.7
Normal map lighting effects on the moon.

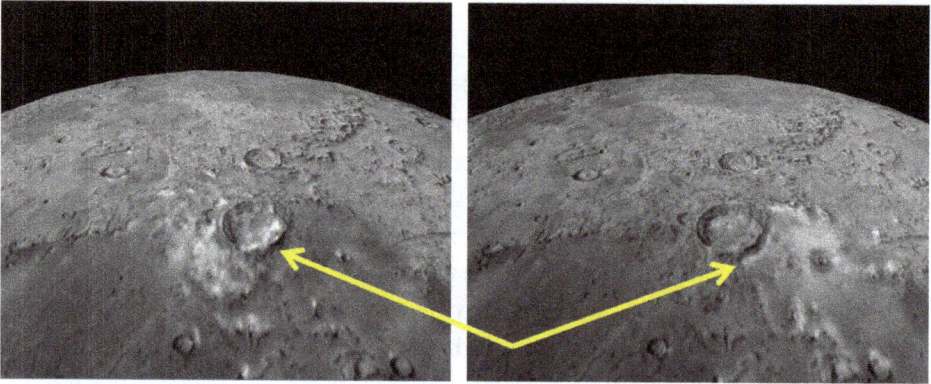

Figure 10.8
Texturing plus normal mapping, with lighting from the left and right.

light source (or camera or object movement). Lighting in the two images is from the left and right sides respectively.

Our program now requires two textures—one for the moon surface image, and one for the normal map—and thus two samplers. The fragment shader blends the texture color with the color produced by the lighting computation as shown in Program 10.3, using the technique described previously in Section 7.6.

Program 10.3 Texturing plus Normal Map

```
// variables and structs as in previous fragment shader, plus:
layout (binding=0) uniform sampler2D s0;       // normal map
layout (binding=1) uniform sampler2D s1;       // texture
```

```
void main(void)
{   // computations same as before, until:

    vec3 N = calcNewNormal();
    vec4 texel = texture(s1,tc);            // standard texture

    . . .
    // reflection computations as before, then blend results:
    fragColor = globalAmbient +
        texel * (light.ambient + light.diffuse * max(cosTheta,0.0)
        + light.specular * pow(max(cosPhi,0.0), material.shininess));
}
```

Interestingly, normal mapping can benefit from *mipmapping*, because the same "aliasing" artifacts that we saw in Chapter 5 for texturing also occur when using a texture image for normal mapping. Figure 10.9 shows a normal-mapped moon, with and without mipmapping. Although not easily shown in a still image, the sphere at the left (*not* mipmapped) has shimmering artifacts around its perimeter.

Anisotropic filtering (AF) works even better, reducing sparkling artifacts while preserving detail, as illustrated in Figure 10.10 (compare the detail on the edge along the lower right). A version combining equal parts texture and lighting with normal mapping and AF is shown alongside, in Figure 10.11.

The results are imperfect. Shadows appearing in the original texture image will still show on the rendered result, regardless of lighting. Also, while normal

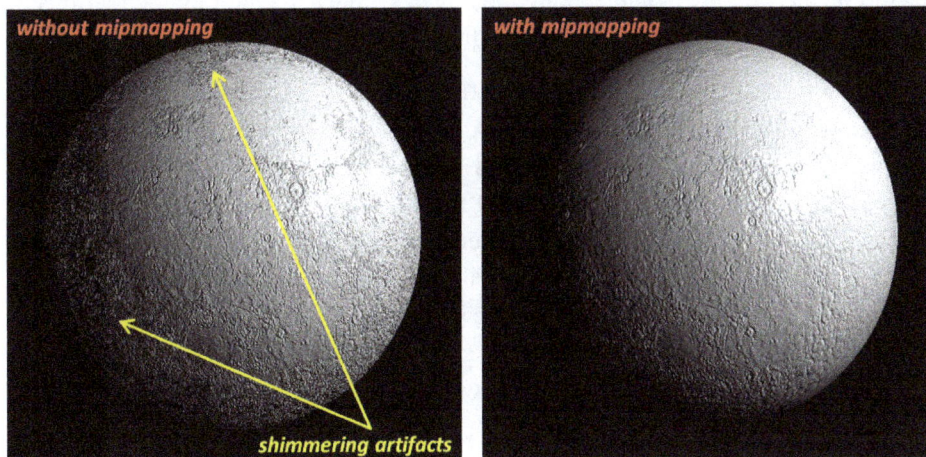

Figure 10.9
Normal mapping artifacts, corrected with mipmapping.

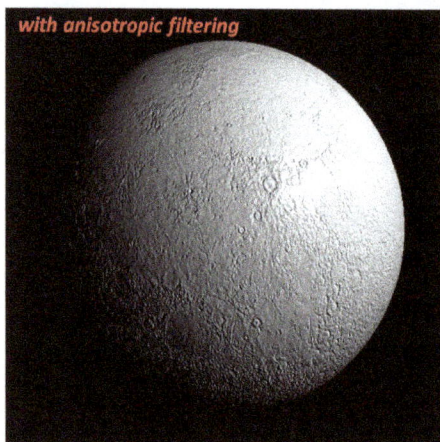

Figure 10.10
Normal mapping with AF.

Figure 10.11
Texturing plus normal mapping with AF.

mapping can affect diffuse and specular effects, it cannot cast shadows. Therefore, this method is best used when the surface features are small.

10.3 HEIGHT MAPPING

We now extend the concept of normal mapping—where a texture image is used to perturb normals—to instead *perturb the vertex locations themselves*. Actually modifying an object's geometry in this way has certain advantages, such as making the surface features visible along the object's edge and enabling the features to respond to shadow-mapping. It can also facilitate building *terrain*, as we will see.

A practical approach is to use a texture image to store *height* values, which can then be used to raise (or lower) vertex locations. An image that contains height information is called a *height map*, and using a height map to alter an object's vertices is called *height mapping*. Height maps usually encode height information as grayscale colors: (0,0,0) (black) = *low* height, and (1,1,1) (white) = *high* height. This makes it easy to create height maps algorithmically or by using a "paint" program. The higher the image contrast, the greater the variation in height expressed by the map. These concepts are illustrated in Figure 10.12 (showing randomly generated maps) and Figure 10.13 (showing a map with an organized pattern).

The usefulness of altering vertex locations depends on the model being altered. Vertex manipulation is easily done in the vertex shader, and when there is a high level of detail in the model vertices (such as in a sphere with sufficiently high precision), this approach can work well. However, when the underlying number of vertices is small (such as the corners of a cube), rendering the object's surface relies on vertex interpolation in the rasterizer to fill in the detail. When there are very few vertices available in the vertex shader to perturb, the heights of many pixels would be interpolated rather than retrieved from the height map, leading to poor surface detail. Vertex manipulation in the fragment shader is, of course, impossible because by then the vertices have been rasterized into pixel locations.

Program 10.4 shows a vertex shader that moves the vertices "outward" (i.e., in the direction of the surface normal) by multiplying the vertex normal by the value retrieved from the height map and then adding that product to the vertex position.

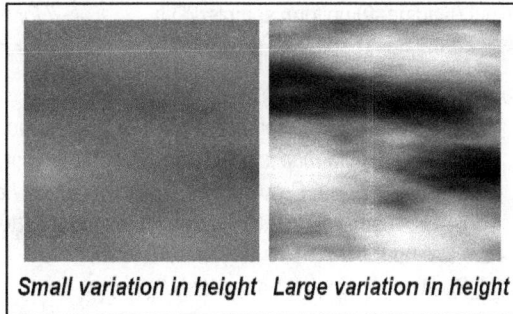

Small variation in height Large variation in height

Figure 10.12
Height map examples.

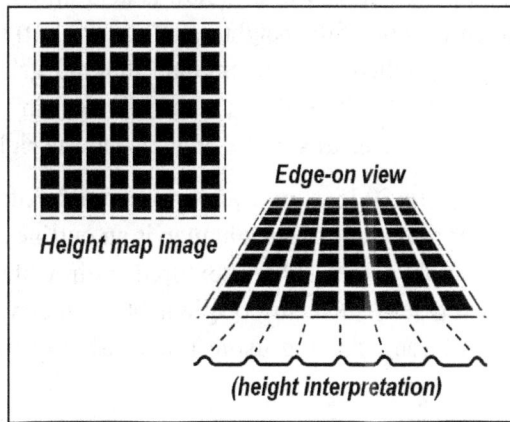

Edge-on view

Height map image

(height interpretation)

Figure 10.13
Height map interpretation.

Program 10.4 Height Mapping in Vertex Shader

```
#version 430

layout (location=0) in vec3 vertPos;
layout (location=1) in vec2 texCoord;
layout (location=2) in vec3 vertNormal;

out vec2 tc;

uniform mat4 mv_matrix;
uniform mat4 p_matrix;
```

```
layout (binding=0) uniform sampler2D t;          // for texture
layout (binding=1) uniform sampler2D h;          // for heightmap

void main(void)
{   // "p" is the vertex position altered by the height map.
    // Since the height map is grayscale, any of the color components can be
    // used (we use "r"). Dividing by 5.0 is to adjust the height.
    vec4 p = vec4(vertPos,1.0) + vec4( (vertNormal * ((texture(h, texCoord).r) / 5.0f)),1.0f );
    tc = tex_coord;
    gl_Position = p_matrix * mv_matrix * p;
}
```

Figure 10.14 shows a simple height map (top left) created by scribbling in a paint program. A white square is also drawn in the height map image. A green-tinted version of the height map (bottom left) is used as a texture. When the height map is applied to a rectangular 100x100 grid model using the shader shown in Program 10.4, it produces a sort of "terrain" (shown on the right). Note how the white square results in the precipice at the right.

Figure 10.15 shows another example of doing height mapping in a vertex shader. This time the height map is an outline of the continents of the world [HT23]. It is applied to a sphere textured with a blue-tinted version of the height map (see top left—note the original black-and-white version is not shown), lit with Blinn-Phong shading using a normal map (shown at the lower left) built using

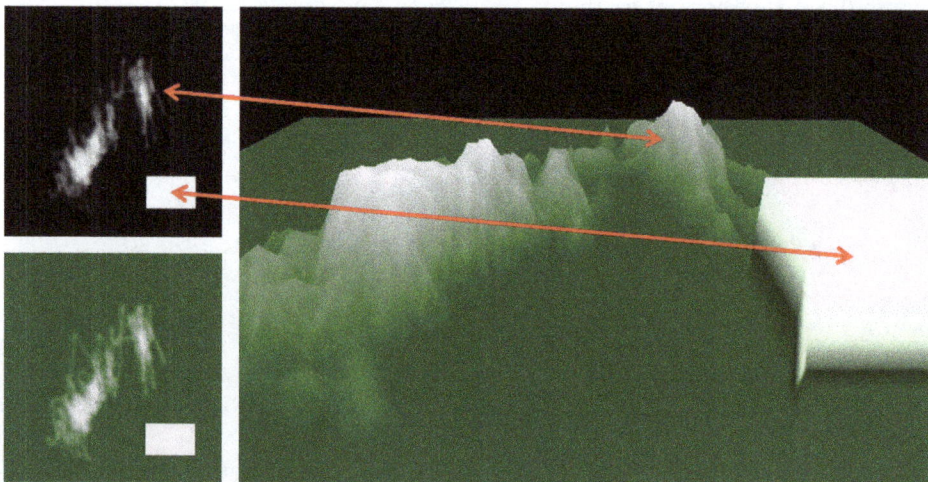

Figure 10.14
Terrain, height-mapped in the vertex shader.

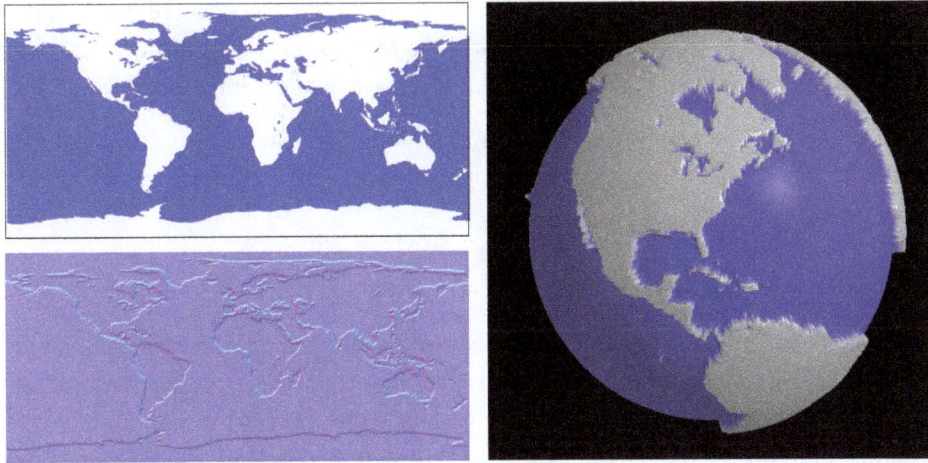

Figure 10.15
Vertex shader-based height mapping, applied to a sphere.

the tool *SSBump Generator* [SS15]. The sphere precision was increased to 500 to ensure that there are enough vertices to render the detail. Note how the raised vertices affect not only the lighting, but also the silhouette edges.

The rendered examples shown in Figure 10.14 and Figure 10.15 work acceptably because the two models (grid and sphere) have a sufficient number of vertices to sample the height map values. That is, they each have a fairly large number of vertices, and the height map is relatively coarse and adequately sampled at a low resolution. However, close inspection still reveals the presence of resolution artifacts, such as along the bottom left edge of the raised box at the right of the terrain in Figure 10.14. The reason that the sides of the raised box don't appear perfectly square, and include gradations in color, is because the 100x100 resolution of the underlying grid cannot adequately align perfectly with the white box in the height map, and the resulting rasterization of texture coordinates produces artifacts along the sides.

The limitations of doing height mapping in the vertex shader are further exposed when trying to apply it with a more demanding height map. Consider the moon image shown back in Figure 10.5. Normal mapping did an excellent job of capturing the detail in the image (as shown previously in Figure 10.9 and Figure 10.11), and since it is grayscale, it would seem natural to try applying it as a height map. However, vertex-shader-based height mapping would be inadequate for this task, because the number of vertices sampled in the vertex shader (even for a sphere with precision=500) is small compared to the fine level of detail in the image. By contrast, normal mapping *was* able to capture the detail impressively, because the normal map is sampled in the fragment shader, at the pixel level.

We will revisit height mapping later in Chapter 12 when we discuss methods for generating a greater number of vertices in a *tessellation shader.*

SUPPLEMENTAL NOTES

One of the fundamental limitations of bump or normal mapping is that, while they are capable of providing the appearance of surface detail in the interior of a rendered object, the silhouette (outer boundary) doesn't show any such detail (it remains smooth). Height mapping, if used to actually modify vertex locations, fixes this deficiency, but it has its own limitations. As we will see later in this book, sometimes a geometry or tessellation shader can be used to increase the number of vertices, making height mapping more practical and more effective.

We have taken the liberty of simplifying some of the bump and normal mapping computations. More accurate and/or more efficient solutions are available for critical applications [BN12].

Exercises

10.1 Experiment with Program 10.1 by modifying the settings and/or computations in the fragment shader and observing the results.

10.2 Using a paint program, generate your own height map and use it in Program 10.4. See if you can identify locations where detail is missing as the result of the vertex shader being unable to adequately sample the height map. You will probably find it useful to also texture the terrain with your height map image file as shown in Figure 10.14 (or with some sort of pattern that exposes the surface structure, such as a grid) so that you can see the hills and valleys of the resulting terrain.

10.3 *(PROJECT)* Add lighting to Program 10.4 so that the surface structure of the height-mapped terrain is further exposed.

10.4 *(PROJECT)* Add shadow-mapping to your code from Exercise 10.3 so that your height-mapped terrain casts shadows.

References

[BL78] J. Blinn, "Simulation of Wrinkled Surfaces," *Computer Graphics* 12, no. 3 (1978): 286–292.

[BN12] E. Bruneton and F. Neyret, "A Survey of Non-Linear Pre-Filtering Methods for Efficient and Accurate Surface Shading," *IEEE Transactions on Visualization and Computer Graphics* 18, no. 2 (2012).

[GI23] GNU Image Manipulation Program, accessed November 2023, http://www.gimp.org

[GN12] GIMP *normalmap plugin*, accessed November 2023, https://code.google.com/archive/p/gimp-normalmap/

[HT23] J. Hastings-Trew, *JHT's Planetary Pixel Emporium*, accessed November 2023, http://planetpixelemporium.com/

[LU16] F. Luna, *Introduction to 3D Game Programming with DirectX 12*, 2nd ed. (Mercury Learning, 2016).

[ME11] E. Meiri, *OGLdev tutorial 26*, 2011, accessed November 2023, https://ogldev.org/www/tutorial26/tutorial26.html

[PH23] Adobe Photoshop, accessed November 2023, https://www.adobe.com/products/photoshop.html

[SS15] SSBump Generator, accessed November 2023, https://sourceforge.net/projects/ssbumpgenerator

PARAMETRIC SURFACES

■ ■ ■ ■ ■

While working at the Renault corporation in the 1950s and 1960s, Pierre Bézier developed software systems for designing automobile bodies. His programs utilized mathematical systems of equations developed earlier by Paul de Casteljau, who was working for the competing Citroën automobile manufacturer [BE72, DC63]. The de Casteljau equations describe curves using just a few scalar parameters, and are accompanied by a clever recursive algorithm dubbed "de Casteljau's algorithm" for generating the curves to arbitrary precision. Now known as "Bézier curves" and "Bézier surfaces," these methods are commonly used to efficiently model many kinds of curved 3D objects.

11.1 QUADRATIC BÉZIER CURVES

A *quadratic Bézier curve* is defined by a set of parametric equations that specify a particular curved shape using three *control points*, each of which is a point in 2D space.[1] Consider, for example, the set of three points $[p_0, p_1, p_2]$ shown in Figure 11.1.

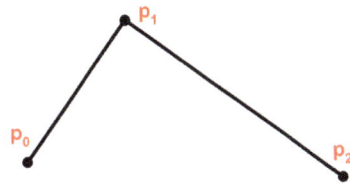

Figure 11.1
Control points for a Bézier curve.

---

[1] Of course, a curve can exist in 3D space. However, a quadratic curve lies entirely within a 2D plane.

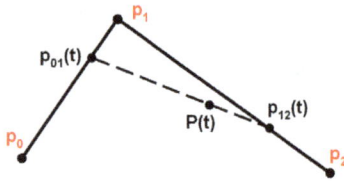

Figure 11.2
Points at parametric position t = 0.75.

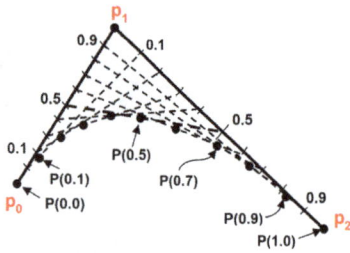

Figure 11.3
Building a quadratic Bézier curve.

By introducing a parameter **t**, we can build a system of parametric equations that define a curve. The **t** represents a fraction of the distance along the line segment connecting one control point to the next control point. Values for **t** are within the range [0..1] for points along the segment. Figure 11.2 shows one such value, t = 0.75, applied to the lines connecting p_0-p_1 and p_1-p_2 respectively. Doing this defines two new points $p_{01}(t)$ and $p_{12}(t)$ along the two original lines. We repeat this process for the line segment connecting the two new points $p_{01}(t)$ and $p_{12}(t)$, producing point P(t) where t = 0.75 along the line $p_{01}(t)$-$p_{12}(t)$. P(t) is one of the points on the resulting curve, and for this reason it is denoted with a capital P.

Collecting many points P(t) for various values of **t** generates a curve, as shown in Figure 11.3. The more parameter values for **t** that are sampled, the more points P(t) are generated, and the smoother the resulting curve.

The analytic definition for a quadratic Bézier curve can now be derived. First, we note that an arbitrary point p on the line segment p_a-p_b connecting two points p_a and p_b can be represented in terms of the parameter **t** as follows:

$$\boldsymbol{p}_{ab}(t) = t\boldsymbol{p}_b + (1-t)\boldsymbol{p}_a$$

Using this, we find the points p_{01} and p_{12} (points on p_0-p_1 and p_1-p_2 respectively) as follows:

$$\boldsymbol{p}_{01}(t) = t\boldsymbol{p}_1 + (1-t)\boldsymbol{p}_0$$
$$\boldsymbol{p}_{12}(t) = t\boldsymbol{p}_2 + (1-t)\boldsymbol{p}_1$$

Similarly, a point on the connecting line segment between these points would be:

$$P(t) = t\boldsymbol{p}_{12}(t) + (1-t)\boldsymbol{p}_{01}(t)$$

Substituting the definitions of p_{12} and p_{01} gives:

$$P(t) = t[tp_2 + (1-t)p_1] + (1-t)[tp_1 + (1-t)p_0]$$

Factoring and combining terms then gives:

$$P(t) = (1-t)^2 p_0 + (-2t^2 + 2t)p_1 + t^2 p_2$$

or,

$$P(t) = \sum_{i=0}^{2} p_i B_i(t)$$

where:

$$B_0(t) = (1-t)^2$$
$$B_1(t) = -2t^2 + 2t$$
$$B_2(t) = t^2$$

Thus, we find any point on the curve by a weighted sum of the control points. The weighting function B is often called a "blending function" (although the name "B" actually derives from Sergei Bernstein [BE23], who first characterized this family of polynomials). Note that the blending functions are all quadratic in form, which is why the resulting curve is called a quadratic Bézier curve.

11.2 CUBIC BÉZIER CURVES

We now extend our model to *four* control points, resulting in a *cubic* Bézier curve as shown in Figure 11.4. Cubic Bézier curves are capable of defining a much richer set of shapes than are quadratic curves, which are limited to concave shapes.

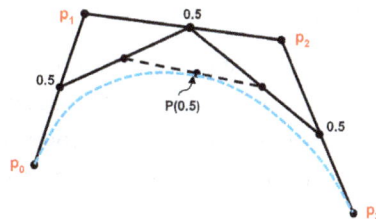

Figure 11.4
Building a cubic Bézier curve.

As for the quadratic case, we can derive an analytic definition for cubic Bézier curves:

$$p_{01}(t) = tp_1 + (1-t)p_0$$
$$p_{12}(t) = tp_2 + (1-t)p_1$$

$$p_{23}(t) = tp_3 + (1-t)p_2$$
$$p_{01-12}(t) = tp_{12}(t) + (1-t)p_{01}(t)$$
$$p_{12-23}(t) = tp_{23}(t) + (1-t)p_{12}(t)$$

A point on the curve would then be:

$$P(t) = tp_{12-23}(t) + (1-t)p_{01-12}(t)$$

Substituting the definitions of $p_{12\text{-}23}$ and $p_{01\text{-}12}$ and collecting terms yields:

$$P(t) = \sum_{i=0}^{3} p_i B_i(t)$$

where:

$$B_0(t) = (1-t)^3$$
$$B_1(t) = 3t^3 - 6t^2 + 3t$$
$$B_2(t) = -3t^3 + 3t^2$$
$$B_3(t) = t^3$$

There are many different techniques for rendering Bézier curves. One approach is to iterate through successive values of *t*, starting at 0.0 and ending at 1.0, using a fixed increment. For instance, if the increment is 0.1, then we could use a loop with *t* values 0.0, 0.1, 0.2, 0.3, and so on. For each value of *t*, the corresponding point on the Bézier curve would be computed, and a series of line segments connecting the successive points would be drawn, as described in the algorithm in Figure 11.5.

Another approach is to use de Casteljau's algorithm to *recursively subdivide* the curve in half, where *t*=½ at each recursive step. Figure 11.6 shows the left side subdivision into new cubic control points (q_0,q_1,q_2,q_3) shown in green, as derived by de Casteljau (a full derivation can be found in [AS14]).

The algorithm is shown in Figure 11.7. It subdivides the curve segments in half repeatedly, until each curve segment is sufficiently straight enough that further subdivision produces no tangible benefit. In the limiting case (as the control points are generated closer and closer together), the curve segment itself is effectively the same as a straight line between the first and last control points (q_0 and q_3). Determining whether a curve segment is "straight enough" can therefore be done

```
drawBezierCurve (controlPointVector C)
{    currentPoint = C[0];   // curve starts at first control point
     t = 0.0;
     while (t <= 1.0)
     {   // compute next point as the sum of the Control Points,
         // weighted by the blending function evaluated at 't'.
         nextPoint = (0,0) ;
         for (i=0; i<=3; i++)
             nextPoint = nextPoint + (blending(i,t) * C[i]);
         drawLine (currentPoint,nextPoint);
         currentPoint = nextPoint;
         t = t + increment;
}   }


blending(i, t)
{    switch (i)
     {   case 0: return ((1-t)*(1-t)*(1-t));      // (1-t)³
         case 1: return (3*t*(1-t)*(1-t));        // 3t(1-t)²
         case 2: return (3*t*t*(1-t));            // 3t²(1-t)
         case 3: return (t*t*t);                  // t³
}   }
```

Figure 11.5
Iterative algorithm for rendering Bézier curves.

by comparing the distance from the first control point to the last control point, versus the sum of the lengths of the three lines connecting the four control points:

$$D_1 = | p_0\text{-}p_1 | + | p_1\text{-}p_2 | + | p_2\text{-}p_3 |$$

$$D_2 = | p_0\text{-}p_3 |$$

Then, if $D_1\text{-}D_2$ is less than a sufficiently small tolerance, there is no point in further subdivision.

An interesting property of the de Casteljau algorithm is that it is possible to generate all of the points on the curve without actually using the previously described blending

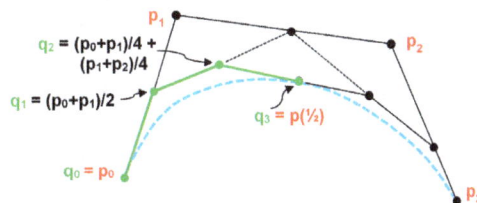

Figure 11.6
Subdividing a cubic Bézier curve.

```
drawBezierCurve(ControlPointVector C)
{    if (C is "straight enough")
          draw line from first to last control point
     else
     {    subdivide(C, LeftC, RightC)
          drawBezierCurve(LeftC)
          drawBezierCurve(RightC)
}    }

subdivide(ControlPointVector p, q, r)
{    // compute left subdivision control points
     q(0) = p(0)
     q(1) = (p(0)+p(1)) / 2
     q(2) = (p(0)+p(1)) / 4 + (p(1)+p(2)) / 4
     // compute right subdivision control points
     r(1) = (p(1)+p(2)) / 4 + (p(2)+p(3)) / 4
     r(2) = (p(2)+p(3)) / 2
     r(3) = p(3)
     // compute "shared" center point at t=0.5
     q(3) = r(0) = (q(2)+r(1)) / 2
}
```

Figure 11.7
Recursive subdivision algorithm for Bézier curves.

functions. Also, note that the center point at p(½) is "shared"; that is, it is both the rightmost control point in the left subdivision, and the leftmost control point in the right subdivision. It can be computed either using the blending functions at t=½, or by using the formula $(q_2 + r_1)/2$, as derived by de Casteljau.

As a side note, we point out that the subdivide() function shown in Figure 11.7 assumes that the incoming parameters p, q, and r are "reference" parameters, and hence the computations in the function modify the actual parameters in the calls from the drawBezierCurve() function listed above it.

11.3 QUADRATIC BÉZIER SURFACES

Whereas Bézier curves define curved *lines* (in 2D or 3D space), Bézier *surfaces* define *curved surfaces* in *3D space*. Extending the concepts we saw in curves to surfaces requires extending our system of parametric equations from one parameter to two parameters. For Bézier curves, we called that parameter *t*. For Bézier surfaces, we will refer to the parameters as **u** and **v**. Whereas our curves were composed of points P(t), our surfaces will comprise points P(u,v), as shown in Figure 11.8.

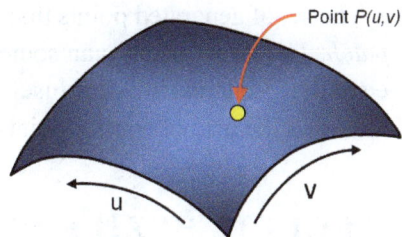

Figure 11.8
Parametric surface.

For quadratic Bézier surfaces, there are three control points on each axis u and v, for a total of *nine* control points. Figure 11.9 shows an example of a set of nine control points (typically called a *control point "mesh"*) in blue, and the associated corresponding curved surface (in red).

The nine control points in the mesh are labeled p_{ij}, where i and j represent the indices in the u and v directions respectively. Each set of three adjacent control points, such as (p_{00}, p_{01}, p_{02}), defines a Bézier curve. Points P(u,v) on the surface are then defined as a sum of two blending functions, one in the u direction and one in the v direction. The form of the two blending functions for building Bézier surfaces then follows from the methodology given previously for Bézier curves:

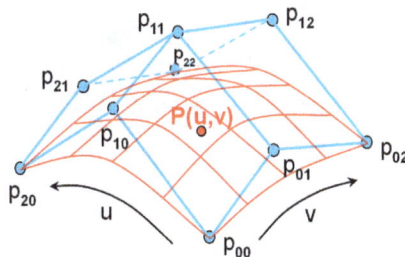

Figure 11.9
Quadratic Bézier control mesh and corresponding surface.

$$B_0(u) = (1-u)^2$$
$$B_1(u) = -2u^2 + 2u$$
$$B_2(u) = u^2$$
$$B_0(v) = (1-v)^2$$
$$B_1(v) = -2v^2 + 2v$$
$$B_2(v) = v^2$$

The points P(u,v) comprising the Bézier surface are then generated by summing the product of each control point p_{ij} and the ith and j^{th} blending functions evaluated at parametric values u and v respectively:

$$P(u,v) = \sum_{i=0}^{2} \sum_{j=0}^{2} p_{ij} * B_i(u) * B_j(v)$$

The set of generated points that comprise a Bézier surface is sometimes called a *patch*. The term "patch" can sometimes be confusing, as we will see later when we study tessellation shaders (useful for actually implementing Bézier surfaces). There, it is the grid of control points that is typically called a "patch."

11.4 CUBIC BÉZIER SURFACES

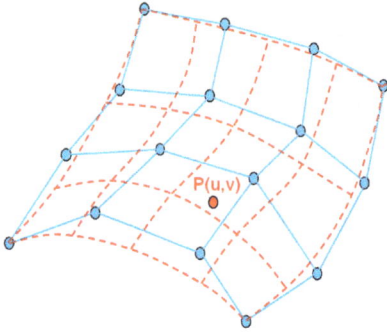

Figure 11.10
Cubic Bézier control mesh and corresponding surface.

Moving from quadratic to cubic surfaces requires utilizing a larger mesh—4x4 rather than 3x3. Figure 11.10 shows an example of a 16-control-point mesh (in blue), and the corresponding curved surface (in red).

As before, we can derive the formula for points P(u,v) on the surface by combining the associated blending functions for cubic Bézier curves:

$$P(u,v) = \sum_{i=0}^{3} \sum_{j=0}^{3} p_{ij} * B_i(u) * B_j(v)$$

where:

$$B_0(u) = (1-u)^3 \qquad\qquad B_0(v) = (1-v)^3$$
$$B_1(u) = 3u^3 - 6u^2 + 3u \qquad B_1(v) = 3v^3 - 6v^2 + 3v$$
$$B_2(u) = -3u^3 + 3u^2 \qquad\quad B_2(v) = -3v^3 + 3v^2$$
$$B_3(u) = u^3 \qquad\qquad\qquad B_3(v) = v^3$$

Rendering Bézier surfaces can also be done with recursive subdivision [AS14], by alternately splitting the surface in half along each dimension, as shown in Figure 11.11. Each subdivision produces four new control point meshes, each containing sixteen points which define one quadrant of the surface.

When rendering Bézier *curves*, we stopped subdividing when the *curve* was "straight enough." For Bézier surfaces, we stop recursing when the *surface* is "flat enough." One way of doing this is to ensure that all of the recursively generated

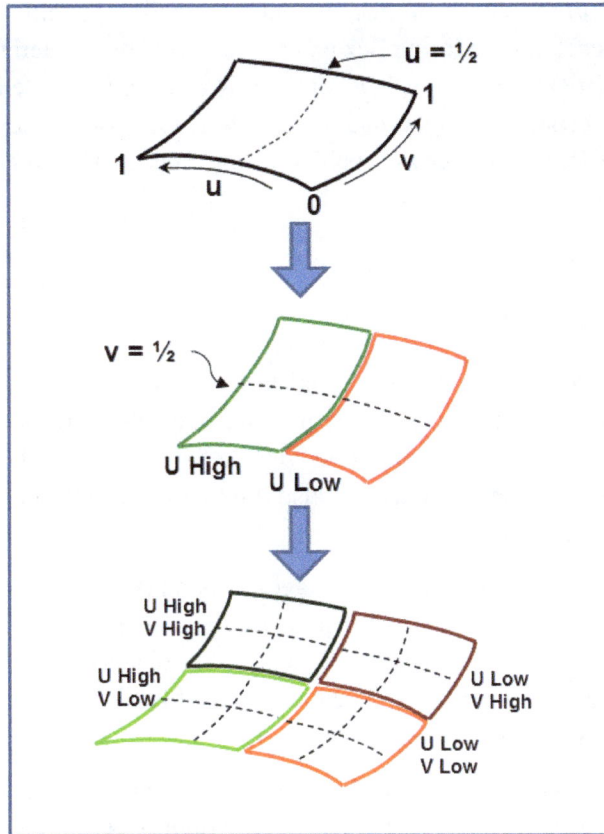

Figure 11.11
Recursive subdivision for Bézier surfaces.

points in a sub-quadrant control mesh are within some small allowable distance from a plane defined by three of the four corner points of that mesh. The distance d between a point (x,y,z) and a plane (A,B,C,D) is:

$$d = abs\left(\frac{Ax + By + Cz + D}{\sqrt{A^2 + B^2 + C^2}} \right)$$

If d is less than some sufficiently small tolerance, then we stop subdividing, and simply use the four corner control points of the sub-quadrant mesh to draw two triangles.

The *tessellation* stage of the OpenGL pipeline offers an attractive alternative approach for rendering Bézier surfaces based on the iterative algorithm in Figure 11.5 for Bézier curves. The strategy is to have the tessellator generate a large grid of vertices, and then use the blending functions to reposition those vertices onto the Bézier surface as specified by the cubic Bézier control points. We implement this in Chapter 12.

SUPPLEMENTAL NOTES

This chapter focused on the mathematical fundamentals of parametric Bézier curves and surfaces. We have deferred presenting an implementation of any of them in OpenGL, because an appropriate vehicle for this is the tessellation stage, which is covered in the next chapter. We also skipped some of the derivations, such as for the recursive subdivision algorithm.

In 3D graphics, there are many advantages to using Bézier curves for modeling objects. First, those objects can, in theory, be scaled arbitrarily and still retain smooth surfaces without "pixelating." Second, many objects made up of complex curves can be stored much more efficiently as sets of Bézier control points, rather than storing thousands of vertices.

Bézier curves have many real-world applications besides computer graphics and automobiles. They can also be found in the design of bridges, such as in the Chords Bridge in Jerusalem [RG12]. Similar techniques are used for building TrueType fonts, which as a result can be scaled to any arbitrary size, or zoomed in to any degree of closeness, while always retaining smooth edges.

Exercises

11.1 A quadratic Bézier curve is limited to defining a curve that is wholly "concave" or "convex." Describe (or draw) an example of a curve that bends in a manner that is neither wholly concave nor convex, and thus could not possibly be approximated by a *quadratic* Bézier curve.

11.2 Using a pen or pencil, draw an arbitrary set of four points on a piece of paper, number them from 1 to 4 in any order, and then try to draw an approximation of the cubic Bézier curve defined by those four ordered control points. Then rearrange the numbering of the control points (i.e., their order, but without changing their positions) and redraw the new resulting cubic Bézier curve. There are numerous online tools for drawing Bézier curves you can use to check your approximation.

References

[AS14] E. Angel and D. Shreiner, *Interactive Computer Graphics: A Top-Down Approach with WebGL*, 7th ed. (Pearson, 2014).

[BE23] S. Bernstein, Wikipedia, accessed November 2023, https://en.wikipedia.org/wiki/Sergei_Bernstein

[BE72] P. Bézier, *Numerical Control: Mathematics and Applications* (John Wiley & Sons, 1972).

[DC63] P. de Casteljau, *Courbes et surfaces à pôles*, technical report (A. Citroën, 1963).

[RG12] R. Gross, "Bridges, String Art, and Bézier Curves", Plus Magazine, accessed November 2023, https://plus.maths.org/content/bridges-string-art-and-bezier-curves

TESSELLATION

■ ▦ ▦ ▦ ▦

The English language term "tessellation" refers to a large class of design activities in which tiles of various geometric shapes are arranged adjacently to form patterns, generally on a flat surface. The purpose can be artistic or practical, with examples dating back thousands of years [TS23].

In 3D graphics, *tessellation* refers to something a little bit different, but no doubt inspired by its classical counterpart. Here, tessellation refers to the generation and manipulation of large numbers of triangles for rendering complex shapes and surfaces, preferably in hardware. Tessellation is a rather recent addition to the OpenGL core, not appearing until 2010 with version 4.0.[1]

12.1 TESSELLATION IN OPENGL

OpenGL support for hardware tessellation is made available through three pipeline stages:

1. the *tessellation control shader*
2. the *tessellator*
3. the *tessellation evaluation shader*

---

[1] The OpenGL Utility library (GLU) had previously included a utility for tessellation much earlier called *gluTess*. In 2001, Radeon released the first commercial graphics card with tessellation support, but there were few tools able to take advantage of it.

The first and third stages are programmable; the intervening second stage is not. In order to use tessellation, the programmer generally provides both a control shader and an evaluation shader.

The tessellator (its full name is *tessellation primitive generator*, or *TPG*) is a hardware-supported engine that produces fixed grids of triangles.[2] The control shader allows us to configure what sort of triangle mesh the tessellator is to build. The evaluation shader then lets us manipulate the grid in various ways. The manipulated triangle mesh is then the source of vertices that proceed through the pipeline. Recall from Figure 2.2 that tessellation sits in the pipeline between the vertex and geometry shader stages.

Let's start with an application that simply uses the tessellator to create a triangle mesh of vertices, and then displays it without any manipulation. For this, we will need the following modules:

1. **C++/OpenGL application:**
   Creates a camera and associated mvp matrix. The view (v) and projection (p) matrices orient the camera; the model (m) matrix can be used to modify the location and orientation of the grid.

2. **Vertex Shader:**
   Essentially does nothing in this example; the vertices will be generated in the tessellator.

3. **Tessellation Control Shader (TCS):**
   Specifies the grid for the tessellator to build.

4. **Tessellation Evaluation Shader (TES):**
   Applies the mvp matrix to the vertices in the grid.

5. **Fragment Shader:**
   Simply outputs a fixed color for every pixel.

Program 12.1 shows the entire application code. Even a simple example such as this one is fairly complex, so many of the code elements will require explanation. Note that this is the first time we must build a GLSL rendering program with components beyond just vertex and fragment shaders. So, a four-parameter overloaded version of createShaderProgram() is implemented.

---

2 Or lines, but we will focus on triangles.

Program 12.1 Basic Tessellator Mesh

C++ / OpenGL application

```cpp
GLuint createShaderProgram(const char *vp, const char *tCS, const char *tES, const char *fp) {
    string vertShaderStr  = readShaderSource(vp);
    string tcShaderStr = readShaderSource(tCS);
    string teShaderStr = readShaderSource(tES);
    string fragShaderStr  = readShaderSource(fp);

    const char *vertShaderSrc = vertShaderStr.c_str();
    const char *tcShaderSrc = tcShaderStr.c_str();
    const char *teShaderSrc = teShaderStr.c_str();
    const char *fragShaderSrc = fragShaderStr.c_str();

    GLuint vShader  = glCreateShader(GL_VERTEX_SHADER);
    GLuint tcShader = glCreateShader(GL_TESS_CONTROL_SHADER);
    GLuint teShader = glCreateShader(GL_TESS_EVALUATION_SHADER);
    GLuint fShader  = glCreateShader(GL_FRAGMENT_SHADER);

    glShaderSource(vShader, 1, &vertShaderSrc, NULL);
    glShaderSource(tcShader, 1, &tcShaderSrc, NULL);
    glShaderSource(teShader, 1, &teShaderSrc, NULL);
    glShaderSource(fShader, 1, &fragShaderSrc, NULL);

    glCompileShader(vShader);
    glCompileShader(tcShader);
    glCompileShader(teShader);
    glCompileShader(fShader);

    GLuint vtfprogram = glCreateProgram();
    glAttachShader(vtfprogram, vShader);
    glAttachShader(vtfprogram, tcShader);
    glAttachShader(vtfprogram, teShader);
    glAttachShader(vtfprogram, fShader);
    glLinkProgram(vtfprogram);
    return vtfprogram;
}
void init(GLFWwindow* window) {
    . . .
    renderingProgram = createShaderProgram("vertShader.glsl",
        "tessCShader.glsl", "tessEShader.glsl", "fragShader.glsl");
}
void display(GLFWwindow* window, double currentTime) {
    . . .
    glUseProgram(renderingProgram);
```

```
     . . .
    glPatchParameteri(GL_PATCH_VERTICES, 1);
    glPolygonMode(GL_FRONT_AND_BACK, GL_LINE);
    glDrawArrays(GL_PATCHES, 0, 1);
}
```

Vertex Shader

```
#version 430
uniform mat4 mvp_matrix;
void main(void)  {  }
```

Tessellation Control Shader

```
#version 430
uniform mat4 mvp_matrix;
layout (vertices = 1) out;

void main(void)
{   gl_TessLevelOuter[0] = 6;
    gl_TessLevelOuter[1] = 6;
    gl_TessLevelOuter[2] = 6;
    gl_TessLevelOuter[3] = 6;
    gl_TessLevelInner[0] = 12;
    gl_TessLevelInner[1] = 12;
}
```

Tessellation Evaluation Shader

```
#version 430
uniform mat4 mvp_matrix;
layout (quads, equal_spacing, ccw) in;

void main (void)
{   float u = gl_TessCoord.x;
    float v = gl_TessCoord.y;
    gl_Position = mvp_matrix * vec4(u,0,v,1);
}
```

Fragment Shader

```
#version 430
out vec4 color;
uniform mat4 mvp_matrix;

void main(void)
{   color = vec4(1.0, 1.0, 0.0, 1.0);        // yellow
}
```

The resulting output mesh is shown in Figure 12.1.

The tessellator produces a mesh of vertices defined by two parameters: *inner level* and *outer level*. In this case, the inner level is 12 and the outer level is 6—the outer edges of the grid are divided into 6 segments, while the lines spanning the interior are divided into 12 segments.

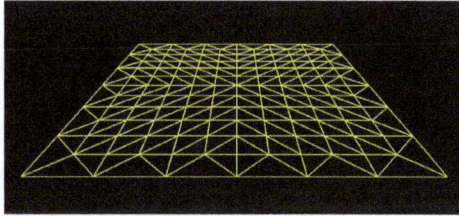

Figure 12.1
Tessellator triangle mesh output.

The specific relevant new constructs in Program 12.1 are highlighted. Let's start by discussing the first portion—the C++/OpenGL code.

Compiling the two new shaders is done exactly the same as for the vertex and fragment shaders. They are then attached to the same rendering program, and the linking call is unchanged. The only new items are the constants for specifying the type of shader being instantiated—the new constants are as follows:

```
GL_TESS_CONTROL_SHADER
GL_TESS_EVALUATION_SHADER
```

Note the new items in the display() function. The glDrawArrays() call now specifies GL_PATCHES. When using tessellation, vertices sent from the C++/OpenGL application into the pipeline (i.e., in a VBO) *aren't rendered*, but are usually *control points*, such as those we saw for Bézier curves. A set of control points is called a "patch," and in those sections of the code using tessellation, GL_PATCHES is the only allowable primitive. The number of vertices in a patch is specified in the call to glPatchParameteri(). In this particular example, there aren't any control points being sent, but we are still required to specify at least one. Similarly, in the glDrawArrays() call we indicate a start value of 0 and a vertex count of 1, even though we aren't actually sending any vertices from the C++ program.

The call to glPolygonMode() specifies how the mesh should be rasterized. The default is GL_FILL. Shown in the code is GL_LINE, which, as we saw in Figure 12.1, caused only connecting lines to be rasterized (so we could see the grid itself that was produced by the tessellator). If we change that line of code to GL_FILL (or comment it out, resulting in the default behavior GL_FILL), we get the version shown in Figure 12.2.

Figure 12.2
Tessellated mesh rendered with GL_FILL.

Now let's work our way through the four shaders. As indicated earlier, the vertex shader has little to do, since the C++/OpenGL application isn't providing any vertices. All it contains is a uniform declaration, to match the other shaders, and an empty main(). In any case, it is a requirement that all shader programs include a vertex shader.

The Tessellation Control Shader specifies the topology of the triangle mesh that the tessellator is to produce. Six "level" parameters are set—two "inner" and four "outer" levels—by assigning values to the reserved words named gl_TessLevel*xxx*. This is for tessellating a large *rectangular* grid of triangles, called a *quad*.[3] The levels tell the tessellator how to subdivide the grid when forming triangles, and they are arranged as shown in Figure 12.3.

Note the line in the control shader that says:

layout (vertices=1) out;

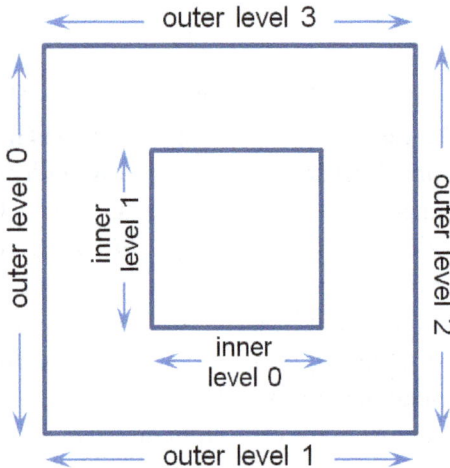

Figure 12.3
Tessellation levels.

This is related to the prior GL_PATCHES discussion and specifies the number of vertices per "patch" being passed from the vertex shader to the control shader (and "out" to the evaluation shader). In this particular program there are none, but we still must specify at least one, because it also affects how many times the control shader executes. Later this value will reflect the number of control points and must match the value in the glPatchParameteri() call in the C++/OpenGL application.

---

[3] The tessellator is also capable of building a *triangular* grid of triangles, but that isn't covered in this textbook.

Next let's look at the Tessellation Evaluation Shader. It starts with a line of code that says:

```
layout (quads, equal_spacing, ccw) in;
```

This may at first appear to be related to the "out" layout statement in the control shader, but actually they are unrelated. Rather, this line is where we instruct the tessellator to generate vertices so they are arranged in a large rectangle (a "quad"). It also specifies the subdivisions (inner and outer) to be of equal length (later we will see a use for subdivisions of unequal length). The "ccw" parameter specifies the winding order in which the tessellated grid vertices are generated (in this case, counter-clockwise).

The vertices generated by the tessellator are then sent to the evaluation shader. Thus, the evaluation shader *may* receive vertices *both* from the control shader (typically as control points) and from the tessellator (the tessellated grid). In Program 12.1, vertices are only received from the tessellator.

The evaluation shader executes once for each vertex produced by the tessellator. The vertex location is accessible using the built-in variable gl_TessCoord. The tessellated grid is oriented such that it lies in the X-Z plane, and therefore gl_TessCoord's X and Y components are applied at the grid's X and Z coordinates. The grid coordinates, and thus the values of gl_TessCoord, range from 0.0 to 1.0 (this will be handy later when computing texture coordinates). The evaluation shader then uses the mvp matrix to orient each vertex (this was done in the vertex shader in examples from earlier chapters).

Finally, the fragment shader simply outputs a constant color yellow for each pixel. We can, of course, also use it to apply a texture or lighting to our scene as we saw in previous chapters.

12.2 TESSELLATION FOR BÉZIER SURFACES

Let's now extend our program so that it turns our simple rectangular grid into a Bézier surface. The tessellated grid should give us plenty of vertices for sampling the surface (and we can increase the inner/outer subdivision levels if we want more). What we now need is to send *control points* through the pipeline, and then use those control points to perform the computations to convert the tessellated grid into the desired Bézier surface.

C++/OpenGL code

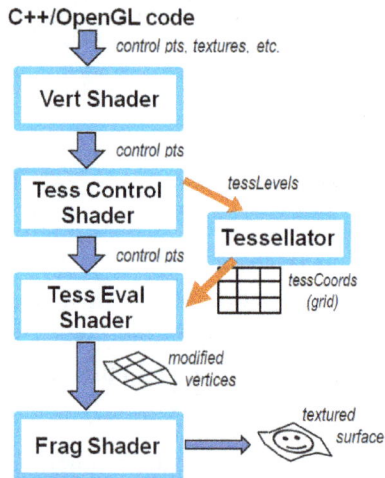

Figure 12.4
Overview of tessellation for Bézier surfaces.

Assuming that we wish to build a *cubic* Bézier surface, we will need sixteen control points. We could send them from the C++ side in a VBO, or we could hardcode them in the vertex shader. Figure 12.4 shows an overview of the process with the control points coming from the C++ side.

Now is a good time to explain a bit more precisely how the tessellation control shader (TCS) works. Similar to the vertex shader, the TCS executes *once per incoming vertex.* Also, recall from Chapter 2 that OpenGL provides a built-in variable called gl_VertexID which holds a counter that indicates which invocation of the vertex shader is currently executing. A similar built-in variable called gl_InvocationID exists for the tessellation control shader.

A powerful feature of tessellation is that the TCS (and also the TES) shader has access to *all* of the control point vertices simultaneously, in arrays. At first, it may seem confusing that the TCS executes once per vertex, when each invocation has access to all of the vertices. It is also counterintuitive that the tessellation levels are specified in assignment statements which are redundantly set at each TCS invocation. Although all of this may seem odd, it is done this way because the tessellation architecture is designed so that TCS invocations can run in parallel.

OpenGL provides several built-in variables for use in the TCS and TES shaders. Ones that we have already mentioned are gl_InvocationID and of course gl_TessLevelInner and gl_TessLevelOuter. Here are some more details and descriptions of some of the most useful built-in variables:

Tessellation Control Shader (TCS) built-in variables:

- **gl_in [ ]** – an array containing each of the incoming control point vertices—one array element per incoming vertex. Particular vertex attributes can be accessed as fields using the "." notation. One built-in attribute is gl_Position—thus, the position of incoming vertex "i" is accessed as gl_in[i].gl_Position.

- **gl_out [ ]** – an array for sending outgoing control point vertices to the TES—one array element per outgoing vertex. Particular vertex attributes can be accessed as fields using the "." notation. One built-in attribute is gl_Position—thus, the position of outgoing vertex "i" is accessed as gl_out[i].gl_Position.

- **gl_InvocationID** – an integer ID counter indicating which invocation of the TCS is currently executing. One common use is for passing through vertex attributes; for example, passing the current invocation's vertex position from the TCS to the TES would be done as follows: gl_out[gl_InvocationID].gl_Position = gl_in[gl_InvocationID].gl_Position;

Tessellation Evaluation Shader (TES) built-in variables:

- **gl_in [ ]** – an array containing each of the incoming control point vertices—one element per incoming vertex. Particular vertex attributes can be accessed as fields using the "." notation. One built-in attribute is gl_Position—thus, incoming vertex positions are accessed as gl_in[*xxx*].gl_Position.

- **gl_Position** – output position of a tessellated grid vertex, possibly modified in the TES. It is important to note that gl_Position and gl_in[*xxx*]. gl_Position are different—gl_Position is the position of an output vertex that originated in the tessellator, while gl_in[*xxx*].gl_Position is a control point vertex position coming into the TES from the TCS.

It is important to note that input and output control point vertices and vertex attributes in the TCS are arrays. By contrast, input control point vertices and vertex attributes in the TES are arrays, but output vertices are scalars. Also, it is easy to become confused as to which vertices are for control points and which are tessellated and then moved to form the resulting surface. To summarize, all vertex inputs and outputs to the TCS are control points, whereas in the TES, gl_in[ ] holds incoming control points, gl_TessCoord holds incoming tessellated grid points, and gl_Position holds output surface vertices for rendering.

Our tessellation control shader now has two tasks: specifying the tessellation levels *and* passing the control points through from the vertex shader to the evaluation shader. The evaluation shader can then modify the locations of the grid points (the gl_TessCoords) based on the Bézier control points.

Program 12.2 shows all four shaders—vertex, TCS, TES, and fragment—for specifying a control point patch, generating a flat tessellated grid of vertices, repositioning those vertices on the curved surface specified by the control points, and painting the resulting surface with a texture image. It also shows the relevant portion of the C++/OpenGL application, specifically in the display() function. In this example, the control points originate in the vertex shader (they are hardcoded there) rather than entering the OpenGL pipeline from the C++/OpenGL application. Additional details follow after the code listing.

Program 12.2 Tessellation for Bézier Surface

Vertex Shader

```
#version 430
out vec2 texCoord;
uniform mat4 mvp_matrix;
layout (binding = 0) uniform sampler2D tex_color;

void main(void)
{   // this time the vertex shader defines and sends out control points:
    const vec4 vertices[ ] =
    vec4[ ] (vec4(-1.0, 0.5, -1.0, 1.0), vec4(-0.5, 0.5, -1.0, 1.0),
             vec4( 0.5, 0.5, -1.0, 1.0), vec4( 1.0, 0.5, -1.0, 1.0),

             vec4(-1.0, 0.0, -0.5, 1.0), vec4(-0.5, 0.0, -0.5, 1.0),
             vec4( 0.5, 0.0, -0.5, 1.0), vec4( 1.0, 0.0, -0.5, 1.0),

             vec4(-1.0, 0.0,  0.5, 1.0), vec4(-0.5, 0.0,  0.5, 1.0),
             vec4( 0.5, 0.0,  0.5, 1.0), vec4( 1.0, 0.0,  0.5, 1.0),

             vec4(-1.0, -0.5,  1.0, 1.0), vec4(-0.5, 0.3,  1.0, 1.0),
             vec4( 0.5, 0.3,  1.0, 1.0), vec4( 1.0, 0.3,  1.0, 1.0) );

    // compute an appropriate texture coordinate for the current vertex, shifted from [-1..+1] to [0..1]
    texCoord = vec2((vertices[gl_VertexID].x + 1.0) / 2.0, (vertices[gl_VertexID].z + 1.0) / 2.0);
    gl_Position = vertices[gl_VertexID];
}
```

Tessellation Control Shader

```
#version 430

in vec2 texCoord[ ];              // The texture coords output from the vertex shader as scalars arrive
out vec2 texCoord_TCSout[ ];   // in an array and are then passed through to the evaluation shader

uniform mat4 mvp_matrix;
layout (binding = 0) uniform sampler2D tex_color;
layout (vertices = 16) out;       // there are 16 control points per patch
```

```
void main(void)
{   int TL = 32;        // tessellation levels are all set to this value
    if (gl_InvocationID == 0)
    {   gl_TessLevelOuter[0] = TL; gl_TessLevelOuter[2] = TL;
        gl_TessLevelOuter[1] = TL; gl_TessLevelOuter[3] = TL;
        gl_TessLevelInner[0] = TL; gl_TessLevelInner[1] = TL;
    }
    // forward the texture and control points to the TES
    texCoord_TCSout[gl_InvocationID] = texCoord[gl_InvocationID];
    gl_out[gl_InvocationID].gl_Position = gl_in[gl_InvocationID].gl_Position;
}
```

Tessellation Evaluation Shader

```
#version 430
layout (quads, equal_spacing,ccw) in;
uniform mat4 mvp_matrix;
layout (binding = 0) uniform sampler2D tex_color;
in vec2 texCoord_TCSout[ ];            // texture coordinate array coming in
out vec2 texCoord_TESout;              // scalars going out one at a time

void main (void)
{   vec3 p00 = (gl_in[0].gl_Position).xyz;
    vec3 p10 = (gl_in[1].gl_Position).xyz;
    vec3 p20 = (gl_in[2].gl_Position).xyz;
    vec3 p30 = (gl_in[3].gl_Position).xyz;
    vec3 p01 = (gl_in[4].gl_Position).xyz;
    vec3 p11 = (gl_in[5].gl_Position).xyz;
    vec3 p21 = (gl_in[6].gl_Position).xyz;
    vec3 p31 = (gl_in[7].gl_Position).xyz;
    vec3 p02 = (gl_in[8].gl_Position).xyz;
    vec3 p12 = (gl_in[9].gl_Position).xyz;
    vec3 p22 = (gl_in[10].gl_Position).xyz;
    vec3 p32 = (gl_in[11].gl_Position).xyz;
    vec3 p03 = (gl_in[12].gl_Position).xyz;
    vec3 p13 = (gl_in[13].gl_Position).xyz;
    vec3 p23 = (gl_in[14].gl_Position).xyz;
    vec3 p33 = (gl_in[15].gl_Position).xyz;

    float u = gl_TessCoord.x;
    float v = gl_TessCoord.y;

    // cubic Bezier basis functions
    float bu0 = (1.0-u) * (1.0-u) * (1.0-u);        // (1-u)^3
    float bu1 = 3.0 * u * (1.0-u) * (1.0-u);        // 3u(1-u)^2
    float bu2 = 3.0 * u * u * (1.0-u);              // 3u^2(1-u)
```

```glsl
float bu3 = u * u * u;                              // u^3
float bv0 = (1.0-v) * (1.0-v) * (1.0-v);            // (1-v)^3
float bv1 = 3.0 * v * (1.0-v) * (1.0-v);            // 3v(1-v)^2
float bv2 = 3.0 * v * v * (1.0-v);                  // 3v^2(1-v)
float bv3 = v * v * v;                              // v^3

// output the position of this vertex in the tessellated patch
vec3 outputPosition =
        bu0 * ( bv0*p00 + bv1*p01 + bv2*p02 + bv3*p03 )
     + bu1 * ( bv0*p10 + bv1*p11 + bv2*p12 + bv3*p13 )
     + bu2 * ( bv0*p20 + bv1*p21 + bv2*p22 + bv3*p23 )
     + bu3 * ( bv0*p30 + bv1*p31 + bv2*p32 + bv3*p33 );
gl_Position = mvp_matrix * vec4(outputPosition,1.0f);

// output the interpolated texture coordinates
vec2 tc1 = mix(texCoord_TCSout[0], texCoord_TCSout[3], gl_TessCoord.x);
vec2 tc2 = mix(texCoord_TCSout[12], texCoord_TCSout[15], gl_TessCoord.x);
vec2 tc = mix(tc2, tc1, gl_TessCoord.y);
texCoord_TESout = tc;
}
```

Fragment Shader

```glsl
#version 430
in vec2 texCoord_TESout;
out vec4 color;
uniform mat4 mvp_matrix;
layout (binding = 0) uniform sampler2D tex_color;

void main(void)
{   color = texture(tex_color, texCoord_TESout);
}
```

C++ / OpenGL application

```cpp
// This time we also pass a texture to paint the surface.
// Load the texture in init() as usual, then enable it in display()
void display(GLFWwindow* window, double currentTime) {

   . . .

   glActiveTexture(GL_TEXTURE0);
   glBindTexture(GL_TEXTURE_2D, textureID);

   glFrontFace(GL_CCW);

   glPatchParameteri(GL_PATCH_VERTICES, 16);       // number of vertices per patch = 16
   glPolygonMode(GL_FRONT_AND_BACK, GL_FILL);
   glDrawArrays(GL_PATCHES, 0, 16);                // total number of patch vertices: 16 x 1 patch = 16
}
```

The vertex shader now specifies sixteen control points (the "patch" vertices) representing a particular Bézier surface. In this example they are all normalized to the range [-1..+1]. The vertex shader also uses the control points to determine texture coordinates appropriate for the tessellated grid, with values in the range [0..1]. It is important to reiterate that the vertices output from the vertex shader are *not* vertices that will be rasterized, but instead are Bézier control points. When using tessellation, patch vertices are *never* rasterized—only tessellated vertices proceed to rasterization.

The control shader still specifies the inner and outer tessellation levels. It now has the additional responsibility of forwarding the control points and texture coordinates to the evaluation shader. Note that the tessellation levels only need to be specified once, and therefore that step is done only during the 0th invocation (recall that the TCS runs once per vertex—thus there are sixteen invocations in this example). For convenience, we have specified thirty-two subdivisions for each tessellation level.

Next, the evaluation shader performs all of the Bézier surface computations. The large block of assignment statements at the beginning of main() extracts the control points from the incoming gl_Position's of each incoming gl_in (note that these correspond to the control shader's gl_out variable). The weights for the blending functions are then computed using the grid points coming in from the tessellator, resulting in a new outputPosition to which the model-view-projection matrix is then applied, producing an output gl_Position for each grid point and forming the Bézier surface.

It is also necessary to create texture coordinates. The vertex shader only provided one for each control point location. But it isn't the control points that are being rendered—we ultimately need texture coordinates for the much larger number of tessellated grid points. There are various ways of doing this—here we linearly interpolate them using GLSL's handy *mix* function. The mix() function expects three parameters: (a) starting point, (b) ending point, and (c) interpolation value, which ranges from 0 to 1. It returns the value between the starting and ending point corresponding to the interpolation value. Since the tessellated grid coordinates also range from 0 to 1, they can be used directly for this purpose.

This time in the fragment shader, rather than outputting a single color, standard texturing is applied. The texture coordinates in the attribute texCoord_TESout are those that were produced in the evaluation shader. The changes to the C++ program are similarly straightforward—note that a patch size of 16 is now specified. The resulting output is shown in Figure 12.5 (a tile texture from [LU16] is applied).

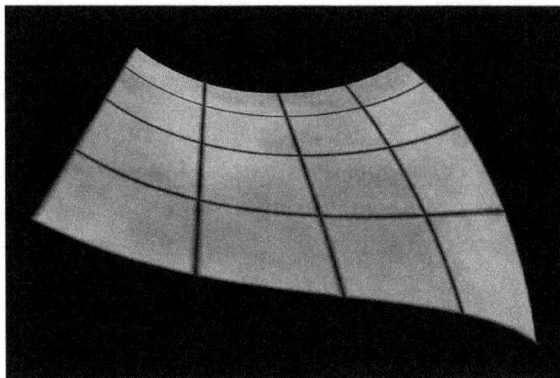

Figure 12.5
Tessellated Bézier surface.

12.3 TESSELLATION FOR TERRAIN / HEIGHT MAPS

Recall that performing height mapping in the vertex shader can suffer from an insufficient number of vertices to render the desired detail. Now that we have a way to generate lots of vertices, let's go back to Hastings-Trew's moon surface texture map (from [HT23]) and use it as a *height map* by raising *tessellated* vertices to produce moon surface detail. As we will see, this has the advantages of achieving vertex geometry that better matches the moon image, along with improved silhouette (edge) detail.

Our strategy is to modify Program 12.1, placing a tessellated grid in the X-Z plane, and use height mapping to set the Y coordinate of each tessellated grid point. To do this a patch isn't needed, because we can hardcode the location of the tessellated grid. So we will specify the required minimum of 1 vertex per patch in glDrawArrays() and glPatchParameteri(), as was done in Program 12.1. Hastings-Trew's moon texture image is used both for color and as the height map.

We generate vertex and texture coordinates in the evaluation shader by mapping the tessellated grid's gl_TessCoord values to appropriate ranges for vertices and textures.[4] The evaluation shader also is where the height mapping is performed, by adding a fraction of the color component of the moon texture to

---

[4] In some applications the texture coordinates are produced externally, such as when tessellation is being used to provide additional vertices for an imported model. In such cases, the provided texture coordinates would need to be interpolated.

the Y component of the output vertex. The changes to the shaders are shown in Program 12.3.

Program 12.3 Simple Tessellated Terrain

Vertex Shader

```
#version 430
uniform mat4 mvp_matrix;
layout (binding = 0) uniform sampler2D tex_color;
void main(void) {}
```

Tessellation Control Shader

```
. . .
layout (vertices = 1) out;        // no control points are necessary for this application

void main(void)
{    int TL=32;
     if (gl_InvocationID == 0)
     {   gl_TessLevelOuter[0] = TL;  gl_TessLevelOuter[2] = TL;
         gl_TessLevelOuter[1] = TL;  gl_TessLevelOuter[3] = TL;
         gl_TessLevelInner[0] = TL;  gl_TessLevelInner[1] = TL;
     }
}
```

Tessellation Evaluation Shader

```
. . .
out vec2 tes_out;
uniform mat4 mvp_matrix;
layout (binding = 0) uniform sampler2D tex_color;

void main (void)
{    // map the tessellated grid vertices from [0..1] onto the desired vertices [-0.5..+0.5]
     vec4 tessellatedPoint = vec4(gl_TessCoord.x - 0.5, 0.0, gl_TessCoord.y - 0.5, 1.0);

     // map the tessellated grid vertices as texture coordinates by "flipping" the Y values vertically.
     // Vertex coordinates have (0,0) at upper left, texture coordinates have (0,0) at the lower left.
     vec2 tc = vec2(gl_TessCoord.x, 1.0 - gl_TessCoord.y);

     // The image is grayscale, so either component (R, G, or B) can serve as height offset.
     tessellatedPoint.y += (texture(tex_color, tc).r) / 40.0;       // Scale down color values.

     // convert the height-map raised point to eye space
     gl_Position = mvp_matrix * tessellatedPoint;
     tes_out = tc;
}
```

Fragment Shader

```
. . .
in vec2 tes_out;
out vec4 color;
layout (binding = 0) uniform sampler2D tex_color;

void main(void)
{   color = texture(tex_color, tes_out);
}
```

The fragment shader is similar to the one for Program 12.2, and simply outputs the color based on the texture image. The C++/OpenGL application is essentially unchanged—it loads the texture (serving as both the texture and height map) and enables a sampler for it. Figure 12.6 shows the texture image (on the left) and the final output of this first attempt, which unfortunately does not yet achieve proper height mapping.

The first results are severely flawed. Although we can now see silhouette detail on the far horizon, the bumps there don't correspond to the actual detail in the texture map. Recall that in a height map, white is supposed to mean "high," and black is supposed to mean "low." The area at the upper right, in particular, shows large hills that bear no relation to the light and dark colors in the image.

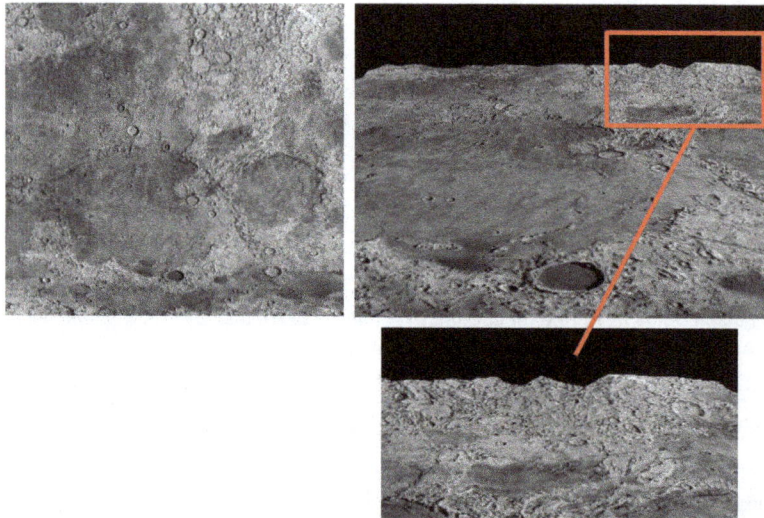

Figure 12.6
Tessellated terrain – failed first attempt, with insufficient number of vertices.

The cause of this problem is the resolution of the tessellated grid. The maximum number of vertices that can be generated by the tessellator is hardware dependent, and a maximum value of at least 64 for each tessellation level is all that is required for compliance with the OpenGL standard. Our program specified a single tessellated grid with inner and outer tessellation levels of 32, so we generated about 32*32, or just over 1000 vertices, which is insufficient to reflect the detail in the image accurately. This is especially apparent along the upper right (enlarged in the figure)—the edge detail is only sampled at 32 points along the horizon, producing large, random-looking hills. Even if we increased the tessellation values to 64, the total of 64*64 or just over 4000 vertices would still be woefully inadequate to do height-mapping using the moon image.

A good way to increase the number of vertices is by using *instancing*, which we saw in Chapter 4. Our strategy will be to have the tessellator generate grids and use instancing to repeat this many times. In the vertex shader we build a patch defined by four vertices, one for each corner of a tessellated grid. In our C++/OpenGL application we change the glDrawArrays() call to glDrawArraysInstanced(). There, we specify a grid of 64 by 64 patches, each of which contains a tessellated mesh with levels of size 32. This will give us a total of 64*64*32*32, or over four million vertices.

The vertex shader starts by specifying four texture coordinates (0,0), (1,0), (0,1), and (1,1). When using instancing, recall that the vertex shader has access to an integer variable gl_InstanceID, which holds a counter corresponding to the glDrawArraysInstanced() call that is currently being processed. We use this ID value to distribute the locations of the individual patches within the larger grid. The patches are positioned in rows and columns, the first patch at location (0,0), the second at (1,0), the next at (2,0), and so on, and the final patch in the first column at (63,0). The next column has patches at (0,1), (1,1), and so forth up to (63,1). The final column has patches at (0,63), (1,63), and so on up to (63,63). The X coordinate for a given patch is the instance ID modulo 64, and the Y coordinate is the instance ID divided by 64 (with integer division). The shader then scales the coordinates back down to the range [0..1].

The control shader is unchanged, except that it passes through the vertices and texture coordinates.

Next, the evaluation shader takes the incoming tessellated grid vertices (specified by gl_TessCoord) and moves them into the coordinate range specified by the incoming patch. It does the same for the texture coordinates. It also applies height mapping in the same way as was done in Program 12.3. The fragment shader is unchanged.

The changes to each of the components are shown in Program 12.4. The result is shown in Figure 12.7. Note that the highs and lows now correspond much more closely to light and dark sections of the image.

Program 12.4 Instanced Tessellated Terrain

C++ / OpenGL application

```
// same as for Bezier surface example, with these changes:
glPatchParameteri(GL_PATCH_VERTICES, 4);
glDrawArraysInstanced(GL_PATCHES, 0, 4, 64*64);
```

Vertex Shader

```
. . .
out vec2 tc;

void main(void)
{   vec2 patchTexCoords[ ] = vec2[ ] (vec2(0,0), vec2(1,0), vec2(0,1), vec2(1,1));

    // compute an offset for coordinates based on which instance this is
    int x = gl_InstanceID % 64;
    int y = gl_InstanceID / 64;

    // tex coords are distributed across 64 patches, normalized to [0..1]. Flip Y coordinates.
    tc = vec2( (x+patchTexCoords[gl_VertexID].x) / 64.0,  (63 - y+patchTexCoords[gl_VertexID].y) / 64.0);

    // vertex locations are the same as texture coordinates, except they range from -0.5 to +0.5.
    gl_Position = vec4(tc.x - 0.5, 0.0, (1.0 - tc.y) - 0.5, 1.0);            // Also un-flip the Y's
}
```

Tessellation Control Shader

```
. . .
layout (vertices = 4) out;
in vec2 tc[ ];
out vec2 tcs_out[ ];

void main(void)
{   // tessellation level specification the same as the previous example
    . . .
    tcs_out[gl_InvocationID] = tc[gl_InvocationID];
    gl_out[gl_InvocationID].gl_Position = gl_in[gl_InvocationID].gl_Position;
}
```

Tessellation Evaluation Shader

```
...
in vec2 tcs_out[ ];
out vec2 tes_out;
void main (void)
{   // map the texture coordinates onto the sub-grid specified by the incoming control points
    vec2 tc = vec2(tcs_out[0].x + (gl_TessCoord.x) / 64.0, tcs_out[0].y + (1.0 - gl_TessCoord.y) / 64.0);

    // map the tessellated grid onto the sub-grid specified by the incoming control points
    vec4 tessellatedPoint = vec4(gl_in[0].gl_Position.x + gl_TessCoord.x / 64.0, 0.0,
                                 gl_in[0].gl_Position.z + gl_TessCoord.y / 64.0, 1.0);

    // add the height from the height map to the vertex:
    tessellatedPoint.y += (texture(tex_height, tc).r) / 40.0;
    gl_Position = mvp_matrix * tessellatedPoint;
    tes_out = tc;
}
```

Now that we have achieved height mapping, we can work on improving it and incorporating lighting. One challenge is that our vertices do not yet have normal vectors associated with them. Another challenge is that simply using the texture image as a height map has produced an overly "jagged" result—in this case because not all grayscale variation in the texture image is due to height. For this particular texture map, it so happens that Hastings-Trew has already produced an improved height map that we can use [HT23]. It is shown in Figure 12.8 (on the left).

To create normals, we could compute them on the fly by generating the heights of neighboring vertices (or neighboring texels in the height map), building vectors connecting them, and using a cross product to find the normal. This requires some tuning, depending on the precision of the scene (and/or the height map image). Here we have instead used the GIMP "normalmap" plugin [GN12] to generate a normal map based on Hastings-Trew's height map, shown in Figure 12.8 (on the right).

Figure 12.7
Tessellated terrain – second attempt, with instancing.

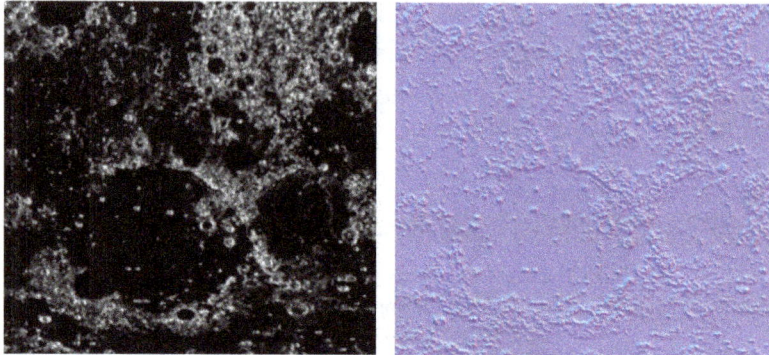

Figure 12.8
Moon surface: height map [HT23] and normal map.

Most of the changes to our code are now simply to implement the standard methods for Phong shading:

- *C++/OpenGL application*

  We load and activate an additional texture to hold the normal map. We also add code to specify the lighting and materials as we have done in previous applications.

- *Vertex shader*

  The only additions are declarations for lighting uniforms and the sampler for the normal map. Lighting code customarily done in the vertex shader is moved to the tessellation evaluation shader, because the vertices aren't generated until the tessellation stage.

- *Tessellation Control shader*

  The only additions are declarations for lighting uniforms and the sampler for the normal map.

- *Tessellation Evaluation shader*

  The preparatory code for Phong lighting is now placed in the evaluation shader:

  ```
  varyingVertPos = (m_matrix * tessellatedPoint).xyz;
  varyingLightDir = light.position - varyingVertPos;
  ```

- *Fragment shader*

  The typical code sections, described previously, for computing Phong (or Blinn-Phong) lighting are done here, as well as the code to extract normals from the normal map. The lighting result is then combined with the texture image with a weighted sum.

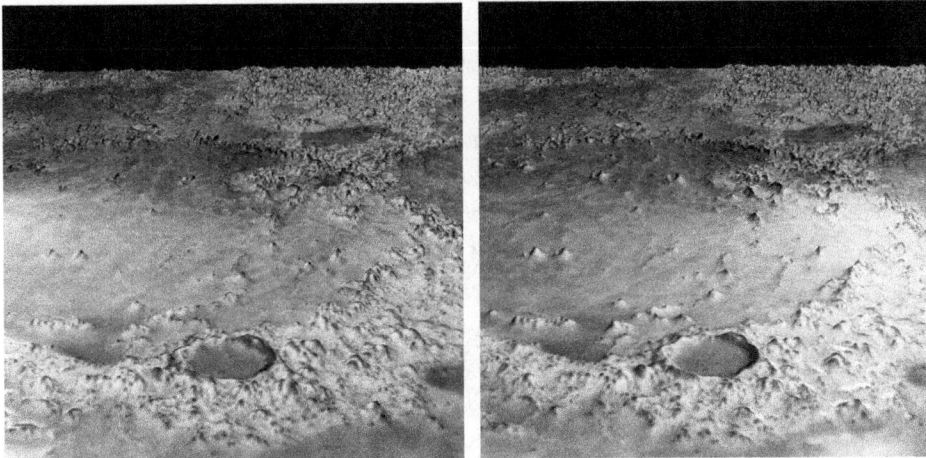

Figure 12.9
Tessellated terrain with normal map and lighting (light source positioned at left and at right respectively).

The final result, with height and normal mapping and Phong lighting, is shown in Figure 12.9. The terrain now responds to lighting. In this example, a positional light has been placed to the left of center in the image on the left, and to the right of center in the image on the right.

Although the response to the movement of the light is difficult to tell from a still picture, the reader should be able to discern the diffuse lighting changes and that specular highlights on the peaks are very different in the two images. This is of course more obvious when the camera or the light source is moving. The results are still imperfect, because the original texture that is incorporated in the output includes shadows that will appear on the rendered result, regardless of lighting.

12.4 CONTROLLING LEVEL OF DETAIL (LOD)

Using instancing to generate millions of vertices in real time, as in Program 12.4, is likely to place a load on even a well-equipped modern computer. Fortunately, the strategy of dividing the terrain into separate patches, as we have done to increase the number of generated grid vertices, also affords us a nice mechanism for reducing that load.

Of the millions of vertices being generated, many aren't necessary. Vertices in patches that are close to the camera *are* important because we expect to discern detail in nearby objects. However, the further the patches are from the camera, the less likely there will even be enough pixels in the rasterization to warrant the number of vertices we are generating!

Changing the number of vertices in a patch based on the distance from the camera is a technique called *level of detail*, or *LOD*. Sellers et al. describe a way of controlling LOD in instanced tessellation [SW15], by modifying the control shader. Program 12.5 shows a simplified version of the approach by Sellers et al. The strategy is to use the patch's perceived size to determine the values of its tessellation levels. Since the tessellated grid for a patch will eventually be placed within the square defined by the four control points entering the control shader, we can use the locations of the control points relative to the camera to determine how many vertices should be generated for the patch. The steps are as follows:

1. Calculate the screen locations of the four control points by applying the MVP matrix to them.
2. Calculate the lengths of the sides of the square (i.e., the width and height) defined by the control points (in screen space). Note that even though the four control points form a square, these side lengths can differ because the perspective matrix has been applied.
3. Scale the lengths' values by a tunable constant, depending on the precision needed for the tessellation levels (based on the amount of detail in the height map).
4. Add 1 to the scaled length values, to avoid the possibility of specifying a tessellation level of 0 (which would result in no vertices being generated).
5. Set the tessellation levels to the corresponding calculated width and height values.

Recall that in our instanced example we are not creating just one grid, but 64*64 of them. So the five steps in the previous list are performed for each patch. Thus, the level of detail varies from patch to patch.

All of the changes are in the control shader and are shown in Program 12.5, with the generated output following in Figure 12.10. Note that the variable gl_InvocationID refers to which vertex in the patch is being processed (not which patch is being processed). Therefore, the LOD computation which tells the tessellator how many vertices to generate occurs during the processing of the 0th vertex in each patch.

Program 12.5 Tessellation Level of Detail (LOD)

Tessellation Control Shader

```
. . .
void main(void)
{   float subdivisions = 16.0;            // tunable constant based on density of detail in height map
    if (gl_InvocationID == 0)
    {   vec4 p0 = mvp * gl_in[0].gl_Position;       // control pt. positions in screen space
        vec4 p1 = mvp * gl_in[1].gl_Position;
        vec4 p2 = mvp * gl_in[2].gl_Position;
        p0 = p0 / p0.w;
        p1 = p1 / p1.w;
        p2 = p2 / p2.w;
        float width = length(p2.xy - p0.xy) * subdivisions + 1.0;    // perceived "width" of tess grid
        float height = length(p1.xy - p0.xy) * subdivisions + 1.0;   // perceived "height" of tess grid
        gl_TessLevelOuter[0] = height;              // set tess levels based on perceived side lengths
        gl_TessLevelOuter[1] = width;
        gl_TessLevelOuter[2] = height;
        gl_TessLevelOuter[3] = width;
        gl_TessLevelInner[0] = width;
        gl_TessLevelInner[1] = height;
    }
    // forward texture coordinates and control points to TES as before
    tcs_out[gl_InvocationID] = tc[gl_InvocationID];
    gl_out[gl_InvocationID].gl_Position = gl_in[gl_InvocationID].gl_Position;
}
```

Applying these control shader changes to the instanced (but not lighted) version of our scene from Figure 12.7, and replacing the height map with Hastings-Trew's more finely tuned version shown in Figure 12.8 produces the improved scene, with more realistic horizon detail, shown in Figure 12.10.

In this example it is also useful to change the layout specifier in the evaluation shader from:

layout (quads, equal_spacing, ccw) in

Figure 12.10
Tessellated moon with controlled level of detail (LOD).

to:

layout (quads, fractional_even_spacing, ccw) in

The reason for this modification is difficult to illustrate in still images. In an animated scene, as a tessellated object moves through 3D space, if LOD is used it is sometimes possible to *see* the changes in tessellation levels on the surface of the object as wiggling artifacts called "popping." Changing from *equal spacing* to *fractional spacing* reduces this effect by making the grid geometry of adjacent patch instances more similar, even if they differ in level of detail. (See Exercises 12.2 and 12.3.)

Employing LOD can dramatically reduce the load on the system. For example, when animated, the scene might be less likely to appear jerky or to lag than could be the case without controlling LOD.

Applying this simple LOD technique to the version that includes Phong shading (i.e., Program 12.4) is a bit trickier. This is because the changes in LOD between adjacent patch instances can in turn cause sudden changes to the associated normal vectors, causing popping artifacts in the lighting! As always, there are tradeoffs and compromises to consider when constructing a complex 3D scene.

SUPPLEMENTAL NOTES

Combining tessellation with LOD is particularly useful in real-time virtual reality applications that require both complex detail for realism and frequent object movement and/or changes in camera position, such as in computer games. In this chapter we have illustrated the use of tessellation and LOD for real-time terrain generation, although it can also be applied in other areas such as in displacement mapping for 3D models (where tessellated vertices are added to the surface of a model and then moved so as to add detail). It is also useful in computer-aided-design applications.

Sellers et al. extends the LOD technique (shown in Program 12.5) further than we have presented, by also eliminating vertices in patches that are *behind the camera* (they do this by setting their inner and outer levels to zero) [SW15]. This is an example of a *culling* technique, and it is a very useful one because of the load that instanced tessellation can still place on the system.

The four-parameter version of createShaderProgram() used in Program 12.1 is added to the Utils.cpp file. Later, we will add additional versions to accommodate the geometry shader stage.

Exercises

12.1 Modify Program 12.1 to experiment with various values for inner and outer tessellation levels, and observe the resulting rendered mesh.

12.2 Test Program 12.5 with the layout specifier in the evaluation shader set to equal_spacing, and then to fractional_even_spacing, as described in Section 12.4. Observe the effects on the rendered surface as the camera moves. You should be able to observe popping artifacts in the first case, which are mostly alleviated in the second case.

12.3 *(PROJECT)* Modify Program 12.4 to utilize a height map of your own design (you could use the one you built previously in Exercise 10.2). Then add lighting and shadow-mapping so that your tessellated terrain casts shadows. This is a complex exercise, because some of the code in the first and second shadow-mapping passes will need to be moved to the evaluation shader.

References

[GN12] GIMP Plugin Registry, *normalmap plugin*, accessed November 2023, https://code.google.com/archive/p/gimp-normalmap

[HT23] J. Hastings-Trew, *JHT's Planetary Pixel Emporium*, accessed November 2023, http://planetpixelemporium.com/

[LU16] F. Luna, *Introduction to 3D Game Programming with DirectX 12*, 2nd ed. (Mercury Learning, 2016).

[SW15] G. Sellers, R. Wright Jr., and N. Haemel, *OpenGL SuperBible: Comprehensive Tutorial and Reference*, 7th ed. (Addison-Wesley, 2015).

[TS23] Tessellation, Wikipedia, accessed November 2023, https://en.wikipedia.org/wiki/Tessellation

CHAPTER **13**

GEOMETRY SHADERS

Immediately following tessellation in the OpenGL pipeline is the *geometry* stage. Here, the programmer has the option of including a *geometry shader*. This stage actually pre-dates tessellation; it became part of the OpenGL core at version 3.2 (in 2009).

Like tessellation, geometry shaders enable the programmer to manipulate *groups* of vertices, in ways that are impossible to do in a vertex shader. In some cases, a task might be accomplished using either a tessellation shader or a geometry shader, as their capabilities overlap in some ways.

13.1 PER-PRIMITIVE PROCESSING IN OPENGL

The geometry shader stage is situated between tessellation and rasterization, within the segment of the pipeline devoted to *primitive processing* (refer back to Figure 2.2). Whereas vertex shaders enable the manipulation of one vertex at a time, and fragment shaders enable the manipulation of one fragment (essentially one pixel) at a time, *geometry shaders enable manipulation of one <u>primitive</u> at a time*.

Recall that primitives are the basic building blocks in OpenGL for drawing objects. Only a few types of primitives are available; we will focus primarily on geometry shaders that manipulate triangles. Thus, when we say that a geometry shader can manipulate one primitive at a time, we usually mean that the shader has access to *all three vertices of a triangle* at a time. Geometry shaders allow you to:

- access all vertices in a primitive at once, then
- output the same primitive unchanged, or
- output the same primitive with modified vertex locations, or
- output a different type of primitive, or
- output additional primitives, or
- delete the primitive (not output it at all).

Similar to the tessellation evaluation shader, incoming vertex attributes are accessible in a geometry shader as *arrays*. However, in a geometry shader, incoming attribute arrays are indexed only up to the primitive size. For example, if the primitives are triangles, then the available indices are 0, 1, and 2. Accessing the vertices themselves is done using the predefined array gl_in, as follows:

gl_in[2].gl_Position   *// position of the 3rd vertex*

Also similar to the tessellation evaluation shader, the geometry shader's output vertex attributes are all *scalars*. That is, the output is a stream of individual vertices (their positions and other attribute variables, if any) that form primitives.

There is a layout qualifier used to set the primitive input/output types and the output size.

The special GLSL command EmitVertex() specifies that a vertex is to be output. The special GLSL command EndPrimitive() indicates the completion of building a particular primitive.

The built-in variable gl_PrimitiveIDIn is available and holds the ID of the current primitive. The ID numbers start at 0 and count up to the number of primitives minus 1.

We will explore four common categories of operations:

- altering primitives
- deleting primitives
- adding primitives
- changing primitive types

13.2 ALTERING PRIMITIVES

Geometry shaders are convenient for changing the shape of an object when that change can be effected through isolated changes to the primitives (typically triangles).

Consider, for example, the torus we rendered previously in Figure 7.12. Suppose that torus represented an inner tube (such as for a tire), and we want to "inflate" it. Simply applying a scale factor in the C++/OpenGL code won't accomplish this, because its fundamental shape wouldn't change. Giving it the appearance of being "inflated" requires also making the inner hole smaller as the torus stretches into the empty center space.

One way of doing this would be to add the surface normal vector to each vertex. While it is true that this could be done in the vertex shader, let's do it in the geometry shader, for practice. Program 13.1 shows the GLSL geometry shader code. The other modules are the same as for Program 7.3, with a few minor changes: the fragment shader input names now need to reflect the geometry shader outputs (for example, varyingNormal becomes varyingNormalG), and the C++/OpenGL application needs to compile the geometry shader and attach it to the shader program prior to linking. The new shader is specified as being a geometry shader as follows:

```
GLuint gShader = glCreateShader(GL_GEOMETRY_SHADER);
```

Program 13.1 Geometry Shader: Altering Vertices

```
#version 430

layout (triangles) in;

in vec3 varyingNormal[ ];            // inputs from the vertex shader
in vec3 varyingLightDir[ ];
in vec3 varyingHalfVector[ ];

out vec3 varyingNormalG;             // outputs through the rasterizer to the fragment shader
out vec3 varyingLightDirG;
out vec3 varyingHalfVectorG;

layout (triangle_strip, max_vertices=3) out;

// matrices and lighting uniforms same as before
. . .
void main (void)
{   // move vertices along the normal, and pass through the other vertex attributes unchanged
```

```
for (int i=0; i<3; i++)
{   gl_Position = p_matrix * v_matrix *
        gl_in[i].gl_Position + normalize(vec4(varyingNormal[i],1.0)) * 0.4;
    varyingNormalG = varyingNormal[i];
    varyingLightDirG = varyingLightDir[i];
    varyingHalfVectorG = varyingHalfVector[i];
    EmitVertex();
}
EndPrimitive();
}
```

Note in Program 13.1 that the input variables corresponding to the output variables from the vertex shader are declared as *arrays*. This provides the programmer a mechanism for accessing each of the vertices in the triangle primitive and their attributes using the indices 0, 1, and 2. We wish to move those vertices outward along their surface normals. Both the vertices and the normals have already been transformed to world space in the vertex shader. We add a fraction of the normal to each of the incoming vertex positions (gl_in[i].gl_Position) and then apply the projection matrix to the result, producing each output gl_Position.

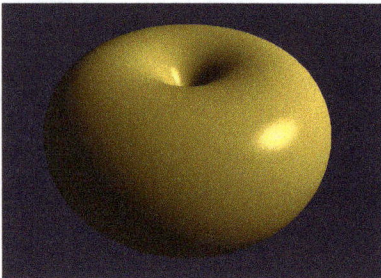

Figure 13.1
"Inflated" torus with vertices altered by geometry shader.

Note the use of the GLSL call EmitVertex() that specifies when we have finished computing the output gl_Position and its associated vertex attributes and are ready to output a vertex. The EndPrimitive() call specifies that we have completed the definition of a set of vertices comprising a primitive (in this case, a triangle). The result is shown in Figure 13.1.

The geometry shader includes two layout qualifiers. The first specifies the input primitive type and must be compatible with the primitive type in the C++-side glDrawArrays() or glDrawElements() call. The options are as follows:

geometry shader input primitive	compatible OpenGL primitives sent from glDrawArrays()	#vertices per invocation
points	GL_POINTS	1
lines	GL_LINES, GL_LINE_STRIP, GL_LINE_LOOP	2

lines_adjacency	GL_LINES_ADJACENCY, GL_LINE_STRIP_ ADJACENCY	4
triangles	GL_TRIANGLES, GL_TRIANGLE_STRIP, GL_TRIANGLE_FAN	3
triangles_adjacency	GL_TRIANGLES_ADJACENCY, GL_TRIANGLE_ STRIP_ADJACENCY	6

The various OpenGL primitive types (including "strip" and "fan" types) were described in Chapter 4. "Adjacency" types were introduced in OpenGL for use with geometry shaders, and they allow access to vertices adjacent to the primitive. We don't use them in this book, but they are listed for completeness.

The output primitive type must be *points*, *line_strip*, or *triangle_strip*. Note that the output layout qualifier also specifies the maximum number of vertices the shader outputs in each invocation.

This particular alteration to the torus could have been done more easily in the vertex shader. However, suppose that instead of moving each vertex outward along its own surface normal, we wished instead to move each *triangle* outward along its surface normal, in effect "exploding" the torus triangles outward. The vertex shader cannot do that, because computing a normal for the triangle requires averaging the vertex normals of all three triangle vertices, and the vertex shader only has access to the vertex attributes of one vertex in the triangle at a time. We can, however, do this in the geometry shader, because the geometry shader *does* have access to all three vertices in each triangle. We average their normals to compute a surface normal for the triangle, then add that averaged normal to each of the vertices in the triangle primitive. Figures 13.2, 13.3, and 13.4 show the averaging of the surface normals, the modified geometry shader main() code, and the resulting output respectively.

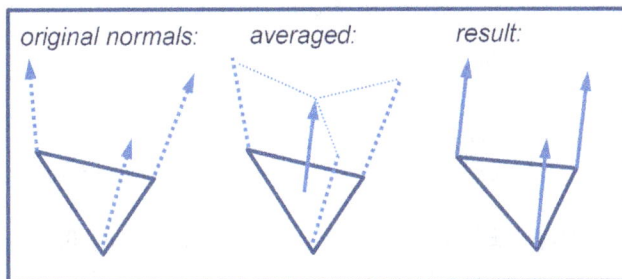

Figure 13.2
Applying averaged triangle surface normal to triangle vertices.

```
void main (void)
{ // average the three triangle vertex normals, creating a single triangle surface normal
  vec4 triangleNormal =
     vec4(((varyingNormal[0] + varyingNormal[1] + varyingNormal[2]) / 3.0),1.0);

  // move all three vertices outward along the same normal
  for (i=0; i<3; i++)
  {  gl_Position = p_matrix * v_matrix * (gl_in[i].gl_Position + normalize(triangleNormal) * 0.4);
     varyingNormalG = varyingNormal[i];
     varyingLightDirG = varyingLightDir[i];
     varyingHalfVectorG = varyingHalfVector[i];
     EmitVertex();
  }
  EndPrimitive();
}
```

Figure 13.3
Modified geometry shader for "exploding" the torus.

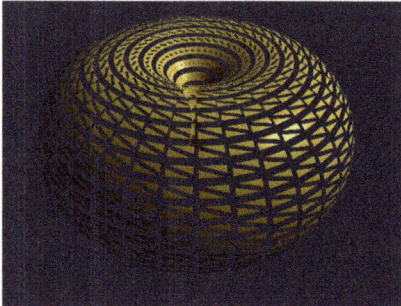

Figure 13.4
"Exploded" torus.

The appearance of the "exploded" torus can be improved by ensuring that the inside of the torus is also visible (normally those triangles are culled by OpenGL because they are "back-facing"). One way of doing this is to render the torus twice, once in the normal manner and once with winding order reversed (reversing the winding order effectively switches which faces are front-facing and which are back-facing). We also send a flag to the shaders (in a uniform) to disable diffuse and specular lighting on the back-facing triangles to make them less prominent. The changes to the code are as follows.

changes to display() function:

```
. . .
// draw front-facing triangles – enable lighting
glUniform1i(lLoc, 1);        // location of uniform for enabling/disabling diffuse/specular light component
glFrontFace(GL_CCW);
glDrawElements(GL_TRIANGLES, numTorusIndices, GL_UNSIGNED_INT, 0);

// draw back-facing triangles – disable lighting
glUniform1i(lLoc, 0);
glFrontFace(GL_CW);
glDrawElements(GL_TRIANGLES, numTorusIndices, GL_UNSIGNED_INT, 0);
```

modification to fragment shader:

```
. . .
if (enableLighting == 1)
{   fragColor = ...       // when rendering front faces, use normal lighting computations
}
else                      // when rendering back faces, enable only the ambient lighting component
{   fragColor = globalAmbient * material.ambient +  light.ambient * material.ambient;
}
```

The resulting "exploded" torus, including back faces, is shown in Figure 13.5.

Figure 13.5
"Exploded" torus including back faces.

13.3 DELETING PRIMITIVES

A common use for geometry shaders is to build richly ornamental objects out of simple ones, by judiciously deleting some of the primitives. For example, removing some of the triangles from our torus can turn it into a sort of complex latticed structure that would be more difficult to model from scratch. A geometry shader that does this is shown in Program 13.2, and the output is shown in Figure 13.6.

Program 13.2 Geometry: Delete Primitives

```
// inputs, outputs, and uniforms as before
. . .
void main (void)
{   if ( mod(gl_PrimitiveIDIn,3) != 0 )
    {   for (int i=0; i<3; i++)
        {   gl_Position = p_matrix * v_matrix * gl_in[i].gl_Position;
            varyingNormalG = varyingNormal[i];
            varyingLightDirG = varyingLightDir[i];
            varyingHalfVectorG = varyingHalfVector[i];
            EmitVertex();
    }   }
    EndPrimitive();
}
```

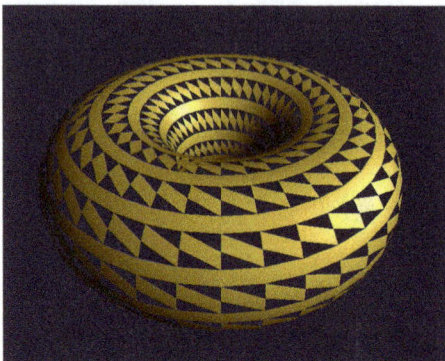

Figure 13.6
Geometry shader: primitive deletion.

Figure 13.7
Primitive deletion showing back faces.

No other changes to the code are necessary. Note the use of the mod function— all vertices are passed through except those in the first of every three primitives, which is ignored. Here too, rendering the back-facing triangles can improve realism, as shown in Figure 13.7.

13.4 ADDING PRIMITIVES

Perhaps the most interesting and powerful use of geometry shaders is for adding additional vertices and/or primitives to a model being rendered. This makes it possible to do such things as increase the detail in an object to improve height mapping, or to change the shape of an object completely.

Consider the following example, where we change each triangle in the torus to a tiny triangular pyramid.

Our strategy, similar to our previous "exploded" torus example, is illustrated in Figure 13.8. The vertices of an incoming triangle primitive are used to define the base of a pyramid. The walls of the pyramid are constructed of those vertices and of a new point (called the "spike point") computed by averaging the normals of the original vertices. New normal vectors are then computed for each of the three "sides" of the pyramid by taking the cross product of two vectors from the spike point to the base.

The geometry shader in Program 13.3 does this for each triangle primitive in the torus. For each incoming triangle, it outputs three triangle primitives, for a total of nine vertices. Each new triangle is built in the function makeNewTriangle(), which

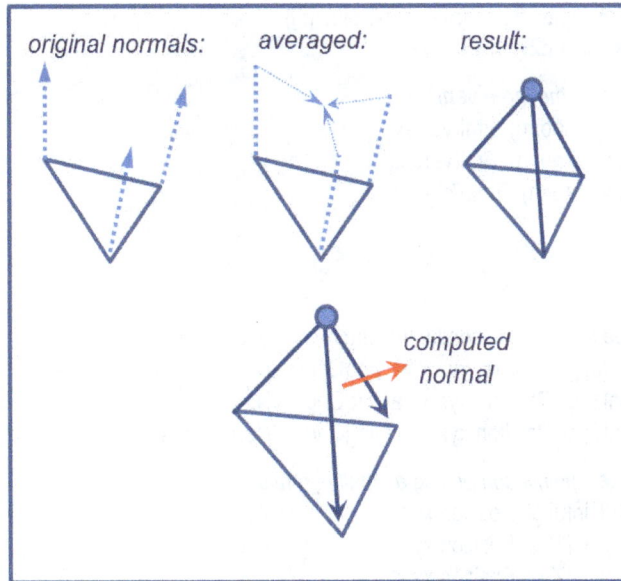

Figure 13.8
Converting triangles to pyramids.

is called three times. It computes the normal for the specified triangle, then calls the function setOutputValues() to assign the appropriate output vertex attributes for each vertex emitted. After emitting all three vertices, it calls EndPrimitive(). To ensure that the lighting is performed accurately, new values of the light direction vector are computed for each newly created vertex.

Program 13.3 Geometry: Add Primitives

```
. . .
vec3 newPoints[9], lightDir[9];
float sLen = 0.01;   // sLen is the "spike length", the height of the small pyramid

void setOutputValues(int p, vec3 norm)
{   varyingNormal = norm;
    varyingLightDir = lightDir[p];
    varyingVertPos = newPoints[p];
    gl_Position = p_matrix * v_matrix * vec4(newPoints[p], 1.0);
}

void makeNewTriangle(int p1, int p2)
{   // generate surface normal for this triangle
    vec3 c1 = normalize(newPoints[p1] - newPoints[3]);
```

```
    vec3 c2 = normalize(newPoints[p2] - newPoints[3]);
    vec3 norm = cross(c1,c2);

    // generate and emit the three vertices
    setOutputValues(p1, norm); EmitVertex();
    setOutputValues(p2, norm); EmitVertex();
    setOutputValues(3, norm); EmitVertex();
    EndPrimitive();
}

void main(void)
{   // offset the three triangle vertices by the original surface normal
    vec3 sp0 = gl_in[0].gl_Position.xyz + varyingOriginalNormal[0]*sLen;
    vec3 sp1 = gl_in[1].gl_Position.xyz + varyingOriginalNormal[1]*sLen;
    vec3 sp2 = gl_in[2].gl_Position.xyz + varyingOriginalNormal[2]*sLen;

    // compute the new points comprising a small pyramid
    newPoints[0] = gl_in[0].gl_Position.xyz;
    newPoints[1] = gl_in[1].gl_Position.xyz;
    newPoints[2] = gl_in[2].gl_Position.xyz;
    newPoints[3] = (sp0 + sp1 + sp2)/3.0;          // spike point

    // compute the directions from the vertices to the light
    lightDir[0] = light.position - newPoints[0];
    lightDir[1] = light.position - newPoints[1];
    lightDir[2] = light.position - newPoints[2];
    lightDir[3] = light.position - newPoints[3];

    // build three new triangles to form a small pyramid on the surface
    makeNewTriangle(0,1);  // the third point is always the spike point
    makeNewTriangle(1,2);
    makeNewTriangle(2,0);
}
```

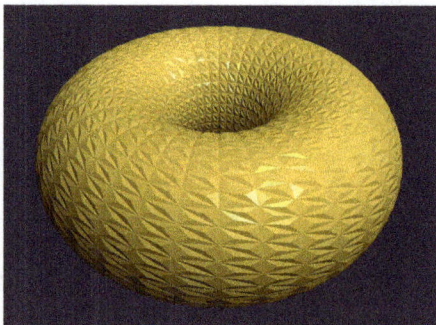

Figure 13.9
Geometry shader: primitive addition.

The resulting output is shown in Figure 13.9. If the spike length (sLen) variable is increased, the added surface "pyramids" would be taller. However, they could appear unrealistic in the absence of shadows. Adding shadow-mapping to Program 13.3 is left as an exercise for the reader.

Careful application of this technique can enable the simulation of spikes, thorns, and other fine surface protrusions, as well as the reverse, such as indentations and craters ([DV23], [KS16]).

13.5 CHANGING PRIMITIVE TYPES

OpenGL allows for switching primitive types in a geometry shader. A common use for this feature is to convert input *triangles* into one or more output *line segments*, simulating fur or hair. Although hair remains one of the more difficult real-world items to generate convincingly, geometry shaders can help make real-time rendering achievable in many cases.

Program 13.4 shows a geometry shader that converts each incoming three-vertex triangle to an outward-facing two-vertex line segment. It starts by computing a starting point for the strand of hair by averaging the triangle vertex locations, thus generating the centroid of the triangle. It then uses the same "spike point" from Program 13.3 as the hair's ending point. The output primitive is specified as a line strip

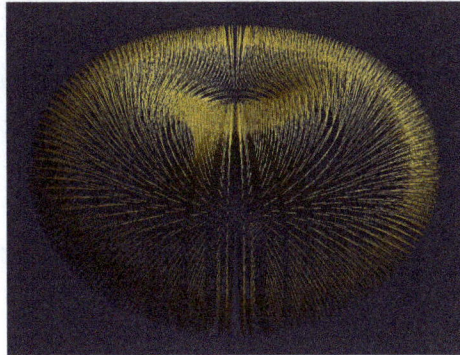

Figure 13.10
Changing triangle primitives to line primitives.

with two vertices, the first vertex being the start point, and the second vertex being the end point. The result is shown in Figure 13.10, for a torus instantiated with a dimensionality of seventy-two slices.

Of course, this is merely the starting point for generating fully realistic hair. Making the hair bend or move would require several modifications, such as generating more vertices for the line strip and computing their positions along curves and/or incorporating randomness. Lighting is complicated by the lack of an obvious surface normal for a line segment; in this example, we simply assigned the normal to be the same as the original triangle's surface normal.

Program 13.4 Geometry: Changing Primitive Types

```
layout (line_strip, max_vertices=2) out;
...
void main(void)
```

```
{   vec3 op0 = gl_in[0].gl_Position.xyz;                              // original triangle vertices
    vec3 op1 = gl_in[1].gl_Position.xyz;
    vec3 op2 = gl_in[2].gl_Position.xyz;
    vec3 ep0 = gl_in[0].gl_Position.xyz + varyingNormal[0]*sLen;      // offset triangle vertices
    vec3 ep1 = gl_in[1].gl_Position.xyz + varyingNormal[1]*sLen;
    vec3 ep2 = gl_in[2].gl_Position.xyz + varyingNormal[2]*sLen;

    // compute the new points comprising a small line segment
    vec3 newPoint1 = (op0 + op1 + op2)/3.0;                           // original (start) point
    vec3 newPoint2 = (ep0 + ep1 + ep2)/3.0;                           // end point

    gl_Position = p_matrix * v_matrix * vec4(newPoint1, 1.0);
    varyingVertPosG = newPoint1;
    varyingLightDirG = light.position - newPoint1;
    varyingNormalG = varyingNormal[0];
    EmitVertex();

    gl_Position = p_matrix * v_matrix * vec4(newPoint2, 1.0);
    varyingVertPosG = newPoint2;
    varyingLightDirG = light.position - newPoint2;
    varyingNormalG = varyingNormal[1];
    EmitVertex();

    EndPrimitive();
}
```

SUPPLEMENTAL NOTES

One of the appeals of geometry shaders is that they are relatively easy to use. Although many applications for which geometry shaders are used *could* be achieved using tessellation, the mechanism of geometry shaders often makes them easier to implement and debug. Of course, the relative fit of geometry versus tessellation depends on the particular application.

Generating convincing hair or fur is challenging, and there is a wide range of techniques employed depending on the application. In some cases, simple texturing is adequate, and/or the use of tessellation or geometry shaders such as the basic technique shown in this chapter. When greater realism is required, movement (animation) and lighting become tricky. One dedicated tool for hair and fur generation is *TressFX*, which was developed by AMD [TR23] for DirectX. An OpenGL port of TressFX is available [GO21]. Examples of using TressFX can be found in [GP14].

Exercises

13.1 Modify Program 13.1 so that it moves each vertex slightly toward the center of its primitive triangle. The result should look similar to the exploded torus in Figure 13.5, but without the overall change in torus size.

13.2 Modify Program 13.2 so that it deletes every other primitive, or every fourth primitive (rather than every third primitive), and observe the effect on the resulting rendered torus. Also, try changing the dimensionality of the instantiated torus to a value that is *not* a multiple of three (such as 40), while still deleting every third primitive. There are many possible effects.

13.3 *(PROJECT)* Modify Program 13.4 to additionally render the original torus. That is, render *both* a lighted torus (as previously done in Chapter 7) *and* the outgoing line segments (using a geometry shader) so that the "hair" looks like it is coming out of the torus.

13.4 *(RESEARCH & PROJECT)* Modify Program 13.4 so that it produces outward-facing line segments with *more than two* vertices, arranged so as to make the line segments appear to bend slightly.

References

[DV20] J. deVries, *LearnOpenGL* (Kendall and Welling, 2020), accessed November 2023, http://www.learnopengl.com/

[GP14] GPU Pro 5: Advanced Rendering Techniques, ed. W. Engel (CRC Press, 2014).

[GO21] TressFX OpenGL, accessed November 2023, https://github.com/Scthe/TressFX-OpenGL

[KS16] J. Kessenich, G. Sellers, and D. Shreiner, *OpenGL Programming Guide: The Official Guide to Learning OpenGL, Version 4.5 with SPIR-V*, 9th ed. (Addison-Wesley, 2016).

[TR23] TressFX Hair, AMD, 2018, accessed November 2023, https://gpuopen.com/tressfx/

CHAPTER 14

OTHER TECHNIQUES

In this chapter, we explore a variety of techniques utilizing the tools we have learned throughout the book. Some we will develop fully, while for others we will offer a more cursory description. Graphics programming is a huge field, and this chapter is by no means comprehensive, but rather an introduction to just a few of the creative effects that have been developed over the years.

14.1 FOG

Usually when people think of fog, they think of early misty mornings with low visibility. In truth, atmospheric haze (such as fog) is more common than most of us think. The majority of the time, there is some degree of haze in the air, and although we have become accustomed to seeing it, we don't usually realize it is there. So we can enhance the realism in our outdoor scenes by introducing fog—even if only a small amount.

Fog also can enhance the sense of depth. When close objects have better *clarity* than distant objects, it is one more visual cue that our brains can use to decipher the topography of a 3D scene.

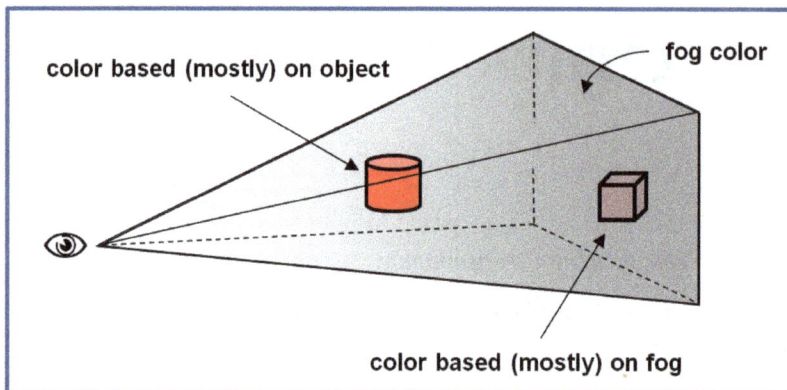

Figure 14.1
Fog: blending based on distance.

There are a variety of methods for simulating fog, from very simple ones to sophisticated models that include light scattering effects. However, even very simple approaches can be effective. One such method is to blend the actual pixel color with another color (the "fog" color, typically gray or bluish-gray—also used for the background color), based on the distance the object is from the eye.

Figure 14.1 illustrates the concept. The eye (camera) is shown at the left, and two red objects are placed in the view frustum. The cylinder is closer to the eye, so it is mostly its original color (red); the cube is further from the eye, so it is mostly fog color. For this simple implementation, virtually all of the computations can be performed in the fragment shader.

Program 14.1 shows the relevant code for a very simple fog algorithm that uses a linear blend from object color to fog color based on the distance from the camera to the pixel. Specifically, this example adds fog to the height mapping example from Program 10.4.

Program 14.1 Simple Fog Generation

Vertex shader

```
. . .
out vec3 vertEyeSpacePos;
. . .
// Compute vertex position in eye space, without perspective, and send it to the fragment shader.
// The variable "p" is the height-mapped vertex, as described earlier in Program 10.4.
vertEyeSpacePos = (mv_matrix * p).xyz;
```

Fragment shader

```
. . .
in vec3 vertEyeSpacePos;
out vec4 fragColor;
. . .
void main(void)
{   vec4 fogColor = vec4(0.7, 0.8, 0.9, 1.0);   // bluish gray
    float fogStart = 0.2;
    float fogEnd = 0.8;

    // the distance from the camera to the vertex in eye space is simply the length of a
    // vector to that vertex, because the camera is at (0,0,0) in eye space.
    float dist = length(vertEyeSpace.xyz);
    float fogFactor = clamp(((fogEnd - dist) / (fogEnd - fogStart)), 0.0, 1.0);
    fragColor = mix(fogColor, (texture(t,tc), fogFactor);
}
```

The variable fogColor specifies a color for the fog. The variables fogStart and fogEnd specify the range (in eye space) over which the output color transitions from object color to fog color, and can be tuned to meet the needs of the scene. The percentage of fog mixed with the object color is calculated in the variable fogFactor, which is the ratio of how close the vertex is to fogEnd to the total length of the transition region. The GLSL clamp() function is used to restrict this ratio to being between the values 0.0 and 1.0. The GLSL mix() function then returns a weighted average of fog color and object color, based on the value of fogFactor. Figure 14.2 shows the addition of fog to a scene with height mapped terrain. (A rocky texture from [LU16] has also been applied.)

Figure 14.2
Fog example.

14.2 COMPOSITING / BLENDING / TRANSPARENCY

We have already seen a few examples of blending—in the supplementary notes for Chapter 7, and just previously in our implementation of fog. However, we haven't yet seen how to utilize the blending (or *compositing*) capabilities that follow after the fragment shader during pixel operations (recall the pipeline sequence shown in Figure 2.2). It is there that *transparency* is handled, which we look at now.

Throughout this book we have made frequent use of the vec4 data type, to represent 3D points and vectors in a homogeneous coordinate system. You may have noticed that we also frequently use a vec4 to store *color* information, where the first three values consist of red, green, and blue, and the fourth element is—what?

The fourth element in a color is called the *alpha channel*, and specifies the *opacity* of the color. Opacity is a measure of how *non*-transparent the pixel color is. An alpha value of 0 means "no opacity," or completely transparent. An alpha value of 1 means "fully opaque," not at all transparent. In a sense, the "transparency" of a color is $1-\alpha$, where α is the value of the alpha channel.

Recall from Chapter 2 that pixel operations utilize the *Z-buffer*, which achieves hidden surface removal by replacing an existing pixel color when another object's location at that pixel is found to be closer. We actually have more control over this process—we may choose to *blend* the two pixels.

When a pixel is being rendered, it is called the "source" pixel. The pixel already in the frame buffer (presumably rendered from a previous object) is called the "destination" pixel. OpenGL provides many options for deciding which of the two pixels, or what sort of combination of them, ultimately is placed in the frame buffer. Note that the pixel operations step is not a programmable stage—so the OpenGL tools for configuring the desired compositing are found in the C++ application, rather than in a shader.

The two OpenGL functions for controlling compositing are glBlendEquation(mode) and glBlendFunc(srcFactor, destFactor). Figure 14.3 shows an overview of the compositing process.

The compositing process works as follows:

1. The *source* and *destination* pixels are multiplied by *source factor* and *destination factor* respectively. The source and destination factors are specified in the glBlendFunc() call.

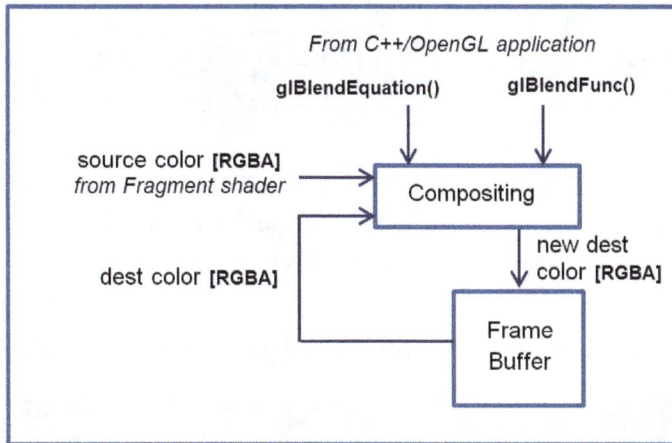

Figure 14.3
OpenGL compositing overview.

2. The specified *blendEquation* is then used to combine the modified source and destination pixels to produce a new destination color. The blend equation is specified in the glBlendEquation() call.

The most common options for glBlendFunc() parameters (i.e., srcFactor and destFactor) are shown in the following table:

glBlendFunc() parameter	resulting srcFactor or destFactor
GL_ZERO	$(0,0,0,0)$
GL_ONE	$(1,1,1,1)$
GL_SRC_COLOR	$(R_{src}, G_{src}, B_{src}, A_{src})$
GL_ONE_MINUS_SRC_COLOR	$(1,1,1,1) - (R_{src}, G_{src}, B_{src}, A_{src})$
GL_DST_COLOR	$(R_{dest}, G_{dest}, B_{dest}, A_{dest})$
GL_ONE_MINUS_DST_COLOR	$(1,1,1,1) - (R_{dest}, G_{dest}, B_{dest}, A_{dest})$
GL_SRC_ALPHA	$(A_{src}, A_{src}, A_{src}, A_{src})$
GL_ONE_MINUS_SRC_ALPHA	$(1,1,1,1) - (A_{src}, A_{src}, A_{src}, A_{src})$
GL_DST_ALPHA	$(A_{dest}, A_{dest}, A_{dest}, A_{dest})$
GL_ONE_MINUS_DST_ALPHA	$(1,1,1,1) - (A_{dest}, A_{dest}, A_{dest}, A_{dest})$
GL_CONSTANT_COLOR	$(R_{blendColor}, G_{blendColor}, B_{blendColor}, A_{blendColor})$
GL_ONE_MINUS_CONSTANT_ COLOR	$(1,1,1,1) - (R_{blendColor}, G_{blendColor}, B_{blendColor}, A_{blendColor})$

GL_CONSTANT_ALPHA	$(A_{blendColor}, A_{blendColor}, A_{blendColor}, A_{blendColor})$
GL_ONE_MINUS_CONSTANT_ALPHA	$(1,1,1,1) - (A_{blendColor}, A_{blendColor}, A_{blendColor}, A_{blendColor})$
GL_ALPHA_SATURATE	$(f, f, f, 1)$ where $f = \min(A_{src}, 1)$

Those options that indicate a "blendColor" (GL_CONSTANT_COLOR, etc.) require an additional call to glBlendColor() to specify a constant color that will be used to compute the blend function result. There are a few additional blend functions that aren't shown in the previous list.

The possible options for the glBlendEquation() parameter (i.e., mode) are as follows:

mode	blended color
GL_FUNC_ADD	result = $source_{RGBA}$ + $destination_{RGBA}$
GL_FUNC_SUBTRACT	result = $source_{RGBA}$ − $destination_{RGBA}$
GL_FUNC_REVERSE_SUBTRACT	result = $destination_{RGBA}$ − $source_{RGBA}$
GL_MIN	result = min($source_{RGBA}$, $destination_{RGBA}$)
GL_MAX	result = max($source_{RGBA}$, $destination_{RGBA}$)

The glBlendFunc() defaults are GL_ONE (1.0) for srcFactor and GL_ZERO (0.0) for destFactor. The default for glBlendEquation() is GL_FUNC_ADD. Thus, by default, the source pixel is unchanged (multiplied by 1), the destination pixel is scaled to 0, and the two are added—meaning that the source pixel becomes the frame buffer color.

There are also the commands glEnable(GL_BLEND) and glDisable(GL_BLEND), which can be used to tell OpenGL to apply the specified blending, or to ignore it.

We won't illustrate the effects of all of the options here, but we will walk through some illustrative examples. Suppose we specify the following settings in the C++/OpenGL application:

- glBlendFunc(GL_SRC_ALPHA, GL_ONE_MINUS_SRC_ALPHA)
- glBlendEquation(GL_FUNC_ADD)

Compositing would proceed as follows:

1. The source pixel is scaled by its alpha value.
2. The destination pixel is scaled by 1-srcAlpha (the *source transparency*).
3. The pixel values are added together.

For example, if the source pixel is red, with 75% opacity: [1, 0, 0, 0.75], and the destination pixel contains completely opaque green: [0, 1, 0, 1], then the result placed in the frame buffer would be:

```
srcPixel * srcAlpha = [0.75, 0, 0, 0.5625]
destPixel * (1-srcAlpha) = [0, 0.25, 0, 0.25]
resulting pixel = [0.75, 0.25, 0, 0.8125]
```

That is, predominantly red, with some green, and mostly solid. The overall effect of the settings is to let the destination show through by an amount corresponding to the source pixel's transparency. In this example, the pixel in the frame buffer is green, and the incoming pixel is red with 25% transparency (75% opacity). So some green is allowed to show through the red.

It turns out that these settings for blend function and blend equation work well in many cases. Let's apply them to a practical example in a scene containing two 3D models: a torus and a pyramid in front of the torus. Figure 14.4 shows such a scene, on the left with an opaque pyramid, and on the right with the pyramid's alpha value set to 0.8. Lighting has been added.

For many applications—such as creating a flat "window" as part of a model of a house—this simple implementation of transparency may be sufficient. However, in the example shown in Figure 14.4, there is a fairly obvious inadequacy. Although the pyramid model is now effectively transparent, an actual transparent pyramid should reveal not only the objects behind it, but also *its own back surfaces*.

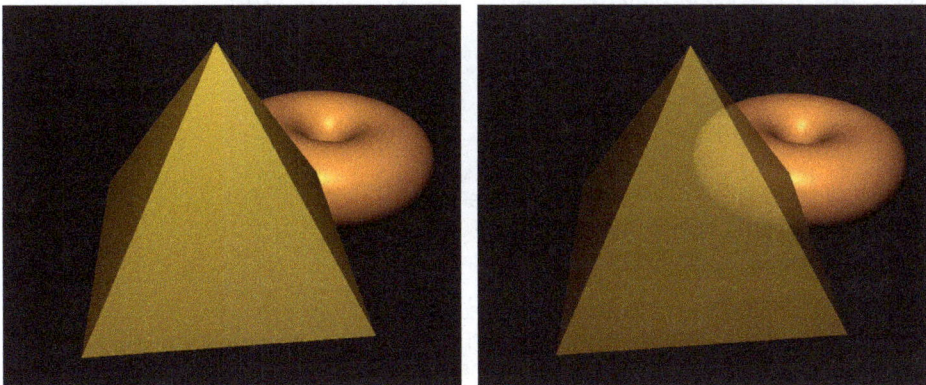

Figure 14.4
Pyramid with alpha=1.0 (left), and alpha=0.8 (right).

Actually, the reason that the back faces of the pyramid did not appear is because we enabled back-face culling. A reasonable idea might be to disable back-face culling while drawing the pyramid. However, this often produces other artifacts, as shown in Figure 14.5 (on the left). The problem with simply disabling back-face culling is that the effects of blending depend on the order that surfaces are rendered (because that determines the source and destination pixels), and we don't always have control over the rendering order. It is generally advantageous to render opaque objects first, as well as objects that are in the back (such as the torus) before any transparent objects. This also holds true for the surfaces of the pyramid, and in this case the reason that the two triangles comprising the base of the pyramid appear different is that one of them was rendered before the front of the pyramid and one was rendered after. Artifacts such as this are sometimes called "ordering" artifacts, and they can manifest in transparent models because we cannot always predict the order in which its triangles will be rendered.

We can solve the problem in our pyramid example by rendering the front and back faces separately, ourselves, starting with the back faces. Program 14.2 shows the code for doing this. We specify the alpha value for the pyramid by passing it to the shader program in a uniform variable, then apply it in the fragment shader by substituting the specified alpha into the computed output color.

Note also that for lighting to work properly, we must flip the normal vector when rendering the back faces. We accomplish this by sending a flag to the vertex shader, where we then flip the normal vector.

Program 14.2 Two-Pass Blending for Transparency

C++ / OpenGL application - in display() for rendering pyramid:

```
. . .
glEnable(GL_CULL_FACE);
. . .
glEnable(GL_BLEND);          // configure blend settings
glBlendFunc(GL_SRC_ALPHA, GL_ONE_MINUS_SRC_ALPHA);
glBlendEquation(GL_FUNC_ADD);

glCullFace(GL_FRONT);        // render pyramid back faces first
glProgramUniform1f(renderingProgram, aLoc, 0.3f);        // back faces very transparent
glProgramUniform1f(renderingProgram, fLoc, -1.0f);       // flip normals on back faces
glDrawArrays(GL_TRIANGLES, 0, numPyramidVertices);
```

```
glCullFace(GL_BACK);        // then render pyramid front faces
glProgramUniform1f(renderingProgram, aLoc, 0.7f);        // front faces slighlty transparent
glProgramUniform1f(renderingProgram, fLoc, 1.0f);        // don't flip normals on front faces
glDrawArrays(GL_TRIANGLES, 0, numPyramidVertices);

glDisable(GL_BLEND);
```

Vertex shader:

```
. . .
if (flipNormal < 0) varyingNormal = -varyingNormal;
. . .
```

Fragment shader:

```
. . .
fragColor = globalAmbient * material.ambient + ... etc.        // same as for Blinn-Phong lighting.
fragColor = vec4(fragColor.xyz, alpha);        // replace alpha value with one sent in uniform variable
```

The result of this "two-pass" solution is shown in Figure 14.5, on the right.

Although it works well here, the two-pass solution shown in Program 14.2 is not always adequate. For example, some more complex models may have hidden surfaces that are *front-facing*, and if such an object were made transparent, our algorithm would fail to render those hidden front-facing portions of the model. Alec Jacobson describes a five-pass sequence that works in a large number of cases [JA12].

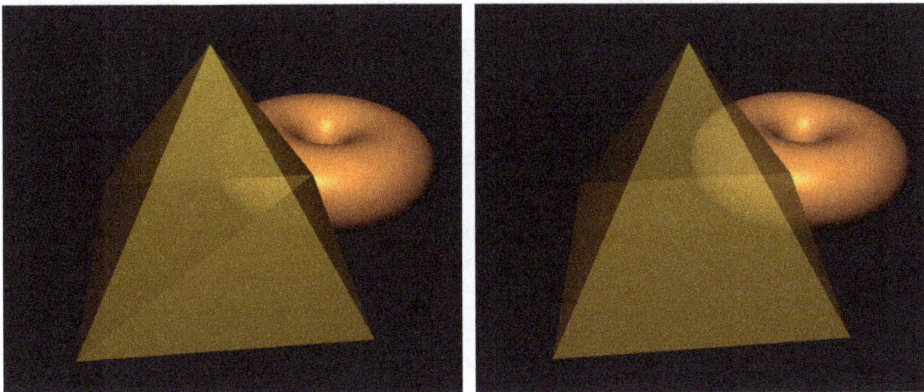

Figure 14.5
Transparency and back faces: ordering artifacts (left) and two-pass correction (right).

14.3 USER-DEFINED CLIPPING PLANES

OpenGL includes the capability to specify clipping planes beyond those defined by the view frustum. One use for a user-defined clipping plane is to slice a model. This makes it possible to create complex shapes by starting with a simple model and slicing sections off of it.

A clipping plane is defined according to the standard mathematical definition of a plane:

$$ax + by + cz + d = 0$$

where a, b, c, and d are parameters defining a particular plane in 3D space with X, Y, and Z axes. The parameters represent a vector (a,b,c) normal to the plane, and a distance d from the origin to the plane. Such a plane can be specified in the vertex shader using a vec4, as follows:

vec4 clip_plane = vec4(0.0, 0.0, -1.0, 0.2);

This would correspond to the plane:

$$(0.0)\ x + (0.0)\ y + (-1.0)\ z + 0.2 = 0$$

The clipping can then be achieved, also in the vertex shader, by using the built-in GLSL variable gl_ClipDistance[ ], as in the following example:

gl_ClipDistance[0] = dot(clip_plane.xyz, vertPos) + clip_plane.w;

In this example, vertPos refers to the vertex position coming into the vertex shader in a vertex attribute (such as from a VBO); clip_plane was defined above. We then compute the signed distance from the clipping plane to the incoming vertex (shown in Chapter 3), which is either 0 if the vertex is on the plane, or is negative or positive depending on which side of the plane the vertex lies. The subscript on the gl_ClipDistance array enables multiple clipping distances (i.e., multiple planes) to be defined. The maximum number of user clipping planes that can be defined depends on the graphics card's OpenGL implementation.

User-defined clipping must then be *enabled* in the C++/OpenGL application. There are built-in OpenGL identifiers GL_CLIP_DISTANCE0, GL_CLIP_DISTANCE1, and so on, corresponding to each gl_ClipDistance[ ] array element. The 0th user-defined clipping plane can be enabled, for example, as follows:

glEnable(GL_CLIP_DISTANCE0);

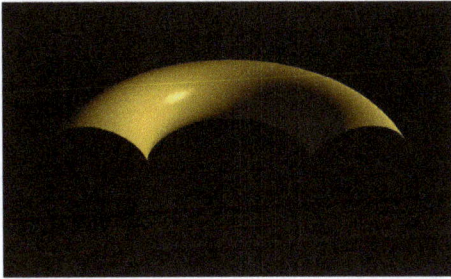

Figure 14.6
Clipping a torus.

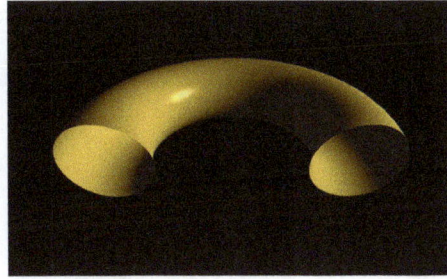

Figure 14.7
Clipping with back faces.

Applying the previous steps to our lighted torus results in the output shown in Figure 14.6, in which the front half of the torus has been clipped. (A rotation has also been applied to provide a clearer view.)

It may appear that the bottom portion of the torus has also been clipped, but that is because the inside faces of the torus were not rendered. When clipping reveals the inside surfaces of a shape, it is necessary to render them as well, or the model will appear incomplete (as it does in Figure 14.6).

Rendering the inner surfaces requires making a second call to gl_DrawArrays(), with the winding order reversed. Additionally, it is necessary to reverse the surface normal vector when rendering the back-facing triangles (as was done in the previous section). The relevant modifications to the C++ application and the vertex shader are shown in Program 14.3, with the output shown in Figure 14.7.

Program 14.3 Clipping with Back Faces

C++ / OpenGL application:

```
void display(GLFWwindow* window, double currentTime) {
    . . .
    flipLoc = glGetUniformLocation(renderingProgram, "flipNormal");
    . . .
    glEnable(GL_CLIP_DISTANCE0);

    // normal drawing of external faces
    glUniform1i(flipLoc, 0);
    glFrontFace(GL_CCW);
    glDrawElements(GL_TRIANGLES, numTorusIndices, GL_UNSIGNED_INT, 0);
```

```
// rendering of back faces with normals reversed
glUniform1i(flipLoc, 1);
glFrontFace(GL_CW);
glDrawElements(GL_TRIANGLES, numTorusIndices, GL_UNSIGNED_INT, 0);
}
```

Vertex shader:

```
. . .
vec4 clip_plane = vec4(0.0, 0.0, -1.0, 0.5);
uniform int flipNormal;          // flag for inverting normal
. . .
void main(void)
{  . . .
    if (flipNormal==1) varyingNormal = -varyingNormal;
    . . .
    gl_ClipDistance[0] = dot(clip_plane.xyz, vertPos) - clip_plane.w;
    . . .
}
```

14.4 ■ 3D TEXTURES

Whereas 2D textures contain image data indexed by two variables, 3D textures contain the same type of image data, but in a 3D structure that is indexed by three variables. The first two dimensions still represent *width* and *height* in the texture map; the third dimension represents *depth*.

Because the data in a 3D texture is stored in a similar manner as for 2D textures, it is tempting to think of a 3D texture as a sort of 3D "image." However, we generally don't refer to 3D texture source data as a 3D image, because there are no commonly used image file formats for this sort of structure (i.e., there is nothing akin to a 3D JPEG, at least not one that is truly three-dimensional). Instead, we suggest thinking of a 3D texture as a sort of substance into which we will submerge (or "dip") the object being textured, resulting in the object's surface points obtaining their colors from the corresponding locations in the texture. Alternatively, it can be useful to imagine that the object is being "carved" out of the 3D texture "cube," much like a sculptor carves a figure out of a single solid block of marble.

OpenGL has support for 3D texture objects. In order to use them, we need to learn how to build the 3D texture and how to use it to texture an object.

Unlike 2D textures, which can be built from standard image files, 3D textures are usually generated *procedurally*. As was done previously for 2D textures, we decide on a resolution—that is, the number of texels in each dimension. Depending on the colors in the texture, we may build a three-dimensional array containing those colors. Alternatively, if the texture holds a "pattern" that could be utilized with various colors, we might instead build an array that holds the pattern, such as with 0s and 1s.

For example, we can build a 3D texture that represents horizontal stripes by filling an array with 0s and 1s corresponding to the desired stripe pattern. Suppose that the desired resolution of the texture is 200x200x200 texels, and the texture is comprised of alternating stripes that are each 10 texels high. A simple function that builds such a structure by filling an array with appropriate 0s and 1s in a nested loop (assuming in this case that width, height, and depth variables are each set to 200) would be as follows:

```
void generate3Dpattern() {
    for (int x=0; x<texWidth; x++) {
        for (int y=0; y<texHeight; y++) {
            for (int z=0; z<texDepth; z++) {
                if ((y/10) % 2 == 0)
                    tex3Dpattern[x][y][z] = 0.0;
                else
                    tex3Dpattern[x][y][z] = 1.0;
            }
        }
    }
}
```

The pattern stored in the tex3Dpattern array is illustrated in Figure 14.8 with the 0s rendered in blue and the 1s rendered in yellow.

Texturing an object with the striped pattern as shown in Figure 14.8 requires the following steps:

1. generating the pattern as already shown
2. using the pattern to fill a byte array of desired colors
3. loading the byte array into a texture object

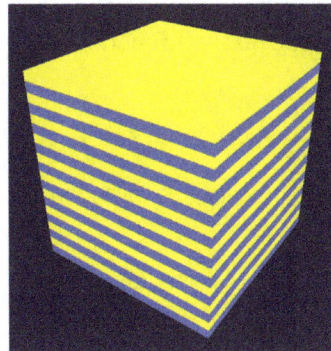

Figure 14.8
Striped 3D texture pattern.

4. deciding on appropriate 3D texture coordinates for the object vertices

5. texturing the object in the fragment shader using an appropriate sampler

Texture coordinates for 3D textures range from 0 to 1, in the same manner as for 2D textures.

Interestingly, step #4 (determining 3D texture coordinates) is usually a lot simpler than one might initially suspect. In fact, it is usually simpler than for 2D textures! This is because (in the case of 2D textures) since a 3D object was being textured with a 2D image, we needed to decide how to "flatten" the 3D object's vertices (such as by UV-mapping) to create texture coordinates. But when 3D texturing, both the object and the texture are of the same dimensionality (three). In most cases, we want the object to reflect the texture pattern, as if it were "carved" out of it (or dipped into it). So the vertex locations themselves serve as the texture coordinates! Usually all that is necessary is to apply some simple scaling to ensure that the object's vertices' location coordinates map to the 3D texture coordinates' range [0..1].

Since we are generating the 3D texture procedurally, we need a way of constructing an OpenGL texture map out of generated data. The process for loading data into a texture is similar to what we saw earlier in Section 5.12. In this case, we fill a 3D array with color values, then copy them into a texture object.

Program 14.4 shows the various components for achieving all of the previous steps in order to texture an object with blue and yellow horizontal stripes from a procedurally built 3D texture. The desired pattern is built in the generate3Dpattern() function, which stores the pattern in an array named "tex3Dpattern". The "image" data is then built in the function fillDataArray(), which fills a 3D array with byte data corresponding to the RGB colors R, G, B, and A, each in the range [0..255], according to the pattern. Those values are then copied into a texture object in the load3DTexture() function.

Program 14.4 3D Texturing: Striped Pattern

C++ / OpenGL application:

. . .

```
const int texWidth = 256;
const int texHeight= 256;
const int texDepth = 256;
double tex3Dpattern[texWidth][texHeight][texDepth];
```

. . .

```
// fill a byte array with RGB blue/yellow values corresponding to the pattern built by generate3Dpattern()
void fillDataArray(GLubyte data[ ]) {
    for (int i=0; i<texWidth; i++) {
        for (int j=0; j<texHeight; j++) {
            for (int k=0; k<texDepth; k++) {
                if (tex3Dpattern[i][j][k] == 1.0) {
                    // yellow color
                    data[i*(texWidth*texHeight*4) + j*(texHeight*4)+ k*4+0] = (GLubyte) 255;   // red
                    data[i*(texWidth*texHeight*4) + j*(texHeight*4)+ k*4+1] = (GLubyte) 255;   // green
                    data[i*(texWidth*texHeight*4) + j*(texHeight*4)+ k*4+2] = (GLubyte) 0;     // blue
                    data[i*(texWidth*texHeight*4) + j*(texHeight*4)+ k*4+3] = (GLubyte) 255;   // alpha
                }
                else {
                    // blue color
                    data[i*(texWidth*texHeight*4) + j*(texHeight*4)+ k*4+0] = (GLubyte) 0;     // red
                    data[i*(texWidth*texHeight*4) + j*(texHeight*4)+ k*4+1] = (GLubyte) 0;     // green
                    data[i*(texWidth*texHeight*4) + j*(texHeight*4)+ k*4+2] = (GLubyte) 255;   // blue
                    data[i*(texWidth*texHeight*4) + j*(texHeight*4)+ k*4+3] = (GLubyte) 255;   // alpha
                }
} } } } }

// build 3D pattern of stripes
void generate3Dpattern() {
    for (int x=0; x<texWidth; x++) {
        for (int y=0; y<texHeight; y++) {
            for (int z=0; z<texDepth; z++) {
                if ((y/10)%2 == 0)
                    tex3Dpattern[x][y][z] = 0.0;
                else
                    tex3Dpattern[x][y][z] = 1.0;
} } } }

// load the sequential byte data array into a texture object
int load3DTexture() {
    GLuint textureID;
    GLubyte* data = new GLubyte[texWidth*texHeight*texDepth*4];

    fillDataArray(data);

    glGenTextures(1, &textureID);
    glBindTexture(GL_TEXTURE_3D, textureID);
    glTexParameteri(GL_TEXTURE_3D, GL_TEXTURE_MIN_FILTER, GL_LINEAR);
    glTexStorage3D(GL_TEXTURE_3D, 1, GL_RGBA8, texWidth, texHeight, texDepth);
    glTexSubImage3D(GL_TEXTURE_3D, 0, 0, 0, 0, texWidth, texHeight, texDepth,
                        GL_RGBA, GL_UNSIGNED_INT_8_8_8_8_REV, data);
    delete[ ] data; return textureID;
}
```

```
void init(GLFWwindow* window) {
    . . .
    generate3Dpattern();            // 3D pattern and texture only loaded once, so done from init()
    stripeTexture = load3DTexture();   // holds the integer texture ID for the 3D texture
}

void display(GLFWwindow* window, double currentTime) {
    . . .
    glActiveTexture(GL_TEXTURE0);
    glBindTexture(GL_TEXTURE_3D, stripeTexture);
    glDrawArrays(GL_TRIANGLES, 0, numObjVertices);
}
```

Vertex Shader:

```
. . .
out vec3 originalPosition;       // the original model vertices will be used for texture coordinates
. . .
layout (binding=0) uniform sampler3D s;

void main(void)
{   originalPosition = position;   // pass original model coordinates for use as 3D texture coordinates
    gl_Position = p_matrix * mv_matrix * vec4(position, 1.0);
}
```

Fragment Shader:

```
. . .
in vec3 originalPosition;        // receive original model coordinates for use as 3D texture coordinates
out vec4 fragColor;
. . .
layout (binding=0) uniform sampler3D s;

void main(void)
{
    fragColor = texture(s, originalPosition/2.0 + 0.5);      // vertices are [-1..+1], tex coords are [0..1]
}
```

In the C++/OpenGL application, the load3Dtexture() function loads the generated data into a 3D texture. Rather than using SOIL2 to load the texture, it makes the relevant OpenGL calls directly, in a manner similar to that explained earlier in Section 5.12. The image data is expected to be formatted as a sequence of bytes corresponding to RGBA color components. The function fillDataArray() does this, applying the RGB values for yellow and blue corresponding to the striped pattern built by the generate3Dpattern() function and held in the tex3Dpattern array. Note also the specification of texture type GL_TEXTURE_3D in the display() function.

Since we wish to use the object's vertex locations as texture coordinates, we pass them through from the vertex shader to the fragment shader. The fragment shader then scales them so that they are mapped into the range [0..1] as is standard for texture coordinates. Finally, 3D textures are accessed via a sam-

Figure 14.9
Dragon object with 3D striped texture.

pler3D uniform, which takes three parameters instead of two. We use the vertex's original X, Y, and Z coordinates, scaled to the correct range, to access the texture. The result is shown in Figure 14.9.

More complex patterns can be generated by modifying generate3Dpattern(). Figure 14.10 shows a simple change that converts the striped pattern to a 3D checkerboard. The resulting effect is then shown in Figure 14.11. It is worth noting that the effect is very different from what the case would be if the dragon's surface had been textured with a 2D checkerboard texture pattern. (See Exercise 14.3.)

```
void generate3Dpattern()
{ int xStep, yStep, zStep, sumSteps;
  for (int x=0; x<texWidth; x++)
  { for (int y=0; y<texHeight; y++)
    { for (int z=0; z<texDepth; z++)
      { xStep = (x / 10) % 2;
        yStep = (y / 10) % 2;
        zStep = (z / 10) % 2;
        sumSteps = xStep + yStep + zStep;
        if ((sumSteps % 2) == 0)
          tex3Dpattern[x][y][z] = 0.0;
        else
          tex3Dpattern[x][y][z] = 1.0;
} } } }
```

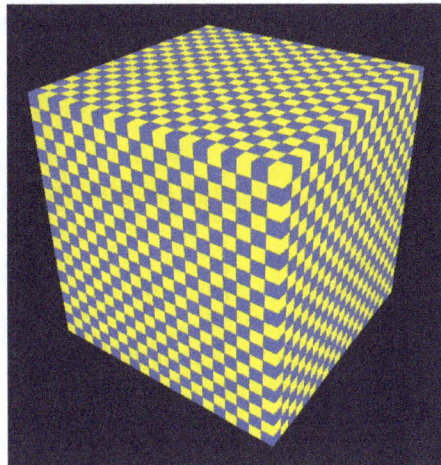

Figure 14.10
Generating a checkerboard 3D texture pattern.

Figure 14.11
Dragon with 3D checkerboard texture.

14.5 ■ NOISE

Many natural phenomena can be simulated using randomness, or *noise*. One common technique, *Perlin Noise* [PE85], is named after Ken Perlin, who in 1997 received an Academy Award[1] for developing a practical way to generate and use 2D and 3D noise. The procedure described here is based on Perlin's method.

There are many applications of noise in graphics scenes. A few common examples are clouds, terrain, wood grain, minerals (such as veins in marble), smoke, fire, flames, planetary surfaces, and random movements. In this section, we focus on generating 3D textures containing noise, and then subsequent sections illustrate using the noise data to generate complex materials such as marble and wood, and to simulate animated cloud textures for use with a cube map or sky-dome. A collection of spatial data (e.g., 2D or 3D) that contains noise is sometimes referred to as a *noise map*.

We start by constructing a 3D texture map out of random data. This can be done using the functions shown in the previous section, with a few modifications. First, we replace the generate3Dpattern() function from Program 14.4 with the following simpler generateNoise() function:

```
#include <random>;
. . .
double noise[noiseWidth][noiseHeight][noiseDepth];
. . .
void generateNoise() {
   for (int x=0; x<noiseWidth; x++) {
      for (int y=0; y<noiseHeight; y++) {
         for (int z=0; z<noiseDepth; z++) {
            noise[x][y][z] = (double) rand() / (RAND_MAX + 1.0);     // computes a double in [0..1]
} } } }
```

---

[1] The Technical Achievement Award, given by the Academy of Motion Picture Arts and Sciences.

Next, the fillDataArray() function from Program 14.4 is modified so that it copies the noise data into the byte array in preparation for loading into a texture object, as follows:

```
void fillDataArray(GLubyte data[ ]) {
  for (int i=0; i<noiseWidth; i++) {
    for (int j=0; j<noiseHeight; j++) {
      for (int k=0; k<noiseDepth; k++) {
        data[i*(noiseWidth*noiseHeight*4)+j*(noiseHeight*4)+k*4+0] =
            (GLubyte) (noise[i][j][k] * 255);
        data[i*(noiseWidth*noiseHeight*4)+j*(noiseHeight*4)+k*4+1] =
            (GLubyte) (noise[i][j][k] * 255);
        data[i*(noiseWidth*noiseHeight*4)+j*(noiseHeight*4)+k*4+2] =
            (GLubyte) (noise[i][j][k] * 255);
        data[i*(noiseWidth*noiseHeight*4)+j*(noiseHeight*4)+k*4+3] =
            (GLubyte) 255;
} } } }
```

The rest of Program 14.4 for loading data into a texture object and applying it to a model is unchanged. We can view this 3D noise map by applying it to our simple cube model, as shown in Figure 14.12. In this example, noiseHeight = noiseWidth = noiseDepth = 256.

This is a 3D noise map, although it isn't a very useful one. As is, it is just *too* noisy to have very many practical applications. To make more practical, tunable noise patterns, we will replace the fillDataArray() function with different noise-producing procedures.

Suppose that we fill the data array by "zooming in" to a small subsection of the noise map illustrated in Figure 14.12, using indexes made smaller by integer division. The modification to the fillDataArray() function is shown below. The resulting 3D texture can be made more or less "blocky" depending on the "zooming" factor used to divide the index. In Figure 14.13, the textures show the result of zooming in by dividing the indices by zoom factors 8, 16, and 32 (left to right respectively).

Figure 14.12
Cube textured with 3D noise data.

Figure 14.13
"Blocky" 3D noise maps with various "zooming in" factors.

```
void fillDataArray(GLubyte data[ ]) {
    int zoom = 8;       // zoom factor
    for (int i=0; i<noiseWidth; i++) {
        for (int j=0; j<noiseHeight; j++) {
            for (int k=0; k<noiseDepth; k++) {
                data[i*(noiseWidth*noiseHeight*4)+j*(noiseHeight*4)+k*4+0] =
                    (GLubyte) (noise [i/zoom] [j/zoom] [k/zoom] * 255);
                data[i*(noiseWidth*noiseHeight*4)+j*(noiseHeight*4)+k*4+1] =
                    (GLubyte) (noise [i/zoom] [j/zoom] [k/zoom] * 255);
                data[i*(noiseWidth*noiseHeight*4)+j*(noiseHeight*4)+k*4+2] =
                    (GLubyte) (noise [i/zoom] [j/zoom] [k/zoom] * 255);
                data[i*(noiseWidth*noiseHeight*4)+j*(noiseHeight*4)+k*4+3] = (GLubyte) 255;
} } } }
```

The "blockiness" within a given noise map can be *smoothed* by interpolating from each discrete grayscale color value to the next one. That is, for each small "block" within a given 3D texture, we set each texel color within the block by interpolating from its color to its neighboring blocks' colors. The interpolation code is shown as follows in the function smoothNoise(), along with the modified fillDataArray() function. The resulting "smoothed" textures (for zooming factors 2, 4, 8, 16, 32, and 64—left to right, top to bottom) then follow in Figure 14.14. Note that the zoom factor is now a double, because we need the fractional component to determine the interpolated grayscale values for each texel.

```
void fillDataArray(GLubyte data[ ]) {
    double zoom = 32.0;
    for (int i=0; i<noiseWidth; i++) {
        for (int j=0; j<noiseHeight; j++) {
```

```
        for (int k=0; k<noiseDepth; k++) {
            data[i*(noiseWidth*noiseHeight*4) + j*(noiseHeight*4) + k*4 +0] =
                (GLubyte) (smoothNoise(zoom, i/zoom, j/zoom, k/zoom) * 255);
            data[i*(noiseWidth*noiseHeight*4) + j*(noiseHeight*4) + k*4 +1] =
                (GLubyte) (smoothNoise(zoom, i/zoom, j/zoom, k/zoom) * 255);
            data[i*(noiseWidth*noiseHeight*4) + j*(noiseHeight*4) + k*4 +2] =
                (GLubyte) (smoothNoise(zoom, i/zoom, j/zoom, k/zoom) * 255);
            data[i*(noiseWidth*noiseHeight*4) + j*(noiseHeight*4) + k*4 +3] = (GLubyte) 255;
} } } }

double smoothNoise(double zoom, double x1, double y1, double z1) {
    // fraction of x1, y1, and z1 (percentage from  current block to next block, for this texel)
    double fractX = x1 - (int) x1;
    double fractY = y1 - (int) y1;
    double fractZ = z1 - (int) z1;

    // indices for neighboring values with wrapping at the ends
    double x2 = x1 - 1; if (x2<0) x2 = round(noiseWidth / zoom) - 1.0;
    double y2 = y1 - 1; if (y2<0) y2 = round(noiseHeight / zoom) - 1.0;
    double z2 = z1 - 1; if (z2<0) z2 = round(noiseDepth / zoom) - 1.0;

    // smooth the noise by interpolating the greyscale intensity along all three axes
    double value = 0.0;
    value += fractX     *  fractY     *  fractZ     *  noise[(int)x1][(int)y1][(int)z1];
    value += (1-fractX) *  fractY     *  fractZ     *  noise[(int)x2][(int)y1][(int)z1];
    value += fractX     *  (1-fractY) *  fractZ     *  noise[(int)x1][(int)y2][(int)z1];
    value += (1-fractX) *  (1-fractY) *  fractZ     *  noise[(int)x2][(int)y2][(int)z1];

    value += fractX     *  fractY     *  (1-fractZ) *  noise[(int)x1][(int)y1][(int)z2];
    value += (1-fractX) *  fractY     *  (1-fractZ) *  noise[(int)x2][(int)y1][(int)z2];
    value += fractX     *  (1-fractY) *  (1-fractZ) *  noise[(int)x1][(int)y2][(int)z2];
    value += (1-fractX) *  (1-fractY) *  (1-fractZ) *  noise[(int)x2][(int)y2][(int)z2];
    return value;
}
```

The smoothNoise() function computes a grayscale value for each texel in the smoothed version of a given noise map by computing a weighted average of the eight grayscale values surrounding the texel in the corresponding original "blocky" noise map. That is, it averages the color values at the eight vertices of the small "block" the texel is in. The weights for each of these "neighbor" colors are based on the texel's distance to each of its neighbors, normalized to the range [0..1]. Values at the ends wrap smoothly to facilitate tiling.

Next, smoothed noise maps of various zooming factors are *combined*. A new noise map is created in which each of its texels is formed by another weighted

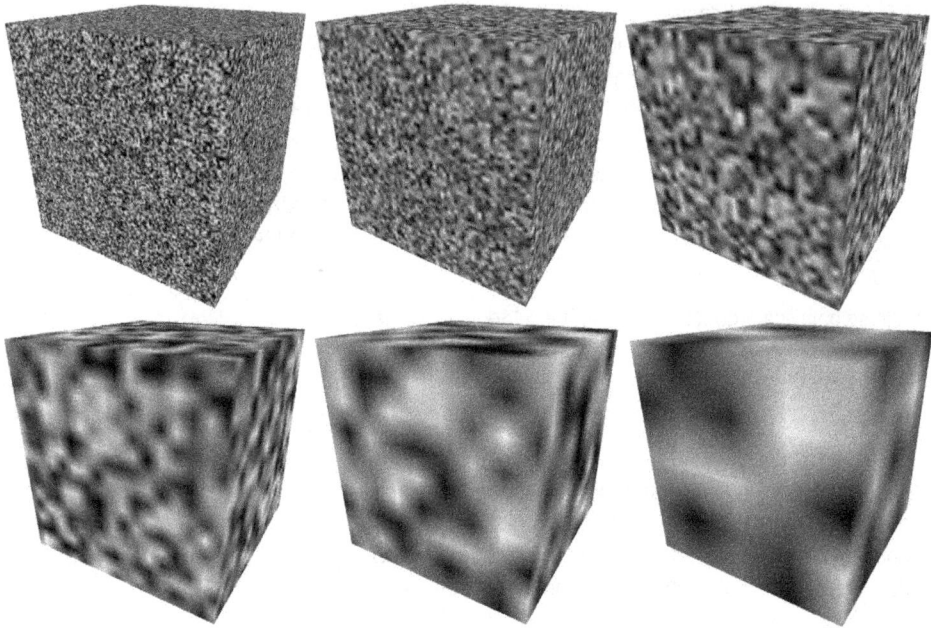

Figure 14.14
Smoothing of 3D textures, at various zooming levels.

average, this time based on the sum of the texels at the same location in each of the "smoothed" noise maps, with the zoom factor serving as the weight. The effect was dubbed "turbulence" by Perlin [PE85], although it is really more closely related to the harmonics produced by summing various waveforms. A new turbulence() function and a modified version of fillDataArray() that specifies a noise map that sums zoom levels 1 through 32 (the ones that are powers of two) are shown as follows, along with an image of a cube textured with the resulting noise map.

```
double turbulence(double x, double y, double z, double maxZoom) {
    double sum = 0.0, zoom = maxZoom;
    while (zoom >= 1.0) {                // the last pass is when zoom=1.
        // compute weighted sum of smoothed noise maps
        sum = sum + smoothNoise(zoom, x / zoom, y / zoom, z / zoom) * zoom;
        zoom = zoom / 2.0;               // for each zoom factor that is a power of two.
    }
    sum = 128.0 * sum / maxZoom;        // guarantees RGB < 256 for maxZoom values up to 64
    return sum;
}
```

```
void fillDataArray(GLubyte data[ ] ) {
    double maxZoom = 32.0;
    for (int i=0; i<noiseWidth; i++) {
        for (int j=0; j<noiseHeight; j++) {
            for (int k=0; k<noiseDepth; k++) {
                data[i*(noiseWidth*noiseHeight*4)+j*(noiseHeight*4)+k*4+0] =
                    (GLubyte) turbulence(i, j, k, maxZoom);
                data[i*(noiseWidth*noiseHeight*4)+j*(noiseHeight*4)+k*4+1] =
                    (GLubyte) turbulence(i, j, k, maxZoom);
                data[i*(noiseWidth*noiseHeight*4)+j*(noiseHeight*4)+k*4+2] =
                    (GLubyte) turbulence(i, j, k, maxZoom);
                data[i*(noiseWidth*noiseHeight*4)+j*(noiseHeight*4)+k*4+3] =
                    (GLubyte) 255;
} } } }
```

3D noise maps can be used for a wide variety of imaginative applications, as we will see in the next sections. It is important to note that because of our use of successive powers of two in building the noise map, it only wraps smoothly on the ends if the dimensions of the map are also a power of two. In all of the examples we present, the dimensions are 256x256x256.

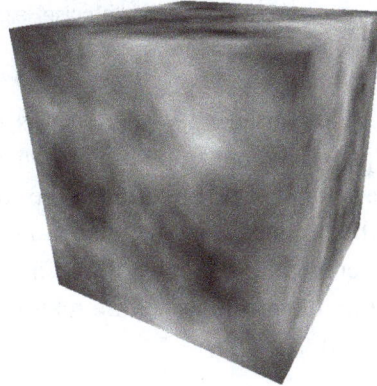

Figure 14.15
3D texture map with combined "turbulence" noise.

14.6 ■ NOISE APPLICATION – MARBLE

By modifying the noise map and adding Phong lighting with an appropriate ADS material as described previously in Figure 7.3, we can make the dragon model appear to be made of a marble-like stone.

We start by generating a striped pattern somewhat similar to the "stripes" example from earlier in this chapter—the new stripes differ from the previous ones, first because they are diagonal, and also because they are produced by a sine wave and therefore have blurry edges. We then use the noise map to perturb those lines, storing them as grayscale values. The changes to the fillDataArray() function are as follows:

```
void fillDataArray(GLubyte data[ ]) {
    double veinFrequency = 2.0;
    double turbPower = 1.5;
    double maxZoom = 64.0;
```

```
for (int i=0; i<noiseWidth; i++) {
    for (int j=0; j<noiseHeight; j++) {
        for (int k=0; k<noiseDepth; k++) {
            double xyzValue = (float)i / noiseWidth + (float)j / noiseHeight + (float)k / noiseDepth
                            + turbPower * turbulence(i,j,k,maxZoom) / 256.0;
            double sineValue = abs(sin(xyzValue * 3.14159 * veinFrequency));

            float redPortion = 255.0f * (float)sineValue;
            float greenPortion = 255.0f * (float)sineValue;
            float bluePortion = 255.0f * (float)sineValue;

            data[i*(noiseWidth*noiseHeight*4)+j*(noiseHeight*4)+k*4+0] = (GLubyte) redPortion;
            data[i*(noiseWidth*noiseHeight*4)+j*(noiseHeight*4)+k*4+1] = (GLubyte) greenPortion;
            data[i*(noiseWidth*noiseHeight*4)+j*(noiseHeight*4)+k*4+2] = (GLubyte) bluePortion;
            data[i*(noiseWidth*noiseHeight*4)+j*(noiseHeight*4)+k*4+3] = (GLubyte) 255;
} } } }
```

The variable veinFrequency is used to adjust the number of stripes, turbSize adjusts the zoom factor used when generating the turbulence, and turbPower adjusts the amount of perturbation in the stripes (setting it to zero leaves the stripes unperturbed). Since the same sine wave value is used for all three (RGB) color components, the final color stored in the image data array is grayscale. Figure 14.16 shows the resulting texture map for various values of turbPower (0.0, 0.5, 1.0, and 1.5, left to right).

We can further control the definition and thickness of the marble veins by modifying the turbulence() function so that it uses a *logistic* function. A logistic (or "sigmoid") function has an S-shaped curve with asymptotes on both ends. Common examples are hyperbolic tangent and $f(x) = 1/(1+e^{-x})$. They are also sometimes called "squashing" functions. Many noise applications utilize a logistic function to push the values in the noise map more towards 0.0 or 255.0, rather than

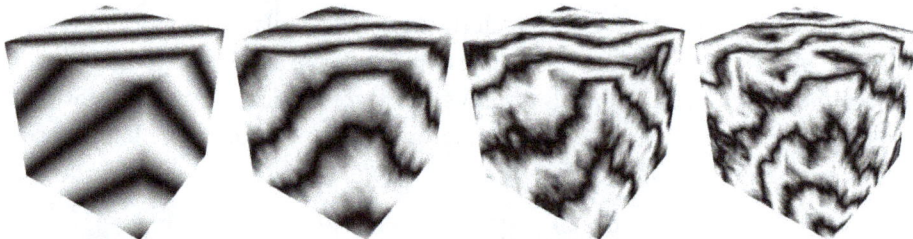

Figure 14.16
Building 3D "marble" noise maps.

values in between. Program 14.5 includes a logistic() function which implements $1/(1+e^{-kx})$, where k is used to tune the degree to which the output is pushed towards 0.0 or 255.0 – in this case, tuning the sharpness of the marble vein edges.

Since we expect marble to have a shiny appearance, we incorporate Phong shading to make a "marble" textured object look convincing. Program 14.5 summarizes the code for generating a marble dragon. The vertex and fragment shaders are the same as used for Phong shading, except that we also pass through the original vertex coordinates for use as 3D texture coordinates (as described earlier). ADS lighting values are the same as specified earlier in Section 7.1, and shininess is set to 0.75. The fragment shader combines the noise result with the lighting result, as described previously in Section 7.6.

Program 14.5 Building a Marble Dragon

C++ / OpenGL application:

```
. . .
void init(GLFWwindow* window) {
    . . .
    generateNoise();
    noiseTexture = load3DTexture();      // same as in Prog 14.4, and which in turn calls fillDataArray()
}
double logistic(double x) {
    double k = 3.0;
    return (1.0 / (1.0 + pow(2.718, -k*x)));
}
void fillDataArray(GLubyte data[ ]) {
    double veinFrequency = 2.0;
    double turbPower = 4.0;
    double maxZoom = 32.0;
    for (int i = 0; i<noiseWidth; i++) {
        for (int j = 0; j<noiseHeight; j++) {
            for (int k = 0; k<noiseDepth; k++) {
                double xyzValue = (float)i / noiseWidth + (float)j / noiseHeight + (float)k / noiseDepth
                        + turbPower * turbulence(i, j, k, maxZoom) / 256.0;

                double sineValue = logistic(abs(sin(xyzValue * 3.14159 * veinFrequency)));
                sineValue = max(-1.0, min(sineValue*1.25 - 0.20, 1.0));  // adjust center to make veins thinner

                float redPortion = 255.0f * (float)sineValue;
                float greenPortion = 255.0f * (float)sineValue;
```

```
            float bluePortion = 255.0f * (float)sineValue;

            data[i*(noiseWidth*noiseHeight * 4) + j*(noiseHeight * 4) + k * 4 + 0] = (GLubyte)redPortion;
            data[i*(noiseWidth*noiseHeight * 4) + j*(noiseHeight * 4) + k * 4 + 1] = (GLubyte)greenPortion;
            data[i*(noiseWidth*noiseHeight * 4) + j*(noiseHeight * 4) + k * 4 + 2] = (GLubyte)bluePortion;
            data[i*(noiseWidth*noiseHeight * 4) + j*(noiseHeight * 4) + k * 4 + 3] = (GLubyte)255;
} } } }
void display(GLFWwindow* window, double currentTime) {
    . . .
    glActiveTexture(GL_TEXTURE0);
    glBindTexture(GL_TEXTURE_3D, noiseTexture);

    glEnable(GL_CULL_FACE);
    glFrontFace(GL_CCW);
    glEnable(GL_DEPTH_TEST);
    glDepthFunc(GL_LEQUAL);
    glDrawArrays(GL_TRIANGLES, 0, numDragonVertices);
}
```

Vertex Shader:

```
//  unchanged from program 14-4
```

Fragment Shader:

```
. . .
void main(void)
{  . . .
    // model vertices are [-1.5..+1.5], texture coordinates are [0..1]
    vec4 texColor = texture(s, originalPosition / 3.0 + 0.5);

    fragColor =
        0.7 * texColor * (globalAmbient + light.ambient + light.diffuse * max(cosTheta,0.0))
        + 0.5 * light.specular * pow(max(cosPhi, 0.0), material.shininess);
}
```

There are various ways of simulating different colors of marble (or other stones). One approach for changing the colors of the "veins" in the marble is by modifying the definition of the Color variable in the fillDataArray() function; for example, by increasing the green component:

```
float redPortion = 255.0f * (float)sineValue;
float greenPortion = 255.0f * (float)min(sineValue*1.5 - 0.25, 1.0);
float bluePortion = 255.0f * (float)sineValue;
```

We can also introduce ADS material values (i.e., specified in init()) to simulate completely different types of stone, such as "jade."

Figure 14.17 shows four examples, the first three using the settings shown in Program 14.5, and the fourth incorporating the "jade" ADS material values shown earlier in Figure 7.3.

Figure 14.17
Dragon textured with 3D noise maps – three marble and one jade.

14.7 ■ NOISE APPLICATION – *WOOD*

Creating a "wood" texture can be done in a similar way as was done in the previous "marble" example. Trees grow in *rings*, and it is these rings that produce the grain we see in objects made of wood. As trees grow, environmental stresses create variations in the rings, which we also see in the grain.

We start by building a procedural "rings" 3D texture map, similar to the "checkerboard" from earlier in this chapter. We then use a noise map to perturb those rings, inserting dark and light brown colors into the ring texture map. By adjusting the number of rings, and the degree to which we perturb the rings, we can simulate wood with various types of grain. Shades of brown can be made by combining similar amounts of red and green, with less blue. We then apply Phong shading with a low level of "shininess."

We can generate rings encircling the Z-axis in our 3D texture map by modifying the fillDataArray() function, using trigonometry to specify values for X and Y that are equidistant from the Z axis. We use a sine wave to repeat this process cyclically, raising and lowering the red and green components equally based on this sine wave to produce the varying shades of brown. The variable sineValue holds the exact shade, which can be adjusted by slightly offsetting one or the other (in this case increasing the red by 80, and the green by 30). We can create more (or fewer) rings by adjusting the value of xyPeriod. The resulting texture is shown in Figure 14.18.

```
void fillDataArray(GLubyte data[ ]) {
    double xyPeriod = 40.0;
    for (int i=0; i<noiseWidth; i++) {
        for (int j=0; j<noiseHeight; j++) {
            for (int k=0; k<noiseDepth; k++) {
                double xValue = (i - (double)noiseWidth/2.0) / (double)noiseWidth;
                double yValue = (j - (double)noiseHeight/2.0) / (double)noiseHeight;
                double distanceFromZ = sqrt(xValue * xValue + yValue * yValue);
                double sineValue = 128.0 * abs(sin(2.0 * xyPeriod * distanceFromZ * 3.14159));

                float redPortion = (float)(80 + (int)sineValue);
                float greenPortion = (float)(30 + (int)sineValue);
                float bluePortion = 0.0f;

                data[i*(noiseWidth*noiseHeight*4)+j*(noiseHeight*4)+k*4+0] = (GLubyte) redPortion;
                data[i*(noiseWidth*noiseHeight*4)+j*(noiseHeight*4)+k*4+1] = (GLubyte) greenPortion;
                data[i*(noiseWidth*noiseHeight*4)+j*(noiseHeight*4)+k*4+2] = (GLubyte) bluePortion;
                data[i*(noiseWidth*noiseHeight*4)+j*(noiseHeight*4)+k*4+3] = (GLubyte) 255;
} } } }
```

The wood rings in Figure 14.18 are a good start, but they don't look very realistic—they are too perfect. To improve this, we use the noise map (more specifically, turbulence) to perturb the distanceFromZ variable so that the rings have slight variations. The computation is modified as follows:

```
double distanceFromZ = sqrt(xValue * xValue + yValue * yValue)
                                  + turbPower * turbulence(i, j, k, maxZoom) / 256.0;
```

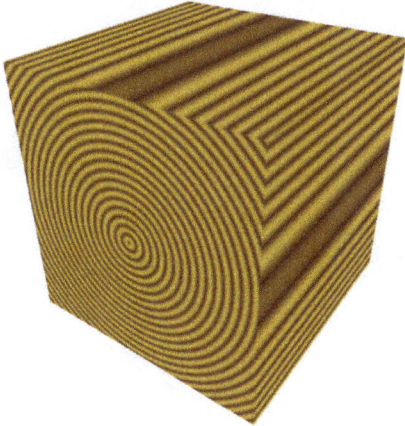

Figure 14.18
Creating rings for 3D wood texture.

Again, the variable turbPower adjusts how much turbulence is applied (setting it to 0.0 results in the unperturbed version shown in Figure 14.18), and max-Zoom specifies the zoom value (32, in this example). Figure 14.19 shows the resulting wood textures for turbPower values 0.05, 1.0, and 2.0 (left to right).

We can now apply the 3D wood texture map to a model. The realism of the texture can be further enhanced by applying a rotation to the originalPosition vertex locations used for texture coordinates; this is because most items carved out of wood don't perfectly align with the orientation of the rings. To accomplish this, we send an additional rotation matrix to the shaders for rotating the texture coordinates. We also add Phong shading, with appropriate wood-color ADS values, and a modest level of shininess. The complete additions and changes for creating a "wood dolphin" are shown in Program 14.6.

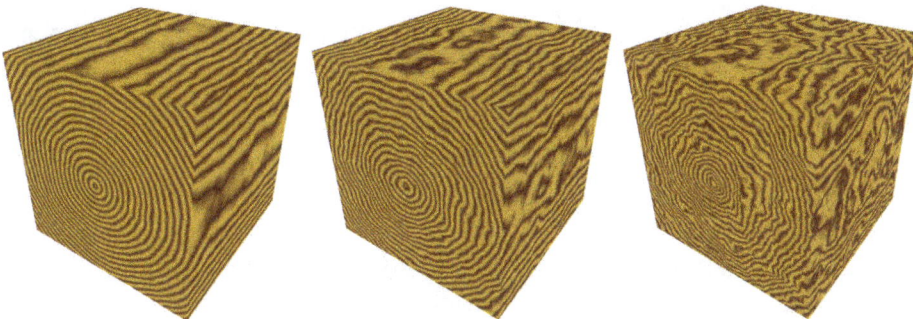

Figure 14.19
"Wood" 3D texture maps with rings perturbed by the noise map.

Program 14.6 Creating a Wood Dolphin

C++ / OpenGL application:

```
glm::mat4 texRot;

//  wood material (brown)
float matAmbient[4] = {0.5f, 0.35f, 0.15f, 1.0f};
float matDiffuse[4] = {0.5f, 0.35f, 0.15f, 1.0f};
float matSpecular[4] = {0.5f, 0.35f, 0.15f, 1.0f};
float matShi = 15.0f;

void init(GLFWwindow* window) {

    . . .
    // rotation to be applied to texture coordinates – adds additional grain variation
    texRot = glm::rotate(glm::mat4(1.0f), toRadians(20.0f), glm::vec3(0.0f, 1.0f, 0.0f));
}

void fillDataArray(GLubyte data[ ]) {
    double xyPeriod = 40.0;
    double turbPower = 0.1;
    double maxZoom = 32.0;
    for (int i=0; i<noiseWidth; i++) {
        for (int j=0; j<noiseHeight; j++) {
            for (int k=0; k<noiseDepth; k++) {
                double xValue = (i - (double)noiseWidth/2.0) / (double)noiseWidth;
                double yValue = (j - (double)noiseHeight/2.0) / (double)noiseHeight;
                double distanceFromZ = sqrt(xValue * xValue + yValue * yValue)
                                    + turbPower * turbulence(i, j, k, maxZoom) / 256.0;
                double sineValue = 128.0 * abs(sin(2.0 * xyPeriod * distanceFromZ * Math.PI));

                float redPortion = (float)(80 + (int)sineValue);
                float greenPortion = (float)(30 + (int)sineValue);
                float bluePortion = 0.0f;

                data[i*(noiseWidth*noiseHeight*4)+j*(noiseHeight*4)+k*4+0] = (GLubyte) redPortion;
                data[i*(noiseWidth*noiseHeight*4)+j*(noiseHeight*4)+k*4+1] = (GLubyte) greenPortion;
                data[i*(noiseWidth*noiseHeight*4)+j*(noiseHeight*4)+k*4+2] = (GLubyte) bluePortion;
                data[i*(noiseWidth*noiseHeight*4)+j*(noiseHeight*4)+k*4+3] = (GLubyte) 255;
} } } }

void display(GLFWwindow* window, double currentTime) {

    . . .
    tLoc = glGetUniformLocation(renderingProgram, "texRot_matrix");
    glUniformMatrix4fv(tLoc, 1, false, glm::value_ptr(texRot));

    . . .
}
```

Vertex shader:

```
. . .
uniform mat4 texRot_matrix;

void main(void)
{  . . .
    originalPosition = vec3(texRot_matrix * vec4(position,1.0)).xyz;
    . . . .
}
```

Fragment shader:

```
. . .
void main(void)
{  . . .
    uniform mat4 texRot_matrix;

    . . .
    // combine lighting with 3D texturing
    fragColor =
        0.5 * ( . . . )
            +
        0.5 * texture(s,originalPosition / 2.0 + 0.5);
}
```

Figure 14.20
Dolphin textured with "wood" 3D noise map.

The resulting 3D textured wood dolphin is shown in Figure 14.20.

There is one additional detail in the fragment shader worth noting. Since we are rotating the model within a 3D texture, it is sometimes possible for this to cause the vertex positions to move beyond the typical [0..1] range of texture coordinates as a result of the rotation. If this were to happen, we could adjust for this possibility by dividing the original vertex positions by a larger number (such as 4.0 rather than 2.0), and then adding a slightly larger number (such as 0.6) to center it in the texture space. Since our noise map wraps, vertex coordinates that move beyond the [0..1] range do not cause a problem.

14.8 NOISE APPLICATION – *CLOUDS*

The "turbulence" noise map built earlier in Figure 14.15 already looks a bit like clouds. Of course, it isn't the right color, so we start by changing it from grayscale to an appropriate mix of light blue and white. A straightforward way of doing this is to assign a color with a maximum value of 1.0 for the blue component and varying (but equal) values between 0.0 and 1.0 for the red and green components, depending on the values in the noise map. The new fillDataArray() function follows:

```
void fillDataArray(GLubyte data[ ]) {
    double maxZoom = 32.0;
    for (int i=0; i<noiseWidth; i++) {
        for (int j=0; j<noiseHeight; j++) {
            for (int k=0; k<noiseDepth; k++) {

                float brightness = 1.0f - (float) turbulence(i, j, k, maxZoom) / 256.0f;

                float redPortion = brightness*255.0f;
                float greenPortion = brightness*255.0f;
                float bluePortion = 1.0f * 255.0f;

                data[i*(noiseWidth*noiseHeight*4)+j*(noiseHeight*4)+k*4+0] = (GLubyte) redPortion;
                data[i*(noiseWidth*noiseHeight*4)+j*(noiseHeight*4)+k*4+1] = (GLubyte) greenPortion;
                data[i*(noiseWidth*noiseHeight*4)+j*(noiseHeight*4)+k*4+2] = (GLubyte) bluePortion;
                data[i*(noiseWidth*noiseHeight*4)+j*(noiseHeight*4)+k*4+3] = (GLubyte) 255;
} } } }
```

The resulting blue version of the noise map can now be used to texture a skydome. Recall that a skydome is a sphere or half-sphere that is textured, rendered with depth-testing disabled, and placed so that it surrounds the camera (similar to a skybox).

One way of building the skydome would be to texture it in the same way as we have for other 3D textures, using the vertex coordinates as texture coordinates. However, in this case, it turns out that using the skydome's 2D texture coordinates instead produces patterns that look more like clouds, because the spherical distortion slightly stretches the texture map horizontally. We can grab a 2D slice from the noise map by setting the third dimension in the GLSL texture() call to a constant value. Assuming that the skydome's texture coordinates have been sent to the OpenGL pipeline in a vertex attribute in the standard way, the following fragment shader textures it with a 2D slice of the noise map:

```
#version 430
in vec2 tc;
out vec4 fragColor;
uniform mat4 mv_matrix;
uniform mat4 p_matrix;
layout (binding=0) uniform sampler3D s;

void main(void)
{   fragColor = texture(s,vec3(tc.x, tc.y, 0.5));      // constant value in place of tc.z
}
```

Figure 14.21
Skydome textured with misty clouds.

The resulting textured skydome is shown in Figure 14.21. Although the camera is usually placed inside the skydome, we have rendered it here with the camera outside, so that the effect on the dome itself can be seen. The current noise map leads to "misty-looking" clouds.

Although our misty clouds look nice, we would like to be able to shape them—that is, make them more or less hazy. Here, again, we can utilize a logistic function, as we did for simulating marble. The modified turbulence() function is shown in Program 14.7, along with an associated logistic() function. The complete Program 14.7 also incorporates the smooth(), fillDataArray(), and generateNoise() functions described earlier.

Program 14.7 Cloud Texture Generation

C++ / OpenGL application:

```
double turbulence(double x, double y, double z, double maxZoom) {
    double sum = 0.0, zoom = maxZoom, cloudQuant;
    while (zoom >= 0.9) {
        sum = sum + smoothNoise(zoom, x/zoom, y/zoom, z/zoom) * zoom;
        zoom = zoom / 2.0;
    }
    sum = 128 * sum / maxZoom;
    cloudQuant = 130.0;        // tunable quantity of clouds
```

```
    sum = 256.0 * logistic(sum - cloudQuant);
    return sum;
}

double logistic(double x) {
    double k = 0.2;                // tunable haziness of clouds, smaller values are more hazy
    return (1.0 / (1.0 + pow(2.718, -k*x)));
}
```

The logistic function causes the colors to tend more toward white or blue, rather than values in between, producing the visual effect of there being more distinct cloud boundaries. The variable cloudQuant adjusts the relative amount of white (versus blue) in the noise map, which in turn leads to more (or fewer) generated white regions (i.e., distinct clouds) when the logistic function is applied. The resulting skydome, now with more distinct cloud formations, is shown in Figure 14.22.

Figure 14.22
Skydome with logistic cloud texture

Lastly, real clouds aren't static. To enhance the realism of our clouds, we should animate them by (a) making them move or drift over time and (b) gradually changing their form as they drift.

One simple way of making the clouds drift is to slowly rotate the skydome. This isn't a perfect solution, as real clouds tend to drift in a straight direction rather than rotating around the observer. However, if the rotation is slow and the clouds are simply for decorating a scene, the effect is likely to be adequate.

Having the clouds gradually change form as they drift may seem tricky. However, given the 3D noise map we have used to texture the clouds, there is actually a very simple and clever way of achieving the effect. Recall that although we constructed a 3D texture noise map for clouds, we have so far only used one "slice" of it, in conjunction with the skydome's 2D texture coordinates (we set the "Z" coordinate of the texture lookup to a constant value). The rest of the 3D texture has so far gone unused.

Our trick will be to replace the texture lookup's constant "Z" coordinate with a variable that changes gradually over time. That is, as we rotate the skydome, we gradually increment the depth variable, causing the texture lookup to use a differ-ent slice. Recall that when we built the 3D texture map, we applied smoothing to the color changes along all three axes. So, neighboring slices from the texture map are very similar, but slightly different. Thus, by gradually changing the "Z" value in the texture() call, the appearance of the clouds will gradually change.

The code changes to cause the clouds to slowly move and change over time are shown in Program 14.8.

Program 14.8 Animating the Cloud Texture

C++ / OpenGL application:

```
. . .
double prevTime = 0.0;
double rotAmt = 0.0;       // Y-axis rotation amount to make clouds appear to drift
float depth = 0.01f;       // depth lookup for 3D noise map, to make clouds gradually change
. . .
void display(GLFWwindow* window, double currentTime) {
    . . .
    // gradually rotate the skydome
    mMat = glm::translate(glm::mat4(1.0f), glm::vec3(domeLocX, domeLocY, domeLocZ));
    rotAmt += (float) ((currentTime – prevTime) * 0.1);
    mMat = glm::rotate(mMat, rotAmt, glm::vec3(0.0f, 1.0f, 0.0f));

    // gradually alter the third texture coordinate to make clouds change
    dOffsetLoc = glGetUniformLocation(program, "d");
    depth += (float) ((currentTime – prevTime) * 0.003f);
    if (depth >= 0.99f) depth = 0.01f;      // wrap-around when we get to the end of the texture map
    glUniform1f(dOffsetLoc, depth);
    . . .
}
```

Fragment Shader:

```
#version 430

in vec2 tc;
out vec4 fragColor;

uniform mat4 mv_matrix;
uniform mat4 p_matrix;
uniform float d;
```

```
layout (binding=0) uniform sampler3D s;

void main(void)
{   fragColor = texture(s, vec3(tc.x, tc.y, d));        // gradually-changing "d" replaces previous constant
}
```

The full implementation in the companion files includes a few additional minor changes to the turbulence() function to enhance the drifting cloud effect. While we cannot show the effect of gradually changing drifting and animated clouds in a single still image, Figure 14.23 shows such changes in a series of snapshots of the 3D generated clouds as they drift across the skydome from right to left and slowly change shape while drifting.

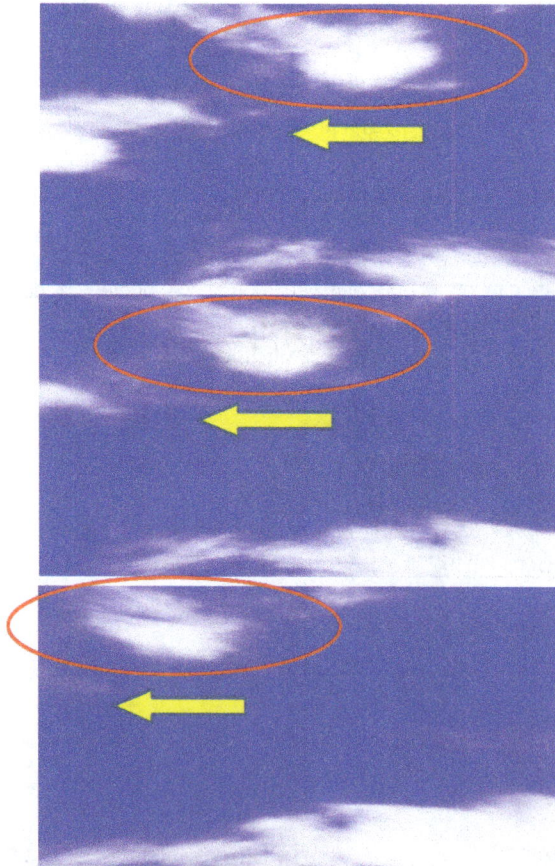

Figure 14.23
3D clouds changing while drifting.

14.9 NOISE APPLICATION – *SPECIAL EFFECTS*

Noise textures can be used for a variety of special effects. In fact, there are so many possible uses that its applicability is limited only by one's imagination.

One very simple special effect that we will demonstrate here is a *dissolve effect*. This is where we make an object appear to gradually dissolve into small particles, until it eventually disappears. Given a 3D noise texture, this effect can be achieved with very little additional code.

To facilitate the dissolve effect, we introduce the GLSL discard command. This command is only legal in the fragment shader, and when executed, it causes the fragment shader to discard the current fragment (meaning not render it).

Our strategy is a simple one. In the C++/OpenGL application, we create a fine-grained noise texture map identical to the one shown back in Figure 14.12, and also a float variable counter that gradually increases over time. This variable is then sent down the shader pipeline in a uniform variable, and the noise map is also placed in a texture map with an associated sampler. The fragment shader then accesses the noise texture using the sampler—in this case, we use the returned noise value to determine whether or not to discard the fragment. We do this by comparing the grayscale noise value against the counter, which serves as a sort of "threshold" value. Because the threshold is gradually changing over time, we can set it up so that gradually more and more fragments are discarded. The result is that the object appears to gradually dissolve. Program 14.9 shows the relevant code sections, which are added to the earth-rendered sphere from Program 6.1. The generated output is shown in Figure 14.24.

Program 14.9 Dissolve Effect Using discard *Command*

C++ / OpenGL application:

```
float threshold = 0.0f;          // gradually-increasing threshold for retaining/discarding fragment
. . .

in Display:

. . .
tLoc = glGetUniformLocation(renderingProgram, "threshold");
threshold = (float) currentTime * 0.1f;
glUniform1f(tLoc, threshold);
. . .
glActiveTexture(GL_TEXTURE0);
glBindTexture(GL_TEXTURE_3D, noiseTexture);
```

```
glActiveTexture(GL_TEXTURE1);
glBindTexture(GL_TEXTURE_2D, earthTexture);
. . .
glDrawArrays(GL_TRIANGLES, 0, numSphereVertices);
```

Fragment Shader:

```
#version 430
in vec2 tc;          // texture coordinates for this fragment
in vec3 origPos;     // original vertex positions in the model, for accessing 3D texture
. . .
layout (binding=0) uniform sampler3D n;        // sampler for noise texture
layout (binding=1) uniform sampler2D e;        // sampler for earth texture
. . .
uniform float threshold;        // threshold for retaining or discarding fragment

void main(void)
{   float noise = texture(n, origPos).x;   // retrieve noise value for this fragment.
    if (noise > threshold)                 // if the noise value > current threshold value,
    {   fragColor = texture(e, tc);        //    render the fragment using the earth texture.
    }
    else
    {   discard;        // otherwise, discard the fragment (do not render it)
    }
}
```

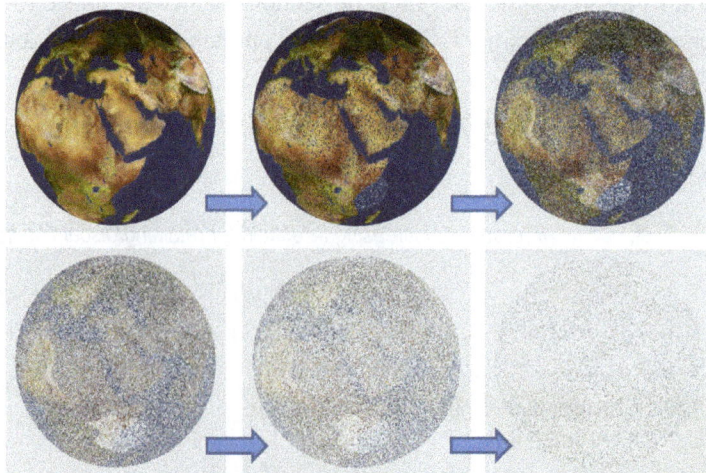

Figure 14.24
Dissolve effect with discard shader.

The discard command should, if possible, be used sparingly, because it can incur a performance penalty. This is because its presence makes it more difficult for OpenGL to optimize Z-buffer depth testing.

SUPPLEMENTAL NOTES

When specifying a user-defined clipping plane for the plane $ax + by + cz + d = 0$, the plane should be "normalized" so that $\sqrt{a^2 + b^2 + c^2} = 1$. The plane that we used in the example shown in Section 14.3 was already normalized in this manner. Alternatively, the distance d can be divided by $\sqrt{a^2 + b^2 + c^2}$.

In this chapter, we used Perlin noise to generate clouds and to simulate both wood and a marble-like stone from which we rendered the dragon. People have found many other uses for Perlin noise. For example, it can be used to create fire and smoke [CC16, AF14] and build realistic bump maps [GR05]; it has been used to generate terrain in the video game Minecraft [PE11].

The noise maps generated in this chapter are based on procedures outlined by Lode Vandevenne [VA04]. There remain some deficiencies in our 3D cloud generation. Occasionally, small horizontal and vertical structures appear that don't look very cloud-like (the enhanced implementation of the turbulence() function in the companion files corrects most of these in the animated example). Another issue is that at the northern peak of the skydome spherical distortion can cause a pincushion effect.

The clouds we implemented in this chapter also fail to model some important aspects of real clouds, such as the way that real clouds scatter the sun's light. Real clouds also tend to be more white on the top and grayer at the bottom. Our clouds also don't achieve a 3D "fluffy" look that many actual clouds have.

Similarly, more comprehensive models exist for generating fog, such as the one described by Kilgard and Fernando [KF03].

While perusing the OpenGL documentation, the reader might notice that GLSL includes some noise functions named noise1(), noise2(), noise3(), and noise4(), which are described as taking an input seed and producing Gaussian-like stochastic output. We didn't use these functions in this chapter because, as of this writing, most vendors have not implemented them. For example, many NVIDIA cards currently return 0 for these functions, regardless of the input seed.

Exercises

14.1 Modify Program 14.2 to gradually decrease the alpha value of an object, causing it to progressively fade out and eventually disappear.

14.2 Modify Program 14.3 to clip the torus along the horizontal, creating a circular "trough."

14.3 Modify Program 14.4 (the version including the modification in Figure 14.10 that produces a 3D cubed texture) so that it instead textures the Studio 522 dolphin. Then observe the results. Many people, when first observing the result (such as that shown on the dragon, but also even on simpler objects) believe that there is some error in the program. Unexpected surface patterns can result from "carving" an object out of 3D textures, even in simple cases.

14.4 The simple sine wave used to define the wood "rings" (shown in Figure 14.18) generate rings in which the light and dark areas are of an equal width. Experiment with modifications to the associated fillDataArray() function with the goal of making the dark rings narrower in width than the light rings. Then observe the effects on the resulting wood-textured object.

14.5 *(PROJECT)* Incorporate the logistic function (from Program 14.7) into the marble dragon from Program 14.5, and experiment with the settings to create more distinct veins.

14.6 Modify Program 14.9 to incorporate the zooming, smoothing, turbulence, and logistic steps described in prior sections. Observe the changes in the resulting dissolve effect.

References

[AF14] S. Abraham and D. Fussell, "Smoke Brush," *Proceedings of the Workshop on Non-Photorealistic Animation and Rendering (NPAR'14)*, 2014, accessed November 2023, https://www.cs.utexas.edu/~theshark/smokebrush.pdf

[AS04] D. Astle, "Simple Clouds Part 1," gamedev.net, 2004 (tutorial by Francis Huang), accessed November 2023, https://www.gamedev.net/tutorials/_/technical/game-programming/simple-clouds-part-1-r2085

[CC16] A Fire Shader in GLSL for your WebGL Games (2016), Clockwork Chilli (blog), accessed November 2023, http://clockworkchilli.com/blog/8_a_ fire_shader_in_glsl_for_your_webgl_games

[GR05] S. Green, "Implementing Improved Perlin Noise," *GPU Gems 2*, NVIDIA, 2005, accessed November 2023, https://http.download.nvidia.com/ developer/GPU_Gems_2/CD/Content/26.zip

[JA12] A. Jacobson, "Cheap Tricks for OpenGL Transparency," 2012, accessed November 2023, http://www.alecjacobson.com/weblog/?p=2750

[KF03] M. Kilgard and R. Fernando, "Advanced Topics," *The Cg Tutorial* (Addison-Wesley, 2003), accessed November 2023, https://developer .download.nvidia.com/CgTutorial/cg_tutorial_chapter09.html

[LU16] F. Luna, *Introduction to 3D Game Programming with DirectX 12*, 2nd ed. (Mercury Learning, 2016).

[PE11] M. Persson, "Terrain Generation, Part 1," *The Word of Notch* (blog), Mar 9, 2011, accessed November 2023, https://www.tumblr.com/n0tch-blog-blog/4231184692/terrain-generation-part-1

[PE85] K. Perlin, "An Image Synthesizer," SIGGRAPH '85 Proceedings of the 12th annual conference on computer graphics and interactive techniques (1985).

[VA04] L. Vandevenne, "Texture Generation Using Random Noise," *Lode's Computer Graphics Tutorial*, 2004, accessed November 2023, http:// lodev.org/cgtutor/randomnoise.html

CHAPTER **15**

SIMULATING WATER

▪ ▪ ■ ▪ ▪

Simulating water is a complex topic, because water is found in so many different settings and takes so many different forms. The technique used depends on the application. The water could be coming out of a kitchen faucet, or out of a lawn sprinkler, or it could be flowing in a river, or in large dark blue ocean waves, or swirling around in a drinking glass. There are too many possibilities to cover all of them here, so in this chapter, we focus on one common scenario: a swimming pool. Our setup will enable viewing the water downwards from above the surface, or upwards from below the surface, and we will tilt the camera accordingly. With minor modifications, it could be modified to instead simulate a lake surface (or an ocean with small waves).

15.1 POOL SURFACE AND FLOOR GEOMETRY SETUP

We start by setting up a very simple scene that includes a flat (horizontal) plane segment and a skybox. The plane is made of two triangles comprising a rectangle, and is textured with a checkerboard procedural texture function similar to (but simpler than) the 3D checkerboard texture described in Chapter 14. (Later, in Program 15.2, we will change the appearance of this plane to instead look like water, and we will move the checkerboard pattern to a second plane at the bottom of the swimming pool. The checkerboard pattern will be used to simulate tiles – if we were instead modeling a lake, then we would of course use a different texture for the bottom.)

Program 15.1 shows the organization of the code. Explanations describing code already presented in previous chapters are not repeated here. Figure 15.1 shows the result when executed.

Program 15.1 – Horizontal Plane Geometry (setup)

C++/OpenGL Application

```
// includes #defines, variables for camera, rendering programs, matrices, and skybox texture as before.
. . .
float cameraHeight = 2.0f, cameraPitch = 15.0f;
float planeHeight = 0.0f;

void setupVertices(void) {
    float PLANE_POSITIONS[18] = {
        -128.0f, 0.0f, -128.0f,  -128.0f, 0.0f, 128.0f,  128.0f, 0.0f, -128.0f,
        128.0f, 0.0f, -128.0f,  -128.0f, 0.0f, 128.0f,  128.0f, 0.0f, 128.0f
    };
    float PLANE_TEXCOORDS[12] = {
        0.0f, 0.0f,  0.0f, 1.0f,  1.0f, 0.0f, 1.0f, 0.0f,  0.0f, 1.0f,  1.0f, 1.0f
    };
    //  cube map vertices, building VAO, VBOs, and loading buffers as before
    . . .
}

void display(GLFWwindow* window, double currentTime) {
    // code for clearing color buffer, perspective matrix, and rendering skybox as before
    // code for drawing the scene is the same as for Program 4.1, but this time for the plane
    vMat = glm::translate(glm::mat4(1.0f), glm::vec3(0.0f, -cameraHeight, 0.0f))
        * glm::rotate(glm::mat4(1.0f), toRadians(cameraPitch), glm::vec3(1.0f, 0.0f, 0.0f));
    . . .
    // code for rendering skybox as before
    . . .
    // render the scene – in this case it is just a plane
    mMat = glm::translate(glm::mat4(1.0f), glm::vec3(0, planeHeight, 0));
    . . .
    glDrawArrays(GL_TRIANGLES, 0, 6);      // plane is 2 triangles, total of 6 vertices
}
. . . // main() and other components as before
```

Vertex Shader (for plane segment)

```
// same as Program 5.1
```

Fragment Shader (for plane segment)

```
//  Similar to previous fragment shaders, except that a checkerboard texture has been added.
//  Incoming texture coordinates are scaled up here to facilitate repeating texture.
#version 430

in vec2 tc;
out vec4 color;

uniform mat4 mv_matrix;
uniform mat4 p_matrix;

vec3 checkerboard(vec2 tc)
{   float tileScale = 64.0;
    float tile = mod(floor(tc.x * tileScale) + floor(tc.y * tileScale), 2.0);
    return tile * vec3(1,1,1);
}

void main(void)
{   color = vec4(checkerboard(tc), 1.0);
}
```

The C++/OpenGL application specifies that the plane is at a height of 0.0, meaning it is level with the XZ plane. The camera is 2.0 units above the plane, and pitched -15° looking downwards towards the plane. Specifying the plane requires 18 floating point values (*2 triangles* x *3 vertices/triangle* x *3 coordinates/vertex*). Computing its procedural "checkerboard" pattern is accomplished in a similar manner as for the 3D example shown previously in Section 14.4. The desired number of

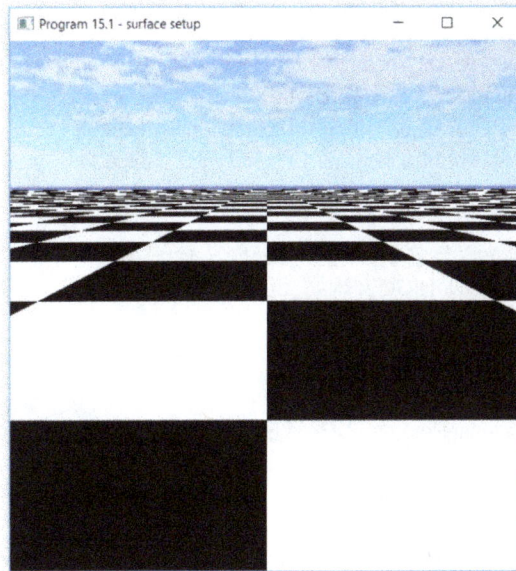

Figure 15.1
Geometry setup for the plane segment surface

squares per side is specified in the variable tileScale, and the pattern is then produced by scaling the texture coordinates up by tileScale and taking that result modulo 2. The result of 0 or 1 is then returned as either color (0,0,0) or (1,1,1) – i.e., black or white – respectively.

We now add a second plane to our scene and build a swimming pool, using the same plane model (PLANE_POSITIONS and PLANE_TEXCOORDS) for both the top surface and bottom floor of the pool. We put the checkerboard pattern on lower plane (the floor), and for the top surface plane, we start with a solid blue color. We also add ADS Phong lighting (covered earlier in Chapter 7). The organization of the C++/OpenGL application for these additions is shown in Program 15.2.

Program 15.2 – Water Geometry (top surface and bottom floor)

C++/OpenGL Application

```
// modifications to Program 15.1 shown here. Code for lighting not shown (see Chapter 7)
. . .
float surfacePlaneHeight = 0.0f;
float floorPlaneHeight = -10.0f;
GLuint renderingProgramSURFACE, renderingProgramFLOOR, renderingProgramCubeMap;

. . .
void setupVertices(void) {
    . . .
    // add normal vectors for top surface and floor lighting (all of them point upwards)
    float PLANE_NORMALS[18] = {
        0.0f, 1.0f, 0.0f,  0.0f, 1.0f, 0.0f,  0.0f, 1.0f, 0.0f,
        0.0f, 1.0f, 0.0f,  0.0f, 1.0f, 0.0f,  0.0f, 1.0f, 0.0f
    };
    . . .
    glBindBuffer(GL_ARRAY_BUFFER, vbo[3]);
    glBufferData(GL_ARRAY_BUFFER, sizeof(PLANE_NORMALS), PLANE_NORMALS, GL_
                                                              STATIC_DRAW);
}

void init(GLFWwindow* window) {
    renderingProgramSURFACE = Utils::createShaderProgram("vertShaderSURFACE.glsl",
                                                  "fragShaderSURFACE.glsl");
    renderingProgramFLOOR = Utils::createShaderProgram("vertShaderFLOOR.glsl",
                                                  "fragShaderFLOOR.glsl");
    renderingProgramCubeMap = Utils::createShaderProgram("vertCShader.glsl", "fragCShader.glsl");
    . . .
}

void display(GLFWwindow* window, double currentTime) {
    // Code for drawing skybox unchanged. Code for surface geometry now done twice, for top surface and floor
    . . .
```

```
// draw water top (surface)
glUseProgram(renderingProgramSURFACE);
mMat.translation(0.0f, surfacePlaneHeight, 0.0f);   // positions the top plane at the specified height
. . .
glBindBuffer(GL_ARRAY_BUFFER, vbo[3]);        // also send normals for lighting
glVertexAttribPointer(2, 3, GL_FLOAT, GL_FALSE, 0, 0);
glEnableVertexAttribArray(2);
. . .
// render the top surface twice, so that it can be viewed from both above and below the surface
if (cameraHeight >= surfacePlaneHeight)
    glFrontFace(GL_CCW);
else
    glFrontFace(GL_CW);
glDrawArrays(GL_TRIANGLES, 0, 6);

// draw water bottom (floor)
glUseProgram(renderingProgramFLOOR);
mMat.translation(0.0f, floorPlaneHeight, 0.0f);   // positions the bottom plane at the specified height
. . .
glBindBuffer(GL_ARRAY_BUFFER, vbo[3]);   // also send normals for lighting
glVertexAttribPointer(2, 3, GL_FLOAT, GL_FALSE, 0, 0);
glEnableVertexAttribArray(2);
. . .
glFrontFace(GL_CCW);     // since the previous setting might have been CW, we set it to CCW here
glDrawArrays(GL_TRIANGLES, 0, 6);
}
. . . // main() and other components as before
```

We have now expanded the previous program to include two plane segments, one for the top surface and one for the bottom surface. We have included normals so that we can use ADS lighting on both surfaces. We have two rendering programs because in this version the top surface is rendered without a texture, and the bottom surface is rendered with the checkerboard texture. Also, the winding order setting for the top surface is based on whether the camera is above or below the water surface (since one or the other side of that plane would then need to be rendered). Figure 15.2 shows the result with the camera both above and below the water surface. A specular highlight is apparent in both cases. In the underwater case, the light-colored band in the distance is the skybox visible beyond the top surface plane. This issue will be resolved later when we add a "fog" effect.

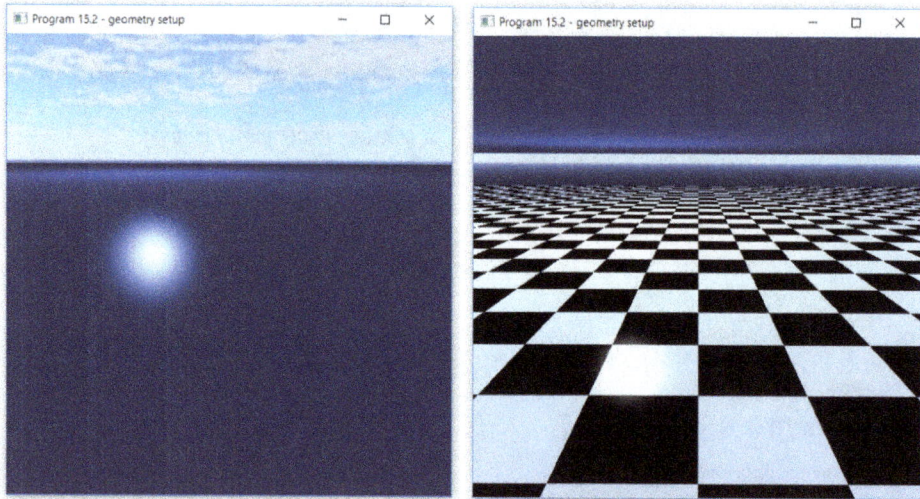

Figure 15.2
Geometry for water top surface and bottom floor, camera above surface (left) and below surface (right)

15.2 ■ ADDING SURFACE REFLECTION AND REFRACTION

Water is complex, and making a completely realistic simulation would require adding the many reflections and refractions that are usually visible in a body of water. A further complication is that different effects are needed depending on whether the camera is above or below the water surface.

We will start by focusing on the first case: the camera *above* the water surface. In Figure 15.2 (the left figure), we can see that so far we have (1) a solid blue surface, (2) a skybox above the water, and (3) lighting on the surface. To start making this look more like water, Program 15.3 adds the following two items:

- *reflection*, so that objects above the water (such as the skybox) are reflected on the water's surface
- *refraction* of the view through the top surface to the bottom floor, so that items under the water (such as the checkerboard floor) are visible when looking down from above the surface of the water

We will accomplish these by rendering the scene to multiple frame buffers, from various vantage points, and then use the resulting frame buffers as textures to apply to the ADS-lighted blue water surface. This is fairly complicated, so we present Program 15.3 in three parts. In part one, we start by reorganizing the code in display()

into separate functions: (1) one that prepares for rendering the skybox, (2) one that prepares for rendering the top surface, and (3) one that prepares for rendering the floor. We then render each of those as before. Later, in part two, we render these items to textures called *reflection* and *refraction* textures, and apply them both to the top surface – but for now we just reorganize the code to help facilitate this future step.

(These same functions will be useful when the camera is below the water surface. But for now, we will concentrate just on the case of the camera being above the water surface.)

The division of the display() function, and the creation of (but not yet filling) the reflection and refraction frame buffers, is shown in Program 15.3. Note that the two framebuffers also include depth attachments (which we saw earlier in Chapter 8 when we studied shadow mapping), which will be useful later.

Program 15.3 – Reflection and Refraction (Part 1: preparation)

C++/OpenGL Application

```
. . .
void createReflectRefractBuffers(GLFWwindow* window) { // called once from init()
    GLuint bufferId[1];
    glGenBuffers(1, bufferId);
    glfwGetFramebufferSize(window, &width, &height);

    // initialize refraction framebuffer
    glGenFramebuffers(1, bufferId);
    refractFrameBuffer = bufferId[0];
    glBindFramebuffer(GL_FRAMEBUFFER, refractFrameBuffer);
    glGenTextures(1, bufferId);               // this is for the color buffer
    refractTextureId = bufferId[0];
    glBindTexture(GL_TEXTURE_2D, refractTextureId);
    glTexImage2D(GL_TEXTURE_2D, 0, GL_RGBA, width, height, 0, GL_RGBA, GL_UNSIGNED_
                                                            BYTE, NULL);
    glTexParameteri(GL_TEXTURE_2D, GL_TEXTURE_MIN_FILTER, GL_LINEAR);
    glTexParameteri(GL_TEXTURE_2D, GL_TEXTURE_MAG_FILTER, GL_LINEAR);
    glFramebufferTexture2D(GL_FRAMEBUFFER, GL_COLOR_ATTACHMENT0, GL_
                                                TEXTURE_2D, refractTextureId, 0);
    glDrawBuffer(GL_COLOR_ATTACHMENT0);
    glGenTextures(1, bufferId);               // this is for the depth buffer
    glBindTexture(GL_TEXTURE_2D, bufferId[0]);
    glTexImage2D(GL_TEXTURE_2D,0,GL_DEPTH_COMPONENT24, width, height, 0, GL_
                                                DEPTH_COMPONENT, GL_FLOAT, NULL);
```

```
glTexParameteri(GL_TEXTURE_2D, GL_TEXTURE_MIN_FILTER, GL_LINEAR);
glTexParameteri(GL_TEXTURE_2D, GL_TEXTURE_MAG_FILTER, GL_LINEAR);
glFramebufferTexture2D(GL_FRAMEBUFFER, GL_DEPTH_ATTACHMENT, GL_
                                                TEXTURE_2D, bufferId[0], 0);

// initialize reflection framebuffer
glGenFramebuffers(1, bufferId);
reflectFrameBuffer = bufferId[0];
glBindFramebuffer(GL_FRAMEBUFFER, reflectFrameBuffer);
(the remainder of this section is identical to the code above for the refraction buffer, but with "reflectTextureID")
. . .
}
void prepForSkyBoxRender() {
    glUseProgram(renderingProgramCubeMap);

    vLoc = glGetUniformLocation(renderingProgramCubeMap, "v_matrix");
    pLoc = glGetUniformLocation(renderingProgramCubeMap, "p_matrix");

    glUniformMatrix4fv(vLoc, 1, GL_FALSE, glm::value_ptr(vMat));
    glUniformMatrix4fv(pLoc, 1, GL_FALSE, glm::value_ptr(pMat));

    // vbo[0] holds the skybox vertices
    glBindBuffer(GL_ARRAY_BUFFER, vbo[0]);
    glVertexAttribPointer(0, 3, GL_FLOAT, GL_FALSE, 0, 0);
    glEnableVertexAttribArray(0);

    glActiveTexture(GL_TEXTURE0);
    glBindTexture(GL_TEXTURE_CUBE_MAP, skyboxTexture);
}
void prepForTopSurfaceRender() {
    glUseProgram(renderingProgramSURFACE);

    mLoc = glGetUniformLocation(renderingProgramSURFACE, "m_matrix");
    vLoc = glGetUniformLocation(renderingProgramSURFACE, "v_matrix");
    pLoc = glGetUniformLocation(renderingProgramSURFACE, "p_matrix");
    nLoc = glGetUniformLocation(renderingProgramSURFACE, "norm_matrix");

    mMat = glm::translate(glm::mat4(1.0f), glm::vec3(0.0f, surfacePlaneHeight, 0.0f));
    invTrMat = glm::transpose(glm::inverse(mMat));

    currentLightPos = glm::vec3(lightLoc.x, lightLoc.y, lightLoc.z);
    installLights(renderingProgramSURFACE);

    // get references to uniform variables
    glUniformMatrix4fv(mLoc, 1, GL_FALSE, glm::value_ptr(mMat));
    glUniformMatrix4fv(vLoc, 1, GL_FALSE, glm::value_ptr(vMat));
    glUniformMatrix4fv(pLoc, 1, GL_FALSE, glm::value_ptr(pMat));
    glUniformMatrix4fv(nLoc, 1, GL_FALSE, glm::value_ptr(invTrMat));
```

```
    //  VBOs 1, 2, and 3 contain the plane vertices, texcoords, and normals
    glBindBuffer(GL_ARRAY_BUFFER, vbo[1]);
    glVertexAttribPointer(0, 3, GL_FLOAT, GL_FALSE, 0, 0);
    glEnableVertexAttribArray(0);

    glBindBuffer(GL_ARRAY_BUFFER, vbo[2]);
    glVertexAttribPointer(1, 2, GL_FLOAT, GL_FALSE, 0, 0);
    glEnableVertexAttribArray(1);

    glBindBuffer(GL_ARRAY_BUFFER, vbo[3]);
    glVertexAttribPointer(2, 3, GL_FLOAT, GL_FALSE, 0, 0);
    glEnableVertexAttribArray(2);
}
void prepForFloorRender() {
    glUseProgram(renderingProgramFLOOR);

    mLoc = glGetUniformLocation(renderingProgramFLOOR, "m_matrix");
    vLoc = glGetUniformLocation(renderingProgramFLOOR, "v_matrix");
    pLoc = glGetUniformLocation(renderingProgramFLOOR, "p_matrix");
    nLoc = glGetUniformLocation(renderingProgramFLOOR, "norm_matrix");

    mMat = glm::translate(glm::mat4(1.0f), glm::vec3(0.0f, floorPlaneHeight, 0.0f));
    invTrMat = glm::transpose(glm::inverse(mMat));

    currentLightPos = glm::vec3(lightLoc.x, lightLoc.y, lightLoc.z);
    installLights(renderingProgramFLOOR);

    // getting the uniform references and preparing plane VBOs – same as prepForTopSurfaceRender()
    . . .
}
void display(GLFWwindow* window, double currentTime) {
    glBindFramebuffer(GL_FRAMEBUFFER, 0);   // enable the default framebuffer to render scene
    . . .
    // draw cube map – most of the code moved to the "prepForSkyBoxRender()" function
    prepForSkyBoxRender();
    glEnable(GL_CULL_FACE);
    glFrontFace(GL_CCW);
    glDisable(GL_DEPTH_TEST);
    glDrawArrays(GL_TRIANGLES, 0, 36);
    glEnable(GL_DEPTH_TEST);

    // draw water top (surface) – most of the code moved to "prepForTopSurfaceRender()" function
    prepForTopSurfaceRender();
    glEnable(GL_DEPTH_TEST);
    glDepthFunc(GL_LEQUAL);
    if (cameraHeight >= surfacePlaneHeight)
```

```
    glFrontFace(GL_CCW);
else
    glFrontFace(GL_CW);
glDrawArrays(GL_TRIANGLES, 0, 6);

// draw water bottom (floor) – most of the code moved to "prepForFloorRender()" function
prepForFloorRender();
glEnable(GL_DEPTH_TEST);
glDepthFunc(GL_LEQUAL);
glFrontFace(GL_CCW);
glDrawArrays(GL_TRIANGLES, 0, 6);
}
```

As previously mentioned, the code for Program 15.3 is spread over three parts, starting with part one, which is listed above. So far, Program 15.3 doesn't actually produce any rendered output different from that produced by Program 15.2. However, it reorganizes the code in a way that will be useful as we proceed, because we have (1) created two custom framebuffers for holding reflection and refraction information, and (2) isolated those sections of display() that prepare particular portions of the scene for rendering (skybox, floor, and surface), facilitating multiple renders.

Now in part two (of Program 15.3), we build the reflection and refraction textures. We do this by repeating some of the actions in display(), but with different view matrices. The strategy is illustrated in Figure 15.3. The camera is above the water's surface looking slightly downwards. Directly below the camera and under the surface is a second camera pointing slightly upwards, which is dubbed the "reflection camera." It is used to render objects above the surface (such as the skybox) to build the reflection texture. It is positioned at a depth equal to the height of the camera above the water, which would be surfacePlaneHeight - cameraHeight. Our camera rotation implementation only includes the pitch (rotation around the X axis), so for the reflection camera, we simply negate the pitch value.

Since the purpose of the reflection camera is to generate a texture containing items reflecting off of the surface, we only render those objects that are above the surface of the water when rendering from the point of view of the reflection camera. Therefore, in this example, we would render the skybox, but we wouldn't render the floor, the top surface, or any objects in the water (such as fish).

The refraction texture is generated from a third camera, dubbed the "refraction camera." It utilizes the same view matrix as the camera's view matrix. Refraction should render everything seen *through* the water. That is, when the main camera is above the surface looking down at the water, refraction should reveal those objects below the surface (such as fish, and in this example, the checkerboard floor object).

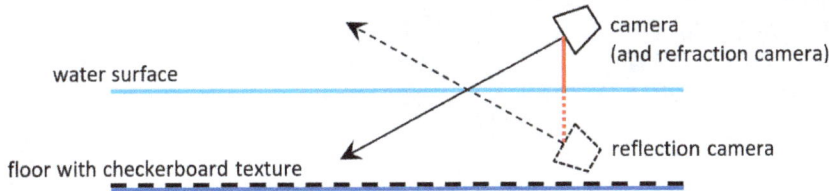

Figure 15.3
Positions for reflection and refraction cameras

Program 15.3 (in part two) adds code for rendering the scene to the reflection and refraction buffers. There are two calls to display() here, one for filling the reflection buffer and one for filling the refraction buffers. (Later, in part three, we add a third call to display() that renders the final scene from the actual camera for building the completed scene. Note that the two display() functions shown here in part two render portions of the scene to the reflection and refraction scenes in preparation for assembling the final scene in part three.) In each case, we bind the respective buffers before rendering the associated relevant elements in the scene. Note that we have now added code to build the appropriate view matrix code in each case, adjusting the pitch as described above for the reflection camera. We have included the subsequent binding of the default framebuffer before assembling the complete scene (those steps are given in part three).

Program 15.3 – Part 2: Filling the Reflection and Refraction Buffers

C++/OpenGL Application

```
. . .
void display(GLFWwindow* window, double currentTime) {

    // compute perspective matrix as before
    . . .
    // render reflection scene to reflection buffer (if camera above surface)
    if (cameraY >= surfaceLocY) {
        // the reflection view matrix negates the camera Y position and pitch
        vMat = glm::translate(glm::mat4(1.0f), glm::vec3(0.0f, -(surfacePlaneHeight - cameraHeight), 0.0f))
            * glm::rotate(glm::mat4(1.0f), toRadians(-cameraPitch), glm::vec3(1.0f, 0.0f, 0.0f));
```

```
    glBindBuffer(GL_FRAMEBUFFER, reflectFrameBuffer);
    glClear(GL_DEPTH_BUFFER_BIT);
    glClear(GL_COLOR_BUFFER_BIT);
    prepForSkyBoxRender();
    glEnable(GL_CULL_FACE);
    glFrontFace(GL_CCW);
    glDisable(GL_DEPTH_TEST);
    glDrawArrays(GL_TRIANGLES, 0, 36);
    glEnable(GL_DEPTH_TEST);
}

// render refraction scene to refraction buffer
// the refraction view matrix is the same as for the regular camera
vMat = glm::translate(glm::mat4(1.0f), glm::vec3(0.0f, -cameraHeight, 0.0f))
    * glm::rotate(glm::mat4(1.0f), toRadians(cameraPitch), glm::vec3(1.0f, 0.0f, 0.0f));

glBindBuffer(GL_FRAMEBUFFER, refractFrameBuffer);
glClear(GL_DEPTH_BUFFER_BIT);
glClear(GL_COLOR_BUFFER_BIT);

// now render the checkerboard floor (and other items below the surface) to the refraction buffer
prepForFloorRender();
glEnable(GL_DEPTH_TEST);
glDepthFunc(GL_LEQUAL);
glDrawArrays(GL_TRIANGLES, 0, 6);

// now switch back to the standard buffer in preparation for assembling the entire completed scene
glBindFramebuffer(GL_FRAMEBUFFER, 0);
    . . .
}
```

Finally, in part three, we complete Program 15.3 by incorporating the reflection and refraction textures (that were built in part two) into the top surface of the water. However, we have a slight problem...

When we rendered the reflection and refraction textures, we did so in the standard manner with 3D perspective, as though they were going to be displayed to a viewer. For example, the checkerboard pattern is rendered in a horizontal plane, making squares nearer the camera larger and those in the distance smaller. But we are used to applying texture images that are "flat" 2D images (i.e., that don't have perspective). So we can't use these reflection and refraction textures in the standard manner using the texture coordinates for the top surface.

Fortunately, correcting for this is surprisingly easy. Consider the case of the camera above the water's surface. Figure 15.4 shows the scene rendered into the refraction buffer (on the left), which contains only the objects below the water's surface (and which is black everywhere else), the reflection buffer (on the right) which contains only the objects above the water's surface (and black everywhere else), and the original scene from Figure 15.2 (repeated in the center of Figure 15.4), which contains the untextured top surface on which we wish to assemble the final rendered scene.

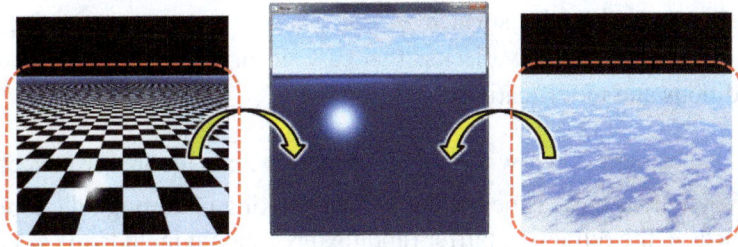

Figure 15.4
Refraction and reflection buffers (left / right) and render scene (center)

Figure 15.4 illustrates that the textures in the reflection and refraction buffers are already in the desired screen position. Therefore, all we need to do is use the *screen coordinates of the object being textured* (in this case, the top water surface), as the coordinates which are used to access the textures in the reflection and refraction buffers. The screen coordinates have already been computed in the vertex shader and are found in the (x,y) portion of the variable gl_Position. We merely need to pass a copy of gl_Position from the vertex shader to the fragment shader (as a varying vertex attribute) and use the .xy portion of that as the texture coordinates.

This technique is a simple case of *projective texture mapping* [WP23], which can be used in cases where some portion of the scene appears on an object. A common example is building a mirror (which, in a sense, we are doing here in the case of the reflection buffer). It is called "projective" because it is similar to projecting a scene onto an object like a projection screen.

We are now ready to complete Program 15.3. In part three, the reflection and refraction textures are incorporated onto the water's top surface. To do this, the C++/OpenGL application needs to make the reflection and refraction buffers available to the shaders for rendering the top surface. The fragment shader for the top surface of the water is where the reflection and refraction textures are applied. The vertex shader copies gl_Position into the new vertex attribute named glp and passes it to the fragment shader, which then uses it as texture coordinates for applying the reflection and refraction textures. Note that the coordinates are converted from the range of screen coordinates to the appropriate [0..1] range for texture coordinates. Notice also that in the case of reflection, the Y texture coordinate is subtracted from 1, because in this case, the reflection off the surface of the water needs to be flipped vertically.

Part three also includes the code that handles the case of the main camera being positioned *below* the surface of the water (i.e., the scene being viewed underwater), and we can now discuss that case. It turns out to only require a few minor additions and modifications:

- If the camera is below the water surface, we can ignore the reflection.
- When the camera is below the surface looking up through the top surface, the refraction buffer (and texture) should include the skybox (as well as objects such as birds and airplanes).
- Code is added to the prepForTopSurfaceRender() and prepForFloorRender() functions that informs the shaders whether the camera is above or below the surface. This is necessary because the fragment shader needs to know whether to include the reflection texture in the top surface.

Thus, in part three, we only compute the reflection if the camera is above the water's surface.

In the fragment shader for the water's top surface, the mixture of the reflection and refraction depends on whether the camera is above or below the water surface. If the camera is above the surface, then both textures are included. If the camera is underwater, then the refraction texture is mixed with the blue water color. The output, both for the camera above and below the water surface, is shown immediately after the code, in Figure 15.5.

Program 15.3 – Part 3: Applying the Reflection/Refraction Textures

C++/OpenGL Application

```
. . .
// added to prepForTopSurfaceRender() and prepForFloorRender():
    aboveLoc = glGetUniformLocation(renderingProgramSURFACE, "isAbove");
    if (cameraHeight >= surfacePlaneHeight)
        glUniform1i(aboveLoc, 1);
```

```
    else
        glUniform1i(aboveLoc, 0);
...
void display(GLFWwindow* window, double currentTime) {

    ...
    // now render the appropriate items to the refraction buffer
    if (cameraHeight >= surfacePlaneHeight) {
        prepForSkyBoxRender();
        glEnable(GL_CULL_FACE);
        glFrontFace(GL_CCW);
        glDisable(GL_DEPTH_TEST);
        glDrawArrays(GL_TRIANGLES, 0, 36);
        glEnable(GL_DEPTH_TEST);
    }
    else {
        prepForFloorRender();
        glEnable(GL_DEPTH_TEST);
        glDepthFunc(GL_LEQUAL);
        glDrawArrays(GL_TRIANGLES, 0, 6);
    }

    ...
    // now switch back to the standard buffer in preparation for assembling the entire completed scene
    glBindFramebuffer(GL_FRAMEBUFFER, 0);
    glClear(GL_DEPTH_BUFFER_BIT);
    glClear(GL_COLOR_BUFFER_BIT);

    ...
    // draw water top (surface)
    prepForTopSurfaceRender();
    glActiveTexture(GL_TEXTURE0);
    glBindTexture(GL_TEXTURE_2D, reflectTextureId);
    glActiveTexture(GL_TEXTURE1);
    glBindTexture(GL_TEXTURE_2D, refractTextureId);

    // the remainder of display() is identical to that shown in part one
    ...
}
```

Vertex Shader (for top surface)

```
...
out vec4 glp;
...
void main(void)
{  ...
```

```
glp = p_matrix * v_matrix * m_matrix * vec4(position,1.0);
gl_Position = glp;
}
```

Fragment Shader (for top surface)

```
. . .
in vec4 glp;
uniform int isAbove;

void main(void)
{   . . . // lighting computations are unchanged from before
    vec4 mixColor, reflectColor, refractColor, blueColor;
    if (isAbove == 1)
    {   refractColor = texture(refractTex, (vec2(glp.x,glp.y))/(2.0*glp.w)+0.5);
        reflectColor = texture(reflectTex, (vec2(glp.x,-glp.y))/(2.0*glp.w)+0.5);
        mixColor = (0.2 * refractColor) + (1.0 * reflectColor);
    }
    else
    {   refractColor = texture(refractTex, (vec2(glp.x,glp.y))/(2.0*glp.w)+0.5);
        blueColor = vec4(0.0, 0.25, 1.0, 1.0);
        mixColor = (0.5 * blueColor) + (0.6 * refractColor);
    }
    color = vec4((mixColor.xyz * (ambient + diffuse) + 0.75*specular), 1.0);
}
```

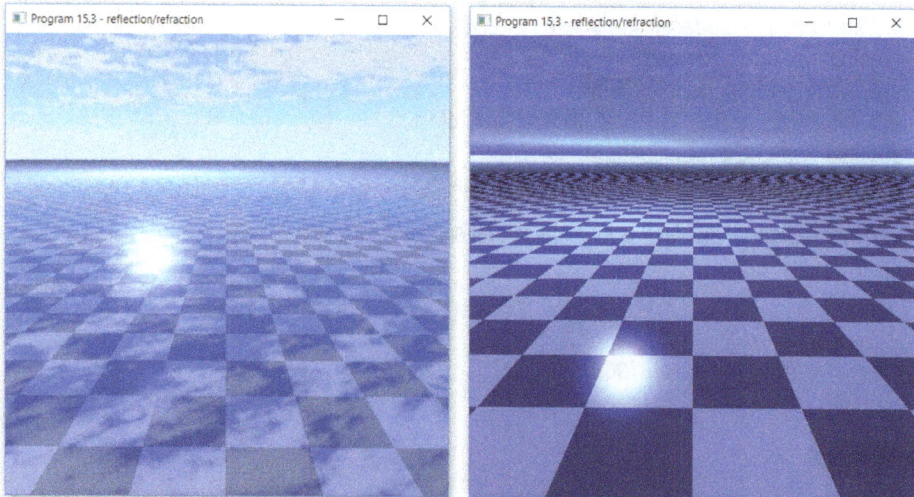

Figure 15.5
Reflection and Refraction - camera above the water's surface (left), and below the water's surface (right)

15.3 ADDING SURFACE WAVES

So far, our simulated water has been perfectly still. We now add movement to the water's surface. There are many ways to do this, depending on whether we wish to simulate tiny ripples, random effects from wind, current flow, or ocean waves. In our example, we simulate modest waves such as might appear if there were a slight breeze, by combining the *normal mapping* technique previously covered in Chapter 10, with a *noise map*. Since waves are not entirely random, the noise map we build for our water's surface will be a combination of the noise that we generated previously in Chapter 14, with the regularity of a sine wave. The noise map will then serve as a sort of height map, but note that we are *not* going to actually modify the water surface geometry as is typically done in height mapping; rather, we will modify the normal vectors (in a manner similar to normal mapping) to make it appear that way. (Techniques exist for actually modifying surface geometry; for example, a geometry shader could be used, as we studied previously in Chapter 13.)

The noise map is built using the code from Section 14.5, with a slight modification to the turbulence() function. Specifically, we add a sine wave that runs diagonally across the XZ plane:

```
double turbulence(double x, double y, double z, double maxZoom) {
    double sum = 0.0, zoom = maxZoom;

    sum = (sin((1.0/512.0)*(8*PI)*(x+z)) + 1) * 8.0;
    while (zoom >= 0.9) {
        sum = sum + smoothNoise(zoom, x/zoom, y/zoom, z/zoom) * zoom;
        zoom = zoom / 2.0;
    }
    sum = 128.0 * sum / maxZoom;
    return sum;
}
```

The diagonal sine wave is accomplished via sin(x+z), with additional factors for scaling (1/512 assuming that the size of the noise map is 256 along the X and Z dimensions), ensuring that the range of values for x+y span a multiple of PI so that the sine wave wraps smoothly at edge boundaries, adding 1 to convert the sine wave from -1..+1 to 0..2, and then scaling the height to the desired amount (in this case, by a factor of 8). Note that since we have been making heavy use of tiling, it is especially important in this application to use a noise map dimension that is a power of 2, so that the noise also wraps smoothly at edge boundaries.

We then pass the noise map to the fragment shader, where we use it to alter the normals by a very small offset. The additions to the code are shown in Program 15.4. The resulting output is shown in Figure 15.6.

Program 15.4 – Adding Surface Waves

C++/OpenGL Application

```
. . .
GLuint noiseTexture;
const int noiseHeight = 256;
const int noiseWidth = 256;
const int noiseDepth = 256;
double noise[noiseHeight][noiseWidth][noiseDepth];
. . .
// generateNoise(), buildNoiseTexture(), fillDataArray(), smoothNoise() same as in Chapter 14
// turbulence() function as described above
. . .
void init(GLFWwindow* window) {
    . . .
    generateNoise();
    noiseTexture = buildNoiseTexture();
}

void display(GLFWwindow* window, double currentTime) {
    . . .
    // draw water top (surface)
    . . .
    glActiveTexture(GL_TEXTURE2);
    glBindTexture(GL_TEXTURE_3D, noiseTexture);
    . . .
}
```

Fragment Shader (for top surface)

```
. . .
layout (binding=2) uniform sampler3D noiseTex;
. . .
vec3 estimateWaveNormal(float offset, float mapScale, float hScale)
{   // estimate the normal using the wave height values stored in the noise texture.
    // Do this by looking up three height values at the specified offset distance around this fragment.
```

```
    // incoming parameters are scale factors for nearness of neighbors, size of noise map relative to
                                                                           scene, and height
    float h1 = (texture(noiseTex, vec3(((tc.s))*mapScale, 0.5, ((tc.t)+offset)*wScale))).r * hScale;
    float h2 = (texture(noiseTex, vec3(((tc.s)-offset)*mapScale, 0.5, ((tc.t)-offset)*mapScale))).r * hScale;
    float h3 = (texture(noiseTex, vec3(((tc.s)+offset)*mapScale, 0.5, ((tc.t)-offset)*mapScale))).r * hScale;

    // build two vectors using the three neighboring height values. The cross product is the estimated normal.
    vec3 v1 = vec3(0, h1, -1);      // neighboring height value #1
    vec3 v2 = vec3(-1, h2, 1);      // neighboring height value #2
    vec3 v3 = vec3(1, h3, 1);       // neighboring height value #3
    vec3 v4 = v2-v1;                // first vector orthogonal to desired normal
    vec3 v5 = v3-v1;                // second vector orthogonal to desired normal
    vec3 normEst = normalize(cross(v4,v5));
    return normEst;
}

void main(void)
{   vec3 L = normalize(varyingLightDir);
    vec3 V = normalize(-varyingVertPos);
    vec3 N = normalize(varyingNormal);
    vec3 N = estimateWaveNormal(.0002, 32.0, 16.0);

    . . .
}
```

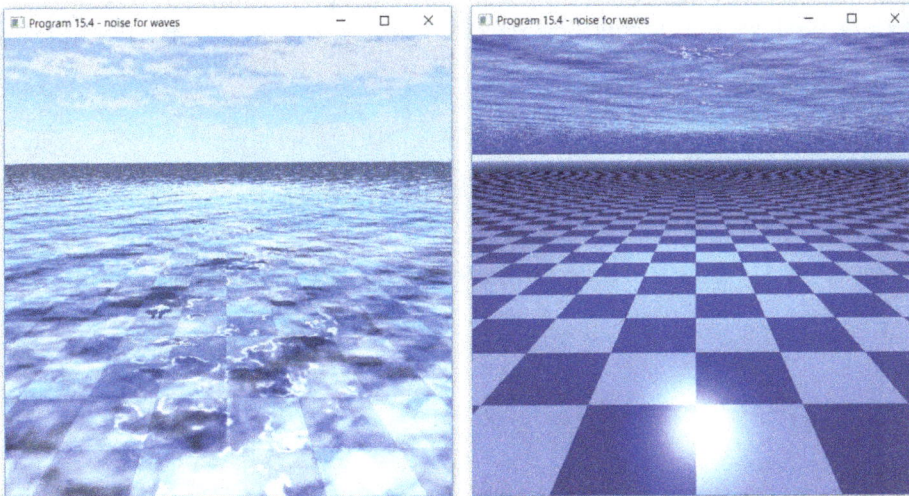

Figure 15.6
Adding surface waves by combining a sine wave and noise map – camera above water surface (left) and below water surface (right)

15.4 ADDITIONAL CORRECTIONS

Take a look at the images in Figure 15.6 and observe the following "flaws" in them:

- When the camera is above the water (left image), we would expect the visible "checkerboard" lines on the floor to be distorted based on the distortions on the water surface – but they are straight.

- When the camera is below the surface (right image), we expect the lighting on the floor to be similarly distorted, but the specular highlight is perfectly round.

- Light is attenuated more rapidly under water, but the floor is equally bright both up close and far away.

- The Fresnel effect is missing. This is a phenomenon in which viewing straight down through a transparent medium (such as water) favors the refraction contribution, while looking across the surface favors the reflection [B01]. Instead, in the image at the left, reflection and refraction are equally apparent across the entire top surface.

Distorting the checkerboard lines when the camera is above the water surface can be done in the portion of the fragment shader that renders the checkerboard. The shader needs the noise map, so we add the following code to the section of the C++/OpenGL application that builds the refraction buffer, to send it the noise texture:

```
glActiveTexture(GL_TEXTURE0);
glBindTexture(GL_TEXTURE_3D, noiseTexture);
```

The revised fragment shader for rendering the floor is shown in Program 15.5.

Program 15.5 – Distorting Objects Under the Water's Surface

Fragment Shader (for floor plane)

```
. . .
layout (binding=0) uniform sampler3D noiseTex;

vec3 checkerboard(vec2 tc)
{   // we use the estimated normals derived from the noise map, as before, but with much less height
    vec3 estN = estimateWaveNormal(.05, 32.0, 0.05);   // this function was described in Section 15.3

    // Compute the amount to distort the color location lookup.
    // The amount of distortion is tunable using the variable distortStrength.
    float distortStrength = 0.1;
```

```
if (isAbove != 1) distortStrength = 0.0;
vec2 distorted = tc + estN.xz * distortStrength;

// adjust the lookup for the color by modifying the axes by the distortion amount
float tileScale = 64.0;
float tile = mod(floor(distorted.x * tileScale) + floor(distorted.y * tileScale), 2.0);
return tile * vec3(1,1,1);
}
```

In Program 15.5, we perturb the normals on the checkerboard floor using small scale factors for height and distortion strength. Experimenting with various distortionStrength values shows that it only takes a very small amount of distortion in the checkerboard color lookup to generate a large visible distortion effect in the lines of the checkerboard. Also note that the test (isAbove!=1) ensures that we only include a distortion factor if the camera is above the surface.

Distorting the underwater *lighting* when the camera is below the water's surface can also be done in the fragment shader that renders the checkerboard. We simply modify the normal vectors for the floor based on the estimated normals from the noise map. In this case, experimentation reveals that larger values for height and distortion strength are needed than were used previously for distorting the lines of the checkerboard itself. The revised fragment shader for rendering the floor is shown in the continuation of Program 15.5.

The output incorporating all of the changes shown in Program 15.5 is shown in Figure 15.7.

Program 15.5 (continued) – Distorting Lighting Under the Water's Surface

Fragment Shader (for floor plane)

```
. . .
void main(void)
{   . . .
    vec3 N = normalize(varyingNormal);
    vec3 estN = estimateWaveNormal(.05, 32.0, 0.5);
    float distortStrength = 0.5;
    vec2 distort = estN.xz * distortStrength;
    N = normalize(N + vec3(distort.x, 0.0, distort.y));
    . . .
    // the rest of the main() is unchanged
}
```

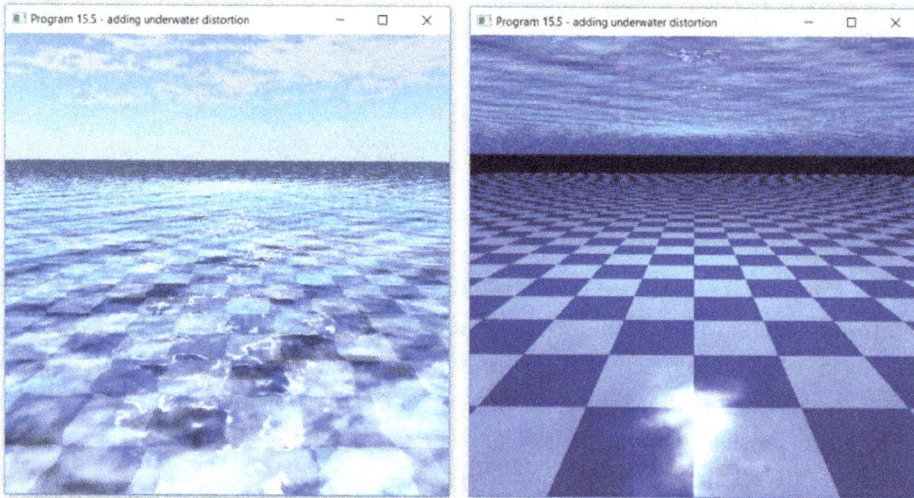

Figure 15.7
Adding distortion to the floor pattern and its lighting – camera above water surface (left, floor pattern distorted), and below water surface (right, lighting distorted)

Making items that are further away become less visible was covered previously in Section 14.1 ("fog"). The code given there works almost verbatim here, and it is only used when the camera is below the water's surface.

A simple Fresnel effect can dramatically enhance realism when the camera is above the top surface, and can be implemented in the fragment shader by computing the angle between the water's surface normal and the view direction, and then mixing the reflection and refraction components based on the magnitude of the angle. We experimented with various offsets and scaling factors and found that, for this scene, shifting the Fresnel factor to smaller values (to increase the refractive contribution), clamping the range to [0..1] (for subsequent use in the mix() function) and raising it to a power of 3 (making the effect nonlinear and sharpening the transition between refractive and reflective dominance) produced a pleasing result. Other scenes may require different adjustments We also observed that the effect is clearest if the original surface normal is used, i.e., without the normals having been perturbed by noise and waves.

The additions for both effects are given in Program 15.6, and the results are shown in Figure 15.8.

Program 15.6 – Adding "fog" and "Fresnel" effects

Fragment Shader (for top surface)

```
. . .
void main(void)
{  // code for determining amount of fog to add – very similar to Section 14.1
    vec4 fogColor = vec4(0.0, 0.0, 0.2, 1.0);
    float fogStart = 10.0;
    float fogEnd = 300.0;
    float dist = length(varyingVertPos.xyz);
    float fogFactor = clamp((((fogEnd-dist) / (fogEnd-fogStart)), 0.0, 1.0);

    . . .
    // angle between normal vector and view vector (for Fresnel effect)
    vec3 Nfres = normalize(varyingNormal);
    float cosFres = dot(V,Nfres);
    float fresnel = acos(cosFres);
    fresnel = pow(clamp(fresnel-0.3, 0.0, 1.0), 3);  // tuning for this particular application

    . . .
    if (isAbove == 1)
    {  // if above the surface, compute reflection and refraction contributions separately, then mix
        refractColor = texture(refractTex, (vec2(glp.x,glp.y))/(2.0*glp.w)+0.5);
        reflectColor = texture(reflectTex, (vec2(glp.x,-glp.y))/(2.0*glp.w)+0.5);
        reflectColor = vec4((reflectColor.xyz * (ambient + diffuse) + 0.75*specular), 1.0);
        color = mix(refractColor, reflectColor, fresnel);
    }
    else
    {  // if below the surface, compute only the refractive contribution, and add fog
        refractColor = texture(refractTex, (vec2(glp.x,glp.y))/(2.0*glp.w)+0.5);
        mixColor = (0.5 * blueColor) + (0.6 * refractColor);
        color = vec4((mixColor.xyz * (ambient + diffuse) + 0.75*specular), 1.0);
        color = mix(fogColor, color, pow(fogFactor,5));
    }
}
```

Fragment Shader (for floor plane)

```
. . .
void main(void)
{  // code for determining amount of fog to add – very similar to Section 14.1
    vec4 fogColor = vec4(0.0, 0.0, 0.2, 1.0);
    float fogStart = 10.0;
    float fogEnd = 300.0;
```

```
float dist = length(varyingVertPos.xyz);
float fogFactor = clamp((((fogEnd-dist) / (fogEnd-fogStart)), 0.0, 1.0);
. . .
if (isAbove != 1) color = mix(fogColor, color, pow(fogFactor,5.0));
}
```

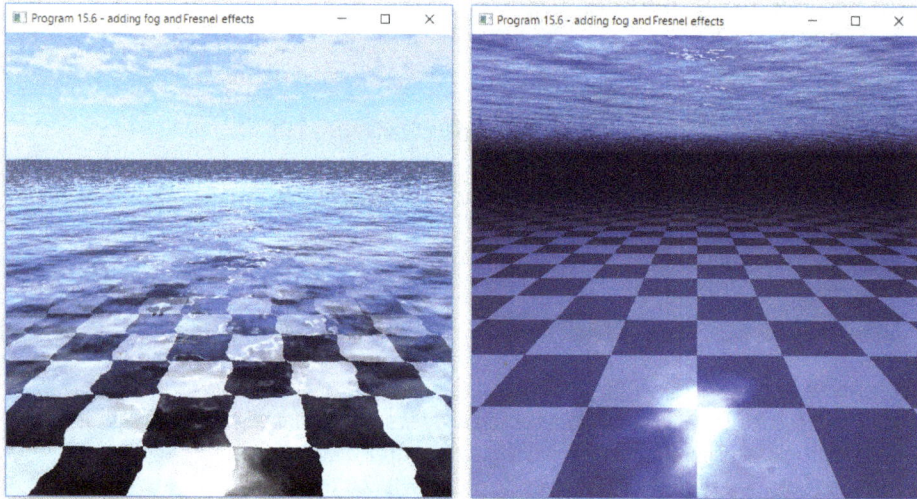

Figure 15.8
Fresnel effect (left, above the water's surface) and fog effect (right, below the water's surface)

15.5 ANIMATING THE WATER MOVEMENT

Animating the water's surface can be done in a similar manner as was done for clouds by taking advantage of the third dimension in the noise map (as yet unused). Recall from Section 14.8 the trick of replacing the texture lookup constant in the third dimension with a variable that changes over time. As the retrieved "slice" of the noise map changes, the noise details change. We can use that same trick here to move the sine wave by adjusting the position along the third axis over time when we look up which "slice" of the noise map to apply.

This modification is given in Program 15.7. Although we cannot adequately show the animation here, some frames showing the changes to the surface and lighting over time are given in Figure 15.9, viewed from both above and below the water's surface. (Or, to see the actual movement, run the code provided in the companion files.)

Program 15.7 – Animating the Water's Surface

C++/OpenGL Application

```
. . .
float depthLookup = 0.0f;
GLuint dOffsetLoc;

double turbulence(double x, double y, double z, double maxZoom) {
    double sum = 0.0, zoom = maxZoom;
    sum = (sin((1.0/512.0)*(8*PI)*(x+z-4*y)) + 1) * 8.0;   // this change moves the sine wave through the noise map
    . . .
}

void prepForTopSurfaceRender() {
    . . .
    dOffsetLoc = glGetUniformLocation(renderingProgramSURFACE, "depthOffset");
    glUniform1f(dOffsetLoc, depthLookup);
    . . .
}

void prepForFloorRender() {
    . . .
    dOffsetLoc = glGetUniformLocation(renderingProgramFLOOR, "depthOffset");
    glUniform1f(dOffsetLoc, depthLookup);
    . . .
}

void display(GLFWwindow* window, double currentTime) {
    depthLookup += (currentTime – prevTime) * .05f;
    prevTime = currentTime;         // prevTime is a global variable initialized to glfwGetTime() in init()
    . . .
}
```

Vertex Shaders (for top surface, and for floor)

```
. . .
uniform float depthOffset;
. . .
```

Fragment Shaders (for top surface, and for floor)

```
. . .
uniform float depthOffset;
vec3 estimateWaveNormal(float offset, float mapScale, float hScale)
{   . . .
```

```
    float h1 = (texture(noiseTex, vec3(tc.s*mapScale, depthOffset, (tc.t + offset)*mapScale))).r * hScale;
    float h2 = (texture(noiseTex, vec3((tc.s-offset)*mapScale, depthOffset, (tc.t - offset)*mapScale))).r * hScale;
    float h3 = (texture(noiseTex, vec3((tc.s+offset)*mapScale, depthOffset, (tc.t - offset)*mapScale))).r * hScale;
    . . .
}
```

In Figure 15.9, when the camera is above the top surface, note the changes in each frame over time, seen in the waves on the surface of the water, the changing light reflections off the surface, and the changing distortions in the lines of the checkerboard. When the camera is below the surface, note the changes in the lighting on the floor, and the changes in the waves and their specular highlights when looking up at the top surface.

Figure 15.9
Animating water effects, both above and below the water's surface. In the top three images, the camera is above the top surface, and in the bottom three images, the camera is below the surface

15.6 UNDERWATER CAUSTICS

It is common to observe curved bands of light on an underwater floor, as light from above the water is transmitted to the floor from the various undulations on the wavy surface. These bands are sometimes called *water caustics* [WC23], and adding them can make an underwater scene more clearly appear underwater. In this section, we only add them to our scene whenever the camera is below the water surface (see Exercise 15.4 for the case where the camera is above the water surface).

Simulating water caustics can be done in a variety of ways. They can be done fairly accurately using ray tracing, although this can be complex and computationally expensive [G07]. However, in most cases, it isn't necessary for the caustics to be perfectly accurate, and even a rough simulation is adequate to convey an underwater effect. In most cases, generating white lines that bend in a manner consistent with the waves on the water surface is sufficient.

We can generate a sort of caustic pattern in the fragment shader, directly from the noise map, as follows. We start by computing the sine of the noise value; the noise value (which ranges between 0 and 1) is first multiplied by 2π so that the sine values cycle smoothly. This results in a value that cycles between -1.0 and 1.0. The absolute value of this cycles between 0.0 and 1.0, but with steep slopes around 0.0 and shallower slopes around 1.0. Subtracting this absolute value from 1.0 then inverts this, resulting in long flat regions around 0.0 and sharp peaks around 1.0. This can be amplified by raising it to an adjustable exponent, using a tunable variable named strength. The result is a function that usually outputs values near 0, but has occasional small regions of output values near 1.0. When applied to the top surface color value at a given world coordinate, it generates periodic patterns that follow the top surface waves, which we can then incorporate into the bottom surface color. Program 15.8 shows this code added to the fragment shader and the resulting computed values added to the color rendered to the floor. The output is shown in Figure 15.10.

Note that the floor color elements after adding the caustic are clamped to the range [0..1] to ensure that they are within the valid range for RGB values.

Program 15.8 – Adding Underwater Caustics

Fragment Shader (for floor)

```
. . .
float getCausticValue(float x, float y, float z)
{   float w = 8;        // frequency of caustic curved bands
    float strength = 4.0;
    float PI = 3.14159;
    float noise = texture(noiseTex, vec3(x*w, y, z*w)).r;
    return pow((1.0-abs(sin(noise*2*PI))), strength);
}
```

```
void main(void)
{   . . .
    color = vec4((mixColor * (ambient + diffuse) + specular), 1.0);

    // add caustics
    if (isAbove != 1)
    {   float causticColor = getCausticValue(tc.s, depthOffset, tc.t);
        float colorR = clamp(color.x + causticColor, 0.0, 1.0);
        float colorG = clamp(color.y + causticColor, 0.0, 1.0);
        float colorB = clamp(color.z + causticColor, 0.0, 1.0);
        color = vec4(colorR, colorG, colorB, 1.0);
    }

    // add fog
    if (isAbove != 1) color = mix(fogColor, color, pow(fogFactor,5.0));
}
```

Figure 15.10
Caustics added when the camera is below the water's surface

SUPPLEMENTAL NOTES

Methods for simulating water in a real-time graphics application is a complex topic, and we have only scratched the surface. We also have only focused on one type of water. Completely different techniques are needed to simulate water spraying from a garden hose or wine splashing in a wine glass.

Even our simulation of a swimming pool or lake surface is limited. For example, only small ripples on the water's surface are possible using the method described. Larger waves would require modifying the surface geometry. One way of doing this would be to use the tessellation stage to increase the number of vertices, and then use height mapping to move them according to the values in the noise map.

Our simulation of the visible distortions on the floor have a fundamental inaccuracy, in that they are based on the noise values for the surface locations directly above the corresponding floor locations. Actually, the distortion for a given floor location should be based on the noise value for the surface location in between the camera and the floor location. However, it is unlikely to make a difference in the perceived realism. There are many simplifications such as this throughout our implementation.

"Fresnel" is pronounced "Fre-nel" – the "s" is silent.

There are numerous papers and resources for readers interested in diving more deeply into the topic of simulating water and other fluids. There are even entire books on the topic [B15].

The technique described in this chapter was patterned closely after an implementation by Chris Swenson (of Havalo, LLC) as part of a special project at California State University, Sacramento. His contributions greatly facilitated our explanations and we appreciate the excellent work that he did generating a nicely coherent step-by-step approach.

Exercises

15.1 Add a flying object such as a bird or airplane (or even the NASA space shuttle model) flying overhead, above the top surface of the water. Then include it in the reflection off the top surface of the water when the camera is above the water's surface and in the refraction through the top surface when the camera is below the water surface.

15.2 Add an object moving underwater, such as a fish or submarine (or even the Studio 522 dolphin) below the top surface of the water. Then include it in the scene when the camera is below the top surface and in the refraction when the camera is above the top surface.

15.3 In exercise 15.2 (above), if you haven't done so already, add water caustics to the underwater object.

15.4 Modify the fragment shader in Program 15.8 so that the water caustics are also rendered when the camera is *above* the top surface as well. Do you think that the scene appears more realistic or less realistic with the caustics included in this case? If the latter, try to find a way to tune the caustics so that they increase realism rather than detracting from it.

References

[B01]   J. Birn (2001), Fresnel Effect, from 3dRender.com, Accessed November 2023, http://www.3drender.com/glossary/index.htm

[B15]   R. Bridson (2015), Fluid Simulation for Computer Graphics, CRC Press.

[G07]   J. Guardado (2007), Rendering Water Caustics, GPU Gems (NVIDIA), Accessed November 2023, https://developer.nvidia.com/gpugems/gpugems/part-i-natural-effects/chapter-2-rendering-water-caustics

[WC23] Caustic (optics) – Wikipedia, 2019. Accessed November 2023, https://en.wikipedia.org/wiki/Caustic_(optics)

[WP23] Projective texture mapping, Wikipedia, Accessed November 2023, https://en.wikipedia.org/wiki/Projective_texture_mapping

CHAPTER **16**

RAY TRACING AND COMPUTE SHADERS

■ ■ ■ ■ ■

In this chapter, we study a method for creating highly realistic lighting effects called *ray tracing*. We studied lighting previously in Chapter 7, and then in Chapter 9 we saw a simple method for simulating reflection called environment mapping. However, all of these methods only partially simulate lighting effects. For example, the ADS lighting model only considers the effect that a light source has on a surface, without regard to the effects of light reflected between objects in the scene. Similarly, environment mapping is limited to modeling the reflection of a cube map, but not neighboring objects. By contrast, ray tracing more closely models the actual paths of light through a scene, considering reflections between objects, shadows, and even refraction through transparent objects. Ray tracing is capable of generating highly detailed and photo-realistic effects, although it requires significant computing resources and cannot always be done in real time.

Ray tracing is motivated by a simple idea: if we can follow the paths of light rays from their source to our eyes, we can faithfully reproduce what we would see. However, in practice this would be infeasible – there are simply too many light rays, most of which don't even end up reaching our eyes (or have only a marginal effect on what we perceive).

A very clever alternative is to reverse this idea. Instead of tracing rays from their source to our eye, we instead trace rays starting from the eye, "bouncing" them some number of times off of the objects in the scene, accumulating and combining whatever lighting effects are noted along the way. In between the eye and the scene, we place a grid of pixels (at the desired resolution) in which we store the rendering of the scene. For each pixel in the grid, we generate one ray, as shown in Figure 16.1. An algorithm for rendering a scene in this manner was first described in 1968 by Arthur Appel, who dubbed it *ray casting* [A68]. The idea was extended in 1979 by Foley and Whitted to include bouncing each ray recursively to simulate reflection, shadows, and refraction [FW79], and this process is called "ray tracing." Today, ray tracing tools and hardware are being introduced into the consumer market (such as Nvidia RTX [RTX23])

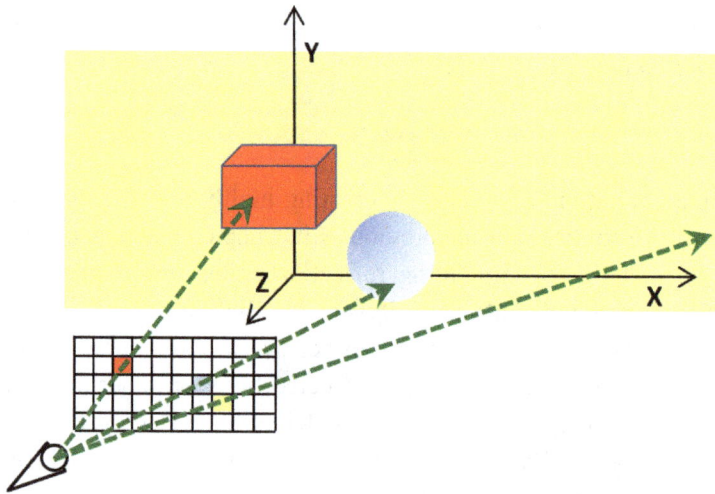

Figure 16.1
Ray Casting

Implementing ray tracing using OpenGL shaders is challenging. The large number of computations that must be done can tax even modern GPUs. Also, as we shall see, a generalized ray tracing algorithm uses recursion, which is not supported in OpenGL (GLSL) shaders. While some simple cases can be done without recursion, implementing a reasonably complete ray tracing algorithm will require us to implement the recursion stack ourselves. Our overall approach will involve a two-phase process:

(phase 1)   Implement the ray-tracing algorithm that builds the pixel grid as an image

(phase 2)   Render the resulting image

Phase 2 will be extremely easy, as we already know how to render an image as a texture. All of the hard work is done in phase 1, and so to help achieve reasonable performance, we will use a *compute shader* for this step.

16.1 COMPUTE SHADERS

GPUs offer extraordinary parallel computing power. Whereas modern CPUs may have 4 or 8 cores, GPUs can have thousands. Therefore, they are often used for computationally-intensive non-graphics tasks. One way of doing this is to use a special-purpose language such as CUDA [NV23], or OpenCL [KR23]. Another way is to use a *compute shader*, which is a variant of the graphics pipeline shaders that we already know. OpenGL compute shaders are programmed in GLSL, so most of the same programming techniques that we have learned so far in the preceding chapters are immediately applicable.

There are many uses for compute shaders. The *OpenGL SuperBible* describes a few, including parallelizing matrix computations, building special-purpose image filters (such as adding depth-of-field), and simulating flocks or particle systems [SW15]. The topic of compute shaders is vast, and we focus only on using them for ray tracing. So, this chapter serves both as an introduction to ray tracing, and to compute shaders.

16.1.1 Compiling and Using Compute Shaders

Compute shaders are just like the other shaders we've seen, except that they are *not* a part of the graphics pipeline. They run independently; that is, they do not interact with, say, vertex or fragment shaders, and have no predefined inputs or outputs. However, they can accept data passed to them, such as in uniform variables, and can generate or modify data in memory. Compute shaders are compiled with glCompileShader(), linked with glLinkProgram(), and made active with glUseProgram() just like any other shader, except that the predefined constant GL_COMPUTE_SHADER is used to specify the shader type. We extend the Utils.cpp file to include a function for compiling a compute shader and building a rendering program from it. The header for this function matches the format of the other functions for compiling shaders, and is:

```
GLuint Utils::createShaderProgram(const char *cS)
```

That is, it accepts *one* string specifying the name of the file containing the compute shader. For example:

```
computeShaderProgram = Utils::createShaderProgram("computeShader.glsl");
```

Setting a particular compute shader program as the current one for execution is then the same as before:

```
glUseProgram(computeShaderProgram);
```

Launching the compute shader invocations is then done using the glDispatch() command, for example:

```
glDispatch(250, 1, 1);
```

The three parameters on the glDispatch() command will be described as we proceed.

16.1.2 Parallel Computing in Compute Shaders

Recall that the exact number of times that a *vertex* shader runs (is "invoked") is typically once per vertex, and is stated explicitly by the programmer as a parameter in the glDrawArrays() command. Similarly, the number of times that a compute shader is invoked is specified explicitly in the parameters to the glDispatch() command.

Let's look at an example of a compute shader to perform a simple parallel computing task. In Program 16.1, we present an application that *sums the corresponding elements of two one-dimensional matrices*. We choose that task because each of the additions are independent, and therefore can be done in parallel. To keep things simple, we will consider only matrices of size six. The strategy is to write a compute shader that simply adds two numbers together, and we run that shader six times, once for each matrix element. This will allow the six executions of the shader to be run in parallel. It is sufficiently simple that we can use it to easily illustrate how to: (1) pass data to a compute shader, (2) perform a simple parallel computation, and (3) pass the result back to the C++/OpenGL application. Details of the code follow the listing.

There are multiple ways of passing data to a compute shader, including many of the normal methods we have already learned such as uniforms, buffers, etc. However, there are only two ways of getting computed data *out* of a compute shader. The first way is to use a special kind of buffer called a *Shader Storage*

Buffer Object (SSBO), which was introduced at OpenGL version 4.3 and is convenient for mathematical applications, such as matrix operations. The second way is to use an *image load/store*, which is more convenient for image processing or graphics applications. For this simple application of summing two matrices, we will use SSBOs. Later, we will use the second method (image load/store) in Section 16.2 when we study ray tracing.

Program 16.1 – Simple Compute Shader example

C++/OpenGL Application

```
// library declarations for stdio, GLEW, GLFW, and Utils are the same as in previous examples
. . .

GLuint buffer[3];
GLuint simpleComputeShader;
int v1[ ] = { 10, 12, 16, 18, 50, 17 };        // these are the two matrices we are adding together
int v2[ ] = { 30, 14, 80, 20, 51, 12 };
int res[6];        // this is the array in which the result will be placed

void init() {
    simpleComputeShader = Utils::createShaderProgram("matrixAdditionComputeShader.glsl");

    glGenBuffers(3, buffer);    // note that each buffer is an SSBO (Shader Storage Buffer) of size 6
    glBindBuffer(GL_SHADER_STORAGE_BUFFER, buffer[0]);
    glBufferData(GL_SHADER_STORAGE_BUFFER, 6, v1, GL_STATIC_DRAW);
    glBindBuffer(GL_SHADER_STORAGE_BUFFER, buffer[1]);
    glBufferData(GL_SHADER_STORAGE_BUFFER, 6, v2, GL_STATIC_DRAW);
    glBindBuffer(GL_SHADER_STORAGE_BUFFER, buffer[2]);
    glBufferData(GL_SHADER_STORAGE_BUFFER, 6, NULL, GL_STATIC_READ);
}

void computeSum() {
    glUseProgram(simpleComputeShader);
    glBindBufferBase(GL_SHADER_STORAGE_BUFFER, 0, buffer[0]); // first input matrix
    glBindBufferBase(GL_SHADER_STORAGE_BUFFER, 1, buffer[1]); // second input matrix
    glBindBufferBase(GL_SHADER_STORAGE_BUFFER, 2, buffer[2]); // buffer to hold output matrix

    glDispatchCompute(6, 1, 1); // invokes the compute shader 6 times – the invocations can run in parallel
    glMemoryBarrier(GL_ALL_BARRIER_BITS); // ensure the compute shader finishes before proceeding
    glBindBuffer(GL_SHADER_STORAGE_BUFFER, buffer[2]); // retrieve the result buffer into array 'res'
    glGetBufferSubData(GL_SHADER_STORAGE_BUFFER, 0, sizeof(res), res);
}
```

```
int main(void) {
    . . . // the start of main() is the same as in other examples
    if (glewInit() != GLEW_OK) { exit(EXIT_FAILURE); }

    init();
    computeSum();  // since we don't use the GL window, we call this "computeSum" instead of "display"

    // display the input matrices, and the computed output matrix retrieved from the output SSBO
    std::cout << v1[0] << " " << v1[1] << " " << v1[2] << " " << v1[3] << " " v1[4] << " " v1[5] << std::endl;
    std::cout << v2[0] << " " << v2[1] << " " << v2[2] << " " << v2[3] << " " v2[4] << " " v2[5] << std::endl;
    std::cout << res[0] << " " << res[1] << " " << res[2] << " " << res[3] << " " res[4] << " " << res[5]
                                                                                        << std::endl;

    . . . // the end of main() is the same as in other examples
}
```

Compute Shader

```
#version 430
layout (local_size_x=1) in;     // sets the number of invocations per work group to 1
layout(binding=0) buffer inputBuffer1 { int inVals1[ ]; };
layout(binding=1) buffer inputBuffer2 { int inVals2[ ]; };
layout(binding=2) buffer outputBuffer { int outVals[ ]; };

void main()
{   uint thisRun = gl_GlobalInvocationID.x;
    outVals[thisRun] = inVals1[thisRun] + inVals2[thisRun];
}
```

Start by looking at the compute shader. Three buffers are declared, two for the input matrices, and one for the output matrix. Next let's consider the preceeding line that says:

layout (local_size_x=1) in;

Compute shader invocations are organized into structures called *work groups*. In this simple example, we don't really utilize work groups, and instead we simply want the shader to run six times. So, this layout command sets the work group size to 1. We will learn more about work groups shortly.

The actual number of times that the compute shader runs is specified in the C++/OpenGL application, specifically in the glDispatchCompute(6,1,1) call. Here we are specifying that the shader will run six times. Note here that the number of compute shader invocations was specified using three parameters comprising a vec3, in this case (6,1,1), and therefore the invocations will be numbered (0,0,0),

(1,0,0), (2,0,0), (3,0,0), (4,0,0), and (5,0,0). (We will see shortly how the other two dimensions of the shader invocation numbering – here both set to one – can be used in more complex situations.)

Now let's look at the main() function in the compute shader. Each time the shader runs, it first retrieves its invocation number by accessing the built-in GLSL variable gl_GlobalInvocationID (which is a vec3). In this case the "x" component of gl_GlobalInvocationID will be either 0, 1, 2, 3, 4, or 5, depending on which of the six invocations it is. It then uses this value as an index into the input SSBOs. Next, the compute shader adds one element from each of the input SSBOs, depending on which invocation ID it has, storing the result in the corresponding element of the output SSBO. In this manner, each invocation of the shader handles one of the six additions, and therefore the six additions can run in parallel.

The code in the C++/OpenGL application is primarily concerned with getting the data in and out of the compute shader. The input matrices v1 and v2 are declared as arrays and initialized to some test values at the top of the code. The output matrix is declared as array res. The buffers themselves are set up in the init() function, very similar to how we created VBOs, except that we specify type GL_SHADER_STORAGE_BUFFER. The three buffers are associated with v1, v2, and res, respectively. Note that in the case of the third buffer, we specify GL_STATIC_READ (instead of GL_STATIC_DRAW), because the C++ program will be retrieving data from that buffer rather than sending data into it. The init() function also compiles and links the shader.

Next, the computeSum() function is called. After making the shader program active, it associates each of the SSBOs with an integer index in a manner similar to what we have been doing with VBOs. In that case, we used the glBindBuffer() command, but since SSBOs aren't inherently indexed, we must use glBindBuffer-Base() to specify both the buffer and an associated index. Observe that the compute shader uses this same index in the binding qualifier to associate each buffer with an array variable (inVals1, inVals2, and outVals).

The computeSum() function next initiates the compute shader invocations by calling glDispatchCompute(). The result will then have been accumulated in the third buffer (i.e., buffer[2]), which can then be extracted into the res array by calling glGetBuffer-SubData(). The reader has probably also noticed the rather cryptic call to glMemory-Barrier() – this is required by OpenGL to ensure that the compute shader invocations fully complete before the code that follows is executed. That is, it ensures that the items produced by the glDispatchCompute() call are all fully available after the call.

The main() simply invokes init() and computeSum(), then prints all three arrays. Note that even though we are not using an OpenGL window, our use of GLFW mandates that a window be created. When run, the output is:

```
10 12 16 18 50  17
30 14 80 20 51  12
40 26 96 38 101 29
```

As expected, the third line contains the sum of the values in the first two lines.

16.1.3 Work Groups

In the previous simple example, we parallelized the matrix addition into six separate integer additions. We did this by specifying that the compute shader run six times, with the glDispatchCompute(6,1,1) call. The shader was written in such a way that each of the six invocations processed a different element of the matrix.

However, the glDispatchCompute() function is more flexible than that. Its three parameters make it possible to spread the computations over a 1D, 2D or 3D grid. In the matrix example, the matrices had dimension 6x1, so it was logical to spread the invocations across a 1D matrix of dimension 6x1x1 (which is what we did). However, soon we will write a compute shader that uses ray tracing to produce a display image, and in that application we will process each pixel in parallel. Since the display is a 2D grid of pixels, it will make more sense to specify the set of computations in a 2D grid. For example, if the GL window was 800x600 pixels, then we could initiate the compute shaders with glDispatchCompute(800, 600, 1), and then each gl_GlobalInvocationID value would correspond directly to the value of a particular pixel's 2D coordinates. The total number of invocations would then be 800x600 = 480,000. OpenGL will assign these 480,000 invocations to as many different processors (running in parallel) as it can.

The setup for compute shader invocations is even more flexible than that! In this last example, the total number 800x600 = 480,000 specified in the glDispatchCompute() call is actually not strictly the number of invocations, but the number of *work groups*. Since in our simple matrix example, the compute shader specified:

layout (local_size_x=1) in;

the work group size was set to 1, meaning that there was one invocation per work-group. Therefore, in this case, the number of work groups equals the number of invocations. This is how we set the work group size in the matrix example, and could also be used in the additional 800x600 example that we just described. It is also how we will set the work group size when we do ray tracing.

If you just want to learn about implementing ray tracing, and don't care to learn more about work groups, you may now bypass the next section and skip ahead to Section 16.2.

16.1.4 Work Group Details

A more complete description of work groups would start by stating that the glDispatchCompute() call distributes the desired computations that are to be done in parallel into work groups, where a work group is a set of invocations that have a need to share some local data. If, for a particular application, all of the invocations can be done completely independently of each other, such as is the case in our matrix or ray tracing applications (i.e., without any of them needing to share any local data), then the work group size may be set to 1, and in that case, the number of invocations is equal to the number of work groups.

The set of all work groups is organized in an abstract 3D grid (if the programmer wishes, one or more of the dimensions may be set to 1, reducing the dimensionality of the grid of workgroups to 2D or 1D). Thus, the numbering scheme used to identify a particular work group is not a single integer, but a *tuple* of three values. Furthermore, the invocations *within* a work group (i.e., in those cases where the work group size is specified to be greater than one) are *also* organized in a 3D grid. Thus, the programmer must specify (1) the size and dimensionality of the grid of work groups and (2) the size and dimensionality of each work group (also organized as a grid). This gives the programmer a huge degree of flexibility in organizing a potentially large set of parallel computations. The entire set of invocations are then initiated in the C++/OpenGL application by calling

glDispatchCompute(x,y,z)

where the x, y, and z parameters specify the size and dimensionality of the abstract grid of the set of work groups. The number of compute shader invocations then executed *within* each work group (and the dimensionality in which they are organized) is specified in the compute shader with the GLSL command

layout (local_size_x = X, local_size_y = Y, local_size_z = Z)

where X, Y, and Z are the dimensions of each work group. The dimensionalities of the set of work groups, and the work groups themselves, need not be the same, and may be 1D, 2D, or 3D. The resulting compute shader invocations can then run in parallel on the GPU.

During execution, a compute shader can determine how many work groups had been dispatched, and in which work group and invocation it is running by querying one or more of the following built-in GLSL variables:

gl_NumWorkGroups	the number of work groups dispatched by the C++ program
gl_WorkGroupID	which work group the current invocation belongs to
gl_LocalInvocationID	which invocation within the current work group this execution represents
gl_GlobalInvocationID	which invocation within the total invocations this execution represents

Let's walk through an example. Suppose the C++ program made the call glDispatchCompute(16,16,4). This would cause the active compute shader to be executed with a total of 16x16x4=1024 work groups. If the compute shader specified the work group size as layout(local_size_x=5, local_size_y=5, local_size_z=1), then the total size of each workgroup is 5x5x1=25, and therefore the total number of times that the compute shader would execute would be 1024x25=5120.

It is then possible to reference a particular work group and invocation being processed via its abstract grid indices. For example, the 1024 work groups dispatched in the previous example would be numbered (0,0,0), (0,0,1), (0,0,2), (0,0,3), (0,1,0), (0,1,1), and so forth, counting up to (15,15,3), and each execution of the compute shader can determine which of these work groups it belongs to by querying the built-in variable gl_WorkGroupID, which will return that value in a vec3. Similarly, in the same example (above), the 25 invocations done within each work group are numbered (0,0,0), (0,1,0), (0,2,0), (0,3,0), (0,4,0), (1,0,0), (1,1,0), (1,2,0), and so forth, counting up to (4,4,0), and each execution of the compute shader can determine which of these invocations it belongs to by querying the built-in variable gl_LocalInvocationID, which also returns a vec3. Note the contrast between how invocations are organized and "counted" in a *vertex* shader using the simple built-in int variable gl_VertexID (or gl_InstanceID in the case of instancing) versus the multidimensional organization (and numbering) of invocations in a compute shader.

The reason that compute shader invocations are organized into grids (actually, grids within grids!) is because many parallel computing tasks lend themselves to being conceptually subdivided into one or more grid structures. If a 3D grid structure is not needed, the programmer can simply set the Z dimensionality in the glDispatchCompute() command to one, reducing the grid to 2D on the remaining X and Y dimensions. And, if the application really only requires a simple series of computations without a grid organization at all, both the Y and Z dimensions can be set to one, producing a one-dimensional numbering of the invocations along the remaining X dimension. Similarly, in the compute shader, the dimensionality of the work group size can be reduced by leaving off the Y and/or Z terms (which is what we did for the matrix example, and what we will do for the ray tracing application).

The reader may still wonder why it can be advantageous to subdivide a solution among work groups, rather than simply making each work group be of size 1 and dispatching a large number of them (or, conversely, one very large work group). The answer depends on the application. Some problems lend themselves to being decomposed into chunks, such as an image blurring filter (described in [SW15]) in which the colors of groups of neighboring pixels are averaged together. In such cases, the need for shared data within a group arises and is supported by OpenGL's *shared local memory* construct (which is not covered in this book). In some cases, there can be performance benefits to selecting a work group size that best utilizes a particular GPU's architecture [Y10].

Our ray tracing application builds a two-dimensional texture image. So, it makes sense to utilize abstract grids that are of 2D dimensionality. For simplicity, we set the work group size to 1 and generate a workgroup for each pixel. For example, if our ray traced texture image is of size 512×512, we would call glDispatchCompute(512, 512, 1), and in the compute shader use layout (local_size_x=1) in; to denote a work group size of (1,1,1). This will generate a compute shader invocation for each pixel. Alternatively, we could subdivide the problem into work groups of size 8×8 by calling glDispatchCompute(64,64,1) and in the compute shader use layout (local_size_x=8, local_size_y=8) in; to denote a workgroup size of (8,8,1). This would also generate a compute shader invocation for each pixel, and result in the same number of total invocations. For this simple application, there are no dependencies between pixel computations, and it doesn't matter in what order the GPU does them (as long as all of them are completed before we try to display the resulting texture image), so either approach would work fine. For simplicity, we will choose the former.

16.1.5 Work Group Limitations

There are limitations on the number and sizes of work groups, and on the number of invocations allowed for each work group, depending on the graphics card. In some cases, these limitations may impact the selection of size and dimensionality of work groups. Those limitations can be determined by querying the built-in variables GL_MAX_COMPUTE_WORK_GROUP_COUNT, GL_MAX_COMPUTE_WORK_GROUP_SIZE, and GL_MAX_COMPUTE_WORK_GROUP_INVOCATIONS. Since these variables are of type vec3, the glGetIntegeri_v command can be used to access the values in each of the X, Y, and Z dimensions. An OpenGL/C++ function for doing this is shown in Figure 16.2 (and added to our Utils.cpp file).

```
void displayComputeShaderLimits() {
    int work_grp_cnt[3];
    int work_grp_siz[3];
    int work_grp_inv;
    glGetIntegeri_v(GL_MAX_COMPUTE_WORK_GROUP_COUNT, 0, &work_grp_cnt[0]);
    glGetIntegeri_v(GL_MAX_COMPUTE_WORK_GROUP_COUNT, 1, &work_grp_cnt[1]);
    glGetIntegeri_v(GL_MAX_COMPUTE_WORK_GROUP_COUNT, 2, &work_grp_cnt[2]);
    glGetIntegeri_v(GL_MAX_COMPUTE_WORK_GROUP_SIZE, 0, &work_grp_siz[0]);
    glGetIntegeri_v(GL_MAX_COMPUTE_WORK_GROUP_SIZE, 1, &work_grp_siz[1]);
    glGetIntegeri_v(GL_MAX_COMPUTE_WORK_GROUP_SIZE, 2, &work_grp_siz[2]);
    glGetIntegerv(GL_MAX_COMPUTE_WORK_GROUP_INVOCATIONS, &work_grp_inv);
    printf("max num of workgroups is: %i  %i  %i\n", work_grp_cnt[0], work_grp_cnt[1], work_grp_cnt[2]);
    printf("max size of workgroups is: %i  %i  %i\n", work_grp_siz[0], work_grp_siz[1], work_grp_siz[2]);
    printf("max local work group invocations %i\n", work_grp_inv);
}
```

Figure 16.2
Querying work group limitations

16.2 RAY CASTING

We start our study of ray tracing by first implementing a very basic *ray casting* algorithm as illustrated previously in Figure 16.1. In ray casting, we initialize a rectangular 2D texture (a grid of pixels), then create a series of rays, one for each pixel, starting from the camera (eye) through the pixel into the scene. Whichever closest object the ray hits, we assign that object's color to the pixel.

Ray casting (and ray tracing, which we will study later) is easiest when the scene contains simple shapes such as spheres, planes, etc., but can also be done on more complex objects comprised of triangle meshes. In this chapter, we limit our scene to spheres, planes, and boxes, In Chapter 17, we will extend the techniques to arbitrary models read in from OBJ files.

16.2.1 Defining the 2D Texture Image

The ray cast image is generated on a 2D texture that is initially defined in the OpenGL/C++ application. The C++ code is shown in Program 16.2. It starts by defining the width and height of the texture on which the ray cast image is built (and ultimately displayed). As explained earlier, there is one work group per pixel, so the X and Y dimensions for the work group abstract grid are set equal to the texture dimensions.

The init() function allocates memory for the texture, and sets each of the entries to color values corresponding to the color pink. Since our algorithm is intended to send a ray through each pixel (and thus calculate the color for each and every one of them), the presence of any remaining pink in the resulting image indicates a likely bug in our implementation. The init() function then creates an OpenGL texture object and associates it with the allocated memory. Next, a rectangle (or "quad") consisting of two triangles is defined that is used for displaying the ray cast texture image; its vertices and corresponding texture coordinates are each loaded into their own buffers. Finally, the two shader programs are generated: (1) the ray casting compute shader program and (2) a simple shader program that displays the ray cast texture image on the rectangular quad.

16.2.2 Building and Displaying the Ray Cast Image

The display() function is broken down into "phase 1" and "phase 2", as outlined earlier. Phase 1 uses the ray casting compute shader program, binds the texture image, and then initiates the shader with glDispatchCompute() as described earlier. Rather than binding the texture image to a sampler, as we did in previous chapters, we used glBindImageTexture() to bind the texture image to an OpenGL *image unit*. Image units are distinct from samplers, and in this case, make accessing the individual pixels from within the shader more convenient. The call to glMemoryBarrier() is there to ensure that, as described previously, we don't try to draw the ray cast image until it is entirely built. Then, phase 2 simply draws that image on the two-triangle quad using the basic techniques described in Chapter 5.

Program 16.2 – Ray Casting

C++/OpenGL Application

```
#define RAYTRACE_RENDER_WIDTH    512     // also set window width & height to these values
#define RAYTRACE_RENDER_HEIGHT  512
int workGroupsX = RAYTRACE_RENDER_WIDTH;
int workGroupsY = RAYTRACE_RENDER_HEIGHT;
int workGroupsZ = 1;
```

```
GLuint screenTextureID;              // The texture ID of the full screen texture
unsigned char *screenTexture;        // The screen texture RGBA8888 color data

GLuint raytraceComputeShader, screenQuadShader;

// other variable declarations for VAOs, VBOs, etc., as before
. . .
void init(GLFWwindow* window) {
    // allocate the memory for the screen texture
    screenTexture = (unsigned char*)malloc(
        sizeof(unsigned char) * 4 * RAYTRACE_RENDER_WIDTH * RAYTRACE_RENDER_HEIGHT);
    memset(screenTexture, 0, sizeof(char) * 4 * RAYTRACE_RENDER_WIDTH *
                                                        RAYTRACE_RENDER_HEIGHT);

    // set the initial texture pixel colors to pink – if pink appears, there might be an error at that pixel
    for (int i = 0; i < RAYTRACE_RENDER_HEIGHT; i++) {
        for (int j = 0; j < RAYTRACE_RENDER_WIDTH; j++) {
            screenTexture[i * RAYTRACE_RENDER_WIDTH * 4 + j * 4 + 0] = 250;
            screenTexture[i * RAYTRACE_RENDER_WIDTH * 4 + j * 4 + 1] = 128;
            screenTexture[i * RAYTRACE_RENDER_WIDTH * 4 + j * 4 + 2] = 255;
            screenTexture[i * RAYTRACE_RENDER_WIDTH * 4 + j * 4 + 3] = 255;
    }  }

    // create the OpenGL Texture on which to ray cast the scene
    glGenTextures(1, &screenTextureID);
    glBindTexture(GL_TEXTURE_2D, screenTextureID);
    glTexParameteri(GL_TEXTURE_2D, GL_TEXTURE_MIN_FILTER, GL_NEAREST);
    glTexParameteri(GL_TEXTURE_2D, GL_TEXTURE_MAG_FILTER, GL_NEAREST);
    glTexImage2D(GL_TEXTURE_2D, 0, GL_RGBA, RAYTRACE_RENDER_WIDTH,
        RAYTRACE_RENDER_HEIGHT, 0, GL_RGBA, GL_UNSIGNED_BYTE, (const void *)screenTexture);
    // create quad vertices and texture coordinates for rendering the finished texture to the window
    const float windowQuadVerts[ ] = {
        -1.0f, 1.0f, 0.3f, -1.0f,-1.0f, 0.3f, 1.0f, -1.0f, 0.3f,
        1.0f, -1.0f, 0.3f, 1.0f, 1.0f, 0.3f, -1.0f, 1.0f, 0.3f
    };

    const float windowQuadUVs[ ] = {
        0.0f, 1.0f, 0.0f, 0.0f, 1.0f, 0.0f,
        1.0f, 0.0f, 1.0f, 1.0f, 0.0f, 1.0f
    };

    glGenVertexArrays(1, vao);
    glBindVertexArray(vao[0]);
    glGenBuffers(numVBOs, vbo);
```

```
    glBindBuffer(GL_ARRAY_BUFFER, vbo[0]); // vertex positions
    glBufferData(GL_ARRAY_BUFFER, sizeof(windowQuadVerts), windowQuadVerts,
                                                        GL_STATIC_DRAW);

    glBindBuffer(GL_ARRAY_BUFFER, vbo[1]); // texture coordinates
    glBufferData(GL_ARRAY_BUFFER, sizeof(windowQuadUVs), windowQuadUVs,
                                                        GL_STATIC_DRAW);

    raytraceComputeShader = Utils::createShaderProgram("raytraceComputeShader.glsl");
    screenQuadShader = Utils::createShaderProgram("vertShader.glsl", "fragShader.glsl");
}
void display(GLFWwindow* window, double currentTime) {

    // ========= Phase 1 invoke the ray tracing compute shader =============
    glUseProgram(raytraceComputeShader);

    // bind the screenTextureID texture to an OpenGL image unit as the compute shader's output
    glBindImageTexture(0, screenTextureID, 0, GL_FALSE, 0, GL_WRITE_ONLY, GL_RGBA8);

    // start the compute shader with the specified number of work groups
    glDispatchCompute(workGroupsX, workGroupsY, workGroupsZ);
    glMemoryBarrier(GL_ALL_BARRIER_BITS);

    // ========= Phase 2 draw the resulting texture =============
    glUseProgram(screenQuadShader);

    glActiveTexture(GL_TEXTURE0);
    glBindTexture(GL_TEXTURE_2D, screenTextureID);

    glBindBuffer(GL_ARRAY_BUFFER, vbo[0]);
    glVertexAttribPointer(0, 3, GL_FLOAT, false, 0, 0);
    glEnableVertexAttribArray(0);

    glBindBuffer(GL_ARRAY_BUFFER, vbo[1]);
    glVertexAttribPointer(1, 2, GL_FLOAT, false, 0, 0);
    glEnableVertexAttribArray(1);

    glDrawArrays(GL_TRIANGLES, 0, 6);
}
// main() as before
```

The phase 2 shaders then fetch the pixels that were put into the texture object by the phase 1 shaders (and subsequently bound to texture unit 0 in the C++/ OpenGL application) and use them to display the ray cast image.

Program 16.2 – Ray Casting (continued)

Vertex Shader

```
#version 430
layout (location=0) in vec3 vert_pos;
layout (location=1) in vec2 vert_uv;
out vec2 uv;

void main(void)
{   gl_Position = vec4(vert_pos, 1.0);
    uv = vert_uv;
}
```

Fragment Shader

```
#version 430
layout (binding=0) uniform sampler2D tex;
in vec2 uv; out vec4 color;

void main()
{   color = vec4( texture2D( tex, uv).rgb, 1.0);
}
```

The phase 1 ray cast compute shader completes Program 16.2. This shader is the heart of the ray casting program. We give the code first, then follow it with detailed explanation of the algorithm and implementation.

Program 16.2 – Ray Casting (continued)

Compute Shader

```
#version 430
layout (local_size_x=1) in;
layout (binding=0, rgba8) uniform image2D output_texture;
float camera_pos_z = 5.0;

struct Ray
{   vec3 start;    // origin of the ray
    vec3 dir;      // normalized direction of the ray
};

struct Collision
{   float t;              // distance along ray at which this collision occurs
    vec3 p;               // world position of the collision
    vec3 n;               // surface normal at the collision point
```

```
    bool inside;        // whether the ray started inside of the object and collided while exiting
    int object_index ;  // index of the object this collision hit
};

float sphere_radius = 2.5;
vec3 sphere_position = vec3(1.0, 0.0, -3.0);
vec3 sphere_color = vec3(0.0, 0.0, 1.0);  // sphere color is blue

vec3 box_mins = vec3(-2.0,-2.0, 0.0);
vec3 box_maxs = vec3(-0.5, 1.0, 2.0);
vec3 box_color = vec3(1.0, 0.0, 0.0);        // box color is red

// ------------------------------------------------------------------------
// Checks if Ray r intersects the box
// ------------------------------------------------------------------------
Collision intersect_box_object(Ray r)
{   // Calculate the box's world mins and maxs:
    vec3 t_min = (box_mins - r.start) / r.dir;
    vec3 t_max = (box_maxs - r.start) / r.dir;
    vec3 t_minDist = min(t_min, t_max);
    vec3 t_maxDist = max(t_min, t_max);
    float t_near = max(max(t_minDist.x, t_minDist.y), t_minDist.z);
    float t_far = min(min(t_maxDist.x, t_maxDist.y), t_maxDist.z);

    Collision c;
    c.t = t_near;
    c.inside = false;

    // If the ray didn't intersect the box, return a negative t value
    if (t_near >= t_far || t_far <= 0.0)
    {   c.t = -1.0;
        return c;
    }

    float intersect_distance = t_near;
    vec3 plane_intersect_distances = t_minDist;

    // if t_near < 0, then the ray started inside the box and left the box
    if (t_near < 0.0)
    {   c.t = t_far;
        intersect_distance = t_far;
        plane_intersect_distances = t_maxDist;
        c.inside = true;
    }

    // Checking which boundary the intersection lies on
    int face_index = 0;
    if (intersect_distance == plane_intersect_distances.y) face_index = 1;
```

```
            else if (intersect_distance == plane_intersect_distances.z) face_index = 2;

            // Create the collision normal
            c.n = vec3(0.0);
            c.n[face_index] = 1.0;

            // If we hit the box from the negative axis, invert the normal
            if (r.dir[face_index] > 0.0) c.n *= -1.0;

            // Calculate the world-position of the intersection:
            c.p = r.start + c.t * r.dir;
            return c;
}

// -----------------------------------------------------------------------
// Checks if Ray r intersects the sphere
// -----------------------------------------------------------------------
Collision intersect_sphere_object(Ray r)
{   float qa = dot(r.dir, r.dir);
    float qb = dot(2*r.dir, r.start-sphere_position);
    float qc = dot(r.start-sphere_position, r.start-sphere_position) - sphere_radius*sphere_radius;

    // Solving for qa * t^2 + qb * t + qc = 0
    float qd = qb * qb - 4 * qa * qc;

    Collision c;
    c.inside = false;

    if (qd < 0.0)   // no solution in this case
    {   c.t = -1.0;
        return c;
    }

    float t1 = (-qb + sqrt(qd)) / (2.0 * qa);
    float t2 = (-qb - sqrt(qd)) / (2.0 * qa);
    float t_near = min(t1, t2);
    float t_far = max(t1, t2);
    c.t = t_near;

    if (t_far < 0.0)    // sphere is behind the ray, no intersection
    {   c.t = -1.0;
        return c;
    }
    if (t_near < 0.0) // the ray started inside the sphere
    {   c.t = t_far;
        c.inside = true;
    }
```

```
    c.p = r.start + c.t * r.dir; // world position of the collision
    c.n = normalize(c.p - sphere_position);      // use the world position to compute the surface normal

    if (c.inside)   // if collision is leaving the sphere, flip the normal
    {   c.n *= -1.0;
    }
    return c;
}

//----------------------------------------------------------------------
// Returns the closest collision of a ray
// object_index == -1 if no collision
// object_index == 1 if collision with sphere
// object_index == 2 if collision with box
//----------------------------------------------------------------------
Collision get_closest_collision(Ray r)
{   Collision closest_collision, cSph, cBox;
    closest_collision.object_index = -1;

    cSph = intersect_sphere_object(r);
    cBox = intersect_box_object(r);

    if ((cSph.t > 0) && ((cSph.t < cBox.t) || (cBox.t < 0)))
    {   closest_collision = cSph;
        closest_collision.object_index = 1;
    }
    if ((cBox.t > 0) && ((cBox.t < cSph.t) || (cSph.t < 0)))
    {   closest_collision = cBox;
        closest_collision.object_index = 2;
    }
    return closest_collision;
}

// -----------------------------------------------------------------------
// This function casts a ray into the scene and returns the final color for a pixel
// -----------------------------------------------------------------------
vec3 raytrace(Ray r)
{   Collision c = get_closest_collision(r);
    if (c.object_index == -1) return vec3(0.0);       // if no collision, return black
    if (c.object_index == 1) return sphere_color;
    if (c.object_index == 2) return box_color;
}

void main()
{   int width = int(gl_NumWorkGroups.x);             // one workgroup = one invocation = one pixel
    int height = int(gl_NumWorkGroups.y);
    ivec2 pixel = ivec2(gl_GlobalInvocationID.xy);
```

```
// convert this pixel's screen space location to world space
float x_pixel = 2.0 * pixel.x / width – 1.0;
float y_pixel = 2.0 * pixel.y / height – 1.0;

// Get this pixel's world-space ray
Ray world_ray;
world_ray.start = vec3(0.0, 0.0, camera_pos_z);
vec4 world_ray_end = vec4(x_pixel, y_pixel, camera_pos_z - 1.0, 1.0);
world_ray.dir = normalize(world_ray_end.xyz - world_ray.start);

// Cast the ray out into the world and intersect the ray with objects
vec3 color = raytrace(world_ray);
imageStore(output_texture, pixel, vec4(color, 1.0));
}
```

The declarations at the top of the compute shader start by setting the workgroup size to 1, as described earlier. A uniform variable for the output texture image is then defined, as well as the camera position (in this example we limit the camera to being positioned along the Z axis, facing in the negative Z direction). Then, structs are declared for defining *rays* (their origins and directions) and *collisions*. Collisions include information about a ray intersecting an object, e.g., the distance along the ray, collision location in world coordinates, which object is hit, and the normal at the surface point of the collision, which will be used later when we add lighting. The declarations conclude by creating variables for the location and color of the objects we intend to draw (in this case, a box and a sphere).

The main() function, shown at the bottom of the code listing, starts by using the work group's invocationID to determine the pixel's X/Y location in the screen-space grid, then converts that from the range [0..width] to the range [-1..+1] corresponding to where the pixel is positioned in the scene's world coordinate system. A ray starting at the camera position and passing through this point is then created, assuming that the render grid is placed a distance of 1.0 (along the Z axis) in front of the camera. main() then calls raytrace(), which accepts a ray and returns the color of the nearest object hit by that ray. main() then stores that color in the image.

The raytrace() function calls get_closest_collision(), which returns a Collision object containing the index of the first object with which the ray collides; raytrace() then returns the color of that object. If the ray doesn't collide with any object in the scene, raytrace() returns the default color (set to black in this example). The get_closest_collision() function works by finding the collision point(s) with the sphere object and the box object (via the functions intersect_sphere_object() and intersect_box_object(), respectively), and returning the collision that has the shortest ray. If there is no colliding object, a special value of -1 is returned.

16.2.3 Ray-Sphere Intersection

Computing the intersection(s) of a ray with a sphere is derived using geometry and is well-documented [S16]. Although the derivation is relatively simple, here we describe only the solution. There are either 0, 1, or 2 intersection points, depending on if the ray misses the sphere, skims the surface, or enters on one side and exits out the other. Given the ray's origin r_s and direction r_d, and the sphere's position s_p and radius s_r, then finding the distance t along the ray at which the intersection(s) occur requires solving the following quadratic equation:

$$(r_d \bullet r_d)t^2 + (2r_d \bullet |r_s - s_p|)t + |r_s - s_p|^2 - s_r^2 = 0 \qquad [1]$$

First, we compute its discriminant[1]:

$$\Delta = (2r_d \bullet |r_s - s_p|)^2 - 4|r_d|^2 (|r_s - s_p|^2 - s_r^2)$$

If $\Delta < 0$, we can stop because the ray misses the sphere (and to avoid attempting to take the square root of a negative number). When Δ is not less than zero, there are then two solutions to equation [1]:

$$t = \frac{(-2r_d \bullet |r_s - s_p|) \pm \sqrt{\Delta}}{2(r_d \bullet r_d)^2}$$

The smaller and larger of the two resulting values of t are denoted t_near and t_far, respectively.

- When both t_near and t_far are negative, the entire sphere is behind the ray and there is no intersection.

- When t_near is negative and t_far is positive, then the ray started inside the sphere and the first intersection point is at t_far.

- When both are positive, the first intersection point is at t_near. Note that this also handles the case of the ray skimming the surface of the sphere, when both t_near and t_far are positive and equal to each other (which occurs when the discriminant Δ is zero).

---

[1] In the code, we sometimes compute the square of the length of a vector $\vec{v}$ by computing $\vec{v} \bullet \vec{v}$, for performance reasons.

Finally, once the value of t has been determined, the corresponding point is easily calculated:

$$collision\ point = r_s + t * r_d$$

Later, we will need the surface normal at the collision point, hereafter called the *collision normal*, which is a vector from the center of the sphere to the intersection point:

$$collision\ normal = normalize(collision\ point - s_p)$$

noting that if the ray started inside the sphere, then the collision normal would need to be negated.

16.2.4 Axis-Aligned Ray-Box Intersection

Computing the intersection(s) of a ray with a box is similarly well-documented and derived using geometry, the most common approach having been derived by Kay and Kajiya [KK86]. Again we describe only the solution, as adapted for GPU vector operations [H89]. And as for the sphere, a ray will intersect a box at 0, 1, or 2 points.

Program 16.2 assumes the box is aligned with the world axes (we handle other orientations later). We define the box using two points at diagonally-opposite corners; i.e., $(x_{min}, y_{min}, z_{min})$ and $(x_{max}, y_{max}, z_{max})$. In Program 16.2, those are box_mins and box_maxs at (-2, -2, 0) and (-0.5, 1, 2), respectively. These two points are then used to identify the six X/Y/Z planes that comprise the box. For example, the two "X" planes are specified as the X values for the two box sides parallel to the YZ plane. Finding the distance t at which the ray intersects each of the six planes can be done efficiently with GLSL vec3 operations (see [S11] for a derivation):

$$t_{mins} = (box_{mins} - r_s)/r_d$$

$$t_{maxs} = (box_{maxs} - r_s)/r_d$$

The resulting t_{mins} and t_{maxs} vectors contain minimum and maximum distances to planes defined by the X, Y, and Z-aligned box sides. The smaller and larger of each of those can then be found efficiently as follows:

$$tminDist = min(t_{mins}, t_{maxs})$$

$$tmaxDist = max(t_{mins}, t_{maxs})$$

(In GLSL, the "min" of two vec3s is a vec3 containing the smaller of each pair of X, Y, and Z elements.)

The vector $t_{minDist}$ then contains (distance r_s to x_{min}, distance r_s to y_{min}, distance r_s to z_{min}).

The vector $t_{maxDist}$ then contains (distance r_s to x_{max}, distance r_s to y_{max}, distance r_s to z_{max}).

Some of the plane collision points are actually outside of the box. The distance from the ray origin to the nearest collision point that is actually on a box surface is the *largest* of the tminDist values, and the distance from the ray origin to the furthest collision point that is on a box surface is the *smallest* of the tmaxDist values:

$$t\_near = \max(tminDist_x, tminDist_y, tminDist_z)$$

$$t\_far = \min(tmaxDist_x, tmaxDist_y, tmaxDist_z)$$

There are then three cases:

- The ray doesn't intersect the box at all, which is the case when t_near > t_far or if t_far ≤ 0.
- There is one collision point when the ray starts inside the box and exits the box, which is the case when t_near < 0 and t_far > 0.
- Otherwise, there are two collision points which occur at distances t_near and t_far.

Computing the world coordinates of the nearest collision is then done the same as for the sphere. Computing the normal at this point is then either (±1,0,0), (0,±1,0) or (0,0,±1), depending on which surface the collision occurs.

16.2.5 Output of Simple Ray Casting Without Lighting

Figure 16.3 shows the output of Program 16.2. The scene contains a red sphere on the right, and a green box on the left. The box is axis-aligned, and is placed slightly closer to the camera than the sphere. Note that lighting has not been applied, so the surfaces appear flat and the sphere just looks like a disk.

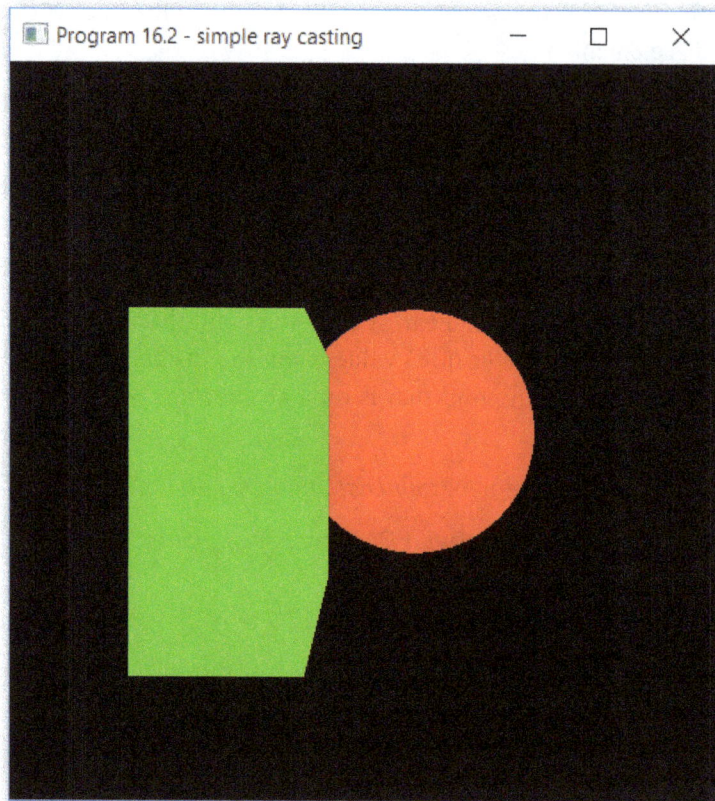

Figure 16.3
Output of Program 16.2, showing simple ray casting without lighting

16.2.6 Adding ADS Lighting

ADS ("ambient-diffuse-specular") lighting was covered in Chapter 7. Here we implement it in the ray casting compute shader by adding code that specifies the global ambient light, the position and ADS characteristics of a positional light, ADS material characteristics of the objects in the scene, and a function to compute the ADS lighting in the same manner as was done in Chapter 7.

Program 16.3 shows the additions and changes to the ray casting compute shader. There are declarations added at the top of the shader, and a new function ads_phong_lighting(). Changes to the raytrace() function are highlighted in yellow, in which the lighting result is multiplied by the color of the object. In this simple example, both the sphere and the box have the same material characteristics. The output is shown in Figure 16.4.

Program 16.3 – Adding Lighting

Compute Shader

```
. . .
vec4 global_ambient = vec4(0.3, 0.3, 0.3, 1.0);

vec4 objMat_ambient = vec4(0.2, 0.2, 0.2, 1.0);
vec4 objMat_diffuse = vec4(0.7, 0.7, 0.7, 1.0);
vec4 objMat_specular = vec4(1.0, 1.0, 1.0, 1.0);
float objMat_shininess = 50.0;

vec3 pointLight_position = vec3(-3.0, 2.0, 4.0);
vec4 pointLight_ambient = vec4(0.2, 0.2, 0.2, 1.0);
vec4 po*tLight_diffuse = vec4(0.7, 0.7, 0.7, 1.0);
vec4 pointLight_specular = vec4(1.0, 1.0, 1.0, 1.0);
. . .
vec3 ads_phong_lighting(Ray r, Collision c)
{   // Compute the ambient contribution from the ambient and positional lights
    vec4 ambient = global_ambient + pointLight_ambient * objMat_ambient;

    // Compute the light's reflection on the surface
    vec3 light_dir = normalize(pointLight_position - c.p);
    vec3 light_ref = normalize( reflect(-light_dir, c.n));
    float cos_theta = dot(light_dir, c.n);
    float cos_phi = dot( normalize(-r.dir), light_ref);

    // Compute the diffuse and specular contributions
    vec4 diffuse = pointLight_diffuse * objMat_diffuse * max(cos_theta, 0.0);
    vec4 specular = pointLight_specular * objMat_specular * pow( max( cos_phi, 0.0),
                                                            objMat_shininess);

    vec4 phong_color = ambient + diffuse + specular;
    return phong_color.rgb;
}

vec3 raytrace(Ray r)
{   Collision c = get_closest_collision(r);
    if (c.object_index == -1) return vec3(0.0);      // if no collision, return black
    if (c.object_index == 1) return ads_phong_lighting(r,c) * sphere_color;
    if (c.object_index == 2) return ads_phong_lighting(r,c) * box_color;
}
```

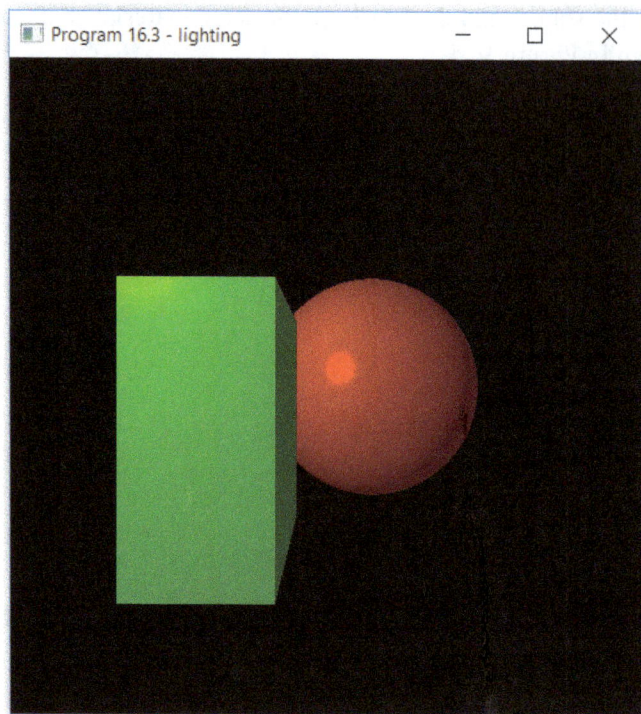

Figure 16.4
Output of Program 16.3, showing simple ray casting with lighting

16.2.7 Adding Shadows

Ray casting provides a remarkably elegant method for detecting whether something is in shadow by leveraging some of the functions we have already written. We do this by defining a "shadow feeler ray" starting at the collision point being rendered, towards the position of the light. We then use our already-developed get_closest_collision() function to determine the closest collider for that ray. If it is closer than the positional light, then there must be an object in between the light and the collision point, and the point must be in shadow.

Recall from Chapter 8 that the way we render the portion of an object that is in shadow is by rendering only the ambient contribution. Therefore, in our compute shader, a convenient place to put our shadow-detecting code is in the ads_phong_lighting() function that we developed in the previous section. Here, the diffuse and specular contributions are initialized to zero, and only computed if the collision point is determined to not be in shadow. Note also that the shadow feeler ray starts at a slight offset away from the object (along the normal) to avoid shadow acne (this is because without this offset, some of the feeler rays will immediately bump into the object itself). The additions are shown in Program 16.4 and highlighted in yellow. The algorithm is considerably simpler than the shadow mapping we learned in Chapter 8! Figure 16.5 shows the program's output. The box is now casting a shadow on the sphere.

Program 16.4 – Adding Shadows

Compute Shader

```
. . .
vec3 ads_phong_lighting(Ray r, Collision c)
{   // Compute the ambient contribution from the ambient and positional lights
    vec4 ambient = worldAmb_ambient + pointLight_ambient * objMat_ambient;

    // initialize diffuse and specular contributions
    vec4 diffuse = vec4(0.0);
    vec4 specular = vec4(0.0);

    // Check to see if any object is casting a shadow on this surface
    Ray light_ray;
    light_ray.start = c.p + c.n * 0.01;
    light_ray.dir = normalize(pointLight_position - c.p);
    bool in_shadow = false;

    // Cast the ray against the scene
    Collision c_shadow = get_closest_collision(light_ray);

    // If the ray hit an object and if the hit occurred between the surface and the light
    if (c_shadow.object_index != -1 && c_shadow.t < length(pointLight_position – c.p))
    {   in_shadow = true;
    }

    // If this surface is in shadow, don't add diffuse and specular components
    if (in_shadow == false)
    {   // Compute the light's reflection on the surface
        vec3 light_dir = normalize(pointLight_position - c.p);
        vec3 light_ref = normalize( reflect(-light_dir, c.n));
        float cos_theta = dot(light_dir, c.n);
        float cos_phi = dot( normalize(-r.dir), light_ref);

        // Compute the diffuse and specular contributions
        diffuse = pointLight_diffuse * objMat_diffuse * max(cos_theta, 0.0);
```

```
    specular = pointLight_specular * objMat_specular * pow( max( cos_phi, 0.0), objMat_shininess);
}
vec4 phong_color = ambient + diffuse + specular;
return phong_color.rgb;
}
```

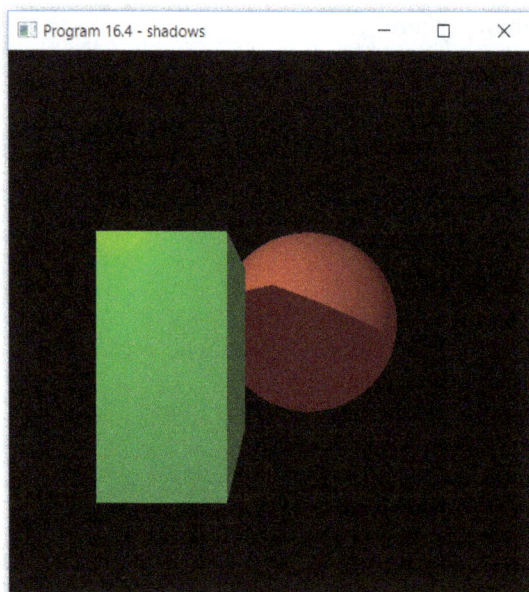

Figure 16.5
Output of Program 16.4, showing simple ray casting with lighting and shadows

16.2.8 Non-Axis-Aligned Ray-Box Intersection

So far, our box has been limited to an orientation where its X, Y, and Z axes are parallel with the world axes. We now show how to include translation and rotation, so that we can orient the box however we wish. Applying translation and rotation on the box is conceptually similar to building a view matrix, as we did in Chapter 4, although the details are slightly different.

We start by making sure that our box_mins and box_maxs variables define a box shape that is centered at the origin. We also specify

- the position where we wish to move the box, as a vec3
- X, Y, and Z rotations around the box origin, as floats

Next, we build translation and rotation transform matrices using the buildTranslate() and buildRotate() functions described back in Section 3.10. The trick is then to use the *inverses* of these matrices to modify the start point and direction of the ray; specifically, we rotate the ray's direction and rotate/translate the ray's starting point. The computations then proceed as before to generate the collision distance (and of course determining whether the ray collides with the box at all). Once the collision distance is determined, it is then used to compute the world collision point as before, based on the actual ray start point and direction. Note that the surface normal also needs to be rotated based on the rotation matrix (actually the inverse-transpose of the rotation matrix, as we learned in Chapter 7).

The changes to intersect_box_object() are shown in Program 16.5 (highlighted in yellow), along with an example set of box parameters for its shape, position, and orientation. The output is shown in Figure 16.6.

Program 16.5 – Non-Axis-Aligned Box Intersection

Compute Shader

```
. . .
vec3 box_mins = vec3(-0.5, -0.5, -1.0);
vec3 box_maxs = vec3( 0.5, 0.5, 1.0);
vec3 box_pos = vec3(-1, -0.5, 1.0);

const float DEG_TO_RAD = 3.1415926535 / 180.0;
float box_xrot = 10.0;
float box_yrot = 70.0;
float box_zrot = 55.0;

Collision intersect_box_object(Ray r)
{   // Compute the box's local-space to world-space transform matrices and their inverses
    mat4 local_to_worldT = buildTranslate(box_pos.x, box_pos.y, box_pos.z);
    mat4 local_to_worldR =
        buildRotateY(DEG_TO_RAD * box_yrot)
        * buildRotateX(DEG_TO_RAD * box_xrot)
        * buildRotateZ(DEG_TO_RAD * box_zrot);
    mat4 local_to_worldTR = local_to_worldT * local_to_worldR;
    mat4 world_to_localTR = inverse(local_to_worldTR);
    mat4 world_to_localR = inverse(local_to_worldR);

    // Convert the world-space ray to the box's local space:
    vec3 ray_start = (world_to_localTR * vec4(r.start,1.0)).xyz;
    vec3 ray_dir = (world_to_localR * vec4(r.dir,1.0)).xyz;
```

```
// Calculate the box's world mins and maxs:
vec3 t_min = (box_mins - ray_start) / ray_dir;
vec3 t_max = (box_maxs - ray_start) / ray_dir;
vec3 t1 = min(t_min, t_max);
vec3 t2 = max(t_min, t_max);
float t_near = max(max(t1.x,t1.y),t1.z);
float t_far = min(min(t2.x, t2.y), t2.z);
. . .
// The computations for determining the collision, which surface of the box
// is intersected, and the normal at the collision are unchanged from before.
// There is one addition to the normal vector computation, shown next in yellow.
. . .
// If we hit the box from the negative axis, invert the normal
if(ray_dir[face_index] > 0.0) c.n *= -1.0;

// now convert the normal back into world space
c.n = transpose(inverse(mat3(local_to_worldR))) * c.n;

// Calculate the world-position of the intersection:
c.p = r.start + c.t * r.dir;

return c;
}
```

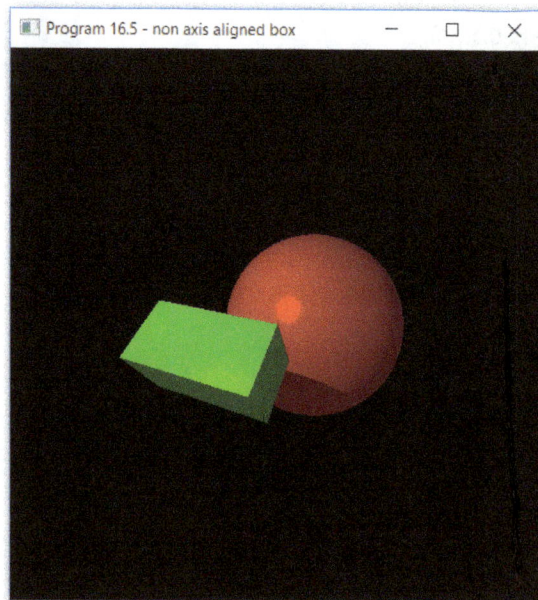

Figure 16.6
Output of Program 16.5 showing simple ray casting with a non-axis-aligned box

16.2.9 Determining Texture Coordinates

If we wish to apply a texture image to the objects in the scene, we need to compute texture coordinates. In previous examples, each texture coordinate corresponded to a vertex in the model, and they were loaded into a VBO either procedurally or by reading them in from an .OBJ file. We cannot do that here, because we aren't using models – we aren't even using vertices! Our shapes are the result of computing ray intersections on mathematically-defined shapes, so we need to extend our computations to determine texture coordinates.

This can be complicated, because the desired layout of the texture coordinates can vary depending on the application. For example, the box might represent a brick wall or it might be a skybox, each of which would require different texture coordinate assignments. In the case of the sphere, it is a bit easier because the layout of the texture images that we have been using (such as for the earth or the moon) is by far the most common.

For the sphere, a clever trick is to use the computed surface normal to specify a point on the surface, along with standard spherical coordinate methods, to find the corresponding point in flattened 2D space. The derivations from classical geometry are well-known [S16] and not repeated here. Given the normal vector N,

$$texCoord_X = 0.5 + \frac{(arcTan(-N_Z,N_X)}{2\pi}$$

$$texCoord_Y = 0.5 - \frac{(arcSin(-N_Y)}{\pi}$$

For the box, our first example assumes the need is to simply apply a texture image evenly over all surfaces, so we will scale it based on the longest box side. One set of steps for doing this is:

1. Compute the collision point, using the world_to_local matrix previously developed.
2. Determine the largest box side length.
3. Convert the X, Y, and Z collision point coordinates to the range [0..1], based on the largest box side.
4. Divide each coordinate by the largest box dimension, so that the image isn't compressed along box sides.
5. Select (X,Y), (X,Z), or (Y,Z) as the texture coordinates, depending on which surface the collision occurred.

Program 16.6 shows the additions and changes to the C++ program and the compute shader. It textures the sphere with the earth image and the box with the brick image. The output is shown in Figure 16.7.

Program 16.6 – Adding Texture Coordinates

C++/OpenGL Application

```
. . .
GLuint earthTexture, brickTexture;        // added to the top-level declarations
. . .
void init(GLFWwindow* window) {
   . . .
   earthTexture = Utils::loadTexture("earthmap1k.jpg");
   brickTexture = Utils::loadTexture("brick1.jpg");
}
void display(GLFWwindow* window, double currentTime) {
   . . .
   glBindImageTexture(0, screenTextureID, 0, GL_FALSE, 0, GL_WRITE_ONLY, GL_RGBA8);

   glActiveTexture(GL_TEXTURE1);
   glBindTexture(GL_TEXTURE_2D, earthTexture);
   glActiveTexture(GL_TEXTURE2);
   glBindTexture(GL_TEXTURE_2D, brickTexture);

   glActiveTexture(GL_TEXTURE0);      // reset of active texture is required when using
                                      // both image store and texture

   glDispatchCompute(workGroupsX, workGroupsY, workGroupsZ);
   . . .
}
```

Compute Shader

```
. . .
layout (binding=1) uniform sampler2D sampEarth;
layout (binding=2) uniform sampler2D sampBrick;
. . .
struct Collision
{  float t;           // value at which this collision occurs for a ray
   vec3 p;            // world position of the collision
   vec3 n;            // normal of the collision
   bool inside;       // whether the collision occurs inside of the object
   int object_index;  // index of the object this collision hit
```

```
    vec2 tc;              // texture coordinates for the object at the collision point
};

. . .

Collision intersect_sphere_object(Ray r)
{  . . .
    c.tc.x = 0.5 + atan(-c.n.z, c.n.x) / (2.0*PI);
    c.tc.y = 0.5 - asin(-c.n.y) / PI;
    return c;
}

. . .

Collision intersect_box_object(Ray r)
{  . . .
    // Compute texture coordinates.
    // Start by computing the position in the box space that the ray collides with
    vec3 cp = (world_to_localTR * vec4(c.p,1.0)).xyz;

    // now compute largest box dimension
    float totalWidth = box_maxs.x - box_mins.x;
    float totalHeight = box_maxs.y - box_mins.y;
    float totalDepth = box_maxs.z - box_mins.z;
    float maxDimension = max(totalWidth, max(totalHeight, totalDepth));

    // convert X/Y/Z coordinates to range [0..1], and divide by largest box dimension
    float rayStrikeX = (cp.x + totalWidth/2.0) / maxDimension;
    float rayStrikeY = (cp.y + totalHeight/2.0) / maxDimension;
    float rayStrikeZ = (cp.z + totalDepth/2.0) / maxDimension;

    // finally, select (X,Y), (X,Z), or (Y,Z) as tex coordinates depending on box face
    if (face_index == 0)
        c.tc = vec2(rayStrikeZ, rayStrikeY);
    else if (face_index == 1)
        c.tc = vec2(rayStrikeZ, rayStrikeX);
    else
        c.tc = vec2(rayStrikeY, rayStrikeX);
    return c;
}
. . .
vec3 raytrace(Ray r)
{  Collision c = get_closest_collision(r);
    if (c.object_index == -1) return vec3(0.0);      // no collision
    if (c.object_index == 1) return ads_phong_lighting(r,c) * (texture(sampEarth, c.tc)).xyz;
    if (c.object_index == 2) return ads_phong_lighting(r,c) * (texture(sampBrick, c.tc)).xyz;
}
```

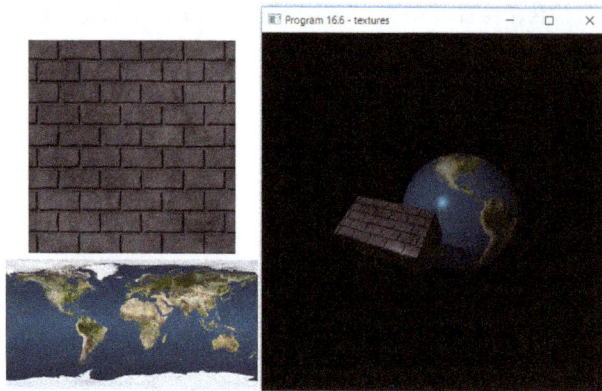

Figure 16.7
Example textures and output of Program 16.6, where texture coordinates are added

If the box is to serve as a room box or skybox, the texture coordinates will need to be computed slightly differently, so as to match the texturing methods we saw in Chapter 9. We can start by adding a second box to the scene, specifically an *axis-aligned* box as described back in Program 16.2, with a solid color. Figure 16.8 shows such a box of size 20x20x20 added to the scene. Because the camera is positioned inside the box, only the inside faces of the box are visible. Note also that in this example the objects in the scene cast shadows on the box, as would be the case for a room box.

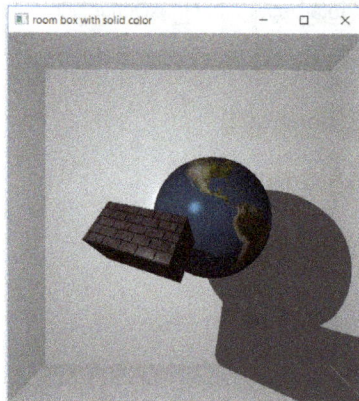

Figure 16.8
Adding a simple axis-aligned room box with solid color[2]

---

[2] Note the seam on the lower right. The .01 offset of light_ray.start (to combat shadow acne) in Program 16.4 is ineffective at the corners because the normal is tangential to an adjoining box side. This isn't an issue for skyboxes because shadows aren't used.

Computing texture coordinates so that we can apply a room box or skybox texture depends on if we wish to use a single texture (such as the one in Figure 9.1) or six separate textures (one for each face of the box). Program 16.7 implements the latter approach, with an additional intersection method specifically to handle room or skyboxes. The changes to both the C++ application and the compute shader are shown. The six textures are loaded and assigned to texture units in the C++ program, sampled in the compute shader, and selected depending on which face the ray collides with. Which of the six faces this is can be easily determined from the normal vector, since each box face has a different normal vector. Texture coordinates are then computed in a manner similar to what was shown in Program 16.6. Finally, note that as we add more and more objects to our scene, the number of tests needed for determining which collision is the closest quickly becomes more complex.

Program 16.7 – Adding Textures to the Skybox

C++/OpenGL Application

. . .

```
GLuint xpTex, xnTex, ypTex, ynTex, zpTex, znTex;        // added to the top-level declarations

void init(GLFWwindow* window) {
    . . .
    xpTex = Utils::loadTexture("cubeMap/xp.jpg");
    xnTex = Utils::loadTexture("cubeMap/xn.jpg");
    ypTex = Utils::loadTexture("cubeMap/yp.jpg");
    ynTex = Utils::loadTexture("cubeMap/yn.jpg");
    zpTex = Utils::loadTexture("cubeMap/zp.jpg");
    znTex = Utils::loadTexture("cubeMap/zn.jpg");
}

void display(GLFWwindow* window, double currentTime) {
    . . .
    glBindImageTexture(0, screenTextureID, 0, GL_FALSE, 0, GL_WRITE_ONLY, GL_RGBA8);
    glActiveTexture(GL_TEXTURE3);
    glBindTexture(GL_TEXTURE_2D, xpTex);
    glActiveTexture(GL_TEXTURE4);
    glBindTexture(GL_TEXTURE_2D, xnTex);
    glActiveTexture(GL_TEXTURE5);
    glBindTexture(GL_TEXTURE_2D, ypTex);
    glActiveTexture(GL_TEXTURE6);
    glBindTexture(GL_TEXTURE_2D, ynTex);
    glActiveTexture(GL_TEXTURE7);
    glBindTexture(GL_TEXTURE_2D, zpTex);
    glActiveTexture(GL_TEXTURE8);
```

```
glBindTexture(GL_TEXTURE_2D, znTex);
glActiveTexture(GL_TEXTURE0);
glDispatchCompute(workGroupsX, workGroupsY, workGroupsZ);
    . . .
}
```

Compute Shader

```
. . .
layout (binding=3) uniform sampler2D xpTex;
layout (binding=4) uniform sampler2D xnTex;
layout (binding=5) uniform sampler2D ypTex;
layout (binding=6) uniform sampler2D ynTex;
layout (binding=7) uniform sampler2D zpTex;
layout (binding=8) uniform sampler2D znTex;
. . .
struct Collision
{   float t;              // value at which this collision occurs for a ray
    vec3 p;              // world position of the collision
    vec3 n;              // normal of the collision
    bool inside;         // whether the collision occurs inside of the object
    int object_index;    // index of the object this collision hit
    vec2 tc;             // texture coordinates for the object at the collision point
    int face_index;      // which box face collides (for textured skybox)
};
. . .
Collision intersect_sky_box_object(Ray r)
{   . . .
    // Calculate face index for collision object (assumes that the normal vectors are of length 1)
    if (c.n == vec3(1,0,0)) c.face_index = 0;
    else if (c.n == vec3(-1,0,0)) c.face_index = 1;
    else if (c.n == vec3(0,1,0)) c.face_index = 2;
    else if (c.n == vec3(0,-1,0)) c.face_index = 3;
    else if (c.n == vec3(0,0,1)) c.face_index = 4;
    else if (c.n == vec3(0,0,-1)) c.face_index = 5;

    // Compute texture coordinates
    float totalWidth = skybox_maxs.x - skybox_mins.x;
    float totalHeight = skybox_maxs.y - skybox_mins.y;
    float totalDepth = skybox_maxs.z - skybox_mins.z;
    float maxDimension = max(totalWidth, max(totalHeight, totalDepth));

    // select tex coordinates depending on box face
    float rayStrikeX = ((c.p).x + totalWidth/2.0)/maxDimension;
    float rayStrikeY = ((c.p).y + totalHeight/2.0)/maxDimension;
    float rayStrikeZ = ((c.p).z + totalDepth/2.0)/maxDimension;
```

```
    if (c.face_index == 0) c.tc = vec2(rayStrikeZ, rayStrikeY);
    else if (c.face_index == 1) c.tc = vec2(1.0-rayStrikeZ, rayStrikeY);
    else if (c.face_index == 2) c.tc = vec2(rayStrikeX, rayStrikeZ);
    else if (c.face_index == 3) c.tc = vec2(rayStrikeX, 1.0-rayStrikeZ);
    else if (c.face_index == 4) c.tc = vec2(1.0-rayStrikeX, rayStrikeY);
    else if (c.face_index == 5) c.tc = vec2(rayStrikeX, rayStrikeY);
    return c;
}
. . .
Collision get_closest_collision(Ray r)
{   . . .
    Collision closest_collision, cSph, cBox, cSBox;

    . . .
    cSBox = intersect_sky_box_object(r);

    . . .
    // determine which collision is the closest
    if ((cSBox.t > 0) && ((cSBox.t < cSph.t) || (cSph.t < 0)) && ((cSBox.t < cBox.t) || (cBox.t < 0)))
    {   closest_collision = cSBox;
        closest_collision.object_index = 3;
    }
    return closest_collision;
}
vec3 raytrace(Ray r)
{   Collision c = get_closest_collision(r);
    if (c.object_index == -1) return vec3(0.0);        // no collision
    if (c.object_index == 1) return ads_phong_lighting(r,c) * (texture(sampEarth, c.tc)).xyz;
    if (c.object_index == 2) return ads_phong_lighting(r,c) * (texture(sampBrick, c.tc)).xyz;

    if (c.object_index == 3) // this example is a skybox, so we return only the texture, without lighting
    {   if (c.face_index == 0) return texture(xnTex, c.tc).xyz;      // sample -X face texture image
        else if (c.face_index == 1) return texture(xpTex, c.tc).xyz;    // sample +X face texture image
        else if (c.face_index == 2) return texture(ynTex, c.tc).xyz;    // sample -Y face texture image
        else if (c.face_index == 3) return texture(ypTex, c.tc).xyz;    // sample +Y face texture image
        else if (c.face_index == 4) return texture(znTex, c.tc).xyz;    // sample -Z face texture image
        else if (c.face_index == 5) return texture(zpTex, c.tc).xyz;    // sample +Z face texture image
    }
}
. . .
```

Notice that in Program 16.7, we did not include ADS lighting when the ray's closest collision is the skybox (this can be seen in the raytrace() function in the compute shader), because a skybox should not respond to lighting. In the case of a room box, we would include ADS lighting, but only if the images of the cube faces strictly correspond to the walls of a room. Figure 16.9 shows the output of

Program 16.7, with and without ADS lighting applied to the skybox (ADS lighting *is* applied to the other objects). Comparing figures 16.8 and 16.9 illustrates why lighting effects are generally appropriate for room boxes, but not for skyboxes.

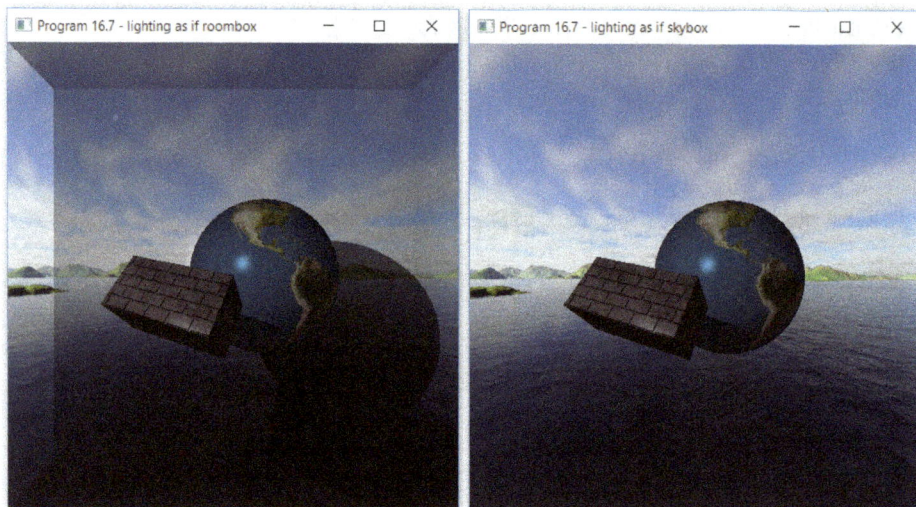

Figure 16.9
Output of Program 16.7 with and without ADS lighting applied to a skybox

16.2.10 Plane Intersection and Procedural Textures

In the previous examples, textures were provided in the form of texture image files. In some cases, a surface texture is sufficiently simple that it can be created procedurally, with the advantage that such textures are less likely to exhibit image-related artifacts.

In Program 16.8, we add a plane object (more precisely, a plane segment) to the scene, serving as a sort of table-top surface below the objects. Shadows are cast onto the plane object, but not onto the skybox. The plane has been textured with a checkerboard pattern, generated procedurally.

Computing the intersection point of a ray with a plane is significantly easier than it was for the sphere and the box because a plane has no "inside" that needs to be considered, so there is always at most one intersection point to consider. The derivation is well documented [S16]. Using standard geometry, the distance t along a ray starting at position with direction when it intersects a horizontal plane centered at the origin with normal $n_p=(0,1,0)$ is:

$$t = (-r_s \bullet n_p)/(r_d \bullet n_p)$$

The intersect point is then, as before,

$$collision\ point = r_s + t * r_d$$

Given the plane's width w (i.e., on the x-axis) and depth d (i.e., on the z-axis), the ray misses the plane segment when

$$|collisionPoint_x| > \frac{w}{2} \qquad or \qquad |collisionPoint_z| > \frac{d}{2}$$

These can be generalized to planes at an arbitrary location and rotation using the non-axis-aligned methods described previously in Section 16.2.8. Similarly, the surface normal at the collision point, which so far has been fixed as (0,1,0), may be rotated if the plane is not aligned with the XZ-axes. Texture coordinates are just the *collisionPoint* x and z coordinates, normalized to the range [0..1].

Computing the procedural checkerboard pattern of white and black colors can be done by scaling the texture coordinates up by the desired number of squares in the checkerboard, and then taking that result modulo 2. The result of 0 or 1 is then returned as either color (0,0,0) or (1,1,1) – i.e., black or white – respectively.

Note that as we increase the number of objects, the test for which collision is the closest (done in the get_closest_collision() function) is becoming increasingly complicated; we improve this design later. The added code for both the plane intersection and the procedural texture are given in Program 16.8, with the resulting output shown in Figure 16.10. All of the changes are in the compute shader.

Program 16.8 – Plane Intersection and Procedural Texturing

Compute Shader

```
. . .
vec3 plane_pos = vec3(0, -2.5, -2.0);   // position of the plane
float plane_width = 12.0;
float plane_depth = 8.0;
float plane_xrot = 0.0;      // rotation of the plane
float plane_yrot = 0.0;
float plane_zrot = 0.0;

. . .
Collision intersect_plane_object(Ray r)
```

```
{   // Compute the plane's local-space to world-space transform matrices and their inverses
    mat4 local_to_worldT = buildTranslate(plane_pos.x, plane_pos.y, plane_pos.z);
    mat4 local_to_worldR = buildRotateY(plane_yrot) * buildRotateX(plane_xrot) *
                                                            buildRotateZ(plane_zrot);
    mat4 local_to_worldTR = local_to_worldT * local_to_worldR;
    mat4 world_to_localTR = inverse(local_to_worldTR);
    mat4 world_to_localR = inverse(local_to_worldR);

    // Convert the world-space ray to the plane's local space:
    vec3 ray_start = (world_to_localTR * vec4(r.start,1.0)).xyz;
    vec3 ray_dir = (world_to_localR * vec4(r.dir,1.0)).xyz;

    Collision c;
    c.inside = false; // there is no "inside" of a plane

    // compute intersection point of ray with plane
    c.t = dot((vec3(0,0,0) - ray_start),vec3(0,1,0)) / dot(ray_dir, vec3(0,1,0));

    // Calculate the world-position and plane-space positions of the intersection:
    c.p = r.start + c.t * r.dir;
    vec3 intersectPoint = ray_start + c.t * ray_dir;

    // If the ray didn't intersect the plane object, return a negative t value
    if ((abs(intersectPoint.x) > (plane_width/2.0)) || (abs(intersectPoint.z) > (plane_depth/2.0)))
    {   c.t = -1.0;
        return c;
    }

    // Create the collision normal, invert it if the ray hits the plane from underneath,
    // and convert to world space
    c.n = vec3(0, 1, 0);
    if(ray_dir.y > 0.0) c.n *= -1.0;
    c.n = transpose(inverse(mat3(local_to_worldR))) * c.n;

    // Compute texture coordinates
    float maxDimension = max(plane_width, plane_depth);
    c.tc = (intersectPoint.xz + plane_width/2.0)/maxDimension;
    return c;
}
Collision get_closest_collision(Ray r)
{   Collision cPlane;
    cPlane = intersect_plane_object(r);
    . . .

    if ((cPlane.t > 0) &&
        ((cPlane.t < cSph.t) || (cSph.t < 0))&&((cPlane.t < cBox.t) || (cBox.t < 0))&&((cPlane.t <
                                                        cRBox.t) || (cRBox.t < 0)))
```

```
    {   closest_collision = cPlane;
        closest_collision.object_index = 4;        // object_index of 4 designates collision with the plane
    }
    . . .
}

vec3 checkerboard(vec2 tc)
{   float tileScale = 24.0;
    float tile = mod(floor(tc.x * tileScale) + floor(tc.y * tileScale), 2.0);
    return tile * vec3(1,1,1);
}

vec3 raytrace(Ray r)
{   . . .
    if (c.object_index == 4) return ads_phong_lighting(r,c) * (checkerboard(c.tc)).xyz;
    . . .
}
```

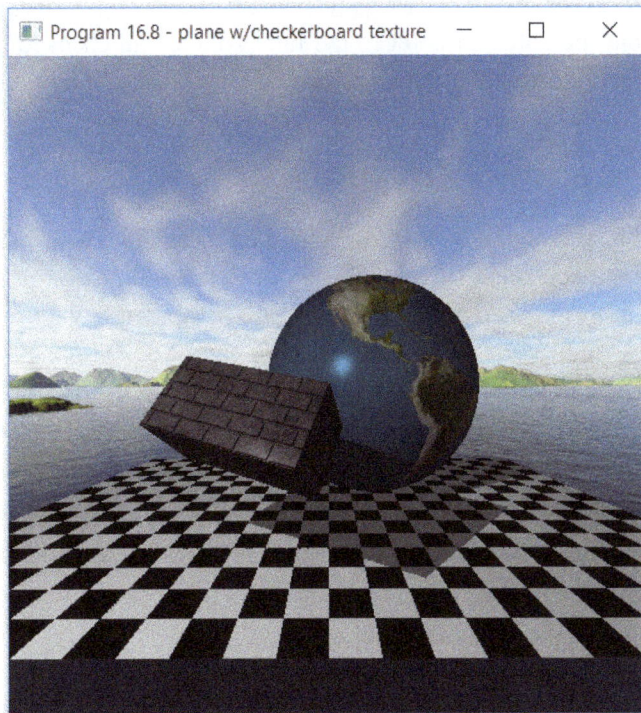

Figure 16.10
Output of Program 16.8, showing the addition of a plane with a procedural checkerboard texture

16.3 RAY TRACING

So far, all of the results we have seen from Programs 16.2 through 16.8 could have been accomplished with the methods described earlier in the book using models and buffers (and probably more efficiently). We now extend our ray casting program to do full ray tracing, which extends the capabilities for lighting and reflection beyond what we have been able to perform up to now.

The ray casting algorithm described in Section 16.2 involved sending out a single ray per pixel, identifying whether (and where) it first encounters an object in the scene, and then painting the pixel accordingly. However, we have the option of generating a new ray from the intersection point (such as a ray that simulates a reflection off of the surface, which we can use the surface normal to generate) and then seeing where that new ray leads. These bounced rays are called *secondary* rays, and these can be used to generate reflections, refractions, and other effects. We have actually already seen one example of a secondary ray: in Program 16.4, when we tested to see if an object was in shadow, we did so by generating a secondary ray from the collision point to the light source and checked to see if that secondary ray collided with an intervening object.

16.3.1 Reflection

Perhaps the most obvious use for secondary rays is to generate reflections of objects off of each other. If we color an object based solely on a secondary reflected ray, it will behave like a pure mirror. Or, we might choose to blend an object's color with the color obtained by a reflected ray, depending on the material qualities we are trying to simulate. We have already seen GLSL's reflect() function, which is useful here. Recall that the reflect() function takes an incident vector and a surface normal and returns the direction of a reflection vector.

In Program 16.9, we extend Program 16.8 so as to generate a single secondary reflection ray when the initial ray collides with the sphere. The sphere color is then set to the color encountered by the secondary ray (also incorporating ADS lighting). The result is shown in Figure 16.11.

Program 16.9 – Adding a Single Secondary Reflection Ray

Compute Shader

. . .

```
vec3 raytrace2(Ray r)
```

```
{   // this function is identical to raytrace() from Program 16.7 (see text for explanation)
    . . .
}
vec3 raytrace(Ray r)
{   Collision c = get_closest_collision(r);
    if (c.object_index == -1) return vec3(0.0);        // no collision
    if (c.object_index == 1)
    {   // in the case of the sphere, determine the color by generating a secondary ray
        Ray reflected_ray;
        // compute start point of secondary ray, offset slightly to avoid colliding with the same object
        reflected_ray.start = c.p + c.n * 0.001;

        reflected_ray.dir = reflect(r.dir, c.n);
        vec3 reflected_color = raytrace2(reflected_ray);
        return ads_phong_lighting(r,c) * reflected_color;
    }
    . . .
}
```

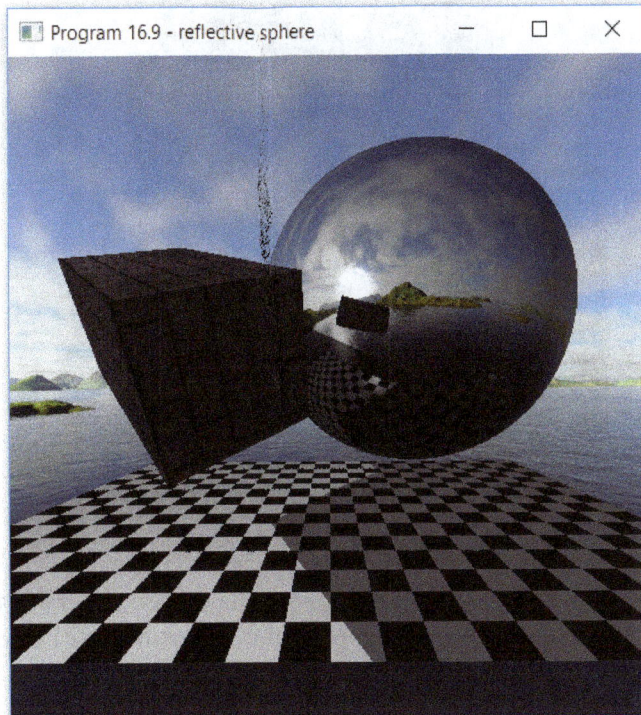

Figure 16.11
Output of Program 16.9 showing a single reflected ray at the sphere object

Note that the sphere is now acting as a mirror, reflecting the surrounding skybox *and* the neighboring brick box and checkerboard plane. Recall that back in Chapter 8, we simulated a reflective object using environment mapping. The drawback there was that the environment-mapped objects were able to reflect the skybox, but not neighboring objects. By contrast, here ray tracing enables the reflective object to reflect all neighboring objects, in addition to the skybox. Also note that the *front* of the skybox (otherwise unseen because it is behind the camera) is now reflected in the sphere.

Figure 16.12 shows the result when we make the box object reflective and use the earth texture for the sphere. We have moved the box object behind the sphere so that its reflections are visible.

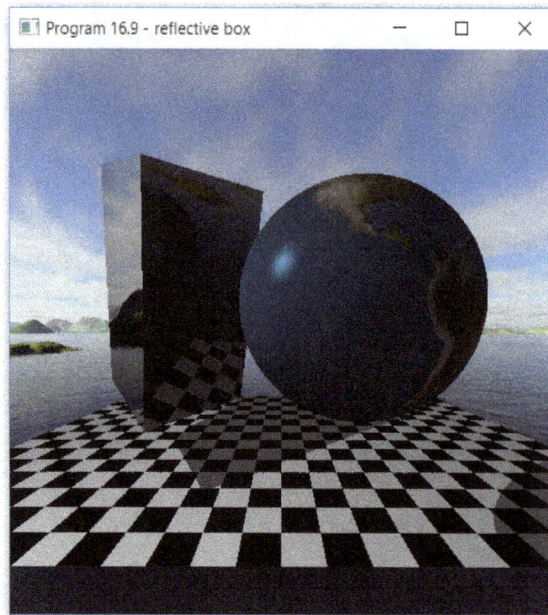

Figure 16.12
Single reflected ray at the box object

In the code shown in Program 16.9, it would have been preferable to eliminate the raytrace2() function altogether and replace the call to raytrace2() with a recursive call to raytrace(). Unfortunately, GLSL doesn't support recursion, so we duplicated the function. Later, as we increase the number of secondary rays, we will build an iterative version of raytrace() that keeps track of recursive ray generation.

It is also worth pointing out one important detail in the code for Program 16.9. The collision point of the initial ray becomes the starting point of the secondary ray, so one would naturally expect the following:

reflected_ray.start = c.p;

However, the code instead contains the following line:

reflected_ray.start = c.p + c.n * 0.001;

This causes the secondary ray to start at a very small distance away, in the direction of the surface normal at the collision point, from the object that was just collided. The purpose of this adjustment is to avoid an artifact very similar to shadow acne (which we saw in Chapter 8). If we were to actually start the reflection ray exactly at c.p, then when the reflection ray is built, rounding errors will sometimes cause it to immediately collide again with the same object (at nearly the exact same point). Figure 16.13 shows the same scene as previously shown in Figure 16.12, except without the correction. Surface acne is now evident on the reflective box object.

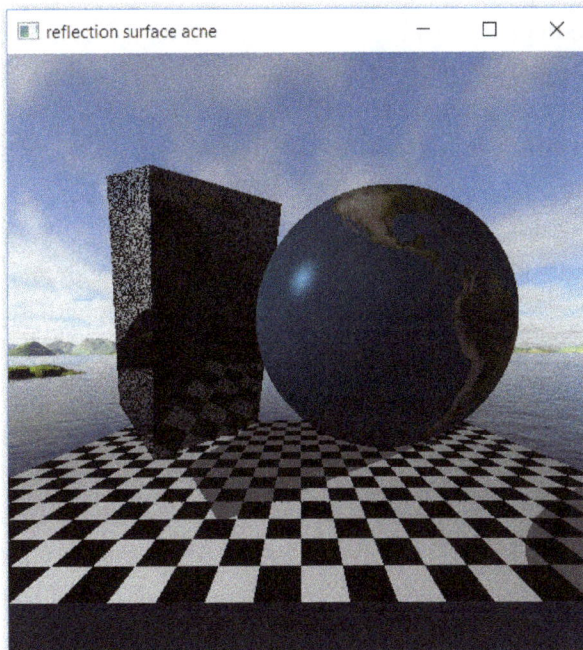

Figure 16.13
Surface acne

16.3.2 Refraction

What happens when an object is transparent? Of course, we expect to see what lies behind it (at least partially). As we saw earlier in Chapter 14, OpenGL has support for rendering with transparency, and there are commands for blending colors to simulate transparency. However, ray tracing can give us the tools to generate some of the more complex aspects of transparency and improve realism. For example, ray tracing allows us to simulate refraction.

Refraction happens when light rays are bent when passing through a transparent object, causing an object's position to appear to "shift" when it is placed behind another transparent object. The amount that the light rays are bent depends on the shape of the transparent object and the material of which it is made. A transparent object is sometimes referred to as the *medium* that the light is passing through, and different transparent media (such as water, glass, or a diamond), will bend light to different degrees. Anyone who has peered through a fishbowl knows how complex refraction can be. We will only discuss some very simple examples.

The amount that a given medium will bend light is called its *index of refraction*, or IOR. We will usually indicate index of refraction with η. IOR is a factor that indicates the degree to which a ray's angle when it hits a medium is altered when the ray continues through the medium (actually, the *sines* of those angles). The IOR of a vacuum is 1, and the IOR of glass is about 1.5. The IOR of air is so close to 1 that it is usually ignored.

In the case of a very thin transparent object, such as a sheet of glass (which we might simulate with a plane object), the amount refraction is usually small. A thicker transparent object, such as a solid glass sphere or pyramid, has a much larger refractive effect. Furthermore, refraction may occur both when the ray enters the object and then again when it exits, and both rays would need to be considered to properly render an object behind a transparent one.

The refractive effect of a solid glass sphere would be very different from that of a hollow glass sphere. For a hollow sphere, a ray enters through the thin front glass surface, travels through the air inside the sphere, and then exits through the thin glass surface at the back. For a solid sphere, the ray travels through glass the entire time, so the refractive effect is much greater. Recreating the precise effect of a hollow sphere would be complex, since technically there are entry and exit points at both the front and back of the sphere, necessitating four secondary rays! A simpler alternative is to treat a hollow sphere the same as a solid sphere, but with a much smaller IOR, which is what we do. In our examples, we use an IOR of 1.5 for a solid glass sphere, and 1.01 or 1.02 for simulating a hollow glass sphere.

Thus, adding refraction to our scene (e.g., making a sphere or a box transparent) requires a sequence of two successive secondary rays, one that refracts from the initial ray into the object and a second one that refracts as the ray exits the object. An example is shown in Figure 16.14, where the current initial ray being processed is labeled I, the normal at the initial collision point is N_1, the first secondary ray is S_1, the normal at the second collision point is N_2, and the second secondary ray is S_2. In a purely transparent object, the color at the final collision point C is the color that would be ultimately be rendered at the collision point of the initial ray "I."

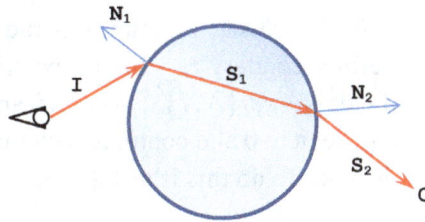

Figure 16.14
Refraction with two secondary rays through a transparent sphere (the angles have been exaggerated for clarity).

The derivation for computing a refraction angle is well-documented [F96], and is as follows:

$$S = \left(\eta_r \left(N \bullet I \right) - \sqrt{1 - \eta_r^2 \left(1 - dot\left(N, I \right)^2 \right)} \right) N - \eta_r I$$

where η_r is the ratio of the IORs of the source and destination media. For a transparent *solid* glass sphere, we would use an IOR at the point of entry equal to $IOR_{air} / IOR_{glass} = 1.0 / 1.5 \approx \mathbf{0.66}$, and at the point of exit, it would be $IOR_{glass} / IOR_{air} = 1.5 / 1.0 = \mathbf{1.5}$. For a transparent *hollow* glass sphere, we would use IOR values of $IOR_{air} / IOR_{glass} = 1.0 / 1.02 \approx \mathbf{0.98}$, and $IOR_{glass} / IOR_{air} = 1.02 / 1.0 = \mathbf{1.02}$ at the points of entry and exit, respectively.

It is tempting to use the GLSL refract() function to implement this formula (and in fact, in a previous edition of this book, we did). GLSL's refract() takes three parameters as input: the incoming vector *I*, the normal vector *N*, and the IOR ratio η_r. It then produces the desired refracted secondary ray *S* as output. This works well for large values of the IOR, such as for the solid glass sphere, but does not work as well for values close to 1, such as for the hollow glass sphere. This is because of how the refract() function, as implemented in OpenGL, handles the square root portion of the formula, specifically how it avoids the potential of having to take the square root of a negative number in the case where $1 - \eta_r^2 \left(1 - dot\left(N, I\right)^2\right)$ is negative. As described in the OpenGL reference [KRF23], the GLSL implementation of refract(), which is otherwise essentially equivalent to the equation from [F96] given above, is as follows:

```
float k = 1.0 – ior * ior * (1.0 - dot(c.n, r.dir) * dot(c.n, r.dir));
if (k<0.0)
  refracted_ray.dir = 0;
else
  refracted_ray.dir = ior * r.dir - (ior * dot(c.n,r.dir) + sqrt(k)) * c.n;
```

Thus, when k equals 0, the refract() function sets the resulting output vector S to 0, which is not a useful secondary ray. In our experience, better results are obtained by computing $1 - \eta_r^2 \left(1 - dot\left(N, I\right)^2\right)$ yourself, and then testing to see if that is less than zero; if it is, set it to 0 and continue with the remainder of the computation to produce S. The code to do this is as follows:

```
float k = 1.0 – ior * ior * (1.0 - dot(c.n, r.dir) * dot(c.n, r.dir));
if (k<0.0) k=0.0;
refracted_ray.dir = ior * r.dir - (ior * dot(c.n,r.dir) + sqrt(k)) * c.n;
```

Program 16.10 converts the sphere to transparent glass using a sequence of two secondary rays to generate the refraction of the brick box and skybox behind it. We also built a third copy of the raytrace() function, so that the two secondary rays can be generated and traced in succession, one entering the sphere and one leaving it (with the appropriate IOR values, as described above). Lighting is included in both the entry and exit points. Since the color and lighting values are all fractions in the range [0..1], and we are multiplying them together, it is common to also scale the resulting color values up or the final result will be too dark; here we have scaled the refracted colors up by a factor of 2.0.

Generating a solid sphere versus a hollow sphere is a simple matter of selecting one or the other corresponding set of IOR values, as described previously. We demonstrate both in the following sections.

Note that the trick we used to avoid surface acne is modified slightly in both functions; instead of adding a small offset along the normal, we subtract the offset. This is because the secondary rays now continue through the collision point rather than rebounding. So, for refracted rays, we must add a small offset along the negative of the normal.

Program 16.10 – Refraction Through a Sphere – Two Secondary Rays

Compute Shader

```
. . .
vec3 raytrace3(Ray r)
{   // this function is identical to raytrace() from Program 16.7
    . . .
}
vec3 raytrace2(Ray r)
{   . . .
    if (c.object_index == 1)     // recall that index==1 indicates collision with the sphere
    {   // generate a second secondary ray for the intersection with the back of the sphere
        Ray refracted_ray;
        refracted_ray.start = c.p – c.n * 0.001;

        float ior = 1.0 / 1.01;     // 1.0/1.01 for hollow sphere, 1.5 for solid glass sphere
        float k = 1.0 – ior * ior * (1.0 - dot(c.n, r.dir) * dot(c.n, r.dir));
        if (k<0.0) k=0.0;
        refracted_ray.dir = ior * r.dir - (ior * dot(c.n, r.dir) + sqrt(k)) * c.n;

        vec3 refracted_color = raytrace3(refracted_ray);
        return 2.0*ads_phong_lighting(r, c) * refracted_color;
    }
    . . .
}
vec3 raytrace(Ray r)
{   . . .
    if (c.object_index == 1)
    {   // generate a secondary ray for the intersection with the front of the sphere
        Ray refracted_ray;
        refracted_ray.start = c.p – c.n * 0.001;

        float ior = 1.01;       // 1.01 for hollow sphere, 1.0/1.5 for solid glass sphere
        float k = 1.0 - ior*ior*(1.0-dot(c.n,r.dir)*dot(c.n,r.dir));
        if (k<0.0) k=0.0;
        refracted_ray.dir = ior*r.dir-(ior*dot(c.n,r.dir)+sqrt(k))*c.n;

        vec3 refracted_color = raytrace2(refracted_ray);
        return 2.0*ads_phong_lighting(r, c) * refracted_color;
    }
    . . .
}
```

Figure 16.15 shows the result, with the "hollow glass" sphere on the left, and the "solid glass" sphere on the right. Notice that the view of the scene through the "hollow" sphere shows the objects behind the sphere to be slightly shifted in position. By contrast, the objects seen through the "solid" glass sphere on the right have been completely flipped vertically and appear upside down. A flipped (and severely curved) version of the brick box is visible in the sphere, as is the checkerboard plane.

Some readers may be skeptical that a glass ball would have this extreme optical effect, but it is commonly observed in the real world [LE16]. To demonstrate this, we obtained an actual solid glass sphere and an actual hollow glass sphere, both approximately the same size. We photographed them in a setting near a river, on a checkerboard surface, similar in style to the one rendered and shown in Figure 16.15. The result is shown in Figure 16.16. Note that similarity in the refraction effects between the real-world photographs and the renderings generated by the code.

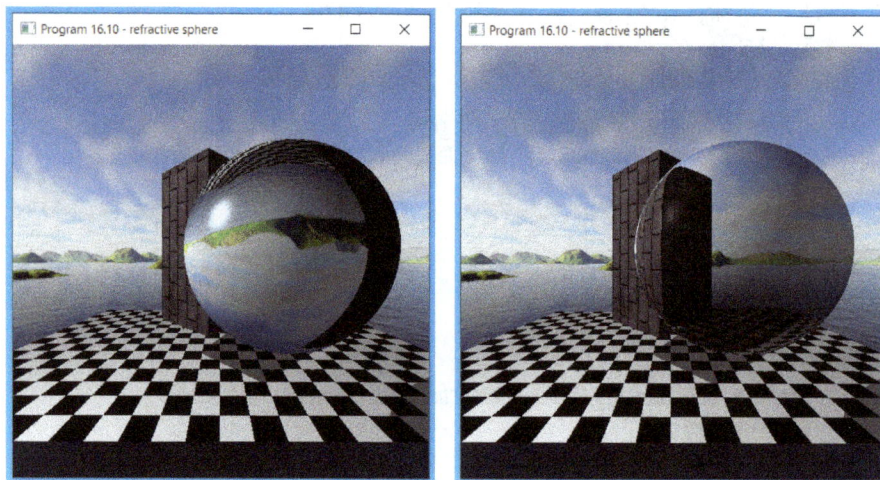

Figure 16.15
Output of Program 16.10 showing refraction through solid and hollow transparent spheres.

It is useful to be aware of the potential for such extreme refraction in thick solid transparent objects such as the solid glass sphere. However, thinner curved surfaces, such as are found in wine glasses and serving pitchers, are likely to be more common in real-world scenes. For the remainder of this chapter, we utilize IOR values that are close to 1, such as values 1.01 and 1.02, as we did here for the hollow glass sphere.

Figure 16.16
Real-world photographs of solid and hollow transparent (glass) spheres.

16.3.3 Combining Reflection, Refraction, and Textures

Transparent objects are also usually slightly reflective. Combining reflection and refraction (as well as textures) can be done in a similar manner as combining lighting and textures, as we did previously in Chapter 7. In Program 16.11, the raytrace() function generates both reflection and refraction rays, combining them using a weighted sum. The degree to which the object is reflective rather than transparent can be tuned by adjusting the weights to get various effects. In this example, we replace the skybox with a blue room box to make the specific effects of reflection and refraction more clearly visible. We also replaced the brick box with a marble-textured slightly reflective box to show an example of combining texturing with reflection. The results are shown in Figure 16.17. Note the interesting propagation of the specular highlights!

Program 16.11 – Combining Reflection and Refraction

Compute Shader

```
. . .
vec3 raytrace(Ray r)
{  . . .
   if (c.object_index == 1)
   {   // generate a refraction ray
       Ray refracted_ray;
       refracted_ray.start = c.p - c.n * 0.001;
       float ior = 1.02;     // 1.02 for hollow sphere, 1.0/1.5 for solid glass sphere
       float k = 1.0 - ior*ior*(1.0-dot(c.n,r.dir)*dot(c.n,r.dir));
```

```
    if (k<0.0) k=0.0;
    refracted_ray.dir = ior*r.dir-(ior*dot(c.n,r.dir)+sqrt(k))*c.n;

    // generate a reflection ray
    Ray reflected_ray;
    reflected_ray.start = c.p + c.n * 0.001;
    reflected_ray.dir = reflect(r.dir, c.n);
    vec3 reflected_color = raytrace3(reflected_ray);        // reflection only requires a single ray

    return clamp(ads_phong_lighting(r,c) *
        ((0.5 * reflected_color) + (1.5 * refracted_color)), 0, 1);    // weighted sum of raytrace collisions
}
    . . .
```

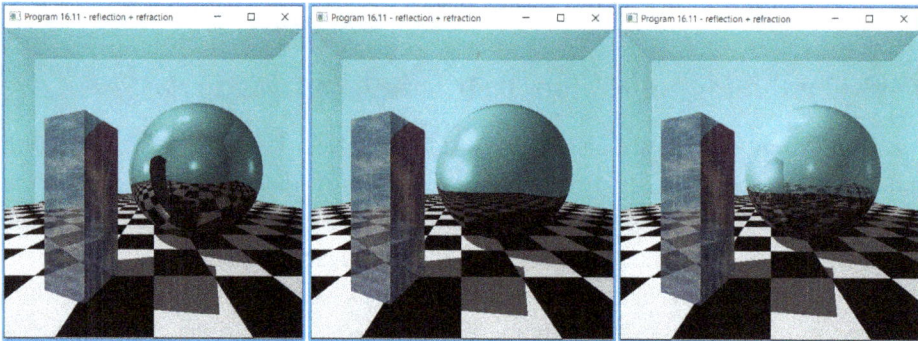

Figure 16.17
Output of Program 16.11, combining reflection, refraction, and textures. Left: sphere with reflection only. Center: sphere with refraction only. Right: sphere with both reflection and refraction

16.3.4 Increasing the Number of Rays

What if we have a transparent object and behind it is another transparent object? Ideally, the ray tracer should generate a series of rays for the first and second transparent objects. Then, whichever surface is encountered behind the second object is what we would see. If the transparent objects were boxes (or spheres), how many rays would be required for the final object to appear? An example is shown in Figure 16.18, in which a green star is viewed through two transparent boxes. Since each transparent object would generally require two secondary rays (one entering the object and one leaving the object), we would need a total of five rays.

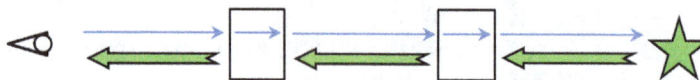

Figure 16.18
Returning an object's color through a sequence of transparent objects.

However, that is not what the code we have built so far will do. Rather, we have hard-coded functions raytrace(), raytrace2(), and raytrace3() that result in a maximum sequence of three rays (plus the shadow ray). In the example shown in Figure 16.18, the sequence of rays would stop at the second transparent object, and we would not see the star at all. As the need for longer and longer sequences of rays increases, we cannot keep making more and more copies of the raytrace() function, as such a solution would not be scalable.

Another similar situation occurs if we have two highly reflective objects facing each other. Anyone who has done this with two mirrors knows the effect as they reflect back and forth between each other. Figure 16.19 shows such an example generated by one of the authors at his home. Our code could only do two reflections, but no subsequent reflections. A much longer sequence of rays is needed to achieve this effect.

We actually faced this situation in the previous example from Program 16.11 and shown in Figure 16.17 because both the box and the sphere were reflective. The effects of any additional rays in that particular example would be negligible, and in such cases, a depth of one or two rays is sufficient. However, in those cases where the additional rays are needed to achieve realistic results, we need a way of generating more rays.

The general solution to this problem is to *recursively* call raytrace(), with the condition that terminates the recursion (the "base case") being whenever a ray encounters a non-reflective or non-transparent surface (or whenever a predetermined maximum depth has been reached) or if the ray collides with no object. Unfortunately, GLSL does not support recursion. To achieve any reasonable simulation of the above effects, we need to keep track of the recursion ourselves.

Building a recursive version of raytrace() in the absence of native support for recursion is not trivial. Our solution requires a stack, defining a structure for items to be pushed onto the stack and building appropriate push and pop operations, as well as a driver that contains the main loop for processing the rays (using stack operations) and a function to process a stack element (which contains the information for an individual ray).

Figure 16.19
Two mirrors facing each other.

Program 16.12 shows these as additions (and replacements) to elements of the previous Program 16.11. There is a struct called Stack_Element that defines the items stored in the stack and functions for raytrace() (which is the driver), push(), pop(), and process_stack_element(). The stack itself is stored as an array of Stack_Elements. Detailed explanations follow the code.

Program 16.12 – Recursive Ray Generation

Compute Shader

```
. . .
struct Stack_Element
{   int type;        // type of ray (1 = reflected, 2 = refracted. Shadow rays are never pushed on stack)
    int depth;       // depth of the recursive raytrace
    int phase;       // which of the five phases of a recursive call is currently being processed
    vec3 phong_color;      // holds the computed ADS color
    vec3 reflected_color;   // holds the reflected color
    vec3 refracted_color;   // holds the refracted color
    vec3 final_color;   // mixture of phong, reflection,and refraction colors (plus texture) for this invocation
    Ray ray;                  // the ray for this raytrace invocation
    Collision collision;      // the collision for this raytrace invocation. Starts with null_collision value.
};
const int RAY_TYPE_REFLECTION = 1;
const int RAY_TYPE_REFRACTION = 2;

// "NULL" values for structs are defined, to make it easier to tell when a value hasn't been assigned
Ray null_ray = {vec3(0.0), vec3(0.0)};
Collision null_collision = { -1.0, vec3(0.0), vec3(0.0), false, -1, vec2(0.0, 0.0), -1 };
Stack_Element null_stack_element = { 0,-1,-1,vec3(0),vec3(0),vec3(0),vec3(0), null_ray, null_collision };

const int stack_size = 100;
Stack_Element stack[stack_size];       // holds the "recursive" stack of raytrace invocations
const int max_depth = 6;   // maximum sequence of rays, which equals maximum recursion depth
int stack_pointer = -1;                      // Points to the top of the stack (-1 if empty)
Stack_Element popped_stack_element;        // Holds the last popped element from the stack

// The "push" function, which schedules a new raytrace by adding it to the top of the stack
void push(Ray r, int depth, int type)
{   if (stack_pointer >= stack_size-1) return;       // if there is no more room on the stack, exit
    Stack_Element element;   // initialize those fields that we already know, and set others to zero or null
    element = null_stack_element;
    element.type = type;
    element.depth = depth;
    element.phase = 0;
```

```
    element.ray = r;
    stack_pointer++;
    stack[stack_pointer] = element;        // add this element to the stack
}

// The "pop" function, which removes a raytrace operation that has been completed
Stack_Element pop()
{   // removes and returns the top stack element
    Stack_Element top_stack_element = stack[stack_pointer];
    stack[stack_pointer] = null_stack_element;
    stack_pointer--;
    return top_stack_element;
}

// Five-phase processing of a given ray: (1) collision, (2) lighting, (3) reflection, (4) refraction, (5) mixing
void process_stack_element(int index)
{   // If there is a popped_stack_element that was previously processed, it holds reflection/refraction
    // information for the current stack element. Store that info, then clear the popped element reference.
    if (popped_stack_element != null_stack_element)   // GLSL supports element-wise comparison of structs
    {   if (popped_stack_element.type == RAY_TYPE_REFLECTION)
            stack[index].reflected_color = popped_stack_element.final_color;
        else if (popped_stack_element.type == RAY_TYPE_REFRACTION)
            stack[index].refracted_color = popped_stack_element.final_color;
        popped_stack_element = null_stack_element;
    }

    Ray r = stack[index].ray;                          // initialized by the initial call
    Collision c = stack[index].collision;              // starts null, gets set in phase 1

    switch (stack[index].phase)
    {   // ========== PHASE 1 - raytrace collision detection
        case 1:
            c = get_closest_collision(r);              // Cast ray into the scene, store collision result
            if (c.object_index != -1)                  // If the ray didn't hit anything, stop.
                stack[index].collision = c;            // otherwise, store the collision result
            break;
        // ========== PHASE 2 – Phong ADS lighting computation
        case 2:
            stack[index].phong_color = ads_phong_lighting(r, c);
            break;
        // ========== PHASE 3 – generate a reflection ray
        case 3:
            if (stack[index].depth < max_depth)        // stop if at max depth
            {   if ((c.object_index == 1) || (c.object_index == 2)) // only sphere and box are reflective
```

```
        {   Ray reflected_ray;
            reflected_ray.start = c.p + c.n * 0.001;
            reflected_ray.dir = reflect(r.dir, c.n);

            // add a raytrace for that ray to the stack, and set its type to reflection
            push(reflected_ray, stack[index].depth+1, RAY_TYPE_REFLECTION);
        }   }
        break;
    // ========== PHASE 4 – generate a refraction ray
    case 4:
        if (stack[index].depth < max_depth)        // stop if at max depth
        {   if (c.object_index == 1)               // only the sphere is transparent
            {   Ray refracted_ray;
                refracted_ray.start = c.p - c.n * 0.001;
                float ior = 1.02;        // 1.02 for hollow sphere, 1.0/1.5 for solid glass sphere
                if (c.inside) ior = 1.0 / ior;

                float k = 1.0 - ior*ior*(1.0-dot(c.n,r.dir)*dot(c.n,r.dir));
                k = max(k, 0.0);
                refracted_ray.dir = ior*r.dir-(ior*dot(c.n,r.dir)+sqrt(k))*c.n;

                // Add a raytrace for that ray to the stack
                push(refracted_ray, stack[index].depth+1, RAY_TYPE_REFRACTION);
            }   }
        break;
    // ========== PHASE 5 – mixing
    case 5:
        if (c.object_index == 1)         // for the sphere, blend refraction, refraction, and lighting
        {   stack[index].final_color = stack[index].phong_color *
                (0.3 * stack[index].reflected_color) + (2.0 * (stack[index].refracted_color));
        }
        if (c.object_index == 2)         // for the box, blend reflection, lighting, and texture
        {   stack[index].final_color = stack[index].phong_color *
                ((0.5 * stack[index].reflected_color) + (1.0 * (texture(sampMarble, c.tc)).xyz));
        }
        if (c.object_index == 3) stack[index].final_color = stack[index].phong_color * rbox_color;
        if (c.object_index == 4) stack[index].final_color = stack[index].phong_color *
                                                            (checkerboard(c.tc)).xyz;

        break;
    // ========== when all five phases are complete, end the recursion
    case 6:
        popped_stack_element = pop();
        return;
    }
    stack[index].phase++;
```

```
    return;    // only process one phase per process_stack_element() invocation
}

// This is the "driver" function that sends out the first ray,
// and then processes secondary rays until all have completed
vec3 raytrace(Ray r)
{   push(r, 0, RAY_TYPE_REFLECTION);
    while (stack_pointer >= 0) // process the stack until it is empty
    {   int element_index = stack_pointer;            // peek at the topmost stack element
        process_stack_element(element_index);   // process next phase of the current stack element
    }
    return popped_stack_element.final_color;      // final color of the last-popped stack element
}
```

In Program 16.12, the stack is an array of structs of type StackElement, where an instance of StackElement contains all of the information necessary to process any given ray. The functions that do the stack pushing and popping, push() and pop(), should be straightforward. The size of the stack must be chosen carefully; if there are many objects that are both reflective and refractive, the number of rays can grow exponentially. (Although, in practice, many rays terminate due to colliding with the skybox before the maximum recursion depth is reached.)

Ray tracing begins in raytrace(). Although all rays require their type to be set (reflection or refraction), the type of the initial ray is not used; we set it to reflection arbitrarily. We then start processing all of the rays in the stack (by repeatedly calling process_stack_element()), and in so doing, secondary (and subsequent) rays may be generated and added to the stack, as well. When all processing for a ray has been completed, its final computed color is then made available to its "parent" ray, which in turn may utilize it to compute its own color.

All of this (the core of the ray trace processing) is done in process_stack_element(), which is organized as a five-phase series of operations. Each of the phases is basically identical to the steps in earlier programs in this chapter. Some of the phases do not require the generation of additional rays (collision detection, lighting/shadows, and texturing). However, the reflection and refraction phases both require generating a new ray, as well as running process_stack_element() on the new ray(s). Since there is no way in GLSL to make such a call recursively, we adjust the contents of the current stack element to keep track of where we left off, push a new stack element containing the new ray to be processed, and then exit process_stack_element(). The driver function (which is the new version of raytrace()) continues iteratively calling process_stack_element() until every stack element (every ray) has had a chance to complete all five phases. The end result is the same as if recursion had been available.

The code in Program 16.12 (the declarations, and the push(), pop(), process_stack_element(), and raytrace() functions) replaces the previous raytrace() function (and its "children" raytrace2() and raytrace3()) from Program 16.11. The remainder of Program 16.12 is unchanged from Program 16.11.

The output of Program 16.12 depends on the max_depth setting. The larger the value, the longer the sequence of rays that can be generated. Figure 16.20 shows the outputs for max_depth values of 0, 1, 2, 3, and 4.

Figure 16.20
The output of Program 16.12: with recursive depth values of 0, 1, 2, 3, and 4 (left-to-right, top-to-bottom).

At depth zero, only direct textures and lighting are visible (and since the sphere is not textured, it has no color). At depth one, immediate reflections are visible, and the very first refraction of the sphere has occurred but had little effect because its ray terminates inside of the sphere. At depth two, the results are essentially equivalent to our previous hard-coded output of Program 16.11 and shown in Figure 16.17. At depths three and four, additional reflections are evident in the sphere, and a second reflection of the box can be seen faintly against the inside back of the sphere. Any differences between depth 3 and depth 4 are negligible for this particular scene.

16.3.5 Generalizing the Solution

Our solution works well, but it is hard-coded for a particular set of four objects: one transparent and partially reflective sphere, one textured and partially reflective box, a procedurally textured plane, and a solid-colored room box. If we wish to alter the set of objects in the scene (perhaps by adding another box or making the sphere textured), we would have to not only change the declarations at the top of the compute shader, but also make significant changes in the process_stack_element() and get_closest_collision() functions. What we really need is a more general solution that allows us to define an arbitrary set of these objects.

To achieve this, we introduce another struct definition for specifying an object in the scene, then build an array of these objects. The get_closest_collision() function iterates through them, taking into account the type of each object. The room box is handled separately as the 0th object, and we assume there is exactly one of those.

Our "more general" solution still has limitations; for example, there are many ways of defining texture coordinates, even for simple shapes. Our solution is still limited to spheres, planes, and boxes with texture coordinates as specified so far, a single room box, global ambient light plus a single positional light (although adding more lights is not difficult), and a fixed camera facing down the negative Z axis. Program 16.13 shows the additions to Program 16.12, along with an example configuration that matches the previous example.

Program 16.13 – More Generalized Object Definition

Compute Shader

```
. . .
struct Object
```

```
{   float   type;           // 0=skybox, 1=sphere, 2=box, 3=plane
    float   radius;         // sphere radius (only relevant if type=sphere)
    vec3    mins;           // box corner (if type=box). If type=plane, X and Z values are width and depth
    vec3    maxs;           // opposite box corner (if type=box)
    float   xrot;           // X component of object rotation (only relevant if type=box or plane)
    float   yrot;           // Y component of object rotation (only relevant if type=box or plane)
    float   zrot;           // Z component of object rotation (only relevant if type=box or plane)
    vec3    position;       // location of center of object
    bool    hasColor;       // whether or not the object has a particular color specified
    bool    hasTexture;     // whether or not the object includes a texture image in computing its color
    bool    isReflective;   // whether or not the object is reflective (generates a secondary ray)
                            // (if the object is a room box, this field is used to enable or disable lighting)
    bool    isTransparent;  // whether or not the object is refractive (generates a secondary ray)
    vec3    color;          // the RGB color specified for the object (only relevant if hasColor is true)
    float   reflectivity;   // percentage of reflective color to include (only relevant if isReflective)
    float   refractivity;   // percentage of refractive color to include (only relevant if isTransparent)
    float   IOR;            // Index of Refraction (only relevant if isTransparent is true)
    vec4    ambient;        // ADS ambient material characteristic
    vec4    diffuse;        // ADS diffuse material characteristic
    vec4    specular;       // ADS specular material characteristic
    float   shininess;      // ADS shininess material characteristic
};

Object[ ] objects =
{   // object #0 is the room box
    { 0, 0.0, vec3(-20, -20, -20), vec3( 20, 20, 20), 0, 0, 0, vec3(0), true, false, true, false, vec3(0.25, 1.0, 1.0),
        0, 0, 0, vec4(0.2, 0.2, 0.2, 1.0), vec4(0.9, 0.9, 0.9, 1.0), vec4(1.0, 1.0, 1.0, 1.0), 50.0
    },
    // object #1 is the checkerboard ground plane
    { 3, 0.0, vec3(12, 0, 16), vec3(0), 0.0, 0.0, 0.0, vec3(0.0, -1.0, -2.0), false, true, false, false, vec3(0),
        0.0, 0.0, 0.0, vec4(0.2, 0.2, 0.2, 1.0), vec4(0.9, 0.9, 0.9, 1.0), vec4(1.0, 1.0, 1.0 ,1.0), 50.0
    },
    // object #2 is the transparent sphere with slight reflection and no texture
    { 1, 1.2, vec3(0), vec3(0), 0, 0, 0, vec3(0.7, 0.2, 2.0), false, false, true, true, vec3(0),
        0.75, 0.6, 1.02, vec4(0.5, 0.5, 0.5, 1.0), vec4(1.0,1.0,1.0,1.0), vec4(1.0, 1.0, 1.0, 1.0), 50.0
    },
    // object #3 is the slightly reflective box with texture
    { 2, 0.0, vec3(-0.25, -0.8, -0.25), vec3(0.25, 0.8, 0.25), 0.0, 70.0, 0.0, vec3(-0.75, -0.2, 3.4),
        false, true, true, false, vec3(0), 0.5, 0.0, 0.0, vec4(0.5, 0.5, 0.5, 1.0), vec4(1.0, 1.0, 1.0, 1.0),
        vec4(1.0, 1.0, 1.0, 1.0), 50.0
    }
} };
int numObjects = 4;
. . .

vec3 getTextureColor(int index, vec2 tc)
```

```
{   // customized for this scene
    if (index==1) return (checkerboard(tc)).xyz;
    else if (index==3) return texture(sampMarble, tc).xyz;
    else return vec3(1,.7,.7);   // return pink if index is for an object other than the plane or box
}
. . .
Collision intersect_plane_object(Ray r, Object o)
{   . . .
    mat4 local_to_worldT = buildTranslate((o.position).x, (o.position).y, (o.position).z);
    mat4 local_to_worldR =
        buildRotateY(DEG_TO_RAD*o.yrot) * buildRotateX(DEG_TO_RAD*o.xrot) *
        buildRotateZ(DEG_TO_RAD*o.zrot);

    . . .
}   // similar object references in other intersection functions also changed to "o.position", "o.mins", etc.

//--------------------------------------------------------------------------
// Returns the closest collision of a ray
// object_index == -1 if no collision
// object_index == 0 if collision with room box
// object_index > 0 if collision with another object
//--------------------------------------------------------------------------
Collision get_closest_collision(Ray r)
{   float closest = 3.402823466e+38;      // initialize to a very large number (max value of a float)
    Collision closest_collision;
    closest_collision.object_index = -1;
    for (int i=0; i<numObjects; i++)
    {   Collision c;
        if (objects[i].type == 0)
        {   c = intersect_room_box_object(r);
            if (c.t <= 0) continue;           // ray didn't collide with this skybox object
        }
        else if (objects[i].type == 1)
        {   c = intersect_sphere_object(r, objects[i]);
            if (c.t <= 0) continue;           // ray didn't collide with this sphere object
        }
        else if (objects[i].type == 2)
        {   c = intersect_box_object(r, objects[i]);
            if (c.t <= 0) continue;           // ray didn't collide with this box object
        }
        else if (objects[i].type == 3)
        {   c = intersect_plane_object(r, objects[i]);
            if (c.t <= 0) continue;           // ray didn't collide with this plane object
        }
```

```
            else continue;    // in case we have any non-collidable object types
            if (c.t < closest)  // we found a collision - now check if it is closer than the current closest
            {   closest = c.t;
                closest_collision = c;
                closest_collision.object_index = i;
        }  }
        return closest_collision;
}
. . .
void process_stack_element(int index)
{      . . .    // phases 1-4 remain unchanged
        // PHASE 5 - Mixing to produce the final color – generalized for any combination of these objects
        if(stack[index].phase == 5)
        {   if (c.object_index > 0)          // we collided with something, and it is not a room box
            {   // first get texture color if applicable
                vec3 texColor = vec3(0.0);
                if (objects[c.object_index].hasTexture)
                    texColor = getTextureColor(c.object_index, c.tc);

                // next, get object color if applicable
                vec3 objColor = vec3(0.0);
                if (objects[c.object_index].hasColor)
                    objColor = objects[c.object_index].color;

                // then get reflected and refractive colors, if they are needed later
                vec3 reflected_color = stack[index].reflected_color;
                vec3 refracted_color = stack[index].refracted_color;

                // Now build the mix of colors – if it is the last color in the chain, just return it without blending
                vec3 mixed_color = objColor + texColor;
                if ((objects[c.object_index].isReflective) && (stack[index].depth<max_depth))
                    mixed_color = mix(mixed_color, reflected_color, objects[c.object_index].reflectivity);
                if ((objects[c.object_index].isTransparent) && (stack[index].depth<max_depth))
                    mixed_color = mix(mixed_color, refracted_color, objects[c.object_index].refractivity);
                stack[index].final_color = mixed_color * stack[index].phong_color;
            }

            if (c.object_index == 0)       // room box object is unique because it might have six textures
            {   vec3 lightFactor = vec3(1.0);   // holds the lighting value if the isReflective flag is set to true
                if (objects[c.object_index].isReflective) lightFactor = stack[index].phong_color;

                if (objects[c.object_index].hasColor) // in this version, a roombox has color or texture,
                                                // but not both
                    stack[index].final_color = lightFactor * objects[c.object_index].color;
                else
                {   if (c.face_index == 0) stack[index].final_color = lightFactor * getTextureColor(5, c.tc);
```

```
            else if (c.face_index == 1) stack[index].final_color = lightFactor * getTextureColor(6, c.tc);
            else if (c.face_index == 2) stack[index].final_color = lightFactor * getTextureColor(7, c.tc);
            else if (c.face_index == 3) stack[index].final_color = lightFactor * getTextureColor(8, c.tc);
            else if (c.face_index == 4) stack[index].final_color = lightFactor * getTextureColor(9, c.tc);
            else if (c.face_index == 5) stack[index].final_color = lightFactor * getTextureColor(10, c.tc);
    } } }
      . . . // other parts of this function are unchanged
} }
```

The definition of the objects array in Program 16.13 corresponds to the example built previously in programs 16.10 and 16.11, and the output matches that shown previously in Figure 16.20. Note that there are still spots in the program (in addition to the definition of the objects array) that might need to be tailored slightly depending on the scene: the camera position, the light position, the texture sampler used for each textured object (or the function to use if procedurally textured – these are all specified in getTextureColor()), recursion depth, and whether shadows are desired (disabling shadows simply requires commenting out the relevant test in the ads_phong_lighting() function). Of course, the program could be generalized further by encapsulating tasks such as ray intersection, texturing, etc. into object subtypes, which would also make it more easily extended.

16.3.6 Additional Examples

Now that the ray tracing program is complete and can be used for various combinations of our basic objects, let's try some of the interesting cases discussed at the beginning of Section 16.3.4. For each configuration, we will need to set the following variables appropriate for the particular scene:

- the objects that comprise the scene (by filling the objects array)
- the number of objects (by setting the variable numObjects)
- the camera position along the Z axis (by setting the variable camera_pos)
- the maximum recursion depth (by setting the variable max_depth)
- the maximum size of the recursion stack (by setting the variable stack_size)
- the location of the positional light (by setting the variable pointLight_position)

For example, can our ray tracer now see an object sitting behind *two* transparent other objects? We can test this by defining the objects array to include two thin refractive boxes and a solid red ball placed behind them, as shown in Program 16.14. The red sphere is centered at 2.0, and the transparent boxes are centered on the positive Z axis at distances 3.0 and 4.0. The camera is also positioned on the positive Z axis at a distance of 5.0.

Program 16.14 – Viewing Through Multiple Transparent Objects

Compute Shader

```
. . .
Object[ ] objects =
{  // object #0 is the room box – this time the room box is white (or grey depending on the lighting)
    { 0, 0.0, vec3(-20, -20, -20), vec3( 20, 20, 20), 0, 0, 0, vec3(0), true, false, true, false, vec3(1.0, 1.0, 1.0),
        0, 0, 0, vec4(0.2, 0.2, 0.2, 1.0), vec4(0.9, 0.9, 0.9, 1.0), vec4(1.0, 1.0, 1.0, 1.0), 50.0
    },
    // red sphere
    { 1, 0.25, vec3(0), vec3(0), 0, 0, 0, vec3(0, 0, 2), true, false, false, false, vec3(1.0, 0.0, 0.0), 0.0, 0.0, 0.0,
        vec4(0.3, 0.3, 0.3, 1.0), vec4(0.7, 0.7, 0.7, 1.0), vec4(1.0, 1.0, 1.0, 1.0), 50.0
    },
    // transparent box with no texture
    { 2, 0, vec3(-0.5, -0.5, -0.1), vec3(0.5, 0.5, 0.01), 0, 0, 0, vec3(0.0, 0.0, 4.0), true, false, false, true,
        vec3(0.9, 0.9, 0.9), 0.0, 0.95, 1.02, vec4(0.8, 0.8, 0.8, 1.0), vec4(1.0, 1.0, 1.0, 1.0), vec4(1.0,
                                                                            1.0, 1.0, 1.0), 50.0
    },
    // transparent box with no texture
    { 2, 0, vec3(-0.5, -0.5, -0.1), vec3(0.5, 0.5, 0.01), 0, 0, 0, vec3(0.0, 0.0, 3.0), true, false, false, true,
        vec3(0.9, 0.9, 0.9), 0.0, 0.95, 1.02, vec4(0.8, 0.8, 0.8, 1.0), vec4(1.0, 1.0, 1.0, 1.0), vec4(1.0,
                                                                            1.0, 1.0, 1.0), 50.0
    }  };
int numObjects = 4;
float camera_pos = 5.0;
const int max_depth = 5;
const int stack_size = 100;
vec3 pointLight_position = vec3(-1,1,3);
. . .
```

The output of Program 16.14 is shown in Figure 16.21. We disabled shadows for this example. Note that at a recursion depth of 3, the red sphere is not visible because the sequence of rays is not sufficient to go through both sides of both boxes and reach the sphere. However, at a recursion depth of 5, the sphere is visible.

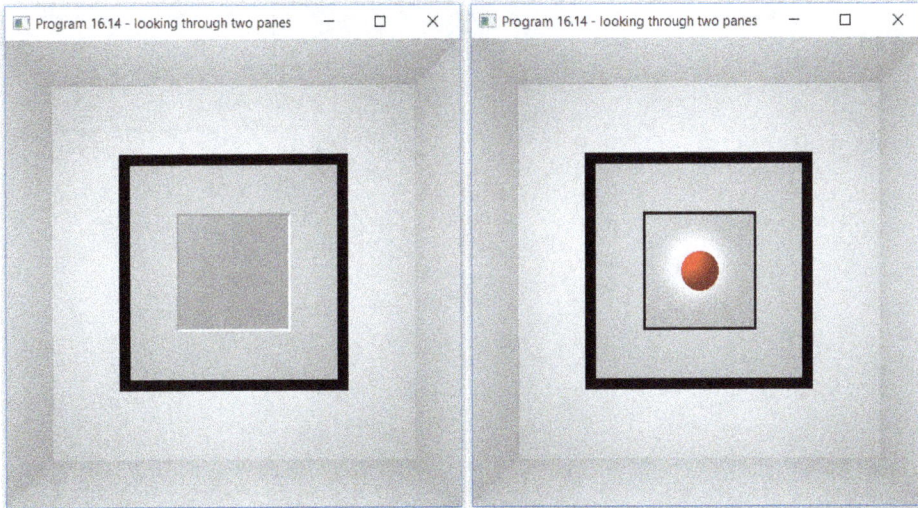

Figure 16.21
The output of Program 16.14. The view of a red ball through two thin transparent boxes. The image on the left has a recursion depth of 3, and the image on the right has a recursion depth of 5.

Another example (discussed previously in Section 16.3.4) is the case of two mirrors facing each other. As illustrated in Figure 16.19, at just the right relative angles between the two mirrors and the viewer, a sort of "recursive tunnel" appears. Can our ray tracer replicate that effect?

We test this by creating two reflective planes (to serve as mirrors) with a red sphere and the camera in between. Figure 16.22 shows the layout of the objects, all of which are placed along the Z axis (slightly offset in some cases), with the camera looking down the negative Z direction. Although the camera (shown in green) would not be able to see an image of the plane that is behind it, it should be able to see an image of the mirror in front of it and the red sphere, including additional images of the red sphere as the reflection bounces back and forth between the two mirrors. Program 16.15 sets up a scene with these objects so oriented.

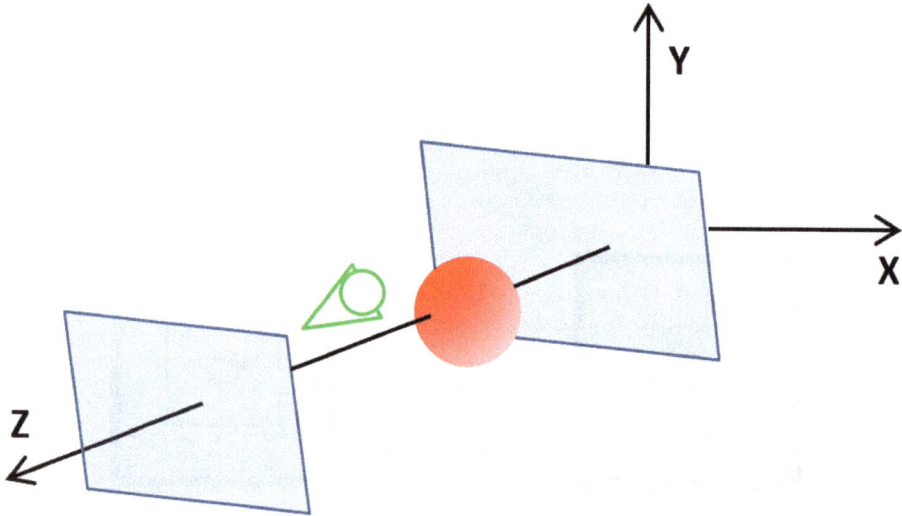

Figure 16.22
Building two mirrors facing each other.

Configuring a scene that reveals a "recursive tunnel" takes some trial-and-error (this can be true with real mirrors in the real world as well). The settings in Program 16.15 represent one such set of object positions and angles that produce a clear example of the desired effect.

Program 16.15 – Two Mirrors Facing Each Other

Compute Shader

. . .

```
Object[ ] objects =
{  // object #0 is the room box
    { 0, 0.0, vec3(-20, -20, -20), vec3(20, 20, 20), 0, 0, 0, vec3(0), true, false, true, false, vec3(0.25,
       1.0, 1.0), 0, 0, 0, vec4(0.2, 0.2, 0.2, 1.0), vec4(0.9, 0.9, 0.9, 1.0), vec4(1.0, 1.0, 1.0, 1.0), 50.0
    },
    // red sphere
    { 1, 0.25, vec3(0), vec3(0), 0, 0, 0, vec3(0, -0.33, 3.3), true, false, false, false, vec3(1.0, 0.0,
       0.0), 0.0, 0.0, 0.0, vec4(0.5, 0.5, 0.5, 1.0), vec4(0.9, 0.9, 0.9, 1.0), vec4(1.0, 1.0, 1.0, 1.0), 50.0
    },
```

```
// first mirror - reflective plane behind camera
{ 3, 0, vec3(4, 0, 4), vec3(0), 90.0, -1.0, 0.0, vec3(0, 0, 3.8), true, false, true, false, vec3(1.0, 1.0,
    1.0), 0.9, 0.0, 0.0, vec4(0.5, 0.5, 0.5, 1.0), vec4(0.9, 0.9, 0.9, 1.0), vec4(1.0, 1.0, 1.0, 1.0), 100.0
},
// second mirror - reflective plane, behind red sphere
{ 3, 0, vec3(.8, 0, .8), vec3(0), 92.0, 0.0, 0.0, vec3(0, 0, 3.1), true, false, true, false, vec3(1.0, 1.0,
    1.0), 0.9, 0.0, 0.0, vec4(0.5, 0.5, 0.5, 1.0), vec4(0.9, 0.9, 0.9, 1.0), vec4(1.0, 1.0, 1.0, 1.0), 100.0
} };
int numObjects = 4;
float camera_pos = 3.7;
const int max_depth = 14;
const int stack_size = 100;
vec3 pointLight_position = vec3(-2, 2, 3);

. . .
```

The red sphere, camera, and mirrors are sitting at various spots along the Z axis, at positions 3.3, 3.7, 3.1, and 3.8, respectively. The red sphere is lowered slightly along the Y axis so that the camera can peer over it. A very light gray color has been specified for the mirrors so that they do not overly darken what they reflect. Since the light has typical ADS characteristics, darkening of off-axis areas slightly increases with each reflection (as was the case in the real-world photo in Figure 16.19). The light has been positioned near the sphere so that shadows cast by the mirrors do not darken it further. The mirror behind the sphere has been tilted down very slightly (by 2.0 degrees on the X axis, to be exact), to make the reflections of the sphere more visible.

Figure 16.23 shows the resulting output for a series of recursion depths. At a recursion depth of 0, only the sphere and one mirror are visible in the scene. At depth=1, the reflection of the sphere in the plane is visible. At depth=2, the reflection of the sphere in the opposite plane has also appeared, and the "tunnel" effect begins to form. Moving forward to a depth of 14, the expected long series of red spheres occurs, and the tunnel effect fully materializes. (The sphere nearest the camera is slightly oblong due to perspective distortion.)

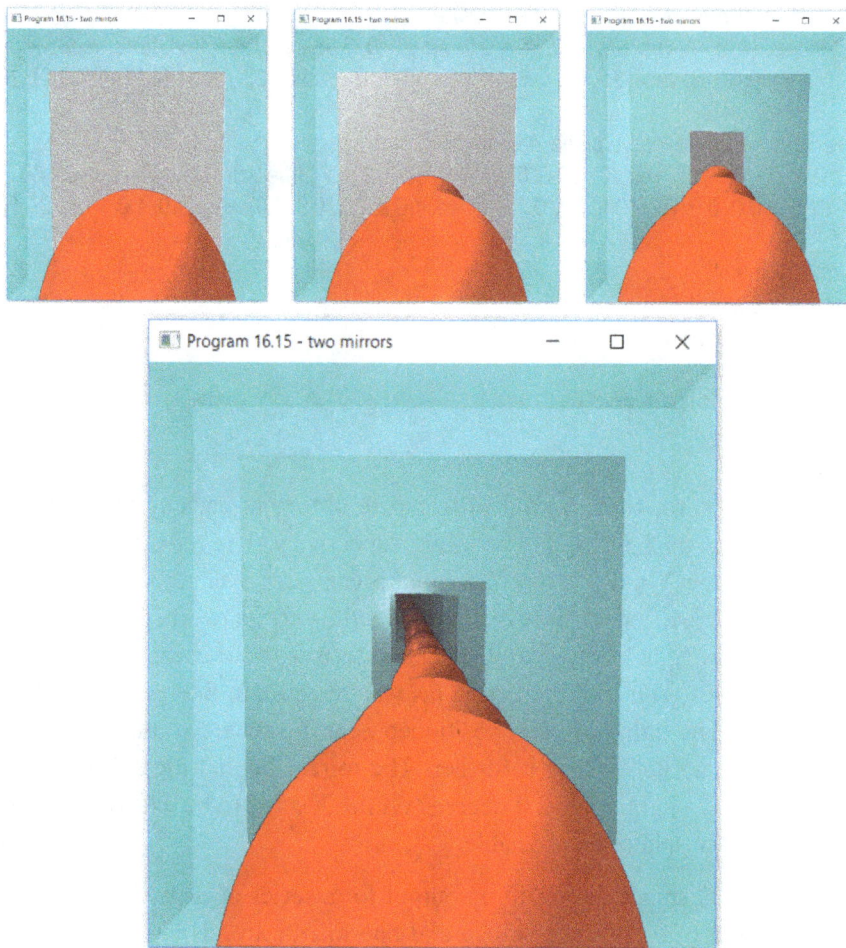

Figure 16.23
The output of Program 16.15 showing two mirrors facing each other. The recursion depth equals 0, 1, 2, and then 14 in the final image.

16.3.7 Blending Colors for Transparent Objects

So far, all of our transparent objects (which we modeled with refracted secondary rays) have had no color (or have been colored white). It is natural to want to make colored transparent objects, such as a tinted window. Even though we have the tools for doing this, there are some rather surprising difficulties that can occur in many cases.

It is a simple matter to declare an object to be transparent and also having a color by simply assigning an RGB value for whatever color we want (such as [1,0,0] for red), and then combining this color with the incoming refracted color as we did in previous examples. However, the results are not always as one would expect! For example, suppose that we declare three planes colored red, yellow, and blue, and stack them in our scene so that we can see the result of mixing the colors as we have been doing, with equal weights where they overlap. The result is shown in Figure 16.24. Is this what you would expect to see if these were real panes of colored glass?

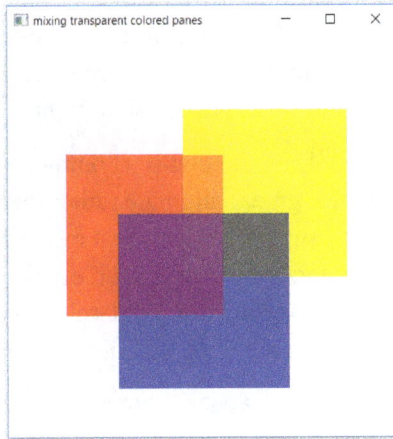

Figure 16.24
A scene with three overlapping colored panes where the colors are mixed equally.

Figure 16.24 was created by defining three overlapping transparent colored panes (red, yellow, and blue) and mixing their colors with a weighted sum:

mixed_color = mix(pane_color, refracted_color, 0.5);

Where the red and yellow overlap, you see orange, and where the red and blue overlap, you see purple, both of which are likely to match your expectations. However, where yellow and blue overlap, you probably expected green, but a sort of gray color appears there instead.

Welcome to the complex world of color models! If those were *real* glass panes, we should indeed see green where the yellow and blue panes overlap. That is because as white light passes through a yellow pane, and then a blue pane, some of the spectrum from the original white light is removed, leaving only the green portion. This is called a *subtractive* color effect, and this is how colors blend when we mix paint or ink.

However, suppose that these panes were actually *emitting* colors, rather than filtering them, such as if a yellow light source was combined (*added*) to a blue light source. In that case, the yellow and blue panes would *not* combine to form green. Thus, depending on what we wish to model, we need to blend colors in different ways.

So far, all of our colors have been expressed using the RGB color model. RGB is an example of an *additive* color model designed for *blending light sources* (the red, green, and blue elements of an RGB computer monitor) by adding them together. That is, the model is designed not to "mix" its colors like paint, but ideally to *add* them. When mixing paint, we expect each successive combined color to *darken* the mix because each successive color subtracts some portion of the light. In an additive model that blends light sources, each successive color *brightens* the mix, moving it closer and closer to white light.

Another aspect of the RGB model that is a common source of confusion is that it uses the primary colors red, green, and blue rather than the familiar red, yellow, and blue primary colors for paints or crayons that most of us learned in elementary school. The RGB primary colors work very well if our three panes are light sources. Suppose, for example, that we replaced the red/yellow/blue panes with red/green/blue panes and simply *added* their colors, without weights, as shown here:

mixed_color = pane_color + refracted_color;

The result is shown in Figure 16.25.

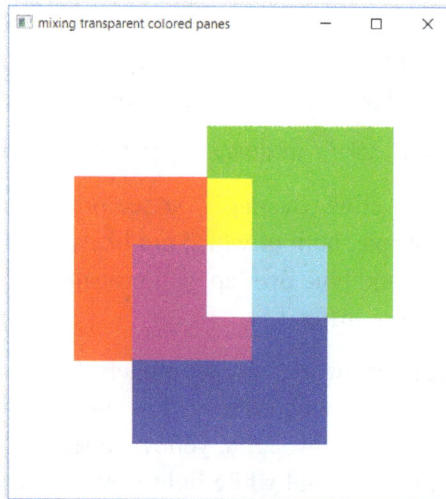

Figure 16.25
A scene with three overlapping colored light sources; colors added together.

To most people new to color models, Figure 16.25 looks very strange (it looks even stranger with red/yellow/blue panes – try it!). The red and blue planes combine to form a sort of light purple called *magenta*, which probably seems fairly reasonable, but few people expect red and green would combine to make yellow. If these panes were *light sources*, believe it or not this is much closer to what would actually happen in the real world. Note, for example, that at the very center, all three red/green/blue primary light colors have been added together, resulting in full spectrum white light. The RGB additive color model is accurate when we use it to blend colored light sources.

What if we want to model colored objects that are not light sources, but are passive colored objects responding to white light sources, such as a colored window pane or a pair of orange sunglasses? Unfortunately, the additive RGB model is not very useful for this task.

If colored transparent objects are desired, rather than light sources, one option is to switch to a subtractive color model, such as CMY (cyan/magenta/yellow). The RGB model designed for computer monitors is composed of tiny red, blue, and green light emitters. The CMY model is commonly used for printers that mix ink to build colors. In the RGB model, [0,0,0] is black and [1,1,1] is white, whereas in CMY, [0,0,0] is white and [1,1,1] is black. Thus, adding colors together in CMY makes them darker. The CMY model matches the real-world observation that when two pigments (such as paint) are mixed together, the resulting substance subtracts out more of the surrounding light and becomes darker. That is why the CMY model is called *subtractive*: the values indicate the amount of light removed from the surrounding light sources, even though we still combine colors by adding them together.

It is easy to convert back and forth between the RGB and CMY models by "inverting" the colors (subtracting them from [1,1,1] or white). One way of blending colors using the CMY model is to invert the RGB colors to generate CMY versions, add them, and then convert them back to RGB values:

$$color1_{CMY} = vec3(1,1,1) - color1_{RGB}$$

$$color2_{CMY} = vec3(1,1,1) - color2_{RGB}$$

$$blend_{CMY} = color1_{CMY} + color2_{CMY}$$

$$result_{RGB} = vec3(1,1,1) - blend_{CMY}$$

This works quite well if the colors of our panes are magenta (RGB=[1,0,1]), yellow (RGB=[1,1,0]), and cyan (RGB=[0,1,1]). Note that it is often necessary to scale the results down so that the final RGB color values do not exceed 1.0. Figure 16.26 shows the resulting blends of colors produced by adding their CMY values.

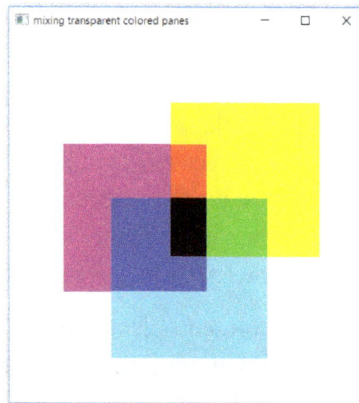

Figure 16.26
Adding cyan, magenta, and yellow panes in CMY color space.

The results are rather similar if we start with these same magenta, yellow, and cyan panes and blend their RGBs with a weighted sum as we did earlier in this chapter (Figure 16.27).

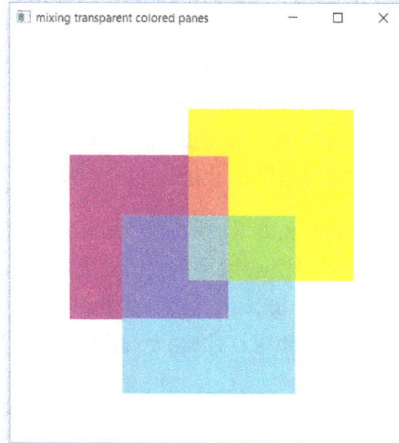

Figure 16.27
Blending cyan, magenta, and yellow panes in RGB color space.

To summarize, we have learned thus far, blending RGB colors for light sources works very well by simply adding the RGB colors, but blending RGB colors for transparent planes (as if we are mixing paint) is more problematic. Depending on the colors being used, some applications may suffice by using one of the two methods just described (that is, either converting the colors to CMY values, adding them, and then converting them back to RGB values or simply blending the two colors in RGB with a weighted sum). Figure 16.28 shows both methods in three scenarios: red/yellow/blue, red/green/blue, and magenta/yellow/cyan panes.

In each of the methods shown in Figure 16.28, there is at least one color combination that would appear incorrect for mixing paint (or stacking glass panes). Therefore, if an application requires correct subtractive blending across the color spectrum, none of the above methods will be adequate. Another method is needed.

A third approach for handling colored planes is to convert the colors from an RGB color model to an *RYB subtractive model* based on the primary colors red/yellow/blue. Precise algorithms for doing this tend to be complex. Sugita and Takahashi [ST15] described a surprisingly simple algorithm for converting between RGB and RYB that is not perfect, but works fairly well across the color spectrum. Program 16.16 shows GLSL implementations of their conversion functions, which may be practical for many cases.

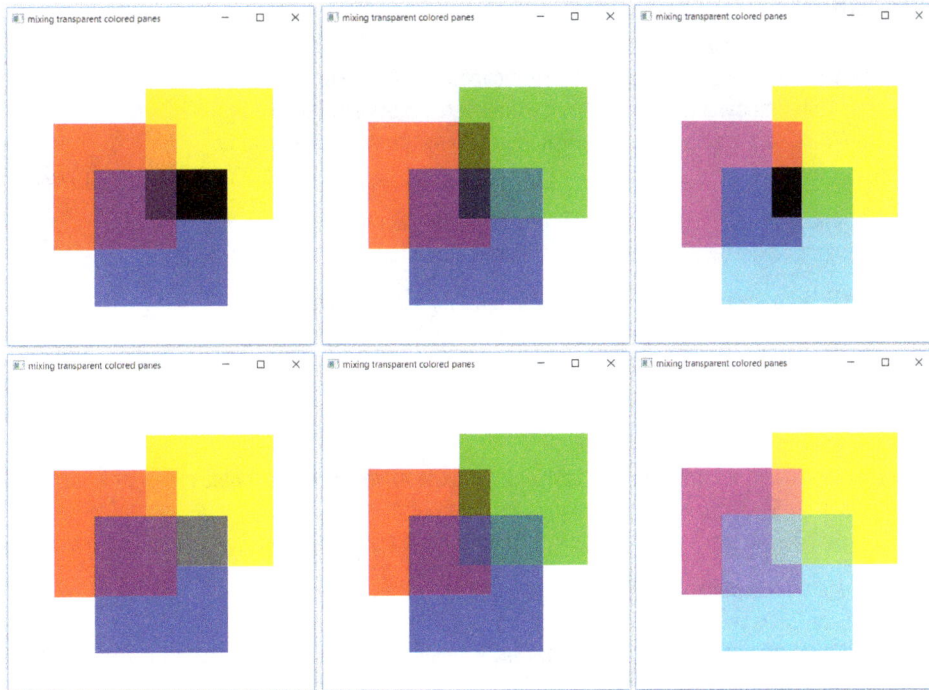

Figure 16.28
Adding in CMY color space (top row), and blending in RGB color space (bottom row).

Program 16.16 – Blending via Conversion to RYB

Compute Shader

```
. . .
void process_stack_element(int index)
{  . . .
        // during phase 4 blending:
            if ((objects[c.object_index].isTransparent)
            {   vec3 mixedRYB = rgb2ryb(mixed_color);
                vec3 refractedRYB = rgb2ryb(refracted_color);
                mixed_color = ryb2rgb(mixedRYB + refractedRYB);
            }
    . . .
}

vec3 rgb2ryb(vec3 rgb)
{   float white = min(rgb.r, min(rgb.g, rgb.b)); // compute white and black contributions for input color
    float black = min((1-rgb.r), min((1-rgb.g), (1-rgb.b))); // assumes colors are clamped to the range [0..1]
    vec3 rgbWhiteRemoved = rgb - white; // remove white from input color before converting to RYB

    // build initial RYB values for the output color
    vec3 buildRYB = vec3(
        rgbWhiteRemoved.r - min(rgbWhiteRemoved.r, rgbWhiteRemoved.g),
        (rgbWhiteRemoved.g + min(rgbWhiteRemoved.r, rgbWhiteRemoved.g)) / 2.0,
        (rgbWhiteRemoved.b + rgbWhiteRemoved.g - min(rgbWhiteRemoved.r,
                                                        rgbWhiteRemoved.g)) / 2.0);

    float normalizeFactor = max(buildRYB.x, max(buildRYB.y, buildRYB.z))
        / max(rgbWhiteRemoved.r, max(rgbWhiteRemoved.g, rgbWhiteRemoved.b));

    buildRYB /= normalizeFactor;        // normalize for similar white level
    buildRYB += black;                  // normalize for similar black level
    return buildRYB;
}

vec3 ryb2rgb(vec3 ryb)
{   float white = min(ryb.x, min(ryb.y, ryb.z));    // compute white and black contributions for input color
    float black = min((1-ryb.x),min((1-ryb.y),(1-ryb.z)));
    vec3 rybWhiteRemoved = ryb - white;    // remove white from input color before converting to RGB

    // build initial RGB values for the output color
    vec3 buildRGB = vec3(
        rybWhiteRemoved.x + rybWhiteRemoved.y - min(rybWhiteRemoved.y, rybWhiteRemoved.z),
        rybWhiteRemoved.y + 2.0 * min(rybWhiteRemoved.y, rybWhiteRemoved.z),
```

```
        2.0 * rybWhiteRemoved.z - min(rybWhiteRemoved.y, rybWhiteRemoved.z));

    float normalizeFactor = max(buildRGB.r, max(buildRGB.g, buildRGB.b))
        / max(rybWhiteRemoved.x, max(rybWhiteRemoved.y, rybWhiteRemoved.z));

    buildRGB /= normalizeFactor;      // normalize for similar white level
    buildRGB += black;                // normalize for similar black level
    return buildRGB;
}
. . .
```

The functions that convert between RGB and RYB are named rgb2ryb() and ryb2rgb(). They both start by computing the amount of "white" and "black" in the input color, as minimum distance from [0,0,0] and [1,1,1] for any of the three color channels (R, G, B, or R, Y, B). They then remove the white portion in all three channels. They then build equivalent values for each of the three channels of the other color model. The approach is based on a proposed subtractive RYB color model where "white" = [0,0,0], "black" = [1,1,1], "red" = [1,0,0], "yellow" = [0,1,0], "blue" = [0,0,1], "green" = [0,1,1], "purple" = [1,0, .5], and "aqua" = [0, .5, 1]. The code for constructing the vectors buildRGB and buildRYB utilizing these proposed colors is based on the equations derived by Sugita and Takahashi and is not included here. Finally, the result is normalized to generate similar white and black levels as the original input color.

The color palette proposed by Sugita and Takahashi is designed to be subtractive, and like the CMY model, its white and black definitions are reversed from the RGB model. Blending colors is again done by simply adding them together, as shown in the changes to the process_stack_element() function in Program 16.16.

The results are shown in Figure 16.29 for the same three scenarios shown in Figure 16.28 (that is, the red/yellow/blue, red/green/blue, and magenta/yellow/cyan panes). In each case, the colors of the panes were defined using the RGB model as described in Program 16.13, converted to RYB using the rgb2ryb() function from Program 16.16, added together (also as shown in Program 16.16), and converted back to RGB values using the ryb2rgb() function before displaying the result. We think that, with slight adjustments, the results in every case are quite close to what one would expect to see when stacking colored transparent planes (or mixing paint) in the real world.

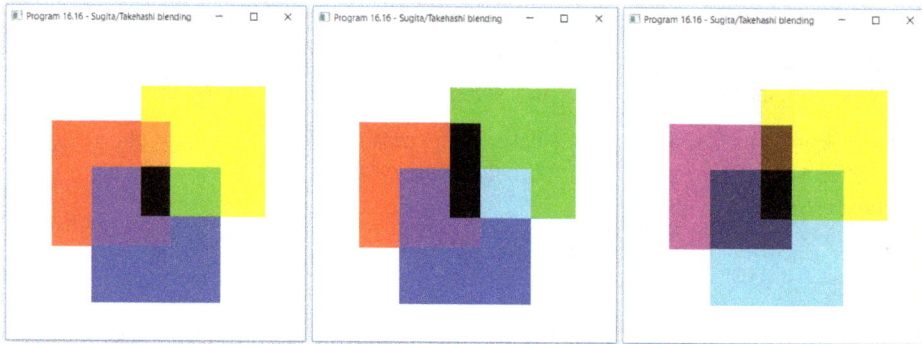

Figure 16.29
The output of Program 16.16, showing blending using the Sugita/Takehashi RYB color conversion.

SUPPLEMENTAL NOTES

Even the simple examples given in this chapter require significant computing cycles, and the later ones (Programs 16.13, 16.14, and 16.15) run very slowly. On a standard laptop, you can expect them to take several seconds or more to render, especially for large depth of recursion settings. On some machines, the default settings for the graphics card may cause OpenGL to "time out," crashing the program before it has a chance to complete. On a Windows machine, the time limit is typically set to 2 seconds, but this can be increased by increasing the TdrDelay registry setting. Instructions for doing this are available on the Web [NO23]. (We set our timeout to 30 seconds.) An appropriate value depends on the machine and the application. Be warned that making this change can also make it a bit more difficult to stop a runaway graphics process.

We have tried to write our compute shader code for readability rather than performance; e.g., our heavy use of conditionals ("if" statements) can slow execution. Tricks for removing conditionals can be found in [H13].

There are a few capabilities we have not implemented in our ray tracer. One is the ability to rotate the sphere. Of course, if the sphere is a solid color or transparent, this is not important. However, if it is textured, such as in the examples utilizing the earth texture, it would be desirable to be able to rotate it to different orientations. Such rotation can be incorporated in the same manner as was done for the box and the plane.

Another deficiency is that we have only implemented hard shadows. Soft shadows for ray tracing are widely used. We just did not address them here. Many resources are available for those interested ([K16], for example).

The most significant technique that we did not cover in this chapter is how to perform ray tracing on 3D models constructed as a triangle mesh, such as models stored in OBJ files. That is discussed in Chapter 17.

Ray tracing is a very rich topic, and there is a wealth of techniques for enhancing realism that we did not describe in this brief introduction. You are encouraged to explore the myriad of textbooks and online resources on ray tracing ([S16] is a particularly nice online overview).

As we saw in Section 16.2, OpenGL has support for blending, including a wide variety of ways to blend colors. However, in this chapter, we did not utilize the rendering pipeline, so we had to blend the colors ourselves.

Much of the code in this chapter was developed by Luis Gutierrez of Lawrence Livermore National Labs as part of a project at California State University, Sacramento. His contributions greatly facilitated our explanations. We appreciate the excellent work that he did distilling these topics into manageable-sized code, especially his code organization for managing the recursion in the non-recursive language of GLSL.

Exercises

16.1 In Program 16.4, shadows can be very easily disabled by commenting out one particular line of code. Identify that line of code.

16.2 Make the following simple changes to Program 16.5:
  (i) Move the box so that it is behind the sphere, but still visible.
  (ii) Change the background color from black to light blue.
  (iii) Modify the properties and position of the light source.

16.3 Make the following changes to Program 16.10:
  (i) Move the box so that it is in front of the sphere.
  (ii) Make the box transparent/refractive and the sphere reflective.
  (iii) Move the checkerboard plane so that it is placed vertically behind the box and sphere. Try to place the objects so that both the sphere and the checkerboard plane are visible through the transparent box.

16.4 In Program 16.12, replace the blue room box with the lake scene skybox. Do not forget to disable lighting on the skybox.

16.5 Modify Program 16.13 to build a scene with a transparent sphere and a transparent box, both of different colors. Include the vertical checkerboard plane behind them as a backdrop. Experiment with the color blending approaches described in Section 16.3.6. Which approach worked best in your scene?

16.6 In Figure 16.29 (the center image), Sugita/Takehashi blending of red and green produces black. Is this a reasonable result? If not, can you devise a workaround that does not compromise other color blends?

References

[A68]   A. Appel (1968), *Some Techniques for Shading Machine Renderings of Solids*, AFIPS Conference Proceedings 32, pp. 37-45.

[F96]   J. D. Foley, (ed.). (1996), *Computer Graphics: Principles and Practice*, Second Edition in C. © 1996 Addison-Wesley Professional.

[FW79]   J. D. Foley and T. Whitted (1979), *An Improved Illumination Model for Shaded Display*, Proceedings of the 6th Annual Conference on Computer Graphics and Interactive Techniques.

[H13]   D. Holden (2013), *Avoiding Shader Conditionals*, Accessed November 2023, http://theorangeduck.com/page/avoiding-shader-conditionals

[H89]   E. Haines et al. (1989), *An Introduction to Ray Tracing*, edited by A. Glassner, © 1989 Academic Press.

[K16]   M. Kissner (2016), *Ray Traced Soft Shadows in Real Time in Spellwrath*, Imagination Technologies Blog, Accessed November 2023, https://blog.imaginationtech.com/ray-traced-soft-shadows-in-real-time-spellwrath/

[KK86]   T. Kay and J. Kajiya (1986), *Ray Tracing Complex Scenes*, SIGGRAPH '86 Proceedings of the 13th Annual Conference on Computer Graphics and Interactive Techniques, pp 269-278.

[KR23]   OpenCL Overview (2023), Khronos Group. Accessed November 2023, https://www.khronos.org/opencl/

[KRF23]   OpenGL Reference on the refract() function. Accessed November 2023, https://registry.khronos.org/OpenGL-Refpages/gl4/html/refract.xhtml

[LE16]   J. Lenton [2016], *Photography Using a Glass Ball – Upside Down Worlds*, in Original Art Photography, Accessed November 2023, https://www.originalartphotography.co.uk/2016/11/photography-using-glass-ball-upside-worlds/

[NO23]   *Extending GPU Timeout Detection*, Notch FAQ, accessed November 2023, https://manual.notch.one/0.9.23/en/docs/faq/extending-gpu-timeout-detection/

[NV23]   About CUDA (2023), NVIDIA Developer. Accessed November 2023, https://developer.nvidia.com/about-cuda

[RTX23]   RTX Ray Tracing (2023), NVIDIA Corp. Accessed November 2023, https://developer.nvidia.com/rtx/ray-tracing

[S11]   H. Shen (2011), *Ray-Tracing Basics*, Accessed November 2023, http://web.cse.ohio-state.edu/~shen.94/681/Site/Slides_files/basic_algo.pdf

[S16]   Scratchapixel (2016, Jean-Colas Prunier), *A Minimal Ray-Tracer*, Accessed November 2023, https://www.scratchapixel.com/lessons/3d-basic-rendering/minimal-ray-tracer-rendering-simple-shapes/parametric-and-implicit-surfaces.html

[ST15]   J. Sugita and T. Takahashi (2015), *Paint-Like Compositing Based on RYB Color Model*, The 42nd International Conference and Exhibition on Computer Graphics and Interactive Techniques (ACM SIGGRAPH), Los Angeles, 2015. Also available (Accessed November 2023) at: http://nishitalab.org/user/UEI/publication/Sugita_IWAIT2015.pdf

[SW15]   G. Sellers, R. Wright Jr., and N. Haemel (2015), *OpenGL SuperBible*: Comprehensive Tutorial and Reference, 7th ed. (Addison-Wesley, 2015).

[Y10]   E. Young (2010), *Direct Compute Optimizations and Best Practices*, GPU Technology Conference, San Jose, CA, Accessed November 2023, https://www.nvidia.com/content/GTC-2010/pdfs/2260_GTC2010.pdf

RAY TRACING OF COMPLEX MODELS

In Chapter 16, we implemented ray tracing and applied it to a few simple shapes. We now extend the ray tracing implementation and apply it to more complex models. Our goal is to render models stored as triangles in OBJ files, such as our Studio 522 dolphin and others, using ray tracing.

Recall that our OBJ model loader, while simple, can input models made of triangles. This means that we will start by formulating a method for detecting *ray-triangle* intersections, and then apply that to all the triangles in a model. Although that is simple in concept, it is common for models to be made of thousands of triangles, leading to serious performance challenges. Fortunately, the number of triangles that need to be tested for intersection with a given ray can be reduced by using a technique called *bounding volume hierarchy* (BVH). In this chapter, we examine and implement the following:

1. Ray-triangle intersection for a single triangle
2. Ray-triangle intersection for all triangles in an OBJ file
3. Rendering a scene with multiple OBJ models
4. BVH for improved performance

17.1 RAY-TRIANGLE INTERSECTION

There are numerous algorithms for finding the intersection of a ray and a triangle. For example, we could adapt the ray-plane algorithm from Chapter 16 to determine whether the ray intersects the plane defined by the triangle, and if so, then perform additional steps to find if that intersection took place within the triangle.

We instead use a more efficient technique called the Möller-Trumbore algorithm, developed by Tomas Möller and Ben Trumbore [MT97]. Their method makes use of *barycentric coordinates*, which are designated by two values u and v, such that $u \geq 0$, $v \geq 0$, and $u+v \leq 1$. Barycentric coordinates can be thought of as a way to uniquely identify points inside of the triangle using two reference values u and v. As we will see, they provide a convenient way of identifying the point where a ray intersects a triangle and for interpolating the corresponding texture coordinates and normal vectors. An excellent and detailed description of barycentric coordinates is available at Scratchapixel [S23]. We summarize the relevant formulas here.

17.1.1 Mathematics for Ray-Triangle Intersection

We will now discuss the formulas derived by Möller and Trumbore [MT97]. As we did in Chapter 16, we start by denoting a ray's origin as $\vec{r_s}$ and its direction as $\vec{r_d}$. If we traverse the ray for a given distance t, we arrive at point:

$$P(t) = \vec{r_s} + t * \vec{r_d} \qquad [1]$$

The three vertices of the triangle are denoted $\vec{V_0}$, $\vec{V_1}$, and $\vec{V_2}$. (Vertex notation is used to make the dimensionality in the resulting formulas clearer.) Points P within the triangle can be determined by the following function:

$$P(u,v) = (1 - u - v)\vec{V_0} + u\vec{V_1} + v\vec{V_2} \qquad [2]$$

where *u* and *v* are the barycentric coordinates for a point *P* inside the triangle. If the ray intersects the triangle, it will do so at the point where the two points *P(t)* and *P(u,v)* are equal, namely, where:

$$(1 - u - v)\vec{V_0} + u\vec{V_1} + v\vec{V_2} = \vec{r_s} + t * \vec{r_d} \qquad [3]$$

Möller and Trumbore solve for t, u, and v (we omit the derivation here), producing:

$$\begin{bmatrix} t \\ u \\ v \end{bmatrix} = \frac{1}{\left| -\vec{r_d}, \vec{E_1}, \vec{E_2} \right|} \begin{bmatrix} \left| \vec{T}, \vec{E_1}, \vec{E_2} \right| \\ \left| -\vec{r_d}, \vec{T}, \vec{E_2} \right| \\ \left| -\vec{r_d}, \vec{E_1}, \vec{T} \right| \end{bmatrix}$$ [4]

where $\vec{E_1} = \vec{V_1} - \vec{V_0}$, $\vec{E_2} = \vec{V_2} - \vec{V_0}$, $\vec{T} = \vec{r_s} - \vec{V_0}$, and the notation $\left| \vec{x}, \vec{y}, \vec{z} \right| = -(\vec{x} \times \vec{z}) \cdot \vec{y}$. The latter is called the *determinant*, and in every case, the elements x, y, and z are 3-element columns, resulting in a square 3x3 matrix.

Once we have determined t, u, and v, it then follows that the ray intersects the triangle if $t > 0$, $u \geq 0$, $v \geq 0$, and $u+v \leq 1$. If those conditions are met, then the intersection point is $\vec{r_s} + t * \vec{r_d}$.

17.1.2 Implementing Ray-Triangle Intersection

We start with the object-generalized compute shader from Program 16.13 and add functionality for defining a triangle. The C++ program does not require modification. Since our ultimate goal is to render models comprised of many triangles, we need a framework that allows us to define a triangle in the same manner as it is specified in an OBJ file (specifically, its vertices, texture coordinates, and normal vectors). Recall that the vertices and normal vectors are defined as vec3, whereas the texture coordinates are defined as vec2.

Program 17.1 starts by defining a framework that includes structs called TriV3, TriT2, and TriN3, for defining the vertices, texture coordinates, and normal vectors of a triangle, respectively. They are so named because the vertices and normal vectors require vec3s, whereas the texture coordinates require vec2s. The struct used to define each object (named Object) is extended to accommodate a triangle object. Since our compute shader is growing in complexity, we also add some predefined constants for readability. We also add predefined constants for filling the triangle fields with zeros for objects that are not triangles (such as spheres or boxes). For this first example, we include two objects: a room box and a single white triangle. The specification of the vertices, texture coordinates, and normal vectors of the triangle is done by hand in this example, and is highlighted in yellow.

Program 17.1 – Ray Tracing a Triangle

Compute Shader

```
. . .
struct TriV3  // for holding the vertices in a triangle
{   vec3 p0;
    vec3 p1;
    vec3 p2;
};

struct TriT2  // for holding the texture coordinates in a triangle
{   vec2 p0;
    vec2 p1;
    vec2 p2;
};
struct TriN3  // for holding the normal vectors in a triangle
{   vec3 p0;
    vec3 p1;
    vec3 p2;
};
// predefined constants for specifying object type
const TriV3 TRIVERTS_ZERO = { vec3(0), vec3(0), vec3(0) };
const TriT2 TRITEXCS_ZERO = { vec2(0), vec2(0), vec2(0) };
const TriV3 TRINORMS_ZERO = { vec3(0), vec3(0), vec3(0) };
const int TYPE_ROOM = 0;
const int TYPE_SPHERE = 1;
const int TYPE_BOX = 2;
const int TYPE_PLANE = 3;
const int TYPE_TRIANGLE = 4;

struct Object
{   int type;  // 0=room, 1=sphere, 2=box, 3=plane, 4=triangle

    . . .
    TriV3  triVerts;  // if type=triangle, these are the vertices
    TriT2  triTCs;    // if type=triangle, these are the texture coordinates
    TriN3  triNorms;  // if type=triangle, these are the normal vectors
};

Object[ ] objects =
{   // object #0 is the room box
    { TYPE_ROOM, 0.0, vec3(-20, -20, -20), vec3(20, 20, 20), 0, 0, 0, vec3(0),
        true, false, true, false, vec3(0.25, 0.5, 0.8), 0, 0, 0,
        vec4(0.2, 0.2, 0.2, 1.0), vec4(0.9, 0.9, 0.9, 1.0), vec4(1, 1, 1, 1), 50.0,
        TRIVERTS_ZERO, TRITEXCS_ZERO, TRINORMS_ZERO
    },
```

```
// object #1 is the white triangle
{ TYPE_TRIANGLE, 0.0, vec3(0), vec3(0), 0.0, 0.0, 0.0, vec3(0),
    true, false, false, false, vec3(1.0, 1.0, 1.0), 0, 0, 0,
    vec4(0.5, 0.5, 0.5, 1.0), vec4(0.5, 0.5, 0.5, 1), vec4(0.5, 0.5, 0.5, 1), 50.0,
    TriV3(vec3(0.0, 0.5, 0.0), vec3(-1.0, -0.5, 0.0), vec3( 0.0, -0.5, 1.0)),
    TriT2(vec2(0.0, 1.0), vec2(0.0, 0.0), vec2(1.0, 0.0)),
    TriN3(vec3(-0.577, 0.577, 0.577), vec3(-0.577, 0.577, 0.577), vec3(-0.577, 0.577, 0.577))
} };
int numObjects = 2;
float camera_pos = 5.0;
const int max_depth = 4;
const int stack_size = 100;
vec3 pointLight_position = vec3(-18.0, 6.0, 3.5);
. . .
```

Functions are added for computing ray-triangle collision using the equations described earlier in Section 17.1.1 in a similar manner as was done for spheres and boxes. When a collision is detected, the collision point is determined using Equation [1], and the interpolated texture coordinates and normal vectors are determined using Equation [2]. A utility function for computing the determinant is also included. The get_closest_collision() function is also extended to utilize the new functions if the object is a triangle, as well as making use of some of the new predefined constants for readability.

The computation of whether the collision occurred "inside" or "outside" the triangle is not relevant for an individual triangle, because like a plane, it is flat and has no volume. Typically, a ray enters and exits at exactly the same point. However, later we will render 3D objects made of many triangles, and in those cases, we will need to know whether the collision occurred "inside" (as it did for spheres and boxes), so we include that computation now. When a ray originates outside of a solid object built of triangles, the first collision point should have a normal that faces in the opposite general direction of the ray, whereas if the ray originates inside a solid object, the first collision point's normal would face in the same general direction of the ray. A simple way of computing this is if their dot product is greater than 0, which means that the angle between them is less than 90°.

The remainder of Program 17.1 is unchanged from Program 16.13, and the output is shown in Figure 17.1.

Program 17.1 (continued)

Compute Shader (continued)

```
. . .
//-------------------------------------------------------------------
// calculates the determinant of the 3x3 matrix with the given columns
//-------------------------------------------------------------------
float det_3x3(vec3 col1, vec3 col2, vec3 col3)
{   return dot(-cross(col1, col3), col2);
}

//-------------------------------------------------------------------
// determines if Ray r intersects the triangle with the given vertices.
//-------------------------------------------------------------------
Collision intersect_triangle(Ray r, TriV3 verts, TriT2 tcs, TriN3 norms)
{   Collision c;
    c.t = -1.0; // t < 0 indicates no collision

    vec3 E1 = verts.p1 - verts.p0;
    vec3 E2 = verts.p2 - verts.p0;
    vec3 T = r.start - verts.p0;

    float det = det_3x3(-r.dir, E1, E2);

    // if the determinant is (effectively) 0, this is a degenerate case in which the ray is parallel to the triangle
    if (det < 1e-9) { return c; }

    float coeff = 1.0 / det;

    // find barycentric u coordinate, and test if u falls inside the triangle
    float u = coeff * det_3x3(-r.dir, T, E2);
    if (u < 0.0 || u > 1.0) { return c; }

    // find barycentric v coordinate, and test if (u,v) falls inside the triangle
    float v = coeff * det_3x3(-r.dir, E1, T);
    if (v < 0.0 || u + v > 1.0) { return c; }

    // calculate distance from ray to intersection
    c.t = coeff * det_3x3(T, E1, E2);
    if (c.t < 0.01)
    {   c.t = -1.0;
        return c;
    }

    // find world point of collision
    c.p = r.start + r.dir * c.t;
```

```
// interpolate normals and texture coordinates
c.n = normalize((1.0 - u - v) * norms.p0 + u * norms.p1 + v * norms.p2);
c.tc = (1.0 - u - v) * tcs.p0 + u * tcs.p1 + v * tcs.p2;

// "inside" if ray and normal point in the same general direction
c.inside = dot(c.n, r.dir) > 0.0;

return c;
}

//------------------------------------------------------------------
// checks if Ray r intersects the Triangle defined by Object o
//------------------------------------------------------------------
Collision intersect_triangle_object(Ray r, Object o)
{   return intersect_triangle(r, o.triVerts, o.triTCs, o.triNorms);
}

//------------------------------------------------------------------
// Returns the closest collision of a ray
// object_index == -1 if no collision
// object_index == 0 if collision with room box
// object_index > 0 if collision with another object
//------------------------------------------------------------------
Collision get_closest_collision(Ray r)
{   ...
    for (int i=0; i<numObjects; i++)
    {   Collision c;

        if (objects[i].type == TYPE_ROOM)
        ...
        else if (objects[i].type == TYPE_SPHERE)
        ...
        else if (objects[i].type == TYPE_BOX)
        ...
        else if (objects[i].type == TYPE_PLANE)
        ...
        else if (objects[i].type == TYPE_TRIANGLE)
        {   c = intersect_triangle_object(r, objects[i]);
            if (c.t <= 0) continue;
        }
        else continue;
        ...
}
```

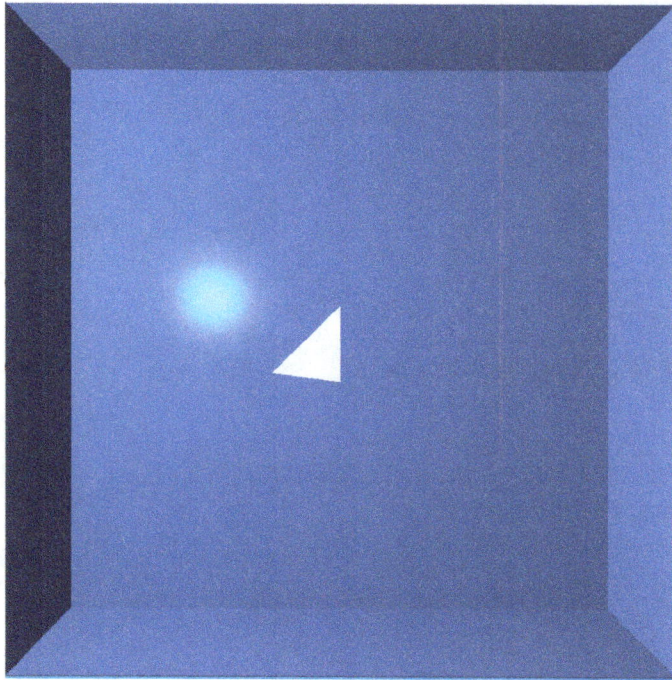

Figure 17.1
Ray tracing a single triangle in a room box.

17.1.3 Ray Tracing Multiple Triangles

Extending Program 17.1 to render multiple triangles is straightforward because the ray tracing framework previously developed for Program 16.13 (on which Program 17.1 is based) already handles an arbitrary number of objects. We simply define the triangles and their properties.

Program 17.2 renders a six-triangle pyramid similar to the one defined previously in Figure 6.15. Texturing and transparency are added, and the reflective sphere and checkerboard plane are also included. We also expand the intersect_triangle_object() function to apply any rotations and translations specified by the programmer, using the same functions (for building translation and rotation matrices) as was done previously for boxes.

The output of Program 17.2 is shown in Figure 17.2 using the ice texture first introduced in Chapter 5.

Program 17.2 – Object with Multiple Triangles

Compute Shader

```
. . .
Object[ ] objects =
{   // object #0 is the room box
    { TYPE_ROOM, 0.0, vec3(-20, -20, -20), vec3( 20, 20, 20), 0, 0, 0, vec3(0),
        true, false, true, false, vec3(0.25, 0.5, 0.8), 0, 0, 0,
        vec4(0.2, 0.2, 0.2, 1.0), vec4(0.9, 0.9, 0.9, 1.0), vec4(1,1,1,1), 50.0,
        TRIVERTS_ZERO, TRITEXCS_ZERO, TRINORMS_ZERO
    },
    // object #1 is the checkerboard ground plane
    { TYPE_PLANE, 0.0, vec3(12, 0, 16), vec3(0), 0.0, 0.0, 0.0, vec3(0.0, -1.0, -2.0),
        false, true, false, false, vec3(0), 0.0, 0.0, 0.0,
        vec4(0.2, 0.2, 0.2, 1.0), vec4(0.9, 0.9, 0.9, 1.0), vec4(1,1,1,1), 50.0,
        TRIVERTS_ZERO, TRITEXCS_ZERO, TRINORMS_ZERO
    },
    // object #2 is a transparent sphere with slight reflection and no texture
    { TYPE_SPHERE, 1.2, vec3(0), vec3(0), 0, 0, 0, vec3(0.7, 0.2, 0.0),
        false, false, true, true, vec3(0,0,0), 0.8, 0.8, 1.02,
        vec4(0.5, 0.5, 0.5, 1.0), vec4(1,1,1,1), vec4(1,1,1,1), 50.0,
        TRIVERTS_ZERO, TRITEXCS_ZERO, TRINORMS_ZERO

    },

    //   the next six objects are triangles that make up a pyramid

    { TYPE_TRIANGLE, 0.0, vec3(0), vec3(0), 0.0, 50.0, 0.0, vec3(-0.8, -0.25, 2.0),
        false, true, false, true, vec3(0,0,0), 0.8, 0.18, 1.02,
        vec4(0.5, 0.5, 0.5, 1.0), vec4(1,1,1,1), vec4(1,1,1,1), 50.0,
        TriV3(vec3(0.75, -0.75, 0.75), vec3(-0.75, -0.75, 0.75), vec3(-0.75, -0.75, -0.75)),
        TriT2(vec2(1.0, 1.0), vec2(0.0, 1.0), vec2(0.0, 0.0)),
        TriN3(vec3(0.0, -1.0, 0.0), vec3(0.0, -1.0, 0.0), vec3(0.0, -1.0, 0.0))
    },
    { TYPE_TRIANGLE, 0.0, vec3(0), vec3(0), 0.0, 50.0, 0.0, vec3(-0.8, -0.25, 2.0),
        false, true, false, true, vec3(0,0,0), 0.8, 0.18, 1.02,
        vec4(0.5, 0.5, 0.5, 1.0), vec4(1,1,1,1), vec4(1,1,1,1), 50.0,
        TriV3(vec3(0.75, -0.75, -0.75), vec3(0.0, 0.75, 0.0), vec3(0.75, -0.75, 0.75)),
        TriT2(vec2(1.0, 0.0), vec2(0.5, 1.0), vec2(0.0, 0.0)),
        TriN3(vec3(0.894, 0.447, 0.0), vec3(0.894, 0.447, 0.0), vec3(0.894, 0.447, 0.0))
    },
    { TYPE_TRIANGLE, 0.0, vec3(0), vec3(0), 0.0, 50.0, 0.0, vec3(-0.8, -0.25, 2.0),
        false, true, false, true, vec3(0,0,0), 0.8, 0.18, 1.02,
        vec4(0.5, 0.5, 0.5, 1.0), vec4(1,1,1,1), vec4(1,1,1,1), 50.0,
```

```
        TriV3(vec3(0.75, -0.75, 0.75), vec3(0.0, 0.75, 0.0), vec3(-0.75, -0.75, 0.75)),
        TriT2(vec2(1.0, 0.0), vec2(0.5, 1.0), vec2(0.0, 0.0)),
        TriN3(vec3(0.0, 0.447, 0.894), vec3(0.0, 0.447, 0.894), vec3(0.0, 0.447, 0.894))
    },
    { TYPE_TRIANGLE, 0.0, vec3(0), vec3(0), 0.0, 50.0, 0.0, vec3(-0.8, -0.25, 2.0),
        false, true, false, true, vec3(0,0,0), 0.8, 0.18, 1.02,
        vec4(0.5, 0.5, 0.5, 1.0), vec4(1,1,1,1), vec4(1,1,1,1), 50.0,
        TriV3(vec3(-0.75, -0.75, 0.75), vec3(0.0, 0.75, 0.0), vec3(-0.75, -0.75, -0.75)),
        TriT2(vec2(1.0, 0.0), vec2(0.5, 1.0), vec2(0.0, 0.0)),
        TriN3(vec3(-0.894, 0.447, 0.0), vec3(-0.894, 0.447, 0.0), vec3(-0.894, 0.447, 0.0))
    },
    { TYPE_TRIANGLE, 0.0, vec3(0), vec3(0), 0.0, 50.0, 0.0, vec3(-0.8, -0.25, 2.0),
        false, true, false, true, vec3(0,0,0), 0.8, 0.18, 1.02,
        vec4(0.5, 0.5, 0.5, 1.0), vec4(1,1,1,1), vec4(1,1,1,1), 50.0,
        TriV3(vec3(0.0, 0.75, 0.0), vec3(0.75, -0.75, -0.75), vec3(-0.75, -0.75, -0.75)),
        TriT2(vec2(0.0, 0.5), vec2(0.0, 0.0), vec2(1.0, 0.0)),
        TriN3(vec3(0.0, 0.447, -0.894), vec3(0.0, 0.447, -0.894), vec3(0.0, 0.447, -0.894))
    },
    { TYPE_TRIANGLE, 0.0, vec3(0), vec3(0), 0.0, 50.0, 0.0, vec3(-0.8, -0.25, 2.0),
        false, true, false, true, vec3(0,0,0), 0.8, 0.18, 1.02,
        vec4(0.5, 0.5, 0.5, 1.0), vec4(1,1,1,1), vec4(1,1,1,1), 50.0,
        TriV3(vec3(0.75, -0.75, -0.75), vec3(0.75, -0.75, 0.75), vec3(-0.75, -0.75, -0.75)),
        TriT2(vec2(1.0, 0.0), vec2(1.0, 1.0), vec2(0.0, 0.0)),
        TriN3(vec3(0.0, -1.0, 0.0), vec3(0.0, -1.0, 0.0), vec3(0.0, -1.0, 0.0))
    }
};

int numObjects = 9;
float camera_pos = 5.0;
const int max_depth = 4;
const int stack_size = 100;
vec3 pointLight_position = vec3(-18.0, 6.0, 3.5);

. . .

Collision intersect_triangle_object(Ray r, Object o)
{   // rotate and translate vertex locations
    mat4 local_to_worldT = buildTranslate((o.position).x, (o.position).y, (o.position).z);
    mat4 local_to_worldR = buildRotateY(DEG_TO_RAD*o.yrot) *
            buildRotateX(DEG_TO_RAD*o.xrot) * buildRotateZ(DEG_TO_RAD*o.zrot);
    mat4 local_to_worldTR = local_to_worldT * local_to_worldR;
    mat4 norm_local_to_worldTR = transpose(inverse(local_to_worldTR));

    vec3 worldVerts0 = (local_to_worldTR * vec4(o.triVerts.p0, 1.0)).xyz;
    vec3 worldVerts1 = (local_to_worldTR * vec4(o.triVerts.p1, 1.0)).xyz;
    vec3 worldVerts2 = (local_to_worldTR * vec4(o.triVerts.p2, 1.0)).xyz;
```

```
TriV3 worldVerts = { worldVerts0, worldVerts1, worldVerts2 };

// apply translations and rotations to normal vectors
vec3 worldNorms0 = (norm_local_to_worldR * vec4(o.triNorms.p0, 1.0)).xyz;
vec3 worldNorms1 = (norm_local_to_worldR * vec4(o.triNorms.p1, 1.0)).xyz;
vec3 worldNorms2 = (norm_local_to_worldR * vec4(o.triNorms.p2, 1.0)).xyz;

TriN3 worldNorms = { worldNorms0, worldNorms1, worldNorms2 };

return intersect_triangle(r, worldVerts, o.triTCs, worldNorms);
}
```

Figure 17.2:
Ray tracing multiple triangles that form a pyramid.

Of course, specifying a large number of triangles by hand is tedious. It also illustrates a shortcoming of our framework, specifically the need to repeatedly specify parameter values that are the same for *all* of the triangles in the pyramid, such as the values for position, transparency, and rotations. We need to solve these in the next section when we read in much larger numbers of triangles specified in OBJ files.

17.2 RAY TRACING AN OBJ MODEL

In Section 6.3, we implemented a class called ImportedModel for loading an OBJ file into arrays of triangle data. We now use that class and then send the loaded triangles to our compute shader for ray tracing. Our strategy on the C++ side is to load the data into three shader storage buffer objects (SSBOs): one for vertices, one for texture coordinates, and one for normal vectors. Then on the GLSL side, we create a new object type called *mesh* that references the three SSBOs.

17.2.1 OBJ Loading for Ray Tracing C++ side

On the C++ side, we begin in init() by generating three SSBOs and storing their IDs. (Recall that OpenGL buffers are referenced by integer IDs that are assigned by OpenGL at the time of creation, and those IDs are placed in an int array.) We create a new function loadModel() that uses the ImportedModel class to load an OBJ model from disk. It places the vertices, texture coordinates, and normal vectors into three vector<float> fields that are in a struct called mdata, which is of type ModelData. The loadModel() function does this by getting the vertices, texture coordinates, and normal vectors from the imported model, and then pushing the individual float values into the corresponding float vectors in mdata. (The utility of this organization will become apparent later when we import multiple OBJ models into a single scene.) This function also displays the number of triangles to the command window, which will be useful later when implementing the compute shader.

The loadModel() function is called from init(), which then places the loaded triangle data into the three SSBOs. It makes use of C++'s built-in function data(), which converts a vector to an array of primitive floats.

Finally, the display() function binds the three buffers with appropriate indices that the compute shader will use to reference them (with layout qualifiers). Since the values 0 and 1 have already been used (for the output image and the texture sampler variable, respectively), we use index values 2, 3, and 4 for the three new buffers.

The added C++ code just described is shown in Program 17.3.

Program 17.3 – Ray Tracing OBJ models (C++ side)

C++/OpenGL Application

```
. . .
GLuint ssbo[3];
```

```
. . .
struct ModelData {
    std::vector<float> pvalues;
    std::vector<float> tvalues;
    std::vector<float> nvalues;
}

ModelData mdata;

void loadModel(std::string filePath) {
    // use ImportedModel from Program 6.3 to load OBJ triangle data
    ImportedModel model(filePath.c_str());
    std::vector<glm::vec3> vert = model.getVertices();
    std::vector<glm::vec2> tex = model.getTextureCoords();
    std::vector<glm::vec3> norm = model.getNormals();
    int numObjVertices = model.getNumVertices();

    // convert the data from glm vec objects to C++ Floats
    for (int i=0; i<numObjVertices; i++) {
        mdata.pvalues.push_back(vert[i].x);
        mdata.pvalues.push_back(vert[i].y);
        mdata.pvalues.push_back(vert[i].z);
        mdata.tvalues.push_back(tex[i].x);
        mdata.tvalues.push_back(tex[i].y);
        mdata.nvalues.push_back(norm[i].x);
        mdata.nvalues.push_back(norm[i].y);
        mdata.nvalues.push_back(norm[i].z);
    }
    std::cout << "Number of triangles in " << filePath << " = " << numObjVertices / 3 << std::endl;
    return;
}

void init(GLFWwindow* window) {

    . . .
    glGenBuffers(3, ssbo);
    loadModel("icosahedron.obj");

    // convert vectors to arrays
    float* pv = mdata.pvalues.data();
    float* tv = mdata.tvalues.data();
    float* nv = mdata.nvalues.data();
    int pvSize = (int) mdata.pvalues.size()*4;
    int tvSize = (int) mdata.tvalues.size()*4;
    int nvSize = (int) mdata.nvalues.size()*4;

    // fill vertex SSBO
    glBindBuffer(GL_SHADER_STORAGE_BUFFER, ssbo[0]);
    glBufferData(GL_SHADER_STORAGE_BUFFER, pvSize, pv, GL_STATIC_DRAW);
```

```
// fill tex coord SSBO
glBindBuffer(GL_SHADER_STORAGE_BUFFER, ssbo[1]);
glBufferData(GL_SHADER_STORAGE_BUFFER, tvSize, tv, GL_STATIC_DRAW);

// fill normal SSBO
glBindBuffer(GL_SHADER_STORAGE_BUFFER, ssbo[2]);
glBufferData(GL_SHADER_STORAGE_BUFFER, nvSize, nv, GL_STATIC_DRAW);   . . .
}

void display(GLFWwindow* window, double currentTime) {

    . . .
    gl.glBindBufferBase(GL_SHADER_STORAGE_BUFFER, 2, ssbo[0]);
    gl.glBindBufferBase(GL_SHADER_STORAGE_BUFFER, 3, ssbo[1]);
    gl.glBindBufferBase(GL_SHADER_STORAGE_BUFFER, 4, ssbo[2]);
    glDispatchCompute(workGroupsX, workGroupsY, workGroupsZ);
    . . .
}
```

17.2.2 OBJ Loading for Ray Tracing GLSL side

On the GLSL side, we start by declaring the three buffers in the shader. Here, we use layout qualifiers to assign values 2, 3, and 4 for referencing the vertices, texture coordinates, and normal vectors, respectively, to correspond with the values assigned in the display() function as described earlier. We define these as float arrays. (Although it is tempting to declare these as vec3 arrays, the OpenGL Wiki recommends against it due to buffer alignment rules and inconsistent vendor implementations [OW22].)

Next, we define a new object type called a *mesh* that will be used to indicate a collection of triangles that form a single model. The addition of the mesh object type necessitates modifying get_closest_collision() to handle the new type. We also add two new fields to the Object struct: one called triCount to hold the number of triangles in the mesh, and another called firstTriIdx to indicate the index of the triangle that begins the mesh. firstTriIdx is always 0 if there is just a single mesh; later we will use it when rendering multiple meshes. If the number of triangles in a particular mesh is not known, one way of determining it is to run the program anyway; although it will not render correctly, it will report the number of triangles in the command window.

Program 17.3 – Ray Tracing OBJ Models (GLSL Side)

Compute Shader

```
#version 430
...
layout (binding=0, rgba8) uniform image2D output_texture;
layout (binding=1) uniform sampler2D sampMarble;
layout (binding=2, std430) buffer vertBuffer { float triVertsBuffer[ ]; };
layout (binding=3, std430) buffer texCoordBuffer { float triTCsBuffer[ ]; };
layout (binding=4, std430) buffer normBuffer { float triNormsBuffer[ ]; };

...
const int TYPE_MESH = 5;
...
struct Object
{  ...
    int firstTriIdx; // if type=mesh
    int triCount;  // if type=mesh
};
...
Collision get_closest_collision(Ray r)
{  ...
    for (int i=0; i<numObjects; i++)
    {  ...
        else if (objects[i].type == TYPE_MESH)
        {   c = intersect_mesh_object(r, objects[i]);
            if (c.t <= 0) continue;
        }
        else continue;
        ...
}
```

We continue building Program 17.3 by implementing the function inter-
sect_mesh_object(), which uses the intersect_triangle_object() developed earlier, and
checks for ray collisions with *all* of the triangles in a mesh object. Starting with
the triangle defined at Object.firstTriIdx, we test the ray for collision with each of the
triangles in the mesh, iterating over all Object.triCount triangles. The closest collision (the one with the shortest distance along the ray) is saved. The computations
for vertex rotations and translations are again done using the same functions as
was done previously for boxes and individual triangle objects.

Extracting and testing triangles from the buffer is handled in intersect_trian-
gle_from_buffer(). This function extracts a triangle from the buffer according to

the index supplied by intersect_mesh_object(), applies the rotation and translation specified for the mesh object, and calls intersect_triangle().

These additions to the compute shader, as well as the object definition for an example mesh (a semi-transparent icosahedron), are shown in Program 17.3. Recursion depth is set to 8.

Program 17.3 (continued)

Compute Shader (continued)

```
. . .
// mesh object for icosahedron OBJ file
{   TYPE_MESH, 0.0, vec3(0), vec3(0), 60.0, 0.0, 0.0, vec3(-2, 0.0, 0.75),
    false, true, false, true, vec3(0,0.7,0.5), 1.0, 0.3, 1.05,
    vec4(0.5, 0.5, 0.5, 1.0), vec4(1,1,1,1), vec4(1,1,1,1), 50.0,
    TRIVERTS_ZERO, TRITEXCS_ZERO, TRINORMS_ZERO, 0, 20,
}


. . .
//------------------------------------------------------------------------
// Checks if Ray r intersects the triangle in the SSBO at the specified index.
// This is done by extracting triangle data from the buffers and passing it to intersect_triangle()
//------------------------------------------------------------------------
Collision intersect_triangle_from_buffer(Ray r, int index, mat4 local_to_worldTR,
                                                  mat4 norm_local_to_worldTR)
{   TriV3 verts;
    TriT2 tcs;
    TriN3 norms;
    Collision c;

    // copy vertices from SSBO (3 vertices in this triangle, each with 3 fields (X,Y,Z) = 9 fields)
    verts.p0.x = triVertsBuffer[index*9+0];
    verts.p0.y = triVertsBuffer[index*9+1];
    verts.p0.z = triVertsBuffer[index*9+2];
    verts.p1.x = triVertsBuffer[index*9+3];
    verts.p1.y = triVertsBuffer[index*9+4];
    verts.p1.z = triVertsBuffer[index*9+5];
    verts.p2.x = triVertsBuffer[index*9+6];
    verts.p2.y = triVertsBuffer[index*9+7];
    verts.p2.z = triVertsBuffer[index*9+8];

    // apply transformations to vertices
    verts.p0 = (local_to_worldTR * vec4(verts.p0, 1.0)).xyz;
    verts.p1 = (local_to_worldTR * vec4(verts.p1, 1.0)).xyz;
    verts.p2 = (local_to_worldTR * vec4(verts.p2, 1.0)).xyz;
```

```
// copy tex coords from SSBO (3 tex coords in this triangle, each with 2 fields (S,T) = 6 fields)
tcs.p0.x = triTCsBuffer[index*6+0];
tcs.p0.y = triTCsBuffer[index*6+1];
tcs.p1.x = triTCsBuffer[index*6+2];
tcs.p1.y = triTCsBuffer[index*6+3];
tcs.p2.x = triTCsBuffer[index*6+4];
tcs.p2.y = triTCsBuffer[index*6+5];

// copy normals from SSBO (3 normals in this triangle, each with 3 fields (X,Y,Z) = 9 fields)
norms.p0.x = triNormsBuffer[index*9+0];
norms.p0.y = triNormsBuffer[index*9+1];
norms.p0.z = triNormsBuffer[index*9+2];
norms.p1.x = triNormsBuffer[index*9+3];
norms.p1.y = triNormsBuffer[index*9+4];
norms.p1.z = triNormsBuffer[index*9+5];
norms.p2.x = triNormsBuffer[index*9+6];
norms.p2.y = triNormsBuffer[index*9+7];
norms.p2.z = triNormsBuffer[index*9+8];

// apply transformations to normals
norms.p0 = (norm_local_to_worldTR * vec4(norms.p0, 1.0)).xyz;
norms.p1 = (norm_local_to_worldTR * vec4(norms.p1, 1.0)).xyz;
norms.p2 = (norm_local_to_worldTR * vec4(norms.p2, 1.0)).xyz;

// test for intersection
c = intersect_triangle(r, verts, tcs, norms);
return c;
}

//----------------------------------------------------------------------
// Checks if Ray r intersects the Mesh defined by Object o.
// This is accomplished by testing every triangle in the mesh and recording the nearest collision
//----------------------------------------------------------------------
Collision intersect_mesh_object(Ray r, Object o)
{   float closest = FLT_MAX;
    Collision c, closest_collision;
    closest_collision.t = -1;

    // build rotation and translation matrices for applying to triangles
    mat4 local_to_worldT = buildTranslate((o.position).x, (o.position).y, (o.position).z);
    mat4 local_to_worldR =
        buildRotateY(DEG_TO_RAD*o.yrot)
        * buildRotateX(DEG_TO_RAD*o.xrot)
        * buildRotateZ(DEG_TO_RAD*o.zrot);
    mat4 local_to_worldTR = local_to_worldT * local_to_worldR;
    mat4 norm_local_to_worldTR = transpose(inverse(local_to_worldTR));

    // iterate over all triangles in the mesh
    for (int i = 0; i < o.triCount; i++)
```

```
{   c = intersect_triangle_from_buffer(r, o.firstTriIdx + i, local_to_worldTR,
                                                      norm_local_to_worldTR);
        if (c.t > 0 && c.t < closest)
        {   closest = c.t;
            closest_collision = c;
    }   }
    return closest_collision;
}
```

The output for Program 17.3 is shown in Figure 17.3, which includes a room box, sphere, checkerboard ground plane, and the simple 20-triangle mesh object loaded in from an OBJ file called "icosahedron.obj." Again, the "ice" texture is applied to the OBJ model.

Figure 17.3
Ray tracing including a single simple semi-transparent OBJ icosahedron model.

17.3 RAY TRACING MULTIPLE OBJ MODELS

Extending Program 17.3 so that multiple different OBJ models can be loaded in and rendered is straightforward, because our code already accommodates multiple meshes. Program 17.4 illustrates this with a simple example.

On the C++ side, we create a new function loadModels() that takes an array of filenames, and calls our previous loadModel() function for each of the OBJ files. The loadModel() function, as already implemented in the previous section, appends all of the data into the existing mdata struct of type ModelData. Note that init() is modified slightly to utilize the new loadModels() function, sending it an array of OBJ filenames.

On the GLSL side, we simply define a mesh object for each OBJ model, in the same manner as we did in Section 17.2. In Program 17.4, we utilize two OBJ files: (1) the 6-triangle pyramid model shown in Figure 6.15, and (2) the 20-triangle icosahedron model used in Section 17.2. Note that in defining the mesh objects, the pyramid is listed first, and therefore has its firstTriIdx value set to 0, and it is triCount set to 6 (because it has 6 triangles). The reflective icosahedron is listed next, and its firstTriIdx value is set to 6, because its position in the buffer is immediately after the pyramid's six triangles.

Program 17.4 – Ray Tracing a Scene with Multiple OBJ models

C++/OpenGL Application

```
. . .
void loadModels(std::string filepaths[ ], int numFiles) {
    // load triangles data for each file
    for (int i=0; i<numFiles; i++) {
        // displays where in the mdata array the next model vertices will be placed
        std::cout << "firstTriIdx for " << filePaths[i] << " = " << (mdata.pvalues.size() / 9) << std::endl;
        loadModel(filePaths[i]);
    }
}

public void init(GLAutoDrawable drawable) {

    . . .
    std::string OBJfilenames[ ] = {
        "pyramid.obj",
        "icosahedron.obj"
    };
    loadModels(OBJfilenames, 2);
    . . .
}
```

Compute Shader

```
. . .
// pyramid
{   TYPE_MESH, 0.0, vec3(0), vec3(0), 0.0, 45.0, 0.0, vec3(1.0, 0.0, 1.5),
    true, false, false, false, vec3(0,0.7,0.5), 0.0, 0.0, 1.0,
```

```
        vec4(0.5, 0.5, 0.5, 1.0), vec4(.5,.5,.5,1), vec4(1,1,1,1), 50.0,
        TRIVERTS_ZERO, TRITEXCS_ZERO, TRINORMS_ZERO, 0, 6,
},
// icosahedron
{   TYPE_MESH, 0.0, vec3(0), vec3(0), 60.0, 0.0, 0.0, vec3(-2, 0.0, 0.75),
    false, true, false, true, vec3(0,0.7,0.5), 1.0, 0.3, 1.05,
    vec4(0.5, 0.5, 0.5, 1.0), vec4(1,1,1,1), vec4(1,1,1,1), 50.0,
    TRIVERTS_ZERO, TRITEXCS_ZERO, TRINORMS_ZERO, 6, 20,
}
. . .
```

The output of Program 17.4 is shown in Figures 17.4 and 17.5. Figure 17.4 shows the output of the C++ command window providing the OBJ model details that were inserted into the compute shader (shown above). Figure 17.5 shows the rendered output.

```
firstTriIdx for pyr.obj = 0
Number of triangles in pyr.obj = 6
firstTriIdx for icosahedron.obj = 6
Number of triangles in icosahedron.obj = 20
```

Figure 17.4
Command window output confirming OBJ model details.

Figure 17.5
Ray tracing two OBJ models

17.4 ■ BOUNDING VOLUME HIERARCHIES (BVH)

The technique presented in the previous sections is adequate for very small OBJ models, but becomes impractical for models containing more than a hundred or so triangles. Even the low-poly version of the Studio 522 dolphin (5664 triangles) by itself takes several minutes to render on our machine. Highly detailed models, like the Stanford dragon that we saw in Chapters 7 and 14, can have hundreds of thousands of triangles. We would like to be able to render such models using ray tracing, but the approach we have employed so far does not scale up to models of that size. This is because every ray is testing for intersection with every triangle, even for triangles that are nowhere near the ray. We need to reduce the number of triangles that each ray needs to consider.

There are many optimization techniques for ray tracing complex scenes. A common approach is to build an "acceleration structure" for each model that contains a large number of triangles. One of the most common is called a *bounding volume hierarchy*, or BVH.

A BVH is a recursively constructed tree of bounding volumes for groups of triangles that comprise the model. At the top level of the tree is a single bounding volume for the entire model. Smaller sets of triangles are grouped into smaller bounding volumes within the larger bounding volume, and within those are still smaller sets, recursively for the entire model. Thus, the set of triangles in a model is subdivided into smaller and smaller sets.

The fully constructed BVH then provides a very efficient way of identifying ray intersections. Rather than testing for ray intersections with every triangle in the model, we instead test for intersection of the ray with the topmost bounding volume. If there is no intersection, we know that the ray does not intersect with any of the triangles in the model and we are done. If, however, it does intersect with the topmost bounding volume, then we recursively test the smaller bounding volumes in that subtree, and the process repeats until the closest triangle is identified, or until it is determined that there is no intersection.

There are many ways to define bounding volumes. A simple approach is to use an axis-aligned bounding box (or "AABB"), which is essentially the same shape that we developed in Section 16.2.4. Other shapes have been developed that can fit more tightly around groups of triangles and are thus more efficient, such as the 8-sided parallelepipeds developed by Kay and Kajiya [KK86]. We will use AABBs.

Likewise, there are many algorithms for subdividing the set of triangles in a model to create the BVH. We will use one of the simplest approaches called *median cut*.

17.4.1 Implementing a BVH – C++ Side

We start by creating a struct called BoundingVolume that stores the six values – the min and max coordinates for the X, Y, and Z axes – necessary to specify an AABB. Included are four utility functions, one for initializing the six values in a BoundingVolume explicitly, one for copying an existing AABB, one for computing the AABB for a given triangle, and one for forming the union of two already existing AABBs.

Program 17.5 – Ray Tracing with BVH – BoundingVolume definition

C++/OpenGL Application

```
. . .
struct BoundingVolume {
    float minX, maxX, minY, maxY, minZ, maxZ;
};

void setBoundingVolume(BoundingVolume &bv, float mnX, float mxX, float mnY, float mxY, float
mnZ, float mxZ) {
    bv.minX = mnX; bv.maxX = mxX;
    bv.minY = mnY; bv.maxY = mxY;
    bv.minZ = mnZ; bv.maxZ = mxZ;
}

void setBoundingVolumeFromBV(BoundingVolume &bv, BoundingVolume bvSource) {
    bv.minX = bvSource.minX; bv.maxX = bvSource.maxX;
    bv.minY = bvSource.minY; bv.maxY = bvSource.maxY;
    bv.minZ = bvSource.minZ; bv.maxZ = bvSource.maxZ;
}

void setBoundingVolumeFromTriangle(BoundingVolume &bv, glm::vec3 p0, glm::vec3 p1,
glm::vec3 p2) {
    bv.minX = std::min(p0.x, p1.x, p2.x);
    bv.maxX = std::max(p0.x, p1.x, p2.x);
    bv.minY = std::min(p0.y, p1.y, p2.y);
    bv.maxY = std::max(p0.y, p1.y, p2.y);
    bv.minZ = std::min(p0.z, p1.z, p2.z);
```

```
    bv.maxZ = std::max(p0.z, p1.z, p2.z);
}

void setBoundingVolumeFromUnion(BoundingVolume &bv, BoundingVolume bv0, BoundingVolume
bv1) {
    bv.minX = std::min(bv0.minX, bv1.minX);
    bv.maxX = std::max(bv0.maxX, bv1.maxX);
    bv.minY = std::min(bv0.minY, bv1.minY);
    bv.maxY = std::max(bv0.maxY, bv1.maxY);
    bv.minZ = std::min(bv0.minZ, bv1.minZ);
    bv.maxZ = std::max(bv0.maxZ, bv1.maxZ);
}
```

Next, we construct a binary tree of BoundingVolume objects to form the BVH. Each node in the tree is an object of struct type BVHNode and contains a reference to its BoundingVolume object, a reference to a triangle (if it is a leaf node), and references to its left and right child nodes (if it is an interior tree node). A utility function is added to initialize a given BVHNode and its BoundingVolume.

Constructing the tree is then done in the function constructBVH(), which implements the median cut algorithm. "Median cut" works by dividing the set of triangles in half along the X axis, then those sets of triangles are each divided in half along the Y axis, and then again along the Z axis, then cycling back to the X axis, and so on, similar to cutting a block of cheese in half, then turning each half 90° and cutting them in half again(although for our application we are dividing in half by quantity, not spatially).

constructBVH() starts by collecting the centroids of each of the triangles in the object, which is done by calling the function getCentroidsWithIndices(). The centroids are stored in a vector of glm type vec4, with the x, y, and z components holding the location of the centroid, and the w component holding the index the triangle it references. It then builds the BVH by calling the recursive function constructBVHRecursively(). This function takes as input parameters for the vertices from which to construct the BVH, a count of the number of those vertices, a sorting axis (X, Y, or Z – coded as an integer 0, 1, or 2), and the min and max range of indices within the centroids array for the portion of the BVH being constructed by this iteration. It then constructs the BVH by performing the following steps:

1. Compute the number of triangles within the min-to-max range of indices for this iteration.

2. If that number is exactly 1, construct a leaf node and its bounding volume object.

3. If that number is 2 or more, construct a BVH interior node as follows:

   a. Sort the indices within the specified min-max range, by their position along the specified axis

   b. Recurse on the first half of those sorted triangles, specifying the next sorting axis.

   c. Recurse in the same manner on the second half.

   d. Compute the BV for this node by taking the union of the BVs of the right and left subtrees

   For Step 3a (above), we utilize the sort() function in the C++ <algorithm> library.

Program 17.5 – Ray Tracing with BVH (continued) – Constructing the BVH

C++/OpenGL Application

```
. . .
struct BVHNode {
    int triangleIdx = -1;
    BoundingVolume bounds;
    BVHNode* left;
    BVHNode* right;
};

std::vector<glm::vec4> centroids;

void initBoundingVolume(BoundingVolume &bv) {
    bv.minX = 0.f; bv.maxX = 0.f;
    bv.minY = 0.f; bv.maxY = 0.f;
    bv.minZ = 0.f; bv.maxZ = 0.f;
}

void initBVHNode(BVHNode &n) {
    n.triangleIdx = -1;
    initBoundingVolume(n.bounds);
}

void getCentroidsWithIndices(glm::vec3 vertices[ ], int numVertices) {
    centroids.clear();
    glm::vec4 centroidWithIndex;
    int triCount = numVertices / 3;

    // for each triangle, compute its centroid by averaging its vertex position values for each axis
    for (int i = 0; i < triCount; i++) {
        glm::vec3 p0 = glm::vec3(vertices[i*3+0]);
```

```
      glm::vec3 p1 = glm::vec3(vertices[i*3+1]);
      glm::vec3 p2 = glm::vec3(vertices[i*3+2]);
      centroidWithIndex.x = (p0.x + p1.x + p2.x) / 3.f;
      centroidWithIndex.y = (p0.y + p1.y + p2.y) / 3.f;
      centroidWithIndex.z = (p0.z + p1.z + p2.z) / 3.f;
      centroidWithIndex.w = (float) i;
      centroids.push_back(centroidWithIndex);
   }
}

void sortCentroids(int axis, int left, int right) {
   std::sort(
      centroids.begin() + left,
      centroids.begin() + right + 1,
      [axis] (const glm::vec4& a, const glm::vec4& b) {
         if (axis == 0) return a.x < b.x;
         else if (axis == 1) return a.y < b.y;
         else return a.z < b.z;
      });
}

BVHNode* constructBVHRecursively(glm::vec3 vertices[ ], int numVertices, int axis, int left, int
right) {
   int count = right - left + 1;

   if (count == 1) {
      BVHNode* node = new BVHNode;
      int i = (int) centroids[left].w;
      node->triangleIdx = i;
      node->left = NULL;
      node->right = NULL;
      BoundingVolume nodeBounds = { 0,0,0,0,0,0 };
      setBoundingVolumeFromTriangle(nodeBounds, vertices[i*3+0], vertices[i*3+1],
      vertices[i*3+2]);
      node->bounds = nodeBounds;
      return node;
   }

   // if there are two or more triangles, this is an interior node
   else {
      sortCentroids(axis, left, right);
      int nextAxis = (axis + 1) % 3;
      int middle = left + count / 2;

      // build the node with its left and right subtrees
      BVHNode* node = new BVHNode;
```

```
    BVHNode* leftnode = new BVHNode;
    BVHNode* rightnode = new BVHNode;

    leftnode = constructBVHRecursively(vertices, numVertices, nextAxis, left, middle-1);
    node->left = leftnode;

    rightnode = constructBVHRecursively(vertices, numVertices, nextAxis, middle, right);
    node->right = rightnode;

    // build the bounding volume for this node
    BoundingVolume bVleft = { 0,0,0,0,0,0 }, bVright = { 0,0,0,0,0,0 };
    setBoundingVolumeFromBV(bVleft, (node->left)->bounds);
    setBoundingVolumeFromBV(bVright, (node->right)->bounds);
    setBoundingVolumeFromUnion(node->bounds, bVleft, bVright);

    node->triangleIdx = -1;
    return node;
}  }
BVHNode constructBVH(glm::vec3 vertices[ ], int numVertices) {
    getCentroidsWithIndices(vertices, numVertices);
    BVHNode* root = constructBVHRecursively(vertices, numVertices, 0, 0, (int) centroids.size()-1);
    BVHNode node = *root;
    delete root;
    return node;
}
```

17.4.2 Transferring the BVH to the Compute Shader

We use a fourth SSBO for transferring the BVH to the compute shader. In order to do this, we must convert the BVH from its existing form – a tree of structs – into a simple series of floats. We start by noting that each node in the tree contains nine floats – a reference to the triangle in the model, a BoundingVolume object (containing the six float values for the bounding volume for this node), and indexes to the root nodes of the left and right subtrees. The entire tree then must be converted to a C++ Vector of floats, made up of groups of nine floats for each node in the BVH.

The function that converts the BVH (tree) into the vector of floats is serialize-BVHRecursively(). The process is recursive, but straightforward. It starts by retrieving the first seven of the nine floats (all but the references to the left and right subtrees) that define the root node of the BVH and appending them into the vector. The values of the two subtree references are not immediately known, so placeholders are inserted for them (to be filled later).

Next, if the node has a left child, it is inserted (by recursively calling serialize-BVHRecursively()), which inserts it immediately after the placeholders. The placeholder for the left subtree is set to that location (i.e., the array index immediately after the placeholders). If there is a right child, it is inserted later, after the entire left subtree has been processed, and its placeholder value will be set to the location immediately after the left subtree.

The vector containing these values is called serialBVHs. An identically-defined field is added to the ModelData class named bvhValues. For each OBJ model that is loaded, its BVH is serialized into serialBVHs, then appended onto the bvhValues field of mdata. Then, after all of the OBJ models have been loaded, mdata's bvhValues field contains the serialized values for *all* of the BVHs.

The two functions that build the BVHs, constructBVH() and serializeBVH(), are called from loadModel() when each OBJ model is read in. The loadModel() function is also responsible for appending the serialized BVH data from serialBVHs to the bvhValues field of mdata. The function loadModels(), which calls loadModel() for each model, is also modified slightly to clear the serialBVHs vector before loading each model, and to display the starting index of each object's BVH within the bvhValues field (useful later when writing the compute shader). The SSBO is generated in init(), which is also where the serialized vector of floats (bvhValues) is copied into the SSBO. The display() function then simply specifies binding index 5 for the SSBO.

Program 17.5 – Ray Tracing with BVH (continued) – Transferring BVH, C++ Side

C++/OpenGL Application

```
. . .
GLuint ssbo[4];
std::vector<float> serialBVHs;

struct ModelData {
    std::vector<float> pvalues;
    std::vector<float> tvalues;
    std::vector<float> nvalues;
    std::vector<float> bvhValues;
};

. . .

void serializeBVHRecursively(BVHNode &node) {
```

```
    // start by adding (to the vector) the index to the triangle associated with this node
    serialBVHs.push_back((float)node.triangleIdx);

    // add the bounding volume associated with this node
    serialBVHs.push_back(node.bounds.minX);
    serialBVHs.push_back(node.bounds.maxX);
    serialBVHs.push_back(node.bounds.minY);
    serialBVHs.push_back(node.bounds.maxY);
    serialBVHs.push_back(node.bounds.minZ);
    serialBVHs.push_back(node.bounds.maxZ);

    // insert placeholders (value = -1) for the pointers to the left and right subtrees
    int indexOfLeftIndex = (int)serialBVHs.size();
    serialBVHs.push_back(-1.f);
    int indexOfRightIndex = (int)serialBVHs.size();
    serialBVHs.push_back(-1.f);

    // if there is a left subtree, add it at the current end of the vector (recursively).
    // Place the index for the start of the left subtree in the appropriate field, replacing the placeholder
    if (node.left != NULL) {
        serialBVHs[indexOfLeftIndex] = (float)serialBVHs.size();
        serializeBVHRecursively(*node.left);
    }

    // if there is a right subtree, add it at the current end of the vector (recursively).
    // Place the index for the start of the right subtree in the appropriate field, replacing the placeholder
    if (node.right != NULL) {
        serialBVHs[indexOfRightIndex] = (float)serialBVHs.size();
        serializeBVHRecursively(*node.right);
    }
}

void loadModel(const char *filePath) {
    . . .
    BVHNode bvhRoot = constructBVH(vert.data(), numOBJvertices);
    serializeBVHRecursively(bvhRoot);
    for (int i = 0; i < serialBVHs.size(); i++) {
        mdata.bvhValues.push_back(serialBVHs[i]);
    }
    . . .
}

void loadModels(char *filePath[ ], int numFiles) {
    // load triangle data for each file
    for (int i=0; i<numFiles; i++) {
        serialBVHs.clear();
```

```
    // displays where in the mdata array the next model vertices will be placed
    std::cout << std::endl << "firstTriIdx for " << filePath[i] << " = " << (mdata.pvalues.size() / 9)
                                                                << std::endl;
    std::cout << "bvhRootIdx for " << filePath[i] << " = " << (mdata.bvhValues.size()) << std::endl;
    loadModel(filePath[i]);
    }
}
void init(GLFWwindow* window) {

    . . .
    // convert vectors to arrays
    float* bv = mdata.bvhValues.data();
    int bvhSize = (int) mdata.bvhValues.size()*4;

    // fill SSBOs with vertex, texture, and normals data for the OBJ file
    glBindBuffer(GL_SHADER_STORAGE_BUFFER, ssbo[3]);
    glBufferData(GL_SHADER_STORAGE_BUFFER, bvhSize, bv, GL_STATIC_DRAW);
}
void display(GLFWwindow* window, double currentTime) {

    . . .
    glBindBufferBase(GL_SHADER_STORAGE_BUFFER, 5, ssbo[3]);
    glDispatchCompute(workGroupsX, workGroupsY, workGroupsZ);
    . . .
}
```

We can see that it took many steps to build the BVH for each model, and load them as a sequence of floats into an SSBO. By contrast, in the compute shader (the GLSL side), it will not be necessary to "unpack" the SSBO. We can traverse the BVH tree(s) as needed directly in the SSBO, as we search for possible ray collisions. Before we can implement that process, we need to set up the structure for referencing the SSBO and the BVHs that it contains in the compute shader.

We specify the buffer containing the SSBO using the binding value 5, as defined in the C++ display() function. We also introduce a new object type for BVH, indicated as TYPE_BVH, with value 6. This necessitates adding an entry to the get_closest_collision() function so we can test whether there are ray collisions with the BVHs.

Program 17.5 – Ray Tracing with BVH (continued) – Transferring BVH, GLSL Side

Compute Shader

```
...
layout (binding=5, std430) buffer nodeBuffer { float bvhNodesBuffer[ ]; };
...
const int TYPE_BVH = 6;

struct Object
{   ...
    int bvhRootIdx; // holds the SSBO index to the root of this BVH, if the type is bvh
};

Collision get_closest_collision(Ray r)
{   ...
    for (int i=0; i<numObjects; i++)
    {   ...
        else if (objects[i].type == TYPE_BVH)
        {   c = intersect_bvh_object(r, objects[i]);
            if (c.t <= 0) continue;
        }
        else continue;
        ...
}
```

17.4.3 Ray-BVH Collision Testing

As described previously (at the start of Section 17.4), to identify collisions with the triangles in a model, we will instead identify collisions with the bounding volumes in the model's BVH tree, starting at the topmost node. This may lead to exploring that node's two children, continuing to traverse the tree until the closest collision is identified (if any). The BVH tree is thus traversed, and when nodes are reached whose bounding volume does not collide with the ray, that entire branch of the tree (and therefore that branch's triangles) are ruled out and do not need to be tested, improving performance considerably.

The process should sound to the reader like a recursive one. However, recall that GLSL does not support recursion. Fortunately, a simple approach exists for traversing the BVH that does not require recursion. Instead, we employ a queue. The queue contains BVH nodes that we wish to test for ray collision. When we test a node, if there is a ray collision, we then add its children to the queue. The process repeats until the queue is empty. It is not necessary to place entire nodes on the queue. Instead, we simply place integer references that point to the starts of nodes in the SSBO into the queue.

We implement the queue as an array of integers. A reference to the BVH root node is placed at the start of the queue. As we traverse the BVH, child nodes are placed at the end of the queue when appropriate. The next node to test is always the one at the front of the queue. Therefore, we will need two integer variables to keep track of the index of the front and the back of the queue. For a binary tree, a relatively small queue should be sufficient – ours is of size 256, which is likely to be much larger than necessary. For convenience, we have included functions for clearing the queue, adding a node to the queue, removing the front element from the queue, and testing to see if the queue is empty (which occurs when the indices of the front and back of the queue are the same, meaning that there are no more nodes to test). In case we overstep the end of the queue, we treat it as a "circular" array by making each reference *mod 256*.

Testing a BVH for collision with a ray is done in intersect_bvh_object(), which is organized in a similar manner as our previous intersection functions. However, it must also utilize the queue and traverse the BVH. It starts by enqueuing the root node of the BVH. It then begins iterating over the nodes in the queue. Note that the SSBO may contain the BVH's for several models, so each reference to a node in the SSBO must be offset by the current object's index offset, which is in the object's bvhRootIdx (which was added to the Object struct in the previous code segment).

After retrieving the BVH node from the SSBO, we test to see if it is an interior node or a leaf node. If it is a leaf node, we test the associated triangle for ray intersection. If the node is internal, we test the ray against the node's bounding volume. If the ray intersects the bounding volume and is not further than the closest triangle found so far, then we add this node's children to the queue, because it is possible that one of them could contain a triangle that is an even closer intersection (although we do not know that yet).

Checking for intersection with a bounding volume, which is done in the function intersect_bounding_volume(), is very similar to intersect_box_object(), which we implemented earlier. The main differences are as follows: (1) it needs to obtain its dimensions from the SSBO, and (2) there are several items that it does not need to compute, such as texture coordinates, normal vectors, and on which face the collision occurred.

Program 17.5 – Ray Tracing with BVH (continued) – BVH Traversal and Collisions

Compute Shader

```
. . .
const int BVH_QUEUE_SIZE = 256;
int bvh_queue[BVH_QUEUE_SIZE];
int bvh_queue_front;
int bvh_queue_end;

void clear_bvh_queue() { bvh_queue_front = bvh_queue_end = 0; }

bool is_bvh_queue_empty() { return bvh_queue_front == bvh_queue_end; }

void enqueue_bvh_node(int index)
{   bvh_queue[bvh_queue_end] = index;
    bvh_queue_end = (bvh_queue_end + 1) % BVH_QUEUE_SIZE;
}

int dequeue_bvh_node()
{   int index = bvh_queue[bvh_queue_front];
    bvh_queue_front = (bvh_queue_front + 1) % BVH_QUEUE_SIZE;
    return index;
}

float intersect_bounding_volume(Ray r, int nodeStartIdx, mat4 world_to_localR,
                                                    mat4 world_to_localTR)

{   vec3 mins =
        vec3(bvhNodesBuffer[nodeStartIdx+1], bvhNodesBuffer[nodeStartIdx+3],
            bvhNodesBuffer[nodeStartIdx+5]);
    vec3 maxs =
        vec3(bvhNodesBuffer[nodeStartIdx+2], bvhNodesBuffer[nodeStartIdx+4],
            bvhNodesBuffer[nodeStartIdx+6]);

    // Convert the world-space ray to the box local space:
    vec3 ray_start = (world_to_localTR * vec4(r.start,1.0)).xyz;
    vec3 ray_dir = (world_to_localR * vec4(r.dir,1.0)).xyz;

    // Calculate the box world mins and maxs (as described in Chapter 16):
    vec3 t_min = (mins - ray_start) / ray_dir;
    vec3 t_max = (maxs - ray_start) / ray_dir;
    vec3 t_minDist = min(t_min, t_max);
    vec3 t_maxDist = max(t_min, t_max);
    float t_near = max(max(t_minDist.x, t_minDist.y), t_minDist.z);
    float t_far = min(min(t_maxDist.x, t_maxDist.y), t_maxDist.z);
```

```
    // If the ray is entering the box, t_near contains the farthest boundary of entry
    // If the ray is leaving the box, t_far contains the closest boundary of exit
    // The ray intersects the box if and only if t_near < t_far, and if t_far > 0.0
    // If the ray did not intersect the box, return a negative t value
    if (t_near >= t_far || t_far <= 0.0 || t_near < 0.0) { return -1.0; }
    return t_near;
}
Collision intersect_bvh_object(Ray r, Object o)
{   const int LEFT_CHILD_OFFSET = 7;
    const int RIGHT_CHILD_OFFSET = 8;
    float closest = FLT_MAX;
    Collision c, closest_collision;
    closest_collision.t = -1;

    // build translation and rotation matrices for applying to bounding box
    mat4 local_to_worldT = buildTranslate((o.position).x, (o.position).y, (o.position).z);
    mat4 local_to_worldR = buildRotateY( DEG_TO_RAD*o.yrot)
                        * buildRotateX(DEG_TO_RAD*o.xrot) * buildRotateZ(DEG_TO_RAD*o.zrot);
    mat4 local_to_worldTR = local_to_worldT * local_to_worldR;
    mat4 norm_local_to_worldTR = transpose(inverse(local_to_worldTR));
    mat4 world_to_localR = inverse(local_to_worldR);
    mat4 world_to_localTR = inverse(local_to_worldTR);

    // initialize the queue, and enqueue the root node of the BVH
    clear_bvh_queue();
    enqueue_bvh_node(0);

    // iterate through the queue of BVH nodes until it is empty
    while (!is_bvh_queue_empty())
    {   int nodeStartIdx = o.bvhRootIdx + dequeue_bvh_node();
        int triangleIdx = int(bvhNodesBuffer[nodeStartIdx]);

        // test to see if the triangle is a leaf node
        if (triangleIdx >= 0)
        {   c = intersect_triangle_from_buffer (r, o.firstTriIdx + triangleIdx, local_to_worldTR,
                                                        norm_local_to_worldTR);

            if (c.t > 0 && c.t < closest)
            {   closest = c.t;
                closest_collision = c;
            }
        }
        else // it is an inner node
        {   float t = intersect_bounding_volume(r, nodeStartIdx, world_to_localR, world_to_localTR);
            if (t > 0 && t <= closest)
            {   // if there is a left child, add it to the queue
```

```
        int leftChildIdx = int(bvhNodesBuffer[nodeStartIdx + LEFT_CHILD_OFFSET]);
        if (leftChildIdx >= 0) { enqueue_bvh_node(leftChildIdx); }

        // if there is a right child, add it to the queue
        int rightChildIdx = int(bvhNodesBuffer[nodeStartIdx + RIGHT_CHILD_OFFSET]);
        if (rightChildIdx >= 0) { enqueue_bvh_node(rightChildIdx); }
  } } }
  return closest_collision;
}
```

An example configuration is shown in the final code segment for Program 17.5, and the output is shown in Figure 17.6. The scene includes a room box, sphere, checkerboard ground plane, a 20-triangle reflective and transparent icosahedron loaded in from the OBJ file "icosahedron.obj," a 6-triangle transparent pyramid loaded in from the OBJ file "pyramid.obj," and the high-poly dolphin loaded in from the OBJ file "dolphinHighPoly.obj."

Program 17.5 – Ray Tracing with BVH (continued) – Example Configuration

Compute Shader

```
. . .
// high-poly textured dolphin
{ TYPE_BVH, 0.0, vec3(0), vec3(0), 0.0, 40.0, 0.0, vec3(-0.3, 0.0, 3.85),
   false, true, false, false, vec3(0), 0.0, 0.0, 0.0,
   vec4(0.5, 0.5, 0.5, 1.0), vec4(.5,.5,.5,1), vec4(.5,.5,.5,1), 50.0,
   TRIVERTS_ZERO, TRITEXCS_ZERO, TRINORMS_ZERO, 0, 0, 0
},
// transparent blue-green pyramid
{ TYPE_BVH, 0.0, vec3(0), vec3(0), 0.0, 60.0, 0.0, vec3(-2.0, 0.0, 1.0),
   true, false, false, true, vec3(0,0.7,0.5), 0.0, 0.3, 1.01,
   vec4(0.5, 0.5, 0.5, 1.0), vec4(.5,.5,.5,1), vec4(.5,.5,.5,1), 100.0,
   TRIVERTS_ZERO, TRITEXCS_ZERO, TRINORMS_ZERO, 32976, 0, 593559
},
// transparent and reflective red icosahedron
{ TYPE_BVH, 0.0, vec3(0), vec3(0), 60.0, 40.0, 10.0, vec3(1.5, 0.0, 2.5),
   true, false, true, true, vec3(1.0,0,0), 0.5, 0.3, 1.0,
   vec4(0.5, 0.5, 0.5, 1.0), vec4(.5,.5,.5,1), vec4(.5,.5,.5,1), 50.0,
   TRIVERTS_ZERO, TRITEXCS_ZERO, TRINORMS_ZERO, 32982, 0, 593658
}
. . .
```

Figure 17.6
Ray tracing several OBJ models with BVH.

17.4.4 Performance Comparison

The performance improvement using BVH is considerable. The "mesh" approach given earlier in Program 17.3, which tested the triangle intersections directly, without using a BVH, included three simple objects and a 20-triangle icosahedron, with recursion depth set to 4. It was quite slow, and took 38 seconds to complete on the authors' laptop. In that example, if we replace the icosahedron with the *low*-poly dolphin model (5664 triangles), it then takes 4 minutes to complete. Replacing the low-poly dolphin with the high-poly dolphin model (32,976 triangles) then takes 20 minutes.

By contrast, the example given in Program 17.5, which makes use of BVH, renders a much more demanding scene. It includes six objects, including both the icosahedron and the *high*-poly dolphin, and an even deeper recursion depth of 8, yet it only takes about 30 seconds to complete, a speedup of more than 20-fold.

SUPPLEMENTAL NOTES

Much can be done to clean up the code presented in this chapter and make it easier for specifying arbitrary scenes. For example, it currently is set up for only one textured object. Specifying more would require modifying the code so that each object definition included a way referencing one of a set of textures (this should be a relatively simple addition).

Although the acceleration structure implemented here worked well, and resulted in dramatic speedup, more can be done to improve performance. Other methods exist for partitioning either the triangles or the render space itself. There are also more sophisticated algorithms for constructing the BVH. Several surveys of existing algorithms are available [AB06, MO21]. Another improvement that can be made is in the queue that we used for traversing the BVH, by prioritizing nodes that are closest to the ray origin.

BVHs are also commonly used for collision detection [E05].

Visualizing the BVH structure itself should be fairly intuitive, but its extent and complexity may not be immediately obvious. Ultimately, every model triangle has its own bounding box, and those boxes are part of a larger binary tree of bounding boxes. So, the BVH generated for a complex model such as the high-poly dolphin will have more bounding boxes than it has triangles (i.e., well over 30,000 boxes for the dolphin). To give an idea of how these boxes are situated, we used the bounding boxes themselves to generate an OBJ file, and opened it in Blender. The result is shown in Figure 17.7.

Much of the code in this chapter was developed initially in Java by Robin O'Connell, an alumnus of California State University, Sacramento. His contributions greatly facilitated our explanations and we appreciate the excellent work that he did implementing the BVH with great clarity, and also for integrating it so well within the framework developed in the previous chapter. He also developed the icosahedron OBJ model used in the latter half of this chapter, and generated the OBJ file containing the BVH visualization shown in Figure 17.7.

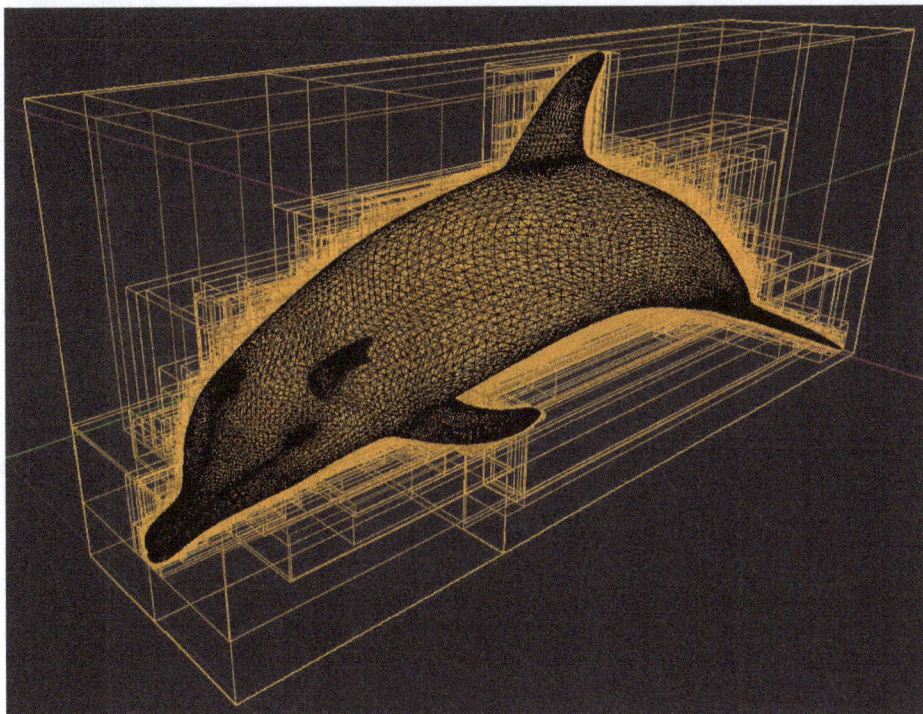

Figure 17.7
Visualizing a BVH for the high-poly dolphin.

Exercises

17.1 Make the following changes to Program 17.5:

(i) replace the room box with a sky box,

(ii) add a second dolphin that is transparent, and

(iii) add a third dolphin that is reflective. You may arrange the dolphins in whatever configuration you like, and you may also move (or remove) the pyramid and icosahedron.

17.2 Modify Program 17.5 so that the dolphin has its texture, and the pyramid uses the brick texture. This will require some changes to how the program associates textures with objects.

References

[AB06] K. Anderson and C. Bay (2006), *A Survey of Algorithms for Construction of Optimal Heterogeneous Bounding Volume Hierarchies*, Department of Computer Science, University of Copenhagen.

[E05] C. Erickson (2005), *Real-Time Collision Detection*. Morgan Kaufmann series in interactive 3D technology.

[KK86] T. Kay and J. Kajiya (1986), *Ray Tracing Complex Scenes*, ACM SIGGRAPH'86, Aug. 1986.

[MO21] D. Meister, S. Ogaki, C. Benthin, M. Doyle, M. Guthe, and J. Bittner (2021), *A Survey on Bounding Volume Hierarchies for Ray Tracing*, Eurographics 2021, volume 40, Number 2.

[MT97] T. Möller and B. Trumbore (1997), *Fast, Minimum Storage Ray/Triangle Intersection*, ACM SIGGRAPH 2005 Courses, also available at https://dl.acm.org/doi/10.1145/1198555.1198746 (accessed November 2023)

[OW22] OpenGL Wiki (Khronos, 2022) – *Interface Block (GLSL), memory layout,* accessed November 2023, https://www.khronos.org/opengl/wiki/Interface_Block_(GLSL)#Memory_layout

[S23] Scratchapixel (2023, Jean-Colas Prunier), *Ray Tracing: Rendering a Triangle*, accessed November 2023. https://www.scratchapixel.com/lessons/3d-basic-rendering/ray-tracing-rendering-a-triangle/barycentric-coordinates

STEREOSCOPY FOR 3D GLASSES AND VR HEADSETS

This entire textbook is about 3D rendering. However, "3D" is an overloaded term. We have been using it to mean displaying scenes using a 3D perspective so that we can realistically perceive their objects at their locations and at their relative sizes. However, "3D" can also mean viewing a scene through a binocular mechanism that creates a fuller illusion of depth, often called *stereoscopy*. For example, you may have seen such techniques at a movie theater, where viewers are given special glasses to see a movie in "3D." In this chapter, we will explore the basics of how to generate stereoscopic renderings using OpenGL.

In the real world, we experience a sensation of depth because our two eyes physically exist in slightly different locations. Our brain is able to combine our two eyes' slightly different viewpoints into a single 3D experience. To replicate this experience mechanically requires providing each eye with a similarly slightly different view of the scene we are rendering. Many approaches for doing this have been invented over the years.

One of the first such devices was produced in the 1800s, consisting of a simple bracket called a "stereoscope" [WST]. This allowed one to view specially-produced photographs – more specifically, image pairs – so that each eye viewed the same subject, but from very slightly different vantage points. These early stereoscopes were the inspiration for the widely popular View-Master® toys that emerged in the mid-1900s, and more recently, for virtual reality headsets (see Figure 18.1). Devices of this sort are often called "side-by-side" viewers.

Figure 18.1
Side-by-side viewers:
1800's stereoscope, 1960's View-Master®, and 2016 Oculus Quest® VR headset.
Photo of 1800's Holmes stereoscope image by Dave Pape:
https://commons.wikimedia.org/wiki/File:Holmes_stereoscope.jpg.
Photo of Oculus Quest by Bryan Clevenger, used with permission.

Side-by-side viewing produces excellent results, however, it has one primary disadvantage – it is only feasible for small images, such as on a personal headset.

Achieving stereoscopy on a larger scale, such as on a movie screen, requires a different approach. The usual method is to project an image that contains both left and right images simultaneously, and then provide a special pair of glasses that only allows the left and right eyes to see their respective images. There are several technologies for achieving this; three currently popular ones are as follows:

- *Anaglyph* – The glasses' lenses are two different colors, typically red and cyan; the left eye sees the red component of the image, and the right eye sees the cyan component. The image is projected such that the left eye's view is rendered in red, and the right eye's view is rendered in cyan.

- *Polarized* – The glasses are split such that one side is polarized vertically and the other side is polarized horizontally. The image is projected such that each eye's view is polarized in one or the other manner.

- *Shutter* – The projected image alternates displaying the left and right images. The glasses alternate allowing the left and right sides to allow the image to pass through.

Each of these technologies has its advantages and disadvantages. Anaglyph is the simplest and least expensive; early "3D movies" used this method. However, the resulting color is often compromised. Polarized does not suffer from color issues, and the glasses are also inexpensive, but projecting a specially-polarized image requires special technology.[1] *Shutter* offers the best quality, but the technology is the most expensive, including the glasses. Figure 18.2 shows an inexpensive cardboard pair of anaglyph glasses.

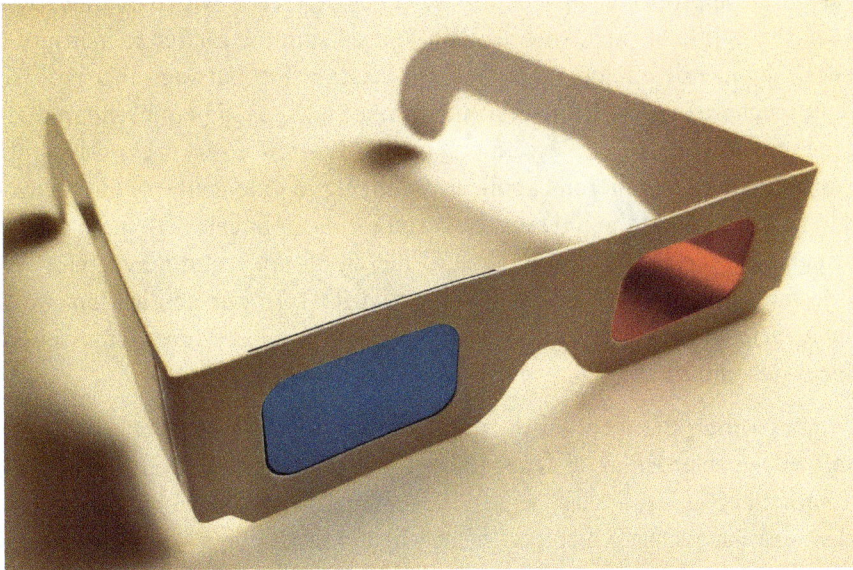

Figure 18.2
Red/cyan anaglyph 3D glasses for cinematic projection.

In this chapter, we introduce the basics of generating 3D stereoscopic images in OpenGL using two techniques: (1) anaglyph, and (2) side-by-side. In both cases, we will first need to learn a few basics regarding the view and projection matrices we will need to properly generate the separate images for each eye.

18.1 ■ VIEW AND PROJECTION MATRICES FOR TWO EYES

The science of how our pair of eyes converge on a particular object and allow us to perceive its distance from us ("stereopsis" or "depth perception") is complex

---

[1] Anaglyph and polarized techniques are called "passive" because the glasses do not need to physically do anything other than filter colors, etc. By contrast, shutter glasses need to dynamically open and close in sync with the projected image, and is therefore referred to as an "active" technology.

[WSS], and a complete discussion is outside the scope of this book. Our implementations will be limited to incorporating only the most basic elements.

Let's consider the vantage point of each eye. Although our eyes are very close together, they are at different points in space. A common approach is to decide on an appropriate *interocular distance* ("IOD"), which is the distance between the pupils of our two eyes. While it is a simple matter to measure this distance, say in millimeters or inches, the relationship between that real-world distance measure (e.g., millimeters) and the axes units used in our rendered scene (i.e., the meaning of "1," "2," etc., along our X, Y, and Z axes) is entirely application-dependent. A commercial application, such as a videogame or movie, would need to make sure that the IOD value chosen for the application domain correctly corresponds to the average human's IOD (about 65 mm), and may even need to provide for the user to adjust for his/her own IOD. In our application, we will define a variable called IOD, and simply decide by trial and error on a value that produces decent results.

We determine the location of each eye as the location of the camera offset by half of the interocular distance. The offset computation would also include any rotation applied to the camera. In the examples in this chapter, the camera is fixed at location (cameraX, cameraY, cameraZ) and faces down the negative Z axis. Therefore, in those cases, ignoring rotation, the eye locations are simply (cameraX ± IOD/2.0, cameraY, cameraZ), and the remainder of computations for computing each eyes' respective view matrix are unchanged.

Deriving accurate perspective projection matrices is complex [N10], although implementing them is fairly simple. While it is possible to get decent results simply using the standard perspective matrix used for the camera, this can lead to undesirable effects at the periphery, namely distant regions that only one eye can see. Figure 18.3 shows frustums applied to both eyes, first using standard perspective transforms, and then with slightly modified perspective transforms that allow both eyes the same distance view while still facing forward. The second approach produces better results, but requires the creation of perspective matrices for asymmetric frustums. GLM provides a function called glm::frustum() that builds such a matrix given the top, bottom, left, and right boundaries of the projection plane. Derivations for various such matrices can be found in [S16].

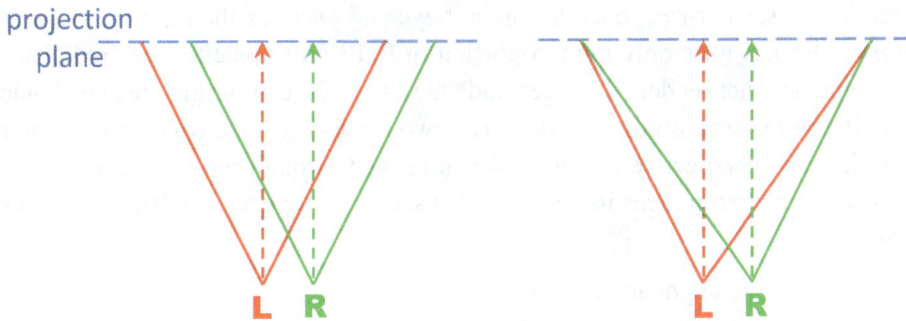

Figure 18.3
Standard and asymmetric frustums for stereoscopic perspective matrices.

Finding the boundaries of the projection plane in the asymmetric case can be accomplished using a bit of geometry, given the field of view, aspect ratio, and near and far clipping planes that we have already been using. Figure 18.4 defines an OpenGL/C++ function computePerspectiveMatrix() that does this. The parameter leftRight is set to -1 for the left eye and +1 for the right eye. All other variables are allocated globally (as before), for reasons of efficiency. The result is placed in the variable pMat.

```
void computePerspectiveMatrix(float leftRight) {
    float top = tan(fov/2.0f) * near;
    float bottom = -top;
    float frustumShift = (IOD / 2.0f) * near / far;
    float left = -aspect * top - frustumShift * leftRight;
    float right = aspect * top - frustumShift * leftRight;
    pMat = glm::frustum(left, right, bottom, top, near, far);
}
```

Figure 18.4
C++/OpenGL function for computing an asymmetric perspective matrix.

18.2 ANAGLYPH RENDERING

Rendering an anaglyph "3D" version of a scene, for viewing with red-blue or red-cyan glasses, is basically the same as we have been doing, except that we need to render the scene *twice*, once for the left eye and once for the right eye. One of these renderings uses only the red portion of RGB color palette (the "red channel"), and the other renders the green and blue channels (combining green and blue in RGB color spaces produces cyan). The two renderings also each employ their own view and perspective matrices. When viewed through red-cyan glasses, the brain fuses the two images into a single 3D scene. An overview of the steps is as follows:

1. Clear the depth and color buffers.
2. Set the OpenGL color mask to enable only the red channel.
3. Call display() to render the scene, using the view and perspective matrices for the left eye.
4. Clear the depth buffer (but not the color buffer).
5. Set the OpenGL color mask to enable only the green and blue channels.
6. Call display() to render the scene, using the view and perspective matrices for the right eye.

The above steps occur in the render loop in main() in a similar manner as we have been doing throughout the book. Note Steps #2 and #5 – it is convenient that OpenGL offers the command glColorMask(), which can be used to restrict the color channels that are written to the color buffer.

We illustrate anaglyph rendering using the "fog" example from Section 14.1 (the scene continually rotates, and this particular image is captured at a different time point than the one shown earlier in Figure 14.2). While we could use almost any example from the preceding chapters, we chose to use a scene that includes fog because incorporating methods that slightly obscure distant objects can further enhance the 3D experience.

Program 18.1 shows the changes and additions to Program 14.1. Explanations follow the code.

Program 18.1 – Anaglyph Rendering of Fog Example

C++/OpenGL Application

```
// includes, #defines, variables for display, rendering programs, init(), matrices, as before.
. . .
```

```
float IOD = 0.01f;    // tunable interocular distance – we chose 0.01 for this scene by trial-and-error
. . .
void computePerspectiveMatrix(float leftRight) {
    // as shown previously in Figures 18.3 and 18.4
}
void display(GLFWwindow* window, double currentTime, int leftRight) {
    . . .
    computePerspectiveMatrix(leftRight);
    vMat = glm::translate(glm::mat4(1.0f), glm::vec3(-(cameraX + (leftRight * IOD / 2.0f)), -cameraY,
                                                                                -cameraZ));

    . . .

}
int main(void) {
    . . .
    // window setup same as before – all changes are in the render loop as follows:
    while (!glfwWindowShouldClose(window)) {
        glColorMask(true, true, true, true);        // all color channels enabled for background color
        glClear(GL_DEPTH_BUFFER_BIT);
        glClearColor(0.7f, 0.8f, 0.9f, 1.0f);       // the fog color is bluish-grey
        glClear(GL_COLOR_BUFFER_BIT);

        glColorMask(true, false, false, false);     // enables only the red channel
        display(window, glfwGetTime(), -1);         // render left eye's view

        glClear(GL_DEPTH_BUFFER_BIT);

        glColorMask(false, true, true, false);      // enables only the green and blue channels
        display(window, glfwGetTime(), 1);          // render right eye's view

        glfwSwapBuffers(window);
        glfwPollEvents();
    }
    . . .
    // other components same as before. Shaders are also unchanged.
}
```

There are very few changes made to the original program 14.1. The interocular distance is set to 0.01, which was arrived at by trial-and-error as described earlier in Section 18.1. Note that the render loop in the main() now calls display() twice, with an additional parameter leftRight, which is set to -1 and then +1, corresponding to the left and right eyes. The display() function then uses this value to offset the camera location used to build the view matrix, to either the left or the right, by half of the interocular distance.

The output of Program 18.1 is shown in Figure 18.5. Note that the output comprises two renderings of the "fog" example, with one in red and the other in cyan, slightly offset horizontally. View this figure through red/cyan glasses to see the resulting 3D stereoscopic effect.

Figure 18.5
Anaglyph rendering of Program 18.1, the fog example.
(best viewed through red/cyan 3D glasses).

18.3 SIDE-BY-SIDE RENDERING

Now that we have seen how to render appropriate left and right eye images using asymmetric perspective matrices, let's adapt these techniques to generating a side-by-side stereoscopic pair for our "fog" example.

If all we desire is a pair of rectangular images for use in a device such as the stereoscope or View-Master®, then the solution is straightforward. We simply use the OpenGL glViewport() function to specify separate halves of the screen (viewports) for each image, then call display() twice, once for each viewport. Program 18.2 shows the changes to Program 14.1. Explanations follow the code.

Program 18.2 – Side-by-Side Rendering of the Fog Example

C++/OpenGL Application

```
// includes, #defines, variables for display, rendering programs, init(), matrices, and IOD as before.
// Addition of the computePerspectiveMatrix() function, and changes to display(), same as Program 18.1
. . .
int sizeX = 1920, sizeY = 1080;
. . .
int main(void) {
    . . .
    // window setup same as before – all changes are in the render loop as follows:
    while (!glfwWindowShouldClose(window)) {
        glViewport(0, 0, sizeX, sizeY);
        glClear(GL_DEPTH_BUFFER_BIT);
        glClear(GL_COLOR_BUFFER_BIT);

        glViewport(0, 0, sizeX/2, sizeY);
        display(window, glfwGetTime(), -1);

        glViewport(sizeX/2, 0, sizeX/2, sizeY);
        display(window, glfwGetTime(), 1);

        glfwSwapBuffers(window);
        glfwPollEvents();
    }
    . . .// remaining code same as before. Shaders are also unchanged.
}
```

The glViewport() function is used to specify a portion of the screen (or "viewport") for rendering. It takes four parameters; the first two specify the X and Y screen coordinates of the lower left corner of the viewport, and the next two specify the width and height of the viewport region (in pixels). We have defined the variables sizeX and sizeY to common dimensions for a modern laptop screen. They should be set to match the machine being used. We then use these values to divide the screen in half, one side for each eye. The resulting output is shown in Figure 18.6. In this example, we have also set the clear color to the fog color, as we did in Program 18.1.

Comparing Figures 18.5 and 18.6, it is clear that the images in 18.6 have been compressed horizontally. With only half of the screen width available for rendering each image, an application would need to take this into account, by changing either the field of view or the aspect ratio. We have ignored that in this simple example.

Figure 18.6
Side-by-side rendering of the Program 18.2 fog example
(best viewed through stereo headset).

18.4 CORRECTING LENS DISTORTION IN HEADSETS

Headsets for viewing side-by-side images utilize high field-of-view lenses that often suffer from lens distortion. Two important types of distortion in lenses are *barrel distortion*, where straight lines bulge outward, and *pincushion distortion*, where straight lines pinch inwards. Figure 18.7 shows a simple grid, and then the same grid having been distorted with both pincushion and barrel distortions.

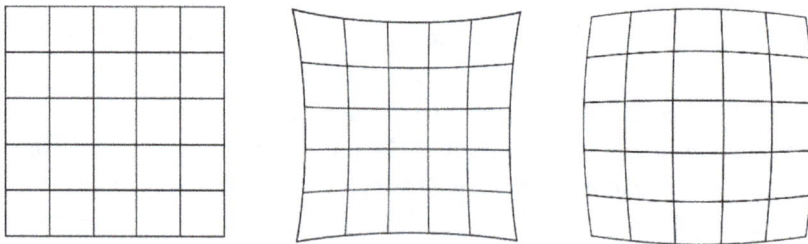

Figure 18.7
Simple grid (left), and the same grid with *pincushion* (center) and *barrel* (right) distortions.

Most headsets utilize high field-of-view lenses that suffer from pincushion distortion. For example, consider the popular stereoscopic headset, the Google Cardboard® [GC23], in which the user places a cell phone inside of a cardboard frame that incorporates a pair of lenses. If the cell phone displays a side-by-side stereoscopic image, it can be viewed in 3D through the Google Cardboard. Figure 18.8 shows a Google Cardboard headset, along with the leftmost grid from Figure 18.7, but actually photographed through one of the Google Cardboard lenses. A pincushion distortion can clearly be observed.

Because headsets tend to use lenses that produce pincushion distortion, applications that target virtual reality headsets usually try to anticipate the pincushion distortion and correct for it by applying a reverse distortion, specifically barrel distortion. Since different headset lenses can have different properties, this *distortion correction* would ideally be tunable for different headsets.

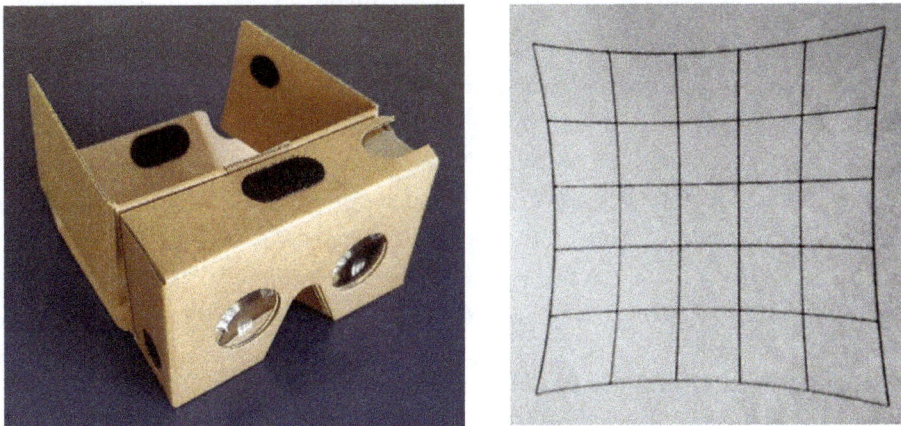

Figure 18.8
Google Cardboard® headset, and a simple grid viewed through one of its lenses, exhibiting pincushion distortion.

Measuring and correcting lens distortion is complex, and a full study is beyond the scope of this book. Instead, we will discuss the steps for a typical example. Specifically, we will apply a barrel distortion correction to our fog example, roughly tuned for the Google Cardboard headset. We also point out some of the tunable parameters along the way. More thorough coverage can be found on the Internet, such as in [BS16].

Applying a distortion correction to a rendered scene can be done in a variety of ways. One of the most efficient methods is called *vertex displacement*, in which the elements in the scene are each rendered with the desired distortion correction applied to the vertices [BS16]. For simplicity, we use an easier, albeit less efficient, *fragment-shader-based* approach. The steps are as follows:

1. Render the entire scene to a framebuffer texture, from the left eye point of view.
2. Use the texture to render a rectangular region to the left half of the screen (the fragment shader applies barrel distortion in this step).
3. Repeat the process for the right eye, to the right half of the screen.

We already studied how to render a scene to a framebuffer texture, for example when we studied shadows. We just learned how to render to the left and right halves of the screen using glViewport(). Now we need to learn how to take a framebuffer texture and render it while distorting the image it contains.

Rendering (and texturing) a rectangular object should be a simple matter, using six vertices comprising two triangles. Applying a corresponding texture would then typically be done in the fragment shader using the texture() function, which expects parameters for the X and Y texture coordinates. Since our rectangle fills the entire viewport, an *undistorted* rendering would be achieved by simply scaling the texture coordinates to the viewport dimensions, such as

fragColor = texture(gl_FragCoord.x / (sizeX/2), gl_FragCoord.y / sizeY);

Instead, we need to modify the X and Y texture lookup values so that they access a different texel, specifically the one that would be at that location (X,Y) if the texture were barrel-distorted. The mathematical derivation of barrel distortion dates back more than 100 years (initially by Conrady [C19], and further refined by Brown [B66]). A simplified model (from [W20]) commonly used in VR systems is as follows:

$$x_u = x_d / \left(1 + K_1 r^2 + K_2 r^4\right)$$

$$y_u = y_d / \left(1 + K_1 r^2 + K_2 r^4\right)$$

where (x_d, y_d) is the original (distorted) texture coordinate location, (x_u, y_u) is the corresponding texture coordinate in an undistorted (corrected) version of the scene, r is the straight-line distance from (x_d, y_d) to the center of the image, and K_1 and K_2 are tunable constants. Even in this simple model, the values for r, K_1, and K_2 require tuning depending on the viewing device, and sometimes even for the person doing the viewing. Commonly-used values for Google Cardboard are -0.55 for K_1, and 0.34 for K_2. For r, we use the Pythagorean Theorem to compute a distance, and then scale that distance by trial-and-error to come up with a reasonably effective result. From here on, we will refer to this barrel distortion as *lens distortion correction*.

Program 18.3 shows the changes made to Program 18.2 in order to render each half screen with lens distortion correction, roughly tuned for Google Cardboard. Note that the existing shaders (unchanged) now render to framebuffer textures, and a new second set of shaders is added to do the final lens distortion correction of these framebuffer textures to their respective half screens. Additional discussion follows the code. The resulting output is then shown in Figure 18.9.

Program 18.3 – Side-by-Side Rendering with Lens Distortion Correction

C++/OpenGL Application

```
// only the changes to Program 18.2 are shown here
. . .
// the 4th VBO (vbo[3]) is the rectangular region for drawing the texture buffer to half of the screen
#define numVBOs 4

GLuint renderingProgram, distCorrectionProgram;
GLuint leftRightBuffer, leftRightTexture;
void setupVertices(void) {
    . . .
    // rectangular region for drawing half of the screen (these vertices are placed in vbo[3])
    float lensQuad[18] = {
        -1.0, 1.0, 0.0, -1.0, -1.0, 0.0, 1.0, 1.0, 0.0,
         1.0, 1.0, 0.0, -1.0, -1.0, 0.0, 1.0, -1.0, 0.0
    };
    glBindBuffer(GL_ARRAY_BUFFER, vbo[3]);
    glBufferData(GL_ARRAY_BUFFER, sizeof(lensQuad), &lensQuad[0], GL_STATIC_DRAW);
}
void setupLeftRightBuffer(GLFWwindow* window) {
    GLuint bufferId[1];
```

```
glGenBuffers(1, bufferId);
glfwGetFramebufferSize(window, &width, &height);

// Initialize Framebuffer for rendering a screen half
glGenFramebuffers(1, bufferId);
leftRightBuffer = bufferId[0];
glBindFramebuffer(GL_FRAMEBUFFER, leftRightBuffer);
glGenTextures(1, bufferId);          // this is for the color buffer
leftRightTexture = bufferId[0];
glBindTexture(GL_TEXTURE_2D, leftRightTexture);
glTexImage2D(GL_TEXTURE_2D, 0, GL_RGBA, width / 2, height, 0, GL_RGBA, GL_UNSIGNED_BYTE,
                                                                                NULL);
glTexParameteri(GL_TEXTURE_2D, GL_TEXTURE_MIN_FILTER, GL_LINEAR);
glTexParameteri(GL_TEXTURE_2D, GL_TEXTURE_MAG_FILTER, GL_LINEAR);
glTexParameteri(GL_TEXTURE_2D, GL_TEXTURE_WRAP_S, GL_CLAMP_TO_BORDER);
glTexParameteri(GL_TEXTURE_2D, GL_TEXTURE_WRAP_T, GL_CLAMP_TO_BORDER);
float blackColor[4] = { 0.0f, 0.0f, 0.0f, 1.0f };
glTexParameterf(GL_TEXTURE_2D, GL_TEXTURE_BORDER_COLOR, *blackColor);
glFramebufferTexture2D(GL_FRAMEBUFFER, GL_COLOR_ATTACHMENT0,
                                          GL_TEXTURE_2D, leftRightTexture, 0);
glDrawBuffer(GL_COLOR_ATTACHMENT0);
glGenTextures(1, bufferId);          // this is for the depth buffer
glBindTexture(GL_TEXTURE_2D, bufferId[0]);
glTexImage2D(GL_TEXTURE_2D, 0, GL_DEPTH_COMPONENT24, width/2, height, 0,
    GL_DEPTH_COMPONENT, GL_FLOAT, NULL);
glTexParameteri(GL_TEXTURE_2D, GL_TEXTURE_MIN_FILTER, GL_LINEAR);
glTexParameteri(GL_TEXTURE_2D, GL_TEXTURE_MAG_FILTER, GL_LINEAR);
glFramebufferTexture2D(GL_FRAMEBUFFER, GL_DEPTH_ATTACHMENT,
                                          GL_TEXTURE_2D, bufferId[0], 0);
}
void init(GLFWwindow* window) {
    . . .
    distCorrectionProgram = Utils::createShaderProgram("vertDistCorrShader.glsl", "fragDistCorrShader.glsl");
}
void copyFrameBufferToViewport(GLFWwindow* window, float leftRight) {
    glUseProgram(distCorrectionProgram);

    // the "leftRight" uniform is the side being rendered, winSizeX and winSizeY are window dimensions
    leftRightLoc = glGetUniformLocation(distCorrectionProgram, "leftRight");
    sizeXLoc = glGetUniformLocation(distCorrectionProgram, "winSizeX");
    sizeYLoc = glGetUniformLocation(distCorrectionProgram, "winSizeY");
    glUniform1f(leftRightLoc, leftRight);
    glUniform1f(sizeXLoc, (float)sizeX/2.0f);
    glUniform1f(sizeYLoc, (float)sizeY);
```

```
    // vbo[3] contains the vertices for the rectangular region (two triangles)
    glBindBuffer(GL_ARRAY_BUFFER, vbo[3]);
    glVertexAttribPointer(0, 3, GL_FLOAT, false, 0, 0);
    glEnableVertexAttribArray(0);

    // the texture containing the rendered scene is sent to the shaders,
    // which will apply lens distortion correction
    glActiveTexture(GL_TEXTURE0);
    glBindTexture(GL_TEXTURE_2D, leftRightTexture);

    glEnable(GL_DEPTH_TEST);
    glDepthFunc(GL_LEQUAL);
    glDrawArrays(GL_TRIANGLES, 0, 6);
}

void clearDisplay() {
    // this is for clearing the actual screen display buffer
    glClearColor(0, 0, 0, 1);
    glBindFramebuffer(GL_FRAMEBUFFER, 0);
    glClear(GL_DEPTH_BUFFER_BIT);
    glClear(GL_COLOR_BUFFER_BIT);
}

void clearBuffer() {
    // this is for clearing the framebuffer texture where the scene is initially rendered
    glClearColor(0.7f, 0.8f, 0.9f, 1.0f);
    glBindFramebuffer(GL_FRAMEBUFFER, leftRightBuffer);
    glClear(GL_DEPTH_BUFFER_BIT);
    glClear(GL_COLOR_BUFFER_BIT);
}

int main(void) {

    . . .

    setupLeftRightBuffer(window);

    while (!glfwWindowShouldClose(window)) {
        clearDisplay();

        // draw left viewport to framebuffer texture
        clearBuffer();
        glBindFramebuffer(GL_FRAMEBUFFER, leftRightBuffer);
        glViewport(0, 0, sizeX/2, sizeY);
        display(window, glfwGetTime(), -1);

        // transfer left viewport framebuffer to the screen
        glBindFramebuffer(GL_FRAMEBUFFER, 0);
        glViewport(0, 0, sizeX/2, sizeY);
```

```
copyFrameBufferToViewport(window, 0.0f);

// draw right viewport to framebuffer texture
clearBuffer();
glBindFramebuffer(GL_FRAMEBUFFER, leftRightBuffer);
glViewport(0, 0, sizeX/2, sizeY);
display(window, glfwGetTime(), 1);

// transfer right viewport framebuffer to the screen
glBindFramebuffer(GL_FRAMEBUFFER, 0);
glViewport(sizeX/2, 0, sizeX/2, sizeY);
copyFrameBufferToViewport(window, 1.0f);

glViewport(0, 0, sizeX, sizeY);
glfwSwapBuffers(window);
glfwPollEvents();
}
glfwDestroyWindow(window);
glfwTerminate();
exit(EXIT_SUCCESS);
}
```

Vertex Shader ("vertDistCorrShader.glsl")

```
// these shaders are for the final rendering of the completed framebuffer texture
// the vertex shader is just a simple pass-through to the fragment shader
#version 430
layout (location=0) in vec3 position;
uniform float leftRight;
uniform float winSizeX;
uniform float winSizeY;
layout (binding=0) uniform sampler2D lensTex;

void main(void)
{   gl_Position = vec4(position, 1.0);
}
```

Fragment Shader ("fragDistCorrShader.glsl")

```
// The fragment shader does all of the lens distortion correction computations
#version 430
out vec4 fragColor;
uniform float leftRight;        // -1 for left, +1 for right
uniform float winSizeX;
uniform float winSizeY;
layout (binding=0) uniform sampler2D lensTex; // the previously rendered framebuffer texture

void main(void)
```

```
{   float K1 = -0.55; // distortion parameters for Google Cardboard
    float K2 = 0.34;

    // compute the location in the half window scaled to (-0.5..+0.5) with (0,0) center
    float xd = (gl_FragCoord.x - winSizeX*leftRight) / winSizeX - 0.5;
    float yd = gl_FragCoord.y / winSizeY - 0.5;

    // compute the distance to the center of the half window
    float ru = sqrt(pow(xd,2.0) + pow(yd,2.0));

    // tune conversion from screen units to physical millimeters
    float mmRatio = 1.3; // ratio of ru/d where d is distance to lens
    float rn = ru * mmRatio;

    // compute the undistorted corresponding location
    float distortionFactor = 1+ K1 * pow(rn,2.0f) + K2 * pow(rn,4.0f);
    float xu = xd / distortionFactor;
    float yu = yd / distortionFactor;

    // move the resulting point by (+0.5, +0.5) to convert to texture space
    fragColor = texture(lensTex, vec2(xu+0.5, yu+0.5));
}
```

In Program 18.3, specifically the C++/OpenGL application, setup of the framebuffer texture (i.e., setting up leftRightBuffer and its associated texture named leftRightTexture) is identical to the "water" example from Program 15.3. There, the buffer was used to store a reflection (later, a second one was used to store a refraction). Here, it is used to store the entire scene, at the same dimensions as the one-half screen window viewport. A second rendering program (called distCorrectionProgram) is created for displaying this buffer to the screen, which happens in the function copyFrameBufferToViewport(), which is called once for the left eye and then again for the right eye. Most of the remaining C++ code is unchanged, including the display() function that renders the scene. The main() is expanded to manage enabling which of the two framebuffers (the screen buffer or the leftRightBuffer) is active.

The actual distortion correction happens in distCorrectionProgram's fragment shader. The GLSL shader code implements (1) the computation of the distance from the location being rendered to the center of the half-screen viewport, (2) the lens distortion correction computations, and (3) the resulting texel lookup in leftRightTexture.

Figure 18.9
Side-by-side rendering of Program 18.3 with lens distortion correction (best viewed through a stereo headset).

18.5 A SIMPLE TESTING HARDWARE CONFIGURATION

There are many ways available today for viewing side-by-side scenes such as the one rendered by Program 18.3. While modern headsets can be expensive, a simple method that the authors have used for preparing the examples in this chapter is to utilize the following set of technologies:

- a reasonably modern cell phone (such as Android or iPhone) connected to the computer
- WiredXDisplay [WX20] (cell phone app), which duplicates the computer screen to the cell phone
- Google Cardboard [GC20] for viewing the cell phone display in split screen format

For readers who already own a smart phone, the total cost for the above solution is under $20. The phone can be connected to a computer using a USB cable. The WiredXDisplay application then transmits the contents of the computer screen to the cell phone, essentially turning the phone into a computer monitor. The phone is then placed inside the Google Cardboard headset, which assumes the left half of the display screen is for the left eye, and the right half is for the right eye. Figure 18.10 shows this configuration being deployed for Program 18.3.

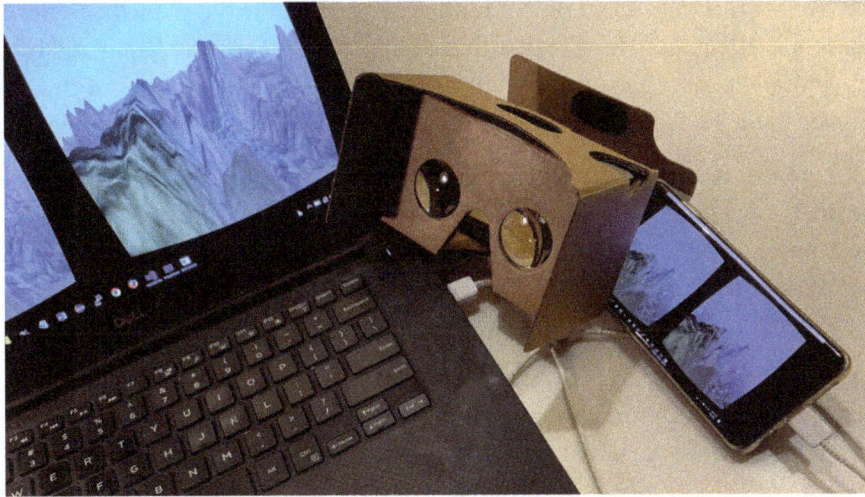

Figure 18.10
Side-by-side output of Program 18.3 using Google Cardboard.

Hardware for testing anaglyph examples, such as the one in Program 18.1, is considerably simpler. We simply use an inexpensive set of cardboard red/cyan glasses, which can be purchased online.

SUPPLEMENTAL NOTES

The stereoscopic techniques described in this chapter constitute only a very basic introduction. Professional systems for movie theaters and VR games and applications typically utilize more sophisticated models and are more carefully tuned for the hardware being used. We have also ignored important related topics, such as retinal blur for depth of field rendering, which would be incorporated in a fully professional deployment. That said, it is fun to use the simple methods shown here to experience the various examples throughout the textbook with full 3D depth perception.

In just a few cases, there are some stumbling blocks. Some of the examples in this textbook utilize user-defined framebuffers for various purposes or render to textures, such as for building shadows, generating water effects, or doing ray tracing. In those cases, the C++ code would need to be further modified to manage the buffers. This is especially tricky in the water examples from Chapter 15, where the reflection and refraction buffers are largely estimated and will not lend themselves to accurate splitting between the two eyes without modification.

We chose the "fog" example for rendering because the "fog" further helps the stereoscopic effect, but also because that example was not overly hampered by the color limitations of red/cyan anaglyph viewing. The colors of some of the other examples in the textbook will not fare as well when viewed in red/cyan anaglyph.

The reader has likely noticed that our side-by-side rendering was horizontally "squished." We did not correct for this to keep the code as simple as possible. A more complete solution would also correct the view frustums so that the aspect ratio is not so radically changed. One drawback of side-by-side viewing is therefore the resulting loss of half of the screen "real estate" when rendering a scene.

Details on the *vertex displacement* method for correcting lens distortion, which has better performance than the simple fragment-shader-based method presented in this chapter, can be found in [K16].

Although we have presented basic approaches to stereoscopic rendering (and viewing) such as are applied for virtual reality systems, there is quite a large set of VR topics that we have not discussed. A full VR system not only displays in stereoscopic 3D, it also includes sensors that enable the user to move and interact more naturally, such as by turning one's head or reaching with the hands. We have focused solely on the graphics.

This chapter also does not discuss how to render for polarized or shutter technologies (although they are mentioned briefly in the beginning of the chapter). Those require more specialized hardware and their solutions are beyond the scope of this introduction.

Exercises

18.1 Modify Program 18.1 to try a variety of different values for IOD. What range of values do you think works the best for this scene? What happens if IOD is set too small? What do you observe as IOD increases, and then what happens when IOD is set too large?

18.2 Convert Program 4.2, specifically the modified version with 100,000 cubes, to both anaglyph and side-by-side stereoscopy.

18.3 Convert Program 12.5, the tessellated moon surface, to both anaglyph and side-by-side stereoscopic rendering. Animate the camera movement so that it skims along and close to the moon surface.

References

[B66]   D. Brown (1966), *Decentering Distortion of Lenses*, Photogrammetric Engineering 32 (3).

[BS16]   B. Smus (2016), *Three Approaches to VR Lens Distortion*. Blog entry, accessed November 2023. https://smus.com/vr-lens-distortion/

[C19]   A. Conrady (1919), *Decentered Lens-Systems*, Monthly notices of the Royal Astronomical Society 79 (1919).

[GC23]   Google Cardboard – accessed November 2023. https://en.wikipedia.org/wiki/Google_Cardboard

[K16]   B. Kehrer (2016), *VR Distortion Correction Using Vertex Displacement* (blog), accessed November 2023. https://www.gamedeveloper.com/programming/vr-distortion-correction-using-vertex-displacement

[N10]   S. Gateau, S. Nash (2010), *Implementing Stereoscopic 3D in Your Applications*, NVIDIA, GPU Technology Conference, San Jose CA, accessed November 2023, https://www.nvidia.com/content/GTC-2010/pdfs/2010_GTC2010.pdf

[S16]   Scratchapixel 2.0 (2016), *The Perspective and Orthographic Projection Matrix*, accessed November 2023, https://www.scratchapixel.com/lessons/3d-basic-rendering/perspective-and-orthographic-projection-matrix/projection-matrix-introduction.html

[W20]   G. Wetzstein (2020), *Head Mounted Display Optics 1*, accessed November 2023, https://stanford.edu/class/ee267/lectures/lecture7.pdf

[WSE]   Wikipedia – Stereoscopy, accessed November 2023, https://en.wikipedia.org/wiki/Stereoscopy

[WSS]   Wikipedia – Stereopsis, accessed November 2020, https://en.wikipedia.org/wiki/Stereopsis

[WST]   Wikipedia – Stereoscope, accessed November 2020, https://en.wikipedia.org/wiki/Stereoscope

[WX20]   WiredXDisplay (cell phone application) – Splashtop.com, accessed November 2023, https://www.splashtop.com/wiredxdisplay

INSTALLATION AND SETUP FOR PC (WINDOWS)

■ ■ ■ ■ ■

As described in Chapter 1, there are a number of installation and setup steps that must be accomplished in order to use OpenGL and C++ on your machine. These steps vary depending on which platform you wish to use. The code samples in this book are designed to be run as-given on a PC (Windows). This appendix provides setup instructions for the Windows platform. Libraries and tools change frequently, so these steps may become outdated.

A.1 INSTALLING THE LIBRARIES AND DEVELOPMENT ENVIRONMENT

A.1.1 Installing the Development Environment

Since we implement several projects throughout the course of the book and there are so many libraries to coordinate in OpenGL, it will be useful to set up your C++ development environment in such a way as to minimize the number of configuration steps needed for each new project. Here, we assume that Visual Studio Community 2022 [VS22] is being used. Similar steps may be possible for other IDEs. If you are installing Visual Studio for the first time, choose the "Desktop development with C++" option.

The first step is to download and install Visual Studio 2022 on your machine. Once this is done, our approach will be to install as many of the necessary libraries as possible in a single shared location, and then create a Visual Studio custom template so that each new project you create will already have the necessary libraries and dependencies in place without having to be redefined each time. We describe creating such a template in Section A.2.1.

A word of warning – Visual Studio is huge. The standard installation can approach 10 Gb.

A.1.2 Installing OpenGL / GLSL

It is not necessary to "install" OpenGL or GLSL, but it is necessary to ensure that your graphics card supports at least version 4.3 of OpenGL. If you do not know what version of OpenGL your machine supports, you can use one of the various free applications (such as GLview [GV23]) to find out.

A.1.3 Preparing GLFW

An overview of the window management library GLFW was given in Chapter 1. As indicated there, GLFW needs to be compiled for the machine on which it will run. (Note that although the GLFW website includes the option of downloading pre-compiled binaries, these frequently do not work adequately.) Compiling GLFW requires first downloading and installing CMAKE (available at https://cmake.org [CM23]). The steps for compiling GLFW are relatively straightforward:

1. Download the GLFW source code (www.glfw.org) [GF20]. Unzip and move the folder to a suitable location. We created a folder called "OpenGL_library_installation" under "Documents" (you can choose a different location if you prefer). We also created the subfolders "download" and "build." We copied the unzipped GLFW folder into the "Download" folder.

2. Download and install CMAKE (https://cmake.org) [CM23]. During the installation, check the box that says *add to system path.*"

3. Run CMAKE and enter the GLFW source location and the desired build destination folder.
   - Specify the source code as the downloaded GLFW folder.
   - Specify the build folder as the "build" folder you created in Step 1 (above).

4. Click "configure." If you had properly installed Visual Studio, it should use that by default. If some of the options are highlighted in red, click "configure" again.

5. Click "generate."

CMAKE produces several files in the "build" folder. One of the files in that folder is named "GLFW.sln." This is a Visual Studio project file. Open it (using Visual Studio), and compile (build) GLFW as a 64-bit application. If this is the first time running Visual Studio on this machine, it might be necessary to choose the "C++" configuration. The box at the top should say "x64." Then choose "Build Solution" under the "Build" menu.

The resulting build produces two items that you will need:

- the glfw3.lib file, which is found in the *src ▶ debug* folder
- the "GLFW" folder, which is found in the original GLFW downloaded source code under the "include" folder. It contains two header files that you will use.

A.1.4 Preparing GLEW

An overview of the GLEW "extension wrangler" library was given in Chapter 1. Download the 64-bit binaries from glew.sourceforge.net [GE17]. The items in particular you will need to obtain are as follows:

- **glew32.lib** (found in the *lib ▶ release ▶ x64* folder) – The name includes "32," but currently these are still the correct files for 64-bit installation.
- **glew32.dll** (found in the *bin ▶ release ▶ x64* folder)
- the **GL** folder, which includes several header files (found in the "include" folder)

A.1.5 Preparing GLM

An overview of the math library GLM was given in Chapter 1. Visit github.com/g-truc/glm [GM23] and download the latest version that includes the release notes. The download folder, after being unzipped, consists of a folder named "**glm**." Inside that folder is another folder also named "**glm**." That folder (and its contents) is the item that you will need to use.

A.1.6 Preparing SOIL2

An overview of the image loading library SOIL2 was given in Chapter 1. Installing SOIL2 [SO23] requires utilizing a tool called "premake" found at https://premake.github.io [PM23]. Although the process involves several steps, they are relatively straightforward:

1. Download and uncompress "premake." The file that we will use is "premake5.exe."

2. Download the SOIL2 source code zip file at https://github.com/SpartanJ/SOIL2 (use the "downloads" link under the "Code" pulldown menu), and uncompress it.

3. Copy the "premake5.exe" file into the SOIL2 folder.

4. Open a command window, navigate to the SOIL2 folder, and enter the following:

   premake5 vs2022

   It should display a number of files that are then created.

5. In the SOIL2 folder, open the "make" folder, then the "windows" folder. Double-click SOIL2.sln.

6. Confirm that the dropdown box at the top says "x64" (not "x86"); then, in the panel on the left, right-click on "soil2-static-lib" and select "build."

7. Close Visual Studio and navigate back to the SOIL2 folder. You should notice two new folders, "lib" and "obj," have been added.

A.1.7 Preparing Shared "lib" and "include" Folders

Choose a location where you would like to house the library files. It could be a folder anywhere you prefer; for example, you could create a folder "C:\OpenGLlibraries." Inside that folder, create subfolders named "lib" and "include."

- In the "lib" folder, place **glew32.lib** and **glfw3.lib**.
- In the "include" folder, place the **GL**, **GLFW**, and **glm** folders described previously.
- Navigate back to the SOIL2 folder, and go into the "*lib▶windows*" folder inside it. Copy the "soil2-debug.lib" file into the "lib" folder (where glew32.lib and glfw3.lib are).
- Navigate back to the SOIL2 folder, then into the "src" folder. Copy the "SOIL2" folder into the "include" folder (where GL, GLFW, and GLM are). This SOIL2 folder contains .c and .h files for SOIL2.

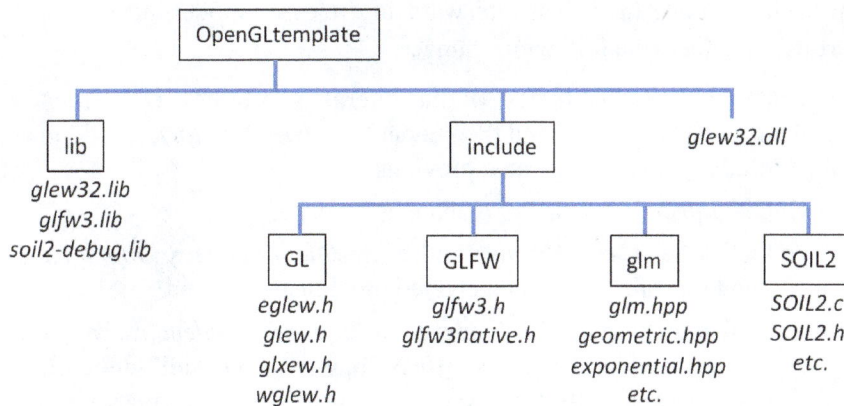

Figure A.1
Suggested library folder structure

- You might find it useful to also place the "**glew32.dll**" file in this "OpenGLtemplate" folder as well, so that you will know where to find it, although that is not strictly necessary.

The complete folder structure is shown in Figure A.1.

A.2 DEVELOPING AND DEPLOYING OPENGL PROJECTS IN VISUAL STUDIO

A.2.1 Creating a Visual Studio Custom Project Template

Because we are using so many special-purpose libraries in our C++/OpenGL programs, creating a Visual Studio template will make it significantly easier to start new OpenGL projects. This section describes the steps for creating and using this template.

Start Visual Studio (we will assume it is the 2022 "Community" version). Create a new, empty C++ project (the name and location for this project do not matter – the default location is fine). At the top center, under the menu bar, there are two pull-down menus next to each other:

- The one on the right allows you to specify "x86" or "x64" – choose "x64."
- The one on the left allows you to specify whether compilation is to be done in "debug" mode or "release" mode. Several steps need to be done for BOTH modes. That is, they should be done in "debug" mode, and then repeated in "release" mode.

In "debug" mode (and then afterward in "release" mode), go into "project properties" and make the following changes:

- Under "*VC++ Directories*" (it may alternatively say "*C/C++*"), then under "*General,*" and then under "*Include Directories,*" add the "**include**" folder you created previously.

- Under "*linker,*" there are two changes to make:
  o Click on "*General,*" then under "*Additional Library Directories,*" add the "**lib**" folder you created previously.
  o Click on "*Input,*" then under "*Additional Dependencies,*" add the following four filenames: **glfw3.lib**, **glew32.lib**, **soil2-debug.lib**, and **opengl32.lib** (this last one should already be available as part of the standard Windows SDK). Separate the four file names with semicolons.

After making the previous changes to the project properties, for both the "debug" and "release" modes, you are ready to create the template. This is done by going into the "*Project*" menu and selecting "*Export template.*" Choose that this is a "project" template, and give the template a useful name, such as "OpenGL project." After doing this, you can close Visual Studio.

A.2.2 Using the Custom Project Template

Once the libraries are installed and the custom template is in place, creating a new OpenGL C++ project is straightforward:

1. Start Visual Studio, and click "Create a new project."
2. Choose your OpenGL template, then click "Next." *Note* – The very first time that you try to use the template, you may need to search for it using the provided search tool.
3. Give your project a name, select a location for the project, then click "Create."
4. Switch from "x86" to "x64" (if necessary) using the dropdown box at the top.
5. Back in Windows, navigate to the folder that Visual Studio created that matches the name of your newly-created project.
6. Copy any files that comprise your application into the subfolder. This includes any **.cpp** source files, **.h** header files, **.glsl** shader files, texture image files, and **.obj** 3D model files that your application uses. It is not

necessary to specify any header files that were already built into the template.

7. Also copy the "**glew32.dll**" file into the same subfolder.

8. In the solution explorer (it could be on the left or the right), right click on "Source Files" and choose *Add▶ Existing item* to load your **main.cpp** file. Repeat this process for other **.cpp** files.

9. Also in the solution explorer, right click on "Header Files" and choose *Add▶ Existing item* to load any header (**.h**) files in your application.

10. You are now ready to build and execute your program.

A.3 DEPLOYING A STAND-ALONE APPLICATION

After developing, testing, and debugging your application, it can be deployed as a stand-alone executable by building the project in "*Release*" mode and then placing the following files in a single folder:

- the **.exe** file generated from building your project
- all shader files used by your application
- all texture images and model files used by your application
- **glew32.dll**

After building the folder, the application can be run by double-clicking the .exe file.

References

[**CM23**] CMake homepage, Accessed November 2023, https://cmake.org

[**GE17**] OpenGL Extension Wrangler (GLEW), accessed November 2020, http://glew.sourceforge.net/

[**GF23**] Graphics Library Framework (GLFW), accessed November 2023, http://www.glfw.org/

[**GM23**] OpenGL Mathematics (GLM), Accessed November 2023, https://github.com/g-truc/glm

[**GV23**] GLview, realtechVR, Accessed November 2023, http://www.realtech-vr.com/home/glview

[PM23] Premake homepage, accessed November 2023, https://premake.github.io/

[SO23] Simple OpenGL Image Library 2 (SOIL2), SpartanJ, accessed November 2023, https://github.com/SpartanJ/SOIL2

[VS22] Microsoft Visual Studio Community, Accessed November 2023, https://visualstudio.microsoft.com/vs/community/

INSTALLATION AND SETUP FOR MACINTOSH

As described in Chapter 1, there are a number of installation and setup steps that must be accomplished in order to use OpenGL and C++ on your machine. These steps vary depending on which platform you wish to use. This appendix provides setup instructions for the Macintosh platform. Libraries and tools change frequently, so these steps may become outdated.

Apple support for OpenGL on the Macintosh has languished over the past several years. For example, modern Macs as of this writing only support up to OpenGL version 4.1. Still, it is possible to run most of the examples in this book with minor modifications. As for preparing the necessary libraries, all of the libraries described in Chapter 1 are cross-platform and available for the Apple Macintosh. We first describe how to install these libraries, and then we discuss the setup for an appropriate development environment.

In addition, since the code samples in this book are designed to be run on a Windows platform with OpenGL 4.3, this appendix also explains how to convert the code samples so that they run correctly on the Macintosh with OpenGL 4.1.

B.1   INSTALLING THE LIBRARIES AND DEVELOPMENT ENVIRONMENT

B.1.1   Preparing and Installing the Libraries

An overview of the purpose and selection of each library was given in Chapter 1. We will not repeat that information here; instead, we focus on how to install each library.

As is the case for Windows, it is not necessary to "install" OpenGL or GLSL, but it is necessary to ensure that your machine supports at least version 4.1 of

OpenGL. Newer Macs should all have this. Apple no longer maintains a list of which Macs include OpenGL. For older Macs, a list is available on the Apple website [AP19].

We start by installing GLEW and GLFW. Probably the easiest way to install these libraries is by using the Homebrew tool. Homebrew is a package manager designed to make the installation of commonly needed utilities on the Mac as easy as possible. The steps for installing Homebrew are as follows:

1. Open the Safari browser, and visit the Homebrew website (**https://brew.sh**).

2. Follow the installation instructions on the Homebrew page. Specifically, copy the line of code given in the center of the page, open a terminal window on the Mac, paste the copied command into it, and press "return." You may need to enter your Mac password. The installation will probably take several minutes to complete.

3. Towards the end of the notifications are the instructions for adding Homebrew to your PATH. Follow those instructions by copying and pasting the given two lines to the command prompt and executing them.

4. Leave the terminal window open; you will use it again in the next steps.

Next, use the newly-installed Homebrew utility to install GLEW and GLFW, as follows:

1. At the terminal prompt, enter the following command: `arch -arm64 brew install glfw`. If your Mac is an older Intel-based variety, instead enter the following: `brew install glfw`

2. Still at the terminal prompt, enter the command: `arch -arm64 brew install glew`. If your Mac is an older Intel-based variety, instead enter `brew install glew`

3. Note that two folders are now in **/opt/homebrew/include**, named **GL** and **GLFW**.

Next, we install the math library GLM. Of the four libraries, this is the simplest. Since GLM is a header-only library, simply (a) download and uncompress the library as described earlier in Section A.1.5, and then (b) copy the resulting "**glm**" folder and its contents to **/opt/homebrew/include**.

Installing SOIL2 is probably the trickiest of the four libraries to install. The steps we have used successfully are as follows:

1. Download and uncompress **SOIL2** as described in Appendix A.

2. Download the Mac version of **premake** (version 5), as described in Appendix A.

3. Uncompress **premake**. In the uncompressed folder is the **premake5** executable.

4. Copy the **premake5** executable into the SOIL2 folder. Move the SOIL2 folder to a location where you have administrator access, such as the "Documents" folder.

5. In a terminal window, navigate to the SOIL2 folder and enter the following:

   ./premake5 gmake

6. Still in the SOIL2 folder, enter cd make/macosx to navigate into the "make" folder, then type:

   make

7. SOIL2 should build successfully (you may get error messages that the test files did not build successfully – that is ok, as the test files are not important to us). The build should produce a "**src/SOIL2**" folder that includes several **.h** files, and a "**lib/macosx**" folder that includes two library files named "**libsoil2-debug.a**" and "**libsoil2-debug.dylib**."

After completing these steps, the file structure should be similar to that shown in Figure B.1.

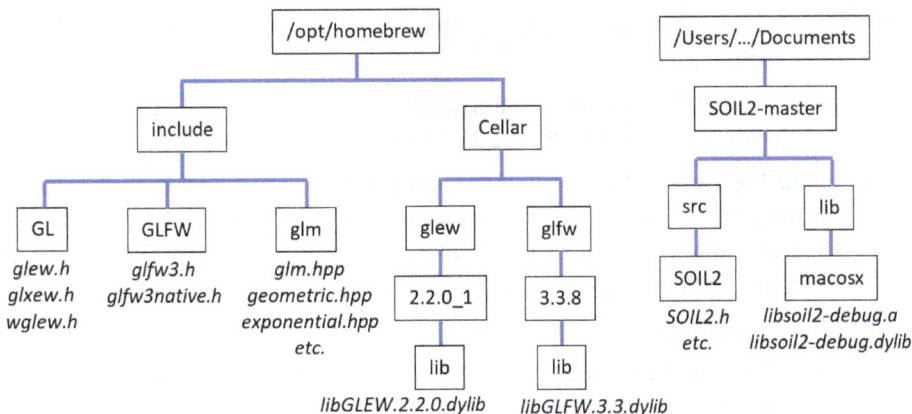

Figure B.1
Directory structure for Macintosh OpenGL C++ libraries

B.1.2 Preparing the Development Environment

We used a popular IDE for the Mac called *Xcode*. If your Mac does not already include Xcode, installing it is a straightforward (albeit rather slow) operation

[XC23]. You may be required to update your operating system in order to install the latest version of Xcode.

After installing Xcode, you will need to configure it to work with OpenGL and with the libraries we are using. Here are the steps we used to successfully set up Xcode for our C++/OpenGL applications:

1. Run Xcode, and have it create a project of type *macOS* ▶ *command line tool*. Set the language to C++.

2. A default **main.cpp** is created that contains a simple "hello world" program. In the Xcode editor, overwrite that code with the desired main.cpp code from one of our C++/OpenGL applications. Several errors in the code might be flagged – ignore those for now.

3. Set up the *header search path* as follows:

    a. At the top of the left panel, click the leftmost icon to open the Project Navigator (if it is not already open).

    b. Click on the project name (at the top of the leftmost panel).

    c. Choose "**Build Settings**" and "**all levels**" tabs at the top center of the main panel.

    d. Scroll down to the "**Search Paths**" section.

    e. Under "**Header Search Paths**," add the following path: /opt/homebrew/include

    f. Also under "Header Search Paths," add the path to SOIL2-master/src (which contains SOIL2/SOIL2.h).

4. Add the path to the folder containing your "libsoil2-debug.a" file to the *library search path*. This is also under "Build Settings," near the header search path section used in the previous step. Ensure that it is added to both the "release" and "debug" categories.

5. Set up the binaries for the *linking phase* as follows:

    a. Click on the project name (at the top of the leftmost panel, in blue), if necessary.

    b. Choose the "**Build Phases**" tab at the top center of the main panel.

    c. Click the little triangle next to *"Link Binary with Libraries"* to open that section.

    d. There should be a "+" next to where it says *"drag to reorder linked binaries."* Click the "+."

    e. A search box should open. Search for "opengl". "**OpenGL Framework**" should appear. Select it and click *"Add"* (note: this OpenGL framework should already exist in the Mac).

f. Click the "+" again, and this time search for "core". "**CoreFoundation Framework**" should appear. Select it and click *"Add"* (this library should also already exist in the Mac).

g. Click the "+" again, and this time click the *"Add Other"* box in the lower left, then choose "add files" on the little popup window that appears.

h. When the browser window opens, enter CMD-SHIFT-G. A go-to folder box should open; enter /opt/homebrew and press enter.

i. In the folder structure shown, navigate to "Cellar," then "glew," then to whatever version number displays, then "lib." Some library files should appear with the ".dylib" extension.

j. Select the appropriate ".dylib" library file. It should be named something like libGLEW.2.2.0.dylib (without an "mx" in it, and without a shortcut arrow). After selecting it, insert it by clicking *"open."*

k. Repeat steps [g] through [j] for the appropriate glfw library. It will also be in /opt/homebrew/Cellar, and then in "glfw," its version number, and "lib." It should be named something like libglfw.3.3.dylib (without a shortcut arrow). After selecting it, insert it by clicking *"open."*

l. Repeat the process for both of the SOIL2 library files (the ones that we created back in section B.1.1). That is, click the "+," click *"Add Other,"* and then navigate to the folder where you placed the libsoil2-debug.a and libsoil2-debug.dylib files. Select and insert both of those files.

m. Choose the "**General**" tab at the top center of the main panel.

n. Click the little triangle next to *"Frameworks and Libraries"* to open that section, if it is not already open. All of the libraries installed in the previous steps should be listed.

o. To the right of the "libsoil2-debug.dylib" library is a small pulldown menu. From that menu, select *"Embed Without Signing."*

6. Set the working directory, as follows: In the "**Product**" menu, under "**Scheme**" - "**Edit Scheme**", then under the "options" tab, check the box labeled *"use custom working directory."* In the adjoining field, copy the path to the project source code folder (the one containing the "main.cpp" file).

7. Copy your supporting files (texture images, shader files, and other support files such as the **Utils.cpp** and **Utils.h** files that we generate over the course of the book) into this same working directory where the "main.cpp" file is located.

8. In the leftmost panel, in the Project Navigator, use the "+" symbol at the lower left to add any additional ".cpp" and ".h" files that are part of your C++/OpenGL application (such as **Utils.cpp**, **Utils.h**, and **Sphere.cpp**) to the project, so that they appear in the left panel alongside "main.cpp."

B.2 MODIFYING THE C++/OPENGL/GLSL APPLICATION CODE FOR THE MAC

For the most part, the C++ programs themselves, as described in this textbook, will run as-is. There are, however, a small number of changes that must be made. Most of the changes are to the "main()" function inside of "main.cpp." You can build it once and duplicate that modified version of main() into each of the other projects. The remaining changes are small, and can be done as needed.

Some of these changes will not make much sense until you have studied the corresponding programming sections in the text. The reader may choose to skip parts of this section and return to it later after learning the material in question. While acknowledging the possible risk of introducing confusion, we have decided to place all of the code changes for the Macintosh here, so that they are assembled in one place.

B.2.1 Modifying the C++ Code

Let's start with the changes that must be made to the "**main.cpp**" file:

- Xcode sometimes generates a huge number of "documentation" warning messages. These can make it inconvenient to find more substantive error messages. There are several ways to stop these messages; one of the simplest is the add the following two lines to the top of "main.cpp:"

  ```
  #pragma clang diagnostic push
  #pragma clang diagnostic ignored "-Wdocumentation"
  ```

- Homebrew installs GLEW as a static library on the Mac, so you will need to add:

  ```
  #define GLEW_STATIC
  ```

  at the top of your program, immediately above the #include <GL/glew.h> command.

- In the glfwWindowHint commands, set the "major" context version to 4, and the "minor" to 1.

You will also need to add two additional glfwWindowHint commands immediately after the two that are already there. They are as follows:

```
glfwWindowHint(GLFW_OPENGL_PROFILE, GLFW_OPENGL_CORE_PROFILE);
glfwWindowHint(GLFW_OPENGL_FORWARD_COMPAT, GL_TRUE);
```

These lines are necessary because they force the Mac to use the latest version of OpenGL available on the hardware (many Macs default to much earlier versions of OpenGL).

* Some Macs, such as those with a *Retina* display, are slightly trickier when it comes to setting up the GLFW rendering window resolution. After creating the window with glfwCreateWindow(), you will need to retrieve the actual screen dimensions from the frame buffer, as follows:

```
int actualScreenWidth, actualScreenHeight;
glfwGetFramebufferSize(window, &actualScreenWidth, &actualScreenHeight);
```

Then, after the glfwMakeContextCurrent(window) command, add the following line:

```
glViewport(0, 0, actualScreenWidth, actualScreenHeight);
```

This will ensure that what is drawn to the framebuffer matches what appears in the GLFW window.

* Finally, immediately before initializing GLEW with glewInit(), add the following line:

```
glewExperimental = GL_TRUE;
```

B.2.2 Modifying the GLSL Code

Some changes will need to be made at various locations in our GLSL shader code (and some of the associated C++/OpenGL code) because of the slightly earlier version of OpenGL (specifically, 4.1) present in Macs:

* The specified version number in the shaders must be changed. Presuming that your Mac supports version 4.1, at the top of each shader locate the line that says

```
#version 430
```

this line of code must be changed to the following:

```
#version 410
```

- Version 4.1 does not support layout binding qualifiers for texture sampler variables. This affects material starting from Chapter 5. You will need to remove the layout binding qualifiers, and replace them with another command that accomplishes the same thing. Specifically, look for lines in the shaders that have the following format:

  layout (binding=0) uniform sampler2D samp;

  The texture unit number specified in the binding clause might be different (it is "0" here), and the name of the sampler variable might be different (it is "samp" here). In any case, you will need to remove the layout clause, and simplify the command so that it just says the following:

  uniform sampler2D samp;

  Then, you will need to add the following command to the C++ program for each texture enabled

  glUniform1i(glGetUniformLocation(renderingProgram, "samp"), 0);

  immediately after the glBindTexture() command in the C++ display() function, where "samp" is the name of the uniform sampler variable, and the "0" in the previous example is the texture unit specified in the binding command that was removed earlier.

B.2.3 Additional Notes

The ray tracing programs shown in Chapter 16 will not run on the Macintosh, because they utilize compute shaders, which were not introduced until version 4.3 of OpenGL.

On some Macs that utilize a *Retina* Display, the pixel count can be inconsistent. For example, in the code described in Section 2.1.6 (with result shown in Figure 2.13), gl_FragCoord.x may return a value twice as big as would be expected based on the window dimensions specified in main(). In that example, change the test value 295 to 590 to produce the desired result.

References

[AP19] Mac computers that use OpenCL and OpenGLgraphics, accessed November 2023, https://support.apple.com/en-us/HT202823

[XC23] Apple Developer site for Xcode, accessed November 2023, https://developer.apple.com/xcode

C

USING THE NSIGHT GRAPHICS DEBUGGER

■ ■ ■ ■ ■

Debugging GLSL shader code is notoriously difficult. Unlike programming in typical languages such as C++ or Java, it is often unclear exactly where a shader program failed. Often, a shader error manifests as a blank screen, offering no clues as to the nature of the error. Even more frustrating is that there is no way to print out the values of shader variables during run time, as one would commonly do when tracking down an elusive bug.

We listed some techniques for detecting OpenGL and GLSL errors in Section 2.2. Despite the help that these techniques provide, the lack of a simple ability to display shader variables is a serious handicap.

For this reason, graphics card manufacturers have sometimes provided capabilities in hardware for extracting information from shaders at run time, and then built tools for accessing the information in the form of a graphics debugger. Each manufacturer's debugging tool(s) work only in the presence of that manufacturer's graphics card. NVIDIA's graphics debugger is part of a larger suite of tools called *Nsight*, and AMD has a similar suite of tools called *CodeXL*. This appendix describes how to get started using Nsight with C++/OpenGL on a PC (Windows) machine.

C.1 ABOUT NVIDIA NSIGHT

Nsight is an NVIDIA suite of tools that includes a graphics debugger, which makes it possible to look inside the shader stages of the OpenGL graphics pipeline while a program is running. It is not necessary to change the code or to add any code.

Simply run an existing program using the Nsight application. Nsight allows examining shaders at runtime, such as seeing the current contents of a shader's uniform variables. Some versions even allow for changing the shader code at runtime.

There are versions of Nsight for Windows and for Linux, including versions that run under Microsoft's Visual Studio and under the Eclipse IDE. We restrict our discussion to the standalone Nsight Graphics application for Windows. (In our "sister" book *Computer Graphics Programming in OpenGL with Java*, we describe using Nsight with Java-based programs.)

Nsight works only with compatible NVIDIA graphics cards; it will not work with Intel or AMD graphics cards. A complete list of supported cards is available on the NVIDIA website [NS23].

Nsight is changing quickly, and the description in our previous (second) edition of this textbook is already outdated. The reader should consider this brief introduction just a starting point, as there are likely to be many more exciting changes and developments in Nsight in the near future.

C.2 SETTING UP NSIGHT

There are various ways of setting up Nsight. In previous editions, we described incorporating Nsight into Visual Studio. This is no longer necessary, as there is now a standalone Nsight graphics debugging tool called **Nsight Graphics** that allows us to use the shader debugger directly while running the application's compiled .exe file.

Start by downloading and installing Nsight Graphics, available at the Nsight Graphics website [NG23] (select "Download for Windows"). We installed version 2023.2.1.

C.3 RUNNING A C++/OPENGL APPLICATION IN NSIGHT

1. Compile your C++/OpenGL application in "Release" mode, and assemble a folder with the files needed to run the application. The steps for doing this were described in Appendix A, Section A.3.

2. Run "Nsight Graphics." A menu comes up, as shown below. Choose "Start Activity."

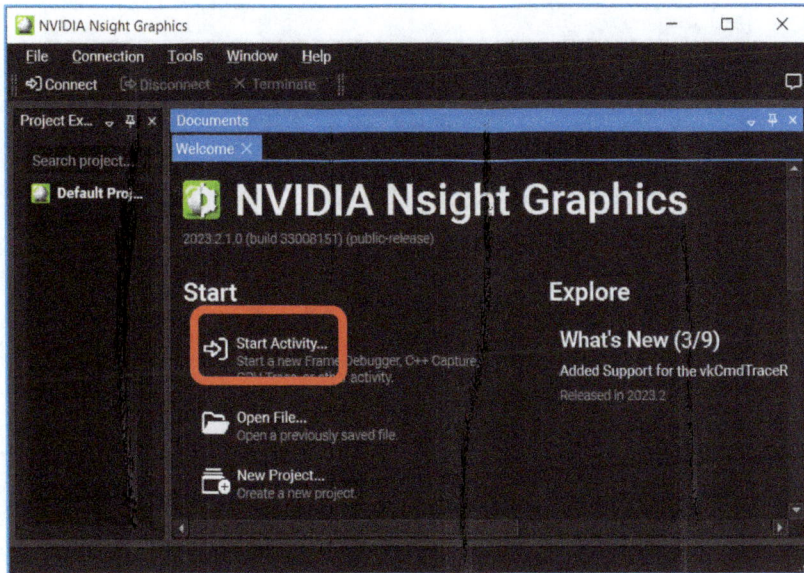

3. A "Target Platform" window should appear. This is where we specify which application we wish to debug using Nsight. Near the top, under "Windows," make sure that the "Launch" selection is highlighted. There are two entries below that that need to be changed:

First, there is a line that says "Application Executable:." In the box to the right of that, replace whatever is there with the path to the .exe executable that you created in Step #1, above. You can browse for this file by clicking the "three dots" at the right of the field. Our executable was here:

C:/Users/gordonvs/Documents/graphics/cubes.exe

Second, in the same pane is a line that says "Working directory:." In the box to the right of that, replace whatever is there with the path to the directory that contains your application. For our example, that was the following:

C:/Users/gordonvs/Documents/graphics/

Here is an example screenshot showing the two entries:

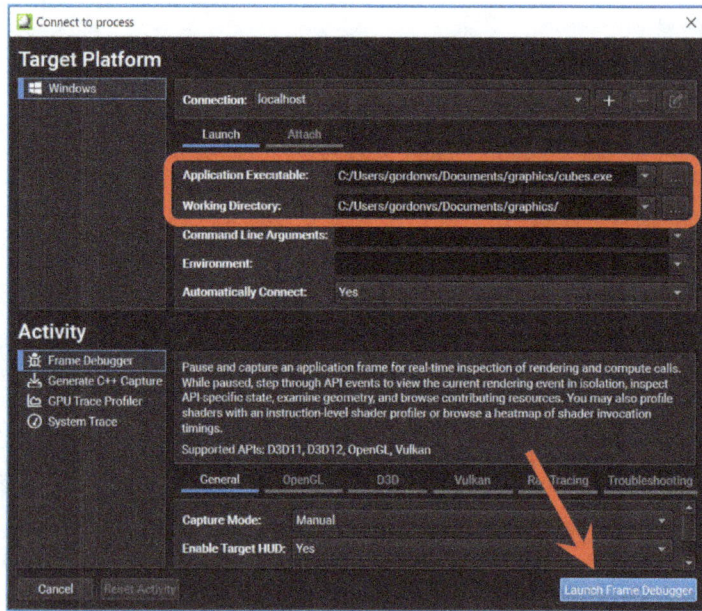

4. Click "Launch Frame Debugger" in the lower right. Your C++/OpenGL program should now execute. Depending on your installation, various windows may appear alongside your running program. Nsight may also superimpose some information over your running program, as shown here:

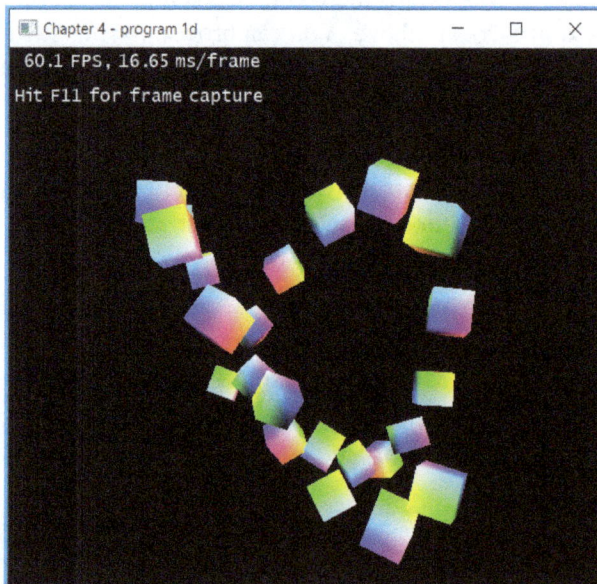

5. Once your program is running, interact with it in whatever area you wish to examine. At that point, you will need to pause the execution by pressing F-11. You should see your program's animation stop and a slider appear at the bottom of the window. Moving the slider shows the progression of OpenGL events that built the current display frame, such as if there were multiple calls to glDrawArrays() as is the case for this particular example.

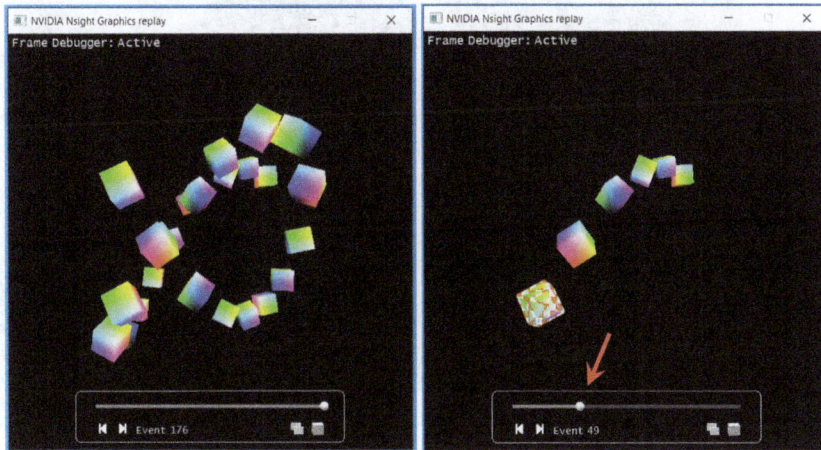

6. The Frame debugger should also appear, with several panels:

- The panel at the left shows the OpenGL events, depending on the slider position.

- At the top is a slider labeled "scrubber" that can also scroll through the events.

- In the center is a left bar with buttons for each shader stage. For example, you can highlight "VS" to view information about the variables in the "Vertex Shader."

- In the large center box to its right, you can scroll down and view the contents of the uniform variables (presuming you have "API inspector" selected above it). In the following screenshot, the small triangles to the left of "mv_matrix" and "proj_matrix" have been opened, revealing the contents of the 4x4 model-view and projection matrices.

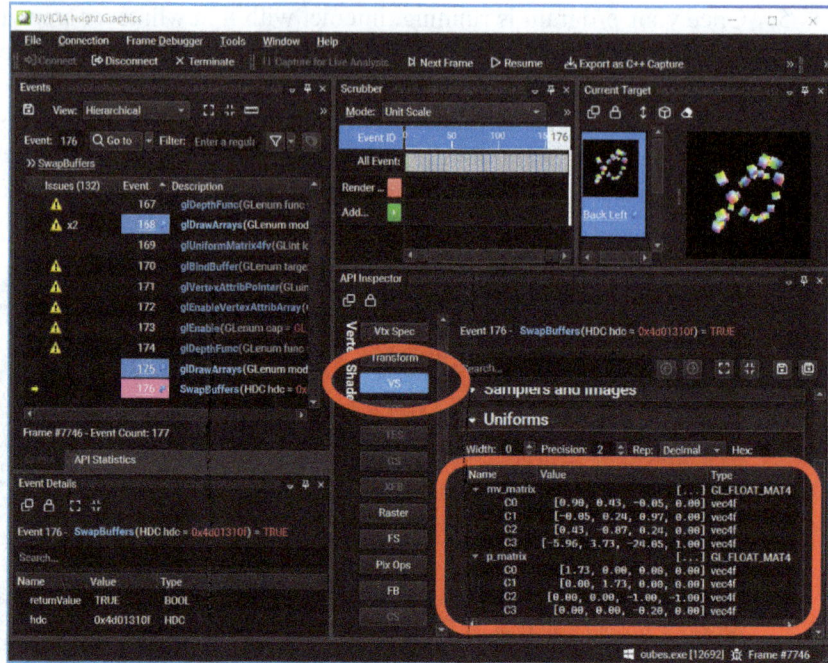

Consult the Nsight documentation for details on how to get the most out of the Nsight tool.

Reference

[NG23] Nsight Graphics, accessed November 2023, https://developer.nvidia.com/nsight-graphics

[NS23] Nsight Graphics GPUs (Full List), accessed November 2023, https://developer.nvidia.com/nsight-graphics-gpus-full-list

BUILDING A SIMPLE
CAMERA CONTROLLER

▪ ▪ ▪ ▪ ▪

Throughout this book, we built our graphics scenes near the origin, and placed the camera at a fixed location somewhere on the positive world Z axis, looking in the direction of the world negative Z axis towards the origin. Because the built-in OpenGL camera already points down the negative Z axis, and we never *turned* the camera, we were able (as described in Chapters 3 and 4) to build a very simple view matrix that took into account only the camera's location, without worrying about the camera's orientation. The command that we used to build this simple view matrix was typically something like the following:

```
vMat = glm::translate(glm::mat4(1.0f), glm::vec3(-cameraX, -cameraY, -cameraZ));
```

As described in Chapter 4, this creates a translation matrix that translates object vertices to the negative of the desired camera position, creating the illusion that we have moved the camera to position (cameraX, cameraY, cameraZ). This works fine as long as there is no change in the orientation of the camera; that is, if there is no need to turn the camera.

However, many common 3D graphics applications allow the user to move and turn the camera. The obvious example is in video games, where the human playing the game moves freely through a virtual 3D world. Video games are typically built using *game engines*, which provide a framework and suite of game-building tools. One such tool is a *camera controller*, which handles the positioning, moving, and turning of the camera.

At the heart of a camera controller is its ability to generate a view matrix that supports both the position and the orientation of the camera. We already described a formula for building such a view matrix in Chapter 3, specifically in Figure 3.13. We just did not use it in the code examples. It is reproduced here:

$$\begin{pmatrix} X_C \\ Y_C \\ Z_C \\ 1 \end{pmatrix} = \begin{bmatrix} \hat{U}_X & \hat{U}_Y & \hat{U}_Z & 0 \\ \hat{V}_X & \hat{V}_Y & \hat{V}_Z & 0 \\ -\hat{N}_X & -\hat{N}_Y & -\hat{N}_Z & 0 \\ 0 & 0 & 0 & 1 \end{bmatrix} * \begin{bmatrix} 1 & 0 & 0 & -C_X \\ 0 & 1 & 0 & -C_Y \\ 0 & 0 & 1 & -C_Z \\ 0 & 0 & 0 & 1 \end{bmatrix} * \begin{pmatrix} P_X \\ P_Y \\ P_Z \\ 1 \end{pmatrix}$$

negative of camera rotation angles — above **R (rotation)**

negative of camera location — above **T (translation)**

point P_C in eye space — **R (rotation)** ... **T (translation)** ... *world point P_W*

V (viewing transform)

The *viewing transform* matrix shown here – instead of the simple code described at the beginning of this appendix – requires us to maintain not only the camera's position C, but also its orientation. As described previously in Chapter 3 (and reflected in the formula from Figure 3.13), the camera's orientation is represented with three mutually orthogonal vectors U, V, and N. This enables us to move the camera (by changing C) and turn the camera (by changing U, V, and N).

It may not be immediately obvious, just by looking at the formula, how to go about moving and turning the camera. This appendix describes how to do this, and thus how to build a simple camera controller. It can be implemented in its own class or file as desired.

D.1 ELEMENTS OF A CAMERA CONTROLLER

A camera controller should include the following:

- Data structures for storing location C and orientation vectors U, V, and N
- Functions for moving the camera by modifying C
- Functions for turning the camera by modifying U, V, and N
- A function that builds a view matrix based on C, U, V, and N

Let's take a close look at each of these elements.

D.1.1 Storing the Location and Orientation Vectors

The camera location C is a designated point in 3D world space, and therefore simply requires three float values C_x, C_y, and C_z. These can be stored in separate variables, or in a single glm vec3. We have already been storing these as float variables, and can continue to do so:

```
float camera, cameraY, cameraZ;
// default camera location on the Z axis
cameraX = 0.0f; cameraY = 0.0f; cameraZ = 8.0f;
```

The orientation vectors U, V, and N can also be stored in float variables (three each), or in glm vec3s. Here we opt for the latter, and utilize the vec3 constructor to initialize them:

```
glm::vec3 cameraU(1.0f, 0.0f, 0.0f);
glm::vec3 cameraV(0.0f, 1.0f, 0.0f);
glm::vec3 cameraN(0.0f, 0.0f, -1.0f);
```

Note that we have taken care to initialize the orientation vectors so as to satisfy the following three requirements (the view matrix computations in Figure 3.13 depend on them):

- They must be of unit length.
- They must be mutually orthogonal.
- They must be arranged as a *left-handed* system.

Specifically in the above example, the right-facing U vector is initialized so that it points down the positive X axis, the up-facing V vector points up the positive Y axis, and the forward-facing N axis points down the *negative* Z axis. This is consistent with the default OpenGL camera orientation as shown back in Chapter 3 (Figure 3.11). Other initial orientations are possible, as long as they obey the three requirements listed above.

It is important that vectors U, V, and N maintain their unit length and mutual orthogonality as the camera moves and turns. We will describe how this is accomplished shortly.

D.1.2 Functions for Moving the Camera

Moving the camera refers to changing its position C, without altering its orientation vectors U, V, and N. The most common camera movements are forward and backward, but other movements are possible. Moving *forward* means that the camera moves along its forward-facing orientation vector N. That is, whichever direction the camera is currently facing, moving "forward" means to change the position C to a different location along that N axis. Note that in so doing, C changes, but N does not change.

A common mistake made by beginners is to assume that moving the camera forward means to move it along the world Z axis. While this is true for the initial camera orientation in the example shown earlier, after turning the camera, it would no longer be correct. Instead, we need to move the camera along its own N orientation vector.

Moving the camera forward requires simple vector arithmetic. If we treat the camera position C as a vector (recalling that a location in space can be treated as a vector from the origin to that location), then simply adding N to C will move the camera forward, as illustrated in Figure D.1. Of course, we typically would want finer control over how far we move the camera forward, so the complete formula is as follows:

$$C' = C + (a*N)$$

where C is the current camera position, N is the forward-facing camera orientation vector, *a* is a floating-point scalar indicating how much movement is desired, and C' is the resulting new camera position. Moving the camera backwards is nearly identical; we simply add -N to C, and the formula becomes $C' = C - (a*N)$. Functions for adding two vectors and for multiplying a vector by a scalar are available in the **glm** math library.

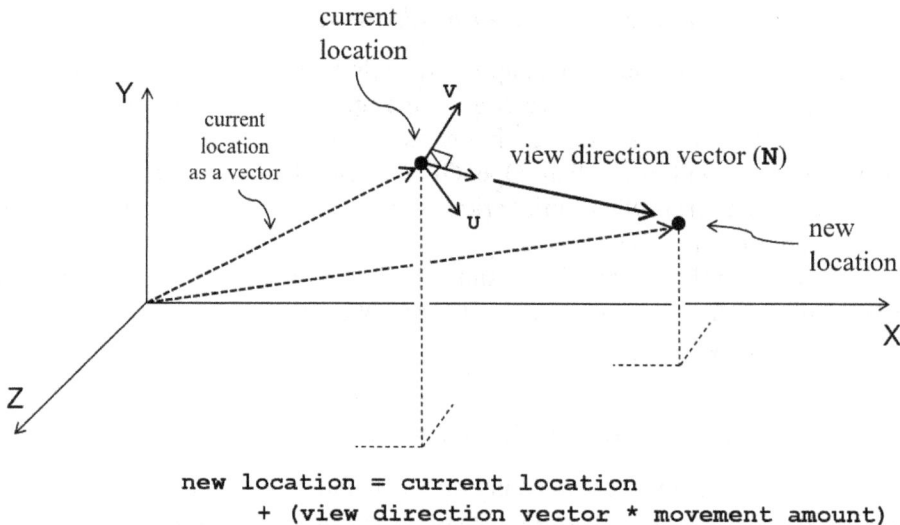

new location = current location
 + (view direction vector * movement amount)

Figure D.1
Moving the camera forward.

Moving the camera right and left uses the same process, except that the right-facing camera orientation vector U is used. The formulas for moving right and left are $C' = C + (a*U)$, and $C' = C - (a*U)$, respectively. It is important to understand the difference between moving right, versus turning right. *Moving right* means sliding the camera to its right, in the direction of its right-facing U vector, without changing the direction it is facing. *Turning right* means to rotate the camera, changing its orientation so that it faces a different direction (we will learn how to do this shortly).

Similarly, moving the camera up and down would be via the formulas $C' = C + (a*V)$ and $C' = C - (a*V)$, respectively.

Enabling the end user to move the camera, such as in a video game, requires capturing user inputs and then calling the desired function. For example, it is common for video games to allow the player to move forward by pressing the "W" key. Fortunately, the GLFW library that we are using makes it easy to capture user keystrokes, and a user guide for doing this is available [GL22]. We thus can use GLFW to capture appropriate keystrokes and call the corresponding functions described above to move the camera as desired.

D.1.3 Functions for Turning the Camera

Turning the camera refers to changing its orientation vectors U, V, and N, without altering its position C. The most common camera turns are *right* and *left*, but other turns are possible. Turning "right" or "left" means that the camera rotates around its upward-facing orientation vector V. That is, whichever direction the camera is currently facing, turning "right" means to change its right-facing U and forward-facing N orientation vectors so that the camera is pointing in a different direction. Note that in so doing, U and N change, but V (and C) do not. Also note that this operation must ensure that the orientation vectors U, V, and N remain orthogonal to each other, and that each remains unit length.

A common mistake made by beginners is to assume that turning the camera to the right means to rotate it around the world Y axis. While this is true for the initial camera orientation in the example shown earlier, for different orientations, it would not be correct. Instead, we need to rotate the camera around its V orientation vector.

Turning the camera requires rotating two of its orientation axes around the third axis. For example, turning the camera right and left (also called "yaw") requires rotating U and N around V. This is illustrated in Figure D.2. Similarly, turning the camera up and down (also called "pitch") requires rotating V and N around U, and "roll" is achieved by rotating U and V around N. In each case, we want to specify the amount of rotation desired (in degrees or radians).

Functions for rotating a vector a specified amount around an axis (i.e., around another vector) are available in the **glm** math library. Note that as long as we rotate the two vectors (U and N) around the third (V) *by the same amount*, the three camera orientation vectors will remain orthogonal to each other, and will retain their left-handed alignment. Also note that simply rotating a vector does not change its length, so they also retain their unit length.

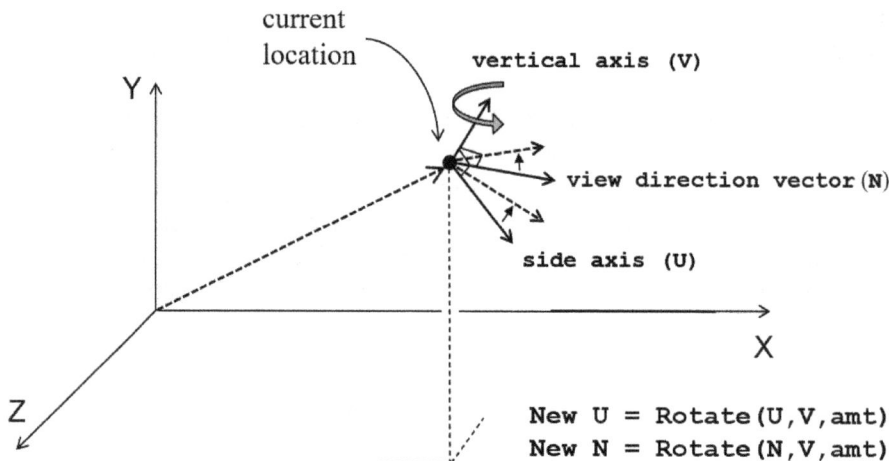

Figure D.2
Turning the camera to the left

As described earlier for moving the camera, it is common for video games to allow the player to "turn left" or "turn right" by performing actions such as pressing the arrow keys. We can use GLFW to capture the desired keystrokes [GL22], and then call the appropriate turning functions to look around and view the scene from different directions.

D.1.4 Building the View Matrix

Now that we have seen the role of the C, U, V, and N vectors in controlling the position and orientation of the camera, building an associated view matrix is simply a matter of applying the formula in Figure 3.13 (and reproduced at the start of this appendix). The steps to do this are as follows:

1. Build the T matrix by inserting the negatives of C_x, C_y, and C_z into an identity matrix, in the rightmost column (thus forming a translation matrix for -C).

2. Build the R matrix by inserting U_x, U_y, U_z, V_x, V_y, V_z, and the negatives of N_x, N_y, and N_z, into an identity matrix, in the positions shown in Figure 3.13.

3. Concatenate (multiply) matrices R and T, forming the view matrix V.

Functions for each of these steps are available in the **glm** math library.

A common error that beginners often make is transposing the R matrix when building it. The T matrix can be built most easily by using one of the translation matrix constructors in **glm**, which ensures that it will be built correctly. However, it is very easy to confuse rows and columns when building the R matrix. Another very common error is to concatenate R and T in the wrong order. They must be multiplied left-to-right as R*T (recall that matrix multiplication is not commutative). Whereas moving and turning the camera are commonly associated with user controls, building the view matrix should happen automatically, typically at every frame. The function that builds the view matrix should therefore be called from display().[1]

D.2 MORE ABOUT CAMERA CONTROLLERS

The controller described in Section D.1 may be adequate for the task of viewing a 3D scene from a variety of vantage points, and it is sometimes called a "flying camera." For example, a CAD tool that enables the user to design a part for an automobile would need to enable the designer to view the part from various angles to ensure that it meets the desired specification. It also may be adequate for offline rendering, such as for a movie, where human interaction is not necessary.

However, video games (and video game engines) typically offer more sophisticated camera controllers. One important reason is that video games often involve a player "avatar," complicating the desired point of view for the camera. For example, it is often useful to include the avatar in the player's view, such as looking over the avatar's shoulder. Or, they may wish to view the world from the avatar's point of view. Two types of camera controllers commonly used in games are as follows:

- *Orbit* or *Targeted* Camera Controller – Here, the camera always looks at the position of the avatar, and as the avatar moves and turns, the camera moves and turns accordingly. The end user is given controls for positioning the camera relative to the avatar, such as its distance from the avatar, and the camera's elevation and angle of view. Implementation often makes use of spherical (polar) coordinates.

- *Chase* or *Tracking* Camera Controller – Here, the camera is always positioned behind and slightly above the avatar, appropriate for example in racing games. As the avatar moves, the camera "chases" it, allowing the end user to watch the avatar as well as the area immediately in front and beside the avatar, as well as other nearby competitors. Chase

---

[1] If camera movement is very infrequent, it could instead be called from the functions that perform the movement.

cameras typically also employ a "spring" system, so that sharp, sudden turns made by the avatar result in a more gradual change to the camera position, so as to avoid motion sickness in the player.

There are numerous online tutorials on how to implement various camera controllers. For example, a good tutorial for building an orbit controller in C++ using **glm** is available online from Megabyte Softworks [MB09].

Reference

[GL22] GLFW Input Guide, accessed November 2023, https://www.glfw.org/docs/3.3/input_guide.html

[MB09] Camera Pt.3 – Orbit Camera, Megabyte Softworks, accessed November 2023, https://www.mbsoftworks.sk/tutorials/opengl4/026-camera-pt3-orbit-camera/

Index

www.ingramcontent.com/pod-product-compliance
Lightning Source LLC
Chambersburg PA
CBHW061923190326
41458CB00009B/2634